NARRATIVE AND METAPHOR IN THE LAW

It has long been recognized that court trials, both criminal and civil, in the common law system, operate around pairs of competing narratives told by opposing advocates. In recent years, however, it has increasingly been argued that narrative flows in many directions and through every form of legal theory and practice. Interest in the part played by metaphor in the law, including metaphors for the law, and for many standard concepts in legal practice, has also been strong, though research under the metaphor banner has been much more fragmentary. In this book, for the first time, a distinguished group of legal scholars, collaborating with specialists from cognitive theory, journalism, rhetoric, social psychology, criminology, and legal activism, explore how narrative and metaphor are both vital to the legal process. Together, they examine topics including concepts of law, legal persuasion, human rights law, gender in the law, innovations in legal thinking, legal activism, creative work around the law, and public debate around crime and punishment.

Michael Hanne founded the Comparative Literature Programme at the University of Auckland, New Zealand and directed it until his retirement in 2010. He has published "Binocular Vision: Narrative and Metaphor in Medicine," in *Genre* (2011) and *Warring with Words: Narrative and Metaphor in Politics* (2014).

Robert Weisberg is Edwin E. Huddleson, Jr. Professor of Law at Stanford. He also founded and now serves as faculty co-director of the Stanford Criminal Justice Center (SCJC). He is co-author (with Guyora Binder) of the book *Literary Criticisms of Law* (2000).

Narrative and Metaphor in the Law

Edited by
MICHAEL HANNE
University of Auckland

ROBERT WEISBERG
Stanford University

CAMBRIDGE UNIVERSITY PRESS

CAMBRIDGE
UNIVERSITY PRESS

University Printing House, Cambridge CB2 8BS, United Kingdom

One Liberty Plaza, 20th Floor, New York, NY 10006, USA

477 Williamstown Road, Port Melbourne, VIC 3207, Australia

314–321, 3rd Floor, Plot 3, Splendor Forum, Jasola District Centre, New Delhi – 110025, India

79 Anson Road, #06–04/06, Singapore 079906

Cambridge University Press is part of the University of Cambridge.

It furthers the University's mission by disseminating knowledge in the pursuit of education, learning, and research at the highest international levels of excellence.

www.cambridge.org
Information on this title: www.cambridge.org/9781108422796
DOI: 10.1017/9781108381734

© Cambridge University Press 2018

This publication is in copyright. Subject to statutory exception and to the provisions of relevant collective licensing agreements, no reproduction of any part may take place without the written permission of Cambridge University Press.

First published 2018

Printed in the United Kingdom by Clays, St Ives plc

A catalogue record for this publication is available from the British Library.

Library of Congress Cataloging-in-Publication Data
NAMES: Hanne, Michael, editor. | Weisberg, Robert, 1946–, editor.
TITLE: Narrative and metaphor in the law / edited by Michael Hanne, Robert Weisberg.
DESCRIPTION: New York : Cambridge University Press, 2018. | Includes bibliographical references and index.
IDENTIFIERS: LCCN 2017053783 | ISBN 9781108422796 (hardback)
SUBJECTS: LCSH: Law – Language. | Semantics (Law) | Metaphor. | BISAC: LAW / General.
CLASSIFICATION: LCC K487.L36 N37 2018 | DDC 340/.14–dc23
LC record available at https://lccn.loc.gov/2017053783

ISBN 978-1-108-42279-6 Hardback

Cambridge University Press has no responsibility for the persistence or accuracy of URLs for external or third-party internet websites referred to in this publication and does not guarantee that any content on such websites is, or will remain, accurate or appropriate.

Contents

List of Contributors		*page* viii
Introduction		1
CONVERSATION I	**NARRATIVE, METAPHOR, AND CONCEPTS OF JUSTICE AND LEGAL SYSTEMS**	13
Editors' Introduction		15
1 On Narrating and Troping the Law: The Conjoined Use of Narrative and Metaphor in Legal Discourse *Greta Olson*		19
2 What's It Like? Native Americans and the Ambivalence of Legal Metaphors *Lawrence Rosen*		37
CONVERSATION II	**NARRATIVE AND METAPHOR IN LEGAL PERSUASION**	55
Editors' Introduction		57
3 Metaphoric Parable: The Nexus of Metaphor and Narrative in Persuasive Legal Writing *Michael R. Smith*		65
4 Embodied Metaphor in Persuasive Legal Narrative *Raymond W. Gibbs, Jr.*		90

CONVERSATION III NARRATIVE AND METAPHOR IN JUDICIAL OPINIONS — 111

   Editors' Introduction — 113

5 Narrative in the Legal Text: Judicial Opinions and Their Narratives — 121
Simon Stern

6 Legal Stories, the Reality Effect, and Visual Narratives: A Response to Simon Stern — 140
Peter Brooks

CONVERSATION IV NARRATIVE, METAPHOR, AND GENDER IN THE LAW — 151

   Editors' Introduction — 153

7 Gender Justice: The Role of Stories and Images — 157
Linda L. Berger and Kathryn M. Stanchi

CONVERSATION V NARRATIVE, METAPHOR, AND INNOVATIONS IN LEGAL THINKING — 193

   Editors' Introduction — 195

8 The "Crime as a Disease" Metaphor: Vision, Power, and Collaboration in Social Problems Research — 200
Roberto H. Potter

9 The Fertility (sic) of the Crime/Disease Linkage for Metaphor and Narrative: Response to Potter — 220
Robert Weisberg

CONVERSATION VI NARRATIVE AND METAPHOR IN PUBLIC DEBATE AROUND CRIME AND PUNISHMENT — 243

   Editors' Introduction — 245

10 Narrative Conventions in Crime Reporting — 251
Dahlia Lithwick

11	Metaphors, Stories, and Media Framing of Crime: Response to Lithwick L. David Ritchie	269
	CONVERSATION VII NARRATIVE AND METAPHOR IN HUMAN RIGHTS LAW	289
	Editors' Introduction	291
12	When Rights-Talk Meets Queue-Talk Katharine G. Young	297
13	The Cutters and the Others Bernadette A. Meyler	319
	CONVERSATION VIII NARRATIVE AND METAPHOR IN CREATIVE WORK BY LAWYERS	325
	Editors' Introduction	327
14	Through Narrative and by Metaphor: Creating a Lawyer-Self in Poetry and Prose Lawrence Joseph	332
15	Secrets of Civility in *Lawyerland* Meredith Wallis	349
	CONVERSATION IX NARRATIVE AND METAPHOR IN LEGAL ACTIVISM	359
	Editors' Introduction	361
16	A Conversation with Mari Matsuda Michael Hanne	367
Bibliography		380
Index		414

Contributors

Linda L. Berger is the Family Foundation Professor of Law at the University of Nevada, Las Vegas, William S. Boyd School of Law. Her research, writing, and teaching converge on the practices of legal rhetoric; her most recent work blends critical rhetorical analysis with computational criticism to explore the making and unmaking of precedent. She is one of the coeditors, with Kathryn Stanchi and Bridget Crawford, of *U.S. Feminist Judgments: Rewritten Opinions of the United States Supreme Court* (Cambridge, 2016), the first volume in an ongoing series. She also is the coauthor, with Kathryn Stanchi, of *Legal Persuasion: A Rhetorical Approach to the Science* (2017).

Peter Brooks is Sterling Professor of Comparative Literature Emeritus at Yale University, where he was the Founding Director of the Whitney Humanities Center. He is currently Andrew W. Mellon Foundation Scholar in the University Center for Human Values and the Department of Comparative Literature, Princeton University. He is the author of several books, including *Reading for the Plot* and *Troubling Confessions: Speaking Guilt in Law and Literature*, and the recently published *Flaubert in the Ruins of Paris*.

Raymond W. Gibbs, Jr. is Distinguished Professor of Psychology at the University of California, Santa Cruz. His research as a cognitive scientist focuses on the interactions between language, thought, and embodied experience. A particular interest within his scholarship is on the ways metaphorical language emerges from enduring metaphorical concepts that are rooted in pervasive bodily actions. Much of his writing extends his empirical findings and theoretical ideas to debates within multiple disciplines including linguistics, philosophy, and literary studies. His most recent books include *Interpreting Figurative Meaning*, with Herb

Colston (2012), and *Metaphor Wars: Conceptual Metaphor in Human Life* (2017), both published by Cambridge University Press.

Michael Hanne founded and, for many years, directed the Comparative Literature program at the University of Auckland, New Zealand. His major research interest has been on the interlocking roles played by narrative and metaphor in a wide range of disciplines. He has coorganized a series of conferences in the United States and Europe on narrative and metaphor in medicine (2010), politics (2012), the law (2016) and education (2017), and coedited volumes stemming from each. *Binocular Vision: Narrative and Metaphor in Medicine* (2011) and *Warring with Words: Narrative and Metaphor in Politics* (with W. Crano and J. S. Mio, 2013) have already appeared. Details of the project are to be found at narrative metaphornexus.weebly.com.

Lawrence Joseph is Tinnelly Professor of Law at St. John's University School of Law, New York, and the author of six books of poems, most recently *So Where Are We?* (2017), and two books of prose, *Lawyerland* (1997), and *The Game Changed: Essays and Other Prose* (2011). Among his awards are fellowships from the National Endowment for the Arts and the Guggenheim Foundation.

Dahlia Lithwick is a senior editor at *Slate*, and in that capacity, writes the "Supreme Court Dispatches" and "Jurisprudence" columns. Her work has appeared in the *New York Times, Harper's, The New Yorker, The Washington Post*, and *Commentary*, among other places. She won a 2013 National Magazine Award for her columns on the Affordable Care Act. She has been twice awarded an Online Journalism Award for her legal commentary and was the first online journalist invited to be on the Reporters Committee for the Freedom of the Press. She received the 2017 Golden Pen Award from the Legal Writing Institute. Ms. Lithwick has testified before Congress about access to justice in the era of the Roberts Court. She has appeared on CNN, ABC, *The Colbert Report*, and is a frequent guest on *The Rachel Maddow Show*.

Mari Matsuda is a law professor at the William S. Richardson School of Law, University of Hawai'i. She is an original member of the group of scholars who developed critical race theory and intersectional feminism. She is also an artist (see marimatsudapeaceorchestra.com). Her books include *Where is Your Body? and Other Essays on Race, Gender, and Law* (1996), *Words That Wound: Critical Race Theory, Assaultive Speech, and the First Amendment* (1993), and *We Won't Go Back: Making the Case for Affirmative Action* (with Charles R. Lawrence III, 1997).

Bernadette A. Meyler is the Carl and Sheila Spaeth Professor of Law at Stanford University. She is the coeditor of *New Directions in Law and Literature* (2017) with Elizabeth Anker and of *The Oxford Handbook of Law and Humanities* (forthcoming) with Simon Stern and Maks Del Mar. She is also the author of the forthcoming *Theaters of Pardoning* and *Common Law Originalism*.

Greta Olson is a professor of English and American Literary and Cultural Studies at the University of Giessen and was Fellow at the Käte Hamburger Center "Law as Culture" in Bonn. She is general editor of the *European Journal of English Studies*, and cofounder of the European Network for Law and Literature Research. She works on projects related to legal pluralism, cultural approaches to law, the politics of narrative form, critical media and American studies, and feminism and sexuality studies. Related publications include "Law's Pluralities" (*German Law Journal*, 2017) and "Narration and Narrative in Legal Discourse" (*Living Handbook of Narratology*, 2014).

Roberto H. Potter is a professor in the Department of Criminal Justice at the University of Central Florida. His research interests lie at the intersections of criminal justice, public and behavioral health, and the mechanisms of social control represented by each of those sectors. In particular, he is interested in the organizational relationships among the various sectors involved in the control of human behavior, including universities. These interests are reflected in *Epidemiological Criminology: A Public Health Approach to Crime and Violence* (2013), and *Criminal Justice Organizations: Structure, Relationships, Control and Planning* (2017).

L. David Ritchie is Professor of Communication at Portland State University, Oregon. His primary research focus is metaphor use, storytelling, metaphorical stories, and humor in naturally occurring discourse. He is the author of three books on metaphor theory, including *Metaphorical Stories in Discourse*, to be issued by Cambridge University Press in September 2017. Other publications include with M. Thomas "A '*glowing marble*': '*brushed with clouds*' or '*parched, scorched, and washed away*'? Obama's use of contrasting metaphors and stories in framing climate change" (*Metaphor and the Social World*, 2015).

Lawrence Rosen has taught at Princeton University for almost forty years and has won all of his university's teaching awards. As a lawyer and adjunct professor of law at Columbia University he has concentrated on comparative law and the rights of indigenous peoples. He has served as a Phi Beta

Kappa Lecturer and was named to the first group of MacArthur Award fellows. The author of a dozen books on law, culture, and Middle East societies, he will be completing a broadscale study of tribes while a visitor next year at the Institute for Advanced Study in Princeton.

Michael R. Smith is a professor of Law and the Founder and Director of The Center for the Study of Written Advocacy at the College of Law, University of Wyoming. He has written extensively on the art and science of persuasive writing, including the groundbreaking article on metaphor in legal discourse, "Levels of Metaphor in Persuasive Legal Writing." He also authored the book, *Advanced Legal Writing: Theories and Strategies in Persuasive Writing* (3rd ed. 2013), which explores strategies in persuasive legal writing based on principles from other disciplines, such as cognitive psychology, classical rhetoric, and narrative theory.

Kathryn M. Stanchi is the Jack E. Feinberg Professor of Litigation and Affiliated Professor of Gender, Sexuality and Women's Studies at Temple University School of Law. She specializes in legal issues related to the intersection of writing, persuasion, and gender. Her scholarship touches on many of the subjects of this volume, notably two recent books *Feminist Judgments: Rewritten Opinions of the United States Supreme Court* (with Linda Berger and Bridget Crawford) (Cambridge, 2016) and *Legal Persuasion: A Rhetorical Approach to the Science* (with Linda Berger) (2017).

Simon Stern is an associate professor of Law and English at the University of Toronto. His current work includes articles on literature and obscenity law, narratives of search and seizure, and the relation between metaphor and metonymy in legal analysis. He is coeditor of the *Routledge Research Companion to Law and Humanities in Nineteenth-Century America* (2017) and of the forthcoming *Oxford Handbook of Law and Humanities*. He is writing a book on the history and theory of legal fictions in common law since the seventeenth century.

Meredith Wallis is an Oakland attorney, finishing her PhD in Modern Thought and Literature at Stanford University. Her practice areas are demonstrations and asylum, and her research is on children's literature as a source of law.

Robert Weisberg, who teaches criminal law at Stanford, has drawn on his pre-law background in addressing themes in law and the humanities. He coauthored (with Guyora Binder) *Literary Criticisms of Law* (Princeton,

2000), a comprehensive assessment of scholarship treating law in regard to such literary phenomena as narrative, rhetoric, and deconstruction. Among his later works in the field is "Law, Literature, and Cultural Unity: Between Celebration and Lament," in *Teaching Law and Literature* (Sarat and Anderson eds., 2012). His writing also examines criminal law from a cultural perspective, as in "Apology, Legislation, and Mercy" (*North Carolina Law Review* 2004), which explores retributive theories related to clemency and the death penalty.

Katharine G. Young is an associate professor at Boston College Law School. She writes in the fields of constitutionalism and human rights, and focuses on, among other issues, the role of narrative, metaphor, and interpretation in the changing nature of legal rights, such as in "Freeing Mohammed Zakari: Rights as Footprints" (with Jeremy Perelman) in *Stones of Hope: How African Activists Reclaim Human Rights to Challenge Global Poverty* (Lucie E. White and Jeremy Perelman, eds., 2011). Two books relevant to these themes are her *Constituting Economic and Social Rights* (2012) and *The Public Law of Gender: from the Local to the Global* (Cambridge, 2016, with Kim Rubenstein).

Introduction

Narrative and Metaphor in the Law

Michael Hanne and Robert Weisberg

Anyone who has even a passing acquaintance with the common law is aware that court trials, both criminal and civil, operate around pairs of competing narratives, with judges and juries tasked with assessing the validity of the stories told by opposing advocates. However, over the last thirty years or so, law scholars and practitioners have come to recognize that narrative flows in many directions and through every form of legal theory and practice.

Law professor Anthony G. Amsterdam and psychologist Jerome Bruner have summarized the role of narrative in the law as follows:

> Law lives on narrative, for reasons both banal and deep... Clients tell stories to lawyers, who must figure out what to make of what they hear. As clients and lawyers talk, the client's story gets recast into plights and prospects, plots and pilgrimages into possible worlds... If circumstances warrant, the lawyers retell their clients' stories in the form of pleas and arguments to judges and testimonies to juries... Next, judges and jurors retell the stories to themselves or each other in the form of instruction, deliberations, a verdict, a set of findings, or an opinion. And then it is the turn of journalists, commentators and critics. This endless telling and retelling, casting and recasting is essential to the conduct of the law. It is how law's actors comprehend whatever series of events they make the subject of their legal actions.[1]

On the larger scale, legal argument in the common-law tradition depends in considerable part on the longer narrative represented by legal precedent, that is, the linking by advocates or judges of the stories under consideration in the current case to decisions made by earlier judges in cases which they argue to be comparable and relevant to the current case. Legal philosopher Ronald

---

[1] Anthony G. Amsterdam and Jerome Bruner, *Minding the Law: How Courts Rely on Storytelling, and How Their Stories Change the Ways We Understand the Law – and Ourselves* (Cambridge, MA: Harvard University Press, 2000), p. 110.

Dworkin describes the line of judicial precedent as a continuing narrative authored by successive judges, best understood as a "chain novel."[2] So, in the words of literary scholar and legal commentator Peter Brooks (a contributor to this volume), "narrative is inevitable and irreplaceable [in the law]: it is not an ornament, it is not translatable into something else."[3]

Narrative, of course, combines the recounting of events (a mere chronicle or annal) with interpretation of those events; as such it is central to all legal processes and the many different kinds of legal story interwoven with each other to form the grand fabric of the law. The last three decades have seen a quite massive proliferation of courses, research, conferences, and publications relating to the part played by narrative in the theory and practice of the law. Most of the courses offered relate broadly to the practical need that attorneys appearing in court have for skills in storytelling and in demonstrating the weaknesses to be found in stories told by opposing counsel. One of the best-known examples over recent years has been the program at the University of Virginia Law School entitled "The Narrative Power of the Law," directed by Peter Brooks. Another long-established course was that offered at New York University School of Law by Anthony Amsterdam and the late Jerome Bruner. These courses may be described as teaching "narrative competence" to (future) attorneys. In this sense, they offer an interesting parallel with courses currently on offer to professionals in other disciplines, such as those offered to present and future doctors by Rita Charon and the Program in Narrative Medicine, at Columbia University.[4]

Moreover, the practical relevance of narrative studies in the law has been taken up in a good number of legal conferences over the last few years, notably the biennial "Applied Legal Storytelling" Conference series in the United States and the United Kingdom. The most recent in this series took place at the Law School of Seattle University, July, 2015, focusing on such topics as: "the scientific research that explains how judges and jurors perceive and are persuaded by narrative. It will then turn to what stories are, what stories are not, and how to incorporate storytelling in all aspects of trial and litigation."[5] In addition, several fine books and articles centered on narrative in the law have been published over the last twenty years, drawing attention to the variety

---

[2] Ronald Dworkin, *Law's Empire* (Cambridge, MA: Harvard University Press, 1986), p. 229.
[3] Peter Brooks, "Narrative transactions—Does the law need a narratology?" *Yale Journal of Law & Humanities*, 18 no. 1 (2006), 1–28.
[4] http://sps.columbia.edu/narrative-medicine.
[5] This is from the abstract of a paper presented by Suparna Malempati, entitled "Constructing the case: Theory, theme, and persuasion from trial advocacy." http://lwionline.org/uploads/FileUpload/2015ASCFinalProgram.pdf.

and complexity of the functions of narrative in the law, some of the most impressive being by Brooks and Gewirtz (1996), Binder and Weisberg (2000), Amsterdam and Bruner (2000), Brooks (2005), and Olson (2014).[6] Several of these authors have contributed essays to this volume.

Finally, a number of different contemporary schools and movements in legal theory have paid particular attention to narrative. The Law and Literature movement has highlighted the extent to which lawyers employ strategies drawn from creative writing, especially from narrative fiction, and, indeed, the extent to which those strategies can be analyzed using insights from literary theory. James Boyd White, whose remarkable book *The Legal Imagination* (1973) laid the foundations for the movement, wrote: "Might it not be suggested that the central act of the legal mind . . . is [the] conversion of the raw material of life . . . into a story that will claim to tell the truth in legal terms?"[7] Other relatively recent movements, including Critical Legal Theory, Feminist Legal Theory, and Critical Race Theory, have raised issues concerning voice, perspective, and story ownership in conventional legal narratives and are centrally concerned with the configurations of power in and around those narratives. For an early broad discussion of these issues, see Richard Delgado's article of 1989, "Storytelling for oppositionists and others: A plea for narrative."[8]

These strands of law-and-narrative scholarship raise, and this volume will explore, very fundamental questions about whether there are qualities or functions inherent in narrative that can guide us in discerning – or predicting – its role in law. One view is that narrative is inherent in all human discourse, so that part of the exercise is to simply uncover what had to have been there all the time – the embedding of narrative in legal discourse. This is an exercise that is especially interesting in the face of the pretenses of the legal system that because of its claim of pure rationality and grounding in fact it does not need, or is undermined by, the possible distortions or emotionality of narrative. Another view is that if narrative is ubiquitous in law, the reason is that it is

---

[6] Peter Brooks and Paul Gewirtz (eds.), *Law's Stories: Narrative and Rhetoric in the Law* (New Haven, CT: Yale University Press, 1996); Guyora Binder and Robert Weisberg, *Literary Criticisms of Law.* (Princeton, NJ: Princeton University Press, 2000), esp. chapter 3, Narrative Criticism of Law; Peter Brooks, "Narrative in and of the law" in James Phelan and Peter J. Rabinowitz (eds.), *A Companion to Narrative Theory* (Malden, MA: Blackwell Publishing, 2005: 415–426; and Greta Olson, "Narration and narrative in legal discourse" in *Living Handbook of Narratology*. Hamburg: Hamburg University Press, 2014. www.lhn.uni-hamburg.de/article/narration-and-narrative-legal-discourse.

[7] James B. White, *The Legal Imagination* (Chicago, IL: University Chicago Press, 1973), p. 859.

[8] Richard Delgado, "Storytelling for oppositionists and others: A plea for narrative," *Michigan Law Review*, 87 no. 8 (August, 1989), 2411–2441.

very purposefully recruited by legal actors to serve instrumental goals, as in making an advocate's argument about the facts at issue in litigation, or characterizing the trajectory of precedent. Still another view picks up the point about the pretense of objective rationality in law to suggest that narrative by its nature shows up in or is inserted in law as a disruptive force. One version of this view is that the rationality pretense is itself inherently conservative, either in the sense of preserving legal tradition or conservative in a broader political sense, so that literary figuration is generally progressive in its orientation or effect. The contestable nature of these perspectives makes narrative in law a very fertile field of study today.

METAPHOR IN THE LAW

The same thirty-year period has also seen quite a strong interest in metaphor and the law, with a number of conferences and publications. Nevertheless, the work done under the metaphor banner has been much more fragmentary. Perhaps one reason is that, while narrative is woven into the fabric of law in several different *contexts* (storytelling in advocacy, precedential reasoning, legal history, etc.), the basic nature of narrative does not fundamentally change among these contexts. By contrast, metaphor tends to operate separately and in distinct ways on several different *levels*. On one level, metaphors are commonly used to define justice in the grand sense in, for instance, the blindfold, scales, and sword associated with figures representing justice. On another level, metaphors are conventionally employed to convey standard concepts in legal practice, for example the contrast between a "chain of evidence" (where, if one link fails, the whole case collapses) and a "rope of evidence" (made up of many strands, where the failure of one or a few strands does not prevent it from supporting the "weight" of the case). And single metaphors may also be used in a tactical manner by an attorney, for instance to capture for the judge or jury a sense of the personality of a defendant ("a schoolyard bully") or of the actions of the opposing attorney ("a fishing expedition").

So obviously, a comparison between narrative and metaphor reveals many differences and similarities. Whereas narratives are necessarily premeditated to some extent, a metaphor is often a flash of intuitive insight. But if we reprise the questions raised above about the inherent role of narrative in law and apply them to metaphor, the picture becomes very mixed. While some may think of metaphor as ornamental artifice, the notion that narrative is an unavoidable part of human discourse is perhaps even truer with metaphor, perhaps because metaphor is much more likely to be spontaneous than premeditated; indeed

Introduction 5

its appearance in any kind of speech may be virtually compulsive. Metaphor may also therefore be less likely to be serving an instrumental goal – unless, ironically, it operates more subtly in that role: metaphor can act subliminally, and it can both highlight and hide. In any event, metaphor is just as subject to the concern that as a literary figure it might be manipulative or overly emotional – this perception is a long hangover from Justice Benjamin Cardozo's much-quoted declaration that "[m]etaphors are to be narrowly watched, for starting as devices to liberate thought, they end often by enslaving it."[9] We can also reprise the question whether metaphor joins narrative as a typically disruptive or progressive force, a challenge to law's rationality pretense. Further, the rival of metaphor is not necessarily abstraction – it can be another form of concreteness, that is, social science data.[10]

Narrative and metaphor may also be evaluated in different ways. We often use the term "stock narrative" for one that is used a great deal, but the term is more descriptive than pejorative. By contrast, we hear the very pejorative term "dead metaphors" for those that have lost their utility, their generative spark or strategic value. The live/dead distinction may be descriptively useful, but let us pause for a moment to consider what follows from it. In the particular context of judicial opinions, perhaps the most vivid metaphors are those used to carry out very vigorous disputes among justices,[11] but the more mundane metaphors are those that last and that guide or control future decisions. Perhaps the key factor is not a matter of life or death but whether a metaphor is so strong as to

---

[9] *Berkey* v. *Third Avenue Railway*, 155 N.E. 58, 61 (N.Y. 1926).
[10] Consider the concept of the Brandeis brief, as exemplified in *Muller* v. *Oregon*, 208 U.S. 412 (1908). There, then-lawyer Brandeis submitted a brief full of huge swaths of statistical data to demonstrate the harms of excessive working hours on women in a laundry. The Court relied on this data in upholding a state labor law against the employer's challenge, which was based on airy abstractions about "liberty of contract." But then consider a recent death penalty case. *Glossip* v. *Gross*, 135 S.Ct. 2726 (2015), Justice Breyer embeds a Brandeis-brief's worth of data in his dissenting opinion. He uses numbers, graphs, and tables about arbitrary and racial and geographic disparities in the infliction of the death penalty, lack of funding for defense counsel, and increasing time between trial and execution (125 S.Ct. at 2255–94) to make the case that the capital punishment has become unconstitutionally cruel and unusual. In his opinion concurring with the majority, Justice Scalia responds to Justice Breyer with mocking invective full of literary tropes. As Scalia puts it, the defendant's arguments have been made before, so "Welcome to Groundhog Day." Justice Breyer and his fellow dissenters cite new disparity studies "as though they have discovered the lost folios of Shakespeare" and their arguments are "gobbldey-gook" (125 S.Ct, at 2746–47).
[11] In his dissent from *United States* v. *Windsor*, 133 S.Ct. 2675 (2013), the same-sex marriage case that struck down part of the Defense of Marriage Act, Justice Scalia denounced the majority opinion of his nemesis, Justice Kennedy, as a "jaw-dropping" decision, that has its "diseased root" and, now infamously, as "argle-bargle" (133 S.Ct. at 2698, 2709).

dominate and freeze a field of legal thought, to pull off a capture that prevents new fresh thinking.

For whatever reason, by contrast to the curricular presence of narrative, there are, to our knowledge, no courses that focus exclusively on metaphor in the law, though there have been a few major conferences, each of which has generated its own published volume. One important conference, "Using Metaphor in Legal Analysis and Communication," was held at Mercer University in 2006, and included a presentation by one of the contributors to the present volume: Michael R. Smith's "Levels of Metaphor in Persuasive Legal Writing,"[12] and David T. Ritchie's "The Centrality of Metaphor in Legal Analysis and Communication: An Introduction."[13] A more recent conference was "Law's Metaphors," held at Southampton University Law School, in September 2015, with papers published the following year.[14] Convenor of the conference David Gurnham makes the useful distinction between: metaphors used *in law*, metaphors *for the law*, and law as a metaphor *for other things*.[15] One of the most original and wide-ranging papers in that collection is by Andreas Philippopoulos-Mihalopoulos, entitled "Flesh of the Law: Material Legal Metaphors," which identifies some of the many ways in which metaphor figures in legal discourse. In regard to the risk that a metaphor will capture and stultify a field of thought, he asserts that "we operate with metaphors on a preconscious level, namely a level where language is accepted unquestioningly. We are so conditioned by the ruling metaphors of law that a) we do not question them and b) we allow them to carry on determining the way we stand in relation to the law, since we cannot even imagine a different way."[16] This observation lies behind a discussion undertaken in this volume, in Conversation 4, about whether a shift of metaphor on a particular legal topic may generate innovative thinking., where we can do thought experiments (or speak-experiments) to isolate the relevant literary variable. Indeed, one can imagine an even bolder thought experiment: try to write a judicial opinion – or even a statute – without any metaphors at all.

Articles on the role of metaphor in law published in the last fifteen years have ranged over many topics: the increasing use of aural metaphors in

---

[12] The proceedings were published as *Mercer Law Review* 58 (Spring 2007).
[13] David T. Ritchie, "The Centrality of Metaphor in Legal Analysis and Communication: an Introduction," *Mercer Law Review* 58 (Spring 2007): 839–843. That David Ritchie should not be confused with L. David Ritchie, who has contributed to this volume.
[14] Special issue of the *Journal of Law and Society*, 43 no. 1 (March 2016).
[15] David Gurnham, "Law's metaphors: Introduction," *Journal of Law and Society*, 43 (2016), 1–7, 2.
[16] Andreas Philippopoulos-Mihalopoulos, "Flesh of the Law: Material Legal Metaphors," *Journal of Law and Society*, 43 (2016), 45–65, 49.

American legal discourse to challenge the traditional dominance of visual metaphors;[17] the part played by metaphors as models in legal theory;[18] the prevalence of sporting and warring metaphors in judicial opinions;[19] the critique of the overuse of the "war" metaphor in relation to terrorism;[20] the distinctive metaphors favored by practitioners in mediation;[21] and the competing metaphors in constitutional theory.[22] Two of the most significant articles are by authors represented in the present volume, Katharine Young and Linda Berger. Young's article examines the implications of using a range of different metaphors for human rights;[23] Berger's studies the power of metaphor in legal persuasion.[24]

There have been only a few attempts by law scholars to depict the full range of ways in which metaphor features in legal theory and practice. Outstanding books on metaphor in/and the law include: Milner S. Ball's, *Lying Down Together: Law, Metaphor, and Theology* (1985),[25] Haig A. Bosmajian's *Metaphor and Reason in Judicial Opinions* (1992),[26] and Steven L. Winter's *A Clearing in the Forest: Law, Life, and Mind* (2001).[27]

There can be little doubt that narrative and metaphor interact, and so one key goal of this volume is to explore the roles played by narrative and metaphor *in combination* in all aspects of the law. Very early on, historian Louis O. Mink asserted the equality of the two, stating: "Narrative is a primary cognitive instrument – an instrument rivalled only by theory and metaphor as irreducible

---

[17] Bernard J. Hibbitts, "Making sense of metaphors: Visuality, aurality, and the reconfiguration of American legal discourse," *Cardozo Law Review* 16 (1994), 229–356.

[18] Finn Makela, "Metaphors and models in legal theory," *Les Cahiers de droit*, 52 nos. 3–4, (September–December 2011), 397–415.

[19] Elizabeth G Thornburg. "Metaphors matter: How images of battle, sports, and sex shape the adversary system," *Wisconsin Women's Law Journal* 10 (1995), 225–281.

[20] Louis Henkin, "War and terrorism: Law or metaphor," *Santa Clara Law Review*, 45 (2005), 817–827.

[21] John Haynes, "Metaphor and mediation." Unpublished manuscript. Available on www.mediate.com/articles.

[22] Vicki C. Jackson, "Constitutions as 'Living Trees'? Comparative constitutional law and interpretive metaphors," *Fordham Law Review*, 75 (2006), 921–960.

[23] Katharine Young and Jeremy Perelman, "Rights as footprints: A new metaphor for contemporary human rights practice," *Northwestern Journal of International Human Rights* 9 no. 27 (2010), 27–58.

[24] Linda L. Berger, "Metaphor and analogy: The sun and moon of legal persuasion," *Journal of Law and Policy*, 22 (2013–2014), 147–195.

[25] Milner S. Ball, *Lying Down Together: Law, Metaphor, and Theology* (Madison, WI; London: University of Wisconsin Press, 1985).

[26] Haig A. Bosmajian, *Metaphor and Reason in Judicial Opinions* (Carbondale, IL SIU Press, 1992).

[27] Steven L. Winter, *A Clearing in the Forest: Law, Life, and Mind*, (Chicago, IL: University of Chicago Press, 2001).

ways of making the flux of experience comprehensible."[28] Our determination traces back to our observation that parallel assertions were made by thinkers from a range of disciplines about thirty years ago for the role of narrative and of metaphor as fundamental devices by which we interpret experience and organize our thoughts and actions.

On the one hand, Hayden White (history), Jerome Bruner (psychology), Roger Schank (cognitive science), Fredric Jameson (literary theory), Theodore Sarbin (psychology), and others asserted the fundamental role of narrative as a device by which human beings structure and give sense to experience. In Jameson's words, narrative is "the all-informing process ... the central function or *instance* of the human mind."[29] On the other hand, such scholars as George Lakoff (linguistics), Mark Johnson (philosophy), Andrew Ortony (cognitive science), Raymond Gibbs (psychology, another contributor to the present volume), and others were making equally grand claims for the fundamental role of metaphor. In the words of Lakoff and Johnson, "our ordinary conceptual system, in terms of which we both think and act, is fundamentally metaphorical in nature."[30]

The way in which modern narrative studies and modern metaphor studies burgeoned separately but alongside each other at this time is nicely epitomized by the holding of key conferences in successive years at the University of Chicago, entitled "Metaphor: The Conceptual Leap" (1978) and "Narrative: The Illusion of Sequence" (1979), with papers from these two conferences being subsequently published as *On Metaphor* (1979)[31] and *On Narrative* (1980–1981).[32] These two volumes serve in many ways as the foundation rocks on which modern metaphor studies and narrative studies have been built.

Thinkers in other fields to hazard opinions on the relationship between narrative and metaphor include: philosopher Paul Ricoeur, who asserted that they were both examples of "semantic innovation"[33] and economic theorist Deirdre (formerly Donald) McCloskey, who insisted that they function in complementary fashion: "there seem to be two ways of understanding things;

---

[28] Louis O. Mink, "Narrative form as a cognitive instrument" in Robert H. Canary and Henry Kosicki (eds.), *The Writing of History: Literary Form and Historical Understanding* (Madison, WI: University of Wisconsin Press, 1978), pp. 129–149, 131.
[29] Frederic Jameson, *The Political Unconscious: Narrative as a Socially Symbolic Act* (Ithaca, NY: Cornell University Press, 1981), p. 13.
[30] George Lakoff and Mark Johnson, *Metaphors We Live By* (Chicago, IL: Chicago University Press, 1980), p. 3.
[31] Sheldon Sacks (ed.), *On Metaphor* (Chicago, IL: University of Chicago Press, 1979).
[32] W.J.T. Mitchell (ed.), *On Narrative* (Chicago, IL: University of Chicago Press, 1981).
[33] Paul Ricoeur, *Time and Narrative*, vol. 1, trans. Kathleen McLaughlin and David Pellauer (Chicago, IL: Chicago University Press, 1984), p. ix.

either by way of narrative or by way of metaphor," and that the relationship between them is "antiphonal" (that is: they sing to each other).[34]

As we have noted previously, research on narrative in the law and research on metaphor in the law have tended to run in parallel with each other. Nevertheless, it should be pointed out that James Boyd White's *The Legal Imagination*, which we have already referred to as one of the earliest sources of interest in narrative and the law, gives almost equal attention to metaphor. Steven L. Winter's *A Clearing in the Forest* likewise explores the interaction of narrative and metaphor in the law. Three of the contributors to the current volume, Laurence Rosen (a legal anthropologist), Linda L. Berger (a scholar in legal rhetoric) and L. David Ritchie (a communications specialist), have all from their various disciplinary standpoints explored aspects of the law employing the narrative perspective and the metaphor perspective in combination.[35]

Linda Berger offers this overview of the function of narrative and metaphor:

> Metaphor and narrative reassure us that things hang together, providing a sense of coherence to the patterns and paths we employ for perception and expression, Without the metaphorical process that allows us to gather them up, group them together, and contain them, our perceptions would scatter like marbles thrown on the ground. Without the ability to tell stories that link discrete events together, place them into a storyline with a beginning and an end, and compose a coherent accounting, our lives would be constructed on "One Damn Thing After Another."[36]

In this collection, we aim to show even more strongly how things "hang together" by combining the narrative perspective and the metaphor perspective.

THE NARRATIVE/METAPHOR NEXUS PROJECT

The conference in early 2016 at Stanford University Law School which spawned the papers collected in this volume is the fourth of a series of five conferences, collectively entitled The Narrative/Metaphor Nexus,[37] exploring

---

[34] Donald McCloskey, "Storytelling in economics" in Cristopher Nash (ed.), *Narrative in Culture: The Uses of Storytelling in the Sciences, Philosophy and Literature* (London; New York, NY: Routledge, 1990), pp. 5–22.

[35] Lawrence Rosen, *Law as Culture: an Invitation* (Princeton, NJ: Princeton University Press, 2006); Linda L. Berger, "The lady or the tiger: A field guide to metaphor and narrative," *Washburn Law Journal*, 50 (2010–2011), 275–318; L. David Ritchie, "'Everybody goes down': Metaphors, stories, and simulations in conversations," *Metaphor and Symbol*, 25 (2010), 123–143.

[36] Berger, "The lady or the tiger," 275.

[37] The website narrativemetaphornexus.weebly.com offers an overview of these conferences and the publications generated by them.

the nature of the narrative-metaphor connection in each of a range of disciplines, from medicine to politics to the law to education. Michael Hanne, one of the editors of this volume, has helped to convene all of these gatherings. Hanne has argued that employing narrative and metaphor in combination allows us to see issues with "binocular vision" (that is, stereoscopically, through the lens of narrative and the lens of metaphor together).

These explorations across several disciplines have revealed considerable commonality among them in their use of narrative and metaphor. So, for instance, there is a tendency for the disciplinary discourse in all fields to be captured by conventional metaphors and stock narratives, which limit innovation in thought and practice. There are, moreover, many striking points of overlap between disciplines, for instance, with medical metaphors being employed by political leaders and metaphors of warfare being found in medical discourse. Indeed, the question arises in more than one of the papers for the present volume as to whether medical metaphors such as "crime as disease" and military metaphors such as "the war on drugs" have value in the legal context.

Nevertheless, there are many examples of divergence among the disciplines. So, in a number of fields, medicine and education, for example, interest in the role of narrative is particularly strong, and study of the role of metaphor is less developed and more fragmentary. We suggest that this has occurred for somewhat the same reasons as the priority given to study of narrative in the law – the many kinds of narrative in all three disciplines are more readily seen as accumulating into a coherent whole than is the case with the rather disparate array of metaphors.[38]

In other disciplines, politics, for example, the study of metaphor is more advanced. This may well be because it is so difficult to bring the many narratives at play in even a single political context together for analysis. Moreover, the main texts employed in the study of political discourse are the speeches, interviews, and writings of political actors and it is relatively easy – and very fruitful – to identify metaphor patterns in such texts.[39]

---

[38] See: Michael Hanne: "The binocular vision project: An introduction" in "Binocular Vision: Narrative and Metaphor in Medicine," special issue of *Genre: Forms of Discourse and Culture*, 44 no. 3 (Fall 2011), 223–237 and the website of the upcoming conference "Look Both Ways: Narrative and Metaphors in Education" https://named2017conference.com/.

[39] See, for instance: Jonathan Charteris-Black, *Politicians and Rhetoric: The Persuasive Power of Metaphor* (Basingstoke; New York, NY: Palgrave Macmillan, 2005) and, more broadly, Michael Hanne, "An introduction to the 'Warring with Words' project" in Michael Hanne, William D. Crano, and Jeffery Scott Mio (eds.), *Warring with Words: Narrative and Metaphor in Politics* (New York, NY; Hove: Psychology Press, 2015), pp. 1–50.

ORGANIZATION OF THIS VOLUME

Papers collected in this volume examine the part played by narrative and metaphor under nine broad headings: Concepts of Justice and Legal Systems, Legal Persuasion, Judicial Opinions, Gender in the Law, Innovations in Legal Thinking, Public Debate around Crime, Human Rights Law, Creative Writing by Lawyers, Legal and Political Activism. This ensures that the spotlight is directed in turn toward each of the areas of theory and practice in the law in which narrative and metaphor feature most prominently.

The contributors are an outstanding team of theorists and practitioners who take up issues within these broad areas and are a mix of: legal scholars who have previously written notable works on narrative or metaphor in the law (only a minority, as we have seen, have previously employed both a narrative lens *and* a metaphor lens on legal issues); and scholars from disciplines as diverse as linguistics, communication studies, literary studies, psychology etc.

The book is set up as a series of "conversations" on topics within these broad areas. The nature of these conversations varies greatly. In some instances, the opening paper is met with a direct response or commentary from the second author; in others, the relation between the two pieces is much looser; in the case of the chapter on "Narrative, Metaphor, and Gender in the Law," the two authors had a prolonged conversation over some months out of which grew a jointly written paper. The last conversation takes the form of an interview, conducted after the Stanford symposium which generated all the other papers, between one of the editors and outstanding social and political activist and law professor Mari Matsuda.

Each "conversation" is preceded by some brief "framing comments" in which the editors seek to locate the specific issues taken up in the conversation itself in relation to the broad heading under which they appear. So, for instance, the pair of papers by Roberto H. Potter and Robert Weisberg explore the theoretical and practical implications of viewing crime as disease, that is, through the lens offered by epidemiology. Their conversation appears under the banner of Narrative, Metaphor, and Innovations in Legal Thinking, so the framing comments that precede the papers draw attention to other metaphors and associated narratives that have been employed innovatively in relation to areas of the law. In addition, the framing comments seek to highlight significant connections, parallels, and conflicts among the various conversations and, indeed, between narrative and metaphor usage in legal contexts and in the usage of disciplines as diverse as medicine and politics.

CONVERSATION I
NARRATIVE, METAPHOR, AND CONCEPTS OF JUSTICE AND LEGAL SYSTEMS

Editors' Introduction

Michael Hanne and Robert Weisberg

As befits its place in the volume, this conversation addresses very foundational questions on our subject.

The notion that law involves, or depends on, narrative has become downright intuitive – even cliché to both those inside and outside the legal system. So the scholarly challenge on that topic is to get past the vague performative utterances about the intimacy of law and narrative and to break down the many varieties of, and contradictions in, that relationship – a challenge many conversations in this volume address. By contrast, the relationship between law and metaphor is not so obvious to many. And yet a legitimate if rhetorical response to someone asking what law has to do with metaphor (or vice versa) is to ask, "How can you even talk about – even conceive – legal principles and legal institutions without metaphor? Indeed, just listen to yourself when you talk about law!"

Consider that over the centuries and across cultures, philosophers and legal scholars have relied on numerous metaphors to capture their sense of the meanings and manifestations of justice ("order," "balance," "uprightness" (Confucius), "harmony," "blindness," " etc.).[1] Equally, metaphor seems indispensable in describing judicial systems, which tend to be broadly distinguished in terms of governing metaphors, e.g., inquisitorial systems (where judges are actively involved in investigating the facts) and adversarial systems (where the judge is primarily an impartial referee between the plaintiff or prosecution and the defendant). In non-Western cultures, other metaphors are employed, e.g. the literal translation of Sharia (law) is "the path to the waterhole." Within Western law, metaphorical nouns such as

---

[1] Milner S. Ball, *Lying Down Together: Law, Metaphor, and Theology* (Madison, WI; London: University of Wisconsin Press, 1985).

"body (of law)," "conflict," "weight," "chains," "contract," "debt (to society)" recur, alongside verbs such as "disobey," "break," "bend," "entrench," etc. Within our own legal system metaphors help us comprehend differences among legal theories. Thus, in American constitutional law we see metaphors drawn from physics and engineering ("balances," "checks," "anchors," "force," "a machine that would go of itself") or organic and biological discourse ("organism," "living breathing being"),[2] and these phrasings also help in comparative constitutional law.

Different metaphors for legal systems or principles are crucial for telling us about the underlying differences among legal cultures. The "living tree doctrine," which holds that the Canadian Constitution should be interpreted in a broad manner, taking account of changing social and cultural conditions, has been entrenched in Canadian constitutional law for over eighty years, in preference to the "frozen rights" approach (or, in the words of Justice Ian Binnie, "a dead tree" approach![3]), whereby the Constitution should be interpreted entirely in terms of the original intent of those who framed it. An alternative metaphor for the "living tree doctrine," uttered in a key 1992 decision in the United States Supreme Court, refers to the constitution as a "a *covenant* running from the first generation of Americans to us and then to future generations ... a coherent succession."[4] The covenant metaphor (with its Judeo-Christian connotations), of course, has a strongly narrative dimension and has been viewed by narrative scholars primarily in terms of its narrative value. So, according to Peter Brooks, it is a "master narrative into which each new narrative episode must be fitted."[5]

So back to narrative. As Greta Olson observes in the first part of this opening conversation, lawyers and legal scholars have embraced the role of narrative in law far more readily than is the case with metaphor. Perhaps the reason is that at least in the common law and adversarial traditions, and particularly because of media depictions of law, we associate law with the narrative drama of the criminal trial, the view of lawyers (including the self-congratulatory view of trial lawyers) as creative rhetorical artists offering competing narratives in trials with judge and jury deciding between them. (And, of course this association

---

[2] Vicki C. Jackson, "Constitutions as 'Living Trees'? Comparative constitutional law and interpretive metaphors," *Fordham Law Review*, 75 (2006), 921–960.
[3] Ian Binnie, "Interpreting the Constitution: The living tree vs. original meaning," *Policy Options* (October 2007), 104–110. http://irpp.org/assets/po/free-trade-20/binnie.pdf.
[4] *Planned Parenthood of Southeastern Pa. v. Casey*, 505 U.S. 833, 901 (1992). (emphasis supplied).
[5] Peter Brooks, "Narrative in and of the Law." *A Companion to Narrative Theory*. James Phelan and Peter J. Rabinowitz (eds.). (Malden, MA: Blackwell Publishing, 2005), pp. 415–426.

invites a useful comparison to the inquisitorial systems, which instead assign the narrative task to the judges, who must construct the most plausible story from evidence presented on both sides.) In addition, at least among common law legal scholars, much attention is paid to the artistry of appellate judges in narrating the facts of cases as an inherent part of the reasoning in the ultimate holding. Further still, the common-law tradition often views the role of precedent in appellate reasoning as a narrative or evolutionary process of iterative refinement of background doctrine in light of new circumstances, as is famously illustrated by Ronald Dworkin's depiction of doctrinal development as a "chain novel."[6]

Greta Olson takes up several major issues in her paper. Intriguingly, she "narrates" the development and consolidation of narrative legal studies since the "narrative turn" which took place more broadly in the social sciences in the 1980s. But she also takes a more abstract conceptual turn in urging legal scholars to advance their understanding of legal narrative by attending to the very vital distinctions made by theoretical narratologists among the concepts of "narrative," "narration," and "narrativity" and between "story" and "discourse." She also contributes to comparative treatment of the subject, detailing the important differences between the operation of narrative in the Anglo-American common law system (where alternative stories are presented in an adversarial context) and narrative in the codified legal systems of Continental Europe (where a tentative narrative must be constructed before the trial begins and amended in an inquisitorial manner as the trial progresses).

As for metaphor, Olson directly addresses the different recent fates of narrative and metaphor in terms of emphasis on or acknowledgment of them in law. For one thing, she takes account of the *suspicion* of metaphor as too distortive, or manipulative, or even frivolous to play a role in the magisterial rationality of law. She thus reviews the many utterances of this sort over the last century by judges and legal scholars in both the common law and codified law systems, yet highlights the extent to which those critics of metaphor themselves resort to lively and effective metaphors in their own writing. On the other hand, Olson underscores the ways in which narrative may be just as culpable as metaphor in distorting reality yet is more readily

---

[6] Stefanie A. Lindquist and Frank B. Cross, "Empirically testing Dworkin's chain novel theory studying the path of precedent," *NYU Law Review*, 80 (October 2005), 1156–1206. www.nyulawreview.org/sites/default/files/pdf/NYULawReview-80-4-Lindquist-Cross.pdf.

accepted by legal commentators. But more importantly, she argues that scholars who consider the role of metaphor in the law have mostly failed to keep pace with developments in metaphor theory among linguists and cognitive scientists, who see metaphor as featuring in every kind of speech, and so, inevitably, in legal discourse.

Olson concludes that the metaphoricity and narrative quality of the law should be embraced equally, because narrative and metaphor are both fundamental devices by which we interpret, and articulate our understanding of, the world. Specifically, she argues that narrative and metaphor feature in combination in the construction of legal fictions and counterfactuals, which are essential to the functioning of the law.

Whereas Olson shows how legal scholars have given favored status to narrative in their discussions and seeks to claim an equal place for metaphor, legal anthropologist Lawrence Rosen, the second contributor to the chapter, insists on the centrality of metaphor, not simply in legal discourse, but in the categories by which a culture conceives of itself. Metaphor, he says, captures what we take to be reality. His paper focuses specifically on the legal consequences of a clash of fundamental metaphors in different cultures.

In particular, he explores in detail the very different metaphors by which Western cultures and indigenous cultures conceive of what we call "property." Whereas Western (especially American) cultures almost uniformly see property of all kinds as individually owned, indigenous cultures employ a wide range of metaphors, including organic and collective metaphors and metaphors of heritage, identity, and relationship. As Rosen shows, each metaphor embodies a rather different implied narrative. International law, he observes, especially law around intellectual property, is usually based narrowly on Western metaphors of individual property, and rarely takes into account the very different metaphorical conceptions of property held by indigenous cultures.

1

On Narrating and Troping the Law: The Conjoined Use of Narrative and Metaphor in Legal Discourse

Greta Olson

In this essay, I want to make a series of six interrelated arguments about the place of narrative and metaphor in law.[1] The first is that there has been a narrative turn in legal studies, whereby what was once considered a problematic quality of narrative, its potential to fictionalize, has now been recognized as a basic part of legal discourse and legal interpretation. In fact, and as a second point, the use of "narrative" to describe any number of phenomena related to law has increased exponentially so that it proves important to differentiate various aspects of narrative definitionally so that these terms can be used with greater precision. A third point concerns the need for contextual specificity when discussing narrative in the law. There are areas in which narrative functions differently in the legal processes that have grown out of the Roman and common-law traditions. Yet the use of narrative also varies in different types of law within a given system. My fourth argument is that, by stark contrast to its narrativity, the metaphoricity of law continues to be largely overlooked in legal studies. Associated with slippage, ideology, and rhetoric, metaphor is figured as law's unconscious, or it is disparaged as a vehicle of distortion. Because the mental leap of metaphorical mapping is immediate rather than sequential and entails the transference of qualities associated with the source domain onto the target one, metaphor usage is viewed generally as a less helpful tool than narrative to explain legal phenomena or to make legal arguments.

I follow on these points with a defense of metaphoricity in law and legal discourse (argument 5) that suggests that it may be helpful to consider tropes and narrative structures as conjoined mental processes and forms of

---

[1] My sincere thanks go to Birte Christ, Franz Reimer, and Natalya Bekhta for their critical comments on earlier iterations of this essay as well as to the editors of this volume. My gratitude also goes to Lisa Beckmann, Maren Walinski, and Madeline Kienzle for research assistance and to Stefanie Rück for proofreading.

articulation rather than separate ones. One of the editors of this volume, Michael Hanne, has termed this complementary focus on narrative and metaphor as a "binocular vision," a perspective largely absent in scholarship, with scholars attesting either to narrative or metaphorical frameworks.[2] In the final and sixth step of this essay, I posit that the use of metaphors functions, like the construction of mental inventions more generally, as a strategy for finding legal solutions where none are immediately in the offing. If framed as a form of fictionality – a rhetorical move to state that something is generally if not specifically true – which I outline in the last part of this essay, then the use of narrative and metaphor can be thought of as strategies for dealing with areas of legal opacity. The sum of these arguments points to what I believe is the intrinsically interrelated nature of metaphor and narrative in law and legal discourse.

THE NARRATIVE TURN

The centrality of narrative elements to law has become a truism in legal studies, most particularly since Peter Brooks made his programmatic call for a legal narratology, suggesting that this had been lacking heretofore.[3] Whereas some still claim that legal practitioners dismiss the importance of understanding narrative,[4] I would argue that this form of analysis has gained widespread credibility. Consensus now has it that narrativization – that is, rendering information into a story consisting of agents, a context, events or plot elements, and the representation of a human-like experience – is central to human sense-making as well as to identity formation. Distinct narrative elements underlie not only constitutions, with their identity-coalescing elements for national collectives. They are also intrinsic to the histories of statutes, ordinances, and cases; and storytelling elements are part of abstract legal norms and hypotheticals, which have to be interpreted using narrative means.[5] Further, the evaluation of competing stories is inherent to common-law trials; and creating

---

[2] Michael Hanne, "The binocular vision project: An introduction," Genre, 44 no. 3 (Fall 2011), 222–237, at 224. The present volume goes toward redressing the absence of such work.
[3] Peter Brooks, "Narrative in and of the law," James Phelan and Peter J. Rabinowitz (eds.), A Companion to Narrative Theory (Malden, MA: Blackwell, 2005), no pag.
[4] Simon Stern, "Legal and literary fictions," in Elizabeth Anker and Bernadette Meyler (eds.) New Directions in Law and Literature (Oxford: Oxford University Press, 2017), pp. 313–326.
[5] Werner Wolf argues that the more linguistically based a text is, the more inherently narrative it is and shall therefore also elicit practices of narrativization. See Wolf, "Narratology and media (lity): The transmedial expansion of a literary discipline and possible consequences," in Greta Olson (ed.), Current Trends in Narratology (Berlin; New York, NY: De Gruyter, 2011), pp. 145–180, and elsewhere.

pre- and posttrial narratives of the "facts" of a given case constitutes part of the investigatory procedure in codified law ones.[6]

A narrative turn occurred during the 1980s in US scholarship. Robert Cover's seminal "Nomos and narrative" (1983) and "Violence and the word" (1986) marked important foundational moments in this passage. Cover's oft-quoted statement that "[n]o set of legal institutions or prescriptions exists apart from the narratives that locate it and give it meaning" is followed by a footnote about the ubiquity of narrative that bears paying close attention to: "It is the diffuse and unprivileged character of narrative in a modern world, together with the indispensability of narrative to the quest for meaning, that is a principal focus of this Foreword."[7] Volumes such as *Law's Stories* (1996) were also widely recognized, and with increasing ubiquity the common-law trial was described to be a "contest of stories."[8]

In particular, Jerome Bruner's work on law and narrative and on the narrative construction of reality was of import. Bruner is widely accredited with having popularized the thesis that identity is constructed through narrative means, with the "Self as a storyteller."[9] By no means uncontroversial, Bruner's narrative thesis has been countered by Galen Strawson, who argues against the implicit moralism in Bruner's model and proposes instead that the self is episodically and non-diachronically constituted.[10] Subsequently, Bruner has analyzed all law as having a narrative structure – "To sum up, law stories are narrative in structure, adversarial in spirit, inherently rhetorical in aim, and justifiably open to suspicion."[11]

I rehearse important moments in the narrative study of law here, yet also want to point out that they cohere with the larger occurrence of understanding the social sciences and scientific commentary to be narratively constructed. Hayden White pointed out that even with the most minimal of evidence, such

---

[6] Greta Olson, "Narration and narrative in legal discourse," in Peter Hühn et al. (eds.), *Handbook of Narratology*, vol. I (Berlin; Boston, MA: de Gruyter, 2014), pp. 371–383. Since the differentiation between "civil law systems" and "common law" ones may be easily confused with the delineation made between civil and criminal law in primarily Anglophone common law systems, I use expressions such as "Civilian law," "Roman law" or "codified law system" in the following.

[7] Robert Cover, "*Nomos* and Narrative," *Narrative, Violence and the Law*, ed. Cover et al. (Ann Arbor, MI: Michigan University Press, 1993 [1983]), pp. 95–172, at 95–96.

[8] Peter Brooks and Paul Gewirtz, *Law's Stories: Narrative and Rhetoric in the Law* (New Haven, CT; London: Yale University Press, 1996).

[9] Jerome Bruner, "Autobiography of the self," *Acts of Meaning* (Cambridge, MA: Harvard University Press, 1990), pp. 99–138, at 111.

[10] Galen Strawson, "Against narrativity," *Ratio*, 18 (2004), 428–452.

[11] Jerome Bruner, *Making Stories: Law, Literature, Life* (Cambridge, MA: Harvard University Press, 1990), p. 43.

as dates listed in annals, historians employ story "and plot elements in historical discourse."[12] That history, which had previously been predicated on the understanding of its results as fact-driven objective accounts rather than as constructed, was now shown to be narratively based, highlighted the narrativity of that other would-be rational domain of human activity, the law. Thus Doris Bachmann-Medick has defined *turns* in scholarship as the juncture at which a new concept or methodology begins to be seen amongst several disciplines simultaneously, suggesting a larger change in ways of conceptualizing.[13]

There are problematic aspects of the narrative turn. One, those interested in narrative may neglect other aspects of law and legal process. Simon Stern argues that non-lawyers, for instance, tend to focus exclusively on legal phenomena that are strongly narrative such as Supreme Court judgments, where they may then exercise their text-exegetical expertise. This occurs to the detriment of attention to less narratively based legal phenomena, such as procedure and ordinances.[14]

Two, in his extensive critique of human rights discourse and its interrelation to the narrative elements of the Bildungsroman, Joseph Slaughter has pointed to the ubiquity and vagueness of the use of "narrative" in legal studies:

> Very often, analyses that invoke narratology tend to reify narrative as the founding articulation of *homo significans*, leaving the structures, capacities and activities of narrative itself unproblematized. In other words, narrative becomes an Archimedean point by positing it as a universal, innate human capacity that is shared by all people, even when it is recognized as contingent upon particular socio-historico-cultural formations.[15]

Like Strawson, Slaughter criticizes the essentialist assumptions about humans as narrating beings that underlie narrative studies of law. Such assumptions, on the one hand, ignore the socio-historical specificity of narrational settings and forms; on the other hand, they occlude the ideological uses of narrative in nation building.

---

[12] Hayden White, "The value of narrativity in the representation of reality," *Critical Inquiry* 1 (1980), 5–27, at 23.
[13] Doris Bachmann-Medick, *Cultural Turns: New Orientations in the Study of Culture*, trans. Adam Blauhut (Berlin/Boston, MA: de Gruyter, 2016).
[14] Simon Stern, "Literary evidence and legal aesthetics," in Austin Sarat, Matthew Anderson, and Catherine O. Frank (eds.), *Teaching Literature and Law: MLA Approaches to Teaching Series* (New York, NY: Modern Language Association, 2011), pp. 244–252.
[15] Joseph Slaughter, *Human Rights, Inc.: The World Novel, Narrative Form, and International Law* (New York, NY: Fordham University Press, 2007), p. 336.

In response to Slaughter's diagnosis of the generalized, uncritical use of *narrative*, I wish to voice a further caveat concerning the narrative turn in legal studies. The lexeme *narrative* is invoked to describe any manner of phenomena. This includes the history of a given legal culture, the aesthetic evocation of a story in a given text, a legal-political trend, as well as the history of a given case or legal norm as well as more specific aspects of legal storytelling, including narration, and what narratologists refer to as *discourse*. This expansive use of *narrative*, I contest, is deleterious to determining the narrational and narrative aspects of law and legal discourse, that is the specific connection between the formal aspect of the telling and its more generalizable function.

DOWN THE RABBIT-HOLE OF NARRATIVE

In a minimalistic overview of insights from the field, a narratologist would distinguish between the following aspects of narrative and narration that are often all loosely referred to as *narrative*. Before the more legally inclined reader turns away her head thinking, what a terminological pain in the ass, let me explain briefly why this is important. A central tenet of narrative theory that has been adapted from its Russian formalist forebears is that isolated narrational forms have quite specific functions that are operable in all settings.

Why is this important? In regarding legal discourse and legal processes critically, it is important to delineate specific aspects of narrative in order to better sort out how minimal elements influence legal processes. On an epistemological level, narrative analysis helps to comprehend specific aspects of the process by which we understand things through storytelling elements. Since storytelling structures shape people's political commitments, the isolation of their discrete forms in law contributes to determining if the effects of these forms function to reify or undermine dominant legal processes.[16]

Narrative and *narration* need to be distinguished from one another as synonyms for story and as the act of telling. The former term may be understood in the following ways in legal discourse. *Narratives* minimally include agents with human-like subjectivity, involve changes or a description of human-like experience, and take place in some identifiable space and time. As in all legal processes, narratives are told by someone (the narrator) to someone else (the narratee or audience) for a specific purpose.[17] Here, it is

---

[16] Greta Olson and Sarah Copland, "Towards a politics of form," *European Journal of English Studies*, 20 no. 3 (2016), 207–221.

[17] I am paraphrasing James Phelan on narrative in James Phelan, *Living to Tell about It: A Rhetoric and Ethics of Character Narration* (Ithaca, NY: Cornell University Press, 2005), p. 15.

appropriate to speak of the entirety of a witness's or a plaintiff's story or the larger stories of law, including the history of a legal case such as, in the US context, *Brown v. Board of Education*, or in the Roman law tradition of the evolving interpretive conceptualization of a given legal concept or norm.

Narrative is used in conjunction with law as follows. To describe

1. the stories told within legal proceedings including non-trial procedures as well as the accounts of those proceedings;
2. *Narratives* are also used to describe examinations of legal discourse as a form of rhetoric.
3. Narrative studies of law also elucidate legal interpretation as a process by which issues such as plain meaning, intentionality, and purposiveness are derived through linguistic and contextual study. In German, this is called *Methodenlehre* (the theory of methods); in Anglo-American common law, this includes general guidelines of interpretation, including the emphasis on coherence, precedent, and analogy, and in constitutional jurisprudence, the tension between originalist, intentionalist, and organic schools of interpretation.
4. Larger narratives about what law does, what might be called law's *grand récit*, are also scrutinized. For instance, does law produce or ameliorate suffering, violence, and conflict, and against which members of a society are legally enforced forms of control directed?

Narration, in contrast to *narrative*, describes the act of relating. In an asylum law case this would be the act of the asylum seeker's telling and later retelling of her story to authorities. Since testimony is essential to cases regarding criminal law, refugee status, and, for instance, domestic violence, the assessment of the coherence of the teller's manner to the generic expectations of how one should bear witness is crucial. Here, as Cover once so wisely wrote, is an illustration of how "[l]egal interpretation takes place in a field of pain and death."[18] The act of telling is separate from what is told and how it is told; the differentiation between the what and how is described narratologically using the terms *story* and *discourse*. This differentiation matters, in turn, because the how of the testimonial telling is intrinsic to the evaluation of its credibility.

Story in narratology denotes what a jurist might call the facts of a case, or the known sequence of events. This might be the tale that the putative asylum seeker tells about the reasons she was forced to leave her country of origin and how she traveled to the place in which she is seeking asylum. *Discourse*, by contrast, describes the form that the narrative takes, including the perspective

---

[18] Robert M. Cover, "Violence and the word," *The Yale Law Journal*, 95 no. 8 (1986), 1601–1629.

from which the story is told, for instance, from a position within or outside of the story world, and in a first- or third-person voice, and from a singular perspective or multiple ones. *Discourse,* or the form of the telling, is typically used in contradistinction to *story* (what happened). The how of her tale might include the pauses the refugee seeker makes when she describes her tale to authorities, the moving backwards and forward in the chronology of events, and the affective level with which she tells her story, etc.

The next two differentiations refer to the cognitive processes by which humans produce and process narratives. *Narrativity* describes the degree to which a text or object possesses qualities that elicit thinking structures that lead people to treat and engage with it as a narrative. As the complementary term, *narrativization* describes the procedure by which a text is processed in someone's mind in response to its story-like qualities. This points to a prototype theory of narrative akin to Eleanor Rosch's insight that rather than a binary system of semantic analysis, in other words "man" is [+ male/ − female, + adult/− child], etc., humans think in terms of things belonging more or less to category types. Thus, in the classic example, some birds such as robins are regarded as more prototypical of the category "bird" or bird-like than are, for instance, ostriches or turkeys, which are both seen as less bird-like.[19] How prototypically narrative-like accounts are adjudged to be determines how they are dealt with in legal processes. Accordingly, the greater the perceived degree of narrativity, the more a given document or a piece of testimony is treated as narrative and likened to other prototypical narratives considered appropriate to the given legal setting.

ON THE NECESSITY OF SPECIFICITY IN NARRATIVE ANALYSES OF THE LAW

As legal systems and cultures become more hybrid and pluralist, or as Russell Miller has argued, even competitive within themselves as to their systemic allegiances,[20] it may be an increasingly strained point to insist on any radical dissimilarities between the uses and functions of narrative in the Roman- and common-law traditions and the legal systems that have grown out of them. The typical binary division of families of law and their trial processes is misleading, because it occludes the adversarial elements that also characterize legal systems not based on common law. Nonetheless, one needs to guard

---

[19] Eleanor Rosch, "Natural categories," *Cognitive Psychology,* 4 (1973), pp. 328–350.
[20] Russell A. Miller, "Germany's German constitution," *Virginia Journal of International Law* 57 (forthcoming), no pag.

against the assumption in so much Anglophone legal scholarship that common-law legal procedures are universal. Thus, in this section, I argue for the need for context-specific narrative analyses of law. On the assumption that readers of this text are more familiar with common law, I shall first concentrate on differences in trial procedures in relation to narrative in different types of German law. I then go on to discuss some large-scale differences.

In civil-law cases in Germany, plaintiffs determine whether or not a given case goes to court. They bear responsibility to provide accounts of the facts – the competing narratives – and the evidence upon which the court will base its decision.[21] This process is comparable to common-law trials in which two alternative narratives are constructed simultaneously by the adversarial parties; if a case goes to trial, these counternarratives are presented synchronically and competitively before a jury and the presiding judge.

In German criminal law, by contrast to civil law, a single narrative about a crime has to be constructed during the pretrial phase, according to the inquisitorial principle. On the basis of the public prosecutor's narrative (her readings of the materials contributing to the putative case), it is established whether or not a certain case is judicable. Then the, in traditional although somewhat misleading terminology, inquisitorial judge or judges examine the materials, conduct any necessary fact-finding, and amend these materials during the trial by examining witnesses, and, in complex cases, also summarizing previous results and findings at key points. Thus the judges behave more like narrators who fulfill the "who says" function in storytelling. By contrast, judges in common-law cases could be described, like jury members, as being more like narratees, those to whom the (competing) stories are told.

John Langbein has described German civil trial procedure as "episodic" rather than, as in common law, "continuous," because the judge narrates the status of the case at important intervals.[22] The judge or judges render judgment subsequently in a written narration of the *Tatbestand* (facts underlying the sentence including the reasons for the application of law that decided the case); thereby a conclusive narrative comes into being in addition to the hearing summaries, which may of course be challenged in appellate decisions.

For a brief overview of such a written judgment in German law, allow me to use the record from the judicial review of a case that had been handled by an

---

[21] This is based on the principle of party presentation (the *Beibringungsgrundsatz*). See Michael Fehling, Berthold Kastner, Rainer Störmer (eds.), *Verwaltungsrecht: VwVfG – VwGO – Nebengesetze, Handkommentar, Vierte Auflage* (Baden-Baden: Nomos, 2016).
[22] John Langbein, "The German advantage in civil procedure," *University of Chicago Law Review* (Fall 1985), no pag. http://chicagounbound.uchicago.edu/uclrev/vol52/iss4/1/. Accessed 17 Feb. 2017.

administrative authority. The original case concerned Azerbaijani plaintiffs who had been granted asylum in Germany several years beforehand and wished to change their first and last names to less foreign-sounding ones.[23] The stated reasons for the desired name change included the family's desire to avoid political persecution from fellow Azerbaijanis, to have an easier time finding jobs in Germany, and to become fully integrated.

The written account of the judicial review begins with a recording of the guiding legal principle that determined the outcome of the case, in this case the statement that "The desire to be integrated does not in itself represent an essential reason for changing a foreign name." The case is then identified with a file number designating the court in which it was tried and the trial date. Then a short narrative of the case is given. In this case, the plaintiffs' efforts to change their name and the administrative authority's rejection of their claim is related. Then the *Entscheidungsgründe* are named, the reasons for the judgment. A reference to the relevant statute in administrative law is given, and all other relevant deeds and orders are named regarding refugee law, permissible legal reasons for changing names, etc. Other precedent cases are named, thus once again demonstrating what might be perceived as an overlap of guiding methodological principles between common-law precedential systems and those resting primarily on the application of codified law. Finally, a summary is given, in which it is stated that the hearing did not change the court's opinion; and therefore the plaintiffs have to carry the costs of the case.[24]

Despite overlaps between systems and internal points of convergence, some general differences between the role of narrative in Continental and common law pertain. For example, the creation of legal narratives in judgment has been described as a more hermeneutical process in judge-driven Continental law courts than in common-law ones. Jeanne Gaakeer depicts this process as a continuous back-and-forth on the judge's part between the legal norm and the case at hand. Therefore, she criticizes Monika Fludernik's contention that legal code disguises its own narrativity to appear objective and to suppress the contingency of individual stories involving the transgression of the rule.[25]

---

[23] German public law is more restrictive than US law regarding name assignments and name changes. First names must reflect a person's gender categorization, family names cannot be used as first names, and fantasy names are not permissible. See Anon, "What's-In-a-Name? German naming laws remain Byzantine," *Spiegel Online*, 5 May 2009. www.spiegel.de/international/ger many/what-s-in-a-name-german-naming-laws-remain-byzantine-a-622912.html. Accessed Feb. 17, 2017.
[24] V. G. Göttingen, Urteil von 25 April 2012, Az. 4 A 18/11. Accessed Feb. 17, 2017.
[25] Monika Fludernik, "A narratology of the law? Narratives in legal discourse," *Critical Analysis of the Law*, 1 no.1 (2014), 87–109.

Gaakeer points out that what are seen as non-narratively organized ordinances in common law have to be understood differently in statute-based Continental settings. In the latter, the judge assumes herself to be the addressee of the ordinance. Her task is then to narrativize the ordinance and apply it to the case at hand. According to Gaakeer, Fludernik confuses common-law jurisdictions and their codes with those based in Roman laws such as those in Continental Europe. In these jurisdictions, "the addressee of the rule is the judge," who has to apply it to the situation (*Tatbestand*) at hand and not to the implicit addressee of the individual citizen, with her or his singular story. Gaakeer thus argues that "European jurisdictions deserve the kind of analysis Fludernik performs on American statutes."[26]

Wilhelm Schapp examined the role of narrative in law in a discussion that long precedes better-known Anglophone ones. In a tellingly entitled monograph *In Geschichten verstrickt: Zum Sein von Mensch und Ding* (1953) (Ensnared in Stories: On the Being of Human and Thing), Schapp explicates the fundamentally narrative quality of law in Continental legal systems. He points out that legal cases can only be extracted from individual human stories through processes of abstraction – a principle of Roman law – in which the humanness of the story is obfuscated even if it remains stubbornly and spectrally present in the case. As he writes, "every case also represents a raped story [...]. On the basis of this insight, one can place civil law under the most general principle of good faith and trust, or one creates, in penal law, the range of sentences that make it possible to pass judgment on 'the same thing' in various ways."[27] I wholly support Gaakeer's call for a more nuanced narratology of law, one that accounts for historical, geographical, and systemic differentiations in narrative use and also for the cultural specificity of the context in which the adjudication takes place.[28]

---

[26] Jeanne Gaakeer, "The perplexity of judges becomes the scholar's opportunity," in Greta Olson and Franz Reimer (eds.), Special Issue on "Law's Pluralities" of the *German Law Journal*, 18, no. 2 (2017), no pag.

[27] Wilhelm Schapp, *In Geschichten verstrickt* (Frankfurt: Klostermann, 1953): "und dass jeder Fall gleichsam eine vergewaltigte Geschichte ist [...]. Aus dieser Einsicht heraus stellt man etwas das bürgerliche Recht unter den allgemeinsten Grundsatz von Treu und Glauben oder schafft man im Strafrecht die Strafrahmen, die es ermöglichen sollen 'Gleiches' verschieden zu beurteilen," at 199.

[28] Greta Olson, "Towards a comparative and localized study of Brazilian law and literature," in Sonja Arnold and Michael Korfmann (eds.), *Direito e Literatura na Virada do Milênio/ Law and Literature at the Turn of the Millennium* (Porto Alegre: Editora Dublinese, 2014), pp. 15–38.

IS METAPHOR UNIVERSAL TO LAW AND LEGAL PROCESSES?

The general turn to narrative in legal studies has gone unmatched by work on metaphor and figuration and law. Only in part have larger changes in scholarship on metaphor theory been reflected on in legal studies. These changes include the following insights. Metaphor is no longer regarded as a lie in contradistinction to "truth-bearing assertions," and metaphor is no longer seen as occurring only in literary language but in every type of speech, including legal discourse. The differentiation between metaphor and metonymy as two distinct types of mental processes that was originally made by Roman Jakobson has been contested.[29] There is no need to draw categorical lines between different forms of figuration. The original terminology for the parts of metaphor – "vehicle," "tenor," and "ground" – has been replaced by "source domain" and "target domain," and the "mapping" process that occurs between them in what might be described as a second generation of cognitive metaphor research.[30]

Changes in metaphor theory have been caused by a first- and second-generation of cognitive research. This research posits that metaphor arises in cognitive processing, and is therefore a basic sense-making structure akin to narrativization. In what is still the most seminal account of the constitutive role of metaphor in general meaning making, George Lakoff and Mark Johnson stress that metaphorical expressions are based in generalizable physical experiences, yet must in their specific realizations cohere to the fundamental values of a given culture, which are themselves expressed in metaphorical models.[31]

A less easy to realize, more abstract thing is understood through its substitution by a mentally more immediate object using mental mapping. For instance in Alina Simone's song "My Love is a Mountain" (2011), "Love" is the mental space onto which various aspects of a "Mountain" are projected. Gilles Fauconnier and Mark Turner's model of mapping also accounts for those complex tropes in which mental mapping includes the projection of the qualities of more than one source domain onto another. According to these cognitivist researchers, metaphors involving one or more source domain allow us to comprehend what has previously been seen as unknowable.[32] The notion

---

[29] Adapted from Monika Fludernik, Donald C. Freeman, and Margaret H. Freeman, "Metaphor and beyond: An introduction," *Poetics Today*, 20 no. 3 (1999), pp. 383–396.
[30] Ibid., at 387.
[31] George Lakoff and Mark Johnson, *Metaphors We Live By* (Chicago, IL; London: University of Chicago Press, 1980), p. 22.
[32] Gilles Fauconnier and Mark Turner, "Conceptual integration networks," *Cognitive Science*, 22 no. 2 (1989), 133–187.

of a legal persona, for instance, combines source qualities from a façade, a role, and an image, as well as a legal construction in a single target domain.

Writing manuals for jurists often describe metaphor as potentially dangerous and misleading. If anything, metaphor and figurative language in general are gendered as seductive and as distracting to the manly and pragmatic business of interpreting and applying the law.[33] Thus in his discussion of the use of metaphor in legal writing, Michael R. Smith points out that while on the one hand metaphor can "put an abstraction into concrete terms," it on the other hand exhibits an "allure combined with its potential pitfalls."[34]

The fear of distortion conveyed by the lexeme "allure" to my mind obfuscates the heuristic value of metaphor, the very reason that these figures are used in legal discourse so readily. Located between the visual and the graphic, metaphors are used to render more tangible what has been discovered and needs to be made known. Warnings to beware of metaphorical language in favor of the supposedly plain language of narrative are therefore misleading. Narrative can never be free of the tropic, since metaphor is intrinsic to language, and narrative is conveyed most readily through linguistic means.[35] Narrative is never plain and non-ideological.

The most frequently quoted prohibition against using metaphor in common law is Benjamin N. Cardozo in his opinion on *Berkey* v. *Third Avenue Railway Co* 244 N.Y. 602 (1927). Here, Cardozo maligns the use of tropic language to obfuscate corporate responsibility and liability:

> Metaphors in law are to be narrowly watched, for starting as devices to liberate thought, they end often by enslaving it. We say at times that the corporate entity will be ignored when the parent corporation operates a business through a subsidiary which is characterized as an 'alias' or a 'dummy.' All this is well enough if the picturesqueness of the epithets does not lead us to forget that the essential term to be defined is the act of operation. (*Berkey* v. *Third Avenue Railway*)

Cardozo argues for using plain language in order to make clear the relations between parent corporations and their subsidiaries. That he couches his claim in the highly figurative language of enslavement and liberation demonstrates the ubiquity of metaphor in legal rhetoric.[36] This metaphor is particularly

---

[33] See Linda L. Berger and Kathryn M. Stanchi, "Metaphor, narrative, and gender in the law" in this volume.
[34] Michael R. Smith, "Levels of metaphor in persuasive writing," *Mercer Law Review*, 58 (2007), 919–947, at 923.
[35] See Wolf, "Narratology and media(lity)."
[36] Smith, "Levels of metaphor in persuasive writing" at 924.

salient given the partial outgrowth of notions of personhood as applied to corporations after the Supreme Court's *Citizens United v. Federal Election Commission* (2010) decision, in which a corporation has been understood to have the status of an individual and hence also the right to free speech.[37]

An accomplished legal stylist, Cardozo maligns his adversaries for indulging in metaphorical obfuscation. Yet, here and elsewhere, he uses arguments that are rich in tropic complexity. The jurist's ease with this rhetorical form can also be seen in the following short excerpts from his opinions on *Wood v. Lucy* and *Baldwin v. Seelig*.

> The law has outgrown its primitive stage of formalism when the precise word was the sovereign talisman, and every slip was fatal. It takes a broader view to-day. (*Wood v. Lucy, Lady Duff-Gordon*, 222 N.Y. 88, 91; 118 N.E. 214 (N.Y. 1917))
>
> This would be to eat up the rule under the guise of an exception. Economic welfare is always related to health, for there can be no health if men are starving. Let such an exception be admitted, and all that a state will have to do in times of stress and strain is to say that its farmers and merchants and workmen must be protected against competition from without, lest they go upon the poor relief lists or perish altogether. (*Baldwin v. Seelig*, 294 U.S. 511, 523 (1935))

In both cases, an extended metaphor illustrates an alternative reality. In *Wood*, the metaphor refers to an earlier time in which contract discourse was interpreted too narrowly and formalistically; and in *Baldwin*, to a country that would ignore the overarching goal of the Constitution to support solidarity, if necessary, also at the expense of individual state rights. The counterfactuals presented in the metaphors have great rhetorical force.[38] They signal that the reader needs to imagine an alternative reality in order to see the danger to the present circumstances that a misinterpretation of legal discourse would bring with it.

We may assume that Cardozo recognizes the power of metaphor as an effective stylistic device in legal discourse but wishes to claim the prerogative to employ the figurative for himself. By contrast, legal manuals such as Klaus F. Röhl and Stefan Ulbrich's overview of visualizations in law display a distrust of the metaphorical. The authors state that "Metaphors are anything other than harmless. In the truest sense of the word, they can subliminally transport

---

[37] Linda L. Berger, "What is the sound of a corporation speaking? How the cognitive theory of metaphor can help lawyers shape the law," *Journal of the Association of Legal Writing Directors*, 2 (2004), 169–208.

[38] Kathryn M. Stanchi, "Feminist legal writing," *San Diego Law Review* 39 (2002), 387–436.

a particular perspective."[39] The emphasis here is on the unconscious effect of the trope, its subliminal character, and this stands in implicit contrast to the presumably consciously recognized relation of perspective that takes place in narrative use.

Rafal Szubert describes the general distaste for metaphor in German jurisprudence as rooted in the ideal of rationality and the desire to differentiate strongly between rational and scientific discourse that is based on literal and unequivocal concepts, and the irrational and metaphorical polysemy of everyday speech, rhetoric, and poetry: "something irrational adheres to metaphor. This stems in particular from the [Cartesian] ideal of rationality, that is that all should be clear and distinct."[40] In different quarters and for different reasons, metaphor has been criticized in both German and US law, while it is used extensively. As a heuristic tool, figuration is also quite common in German legal commentary. For example, metaphor played a central role in a highly controversial discussion of a potential weakening of the *Folterverbot* (the prohibition against torture) in 2003. This prohibition is based on the most fundamental principle of German Basic Law, the inviolability of human dignity (art. 1, para. 1) and it is made explicit in art 104, para 1: "Persons in custody may not be subjected to mental or physical mistreatment."[41] To argue against the long-standing absolute prohibition against torture, Matthias Herdegen describes a core and periphery of the concept of human dignity that would supposedly allow for the legalized use of physical force in some cases.[42]

While not being able to give as complete an overview of metaphor in law as I have done with narrative, I want to refer to Smith's delineation of metaphor as it is used most powerfully in legal discourse in doctrinal interpretation. These

[39] Klaus F. Röhl and Stefan Ulbrich, *Recht anschaulich: Visualisierung in der Juristenausbildung* (Köln: Halem, 2007).
[40] Rafal Szubert, "Ein Beitrag zur Metapher in der Rechtssprache: Am Beispiel 'juristische Person,'" *Zeitschrift des Verbandes Polnischer Germanisten*, 4 no. 2 (2015), 141–157. "Diese als Substitutionstheorie bezeichnete Auffassung beeinflusst die Diskussion über die Metapher bis in die Gegenwart hinein entscheidend und ist dafür verantwortlich, dass der Metapher etwas Irrationales anhaftet. Das kommt besonders in dem Rationalitätsideal der 'idea clara et distincta' zum Ausdruck [...]" at 143.
[41] Basic Law for the Federal Republic of Germany, trans. Christian Tomuschat, David P. Currie, Donald P. Kommers: www.bundestag.de/blob/284870/ceod03414872b427e57fccb703634dcd/basic_law-data.pdf.
[42] Matthias Herdegen, Art 1. Abs. 1 in Maunz/Dürig: Kommentar zum Grundgesetz Band I, Art 1–11. München 2003. See also Verena Krenberger and Greta Olson, "Durchsetzung und Schutz von Menschenrechten mit allen Mitteln? Zur Folterdebatte in Deutschland und in den Vereinigten Staaten," Monika Fludernik and Hans-Helmuth Gander (eds.), *Ethik des Strafens/The Ethics of Punishment* (Wuerzburg: Ergon, 2008), pp. 177–210.

have also been referred to as potentially the most dangerous type of metaphors operating in legal discourse.[43] Additionally, Smith lists metaphors that are employed in descriptions of legal methodology, individual stylistic choices, and in inherent metaphors. Metaphors travel in legal discourse, and when one is used effectively by a single jurist it may be picked up to become a regularized part of legal terminology or what cognitivists might call a conventional metaphor.[44] An example is Cardozo's trope of lifting the veil to describe relations between parent and subsidiary corporations. Metaphors function most resonantly in Constitutional discourse. The wall of separation provides a prominent example of how a leading metaphor offers a template for principles of governance, or for an ideal of interpretation as in the trope of the Constitution as a living tree.[45] Arguably, the trope provides a visual basis for a larger model that is narrativized and then applied in constitutional jurisprudence. I wish to highlight the fact that the uses of metaphor and narrative in law are always conjoined, because narrativization is intrinsic to verbal expression, and metaphor is part of this expression.

METAPHORICAL DIFFERENCE

There is one area of legal interpretation where the tropic as a basis for legal reasoning functions quite differently within the German legal system and common-law ones. This concerns the use of metaphor to describe a rule of legal application. This concerns the *Analogieverbot*, or prohibition of making analogies, in German criminal law. This principle is meant to guard against the danger of an illegitimate use of an analogy to retrospectively penalize the defendant by making her actions punishable. The prohibition is anchored in the Constitution in art. 103, para. 2 which states that "[a]n act may only be punished if it was defined by a law as a criminal offense before it was committed."[46] It belongs to what has been called the "fragmentary quality" of German criminal law that ensures that not every socially deviant action should be penalized.[47] This prohibition is specific to criminal law and not, for instance, to German constitutional interpretation, where, as stated above, metaphors serve as models of interpretation.

---

[43] Smith "Levels of metaphor in persuasive writing," at 924. [44] Ibid., at 941.
[45] Vicki C. Jackson, "Constitutions as 'Living Trees'? Comparative constitutional law and interpretive metaphors," *Fordham Law Review* 75 (2006), 921–960.
[46] Basic Law for the Federal Republic of Germany.
[47] Ingo Bott and Paul Krell, "Der Grundsatz nulla poena sine lege" im Lichte verfassungsgerichtlicher Entscheidungen," *ZJS*, 6 (2010), 694–700, at 694.

The explicit prohibition against judges making analogies in German criminal law is particularly striking in contrast to common-law jurisprudence, where analogical reasoning functions as a basis for interpretation. Where precedential cases are lacking, analogical reasoning allows the common-law jurist to apply the legal principles governing an unrelated case to the one at hand in which the same principle pertains.[48]

NARRATIVE ARRANGEMENT AS DISTORTIVE

In general I wish to argue for the conjoined metaphoricity and narrativity of law, legal processes, and legal discourse. Narrative arrangements made on the discourse level allow for a series of events to be brought together under the aegis of a judgment, and in some cases to be narrativized in written form, as in a Supreme Court opinion or as in a written judgment in systems based on Roman law. These narratives inevitably involve ellipses, highlighting and rearrangement. This can involve the suppression of other stories or parts of the story – narremes – in the interest of a dominant one.

Let me render this less abstract with an example. *Lawrence v. Texas* 2003 is generally hailed as a victory for queers and as an example of the triumph of individual rights to privacy and non-interference by the state. In LGBTQ histories, the case is described as paving the way for the legalization of gay marriage. Yet the details of one of the precedential decisions regarding sodomy used to support the majority position in *Lawrence* are suppressed, namely those of *Powell v. State of Georgia* (1998). What is remembered is that *Powell* was used to argue that since the state could not determine whether an act of sodomy had taken place "with force and against the will" of the object of that act since the action had taken place in a private home (*Powell v. State of Georgia*, 1998), that the same measure of a recognition of privacy had to be accorded to homosexuals. However, the narrative that says that when sodomy takes place privately it is outside of the purview of the law ignores the details of the case: cunnilingus and intercourse occurred in a heterosexual context between an older man and his wife's seventeen-year-old niece. In the original case, the niece testified that the actions in question were anything but consensual. After describing the stiffness of her body as her uncle forced her legs apart, the niece answered the Assistant District Attorney's question as follows:

---

[48] Grant Lamond, "Precedent and analogy in legal reasoning" in Edward N. Zalta (ed.), *The Stanford Encyclopedia of Philosophy* (Spring 2016). https://plato.stanford.edu/entries/legal-re as-prec/ Accessed March 15, 2016.

Q. Now, while he was licking your vaginal area, what were you doing?
A. I was crying. (*Georgia* v. *Anthony San Juan Powell*; quoted in Huffer 2009)

The dominant narrative of *Lawrence* is one of the triumphs of individual (sexual) freedom of expression, and the case is described as the equivalent of *Brown v. Board of Education* for gay rights. The suppressed story about the original charge of rape and non-consensual sodomy is obviated. Counternarratives are obscured in argumentation through precedent via selective highlighting and suppression of information. One of these narratives includes feminist legal scholars' repeated insistence that violence toward women has to be understood differently than assault between men. Another is that gay and feminist legal activism contradict one another. The point here is that the supposed slippage of meaning wrought by the use of metaphor in legal discourse is no more potentially distorting than the typical process of highlighting and eliminating inherent to narrativization in law.

FRAMING AND FICTIONALITY

How can the distrust of metaphor in law be brought into some kind of harmony with the narrative turn in legal studies? I believe that one can look to recent discussions of fictionality for an answer and to suggest that both narrative means and tropic ones are used in legal discourse when other forms of articulation prove inadequate. Fictionality theory comprises the idea that there is no binary separation between the fictional and the non-fictional but only a form of rhetorical framing where whatever is articulated as fictional is an "as if."[49] In light of this intervention, the formerly die-hard distinction between fiction and non-fiction has been deconstructed. Texts have to be reconsidered as existing along a spectrum of their being more or less framed as products of the imagination.[50] This relative fictionality is signaled by paratextual framing, such as calling something a "novel" as well as by clearly signaled elements of what Stefan Iversen and Henrik Skov Nielson call "inventedness."[51]

---

[49] Richard Walsh, *The Rhetoric of Fictionality*, (Columbus, OH: Ohio State University Press, 2007).
[50] Simona Zetterberg Gjerlevsen and Henrik Skov Nielson, "Distinguishing fictionality," C. Maagaard, M. W. Lundholt, and D. Schäbler (eds.). *Fictionality and Factuality: Blurred Borders in Narrations of Identity* (Berlin: Walter de Gruyter, forthcoming), no pag.
[51] Stefan Iversen and Henrik Skov Nielson, "The politics of fictionality in documentary form, *The Act of Killing* and *The Ambassador*" *European Journal of English Studies EJES*, 20, no 3. (2016): 249–262.

Fictionality allows for a kind of imagining of as-if possibilities that non-fictionality does not. These are more generally true propositions rather than ones that are specifically true. Law makes recourse to both narrative means, in this case discourse-level variations, to describe the "facts" at hand, as well as to metaphors in cases where matters are legally inchoate. In such moments when law resorts to the rhetoric of fictionality to explain something coherently – for instance to invent a legal fiction – law is in a moment of transformation. As-if counterfactuals to the current reality are supplied, for instance, by the metaphors that Cardozo uses in his judgments and the narratives that are built around his metaphorizations.

CONCLUSION

This essay first traced the narrative turn in legal studies and claimed that invocations of *narrative* in descriptions of legal processes are used to do all manner of things, to describe in broad terms the stories of legal cultures or the interpretive evolution of given legal concepts. It has argued for a greater precision in the use of these terms. In a move typical of my prior work, I have argued that the definitional understanding of narrative determines the scope of legal practice and that narrative analysis needs to attend carefully not only to differences between Continental and common-law systems but also to differences between types of law within these systems. The essay has also demonstrated that the pooh-poohed use of metaphor in legal discourse is in fact as widespread as that of narrative practices and that metaphorization and narrativization are conjoined.

In conclusion, I have argued that, when used in counterfactual arguments, metaphor and narrative constructions exhibit qualities of what has been called fictionality, the rhetorical framing of a text as not specifically true and thus as generative of wider truths. On this basis, I argue that both metaphoricity and narrative qualities of law need to be recognized as cognitive processes intrinsic to articulation, in general, and therefore also to the business of law, in particular. Just as the underacknowledged metaphoricity of law needs to be better accounted for, so does law's fictionality. Through rhetorical fictionalization, legal discourse can generate general solutions for conflicts for which law does not yet have a name.

2

What's It Like? Native Americans and the Ambivalence of Legal Metaphors

Lawrence Rosen

"[C]ompetition among analogies [is] the essential circumstance of legal reasoning."
Harry Kalven[1]

We are our metaphors. Whether a metaphor originates in just one domain – religion, law, folklore – its spread into other domains is vital to its cultural acceptance. Indeed, it may be argued, if human beings are most distinguishable for their evolved capacity to create the categories of their own experience as a vehicle for adapting to a shifting and uncertain world, and then proliferate those categories across multiple domains until they seem both immanent and natural, metaphor may be the primary instrument through which this integrative process is effected. Which metaphors are employed can make all the difference. To speak of the heart as a pump instead of a furnace, the eye as a receptor instead of a beacon, or the atom as the irreducible unit of matter rather than a miniature planetary system can determine the very course of science, religion, and social relations. Religious metaphors also change with the times. As anthropologist Marshall Sahlins amusingly notes:

> When we were pastoral nomads, the Lord was our shepherd. We were His flock, and He made us to lie down in green pastures, and led us beside the still waters.
> When we were serfs and nobles, the Lord was our king. Sat regnant on the throne of heaven, His shepherd's crook now a jeweled scepter; monarch of feudal monarchs, even to the Prince of Evil, His own contentious baron. But we were mostly peasants, and our comfort and justice no longer lay in the green pastures but in the land. And we would have it. We would inherit the earth.
> Finally we are businessmen – and the Lord is our accountant. He keeps a ledger on us all, enters there our good deeds in black and debits our sins in

---

[1] See also his "Broadcasting, public policy and the First Amendment," *Journal of Law and Economics*, 10 (1967), 15–49, at 38.

red. The Lord useth double-entry bookkeeping; He writeth a man down in fine columns. And when the Great Businessman closes our accounts, to those who show a profit He shall pay eternal dividends; but for those with a life ill spent – well, the Devil take the hindmost.[2]

Indeed, the power of metaphor to capture what we take for the moment as reality is enormous. Politics and policies follow in the wake of our choice of metaphors. If what is required is a "level playing field," if welfare to those on the political left is a "safety net" and to those on the right a 'hammock,'[3] if thoughts exist in "a marketplace of ideas" and even a corporation is a "person," quite different legal protections may apply than if some other analogy is chosen.

How we think of property, production, and ownership is equally susceptible to the power of metaphor. The usual way lawyers in the common-law tradition speak of property ownership is as a "bundle of rights." Even this formulation may be conceptualized as rights I have vis-à-vis a given thing or as the distribution of rights between me and others as it concerns that thing. Either way, two features are immediately noticeable: the emphasis on the individual and the relative lack of emphasis on highly personalized reciprocal obligations that go beyond rights of alienation. For many, the image of property as a field of rights is also deeply entwined with moral precepts, whether phrased in terms of natural prerogatives and affinities, interpersonal duties, or God-given entitlements. Indeed, this cultural orientation is also naturalized, in the sense that only by separating that which is nature's from that upon which mankind places its improvement does the claim of ownership vest. The pervasive power of the property metaphor in American history is well-represented by James Madison's assertion that he even had a property right in his reputation, his religion, and other personal matters.

But how well do the Western concepts and metaphors of property translate to the situation of native peoples, particularly when it concerns intangible productions of knowledge and artistic inspiration? Does a language of property and moral rights, of exclusive ownership or personal control, translate adequately when the place of the individual, family, religious community or tribe may occupy a very different conceptual space for native peoples? And when two often conflicting cultures are involved, which metaphors are most effective and fair?

[2] Marshall D. Sahlins, *Tribesmen* (Englewood Cliffs, NJ: Prentice-Hall, 1968), p. 96.
[3] Ann Cammett, "Deadbeat dads & welfare queens: How metaphor shapes poverty law," *Boston College Journal of Law and Social Justice*, 34 (2014), 233–265.

When it comes to intellectual production and its legal protection, "property" is surely the dominant metaphor, so much so that the phrase "intellectual *property*" and its shorthand IP seem self-evident. But if one accepts the notion of ideas as property-like one may have to accept many attendant features as well. For if "property" implies the exclusive power of alienation it may be difficult to separate individual proprietary interests from the less tangible, but no less heartfelt, aspects of collective attachment. If, too, property implies that a material thing can be separated from the personhood of those identified with it, there may be no clear way of measuring and equating market value with spiritual, sentimental, or nationalistic value. Unlike the never formed part of the common law, civil law countries recognize that certain objects may not enter into commerce (*res extra commercium*), including those objects that are vital to a particular religious or cultural group. In a sense, a similar notion has already been embraced in the Native American Graves Protection Act (NAGPRA) insofar as it requires the return to native groups of human remains and artifacts under certain conditions.[4] By analogizing cultural materials to this concept in civil and international law, one might argue that additional categories of native materials are beyond the scope of commercial trade. Indeed, as many Native Americans argue, if there was no legitimate title in the conqueror to begin with how can it be transferable to another?

Whether some rights should extend beyond the sale of a work also depends on the metaphor one chooses. Under such terms as *droit de suite*, a number of Western countries acknowledge that an artist's interest is not entirely cut off by the work's sale, a portion of each resale being owed to the originator of the work or his heirs.[5] In the United States. there is no comprehensive federal legislation on the practice and no case has reached the Supreme Court addressing the continuing rights of the original artist. California's law on the subject has been the subject of ongoing litigation. That statute, known as the

---

[4] See, O. Metzger, "Making the doctrine of *Res Extra Commercium* visible in United States law," *Texas Law Review*, 74 (1996), 615–653; Silvia Borelli and Federico Lenzerini, eds., *Cultural Diversity: New Developments in International Law* (The Hague: Martinus Nijhoff, 2012); and a Canadian decision ordering the return from buyers of sacred objects belonging to the Catholic Church, as analyzed in Benoît Pelletier, "The case of the Treasures of L'Ange Gardien: An overview," *International Journal of Cultural Property*, 2 no. 2 (1993), 371–382. For the statute relating to the repatriation of Native American burials and artifacts, see NAGPRA, 25 U.S.C. §§ 3001–3013 (2000).

[5] See, e.g., Australia's Resale Royalty Right for Visual Artists Act 2009. This act is presently under review: See http://arts.gov.au/visual-arts/resale-royalty-scheme/review (accessed November 14, 2015). On the experience of the British under a resale royalties law, see Daniel Grant, "Artist resale royalties haven't hindered art trade or helped artists in the U.K.," *Huffington Post*, June 6, 2014.

California Resale Royalties Act (CRRA),[6] requires a 5 percent payment to the artist upon each resale, but only if it occurs within the state.[7] The issue is placed entirely in terms of property and commerce, there being no direct reference by either the legislature or the courts to any "moral" right or aspect of the artist's personality.

Along with tangible, property-like conceptualizations, legal systems often institutionalize control of intangible products through laws of copyright, patent, and trademark. Although such regimes may work well when attached to national and international standards, they can be more problematic when an object or purpose does not fit neatly into categories generated from Western experience. The result is seen by many as a kind of colonization by the West of the concepts to be employed. For example, copyright is for a distinct and limited period of time. But if I or my group creates something, why should our control, like our group's culture, not be entitled to unlimited duration – or at least to our own conception of time – rather than a culturally different measure? Moreover, assigning control over something that holds meaning for an entire culture to an individual artist or producer may wholly displace communal interests. Relying on the metaphor of "heritage" may emphasize collective interests, but designating what shall count as part of a group's heritage is hardly self-evident, particularly if an outside source may be determining what the group involved means by their own heritage.

We also speak of the "theft" or "piracy" of intellectual productions. But what is an idea *like*? Is it like the air, free and unfenced, or is it like the air rights over a building that can in fact be commercialized? Should we envision the entitlement to such products as being like a farmer entitled to reap what he sows?[8] Or should exclusive ownership be replaced by the idea that, like a crop not harvested, an object or idea belongs to whoever makes beneficial use of it? But does that mean that a tribal symbol forced or fallen into disuse may be appropriated by non-natives? Alternatively, we could see the use of another's cultural production as a violation of "the commons" if one can only claim a certain level of usufructory right, perfected by actual use, which must later

---

[6] Cal. Civ. Code §986.
[7] Sam Francis Foundation v. Christie's, 860 F.Supp.2d 1117 (C.D. Cal. 2012), *cert. denied*, 9th Cir., January 11, 2016 (Royalties Act violates the Commerce Clause when it attempts to gain royalties from transactions outside California between non-California parties.)
[8] See generally, Patricia Loughlin, "Pirates, parasites, reapers, sowers, fruits, foxes ... The metaphors of intellectual property," *Sydney Law Review*, 28 (2006), 211–226. See also, Susan Scafidi, *Who Owns Culture? Appropriation and Authenticity in American Law* (New Brunswick, NJ: Rutgers University Press, 2005).

pass to another in the community according to some system of distribution or rotation.[9]

To vary the agricultural metaphor, we could imagine ideas and their production as being like a crop in an unfenced field. But if you think the seed came before the sower a different moral sense may apply than if one attributes all rights to the planter. By that logic if an artist builds on a traditional tribal design she may not have the right to sell it outside of the tribe. And like many patent laws she might have to show that she has really added something new to the original object to perfect her legal control over it. Indeed, American patent law is based on an eighteenth-century image of the "hero inventor" operating independent of all others, whereas the image of the laboratory-based "team as hero" may help to link native peoples to existing laws by conceptualizing their productions, too, as collective entrepreneurship.[10] One question then would be: Who is really doing the inventing, the sowing, or vitalizing the team? Or, to switch metaphors, is this a case of "standing on the shoulders of giants" such that no addition could have existed without that which went before – which must at least be shared and attributed to the predecessor – if legal consequences of ownership are to flow from that analogy?

Copyright protects a tangible form and its original expression, not the idea itself.[11] Patents garnering government approval must demonstrate a new, useful, and non-obvious process or technology. But in the case of native productions, when is the line crossed to originality so as to warrant a change in legal status? And what, if any, duty is owed whoever generated the original design? In the *Bulun Bulun* case, an Australian court held that the artist has a duty to protect the ritual knowledge he has been permitted to use in a bark painting, but it is not a duty that alone vests a financial interest in the tribe when the individual artist's work is used by a commercial textile manufacturer.[12] The court was not prepared to recognize communal title, but it did

---

[9] See Loughlin, "Pirates, parasites, reapers," 223–224.

[10] See Thomas D. Mays, et al., "*Quid Pro Quo*: Alternatives for equity and conservation," in Stephen B. Brush and Doreen Stabinsky, eds., *Valuing Local Knowledge: Indigenous People and Intellectual Property Rights* (Washington, DC: Island Press, 1996), pp. 259–280, at 264; former Secretary of Labor Robert B. Reich, "Entrepreneurship reconsidered: The team as hero," *Harvard Business Review*, 65 no. 3 (May/June 1987), 77–83; and Vinay Prasad, "The folly of big science awards," *New York Times*, October 2, 2015.

[11] For a proposal that some legal protection should be afforded the generator of an idea who has not actually implemented it, see Oren Bar-Gill and Gideon Parchomovsky, "A marketplace for ideas?" *Texas Law Review*, 84 no. 2 (2005), 395–431.

[12] *Bulun Bulun v. R & T Textiles Pty Ltd.*, (Federal Court of Australia 1998), 157 A. L. R. 193. For other cases of traditional design and commentary, see Kimberlee Weatherall, "Culture,

recognize that native law forms part of the "factual matrix" that rendered the relation one of mutual trust and confidence, which, in this particular case, the artist had fulfilled by stopping the textile from being manufactured.

Quite a different set of connotations may flow from thinking of indigenous productions as being like one's "brainchild." Sometimes put in organic terms (the product of a "fruitful mind"), sometimes in the idiom of paternity, such metaphors in the past conveyed not a sense of perpetual ownership but the right to continued acknowledgment and freedom from piracy. Thus, Daniel Defoe in 1710 protested: "[A] book is the Author's Property, 'tis the Child of his Inventions, the Brat of his Brain."As Mark Rose notes, in the usages of the sixteenth and seventeenth centuries, "the paternity metaphor is consonant with the emergence of the individual author in the patriarchal patronage society concerned with blood, lineage, and the dynastic principle that like engenders like."[13] Any intrusion may not only be a violation of a property right but an assault on the person's very identity and self-regard. Many countries refer to this as a "right to publicity," or a "right to personality." It may be considered a property right, with all the legal protections (trespass, etc.) brought in by that analogy. Alternatively, intrusion into this right may be grouped under tort law, thus affording monetary remedies, or as an invasion of privacy, triggering issues of free speech and equitable remedies.[14]

Analogies based on personal identity can take many forms. A number of European countries phrase copyright as a "moral right." Moral rights were first recognized in France and Germany, before they were included in the Berne Convention for the Protection of Literary and Artistic Works in 1928. Article 6bis of the *Berne Convention* protects attribution and integrity, stating: "Independent of the author's economic rights, and even after the transfer of the said rights, the author shall have the right to claim authorship of the work and to object to any distortion, modification of, or other derogatory action in relation to the said work, which would be prejudicial to the author's honor or reputation." While the United States became a signatory to the Berne Convention, it still does not completely recognize moral rights as part of copyright law, but rather as part of other bodies of law, such as defamation or unfair competition. In the United Kingdom, moral claims may be made for

---

autonomy and *Djulibinyamurr*: Individual and community in the construction of rights to traditional designs," *The Modern Law Review*, 64 (2001), 215–242.

[13] Mark Rose, *Authors and Owners: The Invention of Copyright* (Cambridge, MA: Harvard University Press, 1993), p. 39. See also Marilyn Strathern, *Kinship, Law and the Unexpected* (Cambridge, UK: Cambridge University Press, 2005), pp. 58–61.

[14] For other examples on control of one's name or image, see Ray D. Madoff, "The new grave robbers," *New York Times*, March 27, 2011.

property seized by the Nazis and now in public museums, a right that can survive the statutes of limitation. If museums are "ethical guardians," the question arises whether indigenous tribes might also be so conceptualized.

There are other metaphors that relate to one's personal identity. The French speak of the "right to control one's image," while a number of other countries speak of a "right to personality."[15] In the United States, The Visual Artists Rights Act (VARA) takes a somewhat more limited approach. It applies only to works of "recognized stature" where there is some public interest, and allows an artist to bar attribution if (tracking the *Berne* language) such use would be "prejudicial to his or her honor or reputation."[16] Indigenous peoples have somewhat similar ways of putting the matter. In the *Chilkat* case, one Indian said of the tribe's Whale House artifacts: "The primary significance is knowing who you are. When you're selling an artifact you're not only getting rid of a piece of wood, you're getting rid of the music, the song, the dance, and the good, the bad and the ugly."[17] Commercial trademark commenters now speak of "persona" as evoking an image that extends beyond the product proper to include an image that makes the trademark holder feel good about himself. If, say, the tipi symbol of a Kiowa design is seen as imbued with power that extends beyond its immediate referent – if, indeed, it incorporates the deeds and accomplishments no other man should be able to sing about or portray – one could analogize a right to that symbol's persona in the same way trademark law may protect an individual "brand," only in this case the claim of exclusive control would be based on the "medicine" or "vision" that surrounds the production rather than the object per se.[18] Unlike many European countries, US law does not permit an action for group defamation. Yet if one were to extend the analogy of attacks upon one's culture as equivalent to holding one up to public shame or opprobrium – an action that clearly focuses on the collectivity as it affects the individual – cases that have previously failed to gain traction might command a legal basis.[19]

---

[15] For a survey of countries using this concept, see "Personality Rights," *Wikipedia*.
[16] 17 US Code Section 106A(a)(2).
[17] *Chilkat Indian Village v. Johnson*, 870 F.2d 1469 (9th Cir. 1989). The case was remanded to the tribal court: *Chilkat Indian Village, IRA v. Johnson, Indian Law Reporter*, 20, 6127 (Chilkat Tribal Court 1993).
[18] Candace S. Greene and Thomas D. Dresher, "The Tipi with battle pictures: The Kiowa tradition of intangible property rights," *Trademark Reporter*, 84 (1994), 418–433.
[19] So, for example, in the suit brought by successors to Crazy Horse, their attempt to bar the use of his name on a brand of beer failed in the federal court. Vincent Schilling, "Oglala Sioux Tribe's alcohol lawsuit dismissed without prejudice," *Indian Country*, October 3, 2012; and Nell Jessup Newton, "Memory and misrepresentation: Representing Crazy Horse in tribal

The term "intellectual property" tends to place emphasis on the second part of that phrase, building analogies to other forms of real or intangible things. If, however, one focuses on the first word, other analogies may be suggested. For example, control over the presentation, rather than the title, to a native production may become the focus of concern. The question thus arises whether one can strip away the intellectual from the physical aspect of an artifact and fractionate the rights that attend that object just as one limits the use of land or intangible property by dividing the interests of the owner, the state, and other parties accordingly. Such an approach may have the merit of encouraging hybridity and the exchange of information across cultures and may wean intellectual property law away from its emphasis on the property ownership element to the exclusion of the ideational and cultural value. Moreover if one emphasizes metaphors relating to the flow of information, the native originators may be regarded as legally cognizable stewards of the objects, the titleholders being analogized to trust beneficiaries who have a duty of care to the originators as well as to those to whom the objects are displayed.[20]

Finally, one could put matters in terms of human rights. The Covenant on Economic, Social and Cultural Rights is said to protect intellectual creations, and this might even be extended to such intangibles as folklore and songs. However, given the emphasis on persons rather than groups, one would have to interpret these artifacts as extending to collective and not just individual rights.[21] Many of the existing international accords, such as those promulgated through the World Intellectual Property Organization (WIPO) and those embodied in the United Nations Declaration on the Rights of Indigenous Peoples, are, however, in the nature of encouragement to negotiation or consideration, rather than enforceable regulations.[22]

---

court," in Bruce Ziff and Pratima V. Rao, eds., *Borrowed Power: Essays on Cultural Appropriation* (New Brunswick, NJ: Rutgers University Press, 1997), pp. 195–224.

[20] See Kristen A. Carpenter, Sonia Katyal, and Angela Riley, "In defense of property," *Yale Law Journal*, 118 (2009), 1022–1125, the discussion of it in Michael F. Brown, "Culture, property and peoplehood," *International Journal of Cultural Property*, 17 no. 3 (2010), 569–579; and the authors' response, "Clarifying cultural property," Ibid., 581–598.

Cortelyou C. Kenney, "Reframing indigenous cultural artifacts disputes: An intellectual property-based approach," *Cardozo Arts & Entertainment Law Journal*, 28 (2011), 502–552 also suggests that the parties may be analogized to co-authors of a copyrighted work, that the research aspect of such objects places them beyond the ordinary range of property analogies, and that such an image carries with it implication for cooperation and consultation not necessitated by ordinary property law.

[21] A number of declarations have been issued by native peoples concerning their intellectual property. See the listings under the heading of "Indigenous intellectual property" at *Wikipedia*.

[22] See, e.g., Center for International Environmental Law, "The gap between indigenous peoples' demands and WIPO's framework on traditional knowledge" (September 2007).

The analogies discussed so far are drawn mainly from non-native legal regimes. But how do various native peoples analogize their knowledge and products? There is a tendency to imagine that all indigenous groups are based on collective property holding. But ownership, in the sense of undivided control and alienation, is hardly unknown to indigenous peoples. An Australian aborigine may have an exclusive right to his song, while a Melanesian may be far less concerned about its use by others than that its sale or transmission was conducted in an authorized way. Indeed, the sale or purchase may galvanize important social contacts, while the benefits of demonstrating difference, which is vital to forming alliances, may be underscored by acquiring possession of the artifacts of others.[23] From whom knowledge comes most recently may be more important than knowing who initiated it. Thus while most Western metaphors center on the relation of the individual creator to the product, the approach of some indigenous groups may, by contrast, be thought of as concerned with the relations among people, the image being that of "a bundle of relationships, rather than a bundle of economic rights."[24] Similarly, the New Zealand Maori concept of *taonga* expresses the rights and obligations that span generations, and objects that are linked to this concept are not subject to being replaced by money or other objects in the ordinary course of exchange.[25] The dominant metaphor is thus one of kinship and mutuality. Indeed, some anthropologists would argue that a preeminent role of art is less that of expression of religious and aesthetic

---

www.wipo.int/export/sites/www/tk/en/igc/ngo/ciel_gap.pdf. Accessed November 14, 2015. For similarly toothless conventions, see John Hunter and Chris Jones, "Bioprospecting and indigenous knowledge in Australia: Implications of valuing indigenous spiritual knowledge," Bahá'í Library Online, 2006–7. http://bahai-library.com/hunter_jones_bioprospecting_austra lia. Accessed November 14, 2015, and Yano 1993. After reviewing Australia's laws, an attorney concluded: "Australia['s] need to enact much more than a voluntary Code of Conduct in respect of traditional culture is long overdue. The Courts can only do so much to extend the notions of statutory regimes to offer protection which is insufficient and which depends on the facts of a particular case. Australia needs to enact laws which acknowledge, respect and afford legal protection to traditional knowledge." FAL Lawyers, Jenni Lightowlers, "Australian law relating to communal indigenous intellectual property," *Lexology* (February 12, 2013). www.lexology.com/library/detail.aspx?g=073fdf42-e293-4566-bd7e-f936 04e66ae1. Accessed August 10, 2015.

[23] See Simon Harrison, "From prestige goods to legacies: Property and objectification of culture in Melanesia," *Comparative Studies in Society and History*, 42 no. 3 (2000), 662–679.

[24] Erica-Irene Daes, *Protection of the Heritage of Indigenous Peoples* (New York: United Nations, 1997), s. 26. See also Debbora Battaglia, "Retaining reality: Some practical problems with objects as property," *Man*, New Series, 29 no. 3 (1994), 631–644.

[25] Russell Craig, Rawiri Taonui, and Susan Wild, "The concept of *Taonga* in Māori culture: Insights for accounting," *Accounting, Auditing and Accountability Journal*, 25 no. 6 (2012), 1025–1047.

sentiments than that of a set of vehicles to facilitate relationships, whether by demonstrating that persons can be substituted for the things portrayed, that art mediates individual and collective action, or because the contradictions posed by an art object promote creativity in social relationships no less than cosmological orientations.[26]

The emphasis on collective relationships often carries over to conceptions of time. When, for example, a Bamileke chief took office he had his statue carved: "after his death, the statue was respected, but it was slowly eroded by the weather as his memory was eroded in the minds of the people."[27] The intention of natural devolution would be violated were an outsider, then, to lay claim to the object. Clearly native peoples are not the only ones for whom Western concepts may not fit. An analyst of Islamic cultures notes that it is often less the artist than the reception of his work that is important:

> The author, or the artist, may still be recognized, but once the artistic product has been given to the ummah [the community of believers] as a whole, then that product is considered as the product of the Islamic milieu or worldview. This should not be regarded as the negation of the author; rather, the authorship is given to the ummah as a whole, and the center is not the author or artist, but in the Absolute upon which the piece is built.[28]

In each instance, the narrative of the intellectual product is not only wrapped up in the concept of the collective but the extended metaphor of natural decomposition is completely at odds with those of most Western stories that are aimed at the perpetuation of any artistic endeavor.

Indeed, to many indigenous peoples, culturally significant objects may be regarded as possessing life. For example, some Great Lakes Indian groups refer to their creations as living things, and so one approaches these objects – e.g.,

---

[26] Andrew Gell, in *Art and Agency* (Oxford: Oxford University Press, 1998), argues that things provoke attachments – that far from being passive, art is a form of instrumental action influencing the actions of others. Marilyn Strathern, in *The Gender of the Gift: Problems with Women and Problems with Society in Melanesia* (Berkeley: University of California Press, 1988), suggests that relations are substantially between persons and things, with the latter being substituted for the former in a number of instances. Clifford Geertz, taking a more cultural tack, argues against the structural-functional approach, "that is, that works of art are elaborate mechanisms for defining social relationships, sustaining social rules, and strengthening social values ... The central connection between art and collective life does not lie on such an instrumental plane, it lies on a semiotic one ... [Artists] materialize a way of experiencing, bring a particular cast of mind out into the world of objects, where men can look at it." *Local Knowledge* (New York, NY: Basic Books, 1983), p. 99.

[27] Jacques Maquet, *Introduction to Aesthetic Anthropology*, 2nd edition, Malibu, CA: Undena Publications, 1979, p. 14.

[28] Omar W. Nassim, "Toward an Islamic aesthetic theory," *The American Journal of Islamic Social Studies*, 15 no. 1 (1998), 71–90, at 81.

medicine bags, war clubs, drums, pipes – in relational terms. The Ojibwa greeting to such objects, for example, means "hello, all our relations." Similarly, in the *Corrow* case a Navajo anthropologist testified that the medicine bundles were living entities, as were the masks living gods.[29] When seen as living things objects may be regarded as traveling, and because they may not come back soon or ever it may be acceptable to go to a dominant population's museum to visit them. The museum at the University of British Columbia, for example, sets aside a room where native peoples can bring offerings of food to share with the ancestral spirits embodied in the objects housed there.

The relational implications of cultural objects can be very complex. Students of the culture of the Trobriand Islands have suggested that the transfer of such objects as axe blades may actually open up the possibility that expectable exchange may not prove to be reciprocal and thus the seeming inalienability of an object may actually be outstripped by a discourse of possible relationships that go beyond the usual kin boundaries. What might be regarded as a threat to the stability of social ties may, then, operate as a test of existing relationships, an opening for new relationships, or a vehicle for keeping alive the adaptive capacity to form new ties wherever they may prove most efficacious. Under this view, boundaries are constantly being challenged, and an inappropriate regime of legal control – even one that emphasizes relationships over property-like alienation – risks freezing social flexibility in the name of cultural integrity or conservation.[30]

While many legal protections may apply across native and non-native boundaries given their common situations, in many other instances the problems faced by native peoples may pose special problems. In addition to sacred symbols there are various cultural productions that hold special significance for the social and intellectual life of native groups, including music, dance, and folklore. When hip-hop duo OutKast used a Navajo sacred song it caused outrage among the Indians, but unlike New Zealand, where there is protection for such songs, there is none in the United States short of copyrighting the song. To take a case in point, in 2001 several Maori tribal groups threatened legal action against toymaker Lego for allegedly trademarking Maori words that the company was using in its Bionicle products. In response,

---

[29] *United States v. Corrow*, 119 F.2d 796 (10th Cir. 1997).
[30] "The divisive potential of cultural integrity is a danger to be taken into account. The wise lawmaker in this politically charged arena walks a tightrope between proper protection for minority interests, and accusations of apartheid and paternalism." Weatherall, "Culture, autonomy and Djulibinyamurr," 227. Robert Lowie, among many anthropologists, long ago argued that borrowing was common among tribal groups and that the image of tribes as hermetically sealed entities is radically mistaken.

a Lego spokesperson stated that only the term "Bionicle" had been trademarked, but after meeting with tribal representatives the company did agree to change some, but not all, of the words involved.

The use of native genetic material presents a particularly controversial situation.[31] The rule in US law is that if a significant addition is made to a substance in the course of its extraction, a patent may be sought. The question then is what constitutes such an addition. If genetic material is taken from an Indian group and combined with extraneous material, is the result so changed as to be patentable? Native people fear that claims of tribal identity and membership may turn on the findings of such research. In one case the Havasupai settled out of court with Arizona State University, where researchers conducted studies of diabetes with tribal consent but then used the findings for a study of schizophrenia that was not authorized by the tribe.[32]

Similar questions arise for the plants found in native territories, including those from which such medicines as aspirin, digitalis, and scopolamine have been derived.[33] In fact, "77% of all plant related pharmaceutical products, or roughly 25% of the entire pharmaceutical market contains significant elements of direct contribution from the appropriation of indigenous knowledge."[34] The result has been a number of disputes between native peoples and pharmaceutical companies, university researchers, and governmental agencies. The White Earth Ojibwa, for example, were involved in a long-running dispute with the University of Minnesota concerning the wild rice distinctive to their territory.[35] Various international conventions on "genetic prospecting" do exist, but none is pointedly helpful for indigenous peoples.

Even recent expressions of ancient rituals may become the subject of legal suits. In the *Diaz* case a trader in native artifacts took figurines used in a recent ritual from a cave on Indian land and put them up for sale. He was subsequently charged with violating the federal Antiquities Act. He defended by

---

[31] For an example of legislative and popular referendum action on bioprospecting in Costa Rica, see Thomas W. Pearson, "'Life is not for sale': Confronting free trade and intellectual property in Costa Rica," *American Anthropologist*, 115, no. 1 (2013), 58–71. On the Australian experience, see Hunter and Jones 2006–7. See generally the essays in Brush and Stabinsky, 1996.

[32] Interview with Pilar N. Ossorio, a University of Wisconsin law professor who has served as an expert for the tribe, April 2005. See Amy Harmon, "Indian tribe wins fight to limit research of its DNA," *New York Times*, April 21, 2010.

[33] See generally Lester I. Yano, "Protection of the ethnobiological knowledge of indigenous peoples," *UCLA Law Review*, 41 (1993), 443–486.

[34] Hunter and Jones, 2006–7, pp. 4–5.

[35] See, Jake Anders et al., "Genetic research on wild rice and its cultural implications," May 6, 2004. www.d.umn.edu/~ande2927/Report.pdf. Accessed November 14, 2015.

saying that the objects were of recent vintage and thus did not qualify as antiquities. However, the court accepted the argument of an anthropologist that the object of antiquity to be protected was the ancient ritual, of which the contemporary figures were but the most recent expression. In doing so, however, the court declared the statute itself void for vagueness inasmuch as one might not be able to tell in advance when one could be subjected to a criminal penalty if even a recent object could be a surrogate for an ancient ritual.[36]

As technologies change, so do the possibilities for building metaphorical extensions. In the field of software production, for example, the concept of an "open source" license does not, in fact, mean the unconditional use by anyone of material developed by another. It requires that modifiers allow access to any changes they introduce. Moreover, suppliers usually find it more lucrative to charge for software service and support than for the actual software, so the financial incentives are not simply eliminated. One could imagine native productions being seen in the same fashion. Similarly, an analogy could be built from the area of trade secrets, thus treating native designs as proprietary by piggybacking on the concept that prevails in much of non-native commercial law.[37]

Addressing indigenous rights require that we recast some foundational concepts. The basic question may simply be: What is our operative goal? Is it "to preserve meaning and due honor for elements of cultural knowledge and to insure that these traditional universes, and their peoples, maintain their vitality ... [or] to manage the degree and process by which parts of that cultural knowledge are shared with outsiders, and in some instances, to be justly compensated for it"?[38] The *Bulun* Equity Principle, that requires notification of the group affected, might (a) keep firms from buying native designs, thus harming the indigenous people economically, and (b) may limit the communal interest to situations where there are clear tribal laws, where the products are of great social importance, or where the community is uniquely vulnerable in relation to its artists. But applying the *Bulun* principle may be inapplicable, say, to Navajo sand painting given the US courts' reluctance to allow tribes to reach out beyond willing tribal members, particularly if

---

[36] However, *U.S. v. Smyer*, 596 F.2d 939 (10th Cir. 1979), cert. denied 444 U.S. 843 (1979), interpreting The Antiquities Act, 16 U.S.C.A. §§ 431 et seq., found no vagueness in the statute as applied to objects that were 800–900 years old.

[37] For an example of this approach applied to an Alaskan case, see Stuart Schüssel, "Copyright protection's challenges and Alaska Natives' cultural property," *Alaska Law Review*, 92, no. 2 (2012), 313–340.

[38] Paul Kuruk, "Protecting folklore under modern intellectual property regimes: A reappraisal of the tension between individual and communal rights in Africa and United States," *American University Law Review*, 48 (1999), 769–849, at 823.

there are First Amendment problems of restricting artists' expressions.[39] Indeed, who speaks for the entire group is not always straightforward, nor is it straightforward whether group interests should trump those of an individual member.

Put differently, what exactly is the harm of "cultural appropriation"? If the purpose is to allow groups to make collective decisions, analogies based on group interests may be favored over analogies that stress intense individualism. Again, the cultural emphases are important to underscore. We may ask, for example: Are the names of indigenous artists really unknown – or purposely erased? Were their identities irrelevant in their time or intentionally occluded to emphasize, like oral tradition, that the production bespeaks the values of an entire community?

Indeed, should we get rid of copyright and patents altogether? Goulven suggests a form of "equitable copyright" in which a group right would be cognizable, at least to hold matters steady while a longer term solution to respective interests is addressed.[40] Alternatively, should native groups have a right of first refusal for the purchase of an object that comes up for sale, or should certain sales be open only to those who, following purchase, agree to return the object to the native peoples?[41] Would it make greater sense to institute compulsory conciliation, arbitration, or mediation panels, rather than leaving these matters to courts of law? In far too many instances the legislation presently in place, perhaps having been constructed on metaphors of insufficient power, have left much to be desired by way of clarity and equity in the field of indigenous intellectual rights.

---

[39] Amina Para Matlon, "Safeguarding Native American sacred art by partnering tribal law and equity: An exploratory case study applying the *Bulun Bulun* equity to Navajo sandpainting," *Columbia Journal of Law and Arts*, 27 (2003–4), 211–247.

[40] Cited in Weatherall, "Culture, autonomy and *Djulibinyamurr*." at 222.

[41] For example, the Annenberg Foundation paid $530,000 at a Paris auction for twenty-four items they then returned to the Hopi. Alexandria Sage, "U.S. foundation buys Hopi masks at auction to return to tribe," Reuters, December 11, 2013. www.reuters.com/article/2013/12/11/us-france-auction-idUSBRE9B80QJ20131211. Accessed November 14, 2015. Unlike the Hopi, the Navajo have been willing to purchase objects originally from their people at auction. Associated Press, "Navajos reclaim sacred mask at auction," December 16, 2014. www.cbsnews.com/news/navajo-indians-buy-back-sacred-masks-in-france-auction/. Accessed November 14, 2015. In other instances collectors have refused to return objects to the native peoples, preferring a buyer at auction who they believe will better care for the items. See, e.g., Margaret Loke, "Sacred and secular clash at auction," *New York Times*, December 3, 1998. It is also important to remember that: "The market for illicit antiquities – of which indigenous cultural objects are a significant subset – is the third most profitable black market in the world behind drugs and arms." Kenney, "Reframing indigenous cultural artifacts disputes," 517.

The choice and effect of a metaphor may, of course, be deeply entwined with the broader narrative style within which it operates. A story, biography, legal decision, or even a statute may, directly or indirectly, work as an extended metaphor. In the present context, the analogy of intellectual products to "property" is a perfect example of an extended metaphor that has taken on the aura of common sense. What form of narrative now carries our sense of individual and collective well-being? Do our intellectual products seem truer when their story is told as a voyage of discovery but not when narrated as a tiny addition to a collective event envisioned as timeless? When courts choose an extended metaphor, does the entire decision, and the challenge posed to any dissent, not turn on how the narrative employs metaphors to convey and sustain its seemingly obvious result?

Conversely, the choice of metaphor may depend on the style of the narrative. In many societies a truth may be claimed by a circular rather than linear form of telling, where chronological organization is displaced by a constant circling back to a central theme or the repeated iteration of a pattern.[42] So, if native peoples tell their story in a non-linear narrative style, yet are forced by the legal style of narrative into a directional, "progressive" metaphor, the distortion to their sense of the natural order of things may be profound. The result can be a clash of narrative styles that carry in their train the competition for a governing metaphor upon which collective life may depend.

Moreover, metaphors carry profound moral implications. To characterize the stranger as a guest because (as the Hebrew Bible says) we too were "strangers in a strange land" – this is a moral statement no less than a metaphorical one. If we think of museums as "ethical guardians," why not envision the native peoples' control in these terms? If, to some native peoples, certain objects are seen as male or female and should not, therefore, be stored together, is it not a simple matter of respect to honor such beliefs? Indeed, as Joseph Raz has argued, if we have a duty to preserve the items to which *others* attach great importance, should we not fractionate the concept of ownership and regard the intellectual productions of indigenous peoples as objects of mutual concern and control?[43]

Surveying the alternative metaphors for native intellectual production and their implications for the stories that the law narrates through them, we can

---

[42] Our sacred texts also use this style. See, e.g., Mary Douglas, *Thinking in Circles: An Essay on Ring Composition* (New Haven, CT: Yale University Press, 2010), and her *In the Wilderness: The Doctrine of Defilement in the Book of Numbers* (Oxford, UK: Oxford University Press, 2001).

[43] Joseph Raz, *Value, Respect and Attachment* (Cambridge: Cambridge University Press, 2001).

discern several possible conclusions: that a single governing metaphor (like intellectual *property*) neither suits all situations nor fairly addresses the differentials of power that render control over native resources contentious; that thinking in relational rather than possessory terms is far more common in other cultures yet can still be comprehensible to non-native populations, thus forming a possible ground for shared approaches to particular classes of production; that the narrative style may drive the metaphor, rather than the other way around; and that, given the relatively powerless position of many native groups, a version of affirmative action – perhaps in the form of various legal presumptions and rights of first refusal, perhaps under a principle of "equitable copyright" – might (one can never resist a metaphor) level the playing field.

The crucial feature to recognize about native systems of cultural production is that, whatever their differences from dominant Western regimes, they are highly diverse, and no single metaphor may, therefore, fully capture their entire range. Just as some cultures may categorize foods by their taste and others by the way they feel in one's mouth, the intangible regimes of indigenous peoples run the gamut from control over the story being central to the Kiowa to the song of an Aborigine being so central to his personal identity that it cannot be interfered with by any other. Even in the West, so categorizing a legal scholar as Sir William Blackstone stumbled when trying to determine whether water is like land or, being "a moveable, wandering thing must of necessity continue common by the law of nature."[44]

A uniform law of intellectual production is unlikely to suit all situations or to resolve all ambiguities and a single governing metaphor can be as alluring as it can be dangerous. It is ironic that the very imprecision of metaphors may also account for their strength in capturing the terms by which we can live with one another. As one commenter put it: "The motive for metaphor ... is thus not the *evasion* of the law's hard realities, but rather the *revelation* of two of the most basic of those realities: the inability of the law's language to encompass the world it would regulate; and the inescapable link between language and feeling in establishing the hold over opinion that distinguishes law from brute physical coercion."[45]

As competition for its defining metaphors continues to play a critical role in any culture, failure to attend to their implications can leave us with an inappropriately reified and truncated view of both law and culture. Metaphors

---

[44] *Commentaries on the Laws of England*, Book II, Ch, II, 19 (1765–1769).
[45] Thomas C. Grey, *The Wallace Stevens Case: Law and the Practice of Poetry* (Cambridge, MA: Harvard University Press, 1991), p. 65.

invigorate, but they can also ensnare. As Justice Cardozo said: "Metaphors are to be narrowly watched, for starting as devices to liberate thought they end often by enslaving it."[46] Particularly in the legal narratives of relatively powerless native peoples, we need to be sure to capture the situation in the metaphors, rather than allowing the metaphors to hold captive the situation.

---

[46] *Berkey v. 3d Ave. Ry. Co.*, 244 NY 84, 94 (1926). Criminal law and immigration law are two other domains in which the choice of metaphors can have a dramatic, potentially devastating, impact: See, e.g., Sarah Higinbotham, "Bloodletting and beasts: Metaphors of legal violence," *Wake Forest Law Review*, 49 (2014), 727–742; and Keith Cunningham-Parmeter, "Alien language: Immigration metaphors and the jurisprudence of otherness," *Fordham Law Review*, 79 no. 4 (2011), 1545–1598.

CONVERSATION II
NARRATIVE AND METAPHOR IN LEGAL PERSUASION

Editors' Introduction

Michael Hanne and Robert Weisberg

Lawyers are by their very professional identity in the business of persuasion. The persuasive function is most obvious in litigation, with an audience of judges and jurors, but lawyers must also be persuasive in client counseling and negotiation between parties. Moreover, as is argued by the first contributor to this conversation, Michael R. Smith, persuasion is also crucial in judicial opinions, where the audience for persuasion is primarily judges in higher courts (or in their own courts when seeking a majority on a panel). The most venerable literary association of persuasion is of course with classical rhetoric. But as Smith's conversation with Raymond Gibbs illustrates, narrative and metaphor both figure strongly among persuasive devices employed in a legal context and the roles of narrative and metaphor in persuasion have been well documented and analyzed by legal thinkers over the last twenty years and more.

Several very pragmatically-focused textbooks – in effect "lawyer self-help books" – instruct lawyers on how, in terms of psychology, narrative and metaphor are capable of persuading, and also on how lawyers can most effectively deploy narrative and metaphor for the purposes of persuasion. Among the best known, published in several editions are Linda H. Edwards's *Legal Writing: Process, Analysis, and Organization*[1] and Michael R. Smith's *Advanced Legal Writing: Theories and Strategies in Persuasive Writing*.[2] In addition, websites and blogs collect resources to help litigators hone their storytelling skills and their dexterity with metaphor. See for instance, on storytelling: Ken Lopez's "10 Videos to help litigators become

---

[1] Linda H. Edwards, *Legal Writing: Process, Analysis and Organization* (New York, NY: Aspen/Wolters Kluwer Law and Business, 6th edition 2014, 1st edition 1996).

[2] Michael R. Smith, *Advanced Legal Writing: Theories and Strategies in Persuasive Writing* (New York, NY: Aspen/Wolters Kluwer Law and Business, 3rd edition 2013, 1st edition 2002).

better at storytelling"[3] and, on using metaphor and analogy, his "Lists of analogies, metaphors and idioms."[4]

In the common-law adversarial courtroom, opposing sides tell competing stories and, by conventional wisdom, the side that tells the best story wins. (In inquisitorial systems, as Greta Olson demonstrated in the previous conversation, it is the court's responsibility to construct a narrative that corresponds most accurately to the truth, so persuasion by narrative operates somewhat differently.)

In an American or British criminal trial, the opening statement by the prosecutor will usually take the form of a narrative recounting a series of events, detailing the defendant's role in them, and bringing together a cast of characters, agency, likely motivation, context, circumstantial details, and consequence. The lawyer's narrative will not only recount a sequence of events, but interpret the events, and narratives proposed by advocates generally seek to insist on the superiority of that interpretation over any other.

The opening statement by the defense attorney may take either of two approaches. If the best defense claim is that someone else did the crime, or that while the defendant did the act in question he did so with some justification or excuse, she will proffer a counternarrative. A very dramatic example of the latter in recent American law has been the successful "battered spouse" defense. Case law has established that a woman charged with murdering her husband can expand the usual constraints of self-defense doctrine by renarrating the prologue to the intentional killing as an escalating series of abusive acts by the decedent that effectively, if figuratively, trapped her in a situation where killing was the only recourse.[5]

On the other hand, if the defense aims solely to establish reasonable doubt (and thereby take advantage of the heavy burden placed on the prosecution), it may try to undermine the narrative integrity of the prosecution case and argue that the facts alleged defy any effort at a coherent narrative account.[6] Of course these approaches will be reprised in the lawyers' closing arguments, but in between, during the testimony, attorneys elicit narrative fragments to reinforce the strategies outlined in the openings.

---

[3] Ken Lopez, "10 Videos to help litigators become better at storytelling," *The Litigation Report*, 2012: www.a2lc.com/blog/bid/53536/10-Videos-to-Help-Litigators-Become-Better-at-Storytelling.

[4] Ken Lopez, "Lists of Analogies, Metaphors and Idioms for Lawyers," *The Litigation Report*, 2012: www.a2lc.com/blog/bid/54079/Lists-of-Analogies-Metaphors-and-Idioms-for-Lawyers.

[5] *State v. Wanrow*, 559 P.2d 548 (Wash. 1977).

[6] As recounted by Alan Dershowitz, this was the approach by the defense in the O. J. Simpson trial. "Life is not a dramatic narrative," in Peter Brooks and Paul Gewirtz (eds.), *Law's Stories: Narrative and Rhetoric in Law* (New Haven, CT: Yale University Press 1996), pp. 99–105.

The academic research on legal persuasion has surely emphasized narrative far more than metaphor. Indeed, many legal theorists argue that narrative is the primary device by which persuasion occurs in the courtroom. In the words of Chris Rideout, one of the scholars who has written most comprehensively on the topic: "lawyers persuade by telling stories."[7] But perhaps the key theme of this commentary has been about how narrative interacts with analytic reasoning. Robert Burns, in his much cited *A Theory of the Trial* (1999), argued that persuasion at the level of the trial relies equally on two intertwined strands: "One strand is dominated by narrative and the other by informal logical inference or argument. Narrative is the story of events, actors, backgrounds, actions, and motives ... Argument is a logical pattern of propositions ... that must be proven or disproved."[8] Linda Edwards offers a longer taxonomy, distinguishing four modes of legal reasoning: rule-based reasoning, analogical reasoning, policy-based reasoning, and finally narrative reasoning.[9]

In a valuable critical bibliography he has assembled around Applied Legal Storytelling, Rideout identifies a number of related topics: the application of fiction-writing techniques to courtroom storytelling; the ethical issues such storytelling raises; psychology and cognitive science in courtroom storytelling; and the limits of legal storytelling.[10] But just what is the nature of the psychological power of narrative? Outside the legal context, Ross Chambers has asserted that narrative is "seductive," in the sense that it persuades by offering a selective and shaped account of events in the form of a coherent entity, with indications of agency, characterization, causal links, motivation, related by a specific voice and drawing the audience into interpreting it in terms of a specific meaning.[11]

Clearly these functions operate especially well in the legal context, as numerous commentators have shown. Kevin Heller argues that juries, especially, are most readily convinced by a narrative that they can readily imagine: "When an individual is transported by a narrative, all of her mental systems – attentive, imagistic, emotive – converge on its events, with dramatic real-world

[7] Chris Rideout, "Storytelling, narrative rationality, and legal persuasion," *Legal Writing: Journal of the Legal Writing Institute*, 14 (2008), 53–86, 54.
[8] Robert Burns, *A Theory of the Trial* (Princeton, NJ: Princeton University Press, 1999), pp. 36–38.
[9] Linda H. Edwards, *Legal Writing: Process, Analysis and Organization* (1st edition 1999, 6th edition, Alphen aan den Rijn, The Netherlands: Wolters Kluwer Law & Business, 2014), pp. 4–8.
[10] Chris Rideout, "Applied legal storytelling: A bibliography," *Legal Communication and Rhetoric: JALWD*, 12 (2015), 247–264.
[11] Ross Chambers, *Story and Situation: Narrative Seduction and the Power of Fiction* (Minneapolis, MN: Manchester and Minneapolis University Presses, 1984), p. 74.

results: her ability to think critically about the narrative is reduced, making her more likely to believe that it is authentic and less skeptical of the credibility of the author."[12] But a paradox lies here: while some lawyerly creativity can help in fashioning the narrative, the lawyer's goal is often to make her story seem generic rather than dramatically unique. Thus, many scholars have underscored the extent to which the thinking of judges and, especially of jurors, is dominated by stock narrative frames that they bring to the case, and the consequent need for an advocate to shape his/her narrative to fit one of those frames. In the words of Chris Rideout, "The story at trial must correspond to what 'could' happen, or what 'typically' happens, not to what actually happened."[13] The recounting of events will win the credit of the legal audience more if it comfortably fits within the accepted patterns of behavior, causation, and motive. Thus, according to Linda Edwards, "narrative reasoning evaluates a litigant's story against cultural narratives and the moral values and themes these narratives encode."[14] And, according to Anthony Amsterdam and Jerome Bruner, the stock stories draw upon cultural archetypes and represent "both the culture's ordinary legitimacies and possible threats to them."[15]

Complications arise because persuasive narratives are usually composed of several smaller narratives, and they and the relationships among them, may need to be amended as the case progresses. Similarly, stories may not be as single in their possible meaning as the attorney would like – a story may entail or permit multiple perspectives and interpretations.

The solution to this problem of multiple narratives lies in the persuader's ability to guide and unify the strands of story in a theme, "forcing the jury to make comparative judgement[s] about the relative importance of the norms that the two positions represent."[16] And the challenge of setting the theme leads to our next question – about the role of metaphor in enhancing persuasive narrative.

As noted, the role of metaphor in persuasion has gotten less scholarly attention than has narrative, and narrative would indeed seem to have conceptual priority in describing the task of the legal persuader.[17] But notable

---

[12] Kevin Heller, "The cognitive psychology of circumstantial evidence," *Michigan Law Review*, 105 (2006), 1–74, 54.
[13] Rideout, "Storytelling, narrative rationality, and legal persuasion," 67.
[14] Linda H. Edwards, "The convergence of analogical and dialectic imaginations in legal discourse," *Legal Studies Forum*, 20 (1996), 7–50, 11.
[15] Anthony Amsterdam and Jerome Bruner, *Minding the Law* (Cambridge, MA: Harvard University Press, 2000), p. 117.
[16] Burns, *A Theory of the Trial*, p. 172.
[17] While it is often said that the best story told in court wins, it is only occasionally asserted that the side using the best metaphor has won! The exception to test that rule is the case (almost

writers have tackled the subject,[18] and two key and related aspects of metaphoric persuasion have emerged. First, there is the emotive aspect: the "seductive" power of narrative is strengthened by metaphor's "invitation to intimacy."[19] According to Raymond Gibbs, author of the second paper in this conversation, whereas narrative introduces elements of character, events, sequence, and agency into discourse, metaphor leads the reader/listener to absorb the narrative through an imaginative experience that involves simulated physical sensations. This is especially important where the basic narrative of the case is morally neutral or ambiguous, so the advocate may embed metaphors in her version of the story to guide the sorting out of the characters into heroes and villains. The defendant or a witness may be characterized as "a schoolyard bully," testimony may be described as "leaky," the police or the opposing attorney may be described as "going on a fishing expedition."

Second, metaphor also guides the more intellectual or abstract elements of the persuasive discourse, highlighting the steps in logical or precedential argument that favor the persuader's side. So, the metaphor "fruit of the poisonous tree" causes the audience to see that evidence the seizure of which by itself seems legal is tainted by its illegal provenance.[20] The metaphor of the "wall of separation" between religion and the state, enunciated by Thomas Jefferson, is deployed to argue for a categorical interpretation of the otherwise vague concept of the "establishment" of religion under the First Amendment. Also under the First Amendment, a strongly libertarian conception of free speech and tolerance of obnoxious speech find a quasi-economic defense under the metaphor of "a free market of ideas." Moreover, since persuasion in our legal system is usually adversarial, an attorney countering a strong metaphor often finds herself trapped into fighting the metaphor as

certainly apocryphal) cited by Wayne Booth of the attorney representing a small-town utility in a case against a large corporation, who swung the case irreversibly in favor of his client by announcing; "'So now we see what it is. They got us where they want us. They holding us up with one hand, their good sharp fishin' knife in the other, and they sayin' "you jes' sit still little catfish, we're jes going to gut ya."' In the words of the opposing (and eventually losing) attorney, "I was in the hands of a genius of metaphor." Wayne C. Booth, "Metaphor as rhetoric," in Sheldon Sacks (ed.), *On Metaphor* (Chicago, IL: University of Chicago, 1979), pp. 47–70, 50.

[18] E. g., Benjamin L. Berger, "Trial by metaphor: Rhetoric, innovation, and the judicial text" (2002), Michael R. Smith, "Levels of metaphor in persuasive legal writing" (2007), David T. Ritchie, "The centrality of metaphor in legal analysis and communication: An introduction," *Mercer Law Review*, 58 (Spring 2007), 839–843; Linda L. Berger, "Metaphor and analogy: The sun and moon of legal persuasion" (2013–14).

[19] Ted Cohen, "Metaphor and the cultivation of intimacy," in Sheldon Sacks (ed.), *On Metaphor* (Chicago, IL: University of Chicago Press, 1979), pp. 1–10.

[20] First used by Justice Felix Frankfurter in *Nardone v. United States* (1939).

much as the legal argument behind it, thereby yielding a fair amount of advantage to the metaphor's first mover. Of course, the opponent has the option of fighting metaphor with metaphor; so, the prosecution attorney may argue that the evidence in a given case should be regarded as a rope (the cutting of one strand will not invalidate it), and the defense attorney will argue that is rather a chain, where, if one link is broken, it will no longer bear the weight the prosecution seeks to hang on it.

While metaphors thus often serve to enhance the effect of narrative in criminal or perhaps tort cases, they can also operate in more abstracted commercial cases less obviously amenable to narrative in the first place. As Ken Lopez argues, attorneys frequently use vivid metaphors to simplify and concretize complex facts, abstract ideas, or legal concepts.

> In a trial, a lawyer can use a metaphor to show the jury how something works or how an event occurred, based on an analogy to another thing or process that jurors know well from their everyday lives. For example, in an antitrust case, when describing how a group of competitors squeezed another company out of the market by denying it the opportunity to buy a needed product, the lawyer might tell the jury that the conspirators choked the life out of the other company as if they had denied it the air it needed to breathe.[21]

In this vivid example, introduction of the metaphor actually generates a persuasive narrative in a case where one may never have thought narrative could play a role. Thus, in the context of legal persuasion, it sometimes seems that a striking metaphor is capable of generating a fresh (master) narrative,[22] whereas on other occasions it appears that a given narrative will spawn fresh metaphors.

As noted earlier, persuasive narrative tends to work best when it draws on a cultural stock of fairly familiar narrative patterns – after all, the advocate is arguing for the empirical plausibility of her version of the events. Metaphoric persuasion does not face the same constraint, and so, as Linda Berger points out, both fresh metaphors and conventional metaphors may be used to persuade, but they function differently. Fresh metaphors are persuasive if they disturb a stereotype or a conventional way of viewing a topic, generating new knowledge. Hence Berger offers the example of the attorney in a case charging Nike with falsely reporting the conditions under which its products

---

[21] Lopez, "Lists of Analogies, Metaphors and Idioms for Lawyers."
[22] Linda L. Berger, "Metaphor and analogy: The sun and moon of legal persuasion,' *Journal of Law and Policy*, 22 (2013–2014): 147–195, at 189.

were made. The strategy was to recharacterize this manufacturer of sports equipment as "manufacturing" public relations products.[23]

On the other hand, conventional metaphors can avoid the risk of cliché if they are transposed to a fresh context. They "provide categories into which new information is unthinkingly slotted."[24] But in either case, they may "tap into alternative schemas, prompt more reflective comparisons, and activate other persuasive knowledge structures."[25]

Metaphor, however can be a problematic tool. A number of commentators have written on the misuse or overuse of certain types of metaphor for persuasion in legal contexts. Elizabeth Thornburg examines the use of the "fishing" metaphor and argues that "reliance on the metaphor can replace rigorous analysis, disguising the factors that influence the result in a case."[26] She also illustrates the implications of the excessive use of sporting metaphors in the American judicial system, in particular the suggestion that legal process is an exclusively male activity to be understood as adversarial play.[27] The latter trope has played a role in debates about the prosecutor's constitutional duty to disclose potentially exculpatory evidence under the *Brady* doctrine. As the Court once articulated the government's perspective. "[T]he prosecutor remains an adversary, a boxer rather than a referee. If prosecution is a mere game or a sporting event, prosecutors may feel entitled to fight to win at all costs .... But, while he may strike hard blows, he is not at liberty to strike foul ones."[28] But as Professor Stephanos Bibas has explained, in more recent years the Court has suggested the need to relevel the balance: "If the adversarial trial remains a boxing match, at least the prosecutor must fight by the Marquis of Queensbury rules and avoid striking below the Belt."[29] Furthermore, even – or especially – the most striking metaphor can prove to be unstable and risk turning back on the advocate who utters it. So as recounted by Thornburg, the derogatory "fishing" metaphor, deployed to denounce gratuitous and burdensome inquiries by attorneys into information held by the rival side, turned into a virtually honorific term when changes in the Federal Rules of Civil Procedure promoted more open-ended mutual discovery.[30]

---

[23] Ibid., 183.   [24] Ibid., 149.   [25] Ibid., 176.

[26] Elizabeth G. Thornburg, "Just say 'No fishing': The lure of metaphor," *University of Michigan Journal of Law Reform*, 40 (Fall 2006), 1–65, 2.

[27] Elizabeth G. Thornburg, "Metaphors matter: How images of battle, sports, and sex shape the adversary system," Wisconsin Women's Law Journal, 10 (1995), 225–281.

[28] *Berger v. United States*, 295 U.S. 78, 88–89 (1935).

[29] Stephanos Bibas, "The story of Brady v. Maryland: From adversarial gamesmanship toward the search for innocence?" in Carol Steiker (ed.), *Criminal Procedure Stories* (New York, NY: Foundation Press/Thomson/West, 2006), pp. 129–154, 130–131.

[30] Thornburg, "Just Say 'No Fishing,'" 2.

In sum, Linda Berger pinpoints nicely what cognitive psychologists have discovered about this, that when presented with new information "our brain uses a triage-like approach,"[31] applying to that information "a series of scans and frames,"[32] in largely narrative and metaphor form. We organize fresh data into chunks and seek to fit them into frameworks we have developed over time from the historical, cultural, and personal contexts in which we have lived. Juries and judges are therefore constantly trying to fit material presented in court into the frameworks they have in their minds and the persuasive advocate will frequently be seeking to employ narratives and metaphors which either fit or productively disturb those already held by their audience.

In his paper for this conversation, Michael R. Smith examines the form in which narrative and metaphor are most intimately intertwined for persuasive purposes in the trial: parables (that is, metaphorical narratives which serve as succinct didactic stories). He illustrates a host of purposes for which parables may be used in the legal setting: to communicate argument, emotion, entertainment, credibility, and to be memorable. His particular focus is on the use of metaphoric parables in judicial opinions, but they may also be seen in the presentations of advocates on either side in court.

In his response, Raymond Gibbs focuses on the ease with which we process metaphors and metaphorical stories – and their effectiveness therefore in persuading. Context, teller, audience etc. all determine the effect.

---

[31] Berger, "Metaphor and analogy," 152.   [32] Ibid.," 155.

3

Metaphoric Parable: The Nexus of Metaphor and Narrative in Persuasive Legal Writing[*]

Michael R. Smith

INTRODUCTION

Much has been written in recent years about the power of *metaphor* in written legal advocacy.[1] Legal scholars have also written a great deal about the power of *narrative* as a rhetorical strategy in persuasive legal writing.[2] Considering the force of these two writing strategies independently, it would seem to follow

---

[*] I would like to thank (1) Raymond W. Gibbs, Jr., who provided feedback on this project in connection with the Narrative and Metaphor in the Law Conference, (2) the other attendees of the Narrative and Metaphor Conference who provided helpful comments on my topic, (3) conference organizer Hans Lind for inviting me to present an earlier version of this topic at the Yale Conference on Law and Fictional Discourse, (4) the attendees of the Law and Fictional Discourse Conference who gave me many insightful comments on my presentation, and (5) Debra Person of the University of Wyoming College of Law for her research help on this project. I would also like to express my gratitude to the Carl M. Williams Faculty Research Fund for providing summer research funds in support of this project.

[1] Michael R. Smith, "Crafting effective metaphors" in *Advanced Legal Writing: Theories and Strategies in Persuasive Writing*, third edition (New York, NY: Wolters Kluwer Law and Business, 2013), pp. 217–246; Linda L. Berger, "Metaphor and analogy: The sun and moon of legal persuasion," *Journal of Law and Policy*, 22 (2013), 147–195; Linda L. Berger, "What is the sound of a corporation speaking? How the cognitive theory of metaphor can help lawyers shape the law," *Journal of the Association of Legal Writing Directors*, 2 (2004), 169–208; J. Christopher Rideout, "Penumbral thinking revisited: Metaphor in legal argumentation," *Journal of the Association of Legal Writing Directors*, 7 (2010), 155–191; Michael R. Smith, "Levels of metaphor in persuasive legal writing," *Mercer Law Review*, 58 (2007), 919–947.

[2] Michael R. Smith, "Illustrative narratives in rule-based analysis" in *Advanced Legal Writing: Theories and Strategies in Persuasive Writing*, third edition (New York, NY: Wolters Kluwer Law and Business, 2013), pp. 35–64; Kenneth D. Chestek, "Judging by the numbers: An empirical study of the power of story," *Journal of the Association of Legal Writing Directors*, 7 (2010), 1–35; Kenneth D. Chestek, "The plot thickens: The appellate brief as story," *Legal Writing: The Journal of the Legal Writing Institute*, 14 (2008), 127–169; Brian J. Foley and Ruth Anne Robbins, "Fiction 101: A primer for lawyers on how to use fiction writing techniques to write persuasive facts sections," *Rutgers Law Journal*, 32 (2001), 459–483; Ruth Anne Robbins, "Harry Potter, Ruby Slippers and Merlin: Telling the client's story using the characters and paradigm of the archetypal hero's journey," *Seattle University Law Review*, 29 (2006), 767–802.

that a rhetorical device that is both a metaphor and a narrative would be a particularly potent persuasive writing tool. As it turns out, there is a persuasive writing device sitting at the intersection of metaphor and narrative. While the existing literature doesn't give this rhetorical device a specific name, I call it metaphoric parable.

As a persuasive writing device, a metaphoric parable is a short, metaphoric story designed to make a point or teach a lesson. Consider, for example, the metaphoric parable crafted by Justice Jon Sparling of the Texas Court of Appeals in his concurring opinion[3] in the case of *Coyle v. Texas*.[4] In *Coyle*, the Court of Appeals addressed the issue of whether certain statements made by the prosecution during the criminal trial of Mr. Coyle violated the defendant's Fifth Amendment right against self-incrimination. The majority of the court found that the prosecutor's statements did violate the defendant's rights. Although Justice Sparling concurred in the result, he wrote separately to criticize the binding precedential case – a case called *Dickinson*[5] – that served as the basis of the court's decision. Justice Sparling argued that the law in Texas regarding self-incrimination had evolved dramatically from the right's original incarnation in the United States Constitution and that the latest precedent case on which the court relied – i.e., *Dickinson* – bore very little resemblance to the original constitutional right. To highlight how far the law on self-incrimination had drifted from its original constitutional pronouncement, Justice Sparling offered a metaphoric parable:

> I liken this area of the law to the allegory of the woodcutter who attempted to cut firewood in uniform lengths. Instead of measuring each successive log to the original, he measured it to the log cut immediately before. At the end of the cord, he discovered that the last log bore no resemblance in length to the first.
>
> Undoubtedly, the [prosecutor's statement in this case] resembles the [prosecutor's statement] in *Dickinson* – which is the last log cut – and, therefore,

---

[3] Judicial opinions, particularly concurring and dissenting opinions have, long been recognized as a form of persuasive legal writing. Michael R. Smith, "About this book" in *Advanced Legal Writing: Theories and Strategies in Persuasive Writing*, third edition (New York: Wolters Kluwer Law and Business, 2013), p. 6; Anne E. Mullins, "Subtly selling the system: where psychological influence tactics lurk in judicial writing," *University of Richmond Law Review*, 48 (2014), 1111–1156. Although many of the examples of metaphoric parable set out in this paper come from judicial opinions, the device is relevant to persuasive legal writing generally, including court briefs written by practicing attorneys. That being said, my research found that very few legal advocates currently employ metaphoric parable in their briefs to courts. Perhaps that will change with the publication of this paper.
[4] *Coyle v. Texas*, 693 S.W.2d 743 (Tex. App. 1985).
[5] *Dickinson v. Texas*, 685 S.W.2d 320 (Tex. Crim. App. 1984).

must be reversed. I seriously doubt, however, that the framers of our constitution had this extreme in mind when they wrote, "nor shall [any person] be compelled in any criminal case to be a witness against himself." U.S, CONST. Amend. V.[6]

Justice Sparling's woodcutter story adds significant rhetorical force to his passionate concurring opinion in the *Coyle* case. As we will see in this article, the source of this persuasive power comes from the passage's nature as both a narrative and a metaphor.

The woodcutter passage in Justice Sparling's concurrence is clearly a narrative in that it is presented in the form of a short story featuring a protagonist, action that occurs over time, conflict, and a resulting lesson learned.[7] The passage, however, is also metaphoric. The process of cutting logs is not literally akin to the development of case law in a particular legal area. Likewise, the last log cut by the woodcutter in this story is not literally like the *Dickinson* case, as an abstract precedential case is not literally similar to a cut log. However, Justice Sparling's point is that the scenario represented in the woodcutting story is figuratively similar to how the law on self-incrimination developed in Texas. Just as each successive log was measured not against the original model log, but against the immediately preceding cut log, each successive case in the area of self-incrimination in Texas was based not on the original constitutional language, but on the immediately preceding case in the area. And just as the woodcutting procedure resulted in a gradual yet significant departure from the original model log, the Texas courts' process for deciding cases in the area of self-incrimination resulted in a gradual yet ultimately significant departure from the original constitutional pronouncement of the right. Thus, the woodcutting story is presented as a metaphoric narrative designed both to explain and dramatically emphasize Justice Sparling's admonition of the current state of the law in Texas on self-incrimination. Such is the nature of metaphoric parable as a persuasive writing device.

This article explores in detail the rhetorical dimensions of metaphoric parable in persuasive legal writing. The analysis presented here will show that much of the force of metaphoric parable comes from the fact that it

---

[6] *Coyle*, 693 S.W.2d at 745 (Sparling, J., concurring).
[7] The five main characteristics of a story are characters (the individuals in the story), setting (where the action takes place), plot (the chronological events that happen to and by the characters), conflict (the principal problem the main character[s] encounter), and resolution (how the conflict is resolved in the end). Foley and Robbins, "Fiction 101," 465–467 (citing James N. Frey, *How to Write a Damn Good Novel* [New York, NY: St. Martin's Press, 1987] and Josip Novakovich, *Fiction Writer's Workshop* [Cincinnati, OH: Story Press, 1995]).

combines metaphor and narrative and, as such, draws from the power of each. The second part of this article generally defines metaphoric parable as a persuasive writing device and elaborates how metaphoric parable differs from similar types of rhetorical devices such as literal parable, fable, literary allusion, and extended metaphor. We will also see how metaphoric parable differs from legal authority. The third part examines the rhetorical power of metaphoric parable in persuasive legal writing. In this discussion, we will explore the rhetorical functions of metaphor and narrative in written legal advocacy. We will also examine how metaphoric parable, sitting at the nexus of metaphor and narrative, accesses the force of both.

DEFINING METAPHORIC PARABLE AS A PERSUASIVE WRITING DEVICE IN LEGAL ADVOCACY

The General Characteristics of Metaphoric Parables

As a tool of persuasive writing, a metaphoric parable is a very short, metaphoric story inserted into an argument to both communicate and highlight a general point relevant to the argument. Justice Sparling's woodcutter story in the *Coyle* case, which we explored in the Introduction, is a classic example of metaphoric parable as a tool in persuasive legal writing. The main point of Justice Sparling's concurring opinion was that the law in Texas on self-incrimination had gradually and ill-advisedly strayed away from the original constitutional pronouncement of the right. To help communicate and emphasize his point, Justice Sparling used the metaphoric short story of the woodcutter's woes.

Let's look at another example of metaphoric parable as a persuasive writing device, this time from an attorney's brief to an appellate court. In the case of *Hill v. Komar*, Auto-Owners Insurance Company attempted to intervene in the litigation in an effort to recover money it had paid out in connection with the matter.[8] The plaintiff in the case challenged Auto-Owners' right to intervene, and the trial court judge denied Auto-Owners' request. Auto-Owners appealed that decision to the Michigan Court of Appeals. After Auto-Owners filed an Opening Brief in support of its right to intervene, the plaintiff filed an Answer Brief.[9] Auto-Owners subsequently filed a Reply Brief in which it argued that the plaintiff's Answer Brief failed to address Auto-Owners' points of contention.

---

[8] Intervenor-Appellant's Brief on Appeal, *Hill v. Komar* (Mich. Ct. App.) (No. 267959) 2006 WL 6085449, at *3.

[9] Intervenor-Appellant's Reply Brief on Appeal, *Hill v. Komar* (Mich. Ct. App.) (No. 267959) 2006 WL 6085447, at *1.

According to Auto-Owners, the plaintiff's Answer Brief ignored the real issues in the case – issues that posed serious problems for the plaintiff – and instead raised other issues that, although irrelevant, were strong for the plaintiff. In its effort to explain that the plaintiff had inappropriately attempted to shift the focus of the case, Auto-Owners' attorney employed a familiar story:

> There is an old adage about a man looking for his keys under a lamppost. A passing good Samaritan offers to help, and asks where the keys were lost. The man explains that he dropped them somewhere down the street. When the good Samaritan asks why the man is looking under the lamppost, the man responds, "because the light is better over here."[10]

The brief writer continued by expressly applying the metaphoric story to the plaintiff's Answer Brief:

> Plaintiff has not bothered to address, issue-by-issue, the bulk of Auto-Owners' arguments in support of Auto-Owners' claims of error. Instead, ... Plaintiff takes a "the light is better over here" approach, ... presumably in order to redirect the debate to an issue on which Plaintiff believes she can prevail.
>
> Auto-Owners is of the view that the best assistance that it can provide this Court is to ... point out where Plaintiff has mischaracterized Auto-Owners' arguments.[11]

Here again we see the use of metaphoric parable as a persuasive writing device. The theme of Auto-Owners' Reply Brief[12] was that the plaintiff, in her Answer Brief, sought to shift the court's attention away from the real issues of the case, which were weak for the plaintiff, and to redirect that attention to other issues that were irrelevant to the appeal yet substantively strong for the plaintiff. Auto-Owners' attorney highlighted this theme by presenting the lamppost story, which provided the reader with a vivid narrative that was metaphorically akin to the plaintiff's strategy.

Clearly, refocusing a legal argument onto favorable issues is not literally similar to looking for one's keys under a lamppost. The two scenarios, however, are figuratively alike. The man in the lamppost story avoided the arduous task of looking for his keys in the dark part of the street even though that is where he lost them. Instead, the man looked for his keys where the light was better, ignoring the fact that such a search was irrelevant, nonsensical, and

---

[10] Ibid., *2 n.1. This metaphoric parable was presented in a footnote rather than in the text of the brief. I think it would have been even more powerful if the brief writer had included the metaphoric parable directly in the text of the brief.

[11] Ibid., *2.

[12] This discussion in Auto-Owners' brief takes place in the opening paragraphs and presents the theme for the entire brief.

ultimately doomed to failure. Similarly, the plaintiff's Answer Brief in the *Hill* case, according to Auto-Owners' attorney, went out of its way to avoid the arduous task of addressing the real issues in the case. Instead, the Answer Brief addressed issues that were easier for the plaintiff while completely ignoring the fact that those issues were irrelevant to matter before the court. Thus, the metaphoric parable helps the attorney establish the theme of the Reply Brief by asserting that the plaintiff's act of intentionally focusing on the wrong issues in the case is metaphorically comparable to the act of intentionally looking for one's keys in the wrong place.

The argument by Auto-Owner's attorney was persuasive, and ultimately Auto-Owners prevailed.[13] The Michigan Court of Appeals reversed the trial court judge's order denying Auto-Owners the right to intervene, and the case was remanded back to the trial court.

Justice Sparling's woodcutter story and Auto-Owners' lamppost story are examples of the use of metaphoric parable as a persuasive writing device. In both situations, the persuasive writer used a short, metaphoric narrative to explain and highlight an important component of an argument.

I have set out additional examples of metaphoric parable in persuasive legal writing in an Appendix attached to this article. These additional examples are presented without any commentary or analysis.

Metaphoric Parable as a Stylistic Device as Opposed to Authority for an Asserted Legal Proposition

When a metaphoric parable is used effectively as a persuasive legal writing tool, it is not used as *authority* for an asserted proposition. Rather, the metaphoric parable is used only as a stylistic writing device designed to help communicate the substance of a point and, perhaps, to draw attention to it.

All legal writers know that they must cite legal authority, such as case law or a statute, for any legal proposition asserted in a legal argument.[14] Thus, it would be inappropriate and rhetorically unwise for a writer to use a metaphoric parable as support for a legal proposition in lieu of actual legal authority. Instead, metaphoric parable should be used to illustrate an argument or assertion that is otherwise supported by appropriate legal authority. In fact, a

---

[13] *Hill v. L.F. Transportation, Inc., Jan Komar, and Auto-Owners Insurance Company*, 746 N.W.2d 118, 125 (Mich. Ct. App. 2008).

[14] Mary Beth Beazley, *A Practical Guide to Appellate Advocacy*, third edition (New York, NY: Wolters Kluwer Law and Business, 2010), p. 123 ("Generally, you [as a brief writer] must include a citation at the end of every sentence in which you state a legal proposition, refer to a new authority, or quote or paraphrase information from a court opinion or other source.").

legal writer will often use a metaphoric parable to illustrate the theme or thesis of an argument and then support that theme or thesis with an in-depth discussion of the applicable legal authority.

Consider again Justice Sparling's woodcutter metaphoric parable in the *Coyle* case. The theme of Justice Sparling's concurring opinion was that the law in Texas on self-incrimination had strayed too far from the original constitutional right. Justice Sparling introduced this theme with the woodcutter metaphoric parable.[15] He then went on in the rest of the concurrence to prove his assertion using relevant legal authority.[16] Thus, Justice Sparling used the metaphoric parable not as authority but as a stylistic device to help communicate and emphasize the theme of his opinion.

We can see a similar use of metaphoric parable by Auto-Owners' attorney in the *Hill* case. The attorney did not use the lamppost metaphoric parable to prove that the plaintiff's efforts to shift the focus of the appeal were legally inappropriate. Rather, he used the metaphoric parable to set up the theme of the argument.[17] Auto-Owners' attorney then went on in the rest of the Reply Brief to show how this assertion was true using citations to the appellate record and applicable legal authority.[18] So here again we see metaphoric parable used in an appropriate way: as a stylistic device and not as authority for a legal argument.

Levels of Abstraction: Distinguishing Metaphoric Parable from Literal Parable and Fable

Metaphoric parables must be distinguished from other types of short stories – such as literal parables and fables – that may be inserted into a legal argument as a stylistic choice. As a general matter, what sets metaphoric parable apart from all of these other types of short stories is the level of abstraction at which metaphoric parable operates. All of these rhetorical devices are similar in that they are all short narratives that represent an abstract truth or principle. With metaphoric parable, however, the abstraction goes one step further in that the

---

[15] The woodcutter metaphoric parable appears as the second paragraph of Justice Sparling's concurrence and establishes the theme for the ensuing discussion. *Coyle*, 693 S.W.2d at 745 (Sparling, J., concurring).

[16] *Coyle*, 693 S.W.2d at 745–46 (Sparling, J., concurring).

[17] The reference to the lamppost metaphoric parable appears in the first paragraph of the attorney's argument. Intervenor-Appellant's Reply Brief on Appeal, *Hill* v. *Komar* (Mich. Ct. App.) (No. 267959) 2006 WL 6085447, at *2.

[18] Ibid., *2–7.

story is also metaphoric. Literal parables and fables, by contrast, are not metaphoric.[19]

A parable, in a general sense, is "[a]n illustrative story teaching a lesson."[20] Many parables are literal in nature. Thus, metaphoric parables are a subset of parables.

Consider the example of a literal parable in the case of *Powell* v. *Bunn*.[21] In the *Powell* case, the Oregon Court of Appeals was attempting to interpret a statutory term that was not defined in the statute or in the relevant case law. The majority of the court relied on the dictionary to resolve the ambiguity. In a dissenting opinion, Justice Jack Landau criticized the majority for cherry-picking one definition of the word in the dictionary from several available definitions. According to Justice Landau, the majority chose a definition from the dictionary without considering the context in which the word was used in the statute and without considering which of the definitions in the dictionary corresponded with that context. In making this argument, Justice Landau employed a humorous parable:

> I find the majority's proposed construction of the statute unpersuasive. To begin with, the majority relies on an acontextual use of definitions, which—as any lawyer knows—can be employed to make words mean anything ...
>
> I am reminded of the story—probably apocryphal—about an English-Russian translation computer program that, working word by word, translated the King James Biblical passage "the spirit is willing, but the flesh is weak" from English to Russian and back to English. The resulting word-by-word translation was that "the vodka is fine but the meat is rotten."[22]

As is true for all well-used parables, the meaning of this Russian-translation story goes beyond its narrow presentation. The amusing story reveals a more

---

[19] This discussion distinguishing metaphoric parable, literal parable, and fable is designed, at the risk of oversimplification, to highlight the metaphoric nature of metaphoric parable. It is important to note, however, that "the boundaries among these genres are both fuzzy and mutable." Randy Allen Harris and Sarah Tolmie, "Cognitive allegory: An introduction," *Metaphor and Symbol*, 26 (2011), 109–120, 113; see also Peter Crisp, Allegory: Conceptual metaphor in history, *Language and Literature*, 10 (2001), 5–19, 5–8 (discussing the history of the term "allegory").

[20] William Harmon and Hugh Holman, *A Handbook to Literature*, 11th edition (Upper Saddle River, NJ: Pearson Prentice Hall, 2009), p. 397.

[21] *Powell* v. *Bunn*, 108 P.3d 37 (Or. Ct. App. 2005).

[22] Ibid., 61 & n.4 (Landau, J., dissenting, joined by Edmonds and Haselton, JJ.) (citing Ellen P. Aprill, "The law of the word: Dictionary shopping in the Supreme Court," *Arizona State Law Journal*, 30 [1998], 275–336, 285).

general, abstract truth: a word can have many meanings depending on the context in which it is used, and using a particular definition of a word without regard to context can result in the absurd. And it is this general truth that Justice Landau intended to tap into with the use of the story. In this way — as a story that reveals a general truth – the Russian-translation parable is similar to a metaphoric parable. However, Justice Landau's story is unlike a metaphoric parable because the story is not metaphoric. The Russian-translation story is a literal illustration of the point for which it stands, and as such is markedly different from a metaphoric parable.

It is fairly easy to see how the literal Russian-translation story in the *Powell* case is different from the metaphoric nature of a metaphoric parable. Sometimes, however, it is difficult to tell the difference between metaphoric parable and literal parable because the story presented appears on its face to be metaphoric, and its non-metaphoric nature can be seen only upon closer reflection. Consider, for example, the story told by Justice Brian Quinn of the Texas Court of Appeals in the case of *Cismaru v. Radisson Seven Seas Cruises, Inc.*[23] In *Cismaru*, a married couple sued a cruise line in a Texas court alleging that they were falsely imprisoned by cruise line employees during a cruise. In response to the suit, the cruise line filed a motion to dismiss arguing that the terms of the cruise tickets required that the suit be brought in Broward County, Florida. The trial court judge agreed with the cruise line, and the suit was dismissed.

On appeal, the plaintiffs argued, among other things, that the forum selection clause on the cruise tickets was unreasonable because the plaintiffs received the tickets from the cruise line late and they were forbidden under the terms of the tickets to cancel the trip at such late notice without incurring a substantial penalty. Thus, according to the plaintiffs, they were denied a legitimate opportunity to read the terms of the tickets and reject them because they could not do so without being subjected to the prescribed penalty. In response to this argument, the cruise line asserted that, despite the wording on the tickets, the plaintiffs could have in fact rejected the tickets without incurring a penalty if they had asked. To support this contention, the cruise line presented an affidavit from its vice-president of pricing, which had been prepared after the litigation had started. The affidavit stated, "if any passenger were to lodge [an] objection to the forum selection clause in the contract [their] funds ... would be returned [with] impunity."[24] The appellate court

---

[23] *Cismaru v. Radisson Seven Seas Cruises, Inc.*, No. 07–00-00100-CV, 2001 WL 6546, at *3 n.4 (Tex. App. January 2, 2001).
[24] Ibid., *3.

rejected this rebuttal by the cruise line, finding the vice-president's affidavit to be self-serving, untestable, and unpersuasive. In writing this portion of the opinion, Justice Quinn punctuated the court's holding with an amusing story:

> This [affidavit by the cruise line's vice-president] is reminiscent of the story by E. Quinn. A man walks into a hardware store to buy pipe. The storekeeper informs him that it costs 15 cents per foot. The buyer replies that ... down the road, he could acquire it for 10 cents per foot. The storekeeper asks why he didn't buy the pipe down the road. The buyer replies that they were out of it. Hearing this, the storekeeper says that when he is out of pipe he only charges 5 cents per foot. Simply put, blatant self-serving statements that cannot be readily tested are given little credence.[25]

In the end, the Court of Appeals found the forum selection clause on the cruise tickets to be unenforceable. The judgment of the lower court was reversed, and the case was remanded to the Texas trial court for further proceedings.

To many, Justice Quinn's pipe-store story would appear to be a metaphor. After all, what does buying pipe in a hardware store have to do with an affidavit by a cruise line executive? However, upon closer inspection, one can see that the story is not a metaphor at all, but simply a literal illustration of an abstract point regarding human nature. Justice Quinn's point in rejecting the vice-president's affidavit was that untestable self-serving statements are, by their nature, highly suspect. The literal point of the pipe-store story is the same. The statement of the owner of the pipe store down the road – that he sells pipe for 10 cents a foot when he has it – had little credibility in the eyes of the hardware store owner because it was self-serving and untestable. Thus, the story presents a literal example of an untrustworthy statement and, as such, is less a metaphor and more a literal illustration of a general human observation. Thus, Justice Quinn's story should be classified as a literal parable rather than a metaphoric parable.

Metaphoric parables must also be distinguished from the genre of short stories called fables. A fable, like those of the famed Aesop, is a short story designed to teach a moral or lesson and featuring anthropomorphic animals as the characters.[26] What distinguishes a metaphoric parable from a fable is the

---

[25] *Ibid.*, *3 n.4. Despite research attempts, I could not determine who the "E. Quinn" mentioned in this passage refers to. Judging by the last name, my best guess is that it refers to a member of Justice Quinn's family.

[26] Fable, Literary Devices.Net, http://literarydevices.net/fable/ (last visited August 15, 2016) (defining fable and discussing as an example "The Fox and the Crow" from *Aesop's Fables*).

same feature that distinguishes a metaphoric parable from a literal parable: fables are not metaphoric.[27]

We can see the use of a fable as a persuasive device in legal writing in the case of *Sessions v. Southern California Edison*.[28] In this case, Mr. Sessions, a retired employee of Southern California Edison, for many years had received a pension amount that both he and his former employer thought was correct. Years later, when Southern California Edison revised its pension plan for a group of former employees that did not include Mr. Sessions, Mr. Sessions became dissatisfied with the amount of his pension. As a consequence, Mr. Sessions sued his former employer seeking an upward adjustment to his pension payments. When the court looked at the issue, it discovered that Mr. Sessions had actually been overpaid for years and should incur a reduction, not an increase, in his pension payments. In presenting the theme for the legal arguments that followed in the court's opinion, Justice Hanson, writing on behalf of the California Court of Appeal, offered an opening fable:

> The case is a reminder of the fable of the dog with a bone in his mouth who, in crossing a stream, suddenly saw his own reflection in the brook beneath and, annoyed at what he thought was a larger bone in the mouth of another dog, snapped for it, dropped his own bone and so lost all. While it is no doubt unfortunate for the plaintiff, it appears that by his suit he has only shown that he is entitled to a lesser amount than he had before.[29]

The dog-with-a-bone fable in *Sessions* has an abstract moral: greed can lead to loss. Thus, the story, like a metaphoric parable, stands for a point more general than the narrow story itself. The story, however, is not metaphoric. While the story features a dog rather than a person, the story is a literal manifestation of its lesson: the dog lost what he already had due to his greed. Likewise, the story's lesson has a literal application to Mr. Sessions. Mr. Sessions suffered a reduction in his pension payment due to his act of greed.

Most fables are like the dog-with-a-bone fable. While they generally feature animals as the characters, the lessons offered are literal lessons, not metaphoric ones. And in this way, fables are different from metaphoric parables.

---

[27] It is possible for a fable – i.e., a short story that teaches a lesson using anthropomorphic animals – to be used metaphorically rather than for its literal lesson. In such a situation, however, it would be more accurate to characterize the story as a metaphoric parable rather than a fable.
[28] *Sessions v. Southern California Edison*, 118 P.2d 935 (Cal. Ct. App. 1941).   [29] Ibid., 936.

Distinguishing Metaphoric Parable from Metaphoric Literary Allusion

Metaphoric parable is also different from the rhetorical device of literary allusion. Literary allusion occurs when a legal writer includes in an argument a quote or other brief reference to a literary work such as a novel, short story, or poem.[30] Although there are many forms of literary allusion in persuasive legal writing,[31] the form that is closest to metaphoric parable is metaphoric literary allusion. With this type of literary allusion, a legal writer alludes to a literary character, scene, or event in an effort to make a metaphoric comparison between that literary component and some person, event, or aspect in the writer's legal case.[32]

Justice Alan Handler's dissenting opinion in the case of *New Jersey* v. *Muhammad*[33] offers a compelling example of a metaphoric literary allusion. In *Muhammad*, the New Jersey Supreme Court upheld the constitutionality of the state's "victim-impact" statute. This statute allows the prosecution in the sentencing phase of a capital murder case to introduce evidence about the background of the victim and the impact of the victim's death on his or her family. This evidence can then be considered by the jury and the court while deciding whether the convicted murderer will be sentenced to death or to some other type of punishment. In a dissent, Justice Handler argued that, while the statute was innocent enough on its face, it would in its application lead to race discrimination in capital sentencing. In making this argument, Justice Handler employed a metaphoric literary allusion by figuratively comparing the victim-impact statute to the Trojan horse from Virgil's epic Greek poem, *The Aeneid*:

> The introduction of victim-impact evidence unacceptably exacerbates the racial disparities evident in capital sentencing. Victim-impact evidence encourages jurors to examine and use, both consciously and unconsciously, the comparative worth of the defendant and the victim. Race unquestionably influences our perceptions. This evidence will therefore set back our attempts to eliminate racial disparities in capital sentencing. Such discriminatory sentencing cannot be tolerated in New Jersey. "[W]hen an institution of justice fosters either overt or hidden use of constitutionally forbidden criteria such as race, social standing, religion, or sexual orientation, it cannot be defended as just." Victim-impact evidence will be the Trojan horse that will

---

[30] Michael R. Smith, "Literary allusion" in *Advanced Legal Writing: Theories and Strategies in Persuasive Writing*, third edition (New York, NY: Wolters Kluwer Law and Business, 2013) pp. 247–303.
[31] See generally ibid.   [32] Ibid., pp. 251–255.
[33] *New Jersey* v. *Muhammad*, 678 A.2d 164 (N.J. 1996).

bring into every capital prosecution a particularly virulent and volatile form of discrimination.[34]

Justice Handler's reference to the Trojan horse in his dissent is undoubtedly metaphoric. In this passage, Justice Handler equates the victim-impact statute – with its seemingly benign language and its hidden destructive capacity – to the famed wooden horse filled with Greek soldiers during the Trojan War. While the two are not literally alike, they are symbolically alike according to Justice Handler. In the Greek story, the citizens of Troy were fooled by the innocent outward appearance of the horse and brought the horse through the gates of their fortress. Once in, the Greek soldiers exited the horse and defeated the Trojans.[35] According to Justice Handler, the victim-impact statute has a comparable concealed danger.

Metaphoric literary allusion is similar to metaphoric parable in the sense that both devices use a story to create a metaphor. The two devices differ, however, in terms of how the story is used. A metaphoric parable entails the actual telling of a short story from beginning to end. It has a narrative component. Metaphoric literary allusion, by contrast, does not involve the writer telling a complete story. Rather it involves a writer making a brief allusion to a full story that presumably exists in the reader's memory.[36]

Justice Handler, in his dissent, did not tell the whole story of the Trojan horse. He merely made a brief allusion to it. Thus, his figurative use of the Trojan horse story is an example of metaphoric literary allusion, not metaphoric parable.

Distinguishing Metaphoric Parable from Extended Metaphor

Finally, we must explore the difference between a metaphoric parable and an extended metaphor. In my previous writing, I have identified two types of extended metaphors in persuasive legal writing. The first type is *single-comparison extended metaphor*, which is merely a single metaphor "that requires several sentences to communicate it."[37] The following excerpt

---

[34] Ibid., 203–205 (Handler, J., dissenting) (quoting Vivian Berger, "Payne and Suffering: A Personal Reflection and Victim-Centered Critique," *Florida State University Law Review*, 20 [1992], pp. 21–65, 48). I have previously discussed this example of metaphoric literary allusion. Smith, "Literary allusion," pp. 253–254.

[35] Virgil, *The Aeneid*, Bk II:1–56 (A. S. Kline trans. 2002), www.poetryintranslation.com/PITBR/Latin/VirgilAeneidII.htm#anchor_Toc536009309. Accessed August 15, 2016).

[36] Smith, "Literary allusion," pp. 256–258. "By making this type of literary reference, the writer hopes to tap into the reader's mental storehouse of past literary knowledge, thus enabling the reader to bring that information to bear on the new text." Ibid., p. 257.

[37] Smith, "Crafting effective metaphors," p. 227.

from the case of *Anderson v. Litzenberg* includes an example of a single-comparison extended metaphor:

> A metaphor may better illuminate the distinction between contending evidence is irrelevant to prove a claim as opposed to asserting that sufficient evidence was not adduced to prove such claim. Assume that the pieces of two jigsaw puzzles, one of a horse and the other of a ship, were inadvertently commingled. Assume further that we are concerned only with putting together the horse puzzle. By raising a relevancy contention, the objector is effectively claiming that the puzzle builder is using a piece from the ship puzzle to build the horse puzzle. The ship piece does not belong there. A sufficiency of the evidence contention, on the other hand, effectively states that, while the puzzle builder has used only horse pieces to assemble the horse puzzle, the picture is not yet complete.[38]

In this excerpt, Judge Glenn Harrell of the Maryland Court of Special Appeals uses several sentences to set out a single metaphoric comparison. Specifically, the writer uses a puzzle metaphor to explain the difference between the relevancy of evidence and sufficiency of evidence in a legal matter. Because of the complicated nature of the comparison, Judge Harrell needed several sentences to complete the metaphor. Thus, his lengthy metaphor is an example of a single-comparison extended metaphor.

The second type of extended metaphor in persuasive legal writing is *Single-Theme/Multiple-Comparison Extended Metaphor*.[39] With this type of extended metaphor, an initial metaphor is extended and built on with several related metaphors, all of which revolve around the same theme or symbolic concept.[40] We can see an example of this type of extended metaphor in Judge Irving Goldberg's opinion in the Fifth Circuit case of *Shanley v. Northeast Indiana School District*.[41] In *Shanley*, a group of high school students sued school officials on First Amendment freedom of expression grounds after the officials prevented the students from distributing an underground newspaper near the school. The case highlighted the conflict that can occur between the administrative rights of school officials tasked with the responsibility to maintain order in a school and the constitutional rights of free expression of students within the school. A prior Supreme Court case called *Tinker*[42]

---

[38] *Anderson v. Litzenberg*, 694 A.2d 150, 161 n.11 (Md. Ct. Spec. App. 1997), quoted in Smith, "Crafting effective metaphors," p. 227.
[39] Smith, "Crafting effective metaphors," p. 228.   [40] Ibid.
[41] *Shanley v. Northeast Indiana School District*, 462 F.2d 960 (5th Cir. 1972). I have previously discussed the example of an extended metaphor in the *Shanley* case. Smith, "Crafting effective metaphors," pp. 228–229.
[42] *Tinker v. Des Moines Indep. Community Sch. Dist.*, 393 U.S. 503 (1969).

established guidelines for balancing the rights and duties between these two groups. In writing the majority opinion in *Shanley*, Judge Goldberg compared the *Tinker* case to a dam:

> *Tinker*'s dam to school board absolutism does not leave dry the fields of school discipline. This court has gone a considerable distance with the school boards to uphold its disciplinary fiats when reasonable. *Tinker* simply irrigates, rather than floods, the fields of school discipline. It sets canals and channels through which school discipline might flow with the least possible damage to the nation's priceless topsoil of the First Amendment.[43]

In this example of a single theme/multiple comparison extended metaphor, Judge Goldberg extends his initial "dam" metaphor to several related metaphors: "irrigates," "floods," "the fields of school discipline," "canals and channels," and "topsoil of the First Amendment." All of the metaphors revolve around the single theme of farm irrigation.

Both types of extended metaphors differ from metaphoric parable in two important ways. First, extended metaphors such as these are not stories. Although the discussion of the puzzle in the *Anderson* excerpt covers several sentences, it is not a story. The discussion lacks a developed plot, a character encountering conflict, and a resolution of that conflict, all indispensable elements of a story. The *Tinker*'s dam example from the *Shanley* case is even less like a story. This discussion has no characters or plot whatsoever. Thus, as these examples demonstrate, extended metaphors lack the narrative structure of a metaphoric parable.

The second way that extended metaphors differ from metaphoric parables is that, while metaphoric parables contain only metaphoric language, extended metaphors interweave, or "blend," literal language with metaphoric language.[44] In the *Anderson* passage, for example, the metaphoric words "puzzle," "piece," "ship," and "horse" are intermingled with literal words such as "objector," "relevancy contention," and "sufficiency of the evidence contention." Thus, the language of the discussion jumps between the metaphoric and the literal. Similarly, in the *Tinker*'s dam example, metaphoric words such as "dam," "floods," "fields," "canals" are intermingled in the sentences with literal words such as "school board," "school discipline," and "First Amendment." Metaphoric parables, by contrast, contain only metaphoric

---

[43] *Shanley*, 462 F.2d at 978 (citations omitted).
[44] For a similar discussion on how language "blending" distinguishes extended metaphor from allegory, see Peter Crisp, "Between extended metaphor and allegory: Is blending enough?," *Language and Literature*, 17 (2008), 291–308, 291–292; Peter Crisp, "Allegory, blending, and possible situations," *Metaphor and Symbol*, 20 (2005), 115–131, 117.

language throughout their duration. Consider once again Justice Sparling's woodcutter metaphoric parable we discussed in the Introduction. Throughout the entirety of the metaphoric parable, the language about the woodcutter stayed metaphoric. The discussion in Justice Sparling's opinion did not turn literal again until the metaphoric parable had been completely told. This lack of language "blending" in metaphoric parable is a hallmark distinction between metaphoric parable and extended metaphor.

THE RHETORICAL FUNCTIONS OF METAPHORIC PARABLE IN PERSUASIVE LEGAL WRITING

As we have seen, a metaphoric parable in persuasive legal writing is a combination of a metaphor and a narrative. As such, it evokes the persuasive power of both of these rhetorical devices. The best way to appreciate the multifaceted nature of metaphoric parable in persuasion is to analyze it in terms of the fundamental persuasive processes first postulated by the classical rhetoricians. According to classical rhetoric theory, there are three general types or processes of persuasion: logos, pathos, and ethos.[45] Logos refers to efforts to persuade based on appeals to logic and rational thinking.[46] Pathos refers to efforts to persuade based on appeals to emotion.[47] Ethos refers to the process of persuading by establishing credibility in the eyes of one's audience.[48] An effective metaphoric parable, as a metaphor and a narrative, employs all three of these persuasive processes.

The Logos Functions of Metaphoric Parable

Logos – persuading through logic – plays a very big role in the persuasive power of metaphoric parable. According to the scholarship on metaphor as a persuasive legal writing device, metaphors serve an important logos function because they act as figurative analogies for a writer's point.[49] That is, by employing a metaphor, a writer helps to communicate the substance (i.e., logos) of his or her argument by providing the reader with a supportive

---

[45] Michael R. Smith, "The foundations of persuasion: Logos, pathos, and ethos" in *Advanced Legal Writing: Theories and Strategies in Persuasive Writing*, 3rd edition (New York: Wolters Kluwer Law and Business, 2013), pp. 11–13; Edward P. J. Corbett and Robert J. Connors, *Classical Rhetoric for the Modern Student*, 4th edition (New York, NY: Oxford University Press, 1999), pp. 31–32.
[46] Smith, "The foundations of persuasion," pp. 12, 13–14, 28–29.
[47] Ibid., pp. 12, 14–15, 29–31.   [48] Ibid., pp. 12, 15–16, 31.
[49] Smith, "Crafting effective metaphors," p. 231.

analogy.[50] In fact, some points in a legal argument can be difficult to explain in literal terms, and an apt metaphor can even simplify the communication process.[51]

Because a metaphoric parable is a type of metaphor, it serves a clear logos function by operating as a figurative analogy. Consider, once again, Justice Sparling's metaphoric parable about the woodcutter in the *Coyle* case, which we first explored in the Introduction to this article. Justice Sparling's argument was that, with every successive case on the issue, the law of self-incrimination in Texas had drifted away from the original constitutional pronouncement of the right. This abstract concept is difficult to explain in literal terms. Thus, to help communicate the substance of his argument, Justice Sparling employed the metaphoric story of the woodcutter. By implicitly comparing the woodcutter's process to the process of deciding self-incrimination cases in Texas courts, and by implicitly comparing the final log cut to the final Texas case on self-incrimination, Justice Sparling's metaphoric parable helped to communicate the substance of a point that otherwise could have been difficult to convey.

Narrative also serves an important logos function. The best way to appreciate the logos function of narrative is to view narrative and storytelling as a means of communicating information. Narrative, as a mode of communication, differs substantially from communicating through general pronouncements and abstract propositions. While abstract propositions announce their point directly, stories convey their point indirectly by featuring a character that learns a lesson through the resolution of a conflict.[52]

According to narrative theory, stories actually communicate information more effectively than abstract propositions because narrative structure more closely resembles the way the human mind makes sense of the world.

> [A] person learns through story in the same way that he or she learns through experience. Starting at infancy, human beings learn by interacting with and experiencing the world around them. And because life is continual and occurs over the passage of time, much of learning by experience happens as events, ideas, and concepts build on each other. A person is basically the protagonist in the story that is his or her own life. And much of what we learn is learned by chronologically experiencing related events that build on each other.
>
> Story as a mode of communication functions the same way. Just as life involves experiencing the chronological passing of related events, stories too, by definition, involve a chronological telling of related events. When we hear a story, we place ourselves in the role of the protagonist. "We imagine

---

[50] Ibid.   [51] Ibid.   [52] Smith, "Illustrative narratives in rule-based analysis," pp. 38–40.

ourselves as the protagonist and picture ourselves in the protagonist's shoes as we proceed from introduction to conclusion." And we learn from this experience in the same way we learn from our participation in our own lives …

The most fundamental way that we learn and process information is through living the experience. Stories communicate in the same way and thus take advantage of the most fundamental way in which humans process and understand information. For this reason, narrative has a communicative advantage over general propositions. As [Steven] Winter puts it,

The grounding of all human cognition in experience means that there is a greater cognitive "clout" to images from lived experiences as compared to propositional formulations that attempt to "literalize" their meaning. The dramatic image of [narrative] has a communicative power that is unmatched by the "equivalent" propositional statement.[53]

Metaphoric parable gets much of its persuasive power through its narrative structure. A metaphoric parable doesn't communicate its point by stating it as a general proposition. Rather, a metaphoric parable allows a reader to arrive at its point through the process of narrative discovery. Thus, a metaphoric parable helps a writer communicate the substance – i.e., logos – of his or her point by taking advantage of story as an effective mode of communication. In Justice Sparling's concurrence in the *Coyle* case, for example, he could have expressed his objection to the status of self-incrimination law in Texas by stating his point only as a literal, abstract proposition. However, he facilitated the communication of his point by using the story of the woodcutter. As the reader progresses through the woodcutter story, the reader is cognitively transported into the story as the protagonist/woodcutter. When the woodcutter in the end discovers that his log-cutting process has resulted in a pile of irregular logs, the reader vicariously experiences the same discovery. The reader is then allowed to use this vicarious discovery and its attendant lesson to better understand Justice Sparling's description and criticism of Texas' law on self-incrimination. Thus, the story adds significantly to the concurring opinion because it allows Justice Sparling to take advantage of the communicative power of narrative.

The Pathos Functions of Metaphoric Parable

Pathos – persuading through emotion – also plays an important role in metaphoric parable. The process of pathos actually encompasses two separate

---

[53] Ibid., pp. 38–39 (quoting Steven L. Winter, "The cognitive dimension of the agon between legal power and narrative meaning," *Michigan Law Review*, 87 [1989], 2276–2277).

subprocesses of persuasion. In my previous writing, I identified and named these two subprocess *emotional substance* and *medium mood control*.[54] "Persuading through emotional substance involves eliciting an emotional response from the audience regarding the substance of the matter under consideration."[55] Medium mood control, by contrast, involves eliciting a favorable mood in one's audience through the medium of the message as opposed to the substance of the message.[56] Both of the subprocesses of pathos are present in an effective metaphoric parable.

As both a metaphor and a narrative, a well-crafted metaphoric parable can evoke a substantive emotional response in a reader. A metaphor often evokes emotions that correspond with the literal meaning of the metaphoric language.[57] This phenomenon is even more compelling with the parabolic form of metaphor because a metaphoric parable is also a story, and stories have long been praised for their ability to evoke emotions by transporting a reader into their imaginary world.[58] Consider once again Justice Sparling's woodcutter story in the *Coyle* case. This metaphoric parable not only helped Justice Sparling communicate the substance (logos) of his point; it also brought with it the emotional aspects of the story. In the story, the woodcutter discovers at the end of the cord of wood that his cutting process has resulted in a stack of uneven logs. Because the reader is transported into the story as the woodcutter, the reader vicariously experiences the emotions the woodcutter would feel upon making this discovery, emotions such as surprise, dismay, regret, and frustration. The reader then projects these emotions onto Justice Sparling's revelation about the current state of self-incrimination law in Texas. As a consequence, the reader of Justice Sparling's argument, like the woodcutter, feels surprised and dismayed about how the process of deciding cases in Texas has led to the unwitting expansion of the law on self-incrimination. Thus, the metaphoric parable – through the emotional substance component of pathos – works to persuade the reader that Justice Sparling is correct in his criticism of the law.

An effective metaphoric parable also persuades through the medium mood control aspect of pathos. There are several things about a metaphoric parable as a metaphor that help put a reader in a positive and receptive mood. First, as

---

[54] Smith, "The foundations of persuasion," pp. 14–15, 29–31.   [55] Ibid., p. 14.
[56] Ibid., pp. 14–15, 29–31.   [57] Smith, "Crafting effective metaphors," p. 232.
[58] Michael R. Smith, "Literary references for thematic comparison: Summoning dreams and swords" in *Advanced Legal Writing: Theories and Strategies in Persuasive Writing*, third edition (New York, NY: Wolters Kluwer Law and Business, 2013), pp. 291–295 (citing Mark Johnson, *Moral Imagination: Implications of Cognitive Science for Ethics* [Chicago, IL: The University of Chicago Press, 1994], 196–198).

we discussed in the context of logos, the metaphoric nature of a metaphoric parable helps a reader understand a point more easily because the metaphor serves as a supportive analogy. Thus, a metaphoric parable is pleasing to a reader because it facilitates the communication of the writer's point.[59] Second, a metaphoric parable, as a metaphor, is an artistic figure of speech and, as such, can enliven language and even entertain a reader.[60] Like all forms of metaphor, a metaphoric parable captivates a reader by acting as a sort of riddle to be solved.[61] Solving the riddle – i.e., seeing how the metaphoric idea presented in the metaphoric parable is similar to the writer's literal point – can be entertaining to a reader.[62] Similarly, metaphoric parables, as metaphors, "unexpectedly juxtapose two things that the reader may not have thought about as having a symbolic similarity. This unexpected comparison can be entertaining to the reader."[63] Thus, metaphoric parables in persuasive legal writing serve the medium mood control functions that have long been attributed to metaphors generally.

The nature of a metaphoric parable as a short story also serves a medium mood control function. Stories are unquestionably entertaining, as they whisk a reader away from reality and into an imaginary world. This entertaining aspect of stories generally is no less true for parabolic short stories presented in the context of a legal argument. The short story presented in a metaphoric parable mentally transports the reader away from the attendant legal discussion and into the imaginary world of fiction. Because this brief literary experience can be entertaining to a legal reader, a metaphoric parable can help keep the reader in a receptive mood under the medium mood control aspect of pathos.

The Ethos Functions of Metaphoric Parable

The classical rhetorician Aristotle once said that the skill of crafting an effective metaphor "is, in itself, a sign of genius."[64] By this statement, Aristotle was recognizing the ethos dynamic of metaphor.

---

[59] Smith, "Crafting effective metaphors," p. 232.
[60] Michael R. Smith, "Other figures of speech" in *Advanced Legal Writing: Theories and Strategies in Persuasive Writing*, third edition (New York: Wolters Kluwer Law and Business, 2013), p. 310 (discussing the medium mood control function of figures of speech generally.
[61] Smith, "Crafting effective metaphors," p. 232.   [62] Ibid.   [63] Ibid.
[64] Aristotle, *Aristotle's Poetics: A Translation and Commentary for Students of Literature*, Leon Golden (trans.) (Englewood Cliffs, NJ: Prentice-Hall, 1968), p. 41, quoted in Michael Frost, "Greco-Roman analysis of metaphoric reasoning," *Legal Writing: The Journal of the Legal Writing Institute*, 2 (1996), 113–141, 127.

Ethos refers to the process of persuading one's audience by establishing credibility as a trustworthy source of information.[65] An important component of ethos is intelligence. That is, to persuade an audience, a writer must demonstrate that he or she is an intelligent source of information.[66] Classical rhetoricians have long asserted that the ability to construct eloquent language through the effective use of figures of speech is a compelling sign of intelligence.[67] This admiration for eloquent language is particularly true for metaphor. According to classical rhetoric theory, the ability to construct an effective metaphor reflects a higher level of thinking and, as such, speaks to the intelligence of the metaphor's author.

This respect for metaphor undoubtedly applies to the subcategory of metaphor that is metaphoric parable. Although the story related in a metaphoric parable may not be original to the writer, the ability to evoke and apply an apt metaphoric parable to a legal argument evidences both ingenuity and an impressive level of symbolic thinking.

The narrative component of metaphoric parable also enhances the perceived intelligence of a legal writer. By using a metaphoric parable, a writer implicitly represents that he or she has a mental storehouse of illustrative stories at the ready, as well as the ability to deploy these stories to support an argument. This representation evinces both narrative acumen and communicative resourcefulness. Thus, the use of an effective metaphoric parable in persuasive legal writing helps a writer persuade through the ethos function by demonstrating that the writer is an intelligent source of information.

The Rhetorical Style Functions of Metaphoric Parable

An apt metaphoric parable also persuades by capturing the reader's focus and thereby making the corresponding legal argument more memorable to the reader. Although rhetorical figures of speech, like metaphors and similes, are more than stylistic devices, they are nevertheless stylistic tools designed to add eloquence and artistic flair to one's writing.[68] "One of the most fundamental functions of eloquent language is achieving emphasis. Because figures of

---

[65] Michael R. Smith, "Credible character and good will" in *Advanced Legal Writing: Theories and Strategies in Persuasive Writing*, third edition (New York: Wolters Kluwer Law and Business, 2013), pp. 125–127.
[66] Michael R. Smith, "Evincing intelligence" in *Advanced Legal Writing: Theories and Strategies in Persuasive Writing*, 3rd edition (New York: Wolters Kluwer Law and Business, 2013), pp. 149–150.
[67] Ibid., pp. 184–186.   [68] Smith, "Other figures of speech," p. 311.

speech involve unusual or atypical uses of language, they tend to draw readers' attention."[69]

Indeed, metaphoric parables are among the most dramatic and conspicuous figures of speech. They are in no way subtle. With a metaphoric parable, a writer breaks away from the ongoing literal legal discussion and tells a fanciful short tale. The length of a metaphoric parable, its dramatic shift in voice and writing style, and its metaphoric nature, cause it to stand out in the reader's mind. Thus, a metaphoric parable, as a stylistic device, imprints a point in the reader's memory.

CONCLUSION

For over two thousand years, metaphor has been respected as the "supreme ornament" of persuasive communication.[70] Storytelling, too, has long been valued as a tool of persuasion.[71] It should come as no surprise, then, that metaphoric parable, as a metaphoric short story, can be a powerful persuasive device.

Metaphoric parables serve many functions in persuasive legal writing. They help communicate the substance of an argument by providing the reader with an analogical narrative that illustrates the point under discussion. They evoke favorable emotions in the reader. They enhance, in the reader's eyes, the perceived credibility of the writer as an intelligent source of information. And they draw a reader's attention and make an argument more memorable.

All of these persuasive functions can be traced back to the nature of a metaphoric parable as both a metaphor and a narrative. Drawing from the rhetorical power of both of these mechanisms, metaphoric parable occupies a valuable and unique place in the arsenal of the persuasive legal writer.

APPENDIX

Additional Examples of Metaphoric Parable in Persuasive Legal Writing

- *United States* v. *Hudson*, No. 13–20063-01-KHV, 2013 WL 4047145, at *7 (D. Kansas August 9, 2013); Judge Kathryn H. Vratil:

---

[69] Ibid.
[70] Marius Fabius Quintilianus, *Institutio Oratoria*, H. E. Butler (trans.), 3 vols. (Cambridge, MA: Harvard University Press, 1954), vol. 3, 199.
[71] Aristotle, *The Rhetoric of Aristotle*, Lane Cooper (trans.) (New York, NY: D. Appleton and Co., 1932), p. 147–149 (discussing the use of illustrative stories in persuasion).

Defendant presented various witnesses who testified to his nonviolent and peaceable nature. The Court does not necessarily discredit that testimony so much as it recalls the parable of the elephant that is common to many religious traditions. A Jain version of the parable says that six blind men were asked to determine what an elephant looked like by feeling different parts of the elephant's body. The blind man who feels a leg says the elephant is like a pillar; the one who feels the tail says the elephant is like a rope; the one who feels the trunk says the elephant is like a tree branch; the one who feels the ear says the elephant is like a hand fan; the one who feels the belly says the elephant is like a wall; and the one who feels the tusk says the elephant is like a solid pipe. A king explains to them: "All of you are right. The reason every one of you is telling it differently is because each one of you touched the different part of the elephant. So, actually the elephant has all the features you mentioned." Here, defendant may be both generally non-dangerous and highly dangerous to specific individuals in specific situations – the two scenarios are not mutually exclusive.

- *Corcoran v. Astrue*, No. 09–30230-KPN, 2011 WL 2023292, at *9 & n.4 (D. Mass. April 25, 2011) (quoting David Minkoff, Oy!: *The Ultimate Book Of Jewish Jokes* 160 [2007]); Judge Kenneth Neiman:

In the court's estimation, such tailoring by the [Administrative Law Judge] of the vocational expert's testimony seems improperly destined to a conclusion adverse to the Plaintiff …

The quoted testimony reminded the court of the following tale:

[A man] goes to a tailor to try on a new custom-made suit. The first thing he notices is that the sleeves are too long. "No problem," says the tailor. "Just bend them at the elbow and hold them out in front of you. See, now it's fine." "But the collar is up around my ears!" "It's nothing. Just hunch your back up a little … no, a little more … that's it." "But I'm stepping on my cuffs!" [the man] cries in desperation. "No, bend your knees a little to take up the slack. There you go. Look in the mirror – the suit fits perfectly."

- *Montanans for Multiple Use v. Barbouletos*, 542 F. Supp. 2d 9, 15 n.5 (D. D. C. 2008); Chief Judge Thomas Hogan:

The plaintiffs' argument reminds the Court of the parable of the frog and a boiling pot of water. Placed in hot water, the story goes, the frog immediately leaps from the pot in protest. But placed in cool water that is heated one degree at a time, he remains in the pot until – sadly – it is too late and the poor fellow is cooked. Here, the addition of each amendment ratcheted up the forest plan's offensiveness quotient one more click. Before one knows the violation occurred, the administrative appeal procedures have lapsed and their appeal is dead in the water.

- *Kerper* v. *Kerper*, 780 P.2d 923, 941 (Wyo. 1989); Justices Brown and Thomas, concurring in part and dissenting in part:

This incredible holding reminds me of the legend of Adami and Heva. According to this ancient epic, a raging river separated Adami and Heva. The river was not only deep, swift and wide, but was inhabited by piranha-like creatures that would consume an intruder in a single gulp. When confronted with the impregnable river barrier, Adami simply declared that the river was not there and then walked on dry land to Land Bountiful and the waiting arms of Heva.

So it is in this case. The majority avoided an insoluble problem by simply declaring that there was no breach of contract. They made this strange ruling without the support of credible authority or rational analysis.

- *Yaeger* v. *Murphy*, 354 S. E. 393, 396 n.2 (S.C. Ct. App. 1987) (citing P. Trachtman, *The Gunfighters* [1974]); Chief Judge Alex Sanders:

We fully recognize that our opinion from this point on is no more than dictum. As everyone knows, dictum technically does not count because it is outside of what is necessary in resolving a matter. *See* 12 WORDS AND PHRASES, "Dictum," (1954). But those who disregard dictum, either in law or in life, do so at their peril. We are reminded of the apocryphal story of a duel which was about to take place in a saloon. One of the antagonists was an unimposing little man, thin as a rail – but a professional gunfighter. The other was a big, bellicose fellow who tipped the scales at 300 pounds. "This ain't fair," said the big man, backing off. "He's shooting at a larger target." The little man quickly moved to resolve the matter. Turning to the saloon keeper, he said, "Chalk out a man of my size on him. Anything of mine that hits outside the line don't count."

- *Langley* v. *Boyter*, 325 S.E.2d 550, 562, 562 n.20 (S.C. Ct. App. 1984) (citing Lon Fuller, *The Case of the Speluncean Explorers*, 62 HARV. L. REV. 616 [1949]); Chief Judge Alex Sanders:

[W]e feel it is our responsibility to address the arguments which are made for retention of the doctrine [of contributory negligence] and against adoption of the doctrine of comparative negligence.

It is argued that the numerous exceptions to the doctrine of contributory negligence allow juries sufficient flexibility to do substantial justice, and even where no exception is applicable juries often ignore the doctrine when necessary to render justice ...

This argument in support of the doctrine [of contributory negligence] based on its exceptions and lack of uniform application reminds us of the old story about the man who ate a pair of shoes. When asked how he liked them, he replied that the part he liked the best was the holes.

- *Sloviaczek v. Puckett*, 565 P.2d 564, 568–69 (Idaho 1977); Chief Justice Joseph McFadden:

I am reminded in this matter of the Greek legend concerning the Gordian Knot. The knot, tied by King Gordius of Phrygia, was said to be so complex that it could not be undone. The oracles told that only he who would be master of Asia could undo the Gordian Knot. Many tried to untie it and failed. Alexander the Great, however, took one look and then cleaved the knot in half with his sword. This is not different from the approach taken by the majority opinion; faced with a problem of untangling insurance policy provisions, the majority has chosen to disregard the contract provisions of the policies and substitute a result totally unrelated to them. While such an approach to problem solving may lead to greatness in the executive or even the legislative branch of government, it is inappropriate in the judiciary.

- *Weishann v. Kemper*, 27 Ohio N.P. (n.s.) 269, 278, 279 (Common Pleas Ct. 1928); Judge Irving Carpenter:

From the story of the development of the defendant's [junk yard] business which began about in 1915, twelve years ago, and the attitude of the neighborhood tolerating it so long, I am reminded of the fable of the camel and the tent, when the Arab stirred to sympathy for his beast suffering in the cold night air of the desert allowed him to put his head inside the tent, then his shoulders, then a hump and so on until the camel had pre-empted the tent and the Arab was forced to move out.

In view of this overwhelming authority this court is driven to the conclusion that this junk yard in this neighborhood is such a nuisance as calls for the remedy of injunction here sought.

4

Embodied Metaphor in Persuasive Legal Narrative

Raymond W. Gibbs, Jr.

We now recognize the critical importance that metaphor has in legal discourse. It is almost impossible to talk about many abstract legal concepts without metaphor rushing in to give specificity and coherence to ideas that we otherwise struggle to describe in concrete terms. Many legal concepts are not only talked about in various metaphorical ways, but are structured in terms of enduring patterns of metaphorical thoughts seen in other domains of human experience.[1] Abstract ideas can be described as people, plants, and other material objects such that they can be, for example, "fertile," "seminal," "give birth to new ideas," "resurrected," "planted," "harvested," "blossom" or "barren," and can be "packaged," "bought," "sold," "borrowed," and have "value" in the "marketplace of ideas," including the world of law. These metaphorical descriptions of ideas are not dead, because they remain vitally alive given people's continued creative use of these verbal metaphors. Consider one extended discussion of "rights" within critical legal studies in which concepts are conceived of:

> like the organic things that live and die, and this concept is dead, I think. Maybe next month a sprout will suddenly appear in the absolutely driest place on earth in the flowerpot, where you just basically put it down in the cellar thinking it wouldn't even be worth throwing the dirt out. You go down in the cellar, and by God there's a green sprout. And rights analysis once again has got some force and has some meaning for us.[2]

This passage offers a concrete, somewhat novel, instantiation of the source domain PLANTS within the conceptual metaphor IDEAS ARE PLANTS.

---

[1] See, e.g., Raymond W. Gibbs, Jr., *The Poetics of Mind: Figurative Thought, Language, and Understanding* (Cambridge, UK; Cambridge University Press, 1994). Raymond W. Gibbs, Jr., *Metaphor Wars: Conceptual Metaphor in Human Life* (Cambridge, UK; New York, NY: Cambridge University Press, 2017). George Lakoff and Mark Johnson, *Philosophy in the Flesh* (Chicago, IL: University of Chicago, 1999).

[2] Peter Gabel and Duncan Kennedy, "Roll over Beethoven," *Stanford Law Review*, 36: no. 1–2 (1984), 1–55, 40.

Many verbal metaphors, therefore, express the active, even constantly changing, conceptual roots that are at the center of metaphorical imagination and reasoning.

An important empirical development within cognitive science is that metaphors are not only fundamental to abstract thought, but are most typically grounded in human bodily experience.[3] We understand legal ideas as if they were objects, to take one notable instance, given our bodily interactions with objects, both living and inanimate.[4] The embodied motivations for abstract concepts can be revealed through cognitive linguistic analyses of how people talk about intangible ideas, from psycholinguistic experiments showing how tacit bodily knowledge and immediate bodily action underlie people's use and understanding of metaphorical language, and from cognitive neuroscience research demonstrating how sensorimotor brain areas are routinely activated when people employ metaphorical discourse.[5]

The emergence of metaphor as a proper topic for legal scholarship is accompanied by an increasing interest in the narrative qualities of legal documents, especially legal opinions. Narratives enable us to tell stories about the people and events that are the primary focus of legal disputes, yet they are deeply related to various bodily-based reasoning processes that underlie much legal decision-making. Metaphor and narrative are most saliently coupled when we offer stories and myths to explicate the reasons for why we think as we do about particular cases or legal issues. Our conception of a legal argument as being persuasive, for instance, entails embodied metaphorical thinking. Persuading people via narratives to embrace different ideas requires that both writers and readers jointly participate in a metaphorical journey, beginning at a starting point (the source), taking readers along some path (the path), overcoming relevant obstacles along the way, and ending at a particular location or destination (the goal). Confusing narratives may lead readers to wonder about the writer's "point" or where the writer "is headed," thereby again reflecting the essential spatial, journey metaphor underlying our creation and understanding of narratives.

Despite the rise of interest in metaphor and narrative within legal studies, the scholarship still has not yet fully appreciated the active nature of embodied reasoning and imagination in the ways legal narratives are created and interpreted. Many scholars may now be convinced that metaphor is a part of legal

---

[3] Raymond W. Gibbs, Jr. *Embodiment and Cognitive Science* (New York, NY: Cambridge University Press, 2006). Lakoff and Johnson, *Philosophy in the Flesh*.
[4] Stephen Winter, *A Clearing in the Forest: Law, Life, and Mind* (Chicago, IL: University of Chicago Press, 2001).
[5] Gibbs, *Metaphor Wars*.

concepts and reasoning without really acknowledging how they are continuously enacting legal ideas in embodied metaphorical ways. Embodied simulation processes are central to the tacit, fast-acting, unconscious ways that we make sense of both concrete and abstract objects and events in the world, including legal ideas. People automatically imagine themselves participating in the actions alluded to in discourse, even when these refer to abstract activities, which enable them to create an embodied understanding of what speakers and writers aim to communicate in context.[6]

The embodied simulation hypothesis has been applied to various cognitive and linguistic phenomena, including conceptual representations, memory, problem solving, learning, and consciousness. Embodied simulations are a critical part of how many legal concepts are created and interpreted within legal narratives, as well as having distinct persuasive effect in many circumstances. I will now explore this possibility by looking at metaphoric parables as persuasive devices in legal advocacy, as cogently advanced by Michael Smith in his "Parables: The nexus of metaphor and narrative in persuasive legal thinking" in this volume. Parables are familiar stories that teach important lessons, yet are also one of the most exquisite ways in which the embodied metaphorical mind is realized within language. As Smith aptly describes in his writings, metaphoric parable is not infrequent in legal narratives and possibly functions to achieve many persuasive effects. My argument, most generally, is that embodied simulation processes are essential parts of how people interpret metaphors in legal narratives and help give parables their persuasive force.

PARABLE IN LEGAL NARRATIVES

Parables are most typically associated with literature and literary experience. However, Michael Smith makes a compelling case for the importance of parable in legal narratives. He asks us to consider the case of *Coyle* v. *Texas* heard in the Texas Court of Appeals in 1985.[7] The Court of Appeals was asked to consider whether Mr. Coyle's Fifth Amendment rights against self-incrimination were violated during the original trial by the prosecutor when he made various statements about Coyle. The Court of Appeals agreed with this complaint and

---

[6] See, e.g., Benjamin Bergen, *Louder than Words: The New Science of How the Mind Creates Meaning* (New York, NY: Basic Books, 2012); Gibbs, *Metaphor Wars*; Raymond W. Gibbs, Jr. and Herbert L. Colston, *Interpreting Figurative Meaning* (Cambridge, UK; New York, NY: Cambridge University Press, 2012).

[7] Coyle v. Texas, 693. S.M2d 743 (Tex. App. 1985).

overturned Coyle's conviction. Justice Sparling agreed with the majority of justices, but wrote a separate opinion in which he noted a serious problem with the relevant precedent case (i.e., *Dickson v. Texas*). He argued that the case law in Texas regarding self-incrimination had changed over time from adhering to the US Constitution on the matter to something far less exact as seen in the *Dickson* case. For this reason, Justice Sparling argued that the precedent case of Dickson was now inappropriate as the basis for ruling in favor of Coyle. Justice Sparling described the problem with the evolving nature of law via an allegory, or parable, of the woodcutter:

> I liken this area of law to the allegory of the woodcutter who attempted to cut firewood lengths. Instead of measuring each successive log to the original, he measured it to the log cut immediately before. At the end of the cord, he discovered that the last log bore no resemblance in length to the first.

As explained later by Smith, this parable essentially implied, "Just as each successive log was measured not against the original model log, but against the immediately preceding cut log, each successive case in the area of self-incrimination in Texas was based not on the original constitutional language, but on the immediately preceding case in this area."

Parables in legal texts are presumed to be effective in persuading others of a writer's argument through reference to mundane life events that may be readily understandable, even by those outside the legal community. According to Smith, parables may specifically involve three persuasive processes: logos (i.e., efforts to persuade based on appeals to logic and rational thinking), pathos (i.e., efforts to persuade by appeal to emotions), and ethos (i.e., efforts to persuade by establishing a speaker's or writer's credibility with the audience). The woodcutter parable, as applied by Justice Sparling, facilitated understanding of an abstract argument by appeal to the reader's surprise discovery that the last log was different in length from the first, and worked to establish Sparling's credibility by demonstrating him to be an intelligent, even witty, source of wisdom.

Another legal parable, also discussed by Smith, focused on a case where a junkyard owner was sued by his neighbors for spoiling their small community. The defense argued that the neighbors had already endured the situation for twelve years without significant complaint until the present time. Judge Irving Carpenter responded in his ruling against the junkyard owner in the following way:

> I am reminded of the fable of the camel and the tent, when the Arab stirred to sympathy for his beast suffering in the cold night air of the desert allowed him

to put his head inside the tent, then his shoulders, then a hump, and so on until the camel pre-empted the tent as the Arab was forced to move out.

Once again, this parable makes an abstract legal point in concrete, immediate terms and does so in a compelling and credible manner by establishing a metaphorical link between a familiar tale and a particular legal dispute. Even if one did not previously know of the camel and the tent parable, most readers are capable of quickly inferring a system of metaphorical relationships between the two domains (i.e., the parable and the neighbor dispute) and, most importantly, draw further moral inferences that underlie the judge's reasoning in the case. The use of parable in this context was not simply directed at legal minds, but aimed to make clear the logic behind the judge's decision to all concerned parties.

The Bible, of course, is a wonderful repository of parables that apply to a variety of real-world dilemmas. Legal educators even urge that law students be asked to learn different Biblical parables and examine how these may be applied in resolving different legal disputes; what one scholar refers to as "Applying the Bible to think like a lawyer."[8] For example, various aspects of Civil Procedure law can be examined, and more concretely understood, from the study of "The good Samaritan parable," "Pleadings and the Chreia by Jesus," and "Jesus' parable about money."[9] Teaching law students about often cited Biblical parables can make them more sensitive to the persuasive power, and occasional ambiguities, of different forms of metaphoric reasoning in legal argumentation. As one scholar argued, "parables represent a pedagogical methodology that is also available, and distinctly available, to courts because of their institutional characteristics."[10]

Parables need not be described in a complete, full-blown manner to be understood as expressing metaphoric ideas grounded in embodied experiences. People may sometimes briefly refer to the name or a salient part of a familiar parable and leave it to others infer the larger symbolic message. One example of this is provided by Smith in his discussion of Justice Alan Handler's dissenting opinion in the case of *New Jersey v. Irving*.[11] Justice Handler briefly employed a literary allusion when he compared the "victim impact" statute, which was central to this case, to the Trojan horse from *The Aeneid*: "Victim

---

[8] Alfred R. Light, "Civil procedure parables in the first year: Applying the Bible to think like a lawyer." *Gonzaga Law Review*, 37 no. 2 (2001), 282–313.
[9] Light, "Civil procedure parables in the first year."
[10] Robert A. Burt. "Constitutional law and the teaching of parables," *Yale Law Journal*, 93 (1983–84), 455–502.
[11] *New Jersey v. Irving*. A-1094-09T4, State of New Jersey, 2011.

impact evidence will be the Trojan horse that will bring into every capital prosecution a particularly virulent and volatile form of discrimination."

Justice Handler goes on to suggest that allowing victim impact statements may unwittingly lead to racial discrimination in capital sentencing. He need not spell out the complete parable or literary allusion regarding the Trojan horse, because he relies on a certain cultural common ground with others (e.g., knowledge of the Trojan horse story) when justifying the reason for his dissenting opinion.

Parables are often structured in terms of different types of metaphoric reasoning, as seen in some summary metaphors that allude to important legal principles. For instance, some legal opinions introduce parables that have become familiar over time and continue to be the battleground of ongoing legal argumentation. Some notable instances that include the metaphoric ideas of "wall of separation" (i.e., between church and state), "chilling effect" (i.e. the effect of loyalty oaths on freedom of thought and speech), "marketplace of ideas" (i.e., various constitutional rights of free expression and trade), "captive audience" (i.e., free expression in schools, businesses, buses, and airports), and "chain of evidence" (i.e., when one link is broken, the entire case is corrupted) are brief metaphoric descriptions of larger complex arguments.[12] These metaphoric phrases provide familiar, short frames of parabolic thinking in which concrete concepts (e.g., "walls," "marketplaces," and "chains") enable us to conceive of more abstract ideas (e.g., the relationship between religious institutions and the US government) and have become entrenched foci of discussion within legal narratives.

Other parables in law are based on non-legal sources that are applied to particular cases. Within the legal context, for example, former US Supreme Court Justice Anton Scalia employed metaphor, parables, and literary allusion in many of his judicial decisions. For example, in his lone dissenting opinion in *Morrison v. Olson*,[13] a case focusing on the separation of powers within the United States government, Scalia wrote,

> That is what this suit is about. Power. The allocation of power among Congress, the President, and the courts in such fashion as to preserve the equilibrium the Constitution sought to establish ... Frequently an issue of this sort will come before the Court clad, so to speak, in sheep's clothing: the potential of the asserted principle to effect important change in the

---

[12] Haig Bosmajian, *Metaphor and Reason in Judicial Opinion* (Carbondale, IL: Southern Illinois University Press, 1992).
[13] *Morrison v. Olsen*, 487 U.S. 654 (1988).

equilibrium of power is not immediately evident, and must be discerned by a careful and perceptive analysis. But this wolf comes as a wolf.[14]

The biblical allusion to a wolf in sheep's clothing is a metaphor within a broader parable that has been used countless times to convey the message that appearances can be deceiving. In this specific case, however, the metaphor conveys just the opposite in that the "wolf" has no intention to deceive and should be immediately recognized as threatening. Unlike other metaphoric ideas that are quite specific to legal contexts and used widely in legal arguments (e.g., "chain of evidence"), Scalia's use of "a wolf in sheep's clothing" has a more limited use, but nonetheless makes sense given the particular case under consideration in *Morrison v. Olson.*

Furthermore, novel metaphoric ideas may emerge in legal opinions for very specific purposes. Consider, again, the elaborate metaphoric idea employed in a debate over the concept of "rights" in legal discourse:

> like the organic things that live and die, and this concept is dead, I think. Maybe next month a sprout will suddenly appear in the absolutely driest place on earth in the flowerpot, where you just basically put it down in the cellar thinking it wouldn't even be worth throwing the dirt out. You go down in the cellar, and by God there's a green sprout.[15]

Few readers of this narrative segment will have ever previously seen this specific metaphoric instantiation of the general conceptual metaphor IDEAS ARE PLANTS. Still, the novel metaphor at play in this argument is not terribly difficult for readers to understand and apply to the particular legal debate about the concept of "rights," precisely because of the conventional idea that some IDEAS ARE PLANTS. Even though the specific metaphoric language here is novel, people may readily infer a possible parable here regarding the ways that old ideas can sometimes be revitalized, often quite unexpectedly.

The increasing prominence of parable as a persuasive rhetorical device in legal narratives makes perfect sense given parable's various properties. As suggested above, parables differ in the completeness, the extent to which they conventionally apply to legal doctrines, their general familiarity, and the ways that some instantiate familiar ideas in a novel manner. Parable is a poetic form of thinking that is evident in a wide range of mundane life experiences and elaborated upon in great literature and artworks. People

---

[14] *Morrison v. Olsen,* 487 U.S. 654, 699 (1988) (dissenting).
[15] Gabel and Kennedy, "Roll over Beethoven."

cannot help but infer rich connections between the here-and-now of stories they hear, read, and create with larger symbolic meanings, which constitutes part of the "allegorical impulse" that underlies virtually all instances of parable.[16] Let me briefly explore the prominence of parable in human life to set the stage for understanding the ways parable is employed and understood in legal discourse.

THE NEXUS OF METAPHOR AND NARRATIVE: THE ALLEGORICAL IMPULSE

Parable is traditionally studied through the examination of classic literary and religious texts throughout the Western intellectual tradition, such as seen in the Bible, many fairy tales, and numerous contemporary novels and plays. A common theme underlying all parables is the attempt to use smaller stories from both real-life and dream-life events to better understand universal moral, religious, and existential themes. Parable, in this sense, serves as a metonymic device in which particular stories stand for larger enduring life struggles. Most importantly, parables combine metaphor and narrative by using concrete stories to better understand abstract concepts. As literary scholar Mark Turner has emphasized, the human capacity, even our impulse, to tell stories, and project these onto new situations in the form of parables, is a fundamental part of human imagination and reasoning.[17]

Parables often exhibit qualities similar to allegory by linking concrete human events to enduring symbolic life themes. Indeed, parable and allegory are often closely intertwined as narratives rooted in metaphoric reasoning from the concrete to the abstract. Nonetheless, Michael Smith proposes a more careful delineation of parable by distinguishing it from anecdote, fable, metaphorical literary allusion, and extended metaphor. He claims that each of these narrative types possesses different stylistic features, but parable, in particular, operates at the most abstract level, which is critical to its potential persuasive value within the law.

One instance of parable in action was seen in the play *The Crucible* by Arthur Miller, first staged in the United States in 1953. The play presents the story of the infamous Salem Witch trials that took place in Massachusetts in 1692–93 in which nineteen people were put to death for being witches. However, *The Crucible* is widely recognized as a parable or allegory to criticize

---

[16] Raymond W. Gibbs, Jr., "The allegorical impulse," *Metaphor and Symbol*, 26 (2011), 121–130.
[17] Mark Turner, *The Literary Mind* (Princeton, NJ: Princeton University Press, 1996).

the attempts of the United States in the 1950s, to root out Communists from governmental service (i.e., the era of "McCarthyism"). Although one could view the play simply as a tale about a specific historical event, many observers interpreted *The Crucible* as a warning to Americans about the intolerance of the US government in identifying and then prosecuting innocent citizens accused of being Communists.

Parables such as *The Crucible* attract attention for the broader lessons they provide about the vicissitudes of human behavior in changing social contexts. My own view embraces a very liberal understanding of parable, one that properly acknowledges the metaphorical underpinnings of many forms of thinking and speaking about abstract ideas in concrete ways. It may be possible to stylistically distinguish between parable, extended metaphor, fables, anecdotes, parables, metaphoric literary allusions, and even allegory. Yet differences in literary style or form do not imply that people engage in different cognitive processes to use and interpret these varying discourse figures. Each of these devices may be critically grounded in fundamental embodied metaphorical thinking. Parable is not, in my view, simply a literary, communicative device: it is also a pervasive form of human cognition in which people automatically seek connections between mundane reality and larger symbolic life themes, something which has been previously characterized as the "allegorical impulse."[18]

Consider one personal experience that has become a cherished parable in my own life. At age 17, I took a job as a truck driver in Boston, despite being underage and lacking the proper driver's license needed to operate a large truck. Within twenty minutes on that first memorable day, I was trying to drive down this very narrow street in downtown Boston that had parked cars on both sides. I did not believe that my large truck was capable of making it through the parked cars and I felt great panic. Not knowing what to do, and believing at first that I may be stuck, I quickly decided that I should simply look straight ahead and step on the gas. Sure enough, my truck moved forward and soon I was out onto a bigger street. Feeling delighted at this little success, I quickly realized that there was a message to take from this small life experience: When in doubt, look straight ahead and step on the gas! Since that time, I have repeatedly remembered this lesson whenever confronting what appeared to be unrelenting obstacles, both physical and metaphorical. Don't worry about the problems surrounding you, just focus on the goal and continue to move forward without fear of failure.

---

[18] Gibbs, "The allegorical impulse."

The "move forward without fear in the face of obstacles" message is a parable precisely because it draws a larger symbolic theme from an ordinary life story. More specifically, this symbolic theme arises from a metaphoric relationship between the story events (e.g., being stuck in a traffic jam), and the obstacles, both concrete and abstract, which we often encounter in life. In this manner, the stuck in traffic parable is motivated by the common conceptual metaphor LIFE IS A JOURNEY that is grounded in our recurring bodily experiences of taking different journeys (i.e., source-path-goal).

As seen in some legal narratives, parables need not be described in a complete, full-blown manner for these to be understood as expressing metaphoric ideas that are grounded in embodied experiences. People may sometimes briefly refer to the name or a salient part of a familiar parable and have others infer the larger symbolic message.

Everyday discourse highlights the fast and flexible ways in which people give evidence of their embodied metaphoric thinking and communications, including through reference to parables. For example, many common proverbial expressions reflect "mini parables."[19] Consider an exchange in which one speaker says that she is about to invest her limited savings in a scheme to extract crystals from some newly discovered South American mines. The listeners respond with the advice: "You may not want to put all your eggs in one basket." We understand the proverb as expressing a metaphoric theme (e.g., the dangers associated with placing all of one's limited funds in a precarious "get rich" scheme). Thus, the proverb points to one concrete instantiation of the ill-advised investment strategy. The power of proverbial speech across cultures is strong testimony to people's facility with metaphoric thinking about many life situations, with proverbs offering concrete solutions to these dilemmas.

Metaphoric cognition is not an idiosyncratic rhetorical weapon that is only used in certain literary, religious, political, or legal contexts. Human beings, across different cultures and times, are predisposed to link the concrete and the abstract and draw important meaningful correspondences that are often rooted in specific and recurring bodily experiences. Even children exhibit some potential to infer metaphoric messages through their enjoyment of classic fairy tales which also offer symbolic life lessons. As argued by one notable child psychologist, "The child intuitively comprehends that although these stories are *unreal*, they are not *untrue* . . . "[20]

---

[19] Gibbs, "The allegorical impulse."
[20] Bruno Bettelheim, *The Uses of Enchantment: The Meaning and Importance of Fairy Tales*, (New York, NY: Alfred A. Knopf, 1976).

PARABLE INTERPRETATION VIA EMBODIED SIMULATIONS

We can identify parable in legal narratives and within other discourse genres, but is it the case that people are generally able to interpret different parables? Can readers of Justice Sparling's "woodcutter" parable understand the connection between the concrete example and the general legal argument he wished to make about Texas case law on self-incrimination? Did people watching *The Crucible* draw the connection between the play's portrayal of events in the late seventeenth century with those occurring in the mid-twentieth century? Scientific evidence reveals that many ordinary people, including university students, can draw metaphoric mappings to infer larger symbolic messages from a variety of spoken and written discourses.[21] These findings, at the very least, suggest that individuals need not possess special intellectual abilities to interpret many metaphoric parables. One specific possibility, however, is that people understand parables as metaphoric mappings between concrete events and more abstract principles, through embodied simulation processes. This hypothesis asserts that people ordinarily attempt to construct imaginative, embodied reenactments of what some specific discourse must be like to participate in given their own bodily capacities and experiences. For example, people are likely creating coherent metaphorical messages by imagining themselves performing the actions mentioned in a narrative, both when these actions refer to possible and impossible human events.

A great deal of cognitive science research demonstrates that people automatically create simulations of the actions referred to when reading both literal and metaphorical language. For example, experimental studies show that people automatically understand literal statements such as "John opened the drawer" by imagining themselves pulling the drawer toward their bodies, and comprehend "John closed the drawer" by imagining themselves pushing the drawer away from their bodies.[22] People understand "John threw the punch" by imagining themselves making a fist, and "John threw the dart" by imagining themselves pinching an object between their thumbs and forefingers.[23] These results indicate how embodied simulation processes are a critical component in immediate language comprehension.

---

[21] Gibbs (in press). Supra.
[22] Arthur Glenberg and Michael Kaschak, "Grounding language in action," *Psychonomic Bulletin & Review*, 9 (2002), 558–565.
[23] Roberta Klatzky, James Pellegrino, Brian McCloskey, and Stephen Doherty, "Can you squeeze a tomato? The role of motor representations in semantic sensibility judgments," *Journal of Memory and Language*, 28 (1989), 56–77.

Embodied simulation processes help people read metaphorical language referring to actions that are impossible to physically perform in the real world. Consider the simple abstract phrase "John couldn't grasp the concept of infinity." A "concept" is an abstract entity and it seems odd to think that one can physically "grasp" something that does not physically exist. But studies show that having people first make, or even imagine making, a hand movement, such as reaching out to grasp something, subsequently facilitates the speed with which they comprehend a metaphorical phrase such "grasp the concept."[24] Even if people are unable to physically grasp a concept, engaging in relevant bodily actions primes the construction of an embodied simulation to infer the metaphorical meaning of "grasp the concept." Thus, people interpret the word "concept" as a metaphorical object which, when grasped, can be studied and understood. Readers also interpret conventional metaphors such as "The road runs along the coast" by simulating the running action, a form of "fictive motion."[25]

These and many other diverse, experimental results highlight the degree to which people use their perceptual and motor systems for simulation purposes. In some cases, the meaning products that one infers when understanding spoken and written language will be relatively crude, primarily because this set of products will be "good enough" for the purposes at hand. At other times, people may engage in more elaborate, even highly strategic, embodied simulation processes as they tease out numerous meanings and impressions from an extended narrative. For example, consider the following brief narrative that was delivered by Chris Matthews on his American TV political discussion program "Hardball" (Sept 28, 2012).[26] Matthews was commenting on the upcoming TV debate between President Barack Obama and his opponent, Mitt Romney, in the 2012 Presidential contest.

> Let me finish tonight with next week's first debate in Denver.
> I'll be out there to watch the two of them go at it. I have no real idea what to expect. I think Romney will take some hard shots; he may spend the whole 90 minutes blasting away at the President, serving him with one indictment after another, hoping that something will stick.
> I think Obama will play with him, parry the assaults, block the blows, try to keep his head clear so he can avoid getting hurt. I think it will start slow with

---

[24] Nicole Wilson and Raymond W. Gibbs, Jr., "Real and imagined body movement primes metaphor comprehension," *Cognitive Science*, 31 (2007), 721–731.
[25] Teenie Matlock, "Fictive motion as cognitive simulation," *Memory & Cognition*, 32 (2004), 1389–1400.
[26] http://hardballblog.msnbc.com/_nv/more/section/archive?author=chrismatthews.

both men trying to be cautious, neither able to land a punch, not hard enough to register with the tens of millions watching.

Then it will happen: Romney will deliver what is clearly a pre-rehearsed moment, a sound bite. It will be something about Obama not delivering on a promise, something about the economy he said he'd do but hasn't. He will expect the President to defend himself.

When he does, pointing to what he inherited from Bush, Romney will pounce. He'll say that Obama's not running against Bush. This will be the Romney strategy: get Obama to pass the buck on the tough economic recovery and then land his Sunday punch.

People do not understand this narrative simply by reading and interpreting a series of possibly related verbal metaphors (e.g., "Romney will take some hard shots," "blasting away at the President," "Obama will play with him, parry the assaults, block the blows, try to keep his head clear so he can avoid getting hurt," "able to land a punch"). One empirical study showed, in fact, that people make sense of Matthews's text as expressing a larger metaphoric message about the various ways in which political debates are boxing matches.[27] Readers early on started inferring larger metaphoric messages, not needing to first read the entire narrative, which conveyed symbolic ideas about the nuance and shape of political debates. The participants also reported distinct bodily sensations related to different metaphorical actions referred to in the narrative. Thus, they felt themselves blocking blows, throwing punches, and so on even though some reported to not ever engaging in these actions in their own lives.

Finally, many participants suggested that boxing matches are not just physical encounters between two people, with one eventually overcoming the other through physical expertise. Boxing matches are themselves often "symbolic" and "political" in the sense of the two combatants representing different types of people and their larger goals beyond winning the fight itself (e.g., experience, personal appearance, boxing styles, national or ethnic backgrounds, and geographical locations). In this way, people are not simply drawing individual source-to-target domain mappings between boxing and political debates. They are automatically creating embodied simulations to interpret parables regarding political debates.

A different empirical study examined the role that embodied simulations may play in metaphoric literary interpretation, this time in relation to prose

---

[27] Raymond W. Gibbs, Jr., "The allegorical character of political metaphors in discourse," *Metaphor and the Social World*, 5 (2015), 264–282.

fiction.[28] In *The Anthologist* by Nicolson Baker, a poet who is editing a large volume of recent American poetry for a publisher is simply unable to write the introductory essay because he suffers from a terrible case of "writer's block," some of which is due to career and marital problems he has recently experienced.[29] The novel is quite funny, and full of insights, as well as gossip, about literature and the lives of poets. Toward the end of the novel, the poet/editor summarizes his dilemma in the following manner:

> I wish I could spill forth the wisdom of twenty years of reading and writing poetry. But I am not sure I can ... Now it's like I'm on some infinitely tall ladder. You know the way that old aluminum ladders have the texture, that kind of not too appealing roughness of texture, and that kind of cold gray color? I'm clinging to this telescoping ladder that leads up into the blinding blue. The world is somewhere very far below. I don't know how I got here. It's a mystery. When I look up I see people climbing rung by rung. I see Graham. I see Billy Collins. I see Ted Kooser. They're all clinging to the ladder too. And above them, I see Auden, Kunitz. Whoa, way up there. Samuel Daniel, Sara Teasdale, Herrick. Tiny figures clambering, climbing.
>
> The wind comes over, whsssew, and its cold, and the ladder vibrates, and I feel very exposed and high up. Off to one side there's Helen Vendler, in her trusty dirigible, filming our ascent. And I look down and there are many people behind me. They're hurrying up to where I am. They're twenty-three-year-old energetic climbing creatures in their anoraks and goggles, and I'm trying to keep climbing. But my hands are cold and going numb. My arms are tired to tremblement. It's freezing, and it's lonely, and there's nobody to talk to. And what if I just let go? What if I just loosened my grip, and fell to one side, and just – ffffshhhooooww. Let go.

Would that be such a bad thing?

The specific parable here is both novel and complex, but much of it centers around, once again, the common embodied metaphor LIFE IS A JOURNEY. One psychological study indicated that ordinary university students provided consistent evidence of understanding the "climbing ladder" parable through embodied simulation processes.[30] Students read the passage above and immediately wrote out their responses to a series of questions. The results revealed that almost all of the participants readily acknowledged that the "infinitely tall ladder" was symbolic of the LIFE IS A JOURNEY conceptual metaphor. People did not explicitly mention the conceptual metaphor per se, but noted specific aspects of

---

[28] Raymond W. Gibbs, Jr. and Natalia Blackwell, "Climbing the stairs to literary heaven: A case study of allegorical interpretation of fiction," *Scientific Study of Literature*, 2 (2012), 197–217.
[29] Nicholson Baker, *The Anthologist* (New York, NY: Simon & Schuster, 2009), p. 189.
[30] Ibid.

the mapping of journeys onto life, as when they noted how a journey consisted of a source (i.e., the beginning or lower parts of the ladder), a path (i.e., the ladder itself), and a goal (i.e., success, fame, the solution to the problem of writing the introductory essay). Almost all of the participants' responses also alluded to the poet's clinging to the ladder as evidence of insecurity over what he was doing as a poet/editor and his potential for ever achieving fame as a poet. Thus, the poet being stuck on the ladder referred to something larger than just his being unable to make progress in physically climbing the ladder. Participants also widely recognized that the ladder represented the journey toward success such that poets higher up on the ladder (e.g., Auden, Teasdale) were older and more famous, despite not knowing who these people were, with those on the lower parts being younger and less famous.

Most importantly, not only did the participants interpret specific phrases as having metaphorical meaning, they also exhibited significant metaphoric coherence, typical of parables, in their responses to the different questions. For example, when asked about the meaning of "infinitely tall ladder," participants responded as follows: "The function of the ladder is to lead people into the imagination of poetry" and "The ladder provides the link between the realistic, mechanical world and the artistic world." Furthermore, all participants reported having various bodily experiences while reading the passage. Many referred to concrete physical sensations (e.g., feeling cold, tired, stomach sinking), while others noted more general psychological ills (e.g., anxiety, a sense of failure, a fear of competition). These sensations emerged during the actual reading of the story, as noted by some participants, and were not after-the-fact reflections on some preliminary, purely linguistic understanding of the text. Such reports are consistent with the claim that embodied simulations give rise to various bodily effects, many of which are constrained by the objects, actions, and people referred to in the text.

There is clearly much empirical evidence demonstrating that people who are not literature students can easily discern parabolic messages from different types of discourse. Understanding parable involves automatic embodied simulation processes that are similar to those seen in interpreting language more generally, and are critical to many other forms of conscious and unconscious mental experience.

EMBODIED METAPHOR AND PERSUASION

Are parables persuasive in legal narratives? The key facet of metaphorical persuasion rests with the systematic associations that arise from the mappings between source and target domains. Our experiences of LIFE and JOURNEYS do not share the exact same features regarding travelers, paths, destinations, and so on. Instead, the mapping of JOURNEY experiences onto the idea of LIFE creates the specific inferences that people leading a life are travelers, problems in life are physical obstacles along a path, and purposes in life are destinations. Moreover, the mapping of information from a source to a target domain in a conceptual metaphor is generally, but not always, unidirectional. We can understand LIFE in terms of JOURNEYS, but the mapping of LIFE onto JOURNEYS makes less sense. Conventional metaphorical statements are concrete, linguistic manifestations of these different inferences.

Linguists and rhetoricians have long argued that certain metaphors in discourse can be very persuasive, especially in political contexts.[31] Many studies from cognitive and social psychology have, indeed, demonstrated some ways that verbal metaphors can influence people's beliefs, attitudes, and decisions in certain situations.[32] However, the persuasive appeal that any verbal metaphor may have depends on the particular metaphor employed, its relevance to the topic under discussion, who the speaker or writer may be, and the initial beliefs or opinions of the audience, to note just a few of the important constraints on metaphorical persuasion.

Consider, again, Justice Scalia's mention of the wolf in sheep's clothing metaphor in his dissent in *Morrison v. Olsen*. Part of the possible persuasive value of this metaphor is the way Scalia twists the wolf-in-sheep's clothing metaphor back upon itself. Experimental research has shown that contradicting a widely used metaphor can sometimes be a very effective persuasive tool.[33] Yet, critics of Scalia may contend that his use of metaphor is less than persuasive in regard to his analysis of the issues in *Morrison v. Olson*, even if they understand and partly appreciate his aim to distinguish his views from

---

[31] See, e.g., Jonathan Charteris-Black, *Politicians and Rhetoric: The Persuasive Power of Metaphor* (London; New York, NY: Palgrave Macmillan, 2005); George Lakoff, *Moral Politics* (Chicago, IL: University of Chicago Press, 1996); Andreas Musolff, *Metaphor and Political Discourse: Analogical Reasoning in Debates about Europe* (London; New York, NY: Palgrave-Macmillan, 2004).

[32] See, e.g., Michael Hanne, William Crano, and Jeffery Mio (eds.), *Warring with Words: Narrative and Metaphor in Politics* (New York, NY; Hove, UK: Psychology Press, 2015); Mark Landau, Daniel Sullivan and Jeffrey Greenberg, "Evidence that self-relevant motives and metaphoric framing interact to influence political and social attitudes," *Psychological Science*, 20 (2009), 1421–1427; Teenie Matlock, "Framing political messages with grammar and metaphor," *American Scientist*, 100 (2012), 478–483; Paul Thibodeau, "Extended metaphors are the home run of persuasion: Don't fumble the phrase," *Metaphor & Symbol*, 31 (2016), 53–72; Paul Thibodeau and Lera Boroditsky. "Metaphors we think with: The role of metaphor in reasoning," *PLoS ONE* 6(2): e16782. 2011. doi:10.1371/journal.pone.0016782.

[33] Jeffery Mio, "Political metaphors and persuasion" in J. Mio and A. Katz (eds.), *Metaphor: Implications and Applications* (Mahwah, NJ: Lawrence Erlbaum, 1996), pp. 127–146.

the other justices in this, and many other, matters of judicial philosophy, which was one of Scalia's enduring concerns. In this way, the use of parables may be more or less persuasive depending on their literary value, their reliance on familiar stories, conventional metaphorical concepts, their status as extended metaphors, their important moral qualities, and who the audiences are that may read and potentially be influenced by these figurative devices.

Part of the possible persuasive power of parable in legal contexts is the extended manner in which many of these stories are presented in narrative. Asking readers to temporarily immerse themselves in a very specific narrative-world, as seen in even short parables, forces them to engage in extended metaphoric reasoning processes, ones that can, under many circumstances, be effective simply because of mere exposure to the metaphoric ideas at hand. Even when people encounter metaphors that briefly refer to longer parables, or simply summarize metaphoric principles underlying parables (e.g., "wall of separation"), they will typically automatically activate a longer conventional narrative that is far richer in its implications than is the verbal metaphor alone. Many psychological studies demonstrate how the mention of a familiar metaphor can lead people to both reason about abstract topics in particular ways and make narratives containing them memorable, and convincing.[34] The fact that parables and literary allusions often involve extended stories also demands the creation of extended embodied simulation processes, which leads to a more protracted immersive reading experience. Living with the details of metaphorical source domains within parables in this manner increases the possibility that parables may have persuasive impact.

Nonetheless, the use of parable in legal narratives also raises a deeper question regarding what it even means to say that some text is "persuasive." Because of their rich symbolic meanings, parables often function at different communicative levels. For instance, in the woodcutter analogy or parable, Justice Sparling's narrative may be persuasive in terms of (a) calling attention to features of the case that some may not have previously noted, (b) providing a reason for his own opinion in this case that may be convincing to others, and (c) calling attention to how the woodcutter parable is possibly applicable to many, if not all, legal decisions based on previous case law. It is not always clear which of many possible layers of metaphorical meaning one needs to be

---

[34] Victor C. Ottati and Randall A. Enstrom. "Metaphor and persuasive communication: A multifunctional approach," *Social and Personality Compass*, 4 (2010), 783–794.

persuaded about in order for any parable to be thought of as being persuasive.[35]

At the very least, part of what makes some parables especially persuasive is the fact that people typically create enriched embodied simulations to infer what someone has said or written. When Justice Sparling used the woodcutter parable to justify his opinion in *Coyle v. Texas*, readers generally imagined themselves acting as the woodcutter, and perhaps making the mistake of only measuring the next log to be cut in terms of the last one. Therefore, we imaginatively enact the very error that is the basis for Sparling's comparison of the woodcutter to recent self-incrimination law in Texas. Much research in cognitive psychology shows that the mere imagining of both real and fantastic actions (e.g., being bitten on the fingertip by a rat), increases the likelihood of people thinking they have actually experienced those very actions.[36] Imagining an action makes us more likely to believe its feasibility, which, in turn, should push people toward agreeing with the metaphoric meanings of parables within legal narratives.

There is one enduring misunderstanding of metaphor in the legal community, namely long-standing beliefs about conventional and so-called dead metaphors, which lead them to downplay the possible communicative, persuasive value of these tropes. Many legal scholars urge others to avoid clichéd conventional expressions and to certainly not use dead metaphors in attempts to make persuasive arguments.[37] But these admonitions fail to recognize that many conventional verbal metaphors, including those often seen as "dead" by rhetoricians, actually reflect enduring, live metaphoric concepts in the minds of contemporary speakers. Various psycholinguistic studies, for example, show that many so-called dead metaphors, such as idiomatic and proverbial expressions, are connected to cognitively active metaphoric schemes of thought.[38] People tacitly understand that conventional statements like "My marriage is on the rocks" or "We had to overcome many obstacles before getting married" reflect the widespread metaphoric concept ROMANTIC RELATIONSHIPS ARE JOURNEYS. Related research demonstrates that even mundane metaphors, such as "crime is a virus" or "crime is a beast," or "international law is a

---

[35] For more on levels of analysis in legal metaphors, see Michael R. Smith, "Levels of metaphor in persuasive legal writing," *Mercer Law Review*, 58 (2007), 919–947.

[36] Maryanne Garry, Charles Manning, Elizabeth Loftus, and Steven Sherman, "Imagination inflation: imagining a childhood event inflates confidence that it occurred," *Psychonomic Bulletin & Review*, 3 (1996), 208–214.

[37] "Writers should use metaphors sparingly, should wait for the aptest moments, elsewhere using a more straightforward style." Bryan A. Garner, *A Dictionary of Modern Legal Usage*, 2nd edition (New York, NY; Oxford, UK: Oxford University Press, 1995), p. 559.

[38] Raymond W. Gibbs, *The Poetics of Mind*.

two-way street," can have a powerful effect on people's reasoning about different domains (e.g., dealing with crime, international trade agreements) and persuade individuals to adopt new points of view on these topics.[39] One lesson of these studies is that classic rhetorical analyses of metaphoric language, as well as other tropes, often miss the ways that figuration is an active part of human conceptual systems. Even clichéd, conventional metaphors, many of which maintain currency because of their enduring ties to bodily experiences, may be persuasive in certain contexts.

Parables in legal narratives sometimes differ from those seen in most literary (e.g., "The Crucible") and religious (e.g., "The Parable of the Prodigal Son") texts, because writers offering these stories sometimes explicitly comment on their intended meaning and relevance to specific legal cases. The persuasive value that any parable has in law will, therefore, also depend in some cases on the authors' explications of their chosen figures. Justice Sparling's woodcutter parable may be successful, in part, because of his explicit mention of the metaphoric argument (e.g., "I liken this area of law to the allegory of the woodcutter ... "), and Justice Scalia's opinion provides his own interpretation of the wolf in sheep's clothing parable to the case at hand. Surely, the ways jurists openly interpret the relevance of the parables they refer to plays a key role in the success of these parables to persuade others of different legal arguments.

One measure of metaphor's prominence in legal narrative is the degree to which jurists employ specific metaphors, and parables, in their writings. Judicial discourse gives important anecdotal evidence of various widely used metaphors, some of which become the focal point of ongoing legal arguments across different courts. In fact, one project demonstrated that particular metaphors regarding equal access to educational opportunities supported by state governments (e.g., "marketplace of ideas," students as "competitors in the global economy") have been both informally and formally shared across state supreme courts, often in the form of complex social networks.[40] Quantitative documentation of these social networks offers concrete data on the extent to which inter-court metaphors function in how different courts interpret their state constitutions. At the same time, different metaphors become recontextualized depending on the unique circumstances in each legal case, thus making it necessary to better understand how individual metaphors are specifically interpreted in context if we are to fully appreciate the specific ways

---

[39] Gibbs (in press). Supra.
[40] Matt Saleh, *Great Minds Speak Alike: Inter-Court Communication of Metaphor in Education Finance Litigation*. PhD dissertation. Columbia University (2015).

metaphoric language, and parables in particular, may have persuasive value. Most of the experimental research on metaphor in persuasion focuses on examining the role that some metaphors may have in shaping people's opinions after only one reading. Studying the persuasive function of parables, for example, requires that we explore the twists and turns in the use of specific examples in many cases across time and geography, and not just through the analysis of individual judicial decisions.

Finally, Benjamin Cardozo once aptly observed, "Metaphors in law are to be narrowly watched, for starting as devices to liberate thought; they end often by enslaving it."[41] Cardozo's warning about the "enslaving" properties of metaphor raises an important issue for thinking about the persuasive power of parable in legal narratives. Might some parable "enslave" to the point of preventing jurists and other from recognizing alternative ways of thinking about significant legal concepts and arguments? The answer, of course, is yes. However, Cardozo and many other legal theorists are wrong in their implicit assumption that metaphors, sometimes in the form of parables, are optional ways of conceiving certain, often, abstract ideas. Verbal metaphors, once more, are not mere rhetorical flourishes, but reflect fundamental embodied simulative properties of human thought from which there is no escape. Some verbal metaphors and parable may shed light on ways of thinking about some legal argument, and lead people to adopt particular ideological positions as a result, for better or worse. Still, the remedy here is not to dispense with metaphor as it is inherently indispensable within the law. We can, nonetheless, be thoughtful about the metaphoric concepts underlying legal concepts and argumentation, and recognize instances where particular metaphors may blind us to seeing matters in a different light, to use a metaphor. The solution, though, is to awaken sleeping metaphors, turn old metaphors on their heads, or to create new metaphoric ways of thinking about abstract legal ideas.

CONCLUSION

Metaphor is not merely a rhetorical device within legal narratives, but represents a fundamental form of embodied thinking, such as seen in parables, which underlie our understanding of basic legal concepts. Certain embodied metaphors are persuasive because of people's ordinary, and mostly unconscious, embodied simulation processes that give some legal narratives a direct, personal feel. This view of metaphors as embodied actions, both for authors

[41] *Berkey v. Third Ave. Ry. Co.* 155 N.E. 58, 61 (1928). (Cardozo, J).

and readers, highlights a critical feature of narrative more generally. Narratives, and the metaphors within them, are not disembodied texts on paper, but performances, or a type of lived social practice. Legal narratives are examples where judges, for instance, are not simply explaining their decisions – they are enacting them. Our interpretations of these texts also are embodied performances precisely because of the imaginative reenactments of the actions – real and imaginary, literal and metaphorical – that we automatically participate in to understand what is meaningful and perhaps persuasive in what others say or write.

CONVERSATION III
NARRATIVE AND METAPHOR IN JUDICIAL OPINIONS

Editors' Introduction

Michael Hanne and Robert Weisberg

Judges may argue, or pretend, that in their published decisions they need not, and probably should not, rely on literary figures. In the words of Greig Henderson, "With its reliance on the deductive model of particular issue, relevant fact, controlling law, and entailed conclusion, judicial discourse might seem to be the last place where the literary function of language would have any meaningful work to do."[1] But of course that judges rely heavily at least on metaphor is hardly contestable. In this volume, indirect proof comes from the preceding conversations on the role of metaphor in constituting legal doctrine and deploying legal persuasion in arguing for favored legal doctrines. This is because in their published decisions judges are in the business of explaining and adapting legal doctrine, and as those conversations show, metaphor is embedded in legal doctrine. In fact, some of our most important doctrines cannot be imagined or even named without metaphor. Perhaps for that reason, more scholarly and theoretical work has been done on the part played by metaphor in judicial opinions than on the part played by narrative.

Judges regularly employ metaphors in their opinions to characterize individuals and entities who have appeared in front of them, to define the behavior for which these parties have been convicted or absolved, and to describe, whether positively or negatively, the arguments that have been put to them by advocates on either side. But most important is the use of metaphor to simplify complex situations and data and to make abstract legal concepts accessible. As Haig A. Bosmajian states in the major work on metaphor in judicial opinions, *Metaphor and Reason in Judicial Opinions*,[2] "Nonliteral language is often

---

[1] Greig Henderson, "The cost of persuasion: Figure, story, and eloquence in the rhetoric of judicial discourse," *The University of Toronto Quarterly*, 75 no. 4 (Fall 2006), 905–924.
[2] Haig A. Bosmajian, *Metaphor and Reason in Judicial Opinions*. (Carbondale, IL: Southern Illinois University Press, 1992).

needed to explain the abstraction ... that cannot be conveyed as effectively and persuasively through literal language."[3] Bosmajian focuses especially on metaphors coined by judges to crystallize key doctrines in American law for later generations of attorneys and judges, e.g., dangerous speech "setting fire to reason"; suppression of free speech having a "chilling effect'" on public debate. Indeed, as noted by James E. Murray, fundamental legal doctrines whose phrasing has come to sound merely technical are often metaphoric, e.g. "standing" to sue or the "ripeness" of a lawsuit.[4]

One of the most consequential pronouncements in American constitutional law came in the case that identified a "penumbral right" around the set of explicit provisions of the Bill of Rights,[5] a right of personal and bodily privacy that led to *Roe v. Wade*. The continuing debate about the constitutional legitimacy of that holding is inseparable from the debate about whether the metaphor properly infers from the text the framers' intention to articulate an expansive thematic concept of right as well as specific guarantees. Benjamin Berger[6] finds parallels in Canada, such as the metaphor for that country's federalist principle – the "watertight compartments" between the functions of the national and provincial governments. Moreover, while judges often use metaphor to explain doctrine, they also draw on the persuasive use of metaphor to influence each other, or future courts. So, in his dissent in *Lambert v. California*, an unusual civil rights decision that he feared might invalidate a great deal of constitutionally valid legislation, Justice Frankfurter presciently expressed confidence that the majority holding "will turn out to be an isolated deviation from the strong current of precedents – a derelict on the waters of the law."[7]

According to Bosmajian, "Some tropes in judicial opinions appear once or twice and are never heard of again. Others, however, have staying power, become institutionalized and integral to judicial reasoning and decision making."[8] Nevertheless, the practical implications of a given metaphor may be perceived differently in different periods, and an established metaphor may, as Bosmajian shows, come to be challenged and, eventually, replaced. He points out that, for much of the nineteenth century, the US Constitution was referred to as a "machine," a mechanism that could be relied on to go of

---

[3] Bosmajian, *Metaphor and Reason in Judicial Opinions*, p. 47.
[4] James F. Murray, "Understanding law as metaphor," *Journal of Legal Education*, 34 (1984), 714–730.
[5] *Griswold v. Connecticut* 381 US 479 (1965).
[6] Benjamin L. Berger, "Trial by metaphor: Rhetoric, innovation, and the judicial text," *Court Review*, 39 no. 3 (Fall 2002), 30–38.
[7] *Lambert v. California*, 355 U.S. 225, 232 (1957).
[8] Bosmajian, *Metaphor and Reason in Judicial Opinions*, p. 3

itself. From the end of the century, however, it came to be described as "not a machine but a living thing."[9] Had Bosmajian brought his work to the last decade, he would have observed how Justice Scalia formulated his detestation of the idea of a living and changing document: "The only good Constitution is a dead Constitution."[10]

Ironically, it is so evident that judges use metaphors in their decisions that much of the insightful commentary assumes that use as obvious and then focuses on what can go wrong with metaphor. Hence Chad Oldfather alerts us, "A reader who finds that a particular metaphor aptly captures a doctrine, or who does not understand the doctrine apart from its metaphorical formulation, will be likely in the future to think of the doctrine in terms of the metaphor. Even a metaphor that has no virtue apart from being memorable can increase the impact of an opinion."[11] This observation crystallizes a point which will recur in several other conversations in this collection: the potential for a simple metaphor to displace in common thinking the abstract complexity of a legal concept.

It so happens that a key source of this cautionary insight is Benjamin Cardozo, famous for his colorful and often florid metaphors. Cardozo's jurisprudential writings are rife with them, e.g. "Justice is not to be taken by storm. She is to be wooed by slow advances."[12] Metaphors also abound in the text of his opinions, especially those from his years on the New York Court of Appeals. In the legendary "Flopper" case[13] he rejected liability for the alleged malfunctioning of an overtly wild amusement park ride. The customer who bought a ticket for the frightful fun could not complain, because "[t]he antics of the clown are not the paces of the cloistered cleric." But as a further look at that very case shows, Cardozo was hardly an uncritical user of this tool of language. Cardozo was using that phrasing to reject the metaphoric effort of the plaintiff to support his claim with "the facile comment that it threw him with a jerk." Liability could not "rest on something firmer than a mere descriptive epithet, a summary of the sensations of a tense and crowded moment."

And from this concern flows a broader admonition from Cardozo: "Magic words are as fatal to our science as they are to any other. . . . We seek to find

[9] Woodrow Wilson (1908) quoted in Bosmajian, *Metaphor and Reason in Judicial Opinions*, p. 6.
[10] www.nytimes.com/2016/02/15/opinion/justice-antonin-scalia-and-the-dead-constitution.html.
[11] Chad M. Oldfather, "The hidden ball: A substantive critique of baseball metaphors in judicial opinions," *Connecticut Law Review*, 27 no. 1 (Fall 1994), 17–52, 22.
[12] Benjamin Cardozo, *The Growth of the Law* (New Haven: Yale University Press, 1934), p. 132.
[13] *Murphy v. Steeplechase Amusement Park*, 166 N.E. 173 (1929).

peace of mind in the word, the formula, the ritual. The hope is an illusion.'"[14] Cardozo also averred, "The repetition of a catchword can hold analysis in fetters for fifty years or more."[15] (While we hope that judges will rarely succumb to the superficial allure of an inadequate metaphor, it seems clear that members of the public at large will frequently do so, and this is an issue which will be taken up in the conversation between Dahlia Lithwick and L. David Ritchie about narrative and metaphor in public debate around crime.)

One instructive example of the complexity and risk involves perhaps the most cited metaphor in legal doctrine, the "wall of separation" between church and state. As Daniel Dreisbach has shown,[16] once this trope was adopted by Justice Black[17] it became the "high and impregnable wall" that allowed for no breach under any circumstances, yet this ascribed meaning of the term masks bitter legal and philosophical conflicts. Jefferson used the term as a not-very-high minded political maneuver to fend off opponents' attacks on his faith. Moreover, he meant the "wall" to stand not between church and state in general terms but between the federal and state governments, and he was perfectly open to such things as government financing of churches.

As Dreisbach notes, "After two centuries, Jefferson's trope is enormously influential, but it remains controversial. The question bitterly debated is whether the wall illuminates or obfuscates the constitutional principles it metaphorically represents." One side says that total separation is necessary to prevent illegal "establishment," prevents sectarian conflict in attempting to influence government, and ensures freedom of conscience for religious minorities. A competing side views non-establishment and protection of religious liberty as different from separation, and it accepts the Early American assumption that it is healthy for religion-based moral values to influence public policy. An even stronger view is that an "impregnable wall" has often operated to silence the efforts of religious minorities to influence government through expression of their spiritual values. As Dreisbach himself argues, "The uncritical use of the metaphor has unnecessarily injected inflexibility into church-state debate, fostered distortions and confusion, and polarized students of church-state relations, inhibiting the search for common ground and compromise on delicate and vexing issues."

---

[14] Benjamin Cardozo, *The Growth of the Law*, pp. 66–67.
[15] Charles E. Hughes, et al. "Mr. Justice Holmes." *Harvard Law Review*, 44, no. 5, 1931, pp. 677–696 at 682.
[16] Daniel Dreisbach, *The Mythical 'Wall of Separation': How a Misused Metaphor Changed Church–State Law, Policy, and Discourse*, Heritage Foundation Report, Washington, DC (2007).
[17] *Everson v. Board of Education*, 330 U.S. 1 (1947).

As many of the chapters in this volume show, the role of narrative in the law has been a richly mined scholarly subject, yet the role of narrative in the specific context of judicial opinions has been an exception. But why? Consider the defining features of narrative that some believe to be vital in understanding – or operating – the legal system. First, by its very literary nature narrative is not a mere mechanical chronicle or sequence but involves suspense, conflict, and surprise of action; it relies on manipulation of point of view (singular or multiple, to spur understanding of action, and it invites reader or audience to use imagination to extend the narrator's implications. Then there are the claims that narrative brings enhanced epistemological power, authenticity of perception and emotion to overcome the distortions of artifice, and moral improvement through generosity of empathy. And as Binder and Weisberg argue, those claims implicate the paradoxical idea that narrative exists in a relationship of antinomy with law, such that it can serve "to protect, redeem, and subvert" law.[18] So we have descriptive observations about just how narrative manifests itself in law but also normative claims about the salutary things that happen when law gets narrated. On both counts, narrative is surely important in understanding or criticizing law. And even once we turn to something as utilitarian as litigation practice, we see the deployment of key narrative tools for the lawyer, just as we saw in the chapter on legal persuasion, for the purpose of advocating a party's distinct interpretation of events. Then there are the narratable events of the trial process itself – the judgment itself authorizes or requires a narrative of consequence: acquittal, resolution, sentence, penalty.

But most trials do not lead to published judicial opinions – indeed acquittals in criminal cases never do – so the question is whether the context of the formal articulated legal decision is equally amenable to the features and virtues of narrative. And here we find a vigorous debate. One of the most eminent scholars in the field of law and the humanities, James Boyd White,[19] is a strong believer in this amenability and argues that the deft use of narrative in judicial decisions can induce in the reader an imaginative transformation on her apprehension of the ideals and operations of law. Another of our leading law-and-literature scholars, Richard Weisberg[20] boldly affirms and seeks to illustrate that the literary tools of narrative are indeed deployed by

[18] These claims are reviewed in Guyora Binder and Robert Weisberg, *Literary Criticism of Law* (Princeton: Princeton University Press, 2000), pp. 205–209.
[19] James Boyd White, *Heracles' Bow: Essays on the Rhetoric and Poetics of the Law* (Madison, WI: University of Wisconsin Press, 1985), pp. 169–174.
[20] Richard Weisberg, *Poethics and Other Strategies of Law and Literature* (New York: Columbia University Press, 1992) pp. 8–9.

judges, and that the moral and educative power of narrative bears a mutually reinforcing relationship with judicial wisdom. Indeed, he even criticizes famous decisions whose holdings he doubtless agrees with if he sees them as deficient in drawing on narrative. His concern arises in particular with one distinct form – that of background political, economic, or cultural history. Chief Justice Warren's opinion on *Brown* v. *Board of Education* took the unusual step of rooting the case for racial integration in education in the findings of social science. Weisberg disdains reliance on dry social science and asserts that the justices thereby missed the opportunity to write an inspiring emancipation narrative. Thus in the view of these commentators, truly just decisions often reveal their justice through empathetic narrative, and judges who strive to write authentic narratives are more likely to achieve justice.

But in the conversation in this chapter between Simon Stern and Peter Brooks, even the basic descriptive premise is challenged. A key theme of Stern's paper is that the key features of narrative we turn to in exploring the law-narrative connection are necessarily absent in most judicial decision-writing. If we think of such key features as the drama of anticipation through controlled uncertainty, and the pleasure of seeing reality through others' mental states, they are unavailable here. Of course, appellate opinions usually begin with a very bare narrative of the events constituting the case. Then, there will be a narrative account of how the case has proceeded. But sequence of action or evolution of legal doctrine contain no openness of possibility, and point of view is solely a matter of the declaratory authority of the court. As Stern argues, the judge edits the raw chronicle of events to highlight those facts relevant to the conclusion to be reached. While sometimes purporting to tell a story to resolve conflicting narratives proffered by the parties, the judge writes this story with the conclusion already determined – and often the final punch telegraphed.

So, in Stern's view, the most salient thing about narrative in judicial opinion-writing is the exclusion of many of the aspects of narrative that are noted or promoted among those addressing the link between narrative and law. Stern also wryly avers that the feature of literary narrative called the "reality effect" appears to turn up in judicial opinions, but solely as a rhetorical move to enhance the image of authority of the court. Stern only narrows the space between judicial and true narrative by drawing an analogy to Ricoeur's idea of the "quasi-plot" in historical writing, whereby the narrator acknowledges the possibility of an alternative story but solely to make a favorable claim for her own in a competition for the best explanation of the raw facts. And in his part of the conversation, Brooks concedes that the deliberately controlled form of narrative is common for many decisions and is a plausibly realistic standard for judges to hold themselves to. But in his view, judicial narrative all too often (especially on politically and culturally volatile issues) corrupts that standard with gratuitous and often media-like retellings of the facts in a manner that violates the stick-to-the-record norm of appellate judging and all too often mimics the kind of narrative distortions we see in public media.

The normative claims of Richard Weisberg and James Boyd White and others also face ample disagreement. A very blunt example is Greig Henderson's "The Cost of Persuasion: Figure, Story, and Eloquence in the Rhetoric of Judicial Discourse," which insists that "eloquence is no guarantor of virtue and ... beautifully crafted judgments can be morally vicious."[21] And focusing on efficacy and possible unintended consequences of reliance on narrative in a response to Richard Weisberg's critique of the *Brown* decision, Richard Posner has argued that Warren "was right to forgo a narrative of the history of Black People in the South, even though that history is essential background to understand the harm of segregated schooling. Such a narrative would have made it even more difficult for the southern states to accept the decision."[22] And as corollary, Guyora Binder and Robert Weisberg offer a challenge to the assumption that authenticity is inherent in narrative and thereby helps it correct or redeem law, arguing that narrative is a literary artifice, operating under literary conventions, and takes forms subject to historical contingency, including the very legal framework in which narrative would operate.[23]

Thus, we can then situate the Stern-Brooks conversation at the center of a number of conflicting views of the role of narrative in the writings of courts. So, while the conversation stands in counterpoint to many of the more idealized views of judicial narrative, it bears a different, more mixed relationship to the arguments that appear in the later chapter by Linda Berger and Kathryn Stanchi on gender in law. As we will see, Berger and Stanchi might agree with Stern that judicial opinions that recount events rarely match the literary criteria we associate with narrative because, they observe, we have a tradition of decisions on gender-related issues rights that predetermine the flow of events to confirm political and cultural stereotypes. And they might also agree with Brooks that these opinions often distort the reality of events in a way that belies legal prejudice. And yet, they also differ from both Stern and Brooks in suggesting that narrative can be a creative and liberating force in

---

[21] Greig Henderson, 'The cost of persuasion: Figure, story, and eloquence in the Rhetoric of Judicial Discourse,' *The University of Toronto Quarterly*, 75 no. 4 (Fall 2006), 905–924, 905.
[22] Richard Posner, "Judges' writing styles (and do they matter)," *University of Chicago Law Review*, 62 (1995), 142–149.
[23] Binder and Weisberg, *Literary Criticisms*, at 208.

making us rethink – not "pre-think"–the way the American legal system imagines relationships between the genders. They partly align with Richard Weisberg and James Boyd White in their notion of judicial narrative inducing creativity in the reader; for them, the strategic judicial narrator leaves many blanks for the reader to fill in so the reader is persuaded not just by logic and information, but by an imaginative transformation. And Berger and Stanchi also stress that judicial narratives do not get predetermined until the judge comparatively evaluates the narratives proffered by the competing lawyers, so that the creative narration by the adversaries can ultimately influence the judge's final story. Hence literary figurations can be the cause, not the result, of the decision.

5

Narrative in the Legal Text: Judicial Opinions and Their Narratives[*]

Simon Stern

Narrative is essential to numerous aspects of legal practice and writing, from pleading and negotiation to the interpretation of evidence and conflict resolution. Indeed, one of the earliest senses of *narrator* in English, dating from the thirteenth century, refers to a pleader or sergeant-at-law tasked with reciting a party's statement.[1] Yet the law's most familiar and characteristic mode of written expression, the judgment, lacks two of the key ingredients that contribute to the lure of literary narrative – namely, the drive, fueled by uncertainty and anticipation, that propels readers on toward the conclusion, and the pleasure of observing and reflecting on others' mental states, which accounts for a considerable part of fiction's cognitive appeal.[2] The absence of these features should alert us to the questionable premises underlying any treatment of the judgment as simply one more form of narrative, whose fundamental similarity to novels and films can be taken for granted.

---

[*] For invaluable comments on earlier drafts, thanks to Andrew Bricker, Peter Brooks, Monika Fludernik, Catherine Gallagher, Suzanne Keen, Jim Phelan, and Bob Spoo.

[1] Paul Brand, "The language of the English legal profession: The emergence of a distinctive legal lexicon in insular French" in Richard Ingham (ed.), *The Anglo-Norman Language and Its Contexts* (York: York Medieval Press, 2010), pp. 94–101, 97. For an excellent theoretical discussion, see A.C. Spearing, "What is a narrator? Narrator theory and medieval narratives," *Digital Philology*, 4 (2015), 59–105, 67, which notes that in this usage, the narrator is external to the story, "unlike the narrator of modern theory." An external narrator/pleader was strategically desirable, for litigants, because "his words [would] not bind the client until that client ... adopted them," thus allowing for "two chances of pleading correctly" instead of the single chance that a first-person narrative would allow. Sir Frederick Pollock and Frederic William Maitland, *The History of English Law before the Time of Edward I*, 2 vols. (Cambridge, UK: Cambridge University Press, 1895), vol. I, p. 191.

[2] On the ways in which plot and character conspire to allure the reader, see, e.g., David Herman, *Story Logic: Problems and Possibilities of Narrative* (Lincoln, NE: University of Nebraska Press, 2002); Ross Chambers, *Story and Situation: Narrative Seduction and the Power of Fiction* (Minneapolis, MI: University of Minnesota Press, 1990); Lisa Zunshine, *Why We Read Fiction: Theory of Mind and the Novel* (Columbus, OH: Ohio State University Press, 2006).

Narrative, in law, is typically harnessed for the purpose of argument, rather than serving as an end in itself. Sometimes lawyers can achieve that goal by *presenting* a story as an end in itself, and sometimes narrative is not subordinated in this way because it is embedded in the structure of a legal process, such as a trial.[3] To say that a trial is a narrative, however, conveys little about the narrative aspects of a trial judge's decision or any appellate decisions, which seek only to represent certain aspects of the trial for explicit legal ends, such as justifying a finding of liability or showing why a doctrine needs to be modified. Legal decisions offer a prime example of an argumentative form that uses particular narrative resources to advance a set of contentions. In using narrative (as in using rhetoric), judges may be inept or may inadvertently undermine their own aims, but the result is no likelier to yield an engrossing plot. A reader on the lookout for more examples of the judge's blunders has the same kind of analytical distance as a reader who evaluates and accepts the judge's arguments, and both are very different from the reader who is immersed in a story, drawn to its characters, and curious about their fates.

By recognizing that judgments are, in important ways, *unlike* literary narratives, we can gain a better understanding of the features that make judgments narratively distinctive. In what follows, I take a few basic narrative concepts and show how they can suggest new ways of thinking about judgments. First, I comment briefly on the place of narrative studies in legal scholarship, noting that despite its seemingly interdisciplinary orientation, this line of research rarely takes up the questions that narratologists ask. Next, I turn to the narrative qualities of judicial opinions, suggesting that we may consider them as including two related stories: a story about the events leading up to the litigation (the factual story) and the story of its doctrinal resolution (the legal story).[4] These stories often blend; my aim is simply to show how distinguishing them, if only provisionally, alerts us to narratively significant aspects of the judgment that may otherwise escape notice. The work of Todorov and Ricoeur can help to clarify what it means to talk about a plot, in these two stories. Todorov's definition of a plot involves a disturbance to an equilibrium, and this requirement suggests that the treatment of legal issues, in some decisions, is plotless. Ricoeur's concept of "quasi-plot," for certain types of narratives with an

---

[3] For a helpful discussion of the trial's narrative qualities, see Robert Weisberg, "Proclaiming trials as narratives: Premises and pretenses" in Peter Brooks and Paul Gewirtz (eds.), *Law's Stories: Narrative and Rhetoric in the Law* (New Haven and London: Yale University Press, 1996), pp. 61–83.

[4] The analytical section often includes stories about how certain doctrines were created or modified; those narratives would also reward study, but I focus here on narrative features of the analysis in general, regardless of whether it includes doctrinal biographies.

explanatory orientation, offers a means of specifying more precisely what counts as event and character in the decision's legal story; accordingly, this concept allows us to consider how we might read legal cases with an eye to the questions that figure most prominently in the study of narrative – namely, questions concerning the relations between narrator, story, character, and reader.

In the last section, I consider some legal uses of what Barthes calls the "reality effect" – the means by which realist fiction authenticates itself. Seemingly superfluous details, Barthes argues, are included so that they may attest to their own (and the text's) verisimilitude. This idea offers a means of understanding both the extraneous details that arise in the pretrial stages of litigation and the process by which they disappear when those stages end. The shift toward increasingly formal and technical language, with a well-defined structure in which factual details are attached to legal conclusions, reveals an economy of narrative energy that governs the adjudication process. Most of the features that make law narratively compelling belong to the pretrial and trial stages; the ensuing written decisions transpose some of those features into the legal analysis, where their ability to immerse us in the story is purged away, but some of their other functions remain.

Scholarship on law and literature often speaks vaguely about narrative in ways that imply a basic commonality among its legal and literary manifestations. To ask how legal decisions use narrative in a distinctive fashion is not to foreclose this kind of inquiry, but to allow for more precision in exploring both the similarities and differences, opening up an array of new questions about plot and character, and about the law's designs on the reader.

NARRATIVE IN LEGAL SCHOLARSHIP

Although the turn to narrative is hardly a recent development in legal scholarship, this approach has been largely confined to a few areas (e.g., trial advocacy, "outsider" jurisprudence, and occasionally topics such as search and seizure, and the "grand" narratives of constitutional law).[5] Moreover, the

---

[5] For an overview on the research on law and narrative generally, see Greta Olson, "Narration and narrative in legal discourse," in Peter Hühn et al. (eds.), *Handbook of Narratology*, 2nd ed. (Berlin: de Gruyter, 2014), vol. I, pp. 371–383. For helpful discussions of the uses that narrative has served in legal scholarship, see the essays in Brooks and Gewirtz (eds.), *Law's Stories*; Jane Baron and Julia Epstein, "Is law narrative?" *Buffalo Law Review* 45 (1997), 141–187; Jane Baron, "Law, literature, and the problems of interdisciplinarity, " *Yale Law Journal*, 108 (1999), 1059–1085, 1066–1071; Julie Stone Peters, "Law, literature, and the vanishing real," *PMLA*, 120 (2005), 442–453, 446–448; Bernadette Meyler, "The myth of law and literature," *Legal Ethics*, 8 (2005), 318–325.

concept of narrative at work in these discussions remains thin, and rarely considers such basic questions as whether or not the narrator is a character in the story, what kind of access the reader is given to the various characters and events, and what determines the order in which the events are presented. In many instances, these questions would suggest new lines of inquiry that could complement and refine the more conventional doctrinal analysis of the cases under discussion. In other instances, these questions go unasked because they simply do not apply. To recognize that is to see that legal scholars often speak of "narratives" when they mean something else – such as images, conceptions, representations, or ideologies. Frequently, the label means simply that an interpretation is about to follow – the implication being that only narratives call for interpretation, but once the license to interpret has been secured, questions of narrative do not command any further interest. Some forms of interdisciplinary scholarship draw on methods from different fields, and other forms go outside the home discipline for the topic of inquiry rather than for the method; research on law and narrative has tended more toward the latter form, when it attends to narrative at all.

This state of affairs is unfortunate, because some of the key concepts in narratology bear on familiar debates among legal theorists. For example, scholars have long argued over the roles of subjectivity and objectivity in legal analysis and decision-making, and have drawn on various disciplines to explore these issues, but have not asked whether narrative understandings of subjectivity in language could have anything to contribute. One might think that the textual and linguistic manifestations of subjectivity could shed light on how judges actually describe and apply objective and subjective standards. This absence is all the more remarkable because the "reasonable person" is a typical means of expressing those standards; if that figure were not so ubiquitous as to be taken for granted, the personification itself would alert us to the need for narrative inquiry.[6] Most legal standards avoid personification, relying instead on abstractions like "undue burden," "originality," and "rational basis," which strive for objectivity by shunning the human element in their mode of assessment. Legal commentators routinely acknowledge the oddness

---

[6] The concept of subjectivity in language was originally formulated to describe "the capacity of a speaker to posit himself as a 'subject,'" which "creates the category of person." Emile Benveniste, "Subjectivity in language," *Problems in General Linguistics* (Princeton, NJ: Princeton University Press, 1971), p. 224. Thus the very use of the "reasonable person" as the instrument for representing a standard helps to show why Benveniste's concept might have legal significance. For classic discussions of its implications for narrative, see Ann Banfield, *Unspeakable Sentences: Narration and Representation in the Language of Fiction* (London: RKP, 1982); Monika Fludernik, *The Fictions of Language and the Languages of Fiction* (London: Routledge, 1993).

of the personification by referring to the reasonable person as a "character," but have not taken the seemingly obvious step of asking how this figure resembles and differs from the characters that populate literary narratives, nor what the narrative functions of characters might tell us about this one.[7]

Again, although counterfactuals play a significant role in work on legal argumentation and the modeling of legal logic, the narrative study of counterfactuals has yet to inform this area of research. The corpus of textual examples involving legal counterfactuals consists mainly of material taken from cases, not material used in legal advocacy. Without resort to narrative concepts, these two kinds of sources appear identical, but a quick glance shows how different they are. Consider *Worldwide Volkswagen Corporation* v. *Woodson*,[8] in which the US Supreme Court refused to extend the reach of constitutionally permissible "long-arm" jurisdiction to situations in which the defendant's products would foreseeably find their way into another jurisdiction:

> If foreseeability were the criterion, a local California tire retailer could be forced to defend in Pennsylvania when a blowout occurs there, see *Erlanger Mills, Inc.* v. *Cohoes Fibre Mills, Inc.*, 239 F.2d 502, 507 (CA4 1956); a Wisconsin seller of a defective automobile jack could be haled before a distant court for damage caused in New Jersey, *Reilly* v. *Phil Tolkan Pontiac, Inc.*, 372 F.Supp. 1205 (N.J.1974); or a Florida soft-drink concessionaire could be summoned to Alaska to account for injuries happening there, see *Uppgren* v. *Executive Aviation Services, Inc.*, 304 F.Supp. 165, 170–171 (Minn.1969). Every seller of chattels would in effect appoint the chattel his agent for service of process. His amenability to suit would travel with the chattel.[9]

Taken at face value, each *could* invites the reader to entertain the possibility featured in the ensuing scenario, serving precisely the future-oriented, hypothesis-positing function that the legal commentary on counterfactuals typically explores. In fact, the text does no such thing: the citations serve, rhetorically and narratively, to foreclose the option in question by pointing the reader to a case that has already rejected that possibility.

We might consider this pattern in terms of Gerald Prince's work on "disnarrated" events – "events that *do not* happen, but, nonetheless, are referred to

---

[7] However, some literary critics have helpfully explored this idea; for an extremely lucid and provocative discussion, see Elizabeth Fowler, *Literary Character: The Human Figure in Early English Writing* (Ithaca: Cornell University Press, 2003), pp. 24–26; see also my comments in "Law and literature," in Markus Dirk Dubber (ed.), *The Oxford Handbook of Criminal Law* (Oxford, UK: Oxford University Press, 2014), pp. 111–130, 129–130.
[8] 444 U.S. 286 (1980).   [9] Ibid. at 296.

(in a negative or hypothetical mode) by the narrative text."[10] Prince associates certain uses of disnarration with realism (the story rejects far-fetched possibilities to underscore the accuracy of its representations) and with the conditions of tellability itself (the disnarrated is excluded because it would not have generated a plot worth reading).[11] That explanation suggests, by way of analogy, that the Court's disnarrations do not simply refer to what has been repudiated, but also heighten the desirability of the chosen path, which slots the doctrine into a plot that leads somewhere in a legally plausible world – one that is both created and made realistic through contrast with these narrative refusals. That use of the counterfactual differs markedly from one in which competing alternatives are made to sound plausible. Of course, disnarration can gesture toward genuine possibility, as Prince also notes; it is only by contrasting these effects that we can appreciate the different functions of hypotheticals in advocacy and in legal decisions, rather than treating them all as equivalent.

The examples of the reasonable person and the counterfactual suggest two ways of considering how legal decisions incorporate narrative features. First, narrative logic seeps into judicial opinions because it informs various doctrines and the processes of adjudication generally, and judges repeat the same logic when they apply these doctrines and participate in these processes. Second, in mundane ways that can nevertheless have great significance, judicial decisions follow certain narrative conventions and use narrative techniques as means of advancing an argument. Much of the existing research on law and narrative – not all of it expressly presented under that heading – takes the first approach, addressing the narrative logic of law writ large, where the "legal" of "legal narrative" includes doctrines, processes of analysis, and modes of interpretation. Exploring the temporal paradoxes of *retrospective* prophecy, Peter Brooks has shown how the narrative logic of a completed search can foreclose other possible stories about what the search yielded, and has considered the interpretive, evidentiary, and doctrinal manifestations of this logic.[12] Relatedly, David Velleman has argued that the satisfaction created by a fitting conclusion can beguile us into crediting a story, leading us to accept too readily that it has achieved its explanatory aims.[13] Several recent discussions have considered the ways in which the perspective of the omniscient narrator underpins certain aspects of the law of search and seizure, and

---

[10] Gerald Prince, "The disnarrated," *Style*, 22 (1988), 1–8, 2.   [11] Ibid., 5.
[12] Peter Brooks, "Inevitable discovery—Law, narrative, retrospectivity," *Yale Journal of Law & the Humanities*, 15 (2003), 71–102; Peter Brooks, "Narrative transactions—Does the law need a narratology?" *Yale Journal of Law & the Humanities* 18 (2006), 1–38.
[13] J. David Velleman, "Narrative explanation," *Philosophical Review*, 112 (2003): 1–25.

bears on the principles of statutory interpretation.[14] Again, the integrated pattern of an internally consistent and adequately developed story informs various accounts of "narrative coherence" as a criterion for legal fact-finding and analysis: paraphrasing Stanley Fish, we may say that the most successful trial narrative or interpretation of a precedent will be the one that does the most work in explaining and assigning meaning to the details vying for legal significance.[15] The defendant who can ascribe the stray footprint at the crime scene to a rival will do better than the one who can only say, "I was framed."[16]

By contrast with this work on the pervasive influence of narrative logic, the narrative features of judicial decisions have received little attention. Studies of narrative in courtroom discourse have touched on related issues, analyzing testimony and legal argumentation with respect to narrative person, express and implicit markers of attribution, and the like.[17] Those discussions focus on speech, not writing, and they rarely ask how narrative devices relate to legal doctrine, as I propose to do here. One way to assess the significance of these techniques would be to show how perspective, tense, deixis, and narratorial visibility, for example, inflect and condition a decision's doctrinal analysis.

[14] Simon Stern, "The third party doctrine and the third person," *New Criminal Law Review*, 16 (2013), 364–412 (2013); Karen Petroski, "Fictions of Omniscience," *Kentucky Law Review* 103 (2015), 477–528.

[15] Fish explains that an interpretation commands assent by showing a work to exhibit literary qualities "in a greater degree than had hitherto been recognized" (*Is There a Text in This Class?* (Cambridge: Harvard University Press, 1980), p. 351); the usual procedure is to find those qualities in hitherto overlooked details. For treatments of narrative coherence in law, see Bernard S. Jackson, "Narrative Theories and Legal Discourse" in Cristopher Nash (ed.), *Narrative in Culture* (London: Routledge, 1990), pp. 23–50; Nancy Pennington and Reid Hastie, "A cognitive theory of juror decision making: The story model," *Cardozo Law Review*, 13 (1991), 519–557; Neil MacCormick, "Coherence in legal justification" in Aleksander Peczenik et al. (eds.), *Theory of Legal Science* (Dordrecht: Springer, 1984), pp. 235–251. Though not always articulated in terms of narrative, the same ideas have been taken up by commentators on fact-finding more generally, see, e.g., Dan Simon, "A third view of the black box: Cognitive coherence in legal decision making," *University of Chicago Law Review*, 71 (2004), 511–586.

[16] Scholarship on evidence usually considers the story of the frame-up (and the difficulty of evaluating it) in terms of probability, not narrative, but these may be seen as different facets of the same problem. See, e.g., Ronald J. Allen and Michael S. Pardo, "The problematic value of mathematical models of evidence," *Journal of Legal Studies*, 36 (2007): 107–140, 109–110; Lawrence H. Tribe, "Trial by mathematics: Precision and ritual in the legal process," *Harvard Law Review*, 84 (1971), 1329–1393, 1363–1365.

[17] E.g., Jieun Lee, "Interpreting reported speech in witnesses' evidence," *Interpreting*, 12 (2010), 60–82; Elisabetta Cecconi, "Witness narratives in 17th century trial proceedings" in Nicholas Brownlees et al. (eds.), *The Language of Private and Public Communication in a Historical Perspective* (Newcastle upon Tyne, UK: Cambridge Scholars Publishing, 2010), pp. 245–262; Laura Wright, "Third person plural present tense markers in London prisoners' depositions, 1562–1623," *American Speech* 77 (2002), 242–263.

Because of limitations of space, I focus instead on a few theories that have been highly influential in the study of narrative, taken from Todorov, Ricoeur, and Barthes.

NARRATIVE AND THE TRIAL DECISION

From Trial to Judgment

Various forms of legal writing and explanation are imbued with narrative qualities – not to mention the many depictions of law in popular culture – but it is worth focusing specifically on judgments because they figure so prominently, for lawyers and for the public, as the law's own means of justifying its conclusions and describing its operations. Numerous examinations of law and literature attest to the kinship between judgments and imaginative narratives, but these discussions rarely acknowledge the differences that constrain the analogy. One might say that judgments frustrate narrative desire, except that few readers of judgments even begin with the expectations that accompany a novel or a movie, and hence there is no desire to be frustrated. Judgments typically announce the conclusion in advance, and readers will often know the result at any rate, having seen it summarized elsewhere. The reader's curiosity has to do with argumentative technique and evidentiary support, not narrative desire.

Even someone who comes to the recital of facts without any foreknowledge is unlikely to find it narratively engaging. The summary of facts, like the doctrinal analysis, does not tell a story for its own sake: it serves the purposes of argument, first by highlighting the details that will invite a particular doctrinal solution, then by pursuing the analysis that establishes the legitimacy of that solution. As commentators often stress, this means the facts are selected in light of the theory that will resolve the case. Just as important is that the *mode* of delivering the facts also reflects that goal. The recitation of facts therefore admits no space for the techniques that foster readerly engagement with fictional plots – techniques that offer direct access to a character's mental state, or that hint vaguely at an upcoming setback, encouraging readers to speculate about the protagonist's future. Judges write in anticipation of a skeptical reader, and they take the need for support as their primary consideration.[18] The measured and laborious style elicits an attitude of readerly

---

[18] Thus the judge, no less than the lawyers, presents a potentially adversarial narrative, "construct[ed] ... [in] anticipation of one or more alternatives," and open to being "contest[ed] ... from

vigilance, militating against the immersive experience of fictional narrative, the experience of being "lost in a book."

Indeed, the basic distinction between *sjuzhet* and *fabula* seems unproductive as a means of examining the decision's factual narrative, because judges set out the events in a fashion that implies (through the use of tense, perspective, and chronology) that the story on offer simply *is* what happened, and there is no underlying story worth excavating and comparing. Only a naïve reader would accept that, considering the care that goes into crafting the recital; the point is not that anyone believes the decision represents the facts with mimetic accuracy, nor that anyone is being asked to believe that it does, but that the decision eschews any narrative techniques that would elicit another version of the story. Simply by virtue of appearing in such an elaborately processed text, even the plainest of factual narratives cannot help indexing its basis in some rawer material; it simply proposes no means of retrieving it. If *sjuzhet* refers to the effects of narrative artifice, then paradoxically, the judgment offers *sjuzhet* without a *fabula*. The judge has no reason to mark that difference, because it would only cast doubt on the decision's legitimacy.

To be sure, the elaboration of facts has changed significantly over the last century and a half: before the mid-nineteenth century, courts gave those details sporadically and elliptically, and often without sequestering them at the outset. But the evolution of judicial narrative since then has not made the presentation narratively compelling. During the nineteenth century, Anglo-American law became increasingly concerned with exploring mental states as a means of solving various doctrinal problems;[19] these developments had a significant effect on trial advocacy and the trial process (including the rules of evidence), but they did not lead judges to borrow or imitate novelistic devices for representing consciousness. Scholars who have considered the relations between legal decisions and various literary genres have pointedly refrained from analogizing literary and judicial *techniques* of representation (such as flashback and free indirect discourse), focusing instead on questions of rhetoric and structure.[20]

---

a direction not anticipated by [the] narrative's author." James Phelan, "Narratives in contest; or, another twist in the narrative turn," *PMLA*, 123 (2008), 166–175, 168.

[19] Lisa Rodensky, *The Crime in Mind: Criminal Responsibility and the Victorian Novel* (New York, NY: Oxford University Press, 2003) ; Jonathan Grossman, *The Art of Alibi: English Law Courts and the Novel* (Baltimore, MD: Johns Hopkins University Press, 2002); see also Rex Ferguson, *Criminal Law and the Modernist Novel* (New York: Cambridge University Press, 2013).

[20] See, e.g., Robert Ferguson, "The judicial opinion as literary genre," *Yale Journal of Law & the Humanities*, 2 (1990), 201–219.

If legal decisions offer so few of the pleasures that entice the enthusiasts of procedurals, thrillers, and courtroom novels, then why describe law as a narrative enterprise in the first place? Unlike judgments, trials (and the events leading up to them) abound in the features that make narratives absorbing. An unresolved conflict, for which the verdict will be an endpoint, arouses the narrative desires that a written decision would frustrate. Since their inception, trial advocacy manuals have extolled the power of a well-told story. A recent discussion emphasizes that lawyers are most effective when they "consciously ... deploy the tools of the storyteller's craft."[21] A handbook from 1901 recommended that lawyers study "the masters of narration," who teach "the art of telling a story."[22] Nearly a century earlier, a commentator on lawyers' forensic abilities observed that an effective barrister will turn "a long, complicated story, full of minute details," into one that every audience member can easily follow.[23] These examples reflect the understanding that the trial process is a narrative process.

The trial's narrative dimensions, however, are not equally visible to all observers. The narrative's continuity depends on the participant's perspective: the flow of any given witness's testimony may be punctuated by the questions of the lawyer conducting the examination and the objections of the opposing counsel, who may succeed in cutting off a developing narrative array and leaving it entirely stranded. Just as the lawyers seek to capitalize on the narrative potential of their client's case and witnesses, they seek to undermine the power of the narrative being organized on the other side. For the jurors and others in the audience, including the parties themselves, the flow of the testimony may be interrupted by private conferences between the judge and lawyers. Perhaps the best-known way to exploit the narrative potential that some participants glimpse only sporadically is to assemble the materials in a retelling of the trial, with a narrator who has access to all of these partial perspectives.[24] This way of managing conflict and point of view is not limited to courtroom fiction and "true crime" reportage: Alexander Welsh has argued that the trial furnishes a plot and a forensic approach to evidence that played a vital role in the development of the novel, most notably in Henry Fielding's

---

[21] Philip N. Meyer, *Storytelling for Lawyers* (New York, NY: Oxford University Press, 2013), p. 2.
[22] George Rose, "Literature and the bar," *Law Notes*, 5 (1901), 107–110, 110.
[23] John Payne Collier, *Criticisms on the Bar* (London: Simpkin, 1819), p. 159.
[24] For a bibliography of these retellings, see Steve Haste, *Criminal Sentences: True Crime in Fiction and Drama* (London: Cygnus Arts, 1997). For a discussion that usefully compares trial transcripts and modernist fiction, "which abandons the vulgar gratifications of omniscience in order to yield up ... different voices ... speaking for themselves," see Steven Connor, "Transcripts: Law, literature and the trials of the voice," *New Formations*, 32 (1997), 60–76, 67.

Tom Jones (1749).[25] Jonathan Grossman and Lisa Rodensky have shown how nineteenth-century fiction adapted and extended these ways of staging and resolving conflict.[26]

In the movement from trial to judgment, narrative becomes subordinated to argument. Intermittently, perhaps, some vivid or dramatic moments will remain to be savored, like raisins in a pudding – and there is an understandable tendency to isolate those examples and to exaggerate their frequency. Because of the judgment's purpose, however, such moments (on the rare occasions when they occur) fit into a structure aimed at justification, not suspense or curiosity. A case is always a case *of something*, and while that something is open to respecification on appeal, at each juncture the court will concern itself with how the litigants' story fuels the legal one. A case of something is a member of a class, an example on its way to a place in a larger constellation that forms a rule, doctrine, or category, or that may become discernible as one of these. The legal ends, rather than the specific details, account for the case's significance from the judge's point of view.

Catherine Gallagher has suggested that one of the novel's founding justifications involved the claim that made-up characters, though highly individuated (and compelling to readers for that reason), could exemplify truths about general categories of persons.[27] The legal decision furnishes a telling contrast, in which the individual example tilts toward the generalization, allowing particular details to remain insofar as they facilitate an understanding of the dispute's legal contours. The facts are meant to demonstrate a general proposition, to exhibit an abstraction. That exemplary and demonstrative function bridges the story of the parties and the story of the law, accounting for how the former is narrated and how the latter brings both stories to an end.[28]

THE DECISION'S PLOTS

As this discussion has been suggesting, we may think of the factual rendering and the legal analysis as different narratives, with different plots.[29] An important generic feature of the judgment involves the role of tense and plot as they

---

[25] Alexander Welsh, *Strong Representations: Narrative and Circumstantial Evidence in England* (Baltimore, MD: Johns Hopkins University Press, 1992).
[26] Grossman, *The Art of Alibi*; Rodensky, *The Crime in Mind*.
[27] Catherine Gallagher, "George Eliot: Immanent Victorian," *Representations*, 90 (2005), 61–74.
[28] For more on exemplarity and legal narrative, see Maksymilian Del Mar, "Exemplarity and narrativity in the common law tradition," *Law & Literature*, 25 (2013), 390–407.
[29] The requirement that U.S. federal trial courts must separate fact and law, formalized in 1935 in Federal Rule of Civil Procedure 52(a)(1), was borrowed from Equity Rule 70½, promulgated in 1929; see 281 U.S. 773 (1929). Scholarship on the two rules' histories has examined standards

bear on the factual summary and the ensuing legal analysis. Commentators have rightly emphasized the importance of the end-driven structure that guides the judgment's narrative trajectory,[30] but the components of this structure have received less attention. The judgment includes at least two overlapping narratives, with a conclusion that terminates both of them. A story about the parties, narrated in the past tense, gives way to a story about the law, narrated in the present tense. The litigants' story is assimilated to the legal one, meaning that the legal result resolves their conflict, but also that their conflict may become an event in the legal story. That is what it means to say that their dispute is a case "of something." This way of presenting and using the facts/analysis structure links the legal decision to other forms of case study – particularly the research article in the social sciences – and the treatment of narrative here may also have implications for some of these other varieties.[31]

The legal story may be a static one in which the precedents easily dispense with the litigants' conflict, or a dynamic one that requires the judges to draw on policy and analogy as they pit one doctrine against others or modify the law in some way.[32] Todorov's account of the conditions required for the "minimal complete plot" helps to clarify this distinction. According to Todorov, a plot starts with a "stable situation which is disturbed," passes into a "state of disequilibrium," and eventuates in a new equilibrium that is "similar" but "never identical" to the first one.[33] The static (precedent-governed) legal story

of review in law and equity, but has not investigated judicial writing practices before these rules were adopted. A discussion from the late 1940s, however, suggests that trial judges often failed to comply with Rule 52; see "The law of fact: Findings of fact under the federal rules," *Harvard Law Review*, 61 (1948), 1434–1444, 1434–1436.

[30] E.g., Max Radin, "The theory of judicial decision: Or how judges think," *American Bar Association Journal*, 11 (1925), 357–362, 359; Jerome Frank, *Law and the Modern Mind* (New York: Brentano's, 1930), 101; Bruce Anderson, *"Discovery" in Legal Decision-Making* (Dordrecht: Kluwer, 1996), 30; Brooks, "Inevitable Discovery," 99.

[31] See, e.g., Barbara Czarniawska, *Writing Management: Organization Theory as a Literary Genre* (New York, NY: Oxford University Press, 1999), pp. 69–70; John Swales, *Genre Analysis: English in Academic and Research Settings* (Cambridge, UK: Cambridge University Press, 1990), pp. 110–176; Mary S. Morgan, "Case studies: One observation or many? Justification or discovery?" *Philosophy of Science*, 79 (2012), 667–677.

[32] On this contrast, see Frederick Schauer, *Thinking Like a Lawyer* (Cambridge, MA: Harvard University Press, 2009), 91. For a discussion of precedent in narrative terms, see Andrew Bricker, "Is narrative essential to the law? Precedent, case law and judicial emplotment," *Law, Culture & Humanities*, forthcoming.

[33] Tzvetan Todorov, *The Poetics of Prose*, trans. Richard Howard (Ithaca, NY: Cornell University Press, 1977), p. 11. Compare J. Hillis Miller's recipe: "[T]here must be ... an initial situation, a sequence leading to a change or reversal of that situation, and a revelation made possible by the reversal of the situation." J. Hillis Miller, "Narrative" in Frank Lentricchia and Thomas McLaughlin (eds.), *Critical Terms for Literary Study*, 2nd ed. (Chicago, IL: University of

therefore lacks a plot, because the legal equilibrium remains the same throughout.

In most trial and appellate judgments, the text delineates a complete plot for the litigants' tale but not for the legal analysis that resolves it. These are not the cases we usually encounter, however, because such decisions find few readers beyond the parties themselves. The paradigmatic form appears in the unpublished "Memorandum Dispositions" of US federal appellate courts: these easily resolved cases feature a terse style, treating the law's application as entirely perfunctory. They often simply dispense with the facts.[34]

We can appreciate the force of Todorov's definition by contrasting it with E. M. Forster's observation that a plot turns a mere chain of events into a causal sequence.[35] Forster's view finds a plot even in the static analysis that relies entirely on precedent, because legal reasoning always articulates causal relations: a doctrine causes a party's claim to succeed or fail. Todorov's view, on the other hand, suggests that a legal analysis guided by analogy is narratively distinguishable from one governed entirely by precedent. The latter poses no prospect of a threat to the doctrine's stability: it simply offers a demonstration of how the precedent operates. The cases that are anthologized in textbooks and treatises, and reported as news, feature the more complex legal story, in which both phases of the judgment have a complete plot. Those decisions also tend to carry other narratively significant features, because when judges perceive a need to modify the law, they ineluctably locate themselves as narrators in relation to the laws they seek to modify.

If the term "plot" seems to exaggerate the kind of activity that can be discerned in the abstractions of legal analysis, we might instead follow Ricoeur and call it "quasi-plot." In explaining the nature of the causal accounts that historians offer, Ricoeur likens historians to judges: "placed in the real or potential situation of a dispute, they [both] attempt to prove that one given explanation is better than another."[36] Historians do not "explain by recounting"; they proceed by "set[ting] up the explanation itself as a problem in order to submit it to discussion and to the judgment of an audience ... composed first of all of the historian's peers" (1:175). This expectation of critical

---

Chicago Press, 1995), 66–79, 75. This definition imposes nearly the same requirements, and could be applied with much the same effect as Todorov's.

[34] Joseph L. Lemon, Jr., *Federal Appellate Court Law Clerk Handbook* (Chicago, IL: ABA, 2007), pp. 42–44.

[35] E. M. Forster, *Aspects of the Novel* (New York, NY: Harcourt, 1927), p. 130.

[36] Paul Ricoeur, *Time and Narrative*, trans. Kathleen McLaughlin and David Pellauer (Chicago, IL: University of Chicago Press, 1984), vol. 1, p. 175. Further references appear parenthetically.

scrutiny differentiates the historian from the literary narrator (and again recalls the judge's position): the novelist "expects from the public, in Coleridge's familiar expression, a 'willing suspension of disbelief,'" but "[h]istorians address themselves to distrustful readers who expect from them not only that they narrate but that they authenticate their narrative" (1:176). To succeed, Ricoeur writes, the historian's explanation must show why a course of events resulted from "a particular factor *rather than some other*" (1:186). The form of explanation that satisfies this requirement is one that straddles the line between logical proof (according to general laws) and "explanation by emplotment," which depends on understanding rather than on logical entailment (1:181). Ricoeur calls this "transitional structure," which achieves both purposes, "quasi-plot" (1:181), because by arranging matters causally so as to facilitate understanding, it achieves the same function as a literary plot, even though it applies to historical events rather than fictional ones.[37]

In emphasizing that quasi-plot is bound up with "a process of argumentation," Ricoeur again likens historians to judges. Quasi-plot is predicated as argument, but not as matter-of-fact description, because historians "know that we can explain [the result] *in other ways*. They know this because, like a judge, they are in a situation of contestation and of trial, and because their plea is never finished" (1:186). These comments suggest that judicial opinions, even more than the writings of historians, traffic in quasi-plot. Ricoeur also hints at a reason for casting the legal analysis in the present tense. For lawyers, the obvious explanation is that doctrine continues to apply into the future;[38] to this, Ricoeur might add that the present tense can be a way of registering that the judgment's form is one of ongoing contestation.

---

[37] In contrast, Donald Polkinghorne argues that when an explanation refers to "an established law," it cannot be said to proceed "by means of a plot," even if it uses some narrative resources. He writes that when a demonstration refers to an established law, "[t]he power of explanation ... comes from its capacity to abstract events from particular contexts and discover relationships that hold among all instances ... irrespective of the spatial and temporal context," whereas "explanation by means of narrative is [always] contextually related." *Narrative Knowing and the Human Sciences* (Albany: SUNY Press, 1988), 21.

[38] George Coode makes the same point with respect to legislative language, observing that "the law [should] be regarded while it remains in force as *constantly speaking*." George Coode, *On Legislative Expression; or, The Language of the Law* (London: Benning, 1845), p. 63. Consequently, he adds, statutes should use the present tense for circumstances that the legislation covers, and the past tense for "facts precedent to its operation" (e.g., a prior conviction, where the legislation imposes penalties for second and later convictions). The result is that "[n]arration will appear in narrative language," rather than using the "imperious language" of a legislative command; to do otherwise is "to confound *the facts* and *the law*." Ibid., p. 65. Coode thus suggests an approach that resembles the distinctions in tense for facts and law that we find in judgments.

Finally, Ricoeur complements the notion of quasi-plot with "quasi-character," noting that "the role of character can be held by *whoever* or *whatever* is designated in the narrative as the grammatical subject of an action predicate in the basic narrative sentence 'X does R'" (1:197). In historical writing, quasi-character embraces "peoples, nations, [and] classes" (197); in the quasi-plot of the legal analysis, it embraces doctrines, judges (insofar as they take responsibility for making a choice), and also policies and principles – that is, any agents that contribute to the quasi-plot's development. In this way, the legal analysis becomes eligible for the same kinds of questions that we put to fictional stories, such as questions about how the reader is positioned in relation to the characters, which characters are allowed to interact with each other, what kind of information is rendered inaccessible, and why some details are presented directly and others at second-hand. The answers might suggest new ways of seeing legal decisions in terms of genre, and new ways of understanding how certain kinds of problems evoke narrative tendencies that confuse the law instead of clarifying it. One of the most salient problems for any narrative that aims at belief as well as persuasion involves the means of establishing the narrator's authority, and I turn now to one aspect of this question, by considering some legal analogues of Barthes' "reality effect."

THE REALITY EFFECT IN LAW

As we have seen, the potential narrative appeal that circulates before and during the trial diminishes in the course of adjudication. The movement from conflict to litigation to resolution tracks a process in which the participants select certain details to describe to their lawyers, the lawyers select certain details to present in court, and the judge selects certain details to set out in the judgment – each time in accord with the argumentative purpose at hand. Barthes famously observed that the unmotivated detail, the detail that cannot be "assign[ed] ... a place in the structure," creates the "effect of the real": "such notations ... seem to be allied with a kind of narrative *luxury*, lavish to the point of offering many 'futile' details and thereby increasing the cost of narrative information."[39] Yet we revel in those details, Barthes explains, because they "denote what is ordinarily called 'concrete reality.'" Their apparent futility is itself their justification: if no other purpose is served by mentioning the detail, then it must have been included simply because that is

---

[39] Roland Barthes, "The reality effect" (1968) in *The Rustle of Language*, trans. Richard Howard (New York, NY: Hill & Wang, 1986), pp.141–148, 141.

how "it really happened."[40] In the legal pattern just described, the reality effect dwindles because the details become increasingly motivated at each step, as the legal rationales come increasingly to control every aspect of the presentation, such that it would be a generic flaw if the decision included unmotivated details, or lacked sufficient details to motivate the conclusion.[41] The hostility toward useless details in legal writing finds expression in the demand for narrative coherence, mentioned earlier; hence, in the course of the trial, a theory of the case that can redeem some of Barthes's "futile" details will be preferred to one that cannot, and to that extent those details may find their way into the decision, now with their purpose fully evident.

In a sense, any detail that appears at the threshold of legal visibility is potentially motivated; after all, the client's very reason for consulting a lawyer is to consider the advisability of suing, and that purpose informs whatever the client has to say. But that narrative of events nevertheless exhibits some of Barthes's luxury, because although the details cannot be regarded as raw, they have not yet been professionally edited with the aid of doctrinal logic. Moreover, any lawyer who understands how to establish the credibility of a witness will be intent on eliciting some unmotivated details in the course of testimony, for the very reason that Barthes gives: nothing attests to a person's veracity like the trivial point that gets mentioned just because the witness happens to remember it. Again, a lawyer's trial narrative, despite the craft that goes into shaping it, remains experimental and tentative; no one knows which of the details on offer will survive the objections and proof contests that might eliminate them, nor which of the remaining ones the judge will include in the factual summary. By contrast, the judge's decision erases the stray marks punctuating the pleadings and evidence, selects the cognizable claims and supporting arguments, and organizes relevant detail to suit the legal framework being imposed on the case.

The increasing focus on matters of policy and doctrine, as a case is transformed from live dispute to written resolution and then travels up the appellate ladder, suggests a kind of economy of narrative energy in the adjudicative process. In the earlier stages, when it remains unclear which facts will matter, there is a proliferation of narrative energy as the parties enlist witnesses, gather

---

[40] Ibid. p. 146.
[41] For an instance of the latter, consider Justice White's complaint that a draft opinion was "as unsatisfying as ... a bad mystery novel" because the analysis had not paved the way for the proposed doctrinal solution: "[W]e learn on the last page that the victim has been done in by a suspect heretofore unknown, for reasons previously unrevealed." Quoted in Richard Sherwin, "Law frames: Historical truth and narrative necessity in a criminal case," *Stanford Law Review*, 47 (1994), 39–83, 66.

documentary evidence, and consider the various storylines that may result in a legal victory. Some alternatives, and the details that would have supported them, get rejected before the trial, and others are excised in the course of the trial as the judge applies exclusionary rules, the opposing counsel's evidence forecloses certain options, and the lawyers make strategic decisions on the fly.

As the adjudication begins to find textual expression, this energy diminishes. Once the judge has reduced the dispute to writing, most of the teeming narrative energy will be purged from the facts, in a text that enlists them for argumentative purposes. On appeal, the facts may be further pared away. Trial decisions, for example, typically include enough facts to support any of the alternative theories that might justify the judge's conclusions, whereas appellate decisions, zeroing in on a particular doctrinal issue, can be sparer of the operative facts. As narrative energy is leached out of the dispute's factual arena, some of it migrates to the legal analysis, though in a significantly altered form. As noted above, the active agents in that section, which perform the work and may come into conflict or undergo change, are primarily doctrines, not human actors. The judges themselves may figure as both narrators and actors, depending on whether they present the result as compelled by law or deliberately chosen after weighing the alternatives. The narrative energy on display in the analysis is typically subdued, by contrast with the energy that circulates before the trial. Thus the economy does not simply transpose narrative energy from one arena to another: much of it dissipates. Barthes' concept thus offers a useful means of understanding the gestures toward realism that occur during the trial and their transformation in the course of the litigation process.

Although the reality effect is notably absent from the trial and appellate judges' decisions, they offer an analogue, which we might call the "legality effect." If the reality effect in fiction indexes the text's veracity, by the same token it indexes the narrator's reliability or authority. The text that can record "unnecessary" information is a text with access to a wealth of detail; it is a text produced by someone who knows more than the page records. (One could imagine the reality effect in the hands of an unreliable narrator, but if so, the "unnecessary" details would turn out to be motivated after all, serving to make us doubt their accuracy and to look askance at the narrator.) Just as the reality effect testifies to the narrator's comprehensive knowledge about the world of the fiction, the legality effect may serve a parallel function in the analytical part of the judgment.

Despite the earlier suggestion that the unneeded legal detail is regarded as a generic flaw, legal analysis often abounds in unneeded details. For example, courts often opine on matters not strictly before them (which critics characterize as *dicta*) and recite far more doctrine than the case at hand requires, giving mini-lectures in a particular area of law rather than homing in on the legal issues at hand. These gestures are indeed greeted as "increasing the cost of narrative information,"[42] but one may suspect that just as novelists include "futile" details with full awareness of their futility, judges are equally conscious of the demands of the form and are equally deliberate in their efforts. In the early modern period, when the common law was understood as having a separate existence independent from the judges' pronouncements, such material might have served an analogous purpose: elaborating unnecessary doctrinal points could be a way to underscore the text's legal veracity and the judge's comprehensive legal knowledge, affirming his status as an "oracle of the law."

Although contemporary lawyers do not hold the same views about the law's source, the same implications concerning knowledge and authority may nevertheless apply. Formulated in narrative terms, the legality effect reinforces the judge's status as an omniscient narrator with respect to the legal doctrines. That effect reinforces the conventionally omniscient mode that governs the legal analysis, a mode akin to the confident omniscience associated with the Victorian novel. In fictional narratives, various devices – including the reality effect – conspire to create a narrator with privileged access to the characters' histories, thoughts, and motives; correspondingly, the judgment sets up a judicial narrator who can speak confidently about the doctrines' origins, purposes, and limits – a narrator who, by pronouncing that a doctrine serves a particular function, makes it so. The judge's account is inevitably open to challenge, as we noted when considering Ricoeur's quasi-plot, but that simply means that the judge's confidence may prove unwarranted; here we are concerned with how the judgment creates this authority, not with its ability to withstand attack from other judgments, which will use the same techniques to establish their own authority, in turn.

The decision's doctrinal surplusage exhibits "the legal" for the reader, just as the novel's excessive description exhibits "the real." By including legal information that does not form part of a contention, the judge furnishes the reader with a reassuringly accurate and familiar framework to enfold the motivated propositions that constitute the argument. The incontestably true legal details are there to vouch for the soundness of the assertions that follow. Moreover, just as the reality effect has taken on new manifestations over the last century (involving, for example, the use of photographs and other kinds of

---

[42] Barthes, "The reality effect," p. 141.

documentation and pseudo-documentation),[43] so too has the legality effect. During roughly the same period, it became conventional, in American judicial writing, to suffuse the judgment's analytical section with short quotations from a wide array of decisions, in order to validate every single proposition, including those that are so well-accepted as to be banal. Conversely, Canadian judgments developed a tendency to quote other decisions at great length, sometimes amounting to two or three pages at a time, including several levels of nested quotations – and then to make little if any further reference to quoted material. In both cases, the gesture often does nothing to advance the analysis but emphatically attests to the judges' doctrinal fluency. By examining the judgment through the lens of narrative technique, we can find an explanation – if not quite a justification – for what otherwise seems to be a waste of space and a tax on the reader's patience.

Once we consider judgments as having distinctive traits, rather than treating them as interchangeable with the forms of imaginative writing that use plot and character to entice and entertain us, the most fundamental questions in the study of narrative take on new potential. Instead of assuming, without discussion, that the decision's plot corresponds to a novelistic one, we gain the ability to study the problem directly and to distinguish among legal plots. Because this approach has implications for the decision's mode of reasoning and doctrinal conclusions, it raises questions not only for scholars of law and literature (and particularly those who study "law as literature") but also for legal scholars more generally.

---

[43] For some particularly relevant examples, see Todd Herzog, "Crime stories: Criminal, society, and the modernist case history," *Representations*, 80 (2002): 34–61, which appears in revised form as the second chapter of his book *Crime Stories: Criminalistic Fantasy and the Culture of Crisis in Weimar Germany* (New York, NY: Berghahn, 2009).

6

Legal Stories, the Reality Effect, and Visual Narratives: A Response to Simon Stern

Peter Brooks

Simon Stern is right when he demurs from treating the legal judgment "as simply one more form of narrative." To see it as a narrative form would be to lose its generic specificity. I would contend nonetheless that narrative is constitutive of law, an inescapable part of how advocates, juries, and judges think, evaluate, discriminate, convict, and that it therefore needs far more analytic thought than it has received.[1] I will return later to this overarching question, and to my disagreements with Stern. First I want to address his very interesting perceptions about the place of Roland Barthes's "reality effect" as a key rhetorical device in the legal opinion: that element or detail that is there, in Barthes' understanding, to say essentially: "I am the real."[2] The place of the real within the appellate opinion is problematic: what was once reality has here become formalized as part of a judicial logic that works in a hermetic realm. The appellate legal narrative is supposed to be efficient, even minimalist, concerned with rules rather than the impedimenta of reality, whereas according to Barthes the reality effect derives from the superfluous detail.

Yet I think we can all recognize moments where the legal opinion will use details that are not so much legally necessary as they are statements that say – sometimes shout aloud – I am the real. One such case occurs in Chief Justice Rehnquist's opinion in *Payne* v. *Tennessee*, the 1991 case that reversed a decision just four years earlier that Victim Impact Statements had no place in the sentencing phase of capital trials.[3] The VIS typically presents testimony

---

[1] I have written elsewhere about the pervasive presence of narrative in the law. See in particular "Narrative transactions—Does law need a narratology?" *Yale Journal of Law & Humanities* 18 no. 1 (2006), 1–28, and "'Inevitable discovery'—Law, narrative, retrospectivity," *Yale Journal of Law & Humanities*, 15 no. 1 (2003), 101–129.

[2] See Roland Barthes, "L'Effet de réel," in *Le Bruissement de la langue* (Paris: Editions du Seuil, 1984), 167–74; English trans. Richard Howard, "The reality effect," in *The Rustle of Language* (New York, NY: Hill & Wang, 1986), pp. 141–148.

[3] See *Payne* v. *Tennessee*, 501 U.S. 808.

about the harms and pains suffered by victims of crime and their families, and in *Booth* v. *Maryland* (1987) the Court decided this was unduly inflammatory and thus prejudicial. The jury could be presented during the sentencing phase with mitigating but not aggravating evidence. In reversing in *Payne*, Rehnquist writes an opinion which actually says virtually nothing about the sentencing phase of the trial. It's all about the scene of the crime itself – material presented during the guilt phase – and it is as gory as possible:

> Inside the apartment, the police encountered a horrifying scene. Blood covered the walls and floor throughout the unit. Charisse and her children were lying on the floor in the kitchen. Nicholas, despite several wounds inflicted by a butcher knife that completely penetrated through his body from front to back, was still breathing. Miraculously, he survived, but not until after undergoing seven hours of surgery and a transfusion of 1,700 cc's of blood – 400 to 500 cc's more than his estimated normal blood volume. Charisse and Lacie were dead.
>
> Charisse's body was found on the kitchen floor on her back, her legs fully extended. She had sustained 42 direct knife wounds and 42 defensive wounds on her arms and hands. The wounds were caused by 41 separate thrusts of a butcher knife. None of the 84 wounds inflicted by Payne were individually fatal; rather, the cause of death was most likely bleeding from all of the wounds.
>
> Lacie's body was on the kitchen floor near her mother. She had suffered stab wounds to the chest, abdomen, back, and head. The murder weapon, a butcher knife, was found at her feet ... (at 812–813).

I spare you the rest. Rehnquist's legal point seems to be that since this information came to the jury during the guilt phase of the trial, censoring it from the penalty phase accomplishes nothing. But his real point is to make a kind of preemptive factual strike: After such grisly details, is any mitigating evidence conceivable? After such knowledge, what forgiveness? The reality effect of the crime scene trumps everything else.

When the Court has to deal with a narrative that comes to it not as the usual summary verbal narrative but rather in visual form, it appears that the reality effect becomes so powerful that it disables judgment. Such may be the lesson of *Scott* v. *Harris*, a 2007 Supreme Court case which marked the first time, to my knowledge, that the Court posted a video on its website as an appendix to its opinion.[4] It's my contention that eight of the justices are blinded by the reality effect it presents. The reader may want take a look at the video via the link embedded later in this essay. It was taken by cams on the dashboards of

---

[4] *Scott* v. *Harris*, 550 U.S. 372 (2007).

two successive police cruisers pursuing Victor Harris along rural Georgia roads late at night. The pursuit ended when officer Timothy Scott "applied his push bumper to the rear of respondent's vehicle. As a result, respondent lost control of his vehicle, which left the roadway, ran down an embankment, overturned, and crashed. Respondent was badly injured and was rendered a quadriplegic." (at 376)

My quotation comes from Justice Scalia's majority opinion, joined by all the Court except Justice Stevens. In prior proceedings, Harris had sued Scott for violating his Fourth Amendment rights by use of excessive force resulting in an unreasonable seizure; Scott had claimed qualified immunity and moved for summary judgment; the District Court had denied the motion, finding that there were issues of fact that required submission to a jury; and the Eleventh Circuit Court of Appeals had affirmed, allowing Harris' Fourth Amendment claim to go to trial. The Supreme Court now reverses, denying Harris' claim.

Normally the facts of the case would be judged on the appellate level in the light most favorable to the party asserting the injury, as indeed the Eleventh Circuit did. But, says Scalia, there is in this case "an added wrinkle ... existence in the record of a videotape capturing the events in question" (at 378). And: "The videotape quite clearly contradicts the version of the story told by respondent and adopted by the Court of Appeals." In a footnote, disputing Stevens' dissent, Scalia says: "We are happy to allow the videotape to speak for itself" (at 376, n.5). And, in refutation of the opinion from the Eleventh Circuit: "The videotape tells quite a different story" (at 379). The Court can set aside the normal rule of viewing the facts in the light most favorable to Harris because his version of events "is blatantly contradicted by the record, so that no reasonable jury could believe it ..." And: "Respondent's version of events is so utterly discredited by the record that no reasonable jury could have believed him. The Court of Appeals should not have relied on such visible fiction: it should have viewed the facts in the light depicted by the videotape" (at 380–381). Justice Breyer in his concurrence chimes in: "Because watching the video footage made a difference to my view of the case, I suggest that the interested reader take advantage of the link [to the video] in the Court's opinion and watch it" (at 388).[5]

[5] The effect of viewing the video by a sample of 1,350 Americans, and the diverse cognitive biases revealed in their interpretations, have been well studied by Dan M. Kahan, David A. Hoffman, and Donald Braman in "Whose eyes are you going to believe? Scott v. Harris and the perils of cognitive illiberalism," *Harvard Law Review*, 122 (2009), 837–906. While the aim of the authors of that article is different from mine, we agree that the single interpretation claim put forth by the Court majority is untenable.

So on the one hand the "visible fiction" of Harris's claim of excessive force, on the other the visible video which "speaks for itself." Curiously in this case the video itself becomes the central actor, its performance of the truth what trumps all the usual judicial rules, turns the Supreme Court justices into "jurors," as Stevens puts it, and makes viewing of an unfolding action the sole factor of judgment. I am reminded of a pathetic moment at the end of the Rodney King trial in Simi Valley, California, in 1992, where Prosecutor Terry White in his closing argument says over and over to the jury: watch the whole videotape – of the police officers beating Rodney King. Don't pay attention to the dissection of the video by the defense experts; "Trust your own eyes." Here the eight Justices decide to trust their own eyes. I think they are blinded by what may be, to use the words Scalia applies to the erroneous view of the Court of Appeals, a "visible fiction." It is precisely the visuality of the tape – its immediacy, its implicit statement: "I am the real" – that takes over from reasoned analysis here. The reality effect that Barthes finds in certain details of literary narrative is all the more potent in the visual narrative.

To Scalia, the video depicts "a Hollywood-style car chase of the most frightening sort, placing police officers and innocent bystanders alike at great risk of serious injury" (at 380). The respondent poses an "extreme danger to human life" (at 384); "it is clear from the videotape that respondent posed an actual and imminent threat to the lives of any pedestrians who might have been present"; "how does a court go about weighing the perhaps lesser probability of injuring and killing numerous bystanders against the perhaps larger probability of injuring or killing a single person?" (at 384). It was after all Harris who produced "the choice between two evils that Scott confronted." Scalia is caught up in the chase, which has become a version of the streetcar moral dilemma. It's exciting stuff.

It is only in Stevens' lone dissent that things calm down a bit. He notes that when the chase begins, Harris is driving on a four-lane stretch of Highway 34. His speed is clocked at 73 miles per hour in a 55 mph zone when the first officer initiates the chase, which then generates speeds up to 85 mph. Officer Scott picks up the chase on his radio – he does not know why Harris is being pursued – and joins in, then makes himself the lead car, and eventually decides to put an end to it, and to Harris's mobility forever. Stevens argues that a careful viewing of the video in fact "confirms, rather than contradicts, the lower courts' appraisal of the factual questions at issue." And it "surely does not provide a principled basis for depriving the respondent of his right to have a jury evaluate the question whether the police officers' decision to use deadly force to bring the chase to an end was reasonable" (at 390).

So now we have Stevens' analytic reading of the video. It's one that I largely agree with, and I predict that most readers who view the video will too. He makes the point that Harris is at all times in control of his car, that he pulls out to pass other cars only when it is safe to do so, and uses his turn signals, and that the cars he passes seem to have already pulled onto the shoulder, no doubt from the blazing lights and shrieking sirens of the chase, and the two intersections with traffic lights he crosses show only stationary vehicles. Stevens offers a kind of analytic driving lesson to his colleagues. In an interesting footnote, he debunks the majority's "Hollywood chase" designation:

> I can only conclude that my colleagues were unduly frightened by two or three images on the tape that looked like bursts of lightning or explosions, but were in fact merely the headlights of vehicles zooming by in the opposite lane. Had they learned to drive when most high-speed driving took place on two-lane roads rather than superhighways—when split-second judgments about the risk of passing a slowpoke in the face of oncoming traffic were routine—they might well have reacted to the videotape more dispassionately" (at 390, fn 1).

Learn to drive, guys, and stop being so impressed by the Hollywood-style visible fiction.

Stevens also points out that when the cars momentarily move into a mall parking lot, the mall is closed (it's 11 p.m.), and that all those "innocent bystanders" and "pedestrians that might have been present" who worry Scalia don't exist on these rural Georgia roads deep into the night. In sum, Harris' offense is serious, but it is not "a capital offense, or even an offense that justified the use of deadly force" (at 394).

You will see that moment of deadly force toward the end of the video, which might best be viewed at this point of our discussion. My suggestion is that you look first at a couple of minutes from the start of the chase, caught on the cam of Ace Team 078. Then pick up with Ace Team 066 (Officer Scott) around 13 minutes 30 seconds, to view to the end – the very grim moment where you see Scott speed up to bump Harris' car, then that car careen out of control, go off the road and into a telephone pole or a tree.

The video: https://vimeo.com/46603634.

My point, then, is that the viewed video trumps all reason in this case because of its reality *effect* – not because of what it shows, since subjected to analysis it supports as least as much the lower courts' and Stevens' view of what happened as the majority's – but more simply because it says: "I am the real." The Court, again citing Stevens, "used its viewing of the video as an excuse for replacing the rule of law with its ad hoc judgment" (at 394). And then the

Court goes and posts the video on its website as justifying its decision. As if videos were self-interpreting narratives. Which they maybe are if you decide that they show "a Hollywood-style car chase." The generic designation already interprets the narrative. Somehow, Harris and his severely injured state, and even Scott and his decision to "take him out," disappear in the face of the video itself, a reality effect like no other.

This will surely become an increasing problem in the future, as police video cams and bystanders' cell phones are more and more used to provide evidence in encounters of the police with the citizenry. It has been claimed that over one hundred African Americans were shot and killed by the police in 2015.[6] The *Washington Post* estimates that overall, 990 citizens were killed by police officers in that year.[7] The figure as of August for 2016 was 586, including the well-known cases of Alton Sterling and Philandro Castile.[8] The expanding requirement that police wear body cams surely is to be praised, but the notion that video evidence will resolve all factual disputes is a bit naïve. The live streams that we have all seen, such as that of the dying Philandro Castile, are overwhelming evidence – but not necessarily clear and unambiguous evidence. A camera is a point of view. Its context, including what it does not record, needs construction and construal.

It is likely that the generic assumptions we bring to encounters of police and citizenry will in many cases impose an interpretive grid. One can already point to many instances where the police and lay viewers genuinely construct opposed interpretations of shootings recorded for all to see. The overwhelming reality effect of the deadly armed encounter will often result in our reaching for a structuring genre that will interpret it, give it meaning as police brutality on the one hand or the heroic action of the thin blue line on the other. Just as Rehnquist reaches for the hard-boiled crime story in *Payne*, and Scalia resolves his video watching as a "Hollywood-style car chase" in *Scott v. Harris*. If we were to return to the detail in the tale that furnished Roland Barthes's most famous example in "The reality effect" – Madame Aubain's barometer in Flaubert's *A Simple Heart (Un Coeur simple)* – I think we would find something similar: the reader's desire to retrieve and find meaningful that detail within the thematic design of the story. We cannot simply leave details of the real in a thematic no-man's land. We recover them for meaning within the economy of the narrative in which they figure, according to our

---

[6] See http://mappingpoliceviolence.org/unarmed/.
[7] See www.washingtonpost.com/graphics/national/police-shootings/.
[8] See www.huffingtonpost.com/entry/black-people-killed-by-police-america_us_577da633 e4b0c590f7e7fb17.

understanding of the text and its generic markers. That is to say: the simple real, registered as such, does not exist. The human mind must interpret.

The case of *Scott* v. *Harris* seems to me a particularly blinded example of a more general neglect of narrative analysis on the part of judges. Advocates contesting evidence in a courtroom – and those who teach courses in advocacy – know very well that they must tell and critique stories, but on the appellate level it is rare to find a judge who will unpack the narrative that has been formed in courts below. This seems to be what Simon Stern has in mind when he argues that the basic distinction between the story (what the Russian Formalists called the *fabula*) and the narrative discourse that presents it (the *sjuzhet*) has no traction in legal opinions. He writes: "Indeed, the basic distinction between *sjuzhet* and *fabula* seems unproductive as a means of examining the decision's factual narrative, because judges set out the events in a fashion that implies (through the use of tense, perspective, and chronology) that the story on offer simply *is* what happened, and there is no underlying story worth excavating and comparing." That to my mind is precisely the problem. Since "the facts" have been established at trial, the narrative in which they come to courts of appeal may appear inalterable, and the retrieval of any other *fabula* from the given *sjuzhet* impossible.

Yet this cannot be true, since dissents can and do tell the story to a different outcome. The work of post-conviction petitions for relief, for instance, must take a story that appears to have reached a dead end (in many cases a grim pun) and retell it in such a way as to reopen its narrative possibilities. I once had the opportunity of watching Anthony Amsterdam retell the story of Walter Mickens, convicted of aggravated homicide and sentenced to death in Virginia, in such a way as to recast entirely the story made in the trial record, and to bring the case to the United States Supreme Court.[9] There are no facts on the ground without the narratives in which we make them into plausible evidence, narratives of someone having done something. The art of the author of the winning opinion is to display that narrative as seemingly inevitable, the only one that explains. But advocates and judges alike can dispute that inevitability. Alternative versions of reality may be possible: Stevens' dissent in *Scott* v. *Harris* is self-consciously and admirably an attempt to construct one. Such a well-known case as *Rusk* v. *Maryland* and *Maryland* v. *Rusk*, in which a rape conviction was overturned at the first appellate level and then reinstated by the higher court, gives us four

---

[9] See *Mickens* v. *Taylor*, 535 U.S. 162 (2002); and Petition for Writ of Certiorari, *Mickens*, 535 U.S. 162 (No. 00–9285). I speak of this petition as the work of Anthony Amsterdam because I had the good fortune to work with him in his Persuasion Institute at the time he was writing it.

opinions – two for the majorities, two dissents – that retell the same story in differing narrative discourses, as either "consensual sex" or else "rape."[10] The "facts" of what happened weren't in dispute – rather, at issue was how to put the facts together, how to connect the incidents, how to construct the narrative.

In the law, as in other domains of experience, what is often at stake is the "narrative construction of reality," as Jerome Bruner has named it.[11] In Bruner's persuasive view, narrative understanding is part of our basic cognitive tool kit, something that we learn early in life and apply to all sorts of situations that cannot be interpreted without using the successivity of events and the temporality of causes and effects. But narrative construction never seems to have become an analytic optic in appellate decision-making. The only exception that I know of is Justice Souter's opinion in *Johnny Lynn Old Chief* v. *United States* (1997), in a riff on "narrative integrity" as necessary to jurors' decision-making.[12] It is the only moment I've encountered where the Court considers what a student of mine has called the "epistemology of the particular": the way in which stories create certain meanings that cannot otherwise be conveyed.

Souter registers the need for "evidentiary richness and narrative integrity in presenting a case" (at 183). He goes on to say that "making a case with testimony and tangible things ... tells a colorful story with descriptive richness." And he continues:

> Evidence thus has force beyond any linear scheme of reasoning, and as its pieces come together a narrative gains momentum, with power not only to support conclusions but to sustain the willingness of jurors to draw the inferences, whatever they may be, necessary to reach an honest verdict. This persuasive power of the concrete and particular is often essential to the capacity of jurors to satisfy the obligations that the law places on them. (at 187)

Souter's opinion develops into a striking reflection on the nature and the force of narrative:

---

[10] See *Rusk* v. *State*, 43 Md. App. 476 (1979) and *State* v. *Rusk*, 289 Md. 230 (1981). And see the fine essay on Rusk by Jeannie Suk, "'The look in his eyes': The story of *State* v. *Rusk* and Rape Reform," (Harvard Law Sch. Pub. Law & Legal Theory Working Paper Series, Paper No. 10–23, 2010), published in Donna K. Coker & Robert Weisberg (eds.) *Criminal Law Stories* (New York: Foundation Press 2012).

[11] See Jerome Bruner, "The narrative construction of reality," *Critical Inquiry*, 18 no. 1 (1991), 6.

[12] *Johnny Lynn Old Chief* v. *United States*, 519 U.S. 172 (1997).

> A syllogism is not a story, and a naked proposition in a courtroom may be no match for the robust evidence that would be used to prove it. People who hear stories interrupted by gaps of abstraction may be puzzled at the missing chapters ... A convincing tale can be told with economy, but when economy becomes a break in the natural sequence of narrative evidence, an assurance that the missing link is really there is never more than second best. (at 189)

For Souter, the full and convincing tale must be responsive to the jurors' expectations "about what proper proof should be." These expectations preexist service on a jury: jurors bring them to the courthouse, "assuming, for example, that a charge of using a firearm to commit an offense will be proven by introducing a gun in evidence." Failure to meet what we might call jurors' "narrative competence" can undermine the prosecution's proof.

The need for a complete and convincing narrative indeed has an ethical dimension for Souter. Pointing out that jury duty is unsought and often difficult, he writes:

> When a juror's duty does seem hard, the evidentiary account of what a defendant has thought and done can accomplish what no set of abstract statements ever could, not just to prove a fact but to establish its human significance, and so to implicate the law's moral underpinnings and a juror's obligation to sit in judgment. (at 187–188)

Souter seems to be saying that the force of narrative evidence, the kind of evidence of guilty mind and act that it alone can provide, may be tied in a deep way to the very act of passing judgment on one's fellows. He implies that law without narrative would be not only disabled but lacking in moral force.

Yet Souter's interesting and convincing excursus on narrative does not produce the result one might expect in *Old Chief*. His acknowledgment of the force of narrative leads him to the conclusion that the story of Old Chief's prior crime and conviction (on a very similar charge of assault with a weapon) does not belong in the present adjudication. Old Chief should have been allowed to stipulate to the prior crime without having its details introduced into his prosecution. The past crime is part of another story: it is "entirely outside the natural sequence of what the defendant is charged with thinking and doing to commit the current offense" (at 191). Its introduction might "overpersuade" the jury, leading them to convict on the grounds of Old Chief's character rather than the specific deeds alleged in this case. Story is dangerous as well as persuasive. The law needs to keep it channeled or, you might say, under erasure: visible when you look for it but only barely legible. If it is in some way fundamental to the morality of criminal law, to recognize its constitutive force might be to concede that law rests on rhetoric.[13] The narrative constructions of the law might be fundamental to it – something that legal actors do not wish to contemplate.

Souter's rarely cited opinion has not turned Justices into narratologists. It's a pity. While I agree with Simon Stern that judicial opinions can't be classified as forms of narrative – they belong to a different genre – that doesn't conclude the analysis. I am convinced that what Stern calls "narrative logic" is omnipresent in judicial opinions, and throughout the law. That is inevitable, since the law sits in judgment on events alleged to have happened in the world, and these are always subject to narrative logic. While what Stern calls "narrative energy" may dissipate as we move from trial to appeal, that characterizes only the overt clash of stories in the courtroom. Appellate courts, too, must always be telling stories, and how they do so can make all the difference. "The pistol came from the pocket, and from the pistol a single shot, which did its deadly work," writes Benjamin Cardozo in *People* v. *Zackowitz*, denying that the shooting in Brooklyn was premeditated.[14] The language of his narrative – he is one of the masters of summary legal storytelling – tries to close the matter. It may be our job as narrative analysts to open it up again, to revive its potential energy.

Legal decision-making, it seems to me, calls upon narrative paradigms of understanding and ordering events in the world far more than it consciously avows. It cannot eschew narrative because in so many regards its legal logic depends on a logic of events that can only be told in narrative form. There are no facts on the ground until they are put into storied form: they don't make sense until an explanatory narrative makes them available to understanding. This implies that appellate judges should not only be effective storytellers – as often they are – but also keen analysts of the stories they accept, retell, and use as the basis of adjudication. Judges need to be narratologists, though as *Old Chief* demonstrates they are not comfortable validating the place of narrative in law even when it has been recognized. And when confronted with an eye-dazzling visual narrative, as in *Scott* v. *Harris*, they may fall back on a generic Hollywood response. It is easy to fall victim to the visible fiction.

---

[13] I have discussed *Old Chief* at greater length elsewhere. See Brooks, "Law and humanities: Two attempts," *Boston University Law Review*, 93 no. 4 (2013), 1437–1468, at 1451 ff.
[14] *People* v. *Zackowitz*, 254 NY 192 (1930).

CONVERSATION IV

NARRATIVE, METAPHOR, AND GENDER IN THE LAW

Editors' Introduction

Michael Hanne and Robert Weisberg

The various conversations in this collection stand in different relations to the broad topic under which each appears. While some offer a close-up image of a rather specific issue within the broad topic, for instance, Katharine Young's and Bernadette Meyler's wonderfully detailed analysis of the metaphors (and implied narratives) of the "queue" or "line" in human rights law (Conversation 7), others offer a more comprehensive treatment of the broad heading under which they appear.

The present conversation, between Linda Berger and Kathryn Stanchi, falls emphatically into the latter category. It opens with a wide-ranging survey of work done by feminist writers on the ways in which narrative and metaphor have served in all fields on the one hand to reinforce traditional oppression of women, and on the other to foster liberation, before it shifts to a discussion of feminist legal scholarship which has explored the same issues in the context of the law. It then examines in detail a major project by feminist legal scholars to reimagine a number of cases in which women's voices have been silenced and women's interests ignored.

So comprehensive is the Berger-Stanchi discussion about the complex roles of metaphor and narrative with respect to gender in law, that we need not summarize it here. So, these notes will aim rather to draw attention to the numerous connections between this conversation and the other conversations in this volume.

Berger and Stanchi argue that "advocates who thoughtfully engage in metaphor-making and storytelling may alter the law's conceptions of gender justice, and indeed of justice for all." In this respect their work links back to the discussion in Conversation 1, on the role of narrative and metaphor in both the very "constitution" of justice and the organization of legal processes. There, for example, Lawrence Rosen showed how different linguistic figurations manifest very different conceptions of the legal phenomenon of property. Here,

Berger and Stanchi would agree that something as fundamental to a legal system as its relative treatment of women can be discerned from the metaphoric language of law – most obviously in the trope of "separate spheres." Their cultural comparison is between American law as it is or has been and American law as it might be. So, in their treatment of the Feminist Judgments Project they show how a world in which women are not legally subordinated would literally sound in a new language. Moreover, Berger and Stanchi proliferate examples of Rosen's insights about the interrelation of metaphor and narrative. As Rosen shows, and as Berger and Stanchi help demonstrate, extended metaphors can entail narratives, narrative choice can dictate choice of metaphors, and metaphors can enhance and underscore the moral implications of any narrative.

They unabashedly view language as both reflecting and controlling our sense of reality, and they argue that conscious choice of metaphor and narrative can both oppress and liberate. In relying on the Feminist Judgments Project, they confront and counter the common, prejudicial stereotype that reliance on metaphor and narrative by feminists is a marker of reliance on emotion rather than (male-associated) reason. While promoting the emotive capacity of language to critique the supposed ineluctable hardness of reason, they show that the supposed cool logic of traditional law sometimes consciously uses and sometimes falls prey to metaphor and narrative.

Berger and Stanchi have much to say about how narrative and metaphor persuade: "we claim that when it comes to validity and effectiveness, metaphor and narrative stand on equal footing with syllogism and analogy." In this sense, there are clear parallels between their arguments and the discussion in Conversation 2 between Michael Smith and Raymond Gibbs on narrative and metaphor in persuasion. In particular, their discussion of the ways in which we may use alternative narratives and metaphors to induce an audience to "take a second look" meshes well with Raymond Gibbs's assertions about just how we process metaphors. They suggest that some metaphors used in a legal context serve to "make the familiar strange" whereas others serve to "make the strange appear familiar." Indeed, their arguments echo the claims of Ted Cohen for metaphor and of Ross Chambers for narrative (both cited in our introduction) that these devices work by invitation and seduction rather than head-on confrontation. In Berger and Stanchi's words, "we ask them to fill in the details; we hint at possibilities and nudge the observer to step back, tilt her head, and look again. In this way, we say to our readers, 'look do you see what is really going on here?'"

Berger and Stanchi ask us to critique the established metaphors of judicial doctrine (e.g. the "separate spheres") and to enhance the incomplete narratives which judges often present to justify their decisions. In the latter sense, they enter into the arena for debate of Conversation 3, in which Simon Stern and Peter Brooks explore the role of narrative in judicial opinions, and they do so in interestingly complicated ways. For one thing, they suggest that judicial opinions in the area of gender sometimes suppress the very idea of narrative by treating social relations as static and invulnerable to reform. On the other hand, they might agree with Stern that judicial opinions that recount events rarely match the literary criteria we associate with narrative because, they observe, in cases involving gender the articulation of the Court's decisions often reflect and reenforce political and cultural stereotypes. And they might also agree with Brooks that these opinions often distort the reality of events in a way that belies legal prejudice. And yet, they also go beyond both Stern and Brooks in suggesting that narrative can be a creative and liberating force in making us rethink – not "pre-think"- the way the American legal system imagines relationships between the genders. Of course by that measure they might align with Stern in the view that narratives in judicial decisions can be strategically designed to justify an outcome, but they add the element of narrative inducing creativity in the reader: the strategic judicial narrator leaves many blanks for the reader to fill in so the reader is persuaded not just by logic and information, but by an imaginative transformation.

As must already be evident, the narrative and metaphorical strategies they advance for rethinking the conceptions and practice of justice also link closely with the discussion in Conversation 5 between Roberto H. Potter and Robert Weisberg on fresh metaphors and fresh narratives in allowing us to direct a sharper lens on how the subtler dynamics of culture help us both diagnose and improve the social health of our legal system.

While Berger and Stanchi focus on the top levels of the legal system, they write with a premise that legal doctrine has a mutually reinforcing effect with popular notions and tropes of gender, and so their theme aligns with those of Dahlia Lithwick and L. David Ritchie in Conversation 6 concerning public debate around crime and punishment. As Lithwick and Ritchie urge on the media a greater sense of responsibility in not encouraging inaccurate or prejudicial views of the behavior that law affects, so do Berger and Stanchi admonish judges about their professional discourse. On the other hand, whereas Ritchie reviews the empirical skepticism about the actual effect of language figurations on social attitudes, Berger and Stanchi confidently cite the cognitive science indicating that when we embed fresh metaphors and narratives into the legal discourse about gender we indeed induce legal reform.

Berger and Stanchi's observations about how inadequate metaphors and narratives obstruct the just operation of the law in relation to gender are, of course, transferable to all human rights issues discussed by Young and Meyler in Conversation 7.

The observations of Berger and Stanchi are, of course, of extreme relevance also to the topic of Conversation 9, narrative and metaphor as they are to be found in the work of legally trained activists such as Mari Matsuda, who have been concerned with the plight of all groups traditionally regarded as subordinate (indigenous people, manual workers, ethnic and cultural minorities).

7

Gender Justice: The Role of Stories and Images[*]

Linda L. Berger and Kathryn M. Stanchi

INTRODUCTION

If language not only reflects but also creates reality, the language we use to talk about gender needs to change.[1] Feminists know this. They were among the first to critically examine the illusion that language is transparent,[2] and they have taught us that the ways in which we talk about issues affect the ways we think about them. The words we select influence our impressions – and those of our audiences – and thus they limit or expand our later choices. So the language we use to talk about gender – even our choice of whether to say "sex" or "gender" – can lead to progress or it can reinforce the status quo; it can further oppression or advance liberation.

In this chapter, we argue that advocates who thoughtfully engage in metaphor-making and storytelling may alter the law's conceptions of gender justice, and indeed of justice for all. Feminist methods, rhetorical theory, and persuasion science support this argument. Feminist methods depend on unearthing myths and icons that embody the past; they rely equally on employing memorable stories and images to enlighten us about the present and to envision the future. Similarly, rhetoricians recognize and celebrate the duality of metaphor and narrative: although metaphor and narrative may impose constraining labels, they are essential to generating thought, and especially

---

[*] Kathryn Stanchi wishes to thank Marie Loiseau and Sara Mohamed for excellent research assistance.
[1] *See* Joan C. Williams, "Reconstructive feminism: Changing the way we talk about gender and work thirty years after the PDA," *Yale Journal of Law and Feminism*, 21 (2009), 79–117.
[2] Iris Murdoch, *Sartre* (Cambridge, UK: Bowes & Bowes, 1953), p. 27 ("We can no longer take language for granted as a medium of communication..."). *See generally* Dale Spender, *Man Made Language* (Chicago, IL: Pandora, 1998); Lucinda M. Finley, "Breaking women's silence in law: The dilemma of the gendered nature of legal reasoning," *Notre Dame Law Review*, 67 (1989), 886–910, 888; Andrea Nye, "Woman clothed with the sun: Julia Kristeva and the escape from/to language," *Signs: Journal of Women in Culture and Society*, 12 (1987), 664–686.

to finding new ways of looking at problems.[3] Finally, cognitive science emphasizes that our thinking is governed by the comparisons we make to embedded knowledge frameworks, including the stories and images that have become familiar to us because of our experience and culture.[4]

To explore the power to achieve gender justice by changing how we speak about gender, we begin with metaphor and narrative for two reasons. First, metaphor and narrative are central to the work of building common ground between writer and reader, and common ground is essential to establishing the mutual understanding that may lead to persuasion. When, for example, we want to explain something new or unusual, we use concrete images and well-known stories to suggest helpful comparisons that are familiar to both reader and writer. When we want to persuade our readers to perceive and interpret an unfamiliar item in a particular way, in order to achieve a particular outcome, comfortably fitting stories and images may implicitly carry over information, inferences, and expectations from the world we know to the new perception.

Second, and most important for our purpose in this chapter, when we want our readers to take a second look, we suggest alternative stories and images and ask them to fill in the details; we hint at possibilities and nudge the observer to step back, tilt her head, and look again. In this way, we say to our readers, "look, do you see what is really going on here?" When metaphor and narrative are used to frame new information as a part of a coherent and cohesive whole, when the frame is comfortable, and when the reader feels at home, the writer can suggest that the reader consider something new that would not be acceptable if the writer simply presented the information and insisted that the reader take note. Using stories and images, the writer is able to shape something new into an accessible shared perspective.

Only metaphor and narrative ask the reader to join the writer in the imaginative work of seeing one thing as another: the Constitution is a living document, burning the flag is speech, a line of precedents is a journey of progress. This quality of shared imaginative work is unique to metaphor and narrative in legal argument (analogy makes a comparison but the writer does more of the work), but it is emblematic of effective fiction. For example, in Colson Whitehead's book *The Underground Railroad*,[5] the concept that prompts the reader to join in constructing the narrative is that the underground

---

[3] Kenneth Burke, "The range of rhetoric" in *A Rhetoric of Motives* (Berkeley and Los Angeles: University of California Press, 1969), pp. 3–46.

[4] See generally Linda L. Berger, "A revised view of the judicial hunch," *Legal Communication and Rhetoric: J. ALWD*, 10 (2013), 1–39.

[5] Colson Whitehead, *The Underground Railroad* (New York, NY: Doubleday, 2016).

railroad is not a metaphor for a system of way stations and safe houses that helped slaves escape. Instead, *under the ground,* an actual railroad runs from place to place; railroad stations, conductors, and train cars full of passengers literally exist beneath the earth. In Whitehead's book, the switch from metaphorical concept to literal imagining helps Whitehead achieve the novel's task of "saying what only a novel can say." According to one reviewer, the novel does this through "small shifts in perspective: It moves a couple of feet to one side, and suddenly there are strange skyscrapers on the ground of the American South and a railroad running under it, and the novel is taking us somewhere we have never been before."[6] The same shift in perspective that leads to re-conception – a shift that takes advantage of metaphor and narrative's ability to say what only they can say – is what we aim to achieve when we use metaphor and narrative for feminist and social justice advocacy.

THE UNEASY RELATIONSHIP BETWEEN FEMINIST PERSUASION AND ARGUMENT BY METAPHOR AND NARRATIVE

Metaphor and narrative occupy an uncomfortable space in feminist method. While they are often claimed by feminist theorists as tools for resisting patriarchal language, there is no question that they are also tools of oppression. Some feminists have wondered whether metaphor and narrative are versions of the "master's tools" that cannot be used to "dismantle the master's house."[7] Others urge that because they have been the tools of hegemony, it is appropriate that feminists co-opt them as tools of resistance.[8]

Similarly, feminist use of metaphor and narrative to resist patriarchy – and in particular patriarchy's claim on the universal and objective truth – has been a double-edged sword. While these methods have worked many changes and expansions of legal discourse, ironically they have left feminists and other outsider scholars susceptible to the charge that feminists are "politicizing" the objective rules of law.

Turning first to metaphor, the tension is obvious in the feminist scholarship. Metaphor is a fundamental component of what Adrienne Rich referred to as

---

[6] Juan Gabriel Vasquez, "In Colson Whitehead's latest, the Underground Railroad is more than a metaphor," *New York Times Book Review,* August 5, 2016.

[7] Meryl Altman, "How not to do things with metaphors we live by," *College English,* 52 (1990), 495–506, 496 (feminism has "both feared and loved metaphor"); *see* Audre Lorde, "The master's tools will never dismantle the master's house" in *Sister Outsider: Essays & Speeches* (Trumansburg, NJ: Crossing Press Feminist Series, 1984), pp. 110–113.

[8] See, e.g., Sharon Janusz, "Feminism and metaphor, friend or foe," *Metaphor and Symbolic Activity,* 9 (1994), 289–300, 290.

the "oppressor's language."[9] Yet others, Rich included, have seen and used metaphor as a liberating strategy for evading the confines of patriarchal language.[10] Metaphor is seen by some feminists as "inherently subversive" because of the emphasis on logic and objectivity in patriarchal discourse. Because metaphor makes imaginative and imagistic use of language, rather than relying on literal comparisons, its use upsets the fixed "logical" categories of patriarchy.[11] Indeed, metaphor challenges the "logical established frontiers of language in order to bring to light new resemblances the previous classifications [keep] us from seeing."[12]

For these complex and intersecting reasons, it should be no surprise that feminist writers, as diverse as Audre Lorde, Adrienne Rich, and Catharine MacKinnon, often make rich and extensive use of metaphor, expressly to undermine the foundations of patriarchy and patriarchal racism by challenging its epistemology.[13] Think of Catharine MacKinnon's evocative and powerful statement that women's "different" voice is not women's true voice but rather women's voice as distorted by patriarchy: "Take your foot off our necks, then we will hear in what tongue women speak."[14] Or Audre Lorde's brilliant "Black Unicorn" in which she describes the dilemma of embracing identity within the constraints of cultural norms: "The black unicorn is restless / the black unicorn is unrelenting / the black unicorn is not / free."[15]

Adrienne Rich's poem, "Aunt Jennifer's Tigers," was, for many women, an awakening about the terror, damage, and endurance of patriarchy, but also the resilience of women. Many of us experienced the poem as the kind of powerful jolt of shared recognition that can come only from metaphor:

> Aunt Jennifer's tigers prance across a screen,
> Bright topaz denizens of a world of green.
> They do not fear the men beneath the tree;
> They pace in sleek chivalric certainty.

---

[9] Altman, "How not to do things," 496 (referencing both Adrienne Rich and Annette Kolodny regarding the "real world" damage of metaphors about women); see, e.g., Adrienne Rich, "The burning of paper instead of children" in *The Will to Change: Poems 1968–1970* (New York, NY: Norton, 1971).
[10] Altman, "How not to do things," 496.   [11] Janusz, "Feminism and metaphor," 291–292.
[12] Paul Ricoeur, *The Rule of Metaphor: The Creation of Meaning in Language*, (London: Routledge, 1977), p. 197.
[13] Janusz, "Feminism and metaphor," 291.
[14] Catharine MacKinnon, "On difference and dominance" in *Feminism Unmodified: Discourses on Life and Law* (Cambridge, MA: Harvard University Press, 1987), p. 45.
[15] Audre Lorde, "The Black Unicorn" in *The Black Unicorn: Poems* (New York: Norton, 1978).

> Aunt Jennifer's fingers fluttering through her wool
> Find even the ivory needle hard to pull.
> The massive weight of Uncle's wedding band
> Sits heavily upon Aunt Jennifer's hand.
>
> When Aunt is dead, her terrified hands will lie
> Still ringed with ordeals she was mastered by.
> The tigers in the panel that she made
> Will go on prancing, proud and unafraid.[16]

But for every metaphorical articulation that subverts patriarchy, there "lurks another identifiable disempowering articulation."[17] And when feminists "claim" metaphor as a subversive tool, we risk reinforcing the arguments that demean feminist discourse as illogical, frivolous, and politicized.[18] Positing metaphor as an inherent challenge to the purported objective rationality of patriarchal discourse reinforces the common disparagement of metaphor as meaningless decoration. Not surprisingly, metaphor has been associated with femininity because in the dominant discourse, rationality and logic are male; irrational, emotional, and ornamental language is female.[19] Law is certainly not immune to these linguistic stereotypes and feminist legal scholars have been, perhaps rightly, wary of labeling metaphor a uniquely feminist tool.

Narrative method shares some of the same tensions and contradictions. On the one hand, narrative method has been embraced by feminism as a "substantive and methodological challenge" to conventional legal narratives. As Patricia Williams has noted, "[L]egal language flattens and confines in absolutes the complexity of meaning inherent in any given problem."[20] By introducing different story lines and alternative characterizations, counternarrative is a way for feminists to fight the traditional constraints on legal storytelling. Like metaphor, narrative method has been celebrated by feminists, and other

---

[16] Adrienne Rich, "Aunt Jennifer's Tigers" in *Collected Early Poems: 1950–1970* (New York, NY: Norton, 1995).
[17] Janusz, "Feminism and metaphor," 290.
[18] Recall Catharine MacKinnon's anger at the criticism that her antipornography argument was metaphorical in *Only Words*: "[T]o say that pornography is an act against women is seen as metaphorical or magical, rhetorical or unreal, a literary hyperbole or propaganda device." Catharine A. MacKinnon, *Only Words* (Cambridge, MA: Harvard University Press, 1993), p. 11.
[19] Janusz, "Feminism and metaphor," 293. Sometimes, though the feminine is posited as "literal" when "literal" is pejorative. Altman, "How not to do things," 498–499. Steven Winter pointed out the metaphorical nature of claims that "reason is cold; it is rigorous; it is linear; it is clear; it is felt." Steven L. Winter, "Death is the mother of metaphor," *Harvard Law Review*, 105 (1992), 745–772, 749.
[20] Patricia J. Williams, *The Alchemy of Race and Rights* (Cambridge, MA: Harvard University Press, 1991), p. 6.

marginalized groups, as a way of disrupting the conventional narratives, stock stories, and determinations of relevance that are so prevalent in law and that often drive the law's outcomes.[21]

But narrative is hardly an exclusively feminist tool. Law is filled with narrative – not just stories about what happened, but stories about what the law is and what it purports to do. As Linda Edwards has noted, "when we talk about legal authority, using the logical forms of rules and their bedfellows of analogy, policy, and principle, we are actually swimming in a sea of narrative, oblivious to the water around us."[22] Despite the ubiquity of narrative in law, some judges and legal scholars still view narrative as suspect – as a tool that obfuscates and confounds the goals of law to be transparent, rational, and rule-based.[23]

The paradox that metaphor and narrative can be simultaneously tools of patriarchy and liberating tools of feminism has led some feminists to see the use of metaphor and narrative as a kind of linguistic power struggle in which the dominant group uses metaphor and narrative to delineate and reinforce the discourse boundaries and the "out group" uses them to break through those same boundaries. Language creates and reinforces conceptions of reality, and the law is replete with narrative and metaphor that create and reinforce patriarchy. For feminists, similarly, narrative and metaphor are the way we "give name to the nameless so it can be thought."[24] Metaphor and narrative are methods of speaking and creating women's reality. Thus, feminists must put metaphor and narrative to work as catalysts toward change.

METAPHOR AND NARRATIVE, TOGETHER AND APART, IN LEGAL REASONING AND ARGUMENT

Because of the uneasy relationship between feminist methods and the rhetorical practices of metaphor and narrative, feminist arguments provide an appropriate setting to explore how metaphor and narrative interact with one

---

[21] See generally Kathryn Abrams, "Hearing the call of stories," *California Law Review*, 79 (1991), 971–1052; Susan Winnett, "Coming unstrung: Women, men, narrative and principles of pleasure," *PMLA*, 105 (1990), 505–518.

[22] Linda H. Edwards, "Once upon a time in law: Myth, metaphor, and authority," *Tennessee Law Review*, 77 (2010), 883–916, 884; see also Jane B. Baron and Julia Epstein, "Is law narrative?" *Buffalo Law Review*, 45 (1997), 141–187, 144–145.

[23] See Pierre N. Leval, "Judicial opinions as literature" in Peter Brooks and Paul Gewirtz (eds.), *Law's Stories* (New Haven: Yale University Press, 1996); Daniel A. Farber and Susanna Sherry, "Telling stories out of school: An essay on legal narratives," *Stanford Law Review*, 45 (1993), 807–855.

[24] Audre Lorde, "Poetry is not a luxury" in *Sister Outsider: Essays & Speeches* (Trumansburg, NJ: Crossing Press Feminist Series, 1984), p. 37.

another, how they are different, and how they work in legal persuasion. To start with their interaction, stories can be seen as fitting within metaphorical frames,[25] and metaphors often emerge from stories, especially stories that have lived long enough to become deeply embedded in the culture. When that happens, as in the metaphor that men and women exist in *separate spheres*, the metaphorical image constitutes the distilled residue of the story. Spinning off from the original story, these distilled images take on a life of their own. When we think of Rapunzel, for instance, we see long, blond hair falling from a high window, but we recall little of the sequence of events or the conflict of characters that the fairy tale recounted.

As for their distinctiveness, even as a metaphor may contain the murky half-image of a narrative, the metaphor may also move the story to a higher plane of generality, and thus to a broader application, forming a "loft beyond the particular."[26] While narrative is closely allied with the linear telling of chronological time, metaphor is able to capture the turning points and essential moments of kairic time, "nodal points at which the threads of narrative join and divide."[27] When used as the overall frame for an argument, metaphor often is conceptual (the Constitution is a living document), and narrative frequently is sequential (the steps in the evolution of Constitutional interpretation constitute progress toward justice). As a result, the advocate seeking to argue against the status quo may turn more often to metaphor for the work of "imagining as" – projecting a new conception of how things might be. Narrative's more frequent use for the advocate of social change, on the other hand, may be to provide an "accounting for" – telling the full story to account for how things are.

Still, these differences do not change the common persuasive power of metaphor and narrative nor do they diminish their ability to work together.

The Significance of Metaphor and Narrative in Legal Argument

Earlier in the chapter, we made a claim for the uniqueness of metaphor and narrative among legal argument frames. Here, we claim that when it comes to

---

[25] According to Winter, narrative is understood because it arrives in a metaphoric frame: we have constructed an ideal model of a story that includes conceptual schemas that "serve as a kind of genetic material or template for a wide variety of stories in which the plot structure follows a protagonist through an agon to a resolution." Steven L. Winter, *A Clearing in the Forest: Law, Life, and Mind* (Chicago, IL: University of Chicago Press, 2001), pp. 106–113.

[26] Jerome Bruner, *Making Stories: Law, Literature, and Life* (Cambridge, MA: Harvard University Press, 2003), p. 25.

[27] Michael Hanne, "Getting to know the neighbours: When plot meets knot," *Canadian Review of Comparative Literature*, 26 (1999), 35–50.

validity and effectiveness, metaphor and narrative stand on equal footing with syllogism and analogy. In the previous sentence, for example, we recognize *equal footing* as metaphorical, and we may trace the metaphor's narrative past to debates about the original US Constitution's inclusion of each of the states on an "equal footing."[28] There, the metaphor embodied the principle that would govern admission of the Western states to the Union.

Only a few examples are needed to support the assertion that metaphor and narrative are both prevalent and effective in legal persuasion. For instance, after the oral argument before the US Supreme Court in *Zubik* v. *Burwell* in the spring of 2016, many observers pointed to the attention-grabbing metaphor employed by advocate Paul Clement. Clement told the Court that the government's plan through the Affordable Care Act was to "hijack" the health plans provided by organizations affiliated with religious groups so that the government could make sure female employees received contraceptives.[29] Decades earlier, Supreme Court Justice to-be Ruth Bader Ginsburg used a perspective-shifting metaphor in the brief she submitted to the Supreme Court on behalf of the female spouse in *Reed* v. *Reed*, a 1971 case in which the court ruled that an Idaho statute preferring males as the administrators of estates was unconstitutional.[30] Ginsburg wrote that the "pedestal upon which women have been placed has all too often, upon closer inspection, been revealed as a cage,"[31] a phrase repeated two years later in the majority opinion in *Frontiero* v. *Richardson*, where the court held that women who were members of the military could claim their spouses as dependents to receive increased benefits "on an equal footing" with male members of the military.[32] As for narrative, there is increasingly widespread recognition and acceptance of its influence. On both sides of issues ranging from reproductive rights to same-sex marriage, advocates are filing amicus briefs filled with the stories of individuals not in front of the court but designed to persuade the Supreme Court of one perspective or another.[33]

---

[28] *See* Clarence B. Carson, *A Basic History of the United States*, vol. II (Wadley, AL: American Textbook Committee, 1995).

[29] *See* Linda Greenhouse, "A Supreme Court hijacking," *The New York Times*, March 30, 2016. During oral argument, several justices picked up on and seemingly agreed that Clement's metaphor was accurate. The Court eventually ordered the parties to seek a compromise. *Zubik* v. *Burwell*, 578 U.S.136 S. Ct. 1557 (2016).

[30] *Reed* v. *Reed*, 404 U.S. 71 (1971).

[31] *Reed* v. *Reed*, Br. of Appellant, 1971 WL 133596 (U.S.), 21 (U.S., 2004).

[32] Justice Brennan wrote that "[t]raditionally, such discrimination was rationalized by an attitude of 'romantic paternalism' which, in practical effect, put women, not on a pedestal, but in a cage." *Frontiero* v. *Richardson*, 411 U.S. 677, 684 (1973) (Brennan, J.).

[33] *See generally* Linda H. Edwards, "Hearing voices: Non-party stories in abortion and gay rights advocacy," *Michigan State Law Review*, no. 4 (2015), 1327–1356.

Remarkably little quarrel remains with the legitimacy of metaphor and narrative in legal reasoning. Beginning at least with the legal realists, judges, advocates, and scholars have recognized that "the purpose of legal reasoning is not to prove to others the truth of a statement of fact, but is rather to persuade others about how the law ought to be interpreted and applied. Although ... logical in form, in substance it is evaluative."[34] Each of the argument frames employed in legal persuasion – metaphor, narrative, syllogism, and analogy – combines facts and law, the raw materials of legal reasoning. And each depends to a greater or lesser extent on similar mental processes: metaphor and syllogism use categorization; narrative and analogy consider setting, plot, and characterization; metaphor and analogy rely on comparison and differentiation; narrative and syllogism are structured sequentially.

How Metaphor and Narrative Persuade

When we talk about metaphor in this chapter, we are thinking of two general categories.[35] The first is the non-literal comparison through which you are asked to shift your perspective and to "see" one thing as another (*Juliet is the sun*, legislation ostensibly aimed at protecting women instead constitutes a *cage*, the teenager who downloads music without paying is a *pirate*). Most of the metaphors discussed in this chapter fall primarily within the first category. The second category is the use of concrete, visual, or figurative images to explain abstract concepts (*justice is balancing, life is a journey*). These images make it easier to think about and manage abstract or unfamiliar concepts. If the audience accepts the metaphor that copyrights are "property" like real estate, it will transfer inferences and rules from one concept to the other and certain consequences will follow: like real estate, copyrights can be bought and sold, divided, leased, and even protected against trespass. Similarly, if the teenager who downloads a piece of music without paying is a "pirate," then that teenager is an outlaw who should be punished.

Like all category distinctions, these are fuzzy, and a metaphor that starts out in one category easily slips into the next. Some characterize the first

---

[34] See, e.g., Wilson R. Huhn, "Use and limits of syllogistic reasoning in briefing cases," *Santa Clara Law Review*, 42 (2002), 813–862.
[35] We also distinguish conscious and purposeful uses of metaphor, the focus of the chapter, from the automatic and unconscious uses of metaphor well documented by Lakoff and Johnson. See George Lakoff and Mark Johnson, *Metaphors We Live By* (Chicago: University of Chicago Press, 1980); see also James Geary, *I Is an Other: The Secret Life of Metaphor and How It Shapes the Way We See the World* (New York: Harper, 2012), p. 3 ("[W]e utter about one metaphor for every ten to twenty-five words, or about six metaphors a minute.").

category as poetic metaphor; its purpose often is to *make the familiar strange* so that the observer will look again. Like poetry, it disorients the observer, opening up new outlooks and shifting views. The second category is characterized as propositional metaphor; its purpose often is to *make the strange appear familiar* so that the observer can more easily understand. Like literal propositional assertions, it suggests a particular reasoning sequence that leads to a desired outcome.[36]

Whether used to shift perspectives or to encourage large-scale conceptual mapping, metaphor's persuasive power derives from similar thinking processes. First, much of our decision-making is governed by tacit knowledge and unconscious assumptions and inferences.[37] Because tacit knowledge is automatic and constant, it remains unexamined and uncontested. As a result, invoking a deeply embedded conventional metaphor that calls no attention to itself works on a decision-maker in an automatic and unexamined way. Second, thought processes themselves are said to be metaphoric. In other words, metaphor is both a figure of thought and a way of thinking.[38] Many metaphors are derived from bodily experience ("balance" keeps you upright; "more is up" because when you pile things on top of each other, the stack goes up[39]); visual images (the "mouth" of the river, the "long arm" of the law); and stories (the Trojan horse, the sword in the stone, the holy grail). Concepts such as "knowing is seeing" and "understanding is grasping" are directly linked to our learning about the world through the senses of sight and touch.[40] In this way, metaphor helps us to perceive and understand abstract concepts in the same way that we "see" and "grasp" physical ones.

---

[36] Linda L. Berger, "Metaphor in law as poetic and propositional language," Proceedings of the 13th conference of the International Society for the Study of European Ideas (ISSEI) (2012). http://lekythos.library.ucy.ac.cy/bitstream/handle/10797/6172/ISSEIproceedings-Linda%20Berger.pdf?sequence=1&isAllowed=y.

[37] See, e.g., George Lakoff and Mark Johnson, *Philosophy in the Flesh: The Embodied Mind and Its Challenge to Western Thought* (New York, NY: Basic Books, 1999), pp. 9–15. *See also* Dan M. Kahan, "The cognitively illiberal state," *Stanford Law Review*, 60 (2007), 101–140, 115 (discussing the "psychological mechanisms that moor our perceptions of societal danger to our cultural values"); John B. Mitchell, "Narrative and client-centered representation: What is a true believer to do when his two favorite theories collide?" *Clinical Law Review*, 6 (1999), 85–126, 88–89 ("our legal texts float in a sea of varied and often conflicting cultural and historical narratives from which their ultimate meaning is derived.").

[38] Donald A. Schön, "Generative metaphor: A perspective on problem-setting in social policy" in Andrew Ortony (ed.), *Metaphor and Thought* (2nd ed., Cambridge, UK; New York, NY: Cambridge University Press, 1993), p. 137. See *also* George Lakoff, "The contemporary theory of metaphor" in Ortony, ed., *Metaphor and Thought*, p. 203.

[39] Lakoff, "Contemporary theory," 240.   [40] Winter, *A Clearing in the Forest*, pp. 55–56.

Third, logical reasoning appears to be structured analogically and metaphorically.[41] We make sense out of new experiences by placing them into categories[42] and cognitive frames called schemas or scripts.[43] As we go about our lives, we acquire and construct increasingly more sophisticated frames. For example, we experience movement from a beginning along a path to the end, giving rise to the source-path-goal image schema, which in turn leads to more complex conceptual metaphors such as life as a journey.[44] The resulting mental blueprints provide both cognitively effective shortcuts and unexamined stereotypes.

Narrative's persuasive power is related. When we talk about narrative in this chapter, we include stories that organize two or more events through time and that, if they are to be effective, resonate emotionally with an audience.[45] Rather than the "compare" and "categorize" of metaphorical processing, narrative often assigns purpose, sequence, and causation to a series of otherwise-unconnected events. Still, narrative has a similarly tacit and automatic effect. In a successful narrative, once the critical force has been triggered into action, a long line of dominoes collapses as expected.

What Lakoff and Johnson refer to as metaphor's embodiment of human experience has a parallel in the theme of a story that incorporates a seemingly universal plight.[46] Like conventional metaphors, stock stories provide mental blueprints and cognitive shortcuts.[47] Because of their familiarity, such conventional narratives make new experiences more understandable, and they allow an observer to predict what will happen next.[48]

---

[41] Ibid., pp. 56–68.
[42] See Anthony G. Amsterdam and Jerome Bruner, *Minding the Law* (Cambridge, MA: Harvard University Press, 2002), pp. 19–109 (explaining categories and their use at the Supreme Court).
[43] See generally Ronald Chen and Jon Hanson, "Categorically biased: the influence of knowledge structures on law and legal theory," *Southern California Law Review*, 77 (2004), 1103–1254, 1131–1218 (describing the literature showing that categories and schemas are "critical building blocks of the human cognitive process").
[44] Lakoff and Johnson, *Philosophy in the Flesh*, pp. 32–34 and pp. 60–66.
[45] Maksymilian Del Mar, "Exemplarity and narrativity in the common law tradition: Exploring Williams v. Roffey," Queen Mary University of London, School of Law Legal Studies Research Paper No. 139/2013 (available at: http://ssrn.com/abstract=2247937).
[46] Jerome Bruner, "Life as narrative," *Social Research*, 71 (2004), 691–710, 696.
[47] Amsterdam and Bruner, *Minding the Law*, pp. 30–31.
[48] Ibid., p. 117. See also J. Christopher Rideout, "Storytelling, narrative rationality, and legal persuasion," *Journal of Legal Writing*, 14 (2008), 53–86, 55.

How Metaphor and Narrative Contribute to Feminist and Social Justice Advocacy

Metaphor and narrative are unique and complex frames for legal argument. They allow the feminist advocate to invite the reader to try on a new or an alternative conception of how things are or how they should be. Stories and metaphors (both perspective-shifting and large-scale conceptual ones) are particularly effective for this purpose because they can make the new or alternative conception appear to be part of a coherent and cohesive whole, and they can provide the reader with a comfortable world in which the reader feels at home. What qualities give metaphor and narrative the ability to say what only they can say?

First, metaphor and narrative play a crucial role in decision making: they reassure us that things hang together, that discrete items are connected to one another in an understandable way.[49] Cognitive research reinforces our intuitive conclusion that it is easier to make a decision when the evidence and reasons supporting the decision make up a fairly coherent and cohesive package. Metaphor and narrative help us create that package. The metaphorical process allows us to gather up our perceptions, group them together, and "contain" them.[50] The narrative process allows us to link a number of essentially disjointed events together, place them into a story line with a beginning and an end, and compose an accounting.[51]

Second, metaphor and narrative operate with fewer constraints than conventional analogical and syllogistic argument and so are more flexible argument frames. Arguments based on major and minor premises usually must draw on conventional values and beliefs, but the advocate who turns to narrative has the freedom to draw on information and concepts outside the traditional bounds. Stories "can appeal to what is, by convention, still taboo in a culture. Because facts themselves capture and reflect values, what cannot be argued explicitly can be sneaked into a story."[52] In a similar manner, the advocate who turns to metaphor may advance positions without being held to them. When you use a metaphor, the listener usually understands that you have said one thing but that you likely have meant another (Juliet isn't *really* the sun). When you use an analogy, it is hard to deny that you have explicitly

---

[49] See generally Linda L. Berger, "The lady, or the tiger? A field guide to metaphor & narrative," *Washburn Law Review*, 50 (2011), 275–318.
[50] See Linda L. Berger, "Preface," *Journal of the Association of Legal Writing Directors*, 7 (2010), vii. This concept draws on the metaphors that the mind is a container and ideas are objects. See, e.g., Lakoff and Johnson, *Philosophy in the Flesh*, pp. 338, 124–125.
[51] Amsterdam and Bruner, *Minding the Law*, pp. 30–31.
[52] Gerald P. López, "Lay lawyering," *UCLA Law Review*, 32 (1984–85), 1–60, 33.

stated that *the corporation is like a person* and so you may have to provide supporting arguments to establish the similarities.

Perhaps most important, flowing from their role in spurring invention by the writer (and unlike analogy and syllogism), metaphor and narrative are persuasive precisely because they are allusive, leaving something to the imagination. When the reader fills in the gaps, metaphor and narrative become joint constructions, creating shared identity and understanding. As Milner Ball has noted, much of "narrative is inherently communal. A story is shared."[53] Narrative and metaphor thus are most effective when the audience is part of the performance, something that happens naturally with long-established images and stories.

Because both rely on seeing one thing "as" another, metaphor and narrative always carry more (or less) meaning than appears on the surface. Mapping is commonly understood as part of the processing of metaphorical meaning, but understanding narrative also depends on transferring characteristics, reasoning processes, and outcomes from one domain (the familiar plot or the source) to another (the current series of events or the target). In the process, some features are highlighted, but others are eclipsed. So when we view an individual woman through the lens of a metaphorical image left behind by a compelling narrative – a Madonna, a Mary Magdalene, a Jezebel – we get more than we consciously know. And we lose much as well: the opportunity for a fuller accounting, a richer understanding, a broader vision of equity.

This quality of metaphor and narrative crystallizes the dilemma advocates face every time they choose one approach – or even one word – over another. Every choice forecloses another one. Emphasizing one image means that another will not spring to mind. When you ask the listener to see an individual through the lens of a particular characterization (father provider, master criminal) or to see a series of happenings through the filter of a narrative arc that makes them appear to be related in a particular way (the quest, the detective story), you obstruct an alternative view. As you ask the listener to see one thing, you are also asking the listener *not* to see another.

As this discussion suggests, the advocate for social change should understand when certain kinds of images and stories may be most effective for a particular persuasive task. Because metaphor and narrative connect most readily with an audience when the audience member links them to what is already in her mind, well-known or traditional metaphors and established stock stories will be processed more automatically. The audience member will

---

[53] Milner S. Ball, "Stories of origin and constitutional possibilities," *Michigan Law Review*, 87 (1989), 2280–2319.

accept without thinking those images and stories that are so well known they are virtually unnoticed. On the other hand, novel metaphors and individualized or particularized stories – once the audience is inclined to hear them – will require more reflection and generate more resistance. As a result, they may sometimes lead to changed conceptions.[54]

The Disruptive Use of Metaphor and Narrative in Feminism and "Feminist Judgments"

To further explore the relationship between feminism and the rhetorical use of narrative and metaphor, we turn to a recent project that combines the theory of feminism and the rhetoric of judicial decision making. The U.S. Feminist Judgments Project is a collaborative project that has resulted in the rewriting of important and influential cases using feminist reasoning. In its first compilation of rewritten cases, feminist scholars and lawyers reimagined twenty-five critical Supreme Court cases on issues related to gender justice.[55] The authors rewrote and rereasoned these opinions, using the precedent available at the time of the original decision, but also bringing to the precedent a feminist perspective and philosophy.

In the examples below, we explore how metaphor and narrative were used in the original Supreme Court opinions (often unconsciously) to create and reinforce traditional assumptions about gender roles and relationships and how the feminist justices used the same rhetorical practices to challenge and undermine the conventional assumptions and stereotypes of gender embedded in the law.

The Long Tail of the 'Separate Spheres' Metaphor

The history of the metaphor evoking an image of men and women living out their lives in *separate spheres* demonstrates the long-lasting, tangible effects such an image may have on the law and society. Through time, the metaphor has suggested a dichotomy of men's and women's lives: one being mostly public, one primarily private, one going out to work, and one staying in the home with family. This dichotomy has framed legal issues and arguments for centuries.

---

[54] Linda L. Berger, "Metaphor and analogy: The sun and moon of legal persuasion," *Journal of Law and Policy*, 22 (2013), 147–95.

[55] Kathryn M. Stanchi, Linda L. Berger, and Bridget J. Crawford (eds.), *Feminist Judgments: Rewritten Opinions of the United States Supreme Court* (New York, NY: Cambridge University Press, 2016).

Among the most memorable expressions of the metaphor was Justice Bradley's 1873 concurrence in *Bradwell v. Illinois*, the case in which the Supreme Court agreed that nothing in the Constitution, including the new Fourteenth Amendment, precluded Illinois from denying a law license to Myra Bradwell.[56] The majority's grounds were legal – admission to practice in the courts of a state was not a privilege or immunity of the citizens of the United States – but Justice Bradley's concurrence was based almost entirely on metaphor.

Historian Linda Kerber traced the historical roots of the metaphor to prehistoric times: "the habit of contrasting the 'worlds' of men and of women, the allocation of the public sector to men and the private sector (still under men's control) to women is older than western civilization."[57] Kerber pointed out as well that the public-private divide was "deeply embedded in classical Greek thought," with women relegated to the private side, while men "lived in both the private and the public mode." Europeans brought these assumptions with them to America, and in the mid-1800s, Alexis de Tocqueville supplied the image that captured the metaphor. In a description of young middle-class American women, de Tocqueville described the independence they enjoyed until they were married. But when they married, he wrote, "the inexorable opinion of the public carefully circumscribes [her] within the narrow circle of domestic interests and duties and forbids her to step beyond it."[58] Kerber credited this sentence with providing both the concrete image of a circle or sphere and the interpretation that the sphere was limiting.

The social-legal-cultural assumptions captured and reinforced by the metaphor exercised significant influence on the law and public policy well into the twenty-first century: "The fundamental reason that working women's pregnancies or disproportionate load of family work creates gender disadvantage is that we still define the ideal worker as someone who works full force and full time, uninterrupted for thirty years straight – that is, someone supported by a flow of family work from a spouse, which most women never receive."[59]

Justice Bradley's concurrence in *Bradwell* demonstrated the powerful metaphor at the root of the majority's apparently syllogistic legal reasoning about legal protections. Justice Bradley asserted that both the law and "nature

[56] *Bradwell v. Illinois*, 83 U.S. 130 (1873).
[57] Linda K. Kerber, "Separate spheres, female worlds, woman's place: The rhetoric of women's history," *Journal of American History*, 75 (1988), 9–39.
[58] Kerber, "Separate spheres," 10 (quoting Alexis de Tocqueville, *Democracy in America* (New York, 1945), vol. II, bk. 3, ch. 9–12, esp. pp. 201, 211, 214).
[59] Williams, "Reconstructive feminism," 80.

herself" had established that men and women existed, and would always do so, within separate spheres:

> [T]he civil law, as well as nature herself, has always recognized a wide difference in the respective spheres and destinies of man and woman. Man is, or should be, woman's protector and defender. The natural and proper timidity and delicacy which belongs to the female sex evidently unfits it for many of the occupations of civil life.[60]

Recognizing that changes had already occurred in the statutes he relied on, Justice Bradley called on higher authority, determining that families had been constituted in a particular way because of both "divine ordinance" and "nature."

In her feminist revision of *Bradwell*, Professor Phyllis Goldfarb acknowledged the power of the metaphor and attributed its persistence to the long-standing operation of legal norms excluding women from the public sphere.[61] Questioning the metaphor's factual basis, Goldfarb emphasized that "the boundaries of the separate spheres have been much traversed" over a long period of time by, among others, "slave women, pioneer women, women who settled the frontiers of this vast nation, women who managed lands and businesses while men were fighting the Civil War." Using counterexamples that "disprove" the assumptions underlying the metaphor, Goldfarb charged that the justices had allowed the metaphor and the beliefs it represents to displace the rule of law: "Their expressed belief in a hierarchical social order in which men and women should forever and always operate in separate spheres appears to cloud their Fourteenth Amendment vision."

Outside the rewritten feminist judgment, the separate spheres metaphor continued to play a powerful if implicit and unacknowledged role in US law. Only a few years later, in *Muller* v. *Oregon*, the Supreme Court – whose members had just decided that men had a right to contract for their labor without the state's intrusion in the infamous *Lochner* decision – determined that women were different and that their greater need for protection allowed the state to limit their working hours. The influence of the metaphor that men and women live in separate spheres is evident in the Court's reasoning, which centers on women's primary role in the private sphere of motherhood and child rearing: "Even though all restrictions on political, personal, and contractual rights were taken away, and she stood, so far as statutes are concerned,

---

[60] *Bradwell* v. *Illinois*, 83 U.S. at 140 (Bradley, J., concurring).
[61] Phyllis Goldfarb, "Bradwell v. Illinois," in Stanchi, Berger, and Crawford (eds.), *Feminist Judgments*, pp. 60–77.

upon an absolutely equal plane with him, it would still be true that she is so constituted that she will rest upon and look to him for protection." Both "her physical structure and a proper discharge of her maternal functions ... justify legislation to protect her from the greed as well as the passion of man."[62]

In her *Feminist Judgments* revision of *Muller*, Professor Pamela Laufer-Ukeles thus confronted a legal question that was both framed and constrained by the assumption that men and women operate in separate spheres.[63] Because of the metaphor, the question in *Muller* became how to equalize the treatment of persons who exist in different spheres, that is, whether to treat women the same as men, or whether to treat them differently because of their perceived differences. The metaphor's persistence made the male sphere both the norm and the aspiration for *equal* treatment. The metaphor's dominance diminished the advocate's and the judge's ability to imagine and to require a standard that rejected the dichotomy of the spheres.

Decades later, in *Geduldig v. Aiello*,[64] the Supreme Court allowed California to discriminate against pregnant women in a disability insurance program on the basis that the discrimination was between pregnant and non-pregnant persons, and thus was not based on gender. Professor Lucinda Finley, writing the *Feminist Judgments* opinion, pointed out that the persistent separate spheres metaphor kept women from full participation in the workplace: "Women's ability to become pregnant and bear children has long been used as a rationale to deprive them of the economic security and independence, intellectual development, societal opportunity and respect that can come from full participation in the workplace." In particular, Finley pointed to the metaphor's accompanying "[a]ssumptions and stereotypes about the physical and emotional effects of pregnancy and motherhood, about the appropriate role of women in society and the workplace stemming from the physical fact of childbearing, and about the perceived response of women to childbearing."[65]

As late as 2001, the metaphor was still at work in a lawsuit filed by a father complaining of unfair treatment based on long-standing stereotypes about men's and women's roles in caring for children. In *Nguyen v. INS*,[66] the Supreme Court let stand an immigration statute that required fathers to satisfy

---

[62] *Muller* v. *Oregon*, 208 U.S. 412 (1908).
[63] Pamela Laufer-Ukeles, "Muller v. Oregon" in Stanchi, Berger, and Crawford (eds.,), *Feminist Judgments*, pp. 83–97.
[64] *Geduldig* v. *Aiello*, 417 U.S. 484 (1974).
[65] Lucinda Finley, "Geduldig v. Aiello" in Stanchi, Berger, and Crawford (eds.), *Feminist Judgments*, pp. 190–207.
[66] *Nguyen* v. *INS*, 533 U.S. 53 (2001).

more onerous criteria than mothers in order to pass on citizenship to their children born abroad. In her opinion for *Feminist Judgments*, Professor Ilene Durst emphasized the separate spheres ideology underlying the original decision: "The statute as written embodies the unconstitutional presumption that the mother, because of biology, will form ties with the child and ensure that the child forms ties with the United States. In contrast, the presumption is that the unwed citizen father, in the absence of a legal adjudication of paternity, will prefer to abandon or disassociate himself from the child born abroad."[67]

The separate spheres metaphor – said to have been inspired by nature and divine ordinance – has become embedded in the law by generations of lawyers and judges. To cut short its influence, something more than evidence and argument is needed.

Metaphor's New Eyes

When confronted with a tenacious metaphor whose implicit acceptance has constrained the development of the law, what can the feminist advocate do? In her *Feminist Judgments* dissent, Goldfarb demonstrated that Justice Bradley's foundational belief that men and women existed in separate spheres was metaphorical rather than factual. But even if not supported by evidence, well-entrenched metaphors are difficult to overcome. We are unlikely even to talk about the metaphor's existence or its meaning as long as we all share the same unspoken understanding. We are equally unlikely to question the reasoning and results that flow naturally from the associations accompanying the metaphor. Moreover, as discussed earlier, the influence of the separate spheres image has been felt not only in the judicial decision-making process, affecting legal outcomes as in *Bradwell*, but also in the persistent narrowing of subsequent legal questions.

Cognitive psychology and rhetorical theory suggest that if the advocate is able to imagine and employ a novel metaphor (one that begins on a common ground of familiarity or recognition and then shifts a couple of feet to one side), her audience may be better able to consider an alternative reasoning process.[68] Thus, if such a novel metaphor is accepted – not as a substitute but as an alternative – its use may disrupt unconsciously expected outcomes.[69]

[67] Ilene Durst, "Nguyen v. INS" in Stanchi, Berger, and Crawford (eds.), *Feminist Judgments*, pp. 473–484.
[68] Berger, "Metaphor and analogy," 147.
[69] Paul Ricoeur, *The Rule of Metaphor: Multidisciplinary Studies of the Creation of Meaning in Language* (Toronto: University of Toronto Press, 2004), p. 233.

Confronted with the seemingly "natural" metaphor of separate spheres, Goldfarb imagined and employed several novel metaphors. Together, these metaphors established the foundation for an alternative reasoning process. Remember that a novel metaphor may be a new conception or a new expression or both, but often it is simply the use of an already familiar comparison in a new context. Rather than calling attention to itself, as would the suggestion that a corporation is a tiger, a novel metaphor is immediately recognized as something familiar but requiring further thought (for example, a corporation's speech is a manufactured product).

Goldfarb's novel metaphors were these: the new Fourteenth Amendment had *reconstituted* the Constitution. In this way, the Fourteenth Amendment had reconstructed the nation's governing structure, and in particular the relationship between the federal and state governments and their citizens. At the center of this new governance structure and understanding of the federal-state relationship, Goldfarb created a new concept that sounded familiar: any citizen of the United States should be seen as a *federal citizen* who is entitled to protection by the federal government against state incursions into that citizen's rights.

Acceptance of Goldfarb's novel metaphors would have reconfigured the Supreme Court's reasoning. In the original *Bradwell* opinion, the majority had followed the narrow view of the Fourteenth Amendment's Privileges and Immunities Clause that the Court had just adopted in the *Slaughter-House Cases*.[70] If Goldfarb's novel metaphors had been accepted, the Fourteenth Amendment would have been seen instead as a guarantee to all citizens not only of equality but also of an entitlement to the privileges and immunities accruing to any federal citizen. These new metaphors did not seek to change minds about the lives of men and women. Instead, they set up an "ah-ha" moment for the audience: every federal citizen is entitled to the same fundamental rights.

Goldfarb began by offering a new perspective on the Reconstruction Amendments:

> This term marks the Court's first occasion to give meaning to America's new national structure, as enshrined in three Constitutional amendments adopted in 1868 in the aftermath of our terrible and protracted Civil War. Designed to alter the political dynamics of our union, these Amendments establish fundamental freedoms protected by federal power.

---

[70] *Bradwell*, 83 U.S. at 139 (following *Slaughter-House Cases*, 83 U.S. 36 (1873)).

Thus, the amendments had both the explicit purpose and the concrete result of changing the structure and functioning of the nation's governments.

As Goldfarb developed the foundation for a reconstituted national government, she spelled out the "not yet five-year-old text" of Section One of the Fourteenth Amendment, which includes the statement that "No State shall make or enforce any law which shall abridge the privileges and immunities of citizens of the United States," along with the now-more-familiar due process and equal protection guarantees. These moves framed the legal argument in a different way and took it in a wholly new direction:

> What is the meaning of United States citizenship? The second sentence of Section One bears at least part of the answer: citizens have privileges—freedom to do things—and immunities—freedom from state restrictions in exercising their privileges. In short, the Privileges and Immunities Clause tells us that citizens like Bradwell have rights that all states—while showing regard for equal protection and due process of law—must protect. In sum, through the operation of the Fourteenth Amendment, the Constitution now restricts state governments, not just the federal government, from impeding civil rights and individual liberties.

Here, Goldfarb created substantive protections for federal citizens by establishing the Privileges and Immunities Clause as prohibiting state infringements on those rights.

Goldfarb fleshed out the figure of the *federal citizen* by tracing the history of the privileges and immunities clause and emphasizing that the freedoms long thought to be encompassed in citizenship include the "fundamental civil rights found in common law," that is, "protection by the government"; "the enjoyment of life and liberty"; "the right to acquire and possess property"; and the right to "pursue and obtain happiness and safety." In particular, Goldfarb concluded, one of the primary rights of citizenship is the "right to pursue a livelihood," as Bradwell was asserting.

Goldfarb's careful legal arguments cleared the way for audience acceptance of her metaphorical framing of the Fourteenth Amendment as reconstituting the structure of the national government and of the purpose for doing so:

> Beyond oppression by a centralized power, such as the British monarch that America had overthrown, the circumstances that led to the Civil War taught us about decentralized oppression by states as well. Because recent experience has shown that federal power can serve as a check on state tyranny, the Fourteenth Amendment deliberately recalibrates the relationship between the federal government and the states ... I trust that Congress meant what it said when it undertook to grant federal constitutional protection of individual

rights from trespass by the states. In the aftermath of the Civil War, the turbulent circumstances in our nation warrant this important constitutional innovation.

Through her use of novel metaphors, Goldfarb cast the just-adopted Fourteenth Amendment, a product of the Reconstruction era, within a much larger frame than had the original majority in *Bradwell*. Within this frame, the Amendment *reconstituted* the national governance structure to ensure that both the Constitution and the federal government could exercise authority over the states. And this authority was to be exercised to guarantee all federal citizens, whether women or men, full entitlement to the privileges and immunities that are due to all citizens of the United States.

When legal arguments and decisions are confined by unthinking acceptance of the separate spheres metaphor, both the advocate and the judge are likely to respond to arguments like those made by *Bradwell* and *Muller* by seeking to equalize rights across the spheres. The male sphere becomes both the expectation and the aspiration of a successful argument. This might be considered to be progress of a sort. But both the argument and the outcome preclude legal and social actors from imagining a different sort of interpretation of what the Constitution guarantees: a fundamental level of privileges and immunities for all American citizens.[71]

Making the Invisible Visible

Having long critiqued the law for placing limits on storytelling that erase outsider perspectives, feminist scholars have employed storytelling as a tool to expand the law's narrative to include those marginalized by law. It is no secret that the judiciary is not a diverse body – as a matter of race, gender, sexuality, and class. This lack of diversity has a significant, practical impact on the law.

One result of the lack of diversity is to narrow the facts considered relevant or significant in judicial opinions. Judges have a great deal of latitude in choosing what facts to include in the narrative of a case and how to frame and describe them. Like all human beings, judges see facts through the lens of their own experiences and beliefs and that lens can affect and distort how the judges write the narrative of the case. The stories and narratives of judicial opinions will reflect the limited experiences and worldviews of this non-diverse body of writers. Moreover, the law, made by generations of non-diverse judges, will

---

[71] See, e.g., Martha Albertson Fineman, "The vulnerable subject: Anchoring equality in the human condition," *Yale Journal of Law and Feminism*, 20 (2008), 1–23, 23 ("Equality must be a universal resource, a radical guarantee that is a benefit for all.").

also constrain the scope of the facts expected or allowed to be considered. As a result, the factual narrative of judicial opinions can erase certain perspectives and reflect the influence of stock stories and stereotypes.

In a continuous loop, as judges write factual narratives that erase or distort outsider perspectives, the distorted narratives become law's "official story," and those "official stories" will drive future determinations of legal relevance, which will in turn cement that original distorted story as the "true, objective" legal story. Law's "official stories" have a lasting power in a system, like ours, grounded in precedent. And, often, the story drives the application of the rules. Think of the reasonable person and how that stock legal character has influenced the law, often to the detriment of outsiders. As we noted earlier, once the story has been framed and told a certain way, the dominoes will fall in a particular order.[72]

As a result of this continuous loop, the narratives of judicial opinions often will entirely omit facts about race, gender, and sexuality because those facts are "irrelevant" to the official story. Moreover, facts that contribute to a stereotypical image of a group may be included without qualification or reflection. This narrative process has a tremendous effect on the law and its resolution of cases, one that is felt keenly by groups historically marginalized by the law and underrepresented in the judiciary. As an example, one of the most enduring fictions embraced by the law is that of neutrality and objectivity – particularly with regard to race and other status identities. In metaphorical terms, the law is said to be "color blind." Apart from its obvious historical inaccuracy, this fiction contributes to the law's inability to consider implicit bias or historical context in determining outcome in cases involving race, gender and other marginalized groups. It often means that facts about racism and even the race or status identity of the parties are left out as irrelevant, and therefore marked as marginal.

The law's refusal to recognize the relevance of race or gender, for example, can often make it easier for biases and stereotypes to infect the law and its reasoning. The very pervasiveness and systematicity of metaphor and narrative that allow us to see "one aspect of a concept in terms of another" also will "necessarily hide other parts of the concept."[73] The less detail a narrative gives us, the more likely we are to fill gaps in our knowledge with stock stories or stereotypes. Again, here, consider the "domino" metaphor of story – once we erase race from a story, for example, readers might assume that the parties are white, and draw certain conclusions from that. Erasing race from an opinion

---

[72] Baron and Epstein, "Is law narrative?" 142.
[73] Lakoff and Johnson, *Metaphors We Live By*, p. 10.

can also insulate judges from scrutiny about bias, because readers might not know that race is even at play in the case. When an opinion is "color blind" on the surface, it also allows judges to avoid real introspection about the dangers of implicit bias by giving them plausible deniability ("I can prove race didn't matter to me because I didn't even mention it in the opinion").

A stark example of the erasure of race in a judicial decision is the opinion in *Meritor Savings Bank v. Vinson*,[74] the first hostile work environment sexual harassment case decided by the United States Supreme Court. The majority opinion never once mentions the race of the parties. Readers would not know from reading the opinion that both the victim, Mechelle Vinson, and the supervisor accused of sexual harassment, Sidney Taylor, were African American, and that both worked in a predominantly white corporate environment. The reader would also be unaware that Vinson grew up in poverty and violence, had been pregnant as a young teenager, and had held a series of low-paying, low-skill jobs before Taylor, an older, successful middle-class African American man, offered her the opportunity to work at the Bank. None of these facts were part of the law's official story of the case.

Professor Angela Onwuachi-Willig, rewriting the majority opinion in *Meritor*, expanded the facts to show, more deeply, how the intersection of race, class and gender influenced the interaction of the parties and the analysis of the legal issues. Whereas the Supreme Court ignored the race of the parties as irrelevant, Onwuachi-Willig confronted race head-on, explicitly presenting it as central to the legal issues. As Onwuachi-Willig wrote:

> Similarly, as this particular case involves an African-American female complainant, this Court must analyze this claim against the backdrop of a long history of sexual assault, rape, and harassment of African-American women as well as the history of African-American women's extreme vulnerability to sexual misconduct in the workplace and otherwise, both by white and non-white men. Historically, African-American women were viewed as so loose, sexually promiscuous, and lacking in sexual morality that they were deemed legally unrapable.[75]

Because the original Supreme Court opinion in *Meritor* erased any mention of the race of the parties while embracing the shibboleth of the law's color-blindness and objectivity, stereotyped stock stories and metaphors of women infected its narrative and, ultimately, its analysis. The common racialized gender tropes of the sexually promiscuous woman and scorned woman

---

[74] *Meritor Savings Bank v. Vinson*, 477 U.S. 57 (1986).
[75] Angela Onwuachi-Willig, "Meritor Savings Bank v. Vinson" in Stanchi, Berger, and Crawford (eds.), *Feminist Judgments*, pp. 303–321.

underlie several of the Bank's arguments that were ultimately accepted by the Court. For example, the Court found relevant the Bank's evidence and arguments about Vinson's alleged sexual fantasies, sexually provocative dress, and anger at Taylor's rebuffing of her advances.[76] Because the Court did not acknowledge the relevance of race or racism in the case, it was easier for these metaphorical stereotypes to implicitly influence the Justices' view of the facts and law. Moreover, by explicitly endorsing that this racially and sexually stereotyped evidence undercut Vinson's credibility and claims, the *Meritor* opinion enshrined these narratives – the sexually promiscuous Black woman and the angry, vengeful Black woman – as truth, reinforcing them as the law's "official story" of what sexual harassment is and how women, particularly African American women, are. It is a cliché that those who ignore history are doomed to repeat it, but *Meritor* is an excellent example of how those who ignore race and deny the power of racialized gender stereotypes in the law are doomed to succumb to them.

Onwuachi-Willig used narrative to confront the damage of the racialized gender tropes underlying the "official story" of *Meritor* by revealing the race of the parties and thereby making clear that race is and was relevant. By bringing the intersection of race and gender to the forefront of the narrative, Onwuachi-Willig forced the law to confront its own biases. She refused to let the law make Mechelle Vinson into a stock character. Instead, she gave us enough detail to make Vinson a real, three-dimensional human being and challenges us to understand her motivations and fears given her history and the history of our law and culture.

Onwuachi-Willig explicitly recounted, for example, that Vinson's failure to report Taylor's behavior for two years might very well have been the product of the intersection of Vinson's race, gender, and class. She described in detail the invidious intersection of centuries of racism and sexism that has caused African American women to be both statistically more likely to be sexually assaulted or harassed, less likely to report it and less likely to be believed when they do report. By presenting an alternative narrative for Vinson's failure to report, Onwuachi-Willig undercut the stock narrative of white patriarchy, which attributed Vinson's late reporting to her promiscuity or vengefulness.

We can see the work of metaphor in Onwuachi-Willig's counternarrative as well. Onwuachi-Willig was in a difficult position because she had to

---

[76] This trope also surfaced in the Clarence Thomas/Anita Hill hearings, showing its long history and tenacity in the law's "official story" of Black women. That many Congressmen credited this "scorned woman" story in the Hill case shows that Onwuachi-Willig's warnings were spot on.

combat the race and gender stereotypes within an opinion that does not mention race at all. Moreover, she had to speak about an experience unique to African American women in a way that a white male audience might understand. Metaphors are part of her arsenal here. For example, Onwuachi-Willig used bell hooks' metaphor of "dirty laundry" to describe the complex and conflicting feelings Vinson might have had about reporting Taylor. In addition to the conflict of reporting her boss, a successful African American man, to his mostly white supervisors, Vinson also faced the dissonance of having to report an African American man for sexual harassment, a charge that plays into damaging stereotypes about African American male sexuality.

The "dirty laundry" metaphor is not novel language, of course – its genesis is a nineteenth-century French proverb. But as we note above, a conventional metaphor can be transformative when used in a novel context. The significance of Onwuachi-Willig's use of the metaphor is that it refers to the burdens of racism in a United States Supreme Court opinion – a venue in which the existence of racism is rarely explicitly acknowledged, and often denied.

Onwuachi-Willig's use of the familiar metaphor in the new (and unexpected) context explodes the myth of "colorblind" law. "Dirty laundry" links the burden of keeping quiet about sexual harassment to labor traditionally done by African American women, capturing artfully that it is African American women who primarily confront this unique dilemma. The metaphor shows us that it is African American women who must do the unpleasant and onerous work of cleaning and hiding the dirty laundry. It also captures racial stereotypes by connecting sexuality, and particularly the sexuality of African American men and women, with dirtiness, something shameful that must be hidden. It reaches for shared understanding with the common human experience of wanting to hide shameful facts but gives a new layer to this experience. In this way, it powerfully aids the overall narrative of the opinion in making the experience of African American women and their experiences visible in law.

Onwuachi-Willig's narrative, and its attendant metaphors, make Vinson a three-dimensional human being and undercuts the law's relegation of Vinson to a stereotype. It encourages the law and its actors to see sexual harassment for the complex puzzle of human behavior that it is. Her narrative shines a light on the implicit biases that might have infected the story and the rationale and takes steps to change the law's official story about African American women and sexual harassment.

Speaking the Unspeakable

A related feminist use of narrative involves speaking about and uncovering topics about which the law refuses to speak openly because of its adherence to a somewhat old-fashioned modesty about what is proper to speak about in professional company. These topics include sex and sexuality as well as racism and rape. This modesty and forbearance exact a significant cost. The power of the law is, in part, the power to make things exist, both in law and the wider society. When the law ignores a concept, the concept can become invisible or unspeakable.

Because of the domino effect, the law's failure to confront facts related to sex, sexuality, race, racism, and misogyny can change the outcomes in cases involving these issues. More than a few commentators, for example, have noted that the law's shying away from facts about homosexual sex can have a limiting effect on the law's impact, even in cases where the court finds in favor of sexual freedom.[77] Because homophobia is often based in disgust and fear of certain sexual acts, the law's failure to speak about these acts only contributes to the phobia.

In her essay critiquing the reasoning of *Lawrence v. Texas* for its coy treatment of the sexual behavior involved, for example, Professor Mary Ann Case points to two other cases notorious for their evasion of the sexual issues at the heart of the legal issue: *Oncale v. Sundowner*[78] and *Griswold v. Connecticut*.[79] In the *Oncale* majority opinion, Justice Scalia famously refused to detail the disturbing facts at issue in that case, asserting that the details were irrelevant to the legal issues and would tarnish the "dignity" of the Court. Similarly, in *Griswold*, the sex was "hidden under the covers of the marital bed."[80]

The feminist judgments in these two cases, by contrast, confront the details of the sexual acts at the heart of the cases.

In her rewrite of *Oncale*, Professor Ann McGinley asserted outright that it is important to detail the explicit acts of sexual harassment perpetrated against the petitioner in that case, Joseph Oncale.[81] There are a number of important reasons for this. First, the Court's hiding behind "dignity" means that the reader never knows the egregious acts committed in that case, which included

---

[77] See, e.g., Mary Anne Case, "Of 'This' and 'That' in Lawrence v. Texas," *Supreme Court Review*, 55 (2003), 75, 79 ("transparency is not something we associate with polite discussions of sex").
[78] *Oncale v. Sundowner Offshore Svcs.*, 523 U.S. 75 (1998).
[79] *Griswold v. Connecticut*, 381 U.S. 479 (1965)   [80] Case, "Of This and That," 77–78.
[81] Ann McGinley, "Oncale v. Sundowner Offshore Services" in Stanchi, Berger, and Crawford (eds.), *Feminist Judgments*, pp. 414–425.

the forced insertion of a bar of soap into Oncale's rectum. For McGinley, it is important to shock people into awareness and to hold the harassers accountable. The notion that merely writing about these acts damages the Court's dignity reinforces stereotypes about victims of sexual assault and harassment and encourages feelings of shame – the Court is essentially saying "it makes us feel dirty to talk about what happened to you."

Second, it is important to emphasize that the details are, despite Justice Scalia's disclaimer, legally relevant, because as Justice Scalia himself notes later in the opinion, a critical element of sexual harassment is the severity of the conduct. Indeed, in *Oncale*, Justice Scalia addresses severity when he warns that it is important not to "mistake ordinary socializing in the workplace–such as male-on-male horseplay or intersexual flirtation" for discrimination. A common metaphor (with an implied companion narrative) in sexual harassment is that complainants are "thin skulls" – oversensitive prudes who complain about harmless sexual banter and want a sanitized, politically correct workplace devoid of any fun. Professor McGinley's use of expanded narrative undercuts that stock story of sexual harassment.

McGinley's explicit detailing of the sexual abuse against Oncale changes the tone and color of the legal analysis. It puts the minimizing "horseplay" warning in a very different light. In the absence of the detail that McGinley provides, the reader might wonder how serious the behavior was in *Oncale*. By euphemizing what Oncale suffered (Justice Scalia calls it "subjected to sex-related humiliating actions"), the majority invites the reader to fill in the blanks herself. The addition of the "horseplay" warning further undercuts how the reader might view the seriousness of what Oncale endured. The word "horseplay," itself a metaphor that calls forth an image of frisky colts, is a diminishing and euphemizing term especially as applied to sexual harassment and assault. McGinley's version of *Oncale* makes the "horseplay" warning seem out of place and inappropriate in a case that involved such a serious sexual assault.

McGinley's detailed facts derail the myth that what we often call "horseplay" is harmless behavior. She shows that what the Supreme Court and other federal courts often downplay as "rough-housing," "hazing," or "horseplay" can be harassment "because of sex" because it serves to establish masculine boundaries and force a workplace to conform (or continue to conform) to a traditionally macho masculine culture.

Finally, for McGinley, the details of the sexual abuse suffered by Oncale uncover something legally significant about the nature of sexual harassment as a way of policing gender in the workplace. In her view, it is highly relevant that the abuse of Oncale was a way of "feminizing" him, to the extreme of simulated rape. To McGinley, these facts reveal a truth about sexual harassment: that it is not necessarily (or even usually) born of sexual desire, but rather is a complicated fusion of sex, sexuality, and aggression in which sex is the means through which hostility is expressed toward those who violate traditional gender boundaries. This is a significant addition to the law, as federal courts have struggled with sexual harassment cases because of the persistent belief that sexual harassment is a manifestation of sexual desire.[82]

Professor Laura Rosenbury's rewrite of *Griswold* is another example of using factual narrative to speak the unspeakable in law and culture.[83] Her approach to *Griswold's* narrative is unabashedly explicit in talking about the centrality of sex and sexual pleasure to life and liberty. By explicitly tying the legal issue in *Griswold* to issues of sexual pleasure, she revealed the contraceptive ban in *Griswold* for what it really was: the intentional suppression of sexuality, particularly women's sexuality, through patriarchal, misogynist laws. Rosenbury's opinion is bold and positively joyful in its explicitness about sexuality and its importance in the constitutional guarantee of liberty.

Rosenbury wrote:

> Access to contraceptives ... is a necessary prerequisite for many men and women who seek to engage in mutual sexual activity in order to develop their identity, to deepen their relationships, or to simply experience pleasure and release. By criminalizing all use and distribution of contraception, the state of Connecticut has foreclosed this important aspect of liberty or made it unduly risky, therefore limiting individuals' liberty to interact with others in the ways they desire. Although some individuals may choose to develop their identity and relationships through the abstinence urged by the state, others will choose to do so through sexual activity. The state may not use its coercive power to limit this choice.

The sexual explicitness of Professor Rosenbury's opinion is not just narrative window-dressing. It is legally significant. *Griswold*, like the reproductive rights cases, centers on the role of law in regulating the adverse and unintended consequences of sexual activities, particularly for women.[84] Yet none of these cases – not *Griswold*, *Eisenstadt* or *Roe* and its progeny – faces up to the centrality of sexuality, and patriarchal suppression of women's sexuality, to the legal issues in those cases. The regulation of contraception and abortion is

---

[82] *See* Vicki Schultz, "Reconceptualizing sexual harassment," *Yale Law Journal*, 107 (1999), 1683–1805.

[83] Laura Rosenbury, "Griswold v. Connecticut" in Stanchi, Berger, and Crawford (eds.), *Feminist Judgments*, pp. 103–113.

[84] Susan Frelich Appleton, "Toward a 'culturally cliterate' family law?" *Berkeley Journal of Gender Law and Justice*, 23 (2008), 267–337, 275.

intricately intertwined with our cultural views of women's sexuality as shameful, even evil,[85] as something to be hidden and suppressed – and as something for which women should be exposed and punished by being forced to endure unwanted pregnancy. The revulsion toward, and attendant suppression of, women's sexual nature underlies much of the law relating to human sexuality and has a serious impact on rape and sexual harassment law. Yet *Griswold* scarcely mentioned sex.

When women's sexuality as a healthy, normal aspect of women's humanity is unspeakable and unspoken in the legal and cultural discourse, the gap is too easily filled by stereotypes like the Madonna/whore that are essential to the maintenance of patriarchy.[86] By acknowledging the centrality of sexuality and sexual pleasure to the legal issue at hand, Rosenbury paves the way for a future of sexual liberty in which women's sexual agency is celebrated and recognized as a core aspect of liberty, not punished and co-opted.

Like Onwuachi-Willig in *Meritor*, Rosenbury used multiple metaphors to buttress her narrative. As commentator Cynthia Hawkins DeBose wrote, Rosenbury's opinion took sex and women's sexuality out of the "dark recesses" to which law had relegated them. Dismissing the conventional notion of sex as dirty or shameful, Rosenbury sees sex as a beautiful process – of discovery, of human development. The Connecticut contraceptive ban at issue in *Griswold* exemplified the view of sex as a mechanical act purely for the purpose of procreation; in this view woman's sexual pleasure is irrelevant at best. In contrast, sex in Rosenbury's opinion is a journey of "individual discovery" and "development." By writing of sex as an expression of personal identity and self-actualization, Rosenbury also counteracted the narrow traditional view of appropriate sexual behavior: "[s]exual exploration and pleasure" is an "important aspect of individual identity and self-expression." The metaphors in the feminist *Griswold* are of both types: they force us to see one thing as another (sex as a journey of discovery and identity) and figurative images to explain abstract concepts (sexuality as personal evolutionary process).

The metaphors are, in part, what give the opinion its joyful, playful tone with regard to sex. But these happy metaphors also do the serious important work of laying bare the law's complicity in the oppression of women's sexuality and the damage that oppression has wrought in all areas of jurisprudence.

---

[85] Lynne Henderson, "Getting to know: Honoring women in law and in fact," *Texas Journal of Women and Law*, 2 (1993), 41–73, 43; bell hooks, *Ain't I A Woman: Black Women and Feminism* (Boston, MA: South End Press, 1981), pp. 110.

[86] Susan Ekberg Stiritz, "Cultural cliteracy: Exposing the contexts of women's not coming," *Berkeley Journal of Gender, Law and Justice*, 23 (2013), 243–266, 249–53 (describing the treatment of women's sexuality as a kind of "discursive clitoridectomy").

Rosenbury's metaphors of discovery and identity make women's sexual pleasure visible and important. By framing sex beyond the mechanical, as a critical and natural process of human development and identity, Rosenbury makes her point that choices about sexuality are a core aspect of personal liberty. If sex is a mechanical, somewhat distasteful part of humanity, meant to be suppressed and secret, it is quite difficult to see it as a fundamental right. In Rosenbury's framing, sex is central to human development, a source of joy to be celebrated, making it that much easier to see it as a fundamental liberty right shared by all people, men and women alike.

Claiming sexuality as a core liberty interest – not just acceptable, but essential to humanity – has the potential for wide-ranging effects on jurisprudence critical to women's rights as well as LGBTQ rights. Like the "dirty laundry" metaphor, Rosenbury's metaphors challenge us but also bring us together as human beings. Abortion jurisprudence, rape jurisprudence, sexual harassment law – all would look very different in a world in which the Supreme Court had acknowledged women's sexuality and basic humanity.

Building Audience Identification through Emotion

In this final section, we focus on the emotional dimensions of narrative and metaphor.[87] Emotional resonance connects an audience with an image or a story through shared feelings. In narrative, an audience is more receptive to an author's invitation to identify with and enter into a story when, in Walter Fisher's terms, the story "hangs together" – it is coherent and cohesive – and when the story "rings true" – it matches up with what the audience member already knows to be true in the world.[88] In metaphor theory, a novel metaphor is thought to effectively forge an initial link between concepts that are remote from one another when their emotional tones resonate with each other.[89]

---

[87] See Paul Ricoeur, "The metaphorical process as cognition, imagination, and feeling," *Critical Inquiry*, 5 (1978), 143–59 (proposing that metaphor blends cognitive, imaginative, and emotional dimensions). Some scholars are reluctant to emphasize the emotional impact of narrative because doing so seems to support a once-common view that narrative is "a vehicle of emotion, opposed to logic and reasoning." See, e.g., Peter Brooks, "Narrative transactions – Does the law need a narratology?" *Yale Journal of Law and the Humanities*, 18 (2006), 1–28, 2.

[88] Walter R. Fisher, "The narrative paradigm: An elaboration," *Communication Monographs* 52, (1985), no. 4, 347–367, 349.

[89] See, e.g., James R. Averill, "Emotions as mediators and as products of creative activity" in J. Kaufman and J. Baer, eds., *Creativity across Domains: Faces of the Muse* (Mahwah, NJ: Erlbaum, 2005), pp. 225–243 ("the way I feel about lawyers may 'resonate' with the way I feel about broccoli. [The] two resonating tones [may lead] to the formation of an original link between the otherwise remote concepts to which these feeling tones were experientially attached. For example, 'Lawyers are the broccoli of the judicial system.'").

For feminist and social justice advocates, emotional resonance is one of the attributes that help move audience members to different vantage points and may lead to changes in their beliefs or attitudes about specific issues. Transfer of metaphoric meaning, for example, requires audience attention and then *uptake* from the audience (in other words, recognition of a surface familiarity or similarity before moving to deeper levels of interaction). Researchers have found that when individuals are "absorbed into a story or transported into a narrative world," the story may affect their beliefs and attitudes. This sort of narrative transportation is enhanced by melding together elements of attention or focus, images, and feelings.[90]

How might emotional resonance work in legal argument? The US Supreme Court's decision in *Brown* v. *Board of Education* provides a possible example. In *Brown I*, with little directly helpful precedent or legislative history to rely on, Chief Justice Earl Warren declared that segregated schools were inherently unequal and hence unconstitutional.[91] The opinion relied in part on social science research; key components of the research and the court's reliance on it have been consistently criticized.

For the purpose of exploring the quality of narrative transportation, however, the often-maligned "dolls study" may productively be viewed as an influential collection of stories about schoolchildren that conveyed memorable images and may have evoked shared feelings. Nearly sixty years earlier, in *Plessy* v. *Ferguson*, the Supreme Court had belittled the argument that Black children were emotionally harmed by segregation.[92] As one way to counteract that statement, the so-called "dolls study" was one component of the social science research introduced as evidence in several of the cases consolidated in *Brown*. In one of those cases, Dr. Kenneth Clark testified about the questions he asked of sixteen Black children in 1950 in Clarendon County, South Carolina. Considered as narrative, Dr. Clark's testimony invited audience members to *try on* what it felt to be a child in a segregated school. The answers conveyed a world that presumably was much different from the one the justices inhabited.[93]

---

[90] Melanie C. Green and Timothy C. Brock, "The role of transportation in the persuasiveness of public narratives," *Journal of Personality and Social Psychology*, 79 (2000), 701–721.

[91] *Brown* v. *Board of Education*, 347 U.S. 483 (1954).

[92] *Plessy* v. *Ferguson*, 163 U.S. 537, 551 (1896) ("We consider the underlying fallacy of the plaintiff's argument to consist in the assumption that the enforced separation of the two races stamps the colored race with a badge of inferiority. If this be so, it is not by reason of anything found in the act, but solely because the colored race chooses to put that construction upon it.").

[93] Bruce Hay explored Dr. Clark's testimony "as a piece of experimental theater," concluding that the images left behind were "unforgettable." Bruce L. Hay, "The damned dolls," *Law and Literature*, 26 (2014), 321–342, 333.

Dr. Clark testified that he had conducted the tests the previous week at a local elementary school, showing the children Black and white dolls that were identical in every way except their skin color, and asking a series of questions. Dr. Clark began with "Show me the doll that you like best or that you'd like to play with," and moved next to "Show me the doll that is the 'nice' doll," and "Show me the doll that looks 'bad.'" The questions continued: "Give me the doll that looks like a white child," and "Give me the doll that looks like a colored child." Finally, Dr. Clark asked the children to "Give me the doll that looks like a Negro child," and "Give me the doll that looks like you." The testimony continued:

> Q. "Like you?"
> A. "Like you." That was the final question, and you can see why. I wanted to get the child's free expression of his opinions and feelings before I had him identified with one of these two dolls. I found that of the children between the ages of six and nine whom I tested, which were a total of sixteen in number, that ten of those children chose the white doll as their preference; the doll which they liked best. Ten of them also considered the white doll a "nice" doll. And, I think you have to keep in mind that these two dolls are absolutely identical in every respect except skin color. Eleven of these sixteen children chose the brown doll as the doll which looked "bad."[94]

The research on narrative transportation suggests that particular combinations of audience focus, imagery, and feelings can transport the audience into the world of the narrative. Considered as narrative persuasion rather than as proof, Dr. Clark's testimony seems likely to have prompted his audience to venture at least briefly into radically different settings.

In her *Feminist Judgments* revision of the opinion in *Loving v. Virginia*, Professor Teri McMurtry-Chubb wove stories together with stark images drawn from history. The emotional responses evoked by the stories and images resonate with the emotions brought to bear in the legal reasoning that comes late in the opinion.[95] In the original opinion, Chief Justice Earl Warren determined that Virginia's statutes barring marriage between Blacks and whites violated the Constitution's due process and equal protection

---

[94] In *Brown*, the Court agreed with a lower court that "[s]egregation of white and colored children in public schools has a detrimental effect upon the colored children." Citing the Clark study, among others, the Court also said that "[w]hatever may have been the extent of psychological knowledge at the time of *Plessy* v. *Ferguson*, this finding is amply supported by modern authority." *Brown*, 347 U.S. at 494–495.

[95] Teri McMurtry-Chubb, "Loving v. Virginia" in Stanchi, Berger, and Crawford (eds.), *Feminist Judgments*, pp. 119–136.

guarantees.[96] Reading the statutory language alone was sufficient to reveal that there was no reason for these laws except to maintain white supremacy.[97]

McMurtry-Chubb began her feminist revision with a much more detailed and particularized version of the facts than that contained in the original opinion:

> Mildred Delores Jeter, the unnamed African American spouse of the plaintiff in this action, grew up in Central Point, Caroline County, Virginia. Richard Perry Loving, the White man who had become Ms. Jeter's friend through childhood and adolescence and later her husband, also grew up in Central Point, Caroline County, Virginia. This particular locale in Virginia is known for its White and African American residents' habitual practice of interracial coupling and creating children of both European and African descent.

In this opening, McMurtry-Chubb invited the audience to begin to identify with Mildred Jeter and Richard Loving. Her depiction of the couple and their circumstances shortened the distance between the parties and the court, bringing into more familiar territory a marriage and a family that would have seemed unusual to Supreme Court justices at the time. Mildred and Richard were childhood friends who had grown up together in a small town in Virginia. In that small town, there was a practice of "creating children of both European and African descent"; in other words, the Lovings' relationship was customary and not unusual in that "particular locale in Virginia." Through her use of normalizing terms, McMurtry-Chubb established an initial point of contact.

The individualization and particularization of the Lovings continued:

> Mildred Jeter and Richard Loving's friendship began when Mildred was 11 and Richard was 17. The friendship became a courtship and then a romance, consummated and subsequently memorialized by the birth of the couple's son Sidney Clay Jeter on January 27, 1957. Just over a year later, Mildred became pregnant with the couple's second child. At 18 years of age and approximately five months into her pregnancy, Mildred travelled with Richard to Washington, D.C., and on June 2, 1958, the two married legally.

Through these details – likely to have been deemed legally irrelevant – McMurtry-Chubb continued to build audience identification: the Lovings' story is familiar, a story of the progression of love and marriage between

---

[96] *Loving v. Virginia*, 388 U.S. 1 (1967).
[97] *Loving*, 388 U.S. at 11–12 ("The fact that Virginia prohibits only interracial marriages involving white persons demonstrates that the racial classifications must stand on their own justification, as measures designed to maintain White Supremacy.").

friends, culminating in pregnancy and marriage when the young woman was still a teenager. So far, nothing unusual has happened.

But then the Lovings went home: "They travelled back to Caroline County, Virginia where their marriage was illegal." Like any newly married couple, they stayed with Mildred's parents for a few days. And "[o]n ... their tenth day as newlyweds, the two were roused from their marriage bed and arrested on charges of violating Virginia's anti-miscegenation laws." McMurtry-Chubb did not emphasize the racial and gender distinctions in what happened next, simply recounting that the white male, Richard Loving, was released on bail, while the young Black pregnant woman, Mildred, stayed in jail for another four days. According to McMurtry-Chubb's opinion, Mildred gave birth to the couple's second child five days before her hearing was scheduled.

Having established a setting in which the reader came to know the Lovings as individuals, but at the same time, through the lens of a familiar love story that took a sudden and unexpected plot turn, McMurtry-Chubb next detailed the seemingly ordinary facts that became an indictment charging the Lovings with violating Virginia law. The indictment stated:

> [T]he said Richard Perry Loving, being a white person and the said Mildred Dolores [sic] Jeter being a colored person, did unlawfully and feloniously go out of the state of Virginia, for the purpose of being married, and with the intention of returning to the State of Virginia and were married out of the State of Virginia, to-wit, in the District of Columbia on June 2, 1958, and afterwards returned to and resided in the County of Caroline, State of Virginia, cohabitating as man and wife against the peace and dignity of the Commonwealth.

If McMurtry-Chubb has moved the audience into the narrative world of the Lovings, both the exact words of the indictment and the verbatim words of the trial judge will elicit an emotional response. McMurtry-Chubb detailed the trial judge's suspension of the Lovings' sentence based on a condition – that the Lovings leave Virginia and not return – and while making this statement:

> Almighty God created the races white, black, yellow, malay, and red, and he placed them on separate continents. And but for the interference with his arrangement, there would be no cause for such marriages. The fact that he separated the races shows that he did not intend for the races to mix.

From there, McMurtry-Chubb continued to weave new stories with the one left hanging. The Lovings went to live in the District of Columbia and had a third child, and Richard continued to commute back to Virginia for work. In the nation's capital, the Lovings' story became an increasingly significant component of the larger American narrative of progress toward racial justice. While the Lovings were living in the District of Columbia, the civil rights movement was in progress, and one of Mildred's relatives advised her to write to Attorney General Robert F. Kennedy. Kennedy encouraged her to enlist the help of the American Civil Liberties Union (ACLU).

When McMurtry-Chubb returned to the Lovings' story, she next adopted the point of view of Mildred Loving, including the full text of the letter she sent to the ACLU:

Dear Sir,

I am writing to you concerning a problem we have. Five years ago, my husband and I were married here in the District. We then returned to Virginia to live. My husband is White. I am part Negro and part Indian. At the time we did not know there was a law in Virginia against mixed marriages. Therefore we were jailed and tried in a little town of Bowling Green [Virginia]. We were to leave the state to make our home.

The problem is we are not allowed to visit our families. The judge said if we enter the state within the next thirty years, that we will have to spend one year in jail. We know that we can't live there, but we would like to go back once and awhile to visit our families and friends. We have three children and cannot afford an attorney.

We wrote to the Attorney General, he suggested that we get in touch with you. Please help us if you can. Hope to hear from you real soon.

Yours Truly,

Mr. and Mrs. Richard Loving

After accounting for the story of the Lovings in the facts section of the opinion, McMurtry-Chubb turned in her legal argument to unsparingly honest depictions and images of what marriage and family life meant in the context of slavery. Unlike Chief Justice Warren's reliance on the language of the statute alone (and what he assumed everyone knew about the history of Virginia), McMurtry-Chubb's specificity about the historical record made inescapable the tie between the statute and Virginia's goal of maintaining white supremacy.[98]

By weaving together the Lovings' story with the narrative arc of history, the narrative persuasion of the feminist judgment may reach the reader in a different way. The audience's emotional responses to the story of the Lovings and to the history of Black men, women, and children during slavery must include sorrow, anger, sympathy, bitterness, guilt, and fear. To the extent

[98] Some of the judgment recalls Cheryl Harris's stunning examination of whiteness as property. Cheryl I. Harris, "Whiteness as property," *Harvard Law Review*, 106 (1993), 1707–1791.

that the audience members are transported into the world that is formed by these emotions and images of the Lovings and the men and women who were denied marriage and family lives by slavery, they may change their beliefs and attitudes.

We have neither the time nor the space to tell the full story or to paint the whole picture. What's more, the story is still developing and the picture not yet finished. Much remains to be done. What the feminist judgments demonstrate is that judges with diverse experiences and perspectives will fill in the gaps differently, both in conception and expression. Through metaphor and narrative, advocates can help judges hear different voices and perceive new possibilities. They show us a brief glimpse of the future: how the story might unfold and how the picture might be revealed.

CONVERSATION V
NARRATIVE, METAPHOR, AND INNOVATIONS IN LEGAL THINKING

Editors' Introduction

Michael Hanne and Robert Weisberg

Thomas Kuhn's famous description of "paradigm shifts" in scientific domains[1] has been extended to many fields of thought, and philosophers such as Susan Haack have highlighted the value of metaphors for offering a flash of insight in the early stages of rethinking an intellectual field or institutional practice.[2] To take an outstanding example, Darwin's notebooks show him inserting sketches of tree-like structures in the margins of his notebooks[3] very early in the process of developing the narrative theory of biological evolution, which came to displace the traditional narrative whereby God created all species on earth at the same moment. Moreover, as other commentators have shown, the very theory of natural selection is couched in a coherent series of metaphors, which serve to "organize [Darwin's] observations, structure the vague concepts, and ultimately render his observations meaningful and intelligible."[4] These metaphors, including "nature as mother," "life as war," "life as a race," and "evolution as progress," have, in turn, generated endless scientific ideas, as well as political ideas of mixed moral content.[5]

More generally on the side of metaphors, recognition of their reframing power over social issues was taken up strongly by Donald Schön in the 1980s.[6] He

---

[1] Thomas S. Kuhn, *The Structure of Scientific Revolutions* (Chicago, IL: University of Chicago Press, 1962).

[2] Susan Haack, "Dry truth and real knowledge" in Jaakko Hintikka (ed.), *Aspects of Metaphor* (Dordrecht; Boston; London: Kluwer, 1994), pp. 1–22.

[3] Gillian Beer, *Darwin's Plots: Evolutionary Narrative in Darwin, George Eliot and Nineteenth-Century Fiction*, 3rd edition (Cambridge and New York: Cambridge University Press, 2009).

[4] Abdulsalam Al-Zahrani, "Darwin's metaphors revisited: Conceptual metaphors, conceptual blends, and idealized cognitive models in the Theory of Evolution," *Metaphor and Symbol*, 23 (2008), 50–82.

[5] Richard Hofstadter, *Social Darwinism in American Thought* (Boston, MA: Beacon Press, 1944).

[6] Donald A. Schön, "A perspective on problem-setting in social policy," in Andrew Ortony (ed.), *Metaphor and Thought* (Cambridge and New York: Cambridge University Press, 1979), pp. 137–163.

referred to the "generative" force of metaphor in defining any challenge, so that potential solutions to a problem will almost always follow directly from the metaphor chosen to frame it, and such metaphors in turn tend to induce new narratives of policy and practice. Consider Friedrich Froebel's coining of the "horticulture" metaphor for early childhood education in the 1830s, a metaphor which has survived and proliferated in modern educational theory and practice.[7]

As metaphors become established in the minds of experts and the general public, so they may be said to capture, or even monopolize, the discourse; "the history of a scientific discipline can be traced through its changing repertoire of models and metaphors."[8] Of course, the power of metaphor also demands caution from its extenders: So, to use the horticulture-education analogy, we must recognize (a) that only certain features from the source domain are applied to the target domain (e.g. "pruning" growing children is not recommended!) and (b) that over the period since it was coined in the 1830s, the metaphor has been supplemented and combined with a host of other metaphors, such as: "initiation," "liberation," "construction with scaffolding," and "translation."[9]

As shown in the previous chapter about gender, much of the work of narrative legal study in recent years has focused on the alleged impoverishment of the conventional figurations – their failure to reflect the interests and voices of disadvantaged groups. Hence, we hear the call for fresh ways to tell those stories; most notably this has been the mission of the Critical Race Theory movement as applied to law.[10] The implementation of that mission is evidenced in Conversation 9, in the interview with Mari Matsuda.

But as we saw in Conversation 1, metaphor and narrative have been very versatile in capturing and reflecting the most fundamental structures of jurisprudence and legal structures. Key metaphors provide the foundation for many other areas of theory of law, and these both activate and constrain legal practice in important ways, e.g. the "attack" and "defense" pair of metaphors

---

[7] See Chapter 5, "The seed corn and the child: A comparison," in his *Pedagogics of the Kindergarten* http://urweb.roehampton.ac.uk/digital-collection/froebel-archive/pedagogics-kindergarten/index.html.

[8] John Ziman, *Real Science: What It Is and What It Means* (Cambridge, UK; New York, NY: Cambridge University Press, 2000), pp 149–150. This recalls Marshall Sahlin's observations on the changing metaphors employed over the centuries to characterize the relation between Christians and their god, cited in Lawrence Rosen's contribution to Conversation 1.

[9] John Darling, "Education as horticulture: Some growth theorists and their critics," *Journal of Philosophy of Education*, 16 no. 2 (1982), 173–185 and Derek Maus, "The changing metaphors of education," in course notes at Potsdam: www2.potsdam.edu/mausdc/class/601/metaphor.html.

[10] This point is well made in relation to all disadvantaged groups by, for instance, Richard Delgado, "Storytelling for oppositionists and others: A plea for narrative," *Michigan Law Review*, 87 (1989) 2411–2441.

that predominates in the common-law tradition.[11] So, a number of thinkers have proposed alternative metaphors, such as "healing" and "balancing" to promote forms of legal practice such as mediation and restorative justice.[12] Others have contrasted the military metaphors typical of the common law system with the "seeking" and "quest" metaphors of the inquisitorial judicial system. In the words of Thomas Weigend, the "Continental inquisitorial model ... insists that substantive truth can be found if enough effort is made and that the criminal process is ... a search for substantive truth."[13] And, as Ralph Grunewald suggests, the two models favor very different ways for handling and constructing narratives.[14]

To take things a further step, literary analogy is not only used in legal scholarship (as this volume illustrates), but can be used to describe legal scholarship as a phenomenon in itself.

Robert W. Gordon has shown that traditional legal scholarship actually resists narrative in the sense that it is intellectually invested in stasis and order in summarizing and explaining the law. He then offers fascinating observations about how canonical legal scholarship tries to resist the unavoidable manifestations of changes in law either from within legal institutions or imposed from without.[15] The legal historian can engage in denial (hence lending narrative credibility by fearing it); Cartesianism (whereby reluctant credit is given to historical evolution for setting up the principles of law that then become immortal); adaptionism (rationalizing each change as a tinkering); or resignation (thus implicitly narrating a fall from a Golden Age permanence).

When it comes to specific fields of contemporary law, it may be no surprise that the most fertile subject for analysis of metaphor and narrative is litigation (which almost by definition involves contestation and storytelling). And while there have been a few instances in civil litigation – as in Thurman Arnold's hilarious treatment of railroad corporate receivership proceedings as theatrical farce – it is even less surprising that criminal justice has been the dominant locus of this work. The special theatrics of the criminal trial have always

---

[11] Carrie Menkel-Meadow, "The trouble with the adversary system in a postmodern, multicultural world," *William and Mary Law Review*, 38 (1996-7), 5–44.

[12] John Haynes, "Metaphor and Mediation." Unpublished manuscript. Available on www.mediate.com/articles, which argues that conflict is better understood as a journey, rather than a battle.

[13] Thomas Weigend, "Is the criminal process about truth? A German perspective," *Harvard Journal of Law and Public Policy*, 26 (2003), 157–173, 168.

[14] Ralph Grunewald, "The narrative of innocence, or lost stories," *Law and Literature*, 15 no. 3 (2013), 366–389.

[15] Robert W. Gordon, "Historicism in legal scholarship," *Yale Law Journal*, 90 (1981), 1017–1056.

attracted literary and dramatic appreciation,[16] but we see a richer world of metaphor and narrative in law when we turn to criminal justice more broadly – its various institutions as well as the field of criminology, and, still more broadly, even the social perception of crime and law.

A good recent example is the work of Thibodeau and Boroditsky, highlighting the very different public attitudes and policies generated by the contrasting (indeed competing) metaphors of crime as a "predatory beast" or as "a virus."[17] (This point will be taken up in the next conversation, between legal journalist Dahlia Lithwick and communications specialist David L Ritchie, under the heading "Narrative and Metaphor in Public Debate around Crime.") But as shown in the Potter and Weisberg papers in this chapter, those metaphors (along with narratives) are not just expressions of lay public attitude. We see a trend in professional and institutional discourse to identify crime with disease and to devise policies for reducing crime extrapolated from the domain of public health. Potter assesses the adequacy of the metaphor cluster which stems from that identification.

And as Potter shows, influential metaphor clusters often rely on an analogy, not simply between domains, but between the work of practitioners in different disciplines on related topics. Such analogies allow thinkers in the two domains to borrow a range of quite specific insights from each other, e.g., criminologists seek to understand multifactorial causality and the degree of responsibility of people who commit crime, just as epidemiologists seek to understand the same issues in relation to those who experience diseases caused by their chosen modes of living. Of course, we must also be alert to the risk that such laudable interdisciplinary translation might borrow concepts wholesale and uncritically from a metaphorical source domain. e.g. applying the notion of risk factors from epidemiology to criminality too mechanically.[18]

In turn, Weisberg explores the multidimensional implications of the disease-crime analogy and the multiple, and often contradictory, practical policy narratives which such metaphors engender. Moreover, Weisberg also elaborates Potter's striking suggestion that we can apply metaphor and narrative to the work of courts and legislatures as well as to criminals and crime patterns;

---

[16] Two powerful examples are Robert Ferguson, "Story and transcription in the trial of John Brown," *Yale Law Journal of Law and the Humanities*, 6 (1994) 37–74, and Guyora Binder. "Representing Nazism: Advocacy and identity at the trial of Klaus Barbie," *Yale Law Journal*, 98 (1989), 1321–1383.

[17] P.H. Thibodeau and L. Boroditsky, "Metaphors we think with: The role of metaphor in reasoning," *PLoS ONE*, 6 no. 2 (2011).

[18] Kaye Haw, "Risk factors and pathways into and out of crime, misleading, misinterpreted or mythic: From generative metaphor to professional myth," *Australian and New Zealand Journal of Criminology*, 39 no. 3 (2006), 339–353.

thus, we can view judicial doctrine and legislation as organisms that can have a symbiotic or parasitic relation to crime.

For one final context in which metaphor and narrative are part of criminal justice, consider our jurisprudence on the most foundational of criminal justice issues. The classic discourse on the justifying purposes of criminal justice – retribution, rehabilitation, deterrence, and incapacitation – is embodied in a distinct set of metaphors. Arguments around retribution rely heavily on metaphors of "accounting," "paying a debt" to society and so on. Arguments around rehabilitation employ metaphors associated with "ill health," "disability," "return" to full participation in the community. Discussion of deterrence hinges on metaphors associated with "schooling" and "education," though there is always some uncertainty about whether it is the individual concerned or other members of the society who will be deterred. Arguments around incapacitation employ metaphors associated with "risk," "protection," etc.[19] Each of these metaphors imagines and implies a different practical policy narrative and yet also a deeply rooted set of philosophical principles and assumptions.

---

[19] A very early discussion is: Nathaniel Cantor, "Conflicts in penal theory and practice," *Journal of Criminal Law and Criminology*, 26 no. 3 (1935–1936), 330–350.

8

The "Crime as a Disease" Metaphor: Vision, Power, and Collaboration in Social Problems Research

Roberto H. Potter

I told her redneckness has got to be a disease. You catch it on your fingers and it just crawls right up your sleeves.

Lyle Lovett, (1988) "Give Back My Heart" – *Pontiac*

INTRODUCTION

One of the key decisions any society must make is what institutional sector it will use to address the issue of crime.[1] Most industrialized societies have chosen to create a "criminal justice system" that functions to enforce the laws that legislatures have created to govern criminal behaviors and activities. It is to the organizations within this "system" that the State delegates the authority and power to enforce criminal laws, detain, prosecute, and punish/rehabilitate individuals found guilty of violating the criminal law. This includes deprivation of liberty and/or treasure (cash and/or property), and in some instances the use of deadly force. In the minds of most in the United States and many Commonwealth nations, the criminal justice systems we know have seemingly been the same for living memory.

As we move solidly into the twenty-first century there are increasing calls to revisit how we do crime control, as well as reactions to behaviors of criminal justice system(s) organizations. One of the most prominent metaphors being used to make the case for change has been the "crime as disease" metaphor. In essence, it calls for a more health-dominated approach to criminal behaviors than we observed in the previous iteration of the "medical model" of crime

---

[1] David E. Duffee, "Why is criminal justice theory important?" in *Criminal Justice Theory: Explaining the Nature and Behavior of Criminal Justice*, 2nd edition, by Edward R. Maguire and David E. Duffee (New York, NY: Taylor & Francis, 2015), pp. 5–26.

and rehabilitation. This chapter will examine how the crime as disease metaphor has been developed and may influence future thinking about societal responses to behaviors currently labeled "criminal."

We open this chapter with a little "good ole boy" sentiment to demonstrate the metaphor of an undesired condition ("redneckness") as a disease and its acquisition. The ease of transmission ("catch it on your fingers") and the inevitability of developing the disease capture the essence of the crime-disease metaphor succinctly (and, it's a great song). As the song progresses, the adjustment to the redneck lifestyle becomes evident and lifelong.

This is an image that many metaphors linking crime to disease promote. Like a disease, crime invades the community and acts upon it like a cancer, an abscess, or a disfiguring stigma. The mere "exposure" to the criminogenic agent leads to the development of a criminal career and/or crime rates in a community. The only hope for society is the development of some vaccine or procedure to "eliminate" the scourge of the criminal disease state. This is similar to the "labeling" process described by some writers in which a label is applied to an individual and the individual becomes essentially what the label suggests (we will address the fallacy in this characterization of labeling theory later).

While some of the imagery of the "crime as a disease" metaphor is purely symbolic, there are many who have taken the metaphor quite literally. Notions that crime violence, mostly, can be studied with the same methodological and statistical approaches as an infectious disease[2] have been fashionable since the early 1990s.[3] In a later section, we will examine the intertwined history of the methods and approaches of so-called "behavioral epidemiology" and the social science disciplines to study crime.

In this paper we want to provide a brief overview of common disease-crime metaphors. This will include attention to the level of crime and criminal behavior addressed in the metaphor. We will then provide a "life-course" analysis of the disease-crime metaphor. Special attention will be paid to issues of transmission and elimination of the crime disease.

---

[2] Institute of Medicine & National Research Council. *Contagion of Violence: Workshop Summary*. (Washington, DC: National Academies Press, 2013); Gary Slutkin, *Violence is a Contagious Disease* (Chicago: Cure Violence, n.d.); Charles Ransford, Candice Kane and Gary Slutkin, "Cure violence: A disease control approach to reduce violence and change behavior" in Eve Waltermauer and Timothy A. Akers (eds.), *Epidemiological Criminology: Theory to Practice* (New York, NY: Routledge, 2013), pp. 232–242.

[3] James A. Mercy and W. Rodney Hammond, "Preventing Homicide: A Public Health Perspective" in M. Dwayne Smith and Margaret A. Zahn (eds.), *Studying and Preventing Homicide* (Thousand Oaks, CA: Sage, 1999), pp. 274–294.

James A. Mercy and Patrick W. O'Carroll, "New directions in violence prevention: The public health arena," *Violence and Victims*, 3 no. 4 (1988), 285–301.

COMPARING CRIME TO A VIRUS: A "LIFE-COURSE" ANALYSIS

Life-course theories of criminal behavior, combining bio-psycho-social factors, have become increasingly prominent in criminology since the 1990s.[4] In essence, such approaches seek to determine what variables are different in the lives of those who progress through "adolescent-limited" deviance on to "life-course persistent" or career criminal status, when compared with others whose deviance career is not persistent or criminal. The focus is on individuals, while looking for commonalities and identifiable "dynamic" risk factors on which we might intervene to prevent persistent criminal behaviors.

Likewise, we can take a "life-course" approach to criminal laws. We can examine why certain criminal definitions were enacted when they were. There are multiple sociological studies of the role of xenophobia/racism in the enactment of drug laws, for example. The "law in action" can be examined to determine reasons for the maintenance of the "law on the books" – sometimes called policy and/or program analysis. We can also examine why criminal statutes are removed from the books. The paucity of such studies probably reflects the reluctance to take criminal laws off the books, even though they may rarely be enforced. Prosecutors do like their hammers!

In this section, we want to examine the "crime as a disease" metaphor from a life-course perspective. We will follow the criminal law and criminal behaviors from "conception" through "elimination." Special attention will be paid to the issue of "transmission" or "contagion" of crime as a disease. The notion of "elimination" of crime will also be viewed through the public health lens of disease elimination.

IN THE BEGINNING...

Let us begin from the notion of "conception." There is debate about whether "viruses" are alive or in some other state of being.[5] If we take the ability to replicate as a criterion for being alive, then viruses do fit, but only with the assistance of other organisms ("hosts"). If we require that a living organism be able to perform metabolic processes, they are incapable of doing so, and not considered alive. The origin of viruses is open to question, along with whether or not a virus "lives."

---

[4] Terrie E. Moffitt, "Adolescent-limited and life-course-persistent antisocial behavior: A developmental taxonomy," *Psychological Review*, 100 (1993), 674–701.
  David P. Farrington, "Developmental and life-course criminology: Key theoretical and empirical Issues – 2002 Sutherland Award Address." *Criminology*, 19 no. 1 (2003), 221–256.
[5] David R. Wessner, "The origins of viruses," *Nature Education*, 3 no. 9 (2010), 37.

Likewise, the origin of "crime" requires the use of another organizational entity – a legislative body ("host"). Here again we stress that we are discussing contemporary constitutional democracies where laws are developed through some authorized legislative process. A staple of most conflict and societal reaction (labeling) theories of crime is that the cause of crime is the law itself. The birth of a crime begins when an authorized legislative body defines the behavior/situation/act/intent (hereafter "act") as a crime. The behavior may have existed previous to the legal definition (i.e., "mala in se"), but only after the passage of the definition (i.e., "mala prohibita") can it be said to be a crime for which the State may punish an individual.

Switching from the viral/acute metaphor of crime as disease to crime as a chronic disease suggests employing a different lens. Such a metaphor requires that we view the individual as entering society in a healthy state. It is the accumulation of "insults" to the individual, most allegedly as a result of societal and economic deficits, that leads to the person engaging in criminalized acts. The notion of "toxic environments" and other pollution-themed metaphors[6] shifts our focus to extra-individual variables in explaining why individuals and groups of individuals engage in criminal acts. "Risk environments," which include such things as criminalization of substance use, are also called into question by this approach.[7]

In short, the environment creates the problems that lead to criminal behavior. Like many health promotion schemes, educating individuals to make better choices and providing environmental restrictions on the choices available become the approaches of choice to limiting the "spread" of criminality.

At "conception" then, it appears that both a virus and a criminal statute rely on other entities to be "born," or at least to have an effect. Viruses may lie "dormant" (latency; lysogenic phase)[8] under certain circumstances. The "law on the books" may also lie dormant, resurrected selectively by prosecutors. We will return to this theme when we visit the "elimination" phase of our analysis. Using the chronic disease metaphor, the conditions that lead to criminal behavior are sown by larger environmental factors, which may include the

---

[6] Michael J. Lynch, Kimberley L. Barrett, Paul B. Stretsky, Michael A. Long, Melissa L. Jarrell, and Joshua Ozymy, "Crime as pollution? Theoretical, definitional and policy concerns with conceptualizing crime as pollution," *American Journal of Criminal Justice*, 40 (2015), 843–860.

[7] Tim Rhodes, "Risk environments and drug harms: A social science for harm reduction approach." *International Journal of Drug Policy*, 20 no. 3 (2009), 193–201.

[8] Ed Yong, "Dormant viruses can hide in our DNA and be passed from parent to child." http://blogs.discovermagazine.com/notrocketscience/2010/03/27/dormant-viruses-can-hide-in-our-dna-and-be-passed-from-parent-to-child/.

law itself. All of these approaches point to something outside of individuals that contribute to "cause" crime and criminal behaviors.

REPRODUCTION

The effect of a virus is often to cause harm to another organism in order for the virus to replicate. Without another organism, a virus cannot continue to exist. The act "criminalized" by the criminal statute/law may have – like our index virus/bacterium – existed prior to the definition of that act as a crime. The reason for the "replication" of the act is what is of interest. We must also examine whether the act in question is replicated by an individual over a life-course, or whether the act is "transmitted" across individuals, who in turn may replicate the act across individual and collective life-courses.

Just as we would expect a virus or bacterium to mutate as a result of replication, we might expect criminal acts to evolve as societal responses change. Two examples of such change might be seen in the development of "designer drugs" to avoid criminal statutes and the evolution of on-line crimes in response to technological changes. The core question remains – why do acts that have been defined as criminal, and for which there are penalties, persist?

In a similar vein, as criminal acts change so might the societal response (criminal law) to the acts be expected to change. The designer drug example reflects attempts by chemists to develop new variants of substances that were not covered by existing criminal statutes, making their new concoctions, well, not criminal. Legislators have moved to define a broader definition of substances (broad spectrum?) to cover those slight chemical variations. In the area of methamphetamine production (and other substances), the criminalization of possession of certain "precursor" materials or amounts of otherwise legally available drugs (e.g., pseudoephedrine) demonstrates legislative attempts to reduce or eliminate the production of illegal drugs.

New developments in material culture, such as computer networks and tools, may also lead to both the evolution of criminal acts and responses to such. For those of us who were conscious before the advent of the internet, watching certain long-form "cons" (confidence games) adapt to the new environment of the internet and email provides another example of crime adapting to new environments. What used to take several weeks of postal correspondence between the "con artist" and the "mark" can now be reduced in time to a few brief email exchanges. What has not changed is the essential approach and process. The "scourge" persists, but in a new technological format.

The evolution of the "dark web" has also allowed certain criminal activities to move into a different domain. For example, trading in various forms of illegal pornography – especially pornography involving minors – has become in some ways more "hidden" than when bulk packages had to be shipped through postal services. The ability of law enforcement agencies to detect these transactions sometimes outpaces the ability of prosecutors to pursue such transactions because legislatures have not kept up with technological changes in terms of providing intervention tools to law enforcement. Almost everyone agrees that legislative action is much slower than technological innovation that facilitates either the commission of crime or the ability to hide such activities.

THE LAW AS VACCINE

The effect of a criminal statute is to provide a definition under which an authorized organization can act against/on an individual or individuals to protect the interests of the State. Ideally, those interests include the safety of the populace. In this case, the law acts more as a vaccine against the crime it has created. Without an authorized agent of the State to enact the criminal statute, even if the behavior criminalized happens, can we say that the crime exists? Is the mere legal definition enough to say we have "crime," or does it require recognition and reaction from an authorized agent of the State to exist? This is a key component of societal reaction approaches to deviance and crime; without recognition and reaction, there is no crime or deviant act.

Other, more "absolutist" (rather than "relativist") approaches to crime would state that if the law exists and the behavior occurs, there has been a crime. Likewise, as long as a virus has the potential to invade a host, the virus can continue to "live." This is the stage at which the usual analogy to crime as a virus/disease takes off. It should be noted here that the metaphor of crime as a disease is generally seen only in terms of violent acts, or those crimes where physical (and sometimes emotional) injuries are a potential outcome. There has been a reverse use of the "broken windows" metaphor to explain rates of sexually-transmitted infections,[9] but to date there has been little application of the disease metaphor to, say, burglary or car theft. The "crime as a cancer" metaphor may be more widely invoked by politicians than scientists, of course.

---

[9] Deborah Cohen et al., "'Broken windows' and the risk of gonorrhea," *American Journal of Public Health*, 90 no. 2 (2000), 230–236.

At this point, we generally see the idea that a violent act by one individual "transmits" another violent act through an adjacent individual, which then becomes replicated through other individuals until some intervention occurs. It should be noted here that researchers in the public health/biomedical field often lump suicidal behaviors into the "violence" category. Yet, in many Western nations, suicide is not a criminal act. Likewise, self-harm such as "cutting" is not a crime, though the ability to seek what would look like deprivation of liberty through civil remedies available to health professionals may exceed those available to criminal justice actors for interpersonal violence. We will return to this point later.

Most of these transmission theories rely on some form of "contagion" to explain the spread of violent behavior among individuals. Contagion theory has been a topic of debate and research in sociology and collective behavior studies from the time of Le Bon[10] in the late nineteenth century. We do not have time here to outline the various approaches to contagion theory. We want to focus on the central feature of many of them, that the contagion is initially an irrational reaction to an event that releases individuals from their usual bonds to society, that they become suggestible, and commit acts unusual to their behavior. The irrationality and suggestibility of such contagious behavior often stand in stark contrast to the instrumental use of violence in gang-related behavior. Likewise, it overlooks the opportunistic nature of most robbery and non-violent crimes such as theft. While it may be possible to find "clusters" of crimes committed in relatively close proximity and time, much of this is driven by choice of the index event. Broadening the time frame (as well as the proximity variable) may reveal a very different picture from contagion.

A second contagion metaphor employed is the "copycat" effect. This is especially useful in studying suicide clusters.[11] As noted earlier, in most western societies, suicide and other self-injuring behaviors are not criminal offenses[12]. From a crime as disease perspective, then, suicide and other self-directed violence should not be included. When applied to other forms of criminal acts, the evidence on the impact of copycat crimes is weakly supported[13]. Thus, the metaphor of either contagion or copycat crime

---

[10] Gustave LeBon, *The Crowd: A Study of the Popular Mind* (Digireads.com, 1896[2008)].
[11] Madelyn S. Gould, Sylvan Wallenstein, and Collin L. Davidson, "Suicide clusters: A critical review." *Suicide and Life-Threatening Behavior*, 19 no. 1 (2010), 17–29.
[12] Natalie Rezek, "Is self-harm by cutting a constitutionally protected right?" *Quinnipiac Health Law*, 12 (2009), 303–331.
[13] Ray Surette, "Cause or catalyst: The interaction of real world and media crime models," *American Journal of Criminal Justice*, 38 no. 3 (2013), 392–409. Ray Surette, *Media, Crime, and Criminal Justice: Images, Realities and Policies* (Belmont, CA: Cengage, 2015).

to explain the diffusion of criminal behavior in a population is of relatively little empirical value.

ELIMINATION (IN PUBLIC HEALTH TERMS ...)

Stopping the cycle of replication provides the next level of metaphor in the crime as disease metaphor – i.e., a "cure." Whether it is presented as a "vaccination" or an "interrupter"[14] (Slutkin, n.d.), the idea is that something will terminate the transmission of the act so that the "cycle of infection" will be disrupted and the act will cease. But, in practical terms, what does a "cure" look like? This section begins with key public health definitions that are often confused when the crime as disease metaphor is employed. Three key distinctions from the work of Dowdle,[15] generally adopted by national and international bodies, will be examined. These are the differences between "control," "elimination" and "eradication" of a disease:

- *Control:* The reduction of disease incidence, prevalence, morbidity, or mortality to a locally acceptable level as a result of deliberate efforts; continued intervention measures are required to maintain the reduction. Example: diarrheal diseases.
- *Elimination of disease:* Reduction to zero of the incidence of a specified disease in a defined geographical area as a result of deliberate efforts; continued intervention measures are required. Example: neonatal tetanus.
- *Eradication:* Permanent reduction to zero of the worldwide incidence of infection caused by a specific agent as a result of deliberate efforts; intervention measures are no longer needed. Example: smallpox.

People write idealistically and metaphorically "as if" eradication will be the outcome of violence prevention programs (but, rarely other crimes). Yet, the control of crimes, including violence, is the pragmatic goal of most criminal justice efforts.

From the deterrence-focused ideas of the classical philosophers (e.g., Bentham) to the Differential Association/Social Learning (DA/SL) perspectives of sociology,[16] the "interruption" mechanisms that precede the Ceasefire/

---

[14] Slutkin, *Violence is a Contagious Disease.*
[15] Walter R. Dowdle, "The principles of disease elimination and eradication," *Morbidity and Mortality Weekly,* 48 (SU01) (1999), 23–27.
[16] Edwin H. Sutherland, *Principles of Criminology,* 4th edition (Philadelphia, PA: Lippincott, 1947); Ronald L. Akers, *Social Learning and Social Structure: A General Theory of Crime and Deviance* (Boston, MA: Northeastern University Press, 1998).

Cure Violence and all other public health approaches to violence are the same – learning. Whether it is the awareness of penalties for breaking the law (deterrence), or the learning not to break the law through interactions with conventional others (DA/SL), the key element is teaching to and learning by potential offenders of the harms and costs of criminal behavior. Knowledge is the inoculation!

Epidemiologists, some of the driving force behind the crime as disease metaphor, have relied on their "holy trinity" of "host-agent-environment" to make the argument that violence (again, relatively little expansion to other crimes) is transmitted from an agent (offender) to a host (victim) via a vector (gun, knife, etc.) within a particular environment. Akers, Potter, and Hill[17] have criticized the use of this metaphor on the basis of a lack of agency on the part of either the agent or the host. In order for the epidemiological metaphor to work, both agent and host would need to demonstrate almost no ability to resist either the commission or the victimization. Human behavior, especially learned criminal behaviors, would seem to defy this lack of agency. However, when combined with the contagion or copycat metaphor, it would appear that only the ability to commit harm has to be learned. Control, elimination, and eradication are all achieved by simply removing the vector. This ends the problem and brings the life course of crime to a conclusion.

ASSESSING THE METAPHOR

Now that we have examined the life-course of criminal law and criminal behaviors through the health metaphor, we want to turn to the function of metaphor as a way of understanding. The crime as a disease metaphor appears in several of the seminal works on metaphor,[18] as well as a full analysis of both the "crime as disease" and "disease as crime" metaphors by one of the editors of this volume.[19]

The current presentation will draw selectively from those other works in an attempt to expand them for the purposes of examining how metaphors about crime and disease are used to influence social policy around crime. In this

---

[17] Timothy A. Akers, Roberto H. Potter, and Carl V. Hill, *Epidemiological Criminology: A Public Health Approach to Crime and Violence* (San Francisco, CA: Jossey-Bass/Wiley, 2013).

[18] Donald Schön, "'Generative metaphor: A perspective on problem-setting in social policy," in Andrew Ortony (ed.), *Metaphor and Thought*, 2nd edition (Cambridge, UK; New York, NY: Cambridge University Press, 1993), pp. 137–163.

[19] Michael Hanne, "Crime and disease: Contagion by metaphor" in Catherine Stanton & Hannah Quirk (eds.), *Criminalising Contagion: Lethal and Ethical Challenges of Disease Transmission and the Criminal Law* (Cambridge, UK: Cambridge University Press, 2016), pp. 35–54.

sense, our primary interest is in what Schön[20] terms a "generative metaphor." Such an approach

> treats metaphor as central to the task of accounting for our perspectives on the world; how we think about things, make sense of reality, and set problems we later try to solve. In this second sense, 'metaphor' refers both to a certain kind of product – a perspective or frame, a way of looking at things – and to a certain kind of process – a process by which new perspectives on the world come into existence.

Continuing, studying generative metaphor "is nothing less than the question of how we come to see things in new ways . . . "[21]

Schön explores the appeal of the health metaphor in public policy discussions by noting the tendency to conflate "the good life with the healthy life and to make progress synonymous with the eradication of disease."[22] The health metaphor also helps to provide a clear path toward the solution of a social problem such as violence. If the problem can be viewed in terms of a "normative dualism," then "we shall know in what direction to move. Indeed, the diagnosis and the prescription will seem obvious. This sense of the obviousness of what is wrong and what needs fixing is the hallmark of generative metaphor in the field of social policy." In sum, observe, diagnose, treat, monitor, and repeat as necessary.

The concept of generative metaphor now needs to be merged with theories of social action. In the next section, we explore merging social constructionist approaches to social problems in order to examine some of the political implications of the medical generative metaphor applied to crime. Such an analysis will lead further to a discussion of status politics and social movements theories.

SOCIAL PATHOLOGY, SOLUTIONS, AND LEADERSHIP – WHY THE MEDICAL METAPHOR MATTERS

"So follow me, it's good for you, That good old fashioned Medicated Goo, Ooo, ain't it good for you?"
    Winwood and Miller (Traffic), 1969, "Medicated Goo," *Last Exit*

Not only do metaphors for social problems suggest ways of acting to eliminate the problem, they also suggest a narrative of who should provide the leadership

---

[20] Schön, "Generative metaphor: A perspective on problem-setting in social policy," p. 137.
[21] Schön, "Generative metaphor: A perspective on problem-setting in social policy," p. 138.
[22] Ibid., p. 148.

or direction for the problem's solution. This section will take a social problems theory approach to the attempts by public health/biomedical industrial players to "claim" crime as their domain. We will examine the attempts of those players to "frame" the discussion in terms that privilege their professions. Likewise, we will examine how such efforts deprive citizens of fundamental due processes protected by criminal law, but weakened by the use of civil regulatory approaches.

When the author was beginning work in the Division of Violence Prevention at the Centers for Disease Control and Prevention (CDC) in 1998, the Director of the National Center for Injury Prevention and Control, Mark Rosenberg, MD, often reiterated that the criminal justice community had failed to control violence (again, no other crimes were mentioned). It was time for the medical and public health communities to step in and, using the tools of epidemiology, provide the leadership desperately needed.[23] These sentiments were echoed a decade later by physicians such as Slutkin, who parted ways with the police and prosecutor crime control focus of "Cease Fire" to develop the "Cure Violence" approach. The latter has the distinction of being led by physicians and public health professionals rather than criminal justice professionals.

For sociologists working in the specialty area of "social problems," attempts to pathologize and/or medicalize social problems are nothing new.[24] This is especially true of "pathologies" that are clearly or borderline criminal. For criminologists and criminal justice theorists, often overlapping with the sociologists, and in the area of "medicalization" of criminal behaviors and related interventions (including corrections), a whole era of criminal justice intervention is known as the "medical model" era. This takes us back to the development of so-called "scientific criminology" under Cesare Lombroso in the late nineteenth century. The arch-positivism of that approach posits that there are identifiable variables that separate criminals from non-criminals. Treatment following some medical or psychological regime was the most effective

---

[23] Mark L. Rosenberg, Patrick O'Carroll, and, Kenneth E. Powell, "Let's be clear: Violence is a public health problem," *Journal of the American Medical Association*, 267 (1992), 3071–3072; James A. Mercy and W. Rodney Hammond, "Preventing homicide: A public health perspective" in M. Dwayne Smith and Margaret A. Zahn (eds.), *Studying and Preventing Homicide* (Thousand Oaks, CA: Sage, 1999), pp. 274–294; James A. Mercy and Patrick W. O'Carroll, "New directions in violence prevention: The public health arena," *Violence and Victims*, 3 no. 4 (1988), 285–301.

[24] Michael Hanne, "Crime and disease: Contagion by metaphor"; Peter Conrad and Joseph W. Schneider, *Deviance and Medicalization: From Badness to Sickness* (Temple University Press, 1980 [2010]); Erdwin H. Pfuhl, *The Deviance Process*, 2nd edition (Belmont, CA: Wadsworth Publishing, Company, 1986).

manner of intervention with criminals – as opposed to retribution, incapacitation, or deterrence approaches. Even now, those criminologists who work in life-course and criminogenic risk factor approaches find themselves seeking to avoid a similar positivistic and deterministic perspective. Well, some do ...

One of the reasons provided by health-oriented crime controllers for allowing them to take the lead on crime policy resides in the methods and statistics they use to study injury and disease. Bluntly put, the methodology matters more than any theories that might guide our interpretation of the results. My colleagues and I have addressed these claims.[25] In particular, Tim Akers and I have traced the development of methods and statistics used to study disease and crime since the beginning of the "moral statistics" movement of the early nineteenth century to the present. Jeanne Krider and I examined the application of Kurt Lewin's applied science model and the "public health" approach to criminal justice issues as early as the mid-1970s.

Jeff Rosky and I examined the multiple meanings of the "public health model" in attempting to determine how it differs from earlier social science approaches to crime. We were unable to find any substantive differences. In the end it is difficult to understand how one professional sector that uses the same research methods and statistics as another can claim any form of superiority over the other in terms of studying and intervening on a social problem. Yet, the pathology metaphors suggest we should do so. Further, no academic specialty plays more than an advisory role (at best) in the criminal justice process. The functions of criminal justice are carried out by those with State-provided authority to do so.

In *Epidemiological Criminology*,[26] my colleagues and I provided a brief overview of the development of a social problem and how such processes applied to the recognition of diseases and behaviors as public health and/or criminal justice issues. In an earlier text[27] I devoted more space to the definition of social problems following the history of such by theorists such as

---

[25] Timothy A. Akers, Roberto H. Potter, and Carl V. Hill, *Epidemiological Criminology: A Public Health Approach to Crime and Violence* (San Francisco, CA: Jossey-Bass/Wiley, 2013); Roberto H. Potter and Jeanne E. Krider, "Teaching about violence prevention: A bridge between public health and criminal justice educators," *Journal of Criminal Justice Education*, 11 (2000), 339–351; Roberto H. Potter and Jeffrey W. Rosky, "The iron fist in the latex glove: The intersection of public health and criminal justice," *American Journal of Criminal Justice*, 38 (2013), 276–282.
[26] Akers, Potter, and Hill, *Epidemiological Criminology*.
[27] Roberto H. Potter, *Pornography: Group Pressures and Individual Rights* (Sydney: The Federation Press, 1996).

Blumer[28] and Spector and Kitsuse.[29] In that earlier text, I also devoted more attention to the work of Joseph Gusfield[30] on "symbolic crusades" and "status politics."

Briefly, the "social constructionist" (SC) approach to social problems research is grounded in the Symbolic Interactionist approaches to deviance ("Labeling theory") and sociology of knowledge. Its basic premise is that certain social conditions come to be "recognized" as social problems through a process of definition and negotiation by "claims-making groups" which have the social resources necessary to make their definition of the situation the dominant social definition. That is, situations which achieve the status of "social problem" do so through a process of negotiation amongst social groups with varying claims for recognition by the wider society.

Social constructionist approaches often take the form of an analysis of the "career" or "natural history" of a social problem.[31] Spector and Kitsuse built on the "natural history" approach to social problems and Blumer's development of the idea. They defined social problems as "the activities of groups making assertions of grievances and claims to organizations, agencies, and institutions about some putative conditions."[32] They call these complainant groups "claims-makers." It is the job of a theory of social problems to "account for the emergence, maintenance, and history of claim-making and responding activities." They propose a four-stage model, which subsumes some of Blumer's ideas and extends them:

> Stage 1: The attempts by some group(s) to assert the existence of some condition, define it as offensive, harmful, and otherwise undesirable, to publicize the assertions and stimulate controversy and to create a public or political issue over the matter.
>
> Stage 2: The recognition by some official organization, agency or institution of the group('s) legitimate standing. This may lead to an official

---

[28] Herbert Blumer, "Social problems as collective behavior," *Social Problems*, 18 no. 3 (1971), 298–306.

[29] Malcolm Spector and John Kitsuse, "Social problems: A reformulation," *Social Problems* 21 no. 2 (1973), 145–159; Malcolm Spector and John Kitsuse, *Constructing Social Problems* (Hawthorne, NY: Walter de Gruyter, 1987).

[30] Joseph R. Gusfield, *Symbolic Crusade: Status Politics and the American Temperance Movement* (Urbana, IL: University of Illinois Press, 1963); Joseph R. Gusfield, *The Culture of Public Problems: Drinking-Driving and the Symbolic Order* (Chicago, IL: University of Chicago Press, 1981).

[31] Blumer, "Social problems as collective behavior"; Spector and Kitsuse, *Constructing Social Problems*; Spector and Kitsuse, "Social problems: A reformulation."

[32] Spector and Kitsuse *Constructing Social Problems*; Spector and Kitsuse, "Social problems: A reformulation,"146.

investigation of the matter, proposals for reform, and the establishment of an agency to respond to those claims and demands.

Stage 3: The reemergence of claims and demands by the group(s), expressing dissatisfaction with the established procedures for dealing with the imputed conditions, the bureaucratic handling of complaints, and the failure to generate a condition of trust and confidence in the procedures as sympathetic to the complaints, etc.

Stage 4: The rejection by complainant group(s) of the response or lack of response of the agency or institution to their claims and demands, and the development of activities to create alternative, parallel, or counter-institutions as responses to the established procedures.[33]

Spector and Kitsuse extended Blumer's ideas to encompass what happens after claims-making groups become dissatisfied with the almost inevitable perception that official agencies "got it wrong" in their response to the "problem." They are also more direct about the role of relative power amongst groups to bring their claims to public and official notice, as well as to press their claim further.

For this presentation we want to argue that the natural history of the crime as disease metaphor can be most efficiently tracked back to the late 1980s and early 1990s and the dissatisfaction of biomedical/public health professionals with violence control practices of the time. We suggest here that the social problems career approach of the social constructionists is not linear, but it contains feedback loops that may take the process back to the beginning from any point from Stage 2 to Stage 4 in Spector and Kitsuse's stages. For at least the past two decades biomedical/public health professionals have attacked criminal justice practices to control violence – again, devoid of attention to other criminal acts – even in the face of declining incidence and rates of violence in the United States. This is especially true of "mass" casualty and murder incidents.

To complete the analysis, we must also examine how professional and other advocacy groups bring their claims to the public. More importantly, how do such groups bring their complaints and putative solutions to the bodies that matter – legislative bodies? The work of Gusfield on "symbolic crusades" is an early example of the study of how certain groups, in that case temperance groups, mobilize social resources to bring about social and/or legislative changes which favor their definition of how society should operate. Gusfield, in later writing about the efforts to define drunk driving as a criminal act, pointed out that the use of "sociological irony" in the symbolic crusade

---

[33] Spector and Kitsuse, "Social problems: A reformulation," 147.

perspective does not downplay the very real or perceived injuries which those in an aggrieved group might experience (similar to "realist" criminologies). Rather, it aims to examine the processes by which new or modified moral realities are brought about by the activities of claims-making groups. The types of arguments presented by these groups become the data, suspending concern with the validity of the arguments.

In Gusfield's study of the Prohibition movement, two concepts become important for our discussion of the crime as disease metaphor: "symbolic crusades" and "status politics." Alcohol became the *symbol* around which a struggle for "normative dominance" was fought. The idea behind normative dominance is that a particular group's ways of doing things ("norms") become *the* way in which *all* people in the social environment *should* do things. The ability of one group to impose its way of living upon others gives that group the important social resource of *prestige*. Associated with prestige are assumptions about the ways in which members of other groups should act toward the prestigious group, and vice versa. Often these assumptions carry ideas about respect due or deference between members of the various groups. This is especially true when the symbols around which prestige is based involve ethnicity or skin color. The ultimate indicator that a group's norms are those most highly valued in a society comes when those norms are encoded into *law*. Not only is this now a symbolic reference to the superiority of that group's way of acting (morality), but it is now often accompanied by very real penalties for acting in a contrary manner.

Status politics and symbolic crusades are about either protecting or enhancing the social prestige of a particular group: "Status politics is an effort to control the status of a group by acts which function to raise, lower, or maintain the social status of that group vis-à-vis others in the society ... Status movements are collective actions which attempt to raise or maintain the prestige of a group ..."[34] It is the relational aspect of prestige that is important here. Prestige, like power (often closely associated), is a social resource that can wax and wane over time. Social prestige exists in relation to one group's status in comparison with another group.

We would argue that what is unique about the crime as disease metaphor and the movements associated with it is the potential conflict between not only two practice communities – public health/medical services and criminal justice agencies (which includes the legal profession) – but also two academic communities – public health/biomedical sciences versus social science criminology/criminal justice/law. In short, the question is which occupational

---

[34] Gusfield, *Symbolic Crusade*, pp. 19–20.

category will define the problem, provide and direct the programs to control, eliminate, or eradicate the problem, and declare the problem solved? This is an excellent topic around which to conduct academic studies of the civil conflict between occupational groups. To do so requires that we broaden our focus to include the intersection of organizational and social movements/collective behavior[35].

These observations and theoretical approaches suggest a series of hypotheses that might be tested by an enterprising young researcher. The first hypothesis is that there is no "public health" or medical intervention to reduce or eliminate any crime that does not rely on previously attempted social science-informed efforts. This would include a range of learning theory, social bonds/control, and deterrence theories, at a minimum.

A second hypothesis that public health/biomedical attempts to "claim" crime as an area of specialty arise at times when traditional medicine and public health efforts are being viewed as failing or ineffective. For example, the public health focus on violence emerged as an outgrowth of behavioral science interventions coming into play to reduce the transmission of HIV when no biomedical interventions appeared to be effective at stemming the epidemic. Likewise, attention to street and intimate violence arose at the same time as deaths from medical mistakes were coming to be recognized as many times greater annually than deaths from criminal and self-directed violence.

A final hypothesis is that public health/medical attempts to "claim" crime as an area of specialty arise at times when the legitimacy of the criminal justice system is being questioned by society. The elevation of criminal and self-directed violence began at the peak of the crime curve that had begun in the late 1970s and peaked in the mid-1990s. In fact, the curve peaked in the same year the National Center for Injury Prevention and Control (NCIPC) was established at the CDC. The writer is fond of saying that, given some of correlational thinking of epidemiology, it was the founding of the NCIPC that "cured" violence – at least until the mid-2010s.

Our hope is that by putting the life-course/natural history of the crime as disease metaphor (as well as Hanne's disease as crime) into the status of a set of hypotheses, we can begin to predict when such thinking will arise and when it will wane. Criminologists and criminal justice academics and practitioners are well acquainted with the idea of cycles in how we think about crime and corrections and how legislative bodies recycle these ideas in terms of public

---

[35] Gerald F. Davis, Doug McAdam, William Richard, Scott Mayer, and Nathan Zald, (eds.), *Social Movements and Organization Theory* (New York, NY: Cambridge University Press, 2005).

policy and law. Adding the study of which metaphors help to frame these cycles seems to be a worthy effort.

DANGERS OF THE MEDICAL METAPHOR

One of the interesting aspects of metaphor rests in the fact that it always produces this kind of one-sided insight.[36]

Metaphor is inherently paradoxical. It can create powerful insights that also become distortions, as the way of seeing created through a metaphor becomes a way of *not seeing*.[37] (italics in original)

The discussion now turns to two antimedical metaphors my cowriters and I have used in an effort to "disenchant" the crime as disease metaphor. Morgan's statements were developed in his application of metaphorical thinking to the area of organizational studies. We believe they are especially relevant to examining the crime as disease metaphor in terms of social action taken by organized bodies such as professional associations. Our argument here is that the public health/biomedical focus is on outcome – stopping violence (rarely other crimes). The criminal justice focus is not only the outcome of crime prevention and/or control alone, but on the process by which such outcomes are achieved.

VACCINE THINKING

The first is what has been termed the danger of "vaccine thinking,"[38] the notion that what works in any one setting will work in all others – or, a problem of generalizability. When biomedical/public health professionals approach crime – again, violence – their approach is generally one of looking for "the" cure, something that will transcend geographic and social boundaries. The expectation is that one definitive program will be developed that will prevent violence among all those to whom the program is administered, just as a vaccine is expected to deliver immunity to a particular disease among all those vaccinated.

This approach belies one of the major issues with most of the biomedical/public health approaches to preventing crime (again, almost exclusively

---

[36] Gareth Morgan, *Images of Organization*, 4th edition (Thousand Oaks, CA: Sage, 1986), p. 13.
[37] Ibid., p. 5.
[38] Roberto H. Potter, "Jails, public health and generalizability," *Journal of Correctional Health Care*, 16 no. 4 (2010), 263–272.

violence). There is either a complete lack of scholarship in terms of what has been attempted and found effective or lacking; or, there is a complete disregard for what work has preceded the "discovery" of crime by the biomedical/public health community. Returning to the status politics frame discussed earlier, this provides another reason for exploring the hypotheses provided above. Does one professional group believe its perspective, method, and status to be so much more advanced than another that all previous work in an area can be discounted or dismissed? Or, is it simply that there is a lack of belief that intelligent life lies beyond Medline?

IRON FIST IN THE LATEX GLOVE

We have used the illustrative metaphor from early Critical Criminology of the "iron fist in the velvet glove" to explore the public policy implications of moving certain behaviors from the criminal justice to biomedical/public health domains.[39] Among those implications that we explored is the preference of biomedical/public health professionals to move toward regulatory schemes to address currently criminal acts, rather than keeping them in the criminal law domain.[40]

While there are certainly laudable harm reductions that could be achieved using such regulatory tools, there are also some potentially questionable impacts. First among these is the lowering of the threshold for holding persons responsible for their actions. In the criminal justice domain the standard of evidence is "beyond reasonable doubt"; in the regulatory/civil law environment, that standard is "balance of probabilities." Given that, in the United States, 95% of felony (indictable) convictions are the result of a plea agreement,[41] this might not seem to be much of a concern. However, moving certain acts from the criminal to civil domains also strips certain due process protections from the individual in relation to the power of the state.

One cannot forget that, at least ideally, the criminal justice system is set up to protect the liberties of the individual from the power of the State. Public health, in particular among the biomedical sciences, is concerned with the health of the "herd." Reconciling those levels of interest and protection remains an area of contention between these two professional and academic domains.

---

[39] Potter and Rosky, "The iron fist in the latex glove."
[40] Akers, Potter, and Hill, *Epidemiological Criminology*.
[41] Brian A. Reaves, *Felony Defendants in Large Urban Counties, 2009-Statistical Tables* (Washington, DC: Bureau of Justice Statistics, 2013).

The crime as disease metaphor suggests that a particular professional group has the status and knowledge to provide the answers to the problem of crime, and that their judgment exceeds that of the democratic process. We believe these are matters that require substantial deliberation by the citizens and legislative bodies, not something that should be left only to the lobbying efforts of professional groups. There is a matter of democracy and democratic decision-making that comes into play here, as opposed to the elite-driven models of public decision-making associated with certain forms of governance, whether they describe themselves as progressive or conservative. In the end, we suggest this is a greater social harm than anything beyond a miscarriage of justice in the criminal justice process.

CONCLUSION

This exploration of the crime as disease metaphor has wound its way through several themes. The first was an attempt to examine crime and criminal law from the life course perspective in comparison to the life cycle of a virus or other disease. We next moved into an analysis of the metaphor of crime as disease to examine how it shapes our ways of viewing crime causation and control. This included a special emphasis on the process of social problem creation and the interests of claims-making groups to impose their version of proper behavior and control over a society. We ended with an attempt to critique that approach from a number of perspectives, especially the potential removal of crime control policy from a democratic process to one dominated by a particular set of occupational elites.

None of this analysis of the crime as disease metaphor is intended to suggest that there is not a role in the study of criminal behavior and its control for the biomedical/public health occupations. As we noted at the outset by using the life course perspective as our framework, adding the biomedical approach does improve our understanding of the multiple variables that contribute to behavioral outcomes that have been criminalized by legislative bodies. Such voices are also critical as we attempt to remove certain behaviors from the list of criminal offenses over time, as well as improving our responses to those behaviors that remain criminal.

Rather, this analysis of the disease as crime metaphor is intended to bring a balance back into the discussion of crime, especially violent crime, so that the knowledge generated by social science can be effectively melded with that of the biomedical/public health to control crime. Further, the critique is intended to call to attention the need to increase the interdisciplinary approaches to the study of crime. The notions of "team science" and "interdisciplinarity" may be new to those in the biomedical/public health sectors, but they have been key elements of social science approaches to crime and criminal behavior for decades.

Finally, we want to stress that criminal justice deals essentially with a moral dimension of human behavior. The distinction between right and wrong enshrined by the criminal law is fundamentally a moral act. The discussion of status politics brings into view how certain groups use the criminal law (as well as regulatory law) to enshrine their group's morality as the proper way to behave. As Criminal Justice and Criminology academics we seek to overlay at least a patina of science on the effectiveness of the criminal law. We hope that by applying the techniques of science, from social and natural sciences, to the criminal justice process we can improve the effectiveness of the system and enhance the humaneness of that system simultaneously.

One last thought as we close out our discussion of the crime as a disease and other metaphors presented here. It is almost impossible to think about the world of crime and criminal justice without employing some metaphorical frame. Perhaps the best advice for all of our disciplines is never to take your own press seriously.

9

The Fertility (sic) of the Crime/Disease Linkage for Metaphor and Narrative: Response to Potter

Robert Weisberg

INTRODUCTION

My response to the Potter paper will be an instance of praising with faint damn. His treatment of the generativeness of the crime-disease metaphor and accompanying narratives is itself generative[1] and sparks the reader – especially a reader mainly on the criminal justice side of the equation – to imagine and at least tentatively elaborate many possible fruitful extensions of his examination of the metaphoric and narrative strands. And so, if forced to utter a criticism, I can only modestly suggest that Potter has not fully exploited (or appreciated) the implications of his insights along two related dimensions.

One dimension involves the varieties of metaphors and narratives (and the relations between the two) that operate in the linkage between disease and crime. For example, metaphors in the disease/crime context range from self-consciously manipulative media strategems designed to grab attention or instill emotion, to those that are meant as didactic analogy-lessons, to those whose language purports to identify multiple parallels between metaphor and object, and then all the way to figures of speech that are hardly metaphors at all but terms from a purportedly disciplinary vocabulary.

The other dimension involves Potter's brief but provocative diversion about legislators as participants in criminal "disease control." It suggests something that, I believe, merits expansion: the need to divide the "crime" side of the equation between criminology and criminal justice, the latter meaning actual government actors with legal authority, as opposed to social or medical science

---

[1] The premise is that figurative language enhances the important role of much social policy discourse in problem-setting or framing as opposed to direct problem-solving. Donald Schön, "Generative metaphor: A perspective on problem-setting in social policy" in Andrew Ortony (ed.), *Metaphor and Thought* (2d ed.) (Cambridge, UK: Cambridge University Press, 1993), pp. 137–163.

analysts of crime. We get great insights from Potter about metaphor/narrative wars as interprofessional wars, but the distinction for him remains mostly between two types of *analysts* – criminologists/social scientists and medical/public health scientists – who are competitors in *explanation*.[2] The various agents of government that regulate, not explain, crime are deployers of metaphor/narrative, but also, for the various disciplines that study and evaluate the practices of these agents, they are potentially rich *subjects* of metaphoric and narrative analysis. Thus, such agencies as the judiciary, police, and prisons rely on metaphors and their consequent narratives about individual and societal criminality in justifying their own actions, but in some cases their own practices exhibit some patterns that can be described in terms of organic life courses, often with a specific manifestation of health and illness metaphors and trajectories.

Pursuing both these dimensions may enrich our study of metaphor and narrative, and in particular it helps inform us about the practical or political consequences of the use or prominence of particular metaphors and narratives. So my contribution here is actually a series of mini-homages to Potter's paper in which I try to perform further readings of criminal justice as modeled by him.

CRIMINOLOGY, BIOLOGY, AND PUBLIC HEALTH

The scientific explanation and diagnosis of crime receive most of Potter's emphasis; he directly generates some of the key manifestations of the disease metaphor and life-course narrative from the perspective of criminology – abetted by earlier work by Hanne and others[3] – and on this subject I claim only to augment what he has said. There are several criminological takes here, but first I want to briefly allude to how the disease context raises more general questions about priority between and genres of metaphor and narrative.

Now even asking about the "priority" between metaphor and narrative may itself seem like an odd inquiry. For one thing, we would have to clarify whether we mean the term in some very abstract conceptual sense, or in some temporal sense, as when we are tracing the actual emergence of metaphor and narrative in a particular medium or public opinion, or psychologically or neurologically in the sense of the sequencing of human thought.

---

[2] Potter, "The 'crime and disease' metaphor."
[3] Michael Hanne, "Crime and disease: Contagion by metaphor," in Catherine Stanton and Hannah Quirk (eds.) *Criminalising Contagion: Lethal and Ethical Challenges of Disease Transmission and the Criminal Law* (Cambridge, UK: Cambridge University Press, 2016), pp. 35–54; Gary Slutkin, *Violence is a Contagious Disease* (Chicago, IL: Cure Violence, 2013).

Second, one might wonder what, if anything, turns on resolving the question. But as Simon Stern points out, it is always useful to resist the common tendency to loosely elide the two, given that legal scholars sometimes speak of narratives too loosely when they are really referring to images, conceptions, representations, or even ideologies.[4] Of course, how we decide the priority question or even frame the terms in which we ask it depends on context. But even if the outcome is imprecise, we might illuminate the context in which the metaphor and narrative operate. However one might speak in the general or the abstract about metaphors entailing or inspiring narratives, we have to look at the relationship and the nature of the narrative with some specificity, as well as the way that life-course or disease narratives follow from the initial metaphor. And in that regard I suggest that pride of place in the crime-explaining setting goes to metaphor. In so doing, I rely on the major work of Ritchie, who has called on neurology to describe how metaphors become transformed and reconfigured as narratives.[5] The initial metaphor can redirect the way the mind elaborates a temporal story to fulfill the analogy and choose which information to incorporate into its understanding of the original context.

I suggest priority to metaphor here because of the common notion of "crime" as a perennial presence in all social life (or "a" crime as an *event*), of the criminal as a character type, and the success of a particular metaphor for either of these then inspires the user to develop the narrative associated with it. Early continental criminologists often thought of offenders as certain fairly fixed character types[6] and placed little emphasis on psychological development.[7] Moreover, in a prestatistical world, they did not say much about trajectories of crime rates. In modern America, in the sound-bite vocabulary of demagogic politics (the main arena where crime enters public discourse), metaphor works much better and faster in assertion of a favored paradigm.[8]

---

[4] Simon Stern, "Narratives in the legal text: Judicial opinions and their narratives" (in this volume).

[5] His multiple papers on the subject are summarized in L. David Ritchie, "'Justice is blind': A model for analyzing metaphor transformations and narratives in actual discourse" *Metaphor and The Social World*, 1 (2011), 70–89.

[6] Cesare Lombroso, *Criminal Man*, trans. Mary Gibson and Nicole Hahn Rafter (Durham, NC: Duke University Press, 2006 [1876]).

[7] Cesare Beccaria, *On Crimes and Punishments*, trans. David Young (Cambridge, MA: Hackett), 1986) [1764]).

[8] Hence the notorious example of the "superpredator" trope during the high-crime era of some years ago, although the term is itself ambiguous about the "etiology" of the predator identity. See William Bennett, John DiIulio, and John P. Walters, *Body Count* (Simon & Schuster, NY: New York, 1996).

Even with respect to crime rate patterns we are a fairly ahistorical people and often think of change over time chiefly as a lapse from a golden age.[9] Thus, imagistic metaphor probably takes hold in the individual – and collective – mind, then creating an imaginative spur or shock to reconceive the act or the individual, and then certain temporal consequences of that reconception emerge.

Now as for augmenting Potter's classification of metaphors and narratives in the explanatory arena, I can draw on the menus provided by L. David Ritchie and Michael Smith in their previous work but also, happily, in this very volume.[10] Both have helpfully elaborated the varieties of metaphor and narrative (and the relationship between them) at play in law. So let me briefly review and adapt some of their classifications.

Ritchie's taxonomy starts with identifying media maneuvers as story frames, some of which are meant to do no more than use evocative words to gain attention or create emotion, but sometimes go farther in the direction of a conceptual metaphor, where an analogy between one subject domain and another starts with specific metaphors and then spurs a more thematic and image-matching comparison. Then for Ritchie there is the metaphoric story, where an entire plotted narrative as a unit serves as an imaginative and informative parallel to the subject. By contrast there is a story metaphor whereby the unit remains what is in effect a conceptual metaphor but by its nature it requires some elaboration in time, though that elaboration does not involve the kind of human action or suspense or conflict and resolution thereof that inhere in a dramatic narrative.

As described by Smith, what might be a conceptual metaphor can become an extended one if the analogy is complicated (via a single-comparison extended metaphor or a single-theme multiple comparison) and the complications are informative. Often the sustained parallelism has no inherent temporal element other than the time experience of the reader in tracing the parallels, but even if the metaphor describes action, just as with Ritchie's story metaphor that action does not qualify as plot or drama. Smith also describes the metaphoric parable in a way that is close to Ritchie's

---

[9] A staple of research into American attitudes toward crime is that Americans believe that crime rates are unusually high and rising, even when they are relatively low and decreasing. Lauren-Brook Eisen and Oliver Roeder, *America's Faulty Perception of Crime Rates* (New York: Brennan Center for Justice, March 16, 2015). www.brennancenter.org/blog/americas-faulty-perception-crime-rates.

[10] L. David Ritchie, "Metaphors, stories, and media framing of crime: Response to Lithwick" (in this volume), Michael R. Smith, "Metaphoric parable: The nexus of metaphor and narrative in persuasive legal writing" (in this volume).

metaphoric story, and he notes that while it may seem like an allegory, the reading of it is more experiential and less abstract and self-consciously didactic than the stereotypical moralistic allegory. Smith adds the insight that at some point the speaker/writer means to use the metaphor of narrative to claim authority, as if she merits more credibility because of her skill with symbolism.[11]

In the abstract the distinctions among these figures become very subtle. And I hardly will attempt to map these formal categories onto Potter's subject in any systematic way. But I glean from these categories a few questions to keep in mind in considering the fluid movement among types of crime/disease figurations touched on by Potter: Just what is the mix of the literal and the figurative in these categories? How conscious is the reader/listener expected to be about the artifice of the comparison or the abstraction of the lesson? That is, does the writer invite the reader to be knowingly complicit in, or "in on" the artifice? Does the writer want the reader to first be engrossed in the metaphor and then pause in conscious admiration of its vibrancy and then lend more respect to the non-figurative remainder of the exposition? If images in an extended metaphor or metaphoric parable match up well with points in the subject, does the writer expect to receive credit for cleverness, or does she hope to lull the reader into missing the artifice and instead to experience through the metaphoric lens an imaginative transformation of how he sees the subject emotionally or intellectually? Is the writer suggesting that while still analogic, the metaphor or narrative has at least partial substantive significance?[12] Or do we get to a point when to even describe what the writer says as metaphoric at all is wrong from the writer's view? Or does the writer insist that the imagistic-sounding vocabulary actually consists of scientific terms that are called metaphors only because they come from a discipline previously thought to be in a separate conceptual sphere altogether. (As elaborated below, this is the point at which the turf battles depicted by Potter occur.)

In the crime context, surely at one end of a continuum, disease metaphors are used to describe crime in ways that fit the fairly standard notion of an evocative extended metaphor. This is especially true when crime is described in general social terms as a cancer or an epidemic; the use of such metaphors is in no way meant to be literal at all, and the goal is to motivate attitude or action

---

[11] Michael Smith, "Levels of metaphor in persuasive legal writing," *Mercer Law Review* 58 (2007), 919–947, 935–936.

[12] As a side benefit we may get fortuitous discoveries like Hanne's that sometimes disease (e.g. HIV) is precisely the crime being punished. Michael Hanne, "Crime and disease: Contagion by metaphor," pp. 35–54.

such as fright about danger or alarm about social disorder.[13] More benignly, we might describe particular offenders as diseased without any notion of any true connection to medical explanations but as a trope for suggesting sympathy more than condemnation – i.e., possibly as a spur toward general concern for social conditions that might lead to crime or to make a political point.[14] Also this may be where the credibility of the writer,[15] or the susceptibility of the reader,[16] is enhanced by her skill with symbolism relying on ethos as well as pathos, so as to lend more weight to non-metaphoric parts of her argument.

But at a certain point on the continuum, the disease metaphors, while perhaps relied on by their users to achieve certain motivations and emotions, attempt more substantive meaning, with explanatory value. And here I want to attempt another distinction among stages along the continuum. As the writer moves in the direction of metaphors with substantive explanatory value, she may be proffering a hypothesis, a causal story with terms and images borrowed from the discipline that purports to discern causality. But she may be somewhat tentative in this regard, avowedly submitting this hypothesis to a competition with others but claiming it at least provisionally as the most congruent with the facts.[17] For example, if the writer argues that the life-course analogy might help us identify organic changes in the patterns of crime, while still stopping short of applying medical explanations directly, we approach something like Ricoeur's concept of a quasi-plot in capturing historians' discourse.[18]

---

[13] Dahlia Lithwick, "Narrative conventions in crime reporting" (in this volume). In this context the metaphor is not designed to inform but, as Ritchie suggests," to "activate a neural pathway," as in subliminal advertising. Ritchie, "Metaphors, stories, and media framing of crime."

[14] See Lori D. Bougher, "Cognitive coherence in politics: Unifying metaphor and narrative in civic cognition," in Michael Hanne, William D. Crano, and Jeffrey Scott Mio (eds.), *Warring with Words: Narrative and Metaphor in Politics* (Claremont Symposium on Applied Social Psychology Series) (New York, NY and Hove, UK: Psychology Press, 2014), pp. 250–271; Michael R. Smith, "Metaphoric parable: The nexus of metaphor and narrative in persuasive legal writing" (in this volume).

[15] Smith, "Levels of metaphor," 935–936.

[16] For a discussion of how metaphor and narrative can achieve "emotional substance and medium mood control," see Michael R. Smith, "The foundations of persuasion: Logic, pathos and ethos," in *Advanced Legal Writing: Theories and Strategies in Persuasive Writing*, (New York: Wolters Kluwer, 2013), pp. 14–15, 29–31.

[17] On claims of congruence, see the discussion of Kenneth Burke in Barbara Czarniawska, *Narratives in Social Science Research* (New York, NY: Sage, 2011), p. 103.

[18] Paul Ricoeur, *Time and Narrative*, trans. Kathleen McLaughlin and David Pellauer (Chicago, IL: University of Chicago Press, 1984), vol. I, p. 175. Simon Stern, in "Narratives in the legal text," helpfully links this quasi-plot genre to the notion of the "reality effect" depicted by Roland Barthes, "The reality effect" (1968) in *The Rustle of Language*, trans. Richard Howard (New York: Hill & Wang, 1986), pp. 141–148. Stern helpfully interprets Ricoeur and Barthes here. He characterizes the quasi-plot as "straddling the line" between "logical proof" and "explanation by emplotment," fitting the stage of narrative that stops just short of claiming to

Or in a just slightly different vein the writer may offer the metaphor or narrative as a heuristic device designed to cure bad thinking on the subject.

But ultimately, when analysts want us to treat individual criminal behavior as caused by some kind of mental or physical disease, or when they suggest for example that transmissibility of criminal proclivity has some kind of unconscious environmental effect, then the metaphor makes a claim of true analytic superiority. where the user of the metaphor would say that she is not intending a metaphor at all. (For example, psychiatric science could be brought in to explain mechanisms of communication and imitation – even at a basic neurological level – that cause replication of impulsive violent behavior. Whereas the extended metaphor may evoke pathos, we now are at a place where logos joins ethos but replaces pathos, and where each side accuses the other of being merely metaphoric.

So, if we take the most basic crime/disease metaphors, I suspect that they can be cast in any of these calibrations and also see how the genre of metaphor may entail a particular policy implicated by the metaphor – either logically or, well, metaphorically. One is the notion that criminals come prediseased: certain people are genetically predisposed to crime and that the proclivity is absolutely incurable. If we think of a crime gene, then the gene metaphor entails the narrative of the *expression* of a gene.[19] The timing and nature of the expression might produce suspense, because we may not have the science to predict it perfectly, but we know that something bad will eventually happen. If we are agnostic about true genetic cause, we may still be confident that the crime disposition is for some reason inherent as of birth or very early childhood because of an environmental factor. On the theory that opportunity or circumstance still plays a necessary causal role, we do not have a case where

---

be pure science. As shown by Stern in explaining Barthes, the reality effect is achieved not just by the cogency of its argument for congruence but also by the appeal to the audience of the striking presentation of facts. It also has to deal with those parts of the facts that do not easily fit the explanatory narrative, the surplus of "unmotivated detail." In the case of the disease story of about crime, that surplus allows an appearance of honest scientific rigor that acknowledges the noisiness of data that does not defeat statistical significance.

[19] The genetic analogy can of course allow for the complex interactions between genetics and environment. For example, manifestations of disorders relating to such chemicals as serotonin and dopamine could be caused by stressful environmental situations. If environment affects the regulation of gene expression and, in turn, the activity of neurotransmitters that modulate behavior, this kind of interaction may be a significant factor in the development of criminal and antisocial behavior, Gregory R. Bock and Jamie A. Goode, *Genetics of Criminal and Antisocial Behaviour* (Chichester: Wiley, 1996). By the way it is possible that we if we think of at least serious crime as genetically caused, and, if we make the (probably overbroad) assumption that *only* those with the relevant genes can suffer from this disease, then we have at least eliminated concern about the "transmissibility" of the criminal proclivity.

the commission of any particular crime is absolutely inevitable, but is effectively inevitable for any categorically predisposed person who comes of age – a very early age.[20]

Notice all this talk of genetic inevitability can itself be cast in a number of ways. There is the absolutely committed biologically deterministic explanation; there is the partly literal use of "genetic" to refer to some cluster of biological or environmental causes, which we cannot well sort out but where we are confident that a great degree of determinism is in place; and there is the version where the terminology of gene expression is just a metaphoric way of expressing resigned exasperation at how little we know about the cause of apparently inveterate and unavoidable criminal proclivities.[21]

Whatever version is intended, what do we do in the face of a genetic inevitability (or its equivalent)? The strength of the proclivity may require some form of *containment*.[22] Moral issues of culpability may become irrelevant because these criminals are simply feral, and so by virtue of this metaphor we can characterize the governmental response as a "quarantine," not punishment. But in this context the disease metaphor cannot seem to avoid importing moral stigma, any more than leprosy quarantining could be described as non-stigmatic. Further, perhaps, even if this category is based on (pseudo) science in the minds of government, religious notions of taboo and spiritual taint attach to it. Notice here we can see a weird feedback loop where characterizations meant to be scientific can spur some imaginations toward moral and metaphoric versions of the disease model with very different and often troublesome implications.

Of course the extremity of the metaphor serves to justify deprivation of civil liberty, but note one finesse that government can pull off: if we are pretty sure that the predator will commit a crime fairly early, we might safely risk waiting till this happens, convict and punish him with supposed due process, and then

---

[20] For evidence of the peak and expiring ages of offenders for particular crimes, see Robert J. Sampson and John H. Laub. "Life–course desisters? Trajectories of crime among delinquent boys followed to age 70," *Criminology*, 41 (2003), 319–339.

[21] A good example is the supposed diagnosis of the offender as a "psychopath," which some proffer as a scientifically grounded psychiatric or even neurological condition, and some view as a tautological term to describe incorrigibly amoral behavior. See Robert Weisberg, "The unlucky psychopath as death penalty prototype," in Austin Sarat and Karl Shoemaker (ed.), *Who Deserves to Die? Constructing the Executable Subject* (Amherst Mass.: University of Massachusetts Press, 2011), pp. 40–72, 45–52.

[22] For a discussion of how a containment or quarantine for addressing crime not only negates issues of culpability but also can justify detention for a period of time not correlated with the severity of the crime, so long as the social value of the quarantine exceeds its costs, see Scott R. Sehon, *Free Will and Action Explanation: A Non-Causal, Compatibilist Account* (Oxford: Oxford University Press, 2016). p. 10

set a very long sentence (a political art that the United States excels at), because the Eighth Amendment provides little constitutional guidance as to the permissible length of prison sentences.[23] Or we can wait until he commits, say, three crimes, and then habitual offender laws can "quarantine" him forever.[24]

Then there is every possible degree by which this inherent and categorical proclivity is curable or ameliorable – or simply avoidable – if we can prevent any circumstantial trigger. Assume we somehow know that as a result of a gene or some environmental circumstance,[25] the person is at a notably high "risk" of responding to circumstance or opportunity with crime.[26] We then enter the contested areas where the way this disease metaphor operates affects questions of retributive justice and utilitarian control in a different way than is true with the genetic inevitability. The weaker the proclivity, and the more agnostic we are as to whether it is truly genetic or otherwise incurable at all, the more cautious we may be about infringing on civil liberties through preventive detention,[27] and the more we might ascribe blame to the individual. Or we might see the contributing circumstance or opportunity differently – i.e. as viruses that precipitate a latent proclivity toward crime.[28] Do we think of the disease not as a manifestation of willful behavior or moral failure of individuals at all, but as a supraindividual phenomenon of which individuals are helpless instrumentalities? How literally the terminology of disease is meant will determine whether its proponents tilt in the direction of public health disciplines to offer cures or in the direction of political philosophy to suggest morally preferred government policies.

But what if the proclivity is of relatively low probability and at the same time very widely distributed? By one reckoning, in this circumstance the causal effect of the proclivity disease is so weak that we should ignore it

[23] *Harmelin v. Michigan*, 501 U.S. 957 (1991) (deferring to legislatures on proportionality of prison sentences).
[24] *Ewing v. California*, 538 U.S. 11 (2003) (upholding California Three Strikes Law against Eighth Amendment attack).
[25] The environmental cause may be figuratively viewed as a disease germ simply because it produces the symptom – crime. It may be closer to a literal disease, as in the case of lead poisoning or fetal alcohol syndrome which have a high correlation with criminal proclivity.
[26] Pew Center on the States, *Public Safety Performance Project, Risk /Needs Assessment 101: Science Reveals New Tools to Manage Offenders*, Sept. 2011. www.pewtrusts.org/~/media/legacy/uploadedfiles/pcs_assets/2011/pewriskassessmentbriefpdf.pdf.
[27] *Kansas v. Hendricks*, 521 U.S. 346 (1997) (upholding long-term confinement because it does not constitute punishment and so does not require criminal-law related constitutional protections).
[28] Potter, "The 'crime and disease' metaphor."

altogether, blame individuals for their (weakly caused) actions, and ditch the medical model. Conversely, this could be precisely where the public health model should be very appealing.[29] In its strongest form – and here perhaps various psychological theories may compete with biological or neurological conceptions of the disease – would be the idea that we are all born with a certain degree of latent criminality and that bad luck and environmental circumstances could precipitate the criminal symptoms in anyone.[30] Thus we see the tropism toward the non-agent view whereby some social circumstance is the disease and individuals are the mere hosts or carriers. Of course poverty or injustice can be a species of this type of circumstance, but often the culprit is some arguably exogenous and specific force such as the advent of a new addictive drug.[31] Ironically, just as the strict genetic individual model seems to erase volition and responsibility, so the same may be true when our agnosticism about cause leads to this social amelioration approach in a public health frame. So we enter the realm where more emphasis is placed on reducing triggering opportunities, but opportunities may be too broad and diverse to control, and we are urged to work for social justice that in some more foundational way might reduce motives or temptations, if not opportunities. We get the ultimate public health model but one that operates more through emotive political rhetoric than through scientific rigor.[32]

For yet another twist, we can see how the salience of the disease non-agent metaphor may depend on the stage of the justice system we are looking at. So at this moment in America, we see many examples of buyer's remorse for the installation of very severe and rigid sentences in the 1970s that have now led to

---

[29] Timothy B. Akers, Roberto H. Potter, and Carl V. Hill, *Epidemiological Criminology: A Public Health Approach to Crime and Violence* (San Francisco: Jossey-Bass/Wiley, 2013); Roberto H. Potter and Jeffery Rosky, "'The iron fist in the latex glove': The intersection of public health and criminal justice," *American Journal of Criminal Justice* 38 (2013), 276–282.

[30] Bernard Williams, "Moral luck," *Proceedings of the Aristotelian Society*, 1 (1976), 115–135; Thomas Nagel, "Moral luck," in Thomas Nagel, ed. *Mortal Questions* (New York: Cambridge University Press, 1976) pp. 24–38. Peter Arenella, "Convicting the morally blameless: Reassessing the relationship between legal and moral accountability," *UCLA Law Review* 39 (1992) 1511–1622; Peter Arenella, "Character, choice and moral agency: The relevance of character to our moral culpability Judgments," *Social Philosophy & Policy*, 2 (1990): 59–83.

[31] Craig Reinarman and Harry G. Levine, "The crack attack: Politics and media in America's latest drug scare" in Joel Best (ed.), *Images of Issues: Typifying Contemporary Social Problems*. (New York: Aldine de Gruyter, 1989), pp. 115–137.

[32] Potter makes a crucial point that suicide is sometimes declared as a crime and in any event can be a manifestation of the transmissibility of violent proclivities. Potter, "The 'crime and disease' metaphor." When empiricists assessing the consequences of widespread gun ownership in the United States and count suicides along with homicides, they are making a metaphoric point in many senses of the term, including a political point.

overcrowded prisons.[33] So we come to recognize that as we unavoidably reduce imprisonment and release prisoners after they have been withered by their years behind bars, we turn to "risk/needs" language to assist them in the mass reentry that follows mass incarceration.[34] In effect, we shift to the disease treatment metaphor as a manifestation of a great social guilty conscience.

Let me try one final twist: Notice that these criminological strands have a somewhat temporal dimension for the collective, in terms of patterns and crime rates, and also for the individual, in terms of the timing and manner of precipitation of the criminal proclivity. Thus patterns of crime rates allow for narratives built on the analogic figures. But invocation of disease analogies suggests another temporal aspect worth mentioning as a narrative for the individual – the aging process. Old people do not commit violent crimes, and by some reckoning, crime is a self-curing disease, because, depending on the type of crime, people age out of criminal frequency. It may not matter whether we call this a change in proclivity – or of character. Are criminals improved by age? Does the brain change toward curative neurological wisdom? Or is the decaying of the body a kind of exogenous antidote? Obviously, the metaphoric opportunities here are ample. Just as in the collective arena we can speak of an "outbreak" of crime, so for the individual we can speak of "age of onset."

In terms of disease, the question of aging arises in discussions of criminal law's version of "recurrence" of disease – i.e. recidivism. As the United States tries to reverse the drastic increase in incarceration in reentry decades (see below), the vague concept of recidivism has great purchase in public discourse.[35] How to define and measure it is very contestable, and by some definitions it would appear to be "socially constructed" by the actions of government.[36] But the point there is that we may accept an irreducible likelihood of at least a start in criminality by certain diseased individuals, and that attention turns to the therapeutic powers of the punishment system. Whether or not we can prevent the social cancer of crime, perhaps once we identify it we can treat it and promote the opposite of recidivism – "remission"– or project that some diseases of criminal proclivity tend to go away in time.

---

[33] See Robert Weisberg, "How sentencing commissions turned out to be a good idea," *Berkeley Journal of Criminal Law*, 12 (2007), 179–230, 199–201) (reviewing repeal of 1970s mandatory minimum drug laws and bipartisan efforts to reduce prison populations).

[34] James Austin and Patricia Hardyman, "The risks and needs of the returning prisoner population," *Review of Policy Research*, 21 (2005), 13–29.

[35] Robert Weisberg, "Meanings and measures of recidivism," *Southern California Law Review*, 87 (2014) 785–804.

[36] Weisberg, "Meanings and measures of recidivism," 803 (recidivism rate is often a function of number and patterns of practice of probation of police and probation officers).

As noted, the question of recidivism and recurrence of course turns our attention to prisons, but I will get to that a bit later after I open the question of criminal justice agencies of government more generally, and starting with Potter's striking insight about legislatures.

LEGISLATURES – AND COURTS

The analogy to the crime-as-disease narrative works well if we speak of the crime as an epidemic or of the diseased individual as following a life course. On the other hand, as noted below, using metaphor and narrative to capture the "life-course" of legislation is less a serious interdisciplinary explanatory move than an imaginative trope that enlivens a fairly conventional chronicle of the changes in governmental practice. So it provides an opportunity for some thought-experimentation that may seem lighthearted but that may end up fairly illuminating. But why limit the experiment to the legislature?

As Potter shows, legislation is not an explainer of crime as disease, but a participant in a medical narrative we can extrapolate from the crime-as-disease metaphor.[37] We make it possible to prevent the outbreak of harmful behavior, or treat its immediate incidence, by declaring it a crime. But the creativity of antisocial people and the plasticity of the media of science and the economy are such that they constantly adapt their behavior so as to escape the literal statutory prohibition.[38] The legislature must keep trying to refine the nature and dosage of the medication; the legislature is the medical sleuth seeking the magic medicine; the crime is the frighteningly antibiotic-resistant bacterium. Or we might say that legislation is itself a good organism that can defeat the bad organism but must constantly restrategize in this biological duel.

On this subject I want to avoid any chic invocation of social constructionism, the overly clever sociological irony by which we say that government creates crime (not that Potter falls prey to it). I think the idea is more plausible and interesting if more complicated – i.e., there is a real problem of social harm to be dealt with, and it is not unreasonable for the legal system to deploy the special powers of criminalization to fight it. But then criminal justice, in part because of its metaphoric and narrative valence, "takes on a life of its own"

---

[37] Potter, "The 'crime and disease' metaphor."
[38] An interesting episode involves the law requiring a report to the Treasury of all cash transactions with banks of $10,000 or more. Needless to say, people started "structuring" their illicit transactions so that no one transaction exceeded the limit. Then Congress made it a crime to do this structuring with intent to evade the reporting requirement, and in *Ratzlaf* v. *United States*, 510 135 (1994), an offender won reversal of his conviction because this amended law was too obscure for the average person to know it.

and follows some of the life-course paths Potter describes in a complex interaction, a dialectic or symbiosis, between the law and the behavior. In that regard, we begin to observe out-of-control legislation as organic behavior rather than thoughtfully deliberated governmental policy. And in many situations the organic life can be thought of as exhibiting a disease/cure/side effect iteration as well.

But to this picture we need to add the judiciary. So, pause for a moment to consider the relationship between judicial and statutory law, with the deep background of judicial condescension toward statute law as an inferior form of government, indeed as a kind of excrescence on government. Common law is a phenomenon of custom tempered by wisdom. Statute law is the random, arbitrary, literally unprecedented intrusion of political impulse.[39] And so the relationship merits some consideration in regard to metaphor and narrative.

Consider the common law as narrative on its own, nicely described in literary terms by Ronald Dworkin via the chain novel idea: each chapter is partly an innovation and partly an assimilation of and extrapolation from and extension or diversion from the last phase, so there is relative freedom but relative path dependence.[40] On the one hand, even within the paradigm of legitimate statutory vaccination of crime, the judiciary must be a partner in doing the adaptation through interpretation of the statute in specific prosecutions (although the appellate court makes midlevel generalizations about the meaning of the statute) – the dosage regulation. This relationship is apparent in fairly technical criminal legislation (as in Potter's example of designer drugs or in the perennial problem of classifying illegal firearms) where targeting the criminal toxin is a very precise function and near misses occur.[41] But often judicial law must do almost all the work, because while technically criminal law is statutory in a modern democracy,[42] much of the statute law is simply a codification of common law, and the expectation is that the judiciary will do a kind of continuing common law development of the statute law.

A good example is the law of possession. While the range of things illegal to possess has greatly increased over the last century, the statutory definition of

---

[39] According to James Kent, the common law is a "nursing father" while a "statute is like a tyrant," (quoted in David Raack, "'To preserve the best fruits': The legal thought of Chancellor James Kent," *American Journal of Legal History* 33 (1989), 320–366, 354.

[40] Ronald Dworkin, *Law's Empire* (Cambridge, MA: Harvard University Press, 1986), p. 229.

[41] Two perennial examples are laws banning "drug paraphernalia" and those banning "assault" or "semi-automatic weapons." In both cases challengers have occasionally succeeded in claims that these statutory definitions are too vague or too imprecise, or where the statutes attempt greater specificity clever people figure out workarounds.

[42] This is called the principle of Legality, derived from due process. *Keeler v. Superior Court*, 2 Cal. 3d 619 (1970).

possession has hardly advanced beyond the use of that very word. It is then left to the courts to develop notions of "constructive possession" in terms of various ways of exercising "dominion" or "control," and applying such nuanced definitions becomes even more challenging when the dominion can be very indirect and relational among several parties,[43] or, more important, where the thing possessed is essentially intangible – i.e., a computer image. Can one derive the antisocial benefit of a computer image and escape the crime of possession by means of the distinction between merely clicking and viewing on the one hand, and downloading on the other?[44] So the legislature may be the manufacturer of the raw material of the medicine, or the administrator of the cure, but all the medical skill must lie with courts (and prosecutors). Here we see parallels to legislation in certain criminal areas, where the legislature does not adapt. The legislation is the problem, not the cure, and the judiciary must do the healing – usually with creative aesthetic, metaphoric glosses on outmodedly narrow legal terms such as possession or search.

Notably, these possession laws that so well illustrate the medicinal role of the courts are themselves a subset of the definitions of inchoate crimes that are a case of legal vaccination in another sense, because they serve as preemptive strikes on potential social harm.[45] And the more inchoate the crime, the more challenging is the legal art of defining it within constitutional constraints (or, by metaphoric analogy, the greater the challenge in fine-tuning the vaccine).[46]

---

[43] *United States* v. *Maldonado*, 23 F.3d 4(1st Cir. 1994) (defendant never touches drugs but is told to keep guard on room where others have deposited them.).

[44] *State* v. *Barger*, 247 P.3d 309 (Oreg. 2011). The flip side of possession appears in the Fourth Amendment, where the courts must for example rely on old cases about physical "containers" to address rights of privacy in digital information. The difficulty of this extrapolation is laid out in Orin Kerr, "Searches and seizures in a digital world," *Harvard Law Review* 119 (2005), 532–585.

[45] Markus Dubber, "Policing possession: The war on crime and the end of criminal law," *Journal of Criminal Law*, 91 (2001) 829–996.

[46] The example from Hanne of HIV transmission is the strongest version of this – punishing sex by an HIV person as an assault. Assault itself is, like possession, defined by common law in very vague terms (i.e., an attempt or threat to cause a battery), and courts must do all the work in applying it to unforeseen situations. In effect, courts are asked to stretch criminal liability as a way of quarantining the disease through deterrence.

In *State* v. *Smith*, 621 A.2d 495 (N.J. Super. A.D. 1993), a jail inmate who knew he was HIV-positive bit a correctional officer. Upholding his conviction for attempted murder and aggravated assault, the court held there was sufficient evidence that it is possible for the virus to be transmitted through a bite, and that the defendant had been made aware of this possibility. But in *Brock* v. *State*, 555 So. 2d 285 (Ala. Cr. App. 1989) the conviction of attempted murder was overturned for lack of evidence that the defendant believed that HIV virus could be transmitted through a bite.

But if we return to the idea that legislation becomes a phenomenon of organic behavior rather than controlled governmental policy – a symbiotic agent in a biochemical interaction – then courts must sometimes treat the statute itself as a diseased organism that requires treatment or cure, or eradication. We can admire all the technical dexterity and judicial artistry exhibited by courts in the discipline of statutory construction,[47] but at some point we have to see it as stepping in to remedy an abject legislative failure manifested in a sick statute. Sometimes, to mix the medical metaphors, it has to perform major surgery on a statute that either is riddled with vagueness[48] or ambiguity[49] or has fallen into that moribund condition called desuetude.[50] The main "symptom" of that condition is the need for Supreme Court refereeing of a circuit split, whereby lower courts of appeals come to flatly contradictory readings of the same law on effectively the same set of facts (although sometimes the case is taken up because one court flagrantly deviates from settled Supreme Court doctrine).[51] And whether by the Supreme Court or lower courts, sometimes judges must do more than clarify the proper dosage of the crime antidote: they must withdraw the medication altogether as incapable of proper dosing because it is so void for vagueness[52] or overbreadth[53] that

[47] Karl N. Llewellyn, "Remarks on the theory of appellate decision and the rules or canons about how statutes are to be construed, *Vanderbilt Law Review*, 3 (1950), 395–406.
[48] Papachristou v. Jacksonville, 405 U.S. 156 (1972). There the colorful statute defined illegal loiterers as follows: "Rogues and vagabonds, or dissolute persons who go about begging; common gamblers, persons who use juggling or unlawful games or plays, common drunkards, common night walkers, thieves, pilferers or pickpockets, traders in stolen property, lewd, wanton and lascivious persons, keepers of gambling places, common railers and brawlers, persons wandering or strolling around from place to place without any lawful purpose or object, habitual loafers, disorderly persons, persons neglecting all lawful business and habitually spending their time by frequenting houses of ill fame, . . ." The Court found that this law violated due process for failing to give fair notice what behavior is condemned and for giving police unfettered discretion to define its scope.
[49] Yates v. United States, 135 S.Ct. 1074 (2015) (obstruction of justice statute criminalizing destruction of "tangible object" relevant to legal proceeding does not include a fish under that term – only objects used to record information).
[50] In 1825, the Pennsylvania Supreme Court declined to enforce the traditional punishment of ducking for women convicted as common scolds, stating that "total disuse of any civil institution for ages past, may afford just and rational objections against disrespected and superannuated ordinances." Wright v. Crane, 13 Serg. & Rawle 220, 228 (Pa. 1825).
[51] Under Supreme Court Rule 210, in addition to horizontal conflicts among lower courts, the Supreme Court often takes cases where a lower court "has so far departed from the accepted and usual course of judicial proceedings . . . as to call for an exercise of this Court's supervisory power . . ."
[52] Chicago v. Morales, 527 U.S.41 (1999) (despite effort to narrowly tailor gang loitering law to discernable threatening conduct, law too vague to satisfy due process).
[53] Broadrick v. Oklahoma, 413 U.S. 601 (1973) (limit on state employee right to engage in partisan politics covers too much conduct protected by First Amendment)

statutory construction cannot save it, and in the strongest version of judicial doctoring, we find an example of what Potter has described as "eradication" of crime. That is, where certain behavior is a crime solely because the legislature has said so, but where in doing so the legislature has violated the Constitution, then the judiciary converts a crime back into legal behavior.

The reference back to courts and legislatures gives us a chance to consider the issue of control/eradication/elimination.[54] The political currency of criminal justice is usually about "crime rates," with no expectation of a rate of zero but rather attention to things getting better or worse, so a certain degree of disease is expected. But one notable instance of a crime arguably zeroing out involves the crack "epidemic" of a few decades back. On the one hand, the crack disease sort of defeated itself – there is some evidence that its catastrophic harms themselves served as a deterrent to use, and the demise of the crack market was a major contributor to the great crime decline of the 1990s.[55] On the other hand, crack became less criminal when the government decided to finally alter the penalty ratio between crack and power, suggesting a case of partial "constructed eradication."[56] And then we can cite an example of full "constructed eradication" in regard to sodomy. People forget that *Lawrence v. Texas* was a criminal case.[57] We eradicated the crime by ruling the behavior constitutionally protected. But, again to avoid overly chic social constructionism, we might say that there really was a bad behavior or a disease here – it was social prejudice, of which we cured ourselves.

THE POLICE

Law enforcement officers themselves are a fertile subject for application of the disease metaphor and narrative. And while they are government practitioners of criminal justice, they are probably closer to diagnostic criminologists than are other agencies of the system, and so they fit fairly comfortably on the criminological side of Potter's professional pairing. Their job is in part to initiate prosecutions under the rule of law, but more broadly they aim to prevent crime and maintain order, and they are relatively unconstrained by the formal apparatus of legal rules in their core work of investigating or

---

[54] Potter, "The 'crime and disease' metaphor."
[55] Steven Levitt, "Understanding why crime fell in the 1990s: Four factors that explain the decline and six that do not," *Journal of Economic Perspectives*, 18 no. 1 (2004), 163–190.
[56] Fair Sentencing Act, 21 U.S.C. 841(b)(1) (2010).   [57] 539 U.S. 558 (2003).

thwarting crime by their presence.[58] They therefore want to identify the incidence, causes, and cures for crime in a fairly open way. So certainly police officials can participate with politicians, criminologists, and citizens generally in their reliance on metaphors and narratives, including the varieties of disease figurations.

So, it is no surprise that police have become epidemiologists of a sort, especially in recent decades under the broad, misleading and vague rubric of "community policing," where they act to some extent like public health officials. Under one version of this rubric, broken windows policing, they detect and cure the disease of environmental degradation that breeds crime through lowered social morale.[59] (By contrast, order "breeds" more order.) They are exterminators of the sources of infection. The more important subgenre of "community policing" involves Compstat, the computerized system designed to identify the street corners where crime is rampant and then target the dosage of intervention there.[60] To some extent they hope that their mere presence reduces the likelihood of transmission and contagion.[61] To some extent they can actually rely on the public-health vision of the neighborhood as a legally cognizable justification for temporary quarantine, because that is what a stop-and-frisk is.[62] So this "community order" notion, while hardly rejecting the culpability of individual potential offenders, nevertheless enables them to widen their nets.[63]

Whereas as Potter notes, there may not be "copycat" criminals,[64] a version of transmissibility is precisely this practice of identifying crime

---

[58] While the Fourth Amendment constrains the power of police to engage in searches and seizures and the Fifth Amendment does so in regard to interrogations, the police generally need not meet any legal stand in deciding which potential offenders on whom they focus their fact-finding resources or where they should make their deterrent presence known.

[59] George L. Kelling and James Q. Wilson, "Broken windows: The police and neighborhood safety," *The Atlantic Monthly* (March 1982), 29–38; George L. Kelling and William J. Bratton, "Why we need broken windows policing, *City Journal* (Winter 2015).

[60] Compstat: Its origins, evolution, and future in law enforcement agencies, 2013 by Police Executive Research Forum Bureau of Justice Assistance www.policeforum.org/assets/docs/F ree_Online_Documents/Compstat/compstat%20-%20its%20origins%20evolution%20and%2 0future%20in%20law%20enforcement%20agencies%202013.pdf.

[61] In their original article Kelling and Wilson were careful not to claim that broken windows policing would reduce crime – only that it would reduce the environmental sense of disorder. In the retrospective 2015 article, Kelling and Bratton made the stronger claim.

[62] *Terry v. Ohio*, 392 U.S. 1 (1968).

[63] Another set of actors are the supervisors – in effect, the physician assets in the probation and parole departments, who do the follow-up on offenders. They are social workers as well as police.

[64] James Q. Wilson, *Thinking about Crime* (New York: Basic Books (rev. ed. 1983), pp. 45–58. Also, those who argue against selective incapacitation as a sensible goal of punishment note

"hotspots."[65] "Hotspot" is itself is a medical term, and its way of finessing the culpability of individuals helps lend high-tech policing not just high-tech prestige but also some greater claim of fairness. Police are always accused of disproportionately directing their resources at certain vulnerable populations, but Compstat purports to be relying on demonstrable evidence, not hunch or prejudicial assumption, and it also conveys the sense that the culpability lies as much with the local environment as with a set of individuals. On the other hand, since hotpots tend to be in places where poor minorities live and where drug use is more public than it is with wealthier users, it is subject to the charge that it only superficially masks old-fashioned police prejudice. Worse yet, it is accused of fraudulent self-justifications because the more surveillance of hotspots, the more suspicious characters will be stopped and frisked and then possibly arrested, and the hotter the spot will be in police statistics. Thus it can rationalize police searches and seizures by easing the burden on proving reasonable suspicion for a detention where, under Supreme Court law, the very fact of the hotspot enhances suspicion.[66]

THE PRISON

On the one hand, of course, the prison is the key American instrument of intervention to contain the disease of crime and prevent its recurrence. There may remain little faith in the old Pennsylvania model of the rehabilitative prison,[67] but it is still the stated aspiration of prisons.[68] Perhaps because incarceration is so widespread in American society, the transition away from prison has become a major rite of passage in American society[69] and hence

---

that the number of crimes may become more a function of the number of criminal opportunities than the number of criminals – i.e., jail the dealer on Elm Street and he'll be replaced by a new dealer on Elm Street. So what does that make Elm Street in medical terms?

[65] David Weisburd and Lorraine Green Mazerolle, "Crime and disorder in drug hot spots: Implications for theory and practice in policing," *Police Quarterly* 3 (September 2000), 331–349.

[66] Predpol, 5 Myths about predictive policing, www.predpol.com/5-common-myths-predictive-policing-predpol/.

[67] David Rothman, *The Discovery of the Asylum: Social Order and Disorder in the New Republic* (Boston: Little, Brown, 1971), pp. 79–88.

[68] In 1912, California created the California State Detentions Bureau. The name changed in 1951 to the California Department of Corrections. In 2004 Governor Arnold Schwarzenegger renamed it Department of Corrections and Rehabilitation.

[69] Joan Petersilia, *When Prisoners Come Home: Parole and Prisoner Reentry* (New York: Oxford University Press, 2009).

subject to the public health model of the prevention of recurrence. But then the disease metaphor reverses itself. In micro terms, the prison itself is seen as a breeding ground of crime. Some believe in the "school for crime" view of prison whereby transmission of criminal proclivity and skill occurs.[70] More convincingly, some view prison as so interfering with the social health and skill of prisoners as to leave them in a compromised form, with reduced immunity to procrime pressures when they are released.[71]

On a macro level, mass incarceration has become a phenomenon infecting American society. It is viewed as an embarrassing disease of American society, and the very fact that identifying the causal agents or mechanisms is highly contested underscores how it can be viewed as a social ailment. something that has happened to American society. It is metastatic in the sense of the self-reinforcement – as with endless recidivism that reseeds the prison population.[72] It is metastatic in its effect on families and on the futures of released inmates. Again, the judiciary can step in, as in the *Plata* case, where, appropriately enough, the inability of the overcrowded prisons to minimally humanely alleviate actual disease established a violation of the Eighth Amendment.[73]

Incidentally, the disease aspect becomes quite literal. The cost-benefit analysis of keeping aged prisoners in prison involves the social interest in retribution but, in utilitarian terms, the diminishing proclivity versus the increased cost of imprisonment, which is mostly due to the cost of medical care that increases with the aged.

But if we take a broader view of disease, then we see that the United States has been willing to accept a very economically inefficient system of incarcerating sick people for well over a century. That is because, as Bernard Harcourt has shown, the criminal incarceration rate of today closely resembles the incarceration rate that used to include long-term civil commitment of mentally ill people in state-run asylums. Indeed, given overwhelming evidence of the high rate of mental illness among American offenders and inmates, the historical change is to some extent nominal, at least over the last century.[74]

---

[70] Paul Gendreau, Claire Goggin, and Francis T. Cullen, *The Effects of Prison Sentences on Recidivism*, 4–5 (1999), Office of Justice Programs, *available at* www.prisonpolicy.org/scans/e199912.htm.

[71] See Bruce Western, *Punishment and Inequality in America* (New York: Russell Sage Foundation, 2006), pp. 83–163 (summarizing empirical evidence of various economic and social effects of having been incarcerated).

[72] Joan Petersilia, *Understanding California Corrections* (Berkeley: California Policy Research Center, 2006).

[73] *Brown v. Plata*, 563 U.S. 493 (2011).

[74] Bernard Harcourt, "From the asylum to the prison: Rethinking the incarceration revolution," *Texas Law Review*, 84 (2006), 1751–1786.

WHITE COLLAR CRIME

Potter takes pains to locate the disease metaphor in the context of violent crime, and in Dahlia Lithwick's contribution to this book she argues that in journalism, business crime is put on the business page and is rarely the subject of the media's literary flourishes about crime.[75] But why cannot we indeed extend the metaphor/narrative of disease to white collar crime? After all, it is traditionally portrayed as "corruption," the very term suggesting the tainting of a healthy organism, such that all the versions of the disease metaphor can be applied. And it is surely a good example of the "life course of legislation" idea, precisely because the crimes go beyond the "malum in se" crimes we associate with violence, and the expanding variety of fraud and bribery crimes represents an effort like the one Potter has described of legislatures aggressively and sometimes fecklessly trying to isolate and define corrupt actions which are at the border of highly technical regulatory laws.

So for example, the white collar criminal is usually viewed as corrupt because tainted by a specific kind of antisocial motive, such as being the recipient of a bribe. But even when statute law purports to define the precise action which manifests this corruption, it often hedges by adding the wonderfully meaningless or circular term "corruptly" as a mens rea adverb to serve as a requited element.[76] Under the very expressive language of the famous RICO law, what is corrupted is (at least in the original formulation) an otherwise legitimate business enterprise, rendered into diseased form through the infection of money coming from illegal sources or whose operations are conducted in illegal ways.[77] And sometimes the diseased or corrupted organism is the market, because under certain formulations of certain laws, an abuse of fair trading is thought of as infecting the fair operation of the free market even without specific proof of detrimental reliance of financial loss.[78] Indeed, the harm is sometimes viewed as the specter or fear of illicit trading perceived by others in the market that can deter market energy. And in one of the key developments in modern anticorruption law, the body politic is corrupted by the mere receipt of a bribe by a

---

[75] Lithwick, "Narrative conventions in crime reporting."
[76] The term is part of the law proscribing bribery by or of federal officials 18 U.S.C. § 201 (2016) and the basic law of obstruction of justice, 18 U.S.C § 1503 (2016).
[77] See the (literally) Racketeer Influenced and Corrupt Organizations Act, 18 U.S.C. §§ 1961–1964 (2016).
[78] See the discussion of the law's efforts to punish even in the absence of measurable harm to any individual or company in David Mills and Robert Weisberg, "Corrupting the harm requirement in white collar crime," *Stanford Law Review*, 60 (2008), 1371–1446.

public official – it taints the fair exercise of government even without specific proof of malfeasance.[79]

And while many would join with Lithwick in saying that white collar crime is treated as a business problem rather than a criminal problem, at least in popular media, within the realm of federal criminal law prosecutors are viewed as moralistic despots going after alleged criminals with powerful aggression, often through invasive techniques such as wiretaps.[80]

And as with other uprisings of the disease metaphor, reversal is possible. Thus, the public seems to be crying out for criminal prosecutions of the malefactors who caused the 2008 crash of the American economy. And in rationalizing the absence of prosecutions, the government sometimes depicts the problem as so pervasive as to be a kind of economic public health crisis for which the identification of guilty agents is irrelevant or the proof thereof impossible.[81] We are all caught up in the greed of cheap mortgages. The malefactors were often low-level people whose criminal state of mind was more likely a species of recklessness or negligence rather than intentional fraud.[82]

SEXUAL ASSAULT AND COLLEGES

Potter brilliantly demonstrates the "jurisdictional" battle between medially oriented public health and conventional social science for ownership of rights

---

[79] See 18 U.S.C. 1346 (2016) under which a bribe-taking public official commits a crime on the assumption that the bribe distorts her exercise of her duty of good government, even without proof of a specific harm to governmental decision-making under the vague language of "a scheme or artifice to deprive another of the intangible right of honest services."

[80] There is a common *cri de coeur* that federal prosecutors are belligerent abusive bullies and pompous moralists. Radley Balko, "The untouchables: America's misbehaving prosecutors, and the system that protects them," *Huffington Post* (August 6, 2013). www.huffingtonpost.com/2013/08/01/prosecutorial-misconduct-new-orleans-louisiana_n_3529891.html.

[81] William D. Cohan, "A clue to the scarcity of financial crisis prosecutions," *New York Times* (July 26, 2013). www.nytimes.com/2016/07/22/business/dealbook/a-clue-to-the-scarcity-of-financial-crisis-prosecutions.html.

[82] Here is some evocative prose on the subject:

> If you're among those upset that your taxpayer dollars may be spent in volume to rescue people who – for whatever reason – can't make their mortgage payments, Federal Financial Analytics analyst Karen Shaw Petrou recommends thinking about it this way:
> "Preventing foreclosures has a lot in common with treating syphilis. In both cases, you help some who are undeserving, but – in an economic collapse or a public-health emergency – one acts nonetheless."

Mark Felsenthal, "When is a housing crisis like venereal disease?" *Tales from the Trail* (Feb. 20, 2009). http://blogs.reuters.com/talesfromthetrail/2009/02/20/when-is-a-housing-crisis-like-venereal-disease/.

of diagnosis and remedy. I want to address an offshoot of that battle, in a realm that all academics are now very familiar with – the roiling debates about sexual assault on campus. There are several components to this issue. First, does it belong to the universities or to government to police sexual assault? The answer is both because they have dual jurisdiction, but the issue is more complex because they rarely act harmoniously except by mutual deference and default. Universities themselves traditionally took a kind of paternalistic public health approach, putting on seminars for students about "risky" behavior in social and sexual encounters, and focusing on education and counseling.[83] But they always had disciplinary rules, and those have only been enhanced through federal requirements under Title IX. The result is that universities are forced to take on the roles of police and adjudicators at the same time they are trying to treat students as vulnerable young people exposed to risk.

But there is another major component. Alcoholism, or at least alcohol abuse, is a major disease of the young, and it is at least heavily correlated with sexual abuse. So the universities, which, independently of sexual assault, try to take on alcohol, as a "community health" problem and then feel some pressure to treat it as an aspect of sexual assault. But many activists complain that sexual assault is not punished enough – because the police tend to stay away from allegations of non-stranger assaults on campus, thus pushing colleges to act more like police agents, and these activists object to any ascription to alcohol of any causal role. Officials in deans-of-students offices or campus health centers adopt a purportedly "non-judgmental" social model of the public health approach. But the federal government is now turning this approach against the colleges by augmenting requirements for bureaucratic mechanisms to address "risks."[84] And this federal intervention only blurs or complicates the distinctions among criminal law, moral, and health approaches to the problem by mandating protocols for teaching students about good and bad sexual partners, often in bureaucratic prose that sounds half like health advice and half like highly act-specific crime definitions.[85] Ironically, the federal requirement that colleges embed a Title IX office into their administration is all too rife with host/virus metaphor possibilities.

---

[83] Jacob Gersen and Jeannie Suk, "The sex bureaucracy," *California Law Review*, 104 (2016), 881–947.
[84] See Tamara Rice Lave, "Campus sexual assault adjudication: Why universities should reject the Dear Colleague Letter," *Kansas Law Review* 64 (2016) 915–962.
[85] Gersen and Suk, "The sex bureaucracy," 891–897.

CONCLUSION

There is no area of law to which our collective inquiry into the role of metaphor and narrative is irrelevant, but allow me some arrogance in suggesting that crime and criminal justice are close to the ideal arenas for the inquiry. Here are several reasons why the fertility of this area for the uses of metaphor and narrative is so remarkable: the unique power that we constitutionally grant government in the area of criminal punishment; the visceral way that people experience crime; the social salience of the facts of or perceptions about crime; the complex and often conflictual relationships between deontological and utilitarian principles (and among the latter) in justifying punishment; and the susceptibility of crime to such an array of interdisciplinary perspectives. As I have said, Potter has demonstrated the frequency, variety, and power of these figurations in the crime/disease linkage. But his paper also points us toward the great variety of genres of these figurations in the crime/disease area, the different ways the writer induces in her reader an almost irresistible temptation to keep proliferating observations and discoveries about these phenomena. And once we have such variety of examples of and types of metaphor and narrative, we have a superabundance of "data" we can evaluate to see how many genres of these figures there are, how many differences in degree and kind of intended literalness, or of invited complicity between writer and reader or of deliberate strategies by which the writer wants to strategically mystify the reader into reimagining the world. We also then get a sense (to use an economist's cliché – and metaphor!) of the path dependence of these figures in influencing the ways both analysts of crime and practitioners of criminal justice fall prey to, or deliberately implement, the practical entailments of these metaphors and narratives.

CONVERSATION VI
NARRATIVE AND METAPHOR IN PUBLIC DEBATE AROUND CRIME AND PUNISHMENT

Editors' Introduction

Michael Hanne and Robert Weisberg

The previous conversation focused on the ways in which innovative thinking around the law comes about. It was concerned mostly with the ideas of specialists and policy makers. The present conversation is concerned more with public understanding of, and debate around, legal issues, specifically crime, policing and punishment. Of course, policy changes are not generally possible without some degree of public understanding and support. But the difference between these contexts is stark. While academic specialists and policy analysts must work with elected officials, who in turn must rely on the general polity, these thinkers nevertheless are subject to various degrees of formal or informal peer review. Thus, to the extent their work uses or is influenced by metaphor and narrative, standards of social-scientific or medical rigor provide some check on the risk that literary figurations will distort empirical reality. By contrast, the First Amendment bars any check on the accuracy or fairness of the use of metaphor and narrative in popular discourse or commercial media. Moreover, the visceral nature of crime as a cluster of social issues and concerns makes this open arena of depictions of crime and criminal justice especially vulnerable to sensationalistic misrepresentation. One of the oldest clichés about traditional print journalism is, "If it bleeds it leads."

This contrast then in turn imposes an obligation on scholars from the first realm to understand the discourse of the second realm, and then to try to convince the political and media leaders who dominate the second realm to deploy metaphors and narratives with more intellectual honesty. As for the obligation of the political leaders and media, since it cannot be imposed by law, we might point them to principles of political philosophy. Specifically we might point to the argument of Martha Nussbaum that prerequisites for performing fully as a citizen of a democratic society (alongside a capacity for self-criticism) are "narrative imagination" and "empathy,"[1] or that of Lynne Cameron that empathetic citizenship depends crucially on metaphorical processes.[2] From these principles we can derive at least a moral obligation that metaphor and narrative exhibit a fidelity to the complex empirical realities about crime and criminal justice, and to account for the great variety of (and conflict among) social perspectives about these realities.

Public discourse inevitably entails some distillation of these realities about the incidence of crime, how people come to commit crimes, how the police carry out their duties, how criminal trials are conducted, and the effect of penal policy in terms of deterrence, rehabilitation, and reducing recidivism. Renita Coleman, Esther Thorson, and others have argued that news reporting about crime that uses such metaphors, and the narratives they generate, is particularly effective in helping the public to grasp what they call "contextual and base-rate information," contributing social causes of crime and wider consequences of crime, as well as strategies for prevention.[3] The scholarly consensus is that public understanding of, and views on, social and political topics – but perhaps most dramatically crime and punishment – are largely organized in terms of cognitive shortcuts, heuristics, that simplify the processing of complex information[4] and that the conceptual frameworks employed are mainly in narrative and metaphor form.[5] At best, these narrative and metaphorical frames may encapsulate complex issues with rough accuracy; at worst, they grossly disfigure the facts and the issues and are subject to cynical manipulation. The manipulators may be the media, whose chief interest will simply be visibility, or government figures, whose goal is stirring emotion for political gain.

Alas, by-and-large people bring clusters of inadequate metaphors and narratives to bear on their thinking about crime. Two of the clusters take interestingly different forms. One is rooted in the idea that the (very plausible) goal

---

[1] Martha Nussbaum, "Narrative imagination," in her *Cultivating humanity* (Cambridge, MA: Harvard University Press, 1997), Chapter 10.
[2] Lynne Cameron, A talk "Metaphor and Empathy," www.open.ac.uk/researchprojects/living withuncertainty/sites/www.open.ac.uk.researchprojects.livingwithuncertainty/files/pics/d125 010.pdf.
[3] Renita Coleman and Esther Thorson, "The effects of news stories that put crime and violence into context: Testing the public health model of reporting," *Journal of Health Communication*, 7 no. 5 (2002): 401–425.
[4] Charles S. Taber, "Political cognition and public opinion," in Robert Y. Shapiro and Lawrence R. Jacobs (eds.) *The Oxford Handbook of American Public Opinion and the Media* (Oxford, UK; New York, NY: Oxford University Press, 2011), pp. 368–383.
[5] Lori D. Bougher, "Cognitive coherence in politics: Unifying metaphor and narrative in civic cognition," in Michael Hanne, William D. Crano, and Jeffery Scott Mio (eds.), *Warring with Words: Narrative and Metaphor in Politics* (New York, NY and Hove: Psychology Press, 2015), pp. 250–271.

of criminal justice is general deterrence, and it therefore adopts a "rational actor" model of the criminal. In effect, it views the criminal mind as an accounting machine that weighs prospective costs and benefits in deciding whether to commit a crime. This cluster thus leads the public, along with many politicians, to place an unrealistic reliance on punishment (by incarceration) for deterrence. In addition, they employ oversimple "escalation" and cost efficiency models in relation to crime and punishment,[6] viewing criminal justice as a communications system between government and criminals.

The second cluster rejects any notion of rational calculation or even adaptability in the criminal. Rather, by this second view criminals are inherently pathological: they are not insane, but they do exhibit the disorder of antisocial personality or psychopathy, and they have no interest in or ability for controlling their behavior. Thus, the purpose of criminal punishment is not to deter but simply to incapacitate. This cluster leads to the notorious depiction of criminals as "superpredators" or other metaphoric types of monsters. It also leads the public to exaggerate the portion of crime that is violent, and also to feel a special panic when the violence has any sexual component. Racial stereotyping is inherent in this cluster, as is all too well captured in the infamous visual trope of Willie Horton deployed by George H. W. Bush in the 1988 presidential election. As with the first cluster, the public is denied both empirical fact and social nuance.

These different purported understandings of crime (and others, such as the "bad parenting" cluster) underscore – and, unfortunately, reinforce – the public's difficulty in reaching multifactorial explanations for crime, preferring single causes, easily rendered in evocative tropes.[7] These simplistic metaphors and narratives also lead to gross mischaracterizations of both the nature and the volume of crime in the United States. Depictions of violent predatory animals among us cause many people who by virtue of wealth and geography are relatively safe from crime to imagine themselves as highly vulnerable potential victims. Imagery that may be intellectually responsible in the work of social scientists, such as "waves," or "surges," or "epidemics," create hysteria when loosed into public media.

Moreover, easy narratives distort our understanding of the legal system as it deals with crime. Prosecutors and police are depicted either as martial combatants in a war on crime or as opponents in sporting competition with

---

[6] Nathaniel Kendall-Taylor, *Maze and Gears: Using Explanatory Metaphors to Increase Public Understanding of the Criminal Justice System and Its Reform* (Washington, DC: Frameworks Institute, 2013).

[7] James Q. Wilson and Joan Petersilia (eds.), *Crime and Public Policy* (New York, NY: Oxford University Press, 2011).

defense lawyers, and the resolution of a crime is typically depicted in a television-finale-worthy trial verdict. A more accurate picture of the criminal justice system as a multistage and multipart, and often chaotic, bureaucracy, where low-level exercise of official discretion is the deciding factor in outcomes – such a picture lacks media appeal.

In their conversation, Lithwick and Ritchie sharply capture all these problems, demonstrating that the insight of Shanto Iyengar and others in the early 1990s about the media's tendency to "focus on specific episodes, individual perpetrators, victims, or other actors at the expense of more general, thematic information" is even more valid today.[8] Lithwick also observes the arbitrariness of popular definitions of crime, which often exclude white collar crime altogether, or invoke a narrative of the sympathetic white-collar defendant beleaguered by government oppression – an exaggerated opposite of the way "common" criminals are viewed.[9]

Lithwick argues that more responsible public media and public officials would be willing to inform the public of the facts that belie these simplistic images and narratives, or to introduce more accurate competing figurations into the discourse. These can be individually oriented – stories of criminals who are neither accounting machines nor predators but imperfect people who have fallen prey to both external and internal forces and who have some capacity for desistance or rehabilitation. Or they could involve historical narratives that show crime as shifting with social and economic developments and often the "product" of arbitrary legislative definitions.

A move in that direction has come from a group of scholars, around Lois Presser and Sveinung Sandberg, who practice what they have called "narrative criminology." They have sought, by interviewing criminals convicted for a great variety of offenses in many countries, to demonstrate the complexity of the processes by which people actually fall into, and remain in, or abandon, a criminal way of life.[10] Thus, their discussion suggests that the media contribute little to a more sophisticated public understanding of crime and punishment. As a parallel, a number of organizations, notably the Frameworks Institute, have suggested ways in which experts might encapsulate their more sophisticated findings about crime and punishment in more adequate narrative and metaphor frames for the purpose of keeping the public better

---

[8] Shanto Iyengar, *Is Anyone Responsible? How Television Frames Political Issues* (Chicago, IL: University of Chicago Press, 1991).
[9] David O. Friedrichs, *Trusted Criminals: White Collar Crime in Contemporary Society*, 4th edition (Belmont, CA: Wadworth, 2010).
[10] Lois Presser and Sveinung Sandberg (eds.), *Narrative Criminology: Understanding Stories of Crime* (New York, NY; London: New York University Press, 2015).

informed. They suggest recounting: collective stories about the effect of imprisonment on young people; stories about the value of preventive measures; and stories about alternative sentencing and rehabilitation. They also recommend the coining of fresh explanatory metaphors, for example referring to the justice system as a machine with multiple gears, only one of which – long-term prison sentencing – is generally used[11] and to prison as a "dead end."[12]

Ritchie explores the contrasting narratives and metaphors employed by communities (who have experienced major trauma) and the authorities. Here and elsewhere,[13] he highlights the extent to which members of a community in which violent crime is rife will frequently offer a more subtle and complex narrative than that offered by the authorities and the media. His observation is especially salient at a time when the most roiling issues of crime and justice involve interaction of police and African Americans neighborhoods and the much-disputed relationship between mass killings and terrorism. These issues seem to unavoidably generate opposing perspectives, each with attendant imagery and narratives. The simplifying battles between liberal news organizations and right-wing news media distort or avoid the available data relevant to these issues, and indeed even discourage the very collection of such data. Instead, the issues get debated by pundits and popular voices essentially playing caricature roles.[14]

Lithwick and Ritchie enter the debate about whether public attitudes to crime can be shaped by use of this or that single metaphor (including the disease metaphor examined in the preceding chapter). From the various essays in this volume, it may be argued that more important is the extent to which public attitudes to crime are embodied in distinctive clusters of metaphors. The present discussion has the advantage of treating metaphor in combination with narrative, and there can be little doubt that together they have a great influence on public thinking and policy. At the same time, Ritchie and others have offered some highly salutary cautions. Ritchie urges us to take account of the very uncertain scientific basis for our confidence that imagistic and narrative framing have a demonstrable effect on public attitudes. And even

---

[11] Kendall-Taylor, *Mazes and Gears*.
[12] Moira O'Neil, Nathaniel Kendall-Taylor, and Andrew Volmert, *New Narratives: Changing the Frame on Crime and Justice* (Washington, DC: Frameworks Institute, 2016).
[13] L. David Ritchie and Lynne Cameron, "Open hearts or smoke and mirrors: Metaphorical framing and frame conflicts in a public meeting," *Metaphor and Symbol*, 29 (2014), 204–223.
[14] See, for instance, Eric Bradner, "Factcheck: Grim statistics on race and police killings," CNN Politics (December 3, 2014): http://edition.cnn.com/2014/12/02/politics/kristoff-oreilly-police-shooting-numbers-fact-check/index.html.

so strong a promoter of narrative criminology as Sandberg reminds us of the great debate in ethnography as to the accuracy and advantages of direct interviews with narrators of personal experience, as opposed to more removed or generalized approaches. But Sandberg also offers optimism that eclectic reliance on narrative is important for reasons beyond simple positivist representation of fact: it helps us understand how crime and justice happen in a dynamic arena of frames and images and stories that reflect our values and our individual and group identities.[15]

[15] Sveinung Sandberg, "What can 'lies' tell us about life? Notes towards a framework of narrative criminology," *Journal of Justice Education*, 21 no. 4 (2010), 447–465.

10

Narrative Conventions in Crime Reporting

Dahlia Lithwick

Our anxiety over this case has not been due to the facts that are connected with this most unfortunate affair, but to the almost unheard of publicity it has received; to the fact that newspapers all over this country have been giving it space such as they have almost never before given to any case. The fact that day after day the people of Chicago have been regaled with stories of all sorts about it, until almost every person has formed an opinion. And when the public is interested and demands a punishment, no matter what the offense, great or small, it thinks of only one punishment, and that is death. It may not be a question that involves the taking of human life; it may be a question of pure prejudice alone; but when the public speaks as one man, it thinks only of killing.[1]

A newly invented metaphor assists thought by evoking a visual image, while on the other hand a metaphor which is technically "dead" (e.g. *iron resolution*) has in effect reverted to being an ordinary word and can generally be used without loss of vividness. But in between these two classes there is a huge dump of worn-out metaphors which have lost all evocative power and are merely used because they save people the trouble of inventing phrases for themselves.[2]

Without journalists and reporters, most stories about crimes and violence would be brief, isolated, and mostly local, events. It is journalism that takes the story of a crime and attempts to explain what's happened, and why it's happened, and what it says about us as a society. There is a reason that every century will witness dozens of violent criminal events that are later deemed the "crime of the century" by the media. It's not because any one is so spectacularly different or markedly violent. But each of them contains some magical formulation of glamour, horror, mystery, intimacy, and the more we in the media tell about that crime, the more these become the stories we tell about ourselves.

---

[1] Closing argument, delivered by Clarence Darrow, *The State of Illinois* v. *Nathan Leopold & Richard Loeb*, Chicago, Illinois, August 22, 1924.

[2] George Orwell, "Politics and the English language," *Horizon*, 13 no. 76, (1946), pp. 252–265.

I approach this topic not as a scholar in criminal justice, nor as an expert in narrative theory, but as a working journalist in the internet era, often tasked with covering what become iconic crime stories, whether it's the alleged rape cover-up at the University of Virginia, or the police shootings of unarmed Black men. These are stories that demand media coverage within moments of their occurrence, frequently before facts are fully known. Each purports to stand alone as a defining element of the society we have become: in America we turn a blind eye when privileged male athletes assault young women; in America we are unbothered when police officers shoot minorities in ambiguous circumstances. They are less crime stories than national myths. And more and more, the press creates those myths before the story is fully understood.

Why do so many crimes become little more than an entry on a police blotter, while others become national events, featuring wall-to-wall coverage of every twist and turn of the investigation, the charges, and gavel-to-gavel rubbernecking at the trial? The wealth or celebrity of the defendant (Kobe Bryant, O.J. Simpson, the Menendez brothers) explains part of it. But more often than not, a trial becomes yet another "trial of the century" (Scott Peterson, Casey Anthony, Louise Woodward, George Zimmerman) because of the stories they ultimately tell us about us.

We use metaphor and narrative to help us to locate crime in the context of who we are and what we are most afraid of. And it is invariably the press who select the metaphors and the stories and the journalists who create the frames through which these crime stories are understood. This chapter will attempt to survey the role played by journalists in the national discourse around crime, and the ways in which reporters opt to frame the narrative in major criminal cases. It will assess whether what we say in our reporting impacts the policy debates around crime, and whether we are doing a good job of talking about the law, or even about crime, as we translate these stories to the world.

Journalists play a singularly vital role in translating crime stories to the public. "The news media, in particular, provide an important forum in which private troubles are selectively gathered up, invested with broader meaning, and made available for public consumption."[3] How are we doing? In the absence of a compelling metaphor we can settle for this one: meh. We are, as a profession, extremely good at taking a breaking news story and cramming it into a familiar model. We are extremely good at capturing cable news for a few hours of earnest discussion about police brutality or campus sexual assault, or DNA exonerations. We pull out familiar tropes and language and tell familiar

---

[3] Victor F. Sacco, "Media constructions of crime," *Annals of the American Academy of the Political and Social Sciences*, 539 (1995), 141–154.

stories. If it turns out that later we missed some facts, or got something wrong, or elided the larger context, it's invariably ok: the news cycle has moved on.

WHAT CRIME STORIES DO WE CHOOSE TO REPORT?

Journalism has come a long way since the nineteenth century, when "yellow journalism" offered up the most lurid crime stories in the most sensational ways. But how much has journalism changed really? The rule of thumb most often attributed to today's broadcast media remains, "if it bleeds, it leads." As we will learn, print and internet journalism aren't much better.

It has long been understood that journalism selects its news stories not by a metric of importance or urgency, but based on a journalistic standard of newsworthiness, constructed according to internal institutional imperatives. This often has more to do with readership (and increasingly turns on advertising and branding) than it has to do with any editorial rule. We know that there is a fairly standard calculus for what makes a crime story newsworthy.[4] Multiple studies have shown that – at least in the last century – stories are newsworthy if they "appear to disrupt expectations [or are] deviant occurrences." We know that a crime story is far more likely to be reported based on "the level of predictability of the crime"; the readers' sense of how likely they are to be affected by a similar crime; if the crime has a sexual element; if either the offender or victim is a celebrity or high-status person; whether the crime occurred locally, the level of violence, the presence of spectacle or graphic imagery, and whether youth are involved.[5]

This tendency to report so disproportionately on the most unusual, sex-based, gruesome crimes, as opposed to the kinds of everyday property crimes most common in America, creates an effect communications experts have dubbed the "law of opposites," wherein "the characteristics of crime, criminals, and victims represented in the media are in most respects the polar opposite of the pattern suggested by official crime statistics or by crime and victim surveys."[6]

As Jessica Pollak and Charis Kubrin pointed out in reviewing the academic literature in 2007, "Official crime statistics indicate that most crime is non-violent, yet the news media suggests just the opposite, often creating the perception of an 'epidemic of random violence.'"[7] They add that "about

---

[4] Yvonne Jewkes, *Media and Crime* (Thousand Oaks, CA: Sage Publications, 2004).   [5] Ibid.
[6] Jessica M. Pollak and Charis E. Kubrin, "Crime in the news: How crime, offenders and victims are portrayed in the media," *Journal of Criminal Justice and Popular Culture*, 14:1 (2007), 59–83.
[7] Ibid.

two-thirds of crime news stories are primarily about violent or sex offenses, but these account for less than ten percent of crimes recorded by the police." A study by Sheley and Ashkins (1981) found that a St. Louis newspaper gave "crimes against the person" thirty-five times more attention than property crimes and murder ninety times more coverage than other major offenses. At the same time, attention to property crimes in the news has declined "unless they involve celebrities or some highly quirky features," yet property offenses constitute over 90 percent of crimes recorded by the police." They add that the media also have an unnatural and disproportionate fascination with youth offenders: "Relatively few youth are arrested each year for violent crimes, yet the message from the news is that this is a common occurrence. One analysis examining 840 newspaper reports and 109 news segments documented that 40 percent of all newspaper articles on children were about violence, as were 48 percent of television news stories."[8] Needless to say the media are similarly preoccupied with telling crime stories when the criminals are minorities and the victims are white.[9] A 2014 study showed that 37% of the suspects portrayed on television news stories about crime in Los Angeles were black, although blacks made up only 21% of those arrested in the city.[10] Another study found that whites represented 43% of homicide victims in the local news, but only 13% of homicide victims in crime reports.[11]

Summarizing the metastudies, Pollak and Kubrin find that "Overall, the studies taken together indicate that depictions of crime in the news are not reflective of either the rate of crime generally, the proportion of crime which is violent, the proportion of crime committed by people of color, or the proportion of crime committed by youth."[12]

This may be the most telling aspect of the pathology of daily news reporters: we are not interested in white collar crime stories because our readers are not interested in white collar crime stories, because white collar crime is inherently less interesting than rape, robbery and murder. We in the media all-but ignored the Savings and Loan crisis but turn every violent crime that features a minority perpetrator into a national parable about who and what we are. The fact that who and what we are as Americans was amply reflected in the S & L crisis is never considered.

---

[8] Joseph F. Sheley and C.D. Ashkins, "Crime, news, and crime views," *Public Opinion Quarterly*, 45 (1981), 492–506.
[9] Pollak and Kubrin, "Crime in the news."
[10] Richard Prince, "How media have shaped our perception of race and crime,' *The Root* (September 4. 2014). www.theroot.com/blogs/journalisms/2014/09/how_media_have_shaped_our_perception_of_race_and_crime.html.
[11] Ibid. [12] Pollak and Kubrin, "Crime in the news," 63.

There is perhaps no better evidence of the massive rise in American interest in the tick-tock of true crime reporting, than the success of such podcasts as *Serial* (2015), which have invited listeners to relitigate the tiniest details of seemingly mundane cases. In more than one instance, these shows and the public outcry that ensued have resulted in authorities being forced to reopen cases that had been deemed resolved. We as a society are as obsessed with crime as we have ever been. It's just the medium that has changed.

WHAT METAPHORS DO WE USE FOR CRIME REPORTING?

Having established that not all crime stories are created equal and that the media frequently opt to tell stories about outlier events and exotic people, the question is: What types of metaphors they use to affix meaning to these tales? As a journalist, I am at a definitional loss on this front. We can fight all day about what a metaphor is, but perhaps it will suffice to quote Aristotle, who said that a metaphor "consists in giving the thing a name that belongs to something else."

We use metaphors to help us understand that which is inexplicable. Prominent metaphor scholars such as the pathbreaking George Lakoff have argued that metaphors are central to how we reason and make sense of the world around us, and that indeed, metaphors become conceptual frames in policy areas – especially in talking about crime – that go on to influence developments in the policy areas themselves.[13] The study of metaphor and how it constructs our reality has exploded since the time of Lakoff's early work. Wayne Booth once sarcastically calculated that by the year 2039 "there will be more students of metaphor than people."

Why are journalists so apt to use metaphor when we try to explain crime? Perhaps, because crime, especially violent and deviant crime makes us so incredibly uncomfortable. In explaining crime, reporters often turn to metaphor to help us understand (or perhaps more perniciously, to help convey) the fundamentally terrifying notion, that we are all at the mercy of violent and dangerous people who may strike at any time. One prominent study about the relationship between crime and metaphor was conducted in 2011 by two Stanford psychologists, psychology Assistant Professor Lera Boroditsky and doctoral candidate Paul Thibodeau, published in the February 23 edition of *PLoS ONE*.[14] The two researchers wanted to understand the role of metaphor

---

[13] George Lakoff, *Moral Politics: How Liberals and Conservatives Think* (Third edition, Chicago, IL: University of Chicago Press, 2016).
[14] Paul Thibodeau and Lera Boroditsky, "Metaphors we think by: The role of metaphor in reasoning." 6 no. 2 (2011): e16782.

in framing policy discussions of crime and to understand whether metaphor can alter our policy preferences.

The two hypothesized that public discourse about crime is "saturated with metaphor," and that the metaphors we use will inflect upon the policy values we support. As Thibodeau, the study's lead author noted in a subsequent interview, "some estimates suggest that one out of every 25 words we encounter is a metaphor."[15]

What sorts of metaphors do we use when talking about crime? In reviewing the literature the authors observed that we tend to talk about increases in the prevalence of crime as "crime waves, surges or sprees." A spreading crime problem in a region is frequently described as a "crime epidemic," which may be "plaguing a city or infecting a community." They further noted that criminals are most often depicted as wild animals who "prey on unsuspecting victims." And criminal investigations may frequently be spun as police "hunts where criminals are tracked and caught."[16]

We could not practice journalism without such metaphors. As business columnist Peter Coy wrote in a 2013 article for Nieman Reports,[17] entitled "Staggering drunks and fiscal cliffs: How Bloomberg Businessweek uses metaphors in the news," for a journalist, "trying to communicate without using any metaphors would be like trying to complete a paint-by-numbers canvas without red, blue, yellow and green." In my own work reporting on crime, I often use metaphor, sometimes to invoke familiar themes or scripts, and sometimes to tamp down some of my own horror, with tropes that feel familiar. When we write about campus rape – whether it is the famous Duke lacrosse scandal or the UVA story published in 2015 in *Rolling Stone*, the temptation to dip into the rich well of metaphor available to describe pampered Southern athletes is almost unavoidable. We turn again and again to old tropes surrounding sex, race, and violence in America, choosing to describe these events in terms of plantations, predators, and privilege. It's a way of shorthanding for our readers a set of stereotypes they find familiar; of telling them that we are recounting a social formulation they already know and understand.

Metaphors are rife in our system of criminal justice, and in our corresponding reporting about it. We famously fight "wars" on crime, we passionately

---

[15] "Is crime a virus or a beast? When describing crime, Stanford study shows the word you pick can frame the debate on how to fight it." http://news.stanford.edu/news/2011/february/metaphors-crime-study-022311.html.

[16] Thibodeau and Boroditsky, "Metaphors we think by."

[17] Peter Coy "Staggering drunks and fiscal cliffs: How *Bloomberg Businessweek* uses metaphors in the news." http://niemanreports.org/articles/staggering-drunks-and-fiscal-cliffs-how-bloomberg-businessweek-uses-metaphors-in-the-news/.

believe that Justice is "blind." Most commonly, criminals are animals, beasts, monsters. Sexual offenders are predators. Victims are, in the parlance of some researchers, "china dolls."

There is a long history of using the metaphor of monsters to describe violent criminals. In nineteenth-century English prose accounts of crime, rogue pamphlets – the precursor to modern newspapers – offered lurid accounts of crime that catered to readers' fascination with the details of violent incidents. The preferred metaphors of the era, as manifest in these rogue pamphlets, were almost unvarying low animal metaphors. According to researcher Greta Olson, the favored tropes for criminals at the time were "predatory caterpillars, vermin-like birds, parasitical lice, vipers, wandering dogs and licentious pigs."[18] She notes that the tropes used by the pamphleteers would promptly leach into the ways lawyers talked about the defendants at trial, as well as into the laws crafted to address crime at that time.

Why the preoccupation with monsters in nineteenth-century metaphors about criminals? In their 2013 book, *Monstrous Crimes and the Failure of Forensic Psychiatry*, John Douard and Pamela D. Schultz, probe the use of the monster or predator – usually to describe a sexual predator, drug dealer in areas frequented by children, or psychopathic murderer – tracing it back to the nineteenth-century popular obsession with monsters. They argue that the "monster" metaphor has been used to scapegoat certain categories of criminals "for anxieties about our own potential for deviant, and, indeed, dangerous interests."[19] Unlike the metaphors that pervade sports journalism or even political journalism, the media seize upon metaphors that help us think through whether the lone gunman at a school shooting, the child molester, the rapist-murderer is someone like us, or someone so aberrant that he is nothing like us. The critique of so much of the metaphor deployed in crime reporting is, unsurprisingly, that most of it serves to offer up simplistic "us/them" narratives that help us feel both safer, and also psychologically completely differentiated from the criminals that fascinate us. The function of so many of the metaphors that liken crime to disease, or ravening beast, or invader, is to hive off the perpetrator from the rest of us; to reassure ourselves that only deviants and outliers commit crimes and that we can contain them with relative ease. The questions that lurk underneath these metaphors (Who does something like this? Could I do something like this?) are the stuff that would have made Freud weep.

---

[18] Greta Olson, *Criminals as Animals from Shakespeare to Lombroso* (Amsterdam: De Gruyter, 2014).

[19] John Douard and Pamela D. Schultz, *Monstrous Crimes and the Failure of Forensic Psychiatry* (Dordrecht, Heidelberg, New York, NY; London: Springer, 2013).

Perhaps that duality helps explain why the metaphors we deploy for crime victims are as extreme as those we use for the bad guys. Jonathan Simon (2001) points out that perhaps the most compelling modern metaphors are reserved for crime victims, who are idealized and lionized by the policymakers and the media so as to make it easier to declare war on criminals. With respect to the political actors, Simon cites the following remarks made by the then Attorney General Janet Reno in 1997: "I draw most of my strength from victims for they represent America to me: people who will not be put down, people who will not be defeated, people who will rise again and again for what is right ... you are my heroes and heroines. You are but little lower than the angels."[20] But our preoccupation in the media with child victims, from JonBenet Ramsay to the child victims at Columbine, is a way of signaling that the monsters who commit these bad acts are unworthy of the designation, human.

Simon also notes that the metaphor of the "war on crime" – often attributed to Nixon – was in fact a product of the Lyndon Johnson era. In March 1967, signing the Safe Streets Act, he described law enforcement as "the men who wage war on crime day after day."[21] The other metaphors Johnson employed in signing his 1967 crime legislation were those of crime as a stain and crime as a shadow: "I believe this measure, despite its shortcomings, will help to lift the stain of crime and the shadow of fear – from the streets of our communities."[22] Simon theorizes that both the language of stains and shadows created subtle signals both about race and "otherness" that have lingered in our national discourse until today.

What was the net effect of the "war" metaphor as affixed to the fact of crime? Simon theorizes that the costs of this metaphorical framing vastly outweighed the benefits: "The war on crime from as early as the 1968 Safe Streets Act was visibly a war on criminals – those easily mistaken by the police for criminals ... The war on crime and drugs has made the police and the prison system the dominant model of winning."[23]

The same can be said about the metaphors we attach to terrorists. By framing terrorism as a "war," we have set ourselves up for failure. A British study done in 2012 by Alexander Spencer[24] considers the metaphors used to describe terrorism in British tabloid newspapers, and draws out the four metaphors that predominate: terrorism as a "war," a "crime," "uncivilized

---

[20] Jonathan Simon, "Governing through crime metaphors," *Brooklyn Law Review*, 67 (2001), 1035–1070, 1042 Available at: http://scholarship.law.berkeley.edu/facpubs/1342.
[21] Simon, "Governing through crime metaphors," 1053.   [22] Ibid., 1056
[23] Simon, "Governing through crime metaphors," 1065.
[24] Alexander Spencer, "The social construction of terrorism: Media, metaphor and policy implications," *Journal of International Relations and Development*, 15 no. 3 (2012), 393–419 is available online at: http://www.palgravejournals.com/jird/journal/v15/n3/pdf/jird20124a.pdf.

evil," and as a "disease." The use of these metaphors by the papers, says Spencer, makes some policy response options appear more appropriate than others. For example, he posits that understanding terrorism as a war calls for a military reaction, while the constitution of it as a "crime" signals the need for a judicial response. Metaphors that frame terrorists as "uncivilized," "evil" suggest "the tightening of borders and immigration to keep the foreign 'other' out, while the concepts of 'evil' and 'disease' indicate the impossibility of engagement and negotiations with terrorists."

Another fascinating study conducted by Theresa Catalano and Linda R. Waugh looks at the differences in metaphors and metonymy used by the media to depict crimes committed by white collar defendants and Latino immigrants.[25] The authors studied reports on crime between the years 2004 and 2011, comparing reports of corporate crimes to reports of crimes committed by Latinos. They confirm that nearly all publicity about corporate law violations is found in the *business section* of newspapers; that stories about white collar crimes contain fewer quotes from police officers and more from legal people familiar with the sector (such as the Securities and Exchange Commission [SEC]) or lawyers of the defendants. Even though newspapers tend to focus on the worst corporate crimes, their results show "a positive portrayal of CEO's/ corporate criminals convicted or accused of crimes such as fraud." They cite press accounts that characterize Goldman Sachs, for instance, as a "whipping boy" or refer chattily to "Frannie and Freddie" in the white-collar context, and contrast it to references to Latino defendants as "illegals" assaulting "young innocent girls."[26]

Catalano and Waugh conclude that again, these metaphors serve to separate "us" from "them," and that only the powerful get to control the "us" metaphors: "By having access to the media, people in power (such as CEOs, their lawyers, and law enforcement officers) present a positive 'us,' and in many of our examples, replace the discourse of crime with the language of a tragedy or accident. This in turn helps the reader to view the event in a noncriminal way, and allows CEOs and corporate criminals to be seen as unfortunate victims of nature or circumstance. The way these social actors are portrayed plays a large role in how the reader perceives these groups as a whole and the kinds of consequences that result (e.g. prison sentences they serve, government policies that are or are not put in place). Thus, as we know

[25] Theresa Catalano and Linda R. Waugh, "The ideologies behind newspaper crime reports of Latinos and Wall Street/CEOs: A critical analysis of metonymy in text and image," *Critical Discourse Studies*, 10 no. 4 (2013), 406–426. http://digitalcommons.unl.edu/teachlearnfacpub/140.
[26] Ibid.

from various discussions around immigration, in the case of Latino crimes, the negative portrayal of Latinos in crime reports has been used as a rationale for unjust immigration laws and policies."[27] Perhaps unsurprisingly then, "media systems tend to privilege the ideological perspective of the powerful – in particular those of the holders of state power, exponents of establishment politics, and representatives of major capitalist economic interests."[28]

Why Do the Media Report Crime in the Way They Do?

We have suggested earlier that there are tangible benefits to the media from reporting on crime in the sensational ways that they do. Sara Sun Beale[29] points out that the market itself and economic incentives have led to the tendency to overcover the most sensational crimes, because it is cheap and drives traffic to do so. As she explains of local television news:

> This trend results in virtually all channels devoting a disproportionate part of their broadcast to violent crimes, and to many channels adopting a fast-paced, high-crime strategy based on an entertainment model. In the case of network news, this strategy results in much greater coverage of crime, especially murder, with a heavy emphasis on long-running, tabloid-style treatment of selected cases in both the evening news and newsmagazines. Newspapers also reflect a market-driven reshaping of style and content, accompanied by massive staff cuts, resulting in a continued emphasis on crime stories as a cost-effective means to grab readers' attention. These economic and marketing considerations shape the public's exposure to crime in the news media.[30]

This is not a new phenomenon, by the way. As Beale points out, in his 1931 autobiography, celebrated New York muckraker Lincoln Steffens "described typical 'crime waves' that wash over cities and nearly drown the public and the authorities who feel they must explain and cure these extraordinary outbreaks of lawlessness with more law, more arrests, swifter trials, and harsher penalties." As Beale further notes, Steffens famously bragged that he could help generate these waves: "I enjoy crime waves. I made one once."[31]

Television tends to play on emotions over ideas. And no emotion is more motivating than fear. As with regards to emotion, newspapers focus on ideas

---

[27] Ibid.
[28] Paul Schlesinger and Howard Tumber, *Reporting Crime: The Media Politics of Criminal Justice* (Oxford: Clarendon Press; New York, NY: Oxford University Press, 1994), p. 7.
[29] Sara Sun Beale "The news media's influence on criminal justice policy: How market-driven news promotes punitiveness," *William and Mary Law Review*, 48 no. 2 (2006), 397–481. http://scholarship.law.wm.edu/cgi/viewcontent.cgi?article=1103&context=wmlr.
[30] Beale, "The news media's influence on criminal justice policy," 401.   [31] Ibid., 422.

whereas television emphasizes "feeling, appearance, mood... there is a retreat from distant analysis and a dive into emotional and sensory involvement."[32] Also the rare commodity in print is space, whereas in journalism it's time.

We also know that the networks don't only cover aberrant and lurid crime; they also benefit from the subtle suggestion that crime rates are on the rise, even when they are not. Indeed despite the falling crime rates in the last decades, the networks dramatically *increased* the coverage of crime in their dinner-hour newscasts in the 1990s. According to one study, "although they comprise less than two tenths of 1% of all arrests, murders account for between 27% and 29% of all crimes reported on the evening news. Other kinds of illegalities, such as corporate and state crime, tend to be either reported as 'business news' or ignored in favor of violent 'street crime.'"[33]

According to Beale, in 1990 and 1991, the three major networks aired an average of 557 crime stories per year in their evening newscasts. For the rest of the 90s the three networks aired an average of 1,613 such stories per year.[34] As Beale summarizes the data, the true-crime TV phenomenon of the mid-1990s came to overshadow TV network coverage of "real" news including politics and policy: "A snapshot analysis of the programming schedules of three nightly newscasts when a tabloid case was covered revealed that CBS spent 46% of its broadcast on the tabloid crime, and NBC and ABC spent 45% and 31%, respectively." [35] Between 1990 and 1999, the major networks (ABC, NBC, and CBS) devoted more coverage to crime than any other topic on their nightly national newscasts. On local television news, crime consumed 30% of all news time, displacing coverage of other pressing issues. In comparison to crime, topics such as government (11%), health (7%), education (4%), and poverty (2%) received far less attention.[36]

Also, we have seen a proliferation of cable and network shows about spectacular and minor crimes and trials, ranging from 20/20 to *America's Most Wanted* to *Cops*, to cable news shows specifically tracking murders and sexual assaults. Other forms of media follow close behind. According to one content analysis of six print and three broadcast media organizations, "print media present nine crime stories a day, on average, and electronic media four crime stories per day."[37]

Why does real-time, true-crime reporting make so much sense for the media? Because, as my first editor Jack Shafer, once observed, there is nothing

[32] Pollak and Kubrin, "Crime in the news," 65.
[33] Katherine Beckett and Theodore Sasson, "Crime in the media," www.publiceye.org/defendingjustice/overview/beckett_media.html.
[34] Beale, "The news media's influence on criminal justice policy," 423.   [35] Ibid., 423.
[36] Beckett and Sasson, "Crime in the media."   [37] Pollak and Kubrin, "Crime in the news."

cheaper than setting up a cable truck outside a courthouse and paying a reporter to summarize the court proceedings day after day after day. Advertisers love it. Viewers adore it. And, as Susan Bandes has observed, media coverage of violent crime stories can be dramatic, operatic, emotional, and visceral, using repeated images of the crime itself. None of these are hallmarks of the legal process, and rarely do these shows take the time to distinguish – much less explain – the two systems for the viewer.[38]

Moreover, as Katherine Beckett and Theodore Sasson have noted, "crime-related news stories provide detailed accounts of individual criminal events. Comparatively little attention is paid to broader trends in crime, and few stories attempt to put the crime problem in a larger perspective."[39] Reporters rarely step back and tell broader stories than the breathless tale before them. And because newspapers and online magazines are also a business, and their product is created solely to sell advertising, it's hardly a surprise to learn that covering crime in spectacular ways becomes as smart a business move in print as it is in broadcast.

Speaking as a daily journalist I would add only that the news cycle is ever shorter, and that the time needed to fully understand and contextualize a crime story is a luxury afforded to almost none of us. The more we are pressed for time and the more our audiences hunger for breaking crime news, the more likely we are to reach for old metaphors and known tropes on which to hang our stories. More and more the metaphors select the news stories, and not vice versa. We are helping create a feedback loop because there is no time to build a more complicated structure.

DO THE MEDIA INFLUENCE PUBLIC THINKING ABOUT CRIME?

In a time of declining civics education, Americans receive a tremendous proportion of their information about the criminal justice system and the law and constitution from the media. In an American Bar Association survey of 1999 asking respondents to identify "extremely or very important" sources of information on the criminal justice system, 41% of respondents identified television news, 37% identified primetime newsmagazines, and 36% identified local newspapers.[40] Over 75% of the public say they form their opinions about

---

[38] Susan Bandes, "Fear factor: The role of media in covering and shaping the death penalty," *Ohio State Journal of Criminal Law*, 1 no. 2 (2004), 585–597.
[39] Beckett and Sasson, "Crime in the media."
[40] American Bar Association, *Perceptions of the US Justice System* (1999), pp. 94–95 (1999), available at www.abanet.org/media/perception/perceptions.pdf.

crime from what they see on TV or read in the news. That is over three times the number who say they get their primary information on crime from personal experience (22%).[41]

As Beale reports, the effect of the media in shaping public opinion about crime and criminal justice policies is indisputable. "More than 350 empirical studies conducted worldwide support the media's power to set the public's agenda."[42] Moreover, "the influence of media coverage of tabloid crime cases has been found to affect public confidence in the criminal justice system." Researchers have found that respondents primed with reminders of high-profile cases, such as the O.J. Simpson trial or the JonBenet Ramsey murder investigation, expressed lower levels of confidence in the criminal justice system as a whole; and less confidence in individual actors within the system.[43]

One of my long-standing complaints about US broadcast journalism, is that more often than not, coverage of the "law" is limited to coverage of crimes alone. There is very little media attention paid to the law – outside a handful of high profile Supreme Court cases. And that means that what most of the public learns about criminal law happens as a pundit stands at or near a crime scene, speculating about the many things nobody yet knows. Because most of our reporting about spectacularly gruesome and violent crime happens in this fashion, the consumers of news rarely learn about the difference between an arraignment and an indictment, or presumptions of innocence, or what "beyond a reasonable doubt" may mean. There is a widespread assumption in the media that listeners simply know all these things, but in my experience they do not. This raises the question: If most Americans learn most of their law from the media, do they also absorb most of the legal framing they are fed there?

In the seminal study published in 2011 by Stanford's Lera Boroditsky and Paul Thibodeau the question for the authors was simple: Do the metaphors we in the media use when we write about crime influence and inform public opinion?[44] Their findings revealed that the metaphors we choose absolutely impact our policy views. In five related experiments, the subjects' proposed solutions to hypothetical crime problems differed depending on the metaphors to which they were exposed. Participants received two versions of a text about crime in the hypothetical US city of Addison, one opening with the sentence "Crime is a wild beast preying on the city of Addison" while the other

[41] Pollak and Kubrin, "Crime in the news."
[42] Beale, "The news media's influence on criminal justice policy," 445.   [43] Ibid., 446.
[44] Paul Thibodeau, "Is crime a virus or a beast? When describing crime, Stanford study shows the word you pick can frame the debate on how to fight it." http://news.stanford.edu/news/2011/february/metaphors-crime-study-022311.html.

started with "Crime is a virus infecting the city of Addison." Participants were then asked a series of open-ended questions about the policy measures necessary to reduce crime in Addison.

The subjects' responses showed that they generally favored get-tough enforcement measures, but more so when they had seen the "beast" frame than when they had seen the "virus" frame. For instance, 71% of the subjects called for more enforcement in response to: the "beast" metaphor, whereas only 54% did so when crime was described as "a virus." This led Thibodeau and Boroditsky to conclude that the metaphorical frame influences reasoning about a crime problem and its solutions. Subjects who read the text that likened criminals to wild animals ("packs" of youths "preying" on people) tended to favor crime solutions that would deter actual animals ("lock 'em up"). Those who heard "virus" metaphors came up with medical solutions ("clean up our communities"). The authors in fact concluded that the choice of metaphor influenced the subjects even more than their political affiliation.

Perhaps most important, the study revealed that metaphors can matter even when the metaphor itself is forgotten. In a follow-on to the study, the researchers tested the role of "metaphor awareness" in shaping opinions. Postexposure the subjects were asked whether they could remember the framing word ("beast" or "virus") used in their experiment. Since very few subjects could even remember the framing metaphor, Thibodeau and Boroditsky concluded that metaphors covertly influence reasoning. Consumers of news accept the assumptions beneath metaphoric framing, without even knowing there were metaphors at play.

Researchers at Columbia University's Journalism School also studied the ways in which media framing of crime stories affects reader values. In a 2002 study involving 89 college students comparing a public health framing of crime coverage to the more typical episodic framing of crime stories, readers of the public health frame placed more responsibility on society's role/social conditions in crime and violence problems.[45] The study involving 129 college students also compared public health framing to traditional framing, with findings suggesting that reading stories featuring the public health frame was related to decreased blame and criticism directed toward individuals within a story, and greater support for preventive measures before resorting to punitive measures at a societal level. Incidentally, readers of the public health frame also showed greater factual knowledge than readers of a traditionally framed story.[46] Distressingly, the study also found that "Despite potential gains in

---

[45] Sara Tiegreen and Elana Newman, "The effect of news frames." http://dartcenter.org/content/effect-news-frames.

[46] Ibid.

knowledge acquisition and positive perceptions, readers may prefer traditionally written stories that lack such contextual information. In this study readers expressed less interest in public health news stories compared to traditional stories.[47]

Does print really differ from broadcast? In a paper already referred to, the authors compare how television news and newspapers "tell" the same crime stories across these platforms. For this study they collected crime stories from the *Washington Post* and the 11 o'clock local television news from the Washington, DC. ABC affiliate, over a period of several weeks in 2005. They coded stories that appeared in both, and their conclusions support the theory that television tends to present the same news in far more emotional, sensational ways. Among their other observations: "According to our findings, for a crime to be covered in the news, it typically had to be violent in nature; nearly 85 percent of the crimes included in our sample were violent."[48]

They noticed that now familiar themes that emerged in both media included "the portrayal of juvenile offenses as senseless and irrational, the linking of discrete crimes by youth for the purpose of creating a 'juvenile crime wave,' the characterization of juvenile victims as innocent, and a strong emphasis on safety and security following crimes involving youth." Nevertheless, the television reports actively attempted to evoke strong emotional responses: The authors concluded that

> by playing on the viewer's emotions, television reports attempt to instill a sense of fear in consumers and underscore the lack of safety and security. They accomplished this through carefully crafted words and phrases used by the news anchors, statements from witnesses and public officials, and live footage direct from the scene. Whether the crime was a murder, a sexual assault, or a kidnapping, the television news almost always managed to present the story with an additional layer of alarm. This same level of fear was not created in the newspaper reports. Without visuals, witness statements, etc., newspapers are not likely to instill the same sense of fear in readers. [49]

So there we have it. The media, and particularly the broadcast media, are frightening their consumers, misinforming them as to the law, misleading them about risks to their own personal safety, and helping promote certain predetermined policy outcomes with subtle use of framing and metaphor. And we are doing this in the interest of entertainment, advertising, and branding. The remaining question is what journalists might do to counteract these dismaying trends.

[47] Ibid.   [48] Pollak and Kubrin, "Crime in the news," 78.   [49] Ibid.

WHAT MIGHT THE MEDIA DO TO IMPROVE THE STATUS QUO AND WILL METAPHOR HELP?

Donald Schön has argued that when a particular metaphor or cluster of metaphors is deployed to describe a specific social issue, policymakers are apt to respond with solutions which derive from that original metaphor.[50] That is why it is so critical, as Lakoff argues, that creating a frame for complicated political systems, lies in finding the correct metaphors. His own suggestion was to deploy the same metaphors the experts themselves use. He argued the trick lay in figuring out how to distinguish useful frames from the overly simplistic ones.

On the one hand, journalists have a responsibility to translate complex policy. In a 2011 interview, Lakoff said that, "if you have a policy that people don't understand, you're going to lose. What's the point of trying to get support for a major health care reform if no one understands it?"[51] But on the other hand, if we simply repurpose the moral or policy framing of the policymakers we are neither explaining nor questioning their underlying assumptions.

George Orwell argued that lazy journalism consists of repurposing accepted metaphors, which means just passing along the accepted worldview of the time. Orwell warns all journalists: "never use a metaphor, simile, or other figure of speech which you are used to seeing in print."[52] It seems like benign laziness but it reifies certain ideas that need to be thought through very carefully. The risks of allowing a metaphor to pave the way, inexorably, toward a new, more reductive reality are real.

Indeed criminal justice analyst George L. Kelling argues persuasively that the "criminal justice system" itself is a metaphor that disserves the very interests of the system itself. In a 1991 article, he contends that "the system is not a fact but a phrase, a metaphor that attempts to capture the complex and problematic interactions between criminals and police, courts, corrections, and other crime-control agencies."[53] Kelling went on to argue that the metaphor itself all but killed what was best and most effective about community policing: "Transformed into the front end of a system, [the police] were

---

[50] Donald Schön, "'Generative metaphor: A perspective on problem-setting in social policy, in A. Ortony (ed.), *Metaphor and Thought*, 2nd edition (Cambridge and New York: Cambridge University Press, 1993), pp. 137–163.

[51] George Lakoff, American cognitive linguist and professor of linguistics at the University of California, Berkeley, interviewed by Lois Beckett January 31, 2011. http://timtyson.us/word press/wp-content/uploads/2011/pdfs/Explain-Yourself-George-Lakoff.pdf.

[52] Orwell, "Politics and the English language."

[53] George Kelling, "Crime and metaphor: Toward a new concept of policing," *City Journal* 1. www.city-journal.org/story.php?id=1577.

liberated from acting as a city agency, responsible for a broad array of services or for actually solving problems on their own. Instead, their main job was to introduce offenders into a system by arrest, after which they were somebody else's problem. The quantity and quality of arrests became the dominant means of evaluating departments and officers. The score could always be counted at the end of the day."

Kelling's specific complaint lies in the case of a serial rapist attacking eleven girls that was processed by law enforcement over a 15-month period. While conducting their investigation, the police declined to release information that could have been used to prevent future attacks in order to be more likely to trap the offender. In his view the media were also at fault for reporting on the case by using metaphors to frame the offender, victims, and the "hunting" process. He concluded the system itself produced more harm to the victims; that the victims were not only harmed by the rapist, but also by the metaphor. In short, we need to be asking ourselves whether these metaphors that are so entrenched that they become actual things – the "criminal justice system" or the "war on crime" are working toward undermining the very goals they are intended to describe.

Lakoff's prescription for journalists using metaphor is straightforward: he argues that journalists need to restore the real context of policy by trying "to get people in the government and policymakers in the think tanks to understand and talk about what the moral basis of their policy is, and to do this in terms that are understandable."[54] In other words, it seems to me, if metaphors are as powerful drivers of policy and law as the studies suggest, can we as journalists better educate readers by both unpacking the moral underpinning of the metaphors we are handed by our leadership and by using different and more accurate metaphors to sketch out the other side of the story? Instead of falling myopically into the trap of labeling terrorists "animals" or sexual offenders "monsters," we can use our critical abilities to smoke out the agenda behind the creation of these metaphors in the first instance. If the theorists are correct that it takes little more than reimagining crime as a "virus" – it may not be impossible for journalists to help recalibrate the emphasis on capture and excessive punishment that pervades our criminal justice systems.

Peter Coy suggests a similar project: "Readers come to our stories with something in their heads – a mental construct, a way of seeing the world. If I don't manage to dislodge that mental construct by offering what I think is a better one, then all the statistics and charts and authorities that I throw at the reader will slide off like hot butter on Teflon."[55] Our job as journalists is to

[54] Lakoff, "Explain yourself, George Lakoff." [55] Coy, "Staggering drunks."

probe the tedious metaphors we have used about "thugs" and "monsters" as well as to push back on the facile images of victims as china dolls and angels. This language may well obscure far more truths than it reveals. And then we need to create new mental constructs – absent the judgments in the preexisting metaphors – and help our readers think through their policy preferences in an original way. This is not so much a prescription for the journalist as advocate, as it is a *cri de coeur* for the journalist as something more than a sensationalist stenographer. As I write this paragraph, I am well aware that as journalists we have less time, fewer resources, close to no formal editing, and a mounting pressure to feed the beast that is our readership and advertisers what it already knows and wants. I am as guilty as any journalist I know of getting crime stories wrong on the first take, simply because there are no time or resources for getting them right. This is the reality in which we operate, but it is also the problem in a national conversation around crime that assumes violent crime rates are on the rise when they are not.

We have a responsibility when we report on crime to place it in within a context and locate it in the larger trends. The truth is undisputed: violent crime rates are going down. So what benefit is there to report on "sprees" and "waves?" Terrorism isn't an army, so why accept the loaded rhetoric of a "war" on it. Americans are woefully, painfully unaware of how trials happen and what a jury does. So why do we report on trials as if they were sporting events? Cops, prosecutors, judges, and juries are bound by rules of law; so why inflame passions such that the public believes that "justice" is synonymous with "feels right to me?" Trials are not a reality show. The truth is, they aren't even reality. They are a cultural artifice that attempts to approximate "justice" and does so with greater or lesser degrees of success, depending largely on how well informed and sophisticated the populace really is.

Americans consume more media than ever before and somehow they know less about civics than ever. The news media bear a tremendous responsibility for helping to reverse this trend, and one way we can do that is by revisiting the tired old tropes and metaphors around crime that have existed for decades, and replacing them with fresher and more accurate models upon which to build our policy.

11

Metaphors, Stories, and Media Framing of Crime: Response to Lithwick

L. David Ritchie

As Lithwick points out in her excellent paper, the media representation of law and crime, both in general and with respect to specific crimes, has a powerful effect on how the public understands these topics and on public opinion about related policies. The media's use of narrative and metaphors is a central part of that framing. Framing is itself a rather ambiguous word; it has been used by various authors in several ways, most of which fit, in one way or another, the general topic of how media represent crime and law enforcement.

Gamson[1] showed that journalists present issues within *story frames* that reflect journalistic news values, which in turn represent widely accepted ideas about what kind of story will induce customers to buy and read print news, tune in to electronic news, and attend to the sponsors' ads. Musolff[2] showed that media within a particular discourse community draw on a common set of story *scenarios*, often based on one or a combination of conceptual metaphors, to present stories about a particular issue within a coherent overall narrative. For example, he found that coverage of the European Union in British and German newspapers is often organized around metaphors based on LOVE, COURTSHIP, MARRIAGE, AND FAMILY.

Iyengar[3] distinguished between *episodic* and *thematic* frames, arguing that news media prefer to frame crime stories as *episodes*, for example by focusing on particular crimes and confrontations between police officers and civilians and deemphasizing *thematic* issues such as economic and social factors that exacerbate criminal activity and institutional policies and procedures that may

---

[1] William Gamson, *Talking Politics* (Cambridge, UK; New York, NY: Cambridge University Press, 1992).
[2] Andreas Musolff, "Metaphor scenarios in public discourse," *Metaphor and Symbol*, 21 (2006), 23–38.
[3] Shanto Iyengar, *Is Anyone Responsible? How Television Frames Political Issues* (Chicago, IL: University of Chicago Press, 1991).

contribute to patterns of police and prosecutorial behavior that in turn exacerbate police-civilian confrontations. Price, Tewksbury, and Powers[4] examined media framing of issues in terms of relevant *values* such as human interest vs. financial impact and demonstrated that the values implied by language in a headline can strongly influence what readers attend to and recall as well as their subsequent opinions about the topic. The effects of media framing of issues on audience opinions, beliefs, and responses has been well established (see e.g. Pan and Kosicki).[5] Taking a different approach to the topic, Tracy[6] showed that frame conflicts, when interlocutors frame a social interaction in divergent or contradictory ways, can lead to miscommunication and in the extreme to total failure of a communicative interaction.

Combining these approaches, Ritchie and Cameron[7] examined the transcripts of a public meeting about a controversial incident in which police officers killed an unarmed civilian, Kendra James. They found that members and representatives of the community and of the police and city government framed the issue itself as well as the nature of the meeting in contradictory ways. Community members and representatives preferred a *thematic* frame, focusing on this particular incident as part of a pattern of excessive use of force by the police. City and police officials preferred an *episodic* frame, treating Ms. James's death as a unique and "tragic incident." Community members and representatives framed the meeting itself in terms of an *inquest*, in which public officials would address the community's concerns about the overall pattern of police behavior as well as explaining why the officers involved in this particular shooting had not been indicted or held accountable for apparent violations of established procedures and framed the relationship between city officials and the community as one of conflict and accountability. City and police officials framed the meeting as an opportunity to strengthen the city's "community policing initiative," and characterized the relationship between city officials and the community as one of collaboration and amity. Ritchie and Cameron argue that these contradictory frames led to mutual misunderstanding and the total failure of the meeting to satisfy the objectives of either the city officials or the

---

[4] Vincent Price, David Tewksbury, and Elizabeth Powers, "Switching trains of thought: The impact of news frames on readers' cognitive responses," *Communication Research* 24 (1997), 481–506.

[5] Zhongdan Pan and Gerald M. Kosicki, "Framing analysis: An approach to news discourse," *Political Communication*, 10 (1993), 59–79.

[6] Karen Tracy, "Interactional trouble in emergency service requests: A problem of frames," *Research on Language and Social Interaction*, 30 (1997), 315–343.

[7] L. David Ritchie and Lynne Cameron, " Open hearts or smoke and mirrors: Metaphorical framing and frame conflicts in a public meeting," *Metaphor and Symbol*, 29 (2014), 204–223.

community leaders and decreased rather than increased the potential for empathetic understanding.

All of these studies imply that frames exist independently of language, but are readily activated by language – including metaphors and stories. All of them are consistent with Lithwick's claim that journalism has sustained and replicated a lazy and sensationalist framing of legal topics and issues, including crime and terrorism, driven by the audience's appetite for sex and violence and contributing to a distorted understanding of these topics. The accumulated social science research also supports Lithwick's conclusion that it is important to develop metaphorical and narrative frames that place these issues in their historical and social as well as legal context.

Since I largely agree with Lithwick's argument, I will focus my response on the theoretical underpinnings of metaphorical framing, then address some of the recent research findings that indicate a more modest effect of metaphorical framing. I will also expand the discussion of metaphorical framing to encompass the blend of metaphor with narrative in the form of metaphorical stories.

METAPHOR

In traditional approaches, metaphor is often defined as using a word from one domain to talk about a concept or idea from a totally different domain. However, a definition based on Conceptual Metaphor Theory (Lakoff and Johnson)[8] is better suited to Lithwick's overall argument. According to Lakoff and Johnson, metaphors are fundamentally conceptual rather than linguistic, and consist of experiencing one concept (usually more abstract) as or in terms of another concept (usually less abstract) from an entirely different domain of experience. Thus, for example, in *"iron* resolve," the abstract concept of *resolve* is experienced as *made of iron*. To use an example from Lithwick's analysis of metaphors used by journalists: *"smoke out* the *agenda behind* the *creation* of these metaphors" (p. 21) has four metaphors, a verb, noun, preposition, and verb. The noun *"agenda"* could also be classified as a metonym, an intended outcome of an action is experienced as a list of things to accomplish in a meeting. *"Behind"* falls neatly within a common conceptual metaphor, CAUSATION IS MOTION THROUGH SPACE, so a result is experienced as in front of and being pushed by a cause or intention that

---

[8] George Lakoff and Mark Johnson, *Metaphors We Live By* (Chicago, IL: University of Chicago Press, 1980).

is behind it. "*Creation*," a grammatical metaphor[9] based on transformation of the verb *create* to a noun, makes sense only if *metaphor* is also understood by way of the conceptual metaphor MEANING IS AN OBJECT.[10] As a result, formulating a metaphor is "*creating an object.*" "Smoke out" is more complex; it cannot be analyzed independently of the entire phrase, and requires a different approach, combining metaphor and narrative, which I will discuss in the next section.

CONCEPTUAL METAPHORS, METAPHORICAL STORIES, AND STORY METAPHORS

According to Conceptual Metaphor Theory, metaphors consist of correlations between concepts, not substitution of one word for another; the metaphorical words and phrases observed in discourse are manifestations of these underlying conceptual metaphors. A commonplace phrase like "we *look to where we are going* by considering *where we have been*"[11] expresses an underlying conceptual metaphor, LAW IS A JOURNEY, which is itself the product of correlations in experience between the abstract concept of INTERPRETING AND APPLYING LAWS and the more corporeal concept of MOTION THROUGH SPACE. Extensive research over the past several decades has supported this account of metaphor (for a review see Gibbs).[12] The details of Conceptual Metaphor Theory, along with the supporting evidence, have been widely discussed elsewhere. I will focus my own discussion on an extension of Conceptual Metaphors, in which a sequence of events or actions (i.e. a story) from one realm of experience (the topic story) is presented as a story from a different realm of experience (the vehicle story). If the vehicle is narrated as at least a minimal story (a sequence of

---

[9] Michael A. K. Halliday, "Things and relations: Regrammaticising experience as technical knowledge," in James R. Martin and Robert Veel (eds.), *Reading Science: Critical and Functional Perspectives on Discourses of Science* (London; New York: Routledge, 1998), pp. 185–237; L. David Ritchie and Min Zhu, "'Nixon stonewalled the investigation': Potential contributions of grammatical metaphor to conceptual metaphor theory and analysis," *Metaphor and Symbol*, 30 (2015), 118–136.

[10] Michael J. Reddy "The conduit metaphor: A case of frame conflict in our language about language," in Andrew Ortony (ed.), *Metaphor and Thought*, 2nd ed. (New York, NY: Cambridge University Press, 1993), pp. 164–201.

[11] Linda H. Edwards, "Once upon a time in law: Myth, metaphor, and authority." *Tennessee Law Review*, 77, 883–916, 892.

[12] Raymond W. Gibbs, Jr., "Metaphor interpretation as embodied simulation," *Mind and Language*, 21 (2006), 434–458; Raymond W. Gibbs, Jr., "Metaphor and thought: The state of the art," in Raymond W. Gibbs, Jr. (ed.), *The Cambridge Handbook of Metaphor and Thought* (Cambridge University Press, 2008), pp. 3–16; Raymond W. Gibbs, Jr.., this volume.

two or more causally related events) it is a *metaphorical story*; if the story is merely implied or alluded to it is a *story metaphor*.

METAPHORICAL STORIES

A metaphorical story is a story about events in one realm of experience, usually of little or no relevance to the current discourse, that invites or at least permits mapping onto a story about events in a different realm of experience that *is* relevant to the current discourse.[13] Other scholars and researchers have referred to this class of language usage in general as *allegory*,[14] but I think it is useful to reserve the term *allegory* for the narrower class of extended stories, such as *Pilgrim's Progress*, a full-length novel in which characters and places are given philosophically or morally significant names and characters experience events in the physical world that parallel their emotional, spiritual, or moral development.[15] Allegories are occasionally encountered in journalism and political speech (the novel *Animal Farm* is often understood as a political allegory), but metaphorical stories in ordinary discourse tend to be more informal, much more loosely structured, and are often quite terse, leaving it to the audience to fill in crucial details and actions from their knowledge of background contextual information.

"*Smoke out* the *agenda behind the creation* of these metaphors" provides a ready example. At first glance, "*smoke out*" appears to be related to another common metaphor, "*smoke screen*," referring to the way smoke limits visibility and based on the conceptual metaphors TO KNOW IS TO SEE; TO DECEIVE IS TO CONCEAL. But that interpretation is inconsistent with the apparent meaning of the sentence in context, so other uses of "smoke" must be accessed. Readers from a rural or suburban background may recognize the practice of filling the burrow of a rodent or the den of a predator with smoke in order to force the animal into the opening where it can be killed. Most readers will

---

[13] George Lakoff, *The Political Mind* (New York, NY: Penguin, 2008); George Lakoff, "Mapping the brain's metaphor circuitry: Metaphorical thought in everyday reason," *Frontiers of Human Neuroscience* (December 16, 2014); L. David Ritchie, "'Everybody goes down': Metaphors, stories, and simulations in conversations," *Metaphor and Symbol*, 25 (2010), 123–143; L. David Ritchie, "'Born on third base': Stories, simulations, and metaphor comprehension." Presented at the annual conference of Researching and Analyzing Metaphor, Cagliari, Italy (2014).

[14] E.g. Raymond W. Gibbs, Jr. and Erika Boers, "Metaphoric processing of allegorical poetry" in Zouhair Maalej (ed.), *Metaphor and Culture*. (Tunis, Tunisia: University of Manouba Press, 2005).

[15] L. David Ritchie, *Metaphorical Stories in Discourse* (New York, NY: Cambridge University Press, 2017).

have encountered similar practices in war movies and westerns, where a building or other hiding place is filled with smoke to force enemy or outlaw forces to leave the hiding place. The phrase is also used, metaphorically, in card games where a low card may be played to *"smoke out"* higher cards believed to lie in an opponent's hand.

The topic of *"hidden agenda"* is the unacknowledged objectives of people who use particular metaphors; the topic of the metaphorical story is using analysis and criticism to make these unacknowledged private objectives public. How the reader understands the analyst/critic's role and activities will depend on which of the possible vehicle stories the reader activates. It is also possible that a reader will experience no story at all, and that the phrase *"smoke out"* will have no real meaning, in which case the reader may or may not infer the general gist of the sentence from the discourse context. I will return to these issues later in this essay.

Metaphorical stories are sometimes based on culturally commonplace or "typical" stories, like the story about using smoke to force animals or persons to leave a hiding place, discussed above. Sometimes two contrasting versions of the same vehicle story will be contrasted to make a point about the topic story, as when Jim Hightower claimed that "George Bush was *born on third base* (but) *he thought he had hit a triple.*"[16] Sometimes a familiar metaphor is transformed and expanded into a metaphorical story. In a conversation about police-community relations, one participant expanded the conventional metaphor *"all in the same boat"* into a metaphorical story to comment on the effect of adolescent trouble-making on the community: "it's like someone in a boat and saying, 'Well look I'm just gonna *put a hole in the boat* so I can *get me some water.*' No, *everybody goes down. Everybody goes down.*"[17] In another example of a transformed conventional metaphor, a speaker at a public hearing contrasted two metaphorical stories, one based on a metaphorical meaning of *"blind"* and the other on a literal meaning, to comment on the District Attorney's failure to obtain an indictment of a police officer who had shot and killed an unarmed African-American: "Somebody said that 'justice is *blind*,' but we as Portland citizens, we need to know, or I need to know, that our elected and sworn officials are not *taking advantage of her* or us just because she's blind."[18]

---

[16] Ritchie, *Metaphorical Stories*. [17] Ritchie, "'Everybody goes down.'"
[18] L. David Ritchie, "'Justice is blind': A model for analyzing metaphor transformations and narratives in actual discourse," *Metaphor and the Social World*, 1 (2011), 70–89; Ritchie and Cameron, "Metaphorical framing."

STORY METAPHORS

Some metaphors can be satisfactorily explained by reference to a simple conceptual mapping. For example, "After this *panoramic* introductory *view*"[19] expresses KNOWLEDGE IS VISION *and* LEARNING ABOUT IS SEEING. "Set your clocks *ahead* an hour" and "move the meeting *back* a day" both express the conceptual metaphors TIME IS SPACE and THE EXPERIENCE OF TIME IS MOTION THROUGH SPACE, but "[T]he discussion spends some time with the Haley opinion ... "[20] expresses TIME IS MONEY. However, as the passage from which this phrase is taken shows, many metaphors seem to invite the activation of a metaphorical story: "The story *brings us* then to Haley v. Ohio, and *here* the *pace slows*. The discussion *spends some time* with the Haley opinion ... " The passage as a whole combines TIME IS MONEY with NARRATION IS MOTION THROUGH SPACE, and implies a larger story about how an advocate uses narrative to argue a case before the Supreme Court.

Another commonplace example, used both by Edwards and by Berger,[21] "a *tide in* the affairs of men," implies a metaphorical story that is explicitly developed by Edwards, "the *tide* which was to overrule Betts began to *flow* with new vigor"; "there is a *tide* in the affairs of men, and it is this *engulfing tide* which is *washing away* the secret interrogation of the unprotected accused."[22] In another passage, Edwards elaborates the aquatic metaphor in another metaphorical story:

> when we talk about legal authority, using the logical forms of rules and their *bedfellows* of analogy, policy, and principle, we are actually *swimming in a sea* of narrative, oblivious to the *water around* us. It is not surprising that we have failed to consider that narrative pervades the analysis of legal authorities. As the old Buddhist saying goes, we don't know *who discovered the ocean, but it probably wasn't a fish.*[23]

Even *"bedfellows"* implies a metaphorical story about people sharing a bed, presumably within a relationship of some intimacy or at least cooperation, that ordinarily maps onto a story about people who collaborate with others on some activity. Here the conventional metaphorical story is further mapped onto personified logical and legal concepts.

Some metaphors can only be understood in terms of an underlying metaphorical story. Idioms based on parables, fables, and allegories such as *"sour*

---

[19] Edwards, "Once upon a time in law," 893.   [20] Ibid.
[21] Linda L. Berger, "The lady, or the tiger? A field guide to metaphor and narrative." *Washburn Law Journal*, 50 (2010-2011), 275–317.
[22] Edwards, "Once upon a time in law," 895–896.   [23] Ibid, 884.

grapes," "*Good Samaritan*," and "*cry wolf*" have little or no meaning without at least mapping the referenced metaphorical story onto the contextually salient topic story. When an interviewer asked President Lyndon Johnson why he didn't fire FBI Director J. Edgar Hoover, he replied "It's better to have him *inside the tent pissing out* than *outside the tent pissing in*," which makes sense only in terms of two contrasting metaphorical stories.

CONTRASTING METAPHORICAL STORIES

Berger cites a commonplace metaphor "*marketplace* of ideas" and shows how it can be understood in two different senses, based on the classical Greek concept of the *agora*, as simultaneously a place of commerce and trade, and a meeting place where ideas were debated and public policies decided.[24] Each interpretation of the metaphor requires a metaphorical story. One story is about "*selling* and *buying goods*," which maps onto *persuading* and *being persuaded* about *ideas* or *policy proposals*. The alternative is a (metonymic) story about "*meeting in a public square* to debate ideas and proposals," which maps onto *writing* and *reading* or *transmitting* and *watching/listening to* persuasive arguments about ideas and proposals.

Edwards describes and contrasts two different metaphorical stories used to advocate change in legal doctrine, BIRTH and RESCUE.[25] In *Miranda v. Arizona*, an attorney was appointed to represent the accused, Ernesto Miranda, after he had already been questioned for two hours without counsel and signed a confession. The court-appointed attorney, John Paul Frank, related a story about the right to counsel as a story about "*birth* and *development*."[26] After listing a series of previous decisions that had gradually expanded the right to counsel, Frank argued that the right to counsel "had been *growing* for than thirty years."[27] Then at the end of the argument section, Frank quoted Justice Douglas as describing the right to counsel as "yet *unborn*," then referred to the "*birth*" of the right to counsel during interrogation.[28]

In her discussion of the respondent's brief in *Bowers v. Hardwick*, which centered on the right to privacy in intimate relationships, Edwards characterizes the right to privacy as a person who is threatened by another personified abstraction, the State of Georgia, who violently invaded Hardwick's private home to assault the right to privacy.[29] According to Edwards, Hardwick's attorneys presented the story of the state's assault on privacy as a story of

---

[24] Berger, "The lady or the tiger."   [25] Edwards, "Once upon a time in law."
[26] Brief for Petitioner, *Miranda v. Arizona*, 384 U.S. 436 (1966) (No. 65–759), 1966 WL 100543.
[27] Edwards, "Once upon a time in law," 897.   [28] Ibid., 898.   [29] Ibid., 900–901.

"*forcible rape*" and the lower court's decision supporting Hardwick's right to privacy (by overturning his conviction for sodomy by the state of Georgia) as a "*rescue.*" Summing up, Edwards argues that a RESCUE story asks the court to reaffirm existing policy or law but a birth story advocates a change in the law by framing it as "the natural culmination of a normal process."[30] In both cases, the frame is developed to sustain counsel's claim that the position advocated represents continuity rather than a break with precedent, and the rights asserted are either well-established rights (the RESCUE frame) or a logical extension of existing trends in applying well-established rights (BIRTH AND DEVELOPMENT).

METAPHOR AND STORY IN LEGAL JOURNALISM

Quoting Thibodeau and Boroditsky,[31] Lithwick observes that "public discourse about crime is "*saturated* with metaphor" (p. 6; italics added throughout to mark metaphors). Frequent and creative metaphor use certainly characterizes metajournalistic discourse about journalism, as exemplified by this phrase itself. The metaphor invites the reader to experience discourse as a SUBSTANCE and metaphor as LIQUID. Here, a metaphorical story is only weakly implied if at all.

Earlier (p. 2), Lithwick characterizes reporting on certain crimes as "featuring *wall-to-wall coverage* of every *twist and turn* of the investigation, the charges, and gavel-to gavel *rubbernecking* at the trial?" "*Wall-to-wall coverage*" is another common descriptive metaphor, based on an instantiation of a common SPACE metaphor, and at most weakly implies a metaphorical story. The next metaphorical phrase, "every *twist and turn* of the investigation," can be understood either as personifying *investigation* (in which case it might be understood as a metonymic reference to the *investigator* who twists and turns) or, more likely, as an expression of the conceptual metaphor AN INVESTIGATION IS A JOURNEY, which implies a story about investigators "*going after*" something (the truth, one hopes) and maps it onto the cognitive processes of trying to understand what actually happened. The final metaphor, "gavel-to-gavel *rubbernecking*," reinforces the JOURNEY metaphor and dramatically embellishes the implied metaphorical story, using an idiomatic metaphor to cast trial spectators (and viewers of media coverage) in the role of drivers who pass an accident scene and turn their heads (on their pliable, "*rubbery*" necks)

---

[30] Ibid., 908.
[31] Paul Thibodeau and Lera Boroditsky, "Metaphors we think with: The role of metaphor in reasoning," *PLoS ONE*, 6 no. 2 (2011): e16782.

to gawk at the carnage. Thus, the JOURNEY metaphor is joined to an ACCIDENT metaphor to imply a vehicle story about encountering a gory accident while on a journey, and map it onto a topic story about media reporting on a sensational criminal case.

Lithwick explains her own use of metaphor in her writing, "sometimes to *tamp down* some of my own horror" and acknowledges the "temptation to *dip into the rich well* of metaphor ... " (p. 7). "*Tamp down* my horror" expresses horror as a SUBSTANCE, an unpleasant substance that is swelling or rising up out of a container; "*tamp down*" implies a vehicle story in which Lithwick uses an instrument (metaphor) to push the unpleasant substance back into the container and maps that story onto a topic story about using metaphor to control her own emotions. "*Dip into the rich well* of metaphor" expresses metaphor as an abundant supply of water (or another liquid) in an underground reservoir; "*dip into*" implies a vehicle story about dipping a container into a well to bring it up full of valuable liquid and maps the vehicle story onto a topic story about her own writing process. It creates a frame in which metaphors are not created by the writer, but are drawn from a preexisting (and "*underground,*" perhaps subconscious) supply.

Summing up her analysis of the effect of metaphor, Lithwick concludes that "our job as journalists is to *probe* the "*tedious*" metaphors we have used about "*thugs*" and "*monsters*" as well as to *push back on* the facile images of victims as *china dolls and angels.*" "*Probe*" constructs metaphor as an *object* and implies a metaphorical story about journalists using a sharp instrument to discover what is inside the object. This metaphorical story about journalists attempting to discover what is "*inside*" a metaphor continues the "*hidden* meaning" frame established by the "*smoke out the agenda*" metaphorical story discussed earlier in this essay. "*Push back on*" implies a metaphorical story in which "facile images" are "*aggressively pushing*" against a personalized society and journalists defend society by "*pushing* them *back.*" All of these metaphorical stories imply a view of metaphors as particularly active and potent – but in a hidden way that is not apparent until they are "*smoked out*" through journalistic "*probing.*"

STORY METAPHORS ABOUT CRIME AND CRIMINALS

According to several sources cited by Lithwick, many of the metaphors we currently use to talk about crime have a long history. If several sensational crimes are reported within a short time, it is a "*surge*" or a "crime *wave*" that threatens to "*sweep over* and *drown*" the public. The vehicle story invites the audience to experience the story about a series of crimes as an irresistible natural force, a powerful ocean wave, a storm surge or tidal wave that destroys everything in its path.

We frequently *"fight a war on crime,"* drawing on a generic conceptual metaphor X IS WAR. The topic story about routine police work is expressed and experienced as a vehicle story about facing an enemy attack, declaring war, mobilizing military resources, and engaging in violent combat. Lithwick points out that the *"costs* of this metaphorical framing vastly *outweighed the benefits,"* blending a conventional economic metaphor with a conventional balance metaphor. "The war on crime and drugs has made the police and the prison system the dominant model of *winning* . . ." (p. 9).

Lithwick contrasts coverage of crimes committed by poor and minority groups with coverage of white-collar crimes, citing coverage of securities fraud cases that characterized Goldman Sachs as a *"whipping boy,"* a metaphor that simultaneously suggests that Goldman Sachs may not have been responsible for the financial disaster they provoked and that other, unnamed culprits were actually to blame. "*Whipping boy*" is a reference to a practice in feudal times, when it was forbidden to punish a royal prince for his transgressions. A child from the lesser nobility would be selected as a playmate for the prince, and the playmate would be punished for the prince's transgressions. Even for those unfamiliar with the vehicle story, the phrase *"whipping boy"* is likely to imply a story about an innocent person being punished for another's transgressions. Mapped onto the story of crimes committed by Goldman Sachs executives, the story metaphor implies that conventional news coverage establishes a frame in which the real guilt lay elsewhere (without, of course, specifying where). Although Lithwick does not elaborate, her discussion implies a contrast with news coverage of street crime: no one ever describes a petty criminal as a *"whipping boy"* for institutional racism, systematic neglect of deteriorating communities, or organized crime.

ANIMAL and DISEASE metaphors have been used to describe both individual criminals and the abstract issue of crime for centuries. Criminals are *"monsters"* and *"predators"* who *"prey on"* the innocent. Burglaries, carjackings, and random gang violence are all described as *"epidemics."* Lithwick cites an experimental study by Thibodeau and Boroditsky[32] in which *"beast"* and *"virus"* were presented within metaphorical stories. Participants read either a version in which crime was presented as a *"beast preying on"* the city or a *"virus infecting"* the city. Thibodeau and Boroditsky found that the metaphorical framing had a significant influence on participants' views about the most appropriate remedy for crime as well as on their search for

[32] Thibodeau and Boroditsky, "Metaphors we think with."

information about crime. However, Steen, Reijnierse, and Burgers[33] performed a replication of Thibodeau and Boroditsky's experiment, and did not find a metaphorical framing effect. They concluded that "there is another process at play across the board which presumably has to do with simple exposure to textual information" (p. 121).

In a follow-up study, Thibodeau and Boroditsky[34] replicated their 2011 study and also conducted two norming studies to determine how people interpret the response options used in the initial study, as well as in the replication by Steen et al. They discovered that one item, "neighborhood watch programs," was ambiguous, and seems to have undergone a slight change in meaning between the initial 2011 experiments and the 2015 replications. They claim that this change in meaning explains the failure of Steen and his colleagues to replicate their original findings, and emphasize the importance of using current norming studies in experiments of this sort. Both groups used stimulus materials invented for the experiment, rather than drawing from actual discourse that would typically include a cluster of metaphors, which decreases the ecological validity of their conclusions. One clearly supportive study followed by a failure to replicate and another study that seems to explain the non-replication leaves the status of metaphoric framing uncertain – it appears there *is* a metaphoric framing effect at least under some conditions, but the effect may be vitiated by subtle changes in culture and subtle linguistic cues. More research, using stimulus materials drawn from actual discourse and presented in the context in which they appear, is clearly called for.

STORY METAPHORS IN EDITORIAL CARTOONS

Like text journalists, editorial cartoonists need to present a message that is dynamic – an objective most readily achieved by telling a story that viewers can readily connect to. Editorial cartoonists often use visual metaphors or references to commonly known symbols, metaphors, or metaphorical stories to construct a metaphorical story that comments on a topic story from current events. An award-winning cartoon celebrating the Supreme Court's decision

[33] Gerard S. Steen, W. Gudrun Reijnierse, and Christian Burgers, "When do natural language metaphors influence reasoning? A follow-up study to Thibodeau and Boroditsky (2013)," *PLoS One*, 9 no.12 (2014): e113536.
[34] Paul H. Thibodeau and Lera Boroditsky, "Measuring effects of metaphor in a dynamic opinion landscape," *PLoS ONE*, 10 no. 7 (2015): pone.0133939; Paul H. Thibodeau, Peace O. Iyiewaure, and Lera Boroditsky, "Metaphors affect reasoning: Measuring effects of metaphor in a dynamic opinion landscape," *CogSci* (2015).

that struck down the Defense of Marriage Act (DOMA)[35] combined two familiar metaphorical vehicle images, the statue of *"Liberty"* and the statue of *"Justice,"* both depicted as classical goddesses. The image shows the two *"goddesses"* in a passionate embrace, clutching a paper reading "DOMA ruling." Liberty's sword is stuck in the ground, her scales lying next to it as if dropped in haste. The two are out of balance; Justice's legs are off the ground.

This blended image suggests a vehicle story in which Justice saw the ruling, dropped her sword and scales and leapt into the arms of Liberty; it maps readily onto the celebratory joy of the gay and lesbian community. It also potentially maps onto an abstract story about resolving the tension between freedom and equality by allowing freedom and liberty to be *"married."*

A cartoon commenting on the Citizens United and McCutcheon rulings[36] shows a pig dressed in the robes of a Supreme Court justice and seated on a throne, on a dais labeled "SCOTUS," saying "All Americans are equal but some Americans are more equal than others." Readers familiar with the novel *Animal Farm*[37] will recognize the pig as Napoleon (who represented Stalin in the novel), and will recognize the utterance as a modification of the slogan with which the pigs in the novel betrayed the revolution: "All animals are equal, but some animals are more equal than others." It is not easy to guess what a reader, lacking this background cultural and historical knowledge, might make of the cartoon.

El Refaie[38] argues that extensive and detailed contextual knowledge, including relevant cultural knowledge, is required for understanding editorial cartoons, especially those relying on visual metaphors. Even with relevant contextual knowledge many people have difficulty understanding visual metaphors – and cartoonists have remarkably little control over the interpretations people do arrive at. In one pilot study, El Refaie interviewed 8 informants from university communities, all with at least a bachelor's degree and all of whom claimed to be familiar with political cartoons. In a second study she interviewed 25 young people age 16 to 19, including 13 Muslims and 6 white native-born British. She asked each informant to interpret a series of political

---

[35] Nate Beeler, "Lady Justice and Lady Liberty embracing," *Columbus Dispatch* (Thursday, June 27, 2013). www.dispatch.com/content/cartoons/2013/06/beeler0627.html.
[36] Paul Jamiol, "SCOTUS/Animal farm," www.juancole.com/2014/04/supreme-editorial-cartoon.html, 2014.
[37] George Orwell, *Animal Farm* (New York, NY: Harcourt, Brace & World, 1946).
[38] Elizabeth El Refaie, "Metaphor in political cartoons: Exploring audience responses" in Charles J. Forceville and Eduardo Urios-Aparisi (eds.), *Multi-Modal Metaphor* (Berlin; New York, NY: Mouton de Gruyter, 2009), pp. 173–196; Elizabeth El Refaie, "Multiliteracies: How readers interpret political cartoons," *Visual Communication*, 8 (2009), 181–205.

cartoons, which she compared with the cartoonists' intentions, obtained through personal interviews. Most participants recognized depictions of universally familiar conceptual metaphors such as A DECISION IS A CROSSROAD, but only the better-educated native English speakers recognized images depicting metaphorical idioms like *"whitewash"* and *"raspberry."* Even these participants had difficulty with some elements of the more complex cartoons. Some participants became frustrated with the task, and could give no interpretation at all. The majority of the informants gave interpretations that were reasonable, but many were quite different from the cartoonists' intentions.

In my own research, I have also found evidence of a surprising degree of ambiguity in comprehension of metaphors presented in language. For just one example, I have asked several audiences to write down a sentence including the phrase "t– the line" and write down their interpretation. Consistently, the audience is about evenly divided between *"toe"* and *"tow"* – and adherents to each spelling are dismayed to learn how many others "misspell" the word. Moreover, adherents to each spelling arrive at a variety of interpretations: Some identify *"toe"* with a military formation, some with a footrace. Some identify *"tow"* with a tugboat, some with a game of tug-of-war, some with an airplane towing an advertising banner.

DISCUSSION

How we define metaphor is important, since the definition of a concept almost always has theoretical implications for how we understand it: is metaphor use and comprehension a matter of "comparing to" or "experiencing as" (see Gibbs, this volume)? Very likely it can be either or both, depending on the context, and perhaps on the metaphor user or audience, so it is important to be clear about the distinction. In analyzing a complex topic like the framing effect of metaphors in legal journalism, it is important to pay close attention to the nuances of language and image use, as they interact with the context, including the cultural knowledge of source *and* individual members of the audience.

Metaphorical stories have in the past been studied almost exclusively in the context of formal literature, but they also appear with some frequency in ordinary discourse, including public discourse such as journalism. Metaphorical stories in non-literary contexts are often truncated, with minimal narrative development and details left for the audience to fill in – although the degree to which audience members do fill in the details remains to be explored. Metaphors – both conventional idiomatic metaphors and original metaphors – often imply metaphorical stories and in some cases make sense only in the context of a metaphorical story. Accordingly, understanding the framing effects of metaphors requires attention to the implicit and potential metaphorical stories.

In this essay, I have focused primarily on the textual analysis side of metaphor research, and argued for specific attention to metaphorical stories and story metaphors, both in written texts and in visual images. I have given less attention to the cognitive and communicative side of the topic, primarily because there has been so little research on how audience members actually process metaphors in ordinary discourse. It is uncertain whether any particular audience members actually recognize, process, or understand implicit metaphorical stories, and if anything even more uncertain how they understand these tropes. Recent research found that 65–70% of a sample of college students were capable of recognizing and interpreting allegorical elements in written texts[39] but it was not clear how the other 30–35% understood the texts. In the previously described study of visual metaphors, El Refaie found that a significant minority of participants could not interpret the visual metaphors at all, and many of those who did arrive at a reasonable interpretation did not interpret them in a way at all similar to the artist's intentions. The research by Steen et al.[40] also challenges the contention that metaphors, when they are understood, have strong framing effects. From subsequent research by Thibodeau and Boroditsky it appears that metaphors can have framing effects, but they may be subtle and context-dependent.

There is a clear need for more research on how ordinary people interpret both textual and visual metaphors in ordinary discourse (as contrasted with the invented metaphors, presented with little or no context, that have characterized most metaphor research to date). Pending the results of further research we can conclude that members of the audience do not necessarily understand either the metaphors or the implied stories, and those who do understand them often understand them in quite unique ways, based on their own contextual knowledge. The advice to journalists, to be cognizant of the potential implications of the metaphors they use, seems valid as far as it goes, but attention to the potential implications is not nearly enough, as I will discuss in the next section. From the little research that has been published, it appears that authors (writers or visual artists) have little control over how audiences understand the metaphors they use. It is also far from certain

---

[39] Raymond W. Gibbs, Jr. and Erika Boers, "Metaphoric processing of allegorical poetry" in Zouhair Maalej (ed.), *Metaphor and Culture*. (Tunis, Tunisia: University of Manouba Press, 2005).

[40] Steen, Reijnierse, and Burgers, "A follow-up study."

how and to what extent the metaphors journalists use influence the attitudes and beliefs of their audiences.

Given the widespread use (and appreciation) of metaphors, it seems likely that they play more than a merely decorative or whimsical role in discourse. Even if they do not have powerful framing effects, as Steen et al. claim, they may help to attract attention and, if they are sufficiently interesting or rewarding, they may help to motivate at least some members of the audience to process a message more deeply. How they influence the direction such deeper processing takes is yet to be conclusively determined.

ADVICE TO COMMUNICATORS: USING METAPHORS AND METAPHORICAL STORIES TO FRAME LEGAL ISSUES

As noted in the introduction, a long tradition of empirical research supports the claim that nuances of language use can have strong framing effects, including influencing people's judgments about the nature of a communicative interaction)[41] and what issues or values are most relevant to a topic.[42] It can influence audience members to focus on thematic aspects of an issue (e.g. a pattern of occurrences over time and space) or on episodic aspects (e.g., a particular occurrence and the individual characteristics and actions of those involved),[43] and influence the degree to which those involved in an incident are held accountable.[44] There is also evidence that metaphors can have similar effects,[45] but other researchers have challenged these findings,[46] and argued that the apparent framing effects may be an artifact of experiment design rather than an actual effect of the stimulus metaphors.

Other evidence has challenged the expectation that audience members can be relied on to process metaphors extensively, or even to think about them. Evidence also suggests that, when audience members do engage in depth processing they may arrive at interpretations that differ markedly from those of other audience members and from the interpretation intended by the message source. It is possible that the uncertainty and variability of individual metaphor interpretation may account at least in part for the contradictory findings of recent research on metaphorical framing.

[41] Ritchie and Cameron, "Metaphorical framing"; Tracy, "A problem of frames."
[42] Price, Tewksbury, and Powers, "Switching trains of thought"
[43] Iyengar, *Is Anyone Responsible?*
[44] Caitlin M. Fausey and Lera Boroditsky, "Subtle linguistic cues influence perceived blame and financial liability," *Psychonomic Bulletin & Review*, 17 (2010), 644–650.
[45] Thibodeau, & Boroditsky, "Metaphors we think with."
[46] Steen, Reijnierse, and Burgers, "A follow-up study."

In addition to framing, it is likely that metaphors have other important rhetorical effects. It is well established that metaphors at least weakly activate neural systems for perception and muscular activity associated with the metaphor vehicle, interfering with or facilitating comprehension of and response to related messages,[47] but it is not clear to what extent if any these effects influence how messages are actually understood. It is also well established that more detailed (*"depth"*) processing leads to greater message comprehension, recall, and persuasiveness.[48] Similarly, when people are *"transported into"* a story so that they experience it as a virtual participant, they have better recall and are more persuaded by the ideas presented in the story.[49]

For writers, editorial cartoonists, and other message originators, these considerations raise several important questions, including how to encourage intended audience members to think about the message and to arrive at the intended interpretation. For the purposes of this essay, these questions can be more precisely stated: How can metaphors in general and metaphorical stories in particular encourage *"in-depth"* processing? How can audience members be encouraged to *"enter into"* a persuasive story? How can audience members be led to interpret metaphors and metaphorical stories in such a way that they arrive at the intended meanings?

Petty and Cacioppo argue that two factors in particular influence whether people process a message extensively (the *"central route"*) or only at a *"surface"* level (the *"peripheral route"*). One is *ability to process*, which includes lack of distraction, cognitive ability, and knowledge of relevant background information. The other factor is *motivation* to process, which includes personal relevance and what Petty and Cacioppo call "need for cognition," an intrinsic interest in processing and thinking about messages. Petty and Cacioppo conceived of "need for cognition" as an individual trait, but messages themselves differ in the degree to which they seem interesting and intrinsically worth processing.

According to Zwaan,[50] the context, including not only the immediate context of a particular text but also the social, cultural, and political context, including cultural knowledge, determines the balance between purely

---

[47] Gibbs, "Metaphor interpretation as embodied simulation"; Gibbs, "Metaphor and thought"; Gibbs, this volume.
[48] Richard E. Petty and John T. Cacioppo, *Attitudes and Persuasion – Classic and Contemporary Approaches* (Dubuque, IA: W. C. Brown, 1981).
[49] Melanie C. Green, "Transportation into narrative worlds: The role of prior knowledge and perceived realism," *Discourse Processes* 38 (2004): 247–266.
[50] Rolf A. Zwaan, "Embodiment and language comprehension: Reframing the discussion," *Trends in Cognitive Sciences* 18 (2014): 229–234.

semantic interpretation and embodied simulations.[51] Steen[52] claims that characteristics of a metaphor which indicate to the reader whether or not it was used deliberately as a metaphor strongly influence the depth of processing and extent of elaboration. Novel (imaginative and original) metaphors, extended metaphors (in which the writer or speaker develops entailments of the metaphor), and metaphorical stories are particularly likely to be perceived as deliberate and receive more detailed processing. Stories and storytelling is a fundamental part of communication in all cultures, and Schank and Abelson[53] claim that memory consists primarily of stories. It follows that engaging stories, including metaphorical stories, provide a *"fast track"* to memory.

In sum, well-chosen and well-crafted metaphors can increase audience attention and lead to processing a message in greater depth and elaborating the message more extensively, which will in turn lead to greater retention and persuasiveness. These effects in turn depend on the ability and motivation of the audience. Do the metaphors draw on familiar concepts and experiences? Are both the metaphor vehicle and the topic relevant and interesting to audience members? *If* they satisfy these criteria, and *if* they invite audience members to enter into the world of the story, metaphors that either imply or tell a story are particularly likely to be elaborated, remembered, and repeated.

Metaphors and metaphorical stories, presented both in language and in other modes such as visual images, can explain, illustrate, and persuade. However, it is often difficult to predict or control how various audiences will actually interpret these metaphors, and indeed whether any particular audiences will interpret them at all. Audience interpretation is strongly influenced by knowledge and salience of relevant cultural knowledge, including political knowledge. Some of this can be controlled or at least influenced by context-setting elements in preceding or accompanying text and images; knowledge and accurate assessment of an audience's composition and cultural knowledge is necessary, but probably not sufficient. There has been insufficient research to provide definitive answers to any of these questions.

---

[51] Lawrence W. Barsalou, "Grounding symbolic operations in the brain's modal systems" in Gün R. Semin and Eliot R. Smith (eds.), *Embodied Grounding: Social, Cognitive, Affective, and Neuroscientific Approaches* (Cambridge, UK; New York, NY: Cambridge University Press, 2008), pp. 9–42; Gibbs, this volume.

[52] Gerard Steen, "Developing, testing and interpreting Deliberate Metaphor Theory, *Journal of Pragmatics*, 90 (2015), 67–72.

[53] Roger C. Schank and Robert P. Abelson, "Knowledge and memory: The real story" in Robert S. Wyer, Jr. (ed.), *Knowledge and Memory: The Real Story*. Advances in Social Cognition, Vol. VIII (Hillsdale, NJ: Lawrence Erlbaum Associates 1995), 1–86.

CONCLUSION

Although metaphors in general are an important component of public discourse, it isn't at all clear to what extent they drive or even influence policy and law. Metaphorical stories and metaphors that imply metaphorical stories (story metaphors) are common and particularly dynamic elements in public discourse, and we know that context, including the discourse situation and background cultural knowledge, has a strong effect on whether people notice and how they understand metaphors. However, at the present state of research, we have very little idea what actually determines whether people notice metaphors and, if they do notice them, how they interpret them and what they make of them. The advice to journalists (and others engaged in discourse about crime and law) to be attentive to the implications of the metaphors they use, think about the characteristics, and choose metaphors wisely is still good advice. Lithwick closes her essay with the observation that journalists "have a responsibility, when we report on crime, to place it in within a context, and locate it in the larger trends." Given the importance of context in all communication, this is especially good advice.

The accumulating research allows us to elaborate these observations to the extent that audience research needs to address cultural and political knowledge as well as incidental cultural factors that may affect the salience of relevant contextual knowledge, but the research still has little to say about what influences some people to extend and elaborate metaphors and others to let them pass by with scarcely a thought, or what influences various people to interpret images, metaphors, and metaphorical stories in wildly different ways. In sum, a certain degree of humility is required of us when we research, analyze, and comment on metaphors in public discourse.

CONVERSATION VII
NARRATIVE AND METAPHOR IN HUMAN RIGHTS LAW

Editors' Introduction

Michael Hanne and Robert Weisberg

The conversation between Katharine Young and Bernadette Meyler has a very specific scope: it concerns the application by governments and civic authorities of a single metaphor (that of the "queue" or "line") to the allocation of limited resources (immigration, housing, healthcare) in different countries. This depiction and critique of a metaphoric and narrative treatment of a human rights issue is best appreciated against a broader background picture of the role of metaphor and narrative in human rights legal discourse generally.

INTRODUCTION

No legal term is more intuitively appealing to one's sense of morality and justice than "right" or "rights," and yet few are in terms of meaning and ontology so contestable. The contestation derives in part from the complex relationship between law and morals, and between positive law and normative value (or "natural rights.") That last term signifies that rights can be inherent in a Kantian view of morality, or in the conception of a liberal society, or derivable from a theology, and the term implies there are other rights that are not natural – should we call them "artificial?" Another source of contestation is the functional context of right. Does a right only exist against government? Do rights arise in all human relations, with government as a guarantor? Or, as in the American constitutional ethos, do we view rights as existing *against* government? As suggested below, can rights be both active and passive? That is, to use a legal cliché that anticipates the subject of metaphor, can a right be "both sword and shield"?[1] And do rights only belong to the human species?

---

[1] *Harris* v. *New York*, 401 U.S. 222 (1971) (*Miranda* right is a shield to prevent use in prosecution's case-in-chief of statement taken in violation of Fifth Amendment, but cannot be invoked to prevent impeachment of a testifying defendant who might be lying).

But what about the word "human?" What kind of right falls outside that category? To some the adjective suggests hierarchy – "human rights" are the most important and fundamental. To others what makes a right a "human" right is the threat to that right – most obviously threats of massive governmental wrong, ranging from discrimination to slavery to genocide. To others it simply means whatever rights are universally recognized, for whatever reason. These meanings are slippery and greatly overlap, but they implicate different inflections and functions of the term in political, legal, or moral discourse. For example, claims of violation of "human rights" tend to arise not just in formal legal disputes but also in the form of great *cris de coeur* about the sheer scale and scope of an outrageous violation, and the moral claim that it transcends any specific form of government.

So, in this arena of meanings (a metaphor itself), what role do metaphor and narrative play?

METAPHORS FOR RIGHTS

The semantic provenance of "right" brings us directly to the relationship between law and a metaphor of correctness or virtue: according to Steven L. Winter, "The English word 'right' derives most immediately from the German *recht*, which derives in turn from the Latin *rectus* or 'straight.' Thus the notion of a legal right is a conceptual counterpart to the idea of a rule: both are understood in terms of the legally defined behaviors or metaphorical paths marked out by the law."[2] In many European languages, e.g. French, the word for "law" (*le droit*) is the same as the word for "right" (in French, *"les droits de l'homme"*).

But beyond semantics, the perennial debate over the source or status of rights immediately entails metaphor and related locutions. If our rights are inherent in our very existence or in the constitution of our society, then they are a *property* that we "have" and that demand "recognition." If so, the role of government is to protect and defend those rights, but the rights remain even if government ignores or disavows them. If rights are seen as *powers* over others or against government, they are things that we "exercise," and the "rights holder" acts like a sovereign.[3] Further, as we see rights in this relational sense, we learn, by one conceptual reckoning, that there are four basic "elements" to rights: privilege (or

---

[2] Steven L. Winter, *A Clearing in the Forest: Law, Life and Mind* (Chicago, IL: University of Chicago Press, 2001), p.336
[3] H. L. A. Hart, *Essays on Bentham: Studies in Jurisprudence and Political Theory* (Oxford: Clarendon Press, 1982), p. 183.

liberty), claim, power (to), and immunity (from).[4] If we locate a right in a particular set of societal rules, we see it as "granted" by government and therefore historically and culturally contingent.[5] Indeed, a number of scholars have sought to coin metaphors, such as "rights-as-footprints," which draw attention to the local nature of many human rights claims.[6] This last metaphor is spatial, so a right can be "mapped" as territory,"[7] but then it can be "invaded" or "trespassed on." In the words of Leif Wenar, this suggests that "the right of property is the right to keep others at a distance: the legal equivalent of a barbed wire fence."[8]

Each of these metaphor-captured concepts has some relative autonomy in generating legal, political, and cultural entailments. Thus, any linkage to property suggests that they can be inherited, or waived or modified by contract, or, where the right is one of free expression, it can enter the "marketplace of ideas."[9] On the other hand, by some neo-Kantian and neo-Lockean "left libertarian" theorists the idea of the autonomous owner of right as property turns explicitly into the view of a right to "self-ownership," and also to initially equal shares of "world-ownership."[10]

While most associated with such fundamental matters as freedom from violence and persecution, or freedom to practice one's faith, the evocative term "human rights" now gets deployed in such arguably existential claims of rights as those to seek an abortion or to fulfill one's sexual orientation. But then there are rights-claims, such as those to minimum living standards, healthcare, education, and housing, which remain controversial not because they are as morally fraught as abortion or same-sex marriage, but because they demand wealth redistribution often viewed more as matters of legislative policy than deontological entitlement. And then there is the special case of the right to be armed, which in the United States is viewed by some as actually an anachronistic entitlement of obsolete state militias, by some as the most fundamental of

---

[4] Wesley N. Hohfeld, *Fundamental Legal Conceptions*, in W. Cook (ed.), (New Haven, CT: Yale University Press, 1919).
[5] Andrew Fagan, "Human Rights," *The Internet Encyclopedia of Philosophy*, ISSN 2161–0002, www.iep.utm.edu, November 16, 2016.
[6] Katharine Young and Jeremy Perelman, "Rights as Footprints: A New Metaphor for Contemporary Human Rights Practice," *Northwestern Journal of International Human Rights*, 9 no. 27 (2010): 27–58.
[7] Joseph Raz, *The Morality of Freedom* (Oxford: Oxford University Press, 1986), p. 166.
[8] Leif Wenar, "Rights," *The Stanford Encyclopedia of Philosophy* (Fall 2015 Edition), Edward N. Zalta (ed.), http://plato.stanford.edu/archives/fall2015/entries/rights/.
[9] Steven L. Winter, *A Clearing in the Forest: Law, Life and Mind* (Chicago, IL: University of Chicago Press, 2001), p. 280.
[10] Peter Vallentyne and Hillel Steiner, *Left Libertarianism and Its Critics: The Contemporary Debate* (New York, NY: Palgrave Macmillan, 2000); M. Otsuka, 2003, *Libertarianism without Inequality* (Oxford: Oxford University Press, 2003).

fundamental human rights (for both self-defense and defense against tyranny), and by others not as a right at all but as a paranoia-based threat to public safety.

Where rights disputes are between rights-claimants, we need rules for resolution, and metaphors again appear. Ronald Dworkin uses a metaphor from card games to the principle that the fundamental right of one person takes precedence over non-right objectives, e.g. the right to an adequate diet for everyone "trumps" the wish to increase national wealth.[11] But more optimistically, philosophers have discussed not only how rights can conflict, but how they sometimes support one another, which suggests a "scaffolding" or "network" metaphor.[12]

RIGHTS METAPHORS GENERATE RIGHTS NARRATIVES

As was evident in metaphors cited above, many statements of a right suggest an action and thus some degree of agency attributed to a person or group: "A right to life, to speak freely; a right to vote, to work, to strike; to practice a religion, or not."[13] Most rights entitle their holders to active freedom in some sense; indeed, holding a right can entail that one is free in one or more of a variety of senses. The passive incidents entitle their holders to *freedom from* undesirable actions or states.[14] But when a right is conceived in relation to a duty or responsibility,[15] we need a narrative to capture the dynamic between the two: right and duty are concepts which can only be understood in terms of a dynamic narrative: A has the right to walk down the road freely, B has the duty not to assault A, as s/he is walking down the road.

Rights enter law especially in narratives of the interaction we call infringement. The infringer-antagonist can be a government or an individual. But who is the narrator of this narrative? It can be the rights-claimant, herself, or an agent and of course the need for the third-party narrator is greatest when the claimant is voiceless (because of a constraint defined by gender, class, caste, ethnicity, religion, age). But the identity of the narrator may turn on whether the rights infringement becomes a legal cause of action.[16]

Rights narratives can vary in scope, and often the scope itself is a matter of conflict. Thus in trials about major crimes against humanity, the accused will

---

[11] Ronald Dworkin, 1984, "Rights as Trumps," in J. Waldron, J. (ed.), *Theories of Rights*, Oxford: Oxford University Press, 1984), pp. 153–167.
[12] Amartya Sen, *Development as Freedom* (New York, NY: Oxford University Press, 1999).
[13] Wenar, "Rights."   [14] Ibid.
[15] Mary Ann Glendon, *Rights Talk: The Impoverishment of Political Discourse* (New York, NY: The Free Press, 1991).
[16] Hohfeld, *Fundamental Legal Conceptions*.

often seek to explain their own actions in terms of wider historical forces, e.g. in trials relating to killings during the civil war in Yugoslavia, "ancient hatreds" and what is called a "chaos defense" or sometimes the explanation will purport to take the more conventional form (from criminal law) of a "duress defense."[17] When the legal context is a Truth and Reconciliation Commission, the narrative is not just a mechanism for pleading for injunctive, monetary, or punitive relief. Rather, the public narration is itself the legal relief, while deeper forms of relief are supposed to follow once national and international consciousness have been raised and conscience piqued. But even when the Truth and Reconciliation Commission has completed its work, the work of narrative for the victim of human rights abuse continues.[18]

But what about the role of great works of literature in helping societies recognize human rights? Such scholars as Martha Nussbaum, Richard Rorty, and Lynn Hunt argue that the literary form of the European novel in the eighteenth century cultivated our range of felt moral responsibility and empathy.[19] But others, such as Elaine Scarry, argue that sympathetic narratives fail to promote human dignity and that empathy typically fails when migrating from the cultivated literary imagination to the real world of victimization. Inspirational narratives read by privileged peoples may have very little "trickle-down effect" on those victimized by human rights abuses, especially when those narratives valorize the individual experience over that of the group. Richard Rorty laments that we have developed a "human rights culture"[20] whereby rights metaphors and narratives can risk becoming Western literary and philosophical self-indulgences. By this view, we do see a human rights narrative, but, ironically, it is a postcolonial grand narrative, founded on one or another misleading metaphor (e.g. the 'savages-victims-saviors' triangle of Makau Mutua).[21]

---

[17] *Prosecutor v. Erdemovic*, International Criminal Tribunal for the Former Yugoslavia (ICTY) Trial Chamber II, The Netherlands (1998).

[18] Many agencies working with victims of human rights abuses employ "narrative therapy," which assists survivors to reconstruct their lives. They encourage victims not only to narrate their experiences in full, but to draw on metaphors from their own culture to promote healing. See, for instance, *Responding to Survivors of Torture and Suffering: Survival Skill and Stories of Kurdish Families* (Adelaide: Dulwich Centre Foundation International, 2012).

[19] Cited in James Dawes and Samantha Gupta, "On narrative and human rights," *Humanity: An International Journal of Human Rights, Humanitarianism, and Development*, 5: (Spring 2014), 149–156.

[20] See Leonard D. G. Ferry, "Floors without foundations: Ignatieff and Rorty on human rights," *Logos: A Journal of Catholic Thought and Culture*, 10 (Winter 2007), 80–105.

[21] Makau W. Mutua, "Savages, Victims, and Saviors: The Metaphor of Human Rights." *Harvard International Law Journal*, 42 no. 1 (2001), 201–245.

Legal anthropologists such as Lawrence Rosen have studied traditional cultures with radically different legal systems, where narrative (e.g. "the stories our ancestors told") and metaphors (such as "an eye for eye") loom large. Of special interest are the narratives and metaphors which come into play in oral, as opposed to written, cultures and the conflict between local custom and declarations around universal rights.

Against this background, in the conversation between Katharine Young and Bernadette Meyler, the "queue" is a powerful metaphor for the concept of a right at issue in society, especially when it is something so fundamental as the right to habitation, and when its historical context is that of a transition from a monstrous regime of human rights violation to a helpful but struggling new post-Apartheid world. On the one hand, the "queue" is an idealistic metaphor for a right imagined as a fair and equal chance in a world where resources to fulfill that right might be scarce (at least temporarily). But precisely because of the predicate of scarcity, it is not a *categorical* right to have the needs fulfilled. Moreover, because the queue is also an administrative mechanism in a particular social, economic, and political situation, its aura of abstract fairness is potentially tainted by compromises that are unavoidable when a government makes allocation decisions among rights-holders who did not start out with an equal fair chance in the first place.

12

When Rights-Talk Meets Queue-Talk[*]

Katharine G. Young

INTRODUCTION

In 2005, a group of people living in a disused warehouse in inner-city Johannesburg, South Africa, were sent a notice to vacate by the property owner. The group, some eighty-six in number, had occupied the premises informally, over a period of several years, and had, for the most part, paid no rent. They refused to leave. The owner, who had recently purchased the property for the purpose of developing it, applied for an eviction order. In most other liberal capitalist democracies, the eviction would be ordered and the story would end there. In this case, however, the occupiers argued that the eviction would render them homeless. Their lawyers joined the City of Johannesburg to the eviction proceedings, arguing that the state had to supply them with alternative accommodation. The courts, from the High Court, to the Supreme Court of Appeal, to the Constitutional Court, agreed.[1]

The occupiers' claim rested on their right to access housing. South Africa's 1996 Constitution guarantees this right, which must be realized, progressively, by the state.[2] Influenced by international human rights

---

[*] My thanks to Bernadette Meyler, Vlad Perju, and participants of the Narrative and Metaphor Symposium at Stanford Law School, January 2016, and the Prague Colloquium on Philosophy and Social Science, May 2016.
[1] *City of Johannesburg Metropolitan Municipality* v. *Blue Moonlight Properties* 2012 (2) SA 104 (CC); *City of Johannesburg Metropolitan Municipality* v. *Blue Moonlight Properties* 39 (Pty.) Ltd 2011 (4) SA 337 (SCA); *Blue Moonlight Properties 39 (Pty) Limited* v. *Occupiers of Saratoga Avenue* [2008] ZAGPHC 275 (High Court, Witwatersrand Local Division).
[2] Constitution of the Republic of South Africa: 1996, s. 26. Relevant statutes included the Housing Act 107 of 1997 and the Prevention of Illegal Eviction from and Unlawful Occupation of Land Act 19 of 1998 (PIE). Other constitutional provisions relevant to impending homelessness include the right to human dignity (s. 10) and the right to life (s. 11): see *Occupiers of 51 Olivia Road, Berea Township and 197 Main Street, Johannesburg* v. *City of Johannesburg* 2008 (3) SA 208 (CC) [16].

law,[3] as well as the anti-apartheid struggle's professed commitments to human rights,[4] the Constitution guarantees certain economic and social rights, such as access to housing, health care, food, water, social security, and education, alongside the right to property, and the civil and political rights of voting, association, and expression.[5] Thus, in pledging to transform South Africa from its apartheid past in the direction of democracy and human rights,[6] the Constitution recognizes that the state must take positive steps, to "respect, protect, promote and fulfill" the rights in the Bill of Rights.[7] Such steps are constitutionally required, in order to correct the maldistributions of almost half a century of apartheid's racist property and labor restrictions, and in addressing other aspects of inaccess to housing that contradict the Constitution's named values of "human dignity, equality, and freedom."[8]

Read against the text's ambitions, one aspect of the Constitutional Court's resolution of the occupiers' claims is striking. In finding that the City was required to provide accommodation to the occupiers, and that the property owner was required to exercise some (non-compensable) patience before the eviction could proceed, the Court stated that:

> queue jumping is not in issue in this case. The Occupiers do not claim permanent housing, ahead of anyone else in a queue. They have to wait in the queue or join it. What they ask is not to be excluded from the City's provision of temporary housing, even though their situation is an

[3] See, e.g., International Covenant on Economic, Social and Cultural Rights, 16 December 1966, in force 3 January 1976, 993 UNTS 3; John Dugard, "The influence of international human rights law on the South African Constitution," *Current Legal Problems*, 49 (1996), 305–324, at 322.

[4] Freedom Charter of 26 June 1955: reprinted in *Columbia Human Rights Law Review*, 21 (1989), 249–251. See further e.g., Hassen Ebrahim, "The making of the South African Constitution" in Penelope Andrews and Stephen Ellmann (eds.), *The Post-Apartheid Constitutions* (Johannesburg: Witswatersrand University Press, 2001), pp. 85–103, at pp. 95–97.

[5] South African Constitution, ss. 26 (housing), 27 (health care, food, water, and social security), 29 (education); *see also* s. 28(1)(c) (setting out rights of children to basic nutrition, shelter, basic health care services, and social services); s. 25 (property), ss. 16 (freedom of expression), ss. 17–18 (assembly and association), 19 (campaign and vote).

[6] The steps of legal transformation are suggested by Karl E. Klare, "Legal culture and transformative constitutionalism," *South African Journal of Human Rights*, 14 no. 1 (1998), 146–188, which orients much present legal scholarship. For a biographical description, see Deputy Chief Justice Moseneke, "The fourth Bram Fisher Memorial Lecture – transformative adjudication," *South African Journal of Human Rights*, 18, 3 (2002), 309–319.

[7] South African Constitution, s. 7(2).

[8] South African Constitution, s. 7(1). The special importance of the right to housing is described in Hon. Albie Sachs, "The creation of South Africa's Constitution," *New York Law School Law Review*, 41 no. 2 (1997), 669–701, at 671.

emergency ... simply because they are being evicted by a private landowner and not by the City.[9]

In this passage, the Court invoked, and then dismissed as inapplicable, the housing right's queue.[10] By refusing to accept a distinction between occupiers of public and private land, the Court was connecting its language to a persistent political trope in South Africa, employed by politicians, officials, and others commenting on the successes or failures of housing policy and housing rights. In this discourse, the queue is given priority, as the place in which people wait for access to housing according to their constitutional rights. The queue jumpers are those who do not – they cut in line, even when they also claim their constitutional rights. Whatever else it might be, the queue is a metaphor and, like all metaphors, it both distorts and reveals. It is also persistently invoked in human rights contestations that take place far from South Africa's constitutional protections.[11] This chapter argues that "queue-talk" codetermines "rights-talk," particularly for so-called "second-generation," "positive" human rights, distorting our legal concepts of rights and remedies, and revealing the persistent blindspots in our understanding of law's ability to respect human rights.

QUEUE AS METAPHOR

A metaphor involves the transfer of meaning of a word or phrase from its literal application to a new and different object.[12] The metaphor of the queue, or waiting line, tracks the preconceptions that people have about the normative

---

[9] *Blue Moonlight*, (CC), [93].
[10] For other examples of judicial consideration of queue jumping, largely in response to state submissions, see *Government of the Republic of South Africa v. Grootboom* 2001 (1) SA 46 (CC); *Modderfontein Squatters, Greater Benoni City Council v. Modderklip Boerdery (Pty.) Ltd.*; *President of the Republic of South Africa v. Modderklip Boerdery (Pty.) Ltd.* 2004 (6) SA 40 (SCA) [23]-[25] (court rejecting state's submission that queue jumping at issue, finding "no evidence that the occupation took place with the intent to obtain precedence ... [but rather] because the people had nowhere else to go and because they believed that the land, which to them did not appear to have been cultivated, belonged to the municipality"); confirmed in *President of the Republic of South Africa and Another v. Modderklip Boerdery (Pty.) Ltd.* 2005 (5) SA 3 (CC) [32]-[34]; *Port Elizabeth Municipality v. Various Occupiers* (CCT 53/03) [2004] ZACC 7; 2005 (1) SA 217 (CC) [3], [55] (court rejecting state's submission of queue because "occupiers ... are a community who are homeless, who have been evicted once, and who found land to occupy with what they considered to be the permission of the owner where they have been residing for eight years.")
[11] These are analyzed extensively in Katharine G. Young, "Rights and queues: On distributive contests in the modern state," *Columbia Journal of Transnational Law*, 55 no. 1 (2016), 65–137 (comparing Australian, Canadian, and South African "queue talk").
[12] See, e.g., Charles Taylor, *The Language Animal: The Full Shape of the Human Linguistic Capacity* (Cambridge, MA: Harvard University Press, 2016).

priorities involved in addressing questions of resources allocation, particularly in situations of scarcity. This "embodied"[13] knowledge is transferred from the experience of the physical queue, which has become so ubiquitous in modern urban life, from the supermarket and post office, to the ticket booth, to road and air travel, and to the everyday experiences of those who apply for state benefits or services. It also recalls the virtual queue, such as the calling systems, surgery wait lists, or bureaucratic decision-making procedures, which rely on the time of entry to administer the system. While the first usually involves the suspension of other activities for minutes or hours, the second may involve days, weeks, or years in waiting and the continuation of other activities despite significant queueing costs.[14] The queue is a phenomenon of great social complexity, representing a system of physical or virtual ordering which gives priority to the timing of the claim, despite critical differences in the experiences of time in each case, usually following a "first come first served" principle.[15]

While the metaphor of the queue conjures a politics of waiting, connecting time and (scarce) object into a familiar image-schema, the secondary metaphor of queue jumping refers to its corruption. Thus, queues often include an expectation that others observe the priority-norm and "respond critically or even obstructively towards people who flout" it.[16] In many instances, people feel justified in giving social sanction to those who jump the queue, or cut in line, even in the absence of any law. Queue jumping occurs in the physical, visible, queues described above, but also in virtual queues, which provide less opportunity for direct repercussions. The harm of queue jumping can also be different, depending on the type of queue. In

---

[13] For the connections between metaphor and embodiment, and its implication for law, see Steven L. Winter, "Re-embodying law," *Mercer Law Review*, 58 (2006), 869–897.

[14] In a study of prolonged waiting, one geographer distinguished between the different states of "heightened suspense," "lost time," "panic," and "inertia": Craig Jeffrey, "Guest editorial: Waiting," *Environment and Planning D: Society and Space*, 26 no. 6 (2008), 954–958; see further Craig Jeffrey, *Timepass: Youth, Class, and the Politics of Waiting in India* (Stanford, CA: Stanford University Press, 2010).

[15] Such a principle may operate as a default, to be put aside much like an ambulance can flout traffic lines. Much of the ambiguity about queue jumping is really an ambiguity about the default. Less frequently, queues may be administered according to another principle, such as last come, first served, or a variety of priority schemes: *see* Donald Gross, John F. Shortle, James M. Thompson, and Carl M. Harris, *Fundamentals of Queueing Theory*, 4th ed. (Hoboken, NJ: John Wiley & Sons, Inc., 2008), pp. 4–5.

[16] Neil MacCormick, "Norms, institutions and institutional facts," *Law & Philosophy*, 17 no. 3 (1998), 301–345, at 305. A latecomer to the law and social norms literature, the queue has recently been analyzed by David Fagundes, "The social norms of waiting in line," (forthcoming) *Law and Social Inquiry*, may be read at: http://onlinelibrary.wiley.com/journal/10.1111/(ISSN)1747-4469/earlyview.

simple distribution queues, people may be queueing to receive the same good before others.[17] But queues may also determine the quality of the good, service, or opportunity, its price at point of provision, or indeed whether it is received at all.[18] In the latter instance, queue jumping may be perceived as even more egregious. And in both cases, the harm of queue jumping includes both the private injury to all individuals who stand behind the point of intrusion, and a public injury, in the form of its connoted disrespect, to the entire normative order of the queue.[19]

This overarching image generates different understandings of rights. For South Africa's housing rights, the queue stands in as a metaphor for access to housing, from two standpoints – as the housing waiting list and as the sequence of steps toward the progressive realization of the housing rights guaranteed by the South African Constitution. Jumping the queue implies any perversion of housing delivery, in both senses, such as through "occupying" vacant lots earmarked for development, or empty buildings, and then using anti-eviction rules and courts to defend that occupation.[20] At the same time, there is also a perception that some "will torch their shacks and backyard shanties to jump the queue,"[21] and others will "pay and jump to the front of the queue,"[22] which signals a general distrust of the system. Under the queue-jumping metaphor – which also, incidentally, operates much like a narrative – the resulting harm falls on those waiting for housing allocation or support (recorded as some 1.8

---

[17] For example, the Pacific Telegraph Act of 1860 facilitated communication by transmitting in order of reception, "excepting that dispatches of the government shall have priority": thus the queue determined the order in which one's claim was processed, rather than the quality of service or whether one got it at all.

[18] Ronen Perry and Tal Z. Zarsky, "Queues in law," *Iowa Law Review*, 99 no. 4 (2014), 1595–1620, at 1601 (referring to first-in-time, first-in-right rules in property law as "winner takes all," entitlement-determining queues).

[19] Kevin Gray, "Property in a queue" in Gregory S. Alexander and Eduardo M. Peñalver (eds.), *Property and Community* (Oxford, UK; New York, NY: Oxford University Press, 2010), pp 165–195, at 184–185.

[20] Kate Tissington, Naadira Munshi, Gladys Mirugi-Mukundi, and Ebenezer Durogaye, "'Jumping the queue,' waiting lists and other myths: Perceptions and practice around housing demand and allocation in South Africa," report, Community Law Centre, University of the Western Cape & Socio-Economic Rights Institute of South Africa (2013).

[21] Rowan Philp and Nashira Davids, "South Africa: Jumping the Housing Queue," Africa News Service, May 9, 2005, available at http://allafrica.com/stories/200505091640.html.

[22] Lauren Royston and Ronald Eglin, "Allocation thought piece for managed land settlement," unpublished draft (Dec. 5, 2011), available at www.incrementalsettlement.org.za/files/uploads/files/1323332855-allocation-thought-piece-for-managed-land-settlement.pdf (suggesting "people don't believe in waiting lists as the allocation mechanism in practice – views are widely held that they are corrupt and that people can pay and jump to the front of the queue"); Tissington et al., "Jumping the queue," at 72.

million households[23]), as well as on property holders, the government, and the general public, from perceptions of corruption and patronage, and the breakdown of the rule of law.

In the first image, the metaphor has an institutional allusion: it refers to the housing register that most low-income South Africans join as a rite of passage.[24] This register was established in 1994, when the 1994 White Paper on Housing committed the government to provide housing for all its citizens, mainly through the construction of new houses on greenfield, previously undeveloped land.[25] This scheme has, according to government reports, resulted in the construction of "over 2.7 million homes for South Africans, giving shelter to more than 13 million people."[26] State-subsidized housing is delivered based on various criteria such as location, special needs, age, along with, importantly, time spent on the "waiting list." Integral to the human rights hopes of the new, post-apartheid South Africa, the "eradication of the housing backlog" is described as both a political target and a broader goal for development.[27]

In the second image, the metaphor is doctrinal;[28] it concretizes the positive steps required of government, to "achieve the progressive realization of this right."[29] Under this understanding, the queue metaphor fills the doctrinal vacuum in the law of human rights, as to what this abstract, open, positive obligation entails.[30] Unlike obligations to respect rights, which are more usually equated with civil and political rights and are understood to take

---

[23] Of this national figure, around 25% live in shacks in informal settlements, 45% live in a dwelling or other structure on a separate stand, 12% live in a traditional dwelling and 10% live in a backyard shack. Housing Development Agency (HDA), South Africa: Informal Settlements Status 47 (2012); Tissington et al., "Jumping the queue," at 27.

[24] Discussion with Gauteng NGO, noted in Tissington et al., "Jumping the queue," at 59 (noting that registering one's name was "a rite of passage for people when they turn 18," with no sense of how long they will wait or what options are available to them during this time.

[25] White Paper on Housing (1994) (Sth. Afr.) The Reconstruction and Development Programme of 1994 transitioned into the Breaking New Ground (BNG) plan in 2004.

[26] While the government has reported these figures (available at www.info.gov.au/aboutsa/housing.htm) these figures are disputed, with less than 1.44 million state-subsidized properties registered since 1994. See Tissington et al., "Jumping the queue," at 23.

[27] Marie Huchzermeyer, "Pounding at the tip of the iceberg: The dominant politics of informal settlement eradication in South Africa," *Politikon: The South African Journal of Political Science*, 37 no. 1 (2010), 129–148.

[28] For pertinent studies of the role of metaphor in shaping legal doctrine, see, e.g., Vicki C. Jackson, "Constitutions as 'living trees'? Comparative constitutional law and interpretive metaphors," *Fordham Law Review*, 75 no. 2, (2006), 921–960; David Cole, "Agon at Agora: Creative misreadings in the first amendment tradition," *Yale Law Journal*, 95, 5 (1986), 857–905.

[29] South African Constitution, s. 26(2); see also s. 27(2).

[30] That is not to say that more suitable metaphors are not available. For example, the metaphor of "the bridge" was applied to South Africa's Interim Constitution, in a seminal reading of the

immediate effect, progressive realization is a way to give legal latitude to a country's socio-economic policy.[31] In this sense, the queue refers to "the sequence of steps in [the state's] housing policy directed at the progressive realization of housing rights, namely, from emergency housing to temporary accommodation and then finally to permanent accommodation."[32] After the famous *Grootboom* decision of the Constitutional Court, the right to housing, at the very least, requires that the state cater to those in crisis conditions, by providing emergency accommodation in its housing policy.[33] But the constitutional guarantee is no less concerned with the reasonable administration of a housing policy for all classes of claimants.[34] Jumping the queue is the metaphor that names the act of seeking the wrong stage of entitlement, as one progresses through this hierarchy.

Due to the hold of the metaphor in both contexts, and the curious ambiguity that flows from their combined effect, the metaphor distorts the understanding, and operation, of housing rights. First, as South African commentators have shown, the idea of a housing wait list is a myth.[35] At

---

legal obligations (and legal possibilities) of economic and social rights: Etienne Mureinik, "Beyond a charter of luxuries: Economic rights in the constitution," *South African Journal on Human Rights*, 8 no. 4 (1992) 464–474. See also the "living tree" approach to interpretation: Jackson, "Constitutions as 'living trees.'"

[31] Compare International Covenant on Civil and Political Rights, 16 December 1966, 999 UNTS 171 (entered into force 1976), art. 2(1) (obligations to "respect and to ensure" all rights; and art. 2(2) (obligations to take the necessary steps); with International Covenant on Economic, Social and Cultural Rights, 16 December 16, 1966, 993 UNTS 3 (entered into force 1976), art. 2(1) (obligation "to take steps, to the maximum of available resources, with a view of achieving progressively the full realization of the rights"). See also UN Committee on Economic, Social and Cultural Rights (CESCR), *General Comment No. 3: The Nature of States Parties' Obligations (Art. 2, Para. 1, of the Covenant)*, December 14, 1990, E/1991/23, para. 9, available at: www.refworld.org/docid/4538838e10.htm. While later covenants, which combined civil, political, economic, social and cultural rights together, eschewed this formulation, the Convention on the Rights of Persons with Disabilities, December 13, 2006, 2515 UNTS 3 (entered into force 2008) has reverted to the progressive realization formula for economic and social rights: art. 4(2). But for the suggestion that the "minimum essential level of enjoyment" requires immediate respect, see UN Office for the High Commissioner for Human Rights, Monitoring the Convention on the Rights of Persons with Disabilities, Guidance for Human Rights Monitors (Professional Training Series No. 17, New York and Geneva, 2010), 28.

[32] *Blue Moonlight*, (SCA), para. 21 (reflecting the City of Johannesburg's submissions).

[33] *Government of the Republic of South Africa v. Grootboom* 2001 (1) SA 46 (CC).

[34] Theunis Roux, "Understanding Grootboom—A response to Cass R. Sunstein," *Constitutional Forum*, 12 no. 2 (2002) 41–51, at 46–47; Danie Brand, "The proceduralization of South African socio-economic rights jurisprudence" in Henk Botha, Andre van der Walt, and Johan van der Walt (eds.), *Rights and Democracy in a Transformative Constitution* (Stellenbosch, South Africa: Sun Press, 2003), p. 33–56.

[35] Tissington et al., "Jumping the queue."

most a metonym, naming (and unduly enlarging the relevance of[36]) a very minor aspect of housing delivery in South Africa, the queue metaphor creates the impression of a rationally administered housing system, which rests on temporal prioritization. The register itself is made up of a series of names, first drawn up (and segregated) during apartheid.[37] In merging these lists and creating new databases, housing claimants were asked to fill in a form with details such as ID number, gender, age, and number of dependents, and were given a receipt with the date in which they had registered.[38] Yet while the expectation was that this list would work on a "first come first served" basis, and applicants would receive a house when their name made its way to the top,[39] other factors quickly became more relevant, such as location and "catchment" for an intended housing project, or applicant's income. Some municipalities also created random selection or "lottery" systems, and discrete application processes for advertised, project-based opportunities.[40] Moreover, the list itself became mired by allegations of corruption: during the auditing of one list, for example, "it was discovered that 50% of beneficiaries' ID numbers were invalid, while 65% did not match the applicants' records."[41] Since 2008, public guidelines have been drawn up to facilitate "fair, equitable, transparent and inclusive selection and housing subsidy application approval processes" for certain housing applications, although their practical effect has been unclear.[42] In this respect, the queue metaphor distorts what the state is doing (rather than what it is saying[43]), in order to secure housing for all.

Secondly, in relation to doctrine, the queue metaphor misleads as to how a court can conceptualize the right to housing, in which it must take an appropriately deferential stance. As courts have neither the information

---

[36] Metonymy indicates a contiguity between target and source: see, e.g., Linda L. Berger, "Of metaphor, metonymy, and corporate money: Rhetorical choices in Supreme Court decisions on campaign finance regulation," *Mercer Law Review*, 58 no. 3 (2007), 949–990.

[37] Sophie Oldfield and Saskia Greyling, "Waiting for the state: A politics of housing in South Africa," *Environment and Planning A*, 47 no. 5 (2015), 1100–1112, at 1106 (noting how, in Cape Town, individuals formerly classified as "coloured" (mixed race) were placed on waiting lists in the segregated group areas, but families classified as "African" [the majority] were excluded from access. This meant the place on the list reflected different dates of insertion.)

[38] Tissington et al., "Jumping the queue," at 25.

[39] Ibid.; Oldfield and Greyling, "Waiting for the state," at 1107.

[40] Tissington et al., "Jumping the queue."

[41] Ibid. at 61 (citing Press Release, Gauteng Dept. of Local Gov't and Housing, A Call to Update Your Details on Demand Database, May 21, 2009).

[42] Ibid. at 33 (referring to Department of Human Settlements, Strategy for the Allocation of Housing Opportunities Created through the National Housing Programmes [2008]).

[43] See also Oldfield and Greyling, "Waiting for the state," at 1107 (noting that, based on "sustained and repeated promises from the state, putting yourself on the housing list remains the most likely route to obtain a formal house").

resources nor the democratic accountability to restructure a government's socio-economic policy, they tend to provide a more flexible standard of review, and a more open remedy, in economic and social rights cases.[44] Such an approach also helps to ensure that "those individuals with the sharpest elbows (and the best lawyers)"[45] do not get priority access to scarce resources through litigation. Thus, in its first economic and social rights decision, the Court indicated that it would be slow to interfere with funding priorities.[46] The Court uses the test of "reasonableness" as its yardstick, which allows for a broad range of actions.[47] Notwithstanding that the Court has not incorporated a "minimum core" entitlement,[48] the test of reasonableness requires that the needs of the most vulnerable be addressed.[49] And while the South African Constitutional Court has acted more decisively in overruling socio-economic laws indicating formal discrimination,[50] or health policies based on irrationality,[51] neither requires a sequence of steps for the government to provide evidence of, nor a sequence of steps as remedy.

In *Blue Moonlight*, the Court unusually ventured into reviewing the City's budget, finding that moneys had been apportioned in a way that was contrary to the constitutional right.[52] Thus, it found inappropriate line-drawing

---

[44] This tendency is not the same everywhere. I discuss the immense variability of courts, in this respect, in Katharine G. Young, *Constituting Economic and Social Rights* (Oxford: Oxford University Press, 2012) (comparing the Indian Supreme Court, the Colombian Constitutional Court, and the South African Constitutional Court); see also Mark Tushnet, *Weak Courts, Strong Rights* (Princeton, NJ: Princeton University Press, 2008); Roberto Gargarella, Pilar Domingo, and Theunis Roux (eds.), *Courts and Social Transformation in New Democracies: An Institutional Voice for the Poor?* (Burlington, VT; Aldershot, UK: Ashgate: 2006).

[45] Albie Sachs, *The Strange Alchemy of Life and Law* (Oxford, UK; New York, NY: Oxford University Press, 2009), pp. 181–182.

[46] *Soobramoney v. Minister of Health (Kwazulu-Natal)* 1998 (1) SA 765 (CC) [29].

[47] *Grootboom*; see also *Blue Moonlight* [83]; see generally Sandra Liebenberg, *Socio-Economic Rights: Adjudication under a Transformative Constitution* (Claremont, South Africa: Juta & Co., 2010).

[48] General Comment No. 3, para. 10. For the challenge of establishing this minimum, see Katharine G. Young, "The minimum core of economic and social rights: A concept in search of content," *Yale Journal of International Law*, 33 no. 1 (2008), 113–175.

[49] *Grootboom* (CC), [44]:

> To be reasonable, measures cannot leave out of account the degree and extent of the denial of the right they endeavour to realise. Those whose needs are the most urgent and whose ability to enjoy all rights therefore is most in peril, must not be ignored by the measures aimed at achieving realisation of the right. It may not be sufficient to meet the test of reasonableness to show that the measures are capable of achieving a statistical advance in the realisation of the right. Furthermore, the Constitution requires that everyone must be treated with care and concern.

[50] *Khosa v. Minister of Social Development* 2004 (6) SA 505 (CC).

[51] *Minister of Health v. Treatment Action Campaign* 2002 (5) SA 721 (CC).

[52] *Blue Moonlight*, (CC), [74].

between occupiers of public property, on the one hand, who were allocated temporary accommodation in situations of need that arose beyond their control,[53] and occupiers of private property, on the other, who were not.[54] This, the Court held, was unreasonable, where pending homelessness was the relevant issue. It ordered the occupiers' eviction to occur only once temporary accommodation had been provided, as close to the original location as possible.[55] In a follow-up case (and there were many[56]), it noted the general requirement for the parties to engage meaningfully on the nature of the temporary accommodation, before the eviction.[57] The flexibility of this open-ended, dialogical remedy, further unsettles the queue metaphor, except in the general sense that people who have access to courts may have secured an advantage (of a guaranteed participation in decision-making) over those who do not. In this latter sense, the conundrum between the advantage secured by successful litigants and those similarly situated non-litigants who must

---

[53] National Housing Code, Chapter 12, s. 12.3.1, defining "Emergencies" applicable to people who:

   a. Owing to situations beyond their control:
   - have become homeless as a result of a declared state of disaster;
   - are evicted or threatened with imminent eviction from land or from unsafe buildings, or situations where pro-active steps ought to be taken to forestall such consequences;
   - whose homes are demolished or threatened with imminent demolition, or situations where proactive steps ought to be taken to forestall such consequences; or...
   - live in conditions that pose immediate threats to life, health and safety and require emergency assistance.

   b. Are in a situation of exceptional housing need, which constitutes an Emergency that can reasonably be addressed only by resettlement or other appropriate assistance, in terms of this Programme.

[54] *Blue Moonlight*, (CC), [92]–[97] For background to the municipality's encouragement to the private sector to evict inner city occupiers, see Stuart Wilson, "Curing the poor: State housing policy in Johannesburg after Blue Moonlight," *Constitutional Court Review*, 5 (2013), 280–296, at 283; Janke Strydom and Sue-Mari Viljoen, "Unlawful occupation of inner-city buildings: A constitutional analysis of the rights and obligations involved," *Potchefstroom Electronic Law Journal*, 17 no. 4 (2014), 1206–1261, at 1210.

[55] *Blue Moonlight*, (CC), para. 104.

[56] Wilson, "Curing the poor," (outlining various sequels in the fortunes of those living at Saratoga Ave., including 30 forced into "managed care" arrangements that, he argues, are at odds with human rights.)

[57] *Occupiers of Saratoga Avenue v. City of Johannesburg Metropolitan Municipality and Another* 2012 (9) BCLR 951 (CC) (24 May 2012). For further description of "meaningful engagement," see *Occupiers of 51 Olivia Road, Berea Township and 197 Main Street, Johannesburg v. City of Johannesburg* 2008 (3) SA 208 (CC); *Residents of Joe Slovo Community, Western Cape v. Thubelisha Homes* 2010 (3) SA 454.

wait for a less directly supervised response, remains best addressed – if not completely resolved – by remedy.[58]

Thus, in each case, analysis of the queue uncovers the conceptual distortions that accompany the right to housing, when the right is formalized as law. These distortions apply to other human rights, particularly when positive obligations are at issue. Indeed, the queue is frequently invoked in other rights contestations, from the right of refugees to be free from political persecution, to rights to health care.[59] For example, in Australia, the image of queue jumpers is assigned to those who seek asylum by arriving to the border by boat, invoking Australia's human rights responsibilities under the 1951 Refugee Convention, in front of those waiting for processing in camps abroad.[60] In Canada the image of queue jumpers is assigned to those who seek access to health care by paying for treatment, in front of those waiting under the Canada Health Act.[61] This discourse separates insiders and outsiders, or the deserving and undeserving, but does so in a way that is different from other metaphors of exclusion. For example, a comparison of the discourses reveals that the pejorative term is used against the poor and politically unpopular in some cases, and the privileged and politically connected in others.[62] While this comparison is taken up elsewhere, this chapter explores why queue-talk has become so integral to rights-talk, and what the metaphor reveals more generally about the possibilities and limits of human rights law.

---

[58] This conundrum arises persistently in economic and social rights cases, although it applies more broadly. See, e.g., Young, *Constituting Economic and Social Rights* (describing the basic tension of *Grootboom's* weak, declaratory remedy along with public law litigation in general). The challenge of maintaining due recognition for the success of the litigants' claims, with due acknowledgment that their situation is shared by many, has led to support for "dialogical" remedies: see Kent Roach, "Polycentricity and queue jumping in public law remedies: A two-track response," *University of Toronto Law Journal*, 66, 1 (2016), 3–52. See further *Port Elizabeth Municipality v. Various Occupiers* 2005 (1) SA 217 (CC); Lilian Chenwi, "Democratizing the socio-economic rights enforcement process" in Helena Alviar García, Karl E. Klare, and Lucy A. Williams (eds.), *Social and Economic Rights in Theory and Practice: Critical Inquiries* (New York: Routledge, 2015), pp. 178–197 (analyzing the remedial possibilities, and shortcomings, of requiring "meaningful engagement").
[59] These uses are analyzed in Young, "Rights and queues."
[60] Jane McAdam, "Editorial: Australia and asylum seekers," *International Journal of Refugee Law*, 25 no. 3 (2013), 435–448, at 438; Katherine Gelber, "A fair queue? Australian public discourse on refugees and immigration," *Journal of Australian Studies*, 27 no. 77 (2003), 23–30.
[61] *Chaoulli v. Quebec (Att'y Gen)* [2005] 1 SCR 791 (Can.); Canada Health Act, R.S.C. c C-6 (1985) (support for "medically necessary" hospital care and "medically required" physician services).
[62] Young, "Rights and queues."

WHEN QUEUE-TALK MEETS RIGHTS-TALK

As a discourse, human rights have recently been described as our "ethical lingua franca."[63] From natural rights, to civil rights, to human rights, rights-talk involves an appeal to rights (and often, an appeal to litigation) to settle a political argument.[64] While the "vernacularization" of human rights has helped explain its global appeal,[65] the resulting discourse helps generate other idioms of moral judgment, that also call for analysis. Queue-talk may indeed be an inevitable accompaniment to rights-talk, as rights appear to require, or at the very least permit, queues, in order to be realized.[66] In that sense, the institutionalization of human rights in *law* – whose language, as Nicola Lacey demonstrates, has an "inevitably metaphorical tinge"[67] – compels the discourse to connect with social and moral understandings across different groups. The relation between rights-talk and queue-talk is both symbiotic and contradictory, as a deeper study of metaphor and narrative reveals.

Indeed, the relationship between rights and metaphor is itself worthy of analysis. John Locke condemned metaphor and other figurative speech as "perfect cheat,"[68] existing only "to insinuate wrong ideas, move the passions, and thereby mislead the judgment." Like narrative, metaphor sits uneasily against the truth claims of rights.[69] But cognitive and linguistic researchers now claim that

[63] John Tasioulas, "The moral reality of human rights," in Thomas Pogge, (ed.), *Freedom from Poverty as a Human Right: Who Owes What to the Very Poor* (Paris: UNESCO; Oxford; New York: Oxford University Press, 2007), pp. 75–103 (noting the "discourse of human rights [has attained] in recent times ... the status of an ethical lingua franca").
[64] Mary Ann Glendon, *Rights Talk: The Impoverishment of Political Discourse* (New York, NY: The Free Press, 1991); cf. Jeremy Waldron, "Rights and needs, the myth of disjunction," in Austin Sarat and Thomas Kearns (eds.), *Legal Rights: Historical and Philosophical Perspectives* (Ann Arbor, MI: University of Michigan Press, 1996), pp. 87–110.
[65] Sally Engle Merry, *Human Rights and Gender Violence: Translating International Law into Local Justice*, Chicago Series in Law and Society (Chicago, IL: University of Chicago Press, 2006); Kay Schaffer and Sidonie Smith, *Human Rights and Narrated Lives: The Ethics of Recognition* (New York, NY: Palgrave Macmillan, 2004); for a different account of the influence of language on human rights, this time via the epistolary novel, see Lynn Hunt, *Inventing Human Rights* (New York, NY: W.W. Norton & Company, 2007).
[66] Young, "Rights and queues."
[67] Nicola Lacey, "The metaphor of proportionality," *Journal of Law and Society*, 43 no. 1 (2016), 27–44, at 29 (pointing to the example of "contract," which is a term applicable to a discrete legal relationship as well as a broader social one). See also see Stuart Scheingold, *The Politics of Rights: Lawyers, Public Policy and Political Change* (New Haven, CT: Yale University Press, 1974) (applying similar insights to the "myth" of rights).
[68] Peter H. Nidditch (ed.), *John Locke: An Essay concerning Human Understanding* (Oxford: Clarendon Press, 1975), p. 508 (bk. 3, ch. 10).
[69] The claims of rights to truth are a matter of philosophical disagreement that is not necessary to settle here. Compare the skillful disassembling of "loose talk" in Amartya Sen, "Elements of a theory of human rights," *Philosophy & Public Affairs*, 32 no. 4 (2004), 315–356, with Michael

metaphor (along with metonymy and analogy) serves as a fundamental building block of human reasoning.[70] Metaphors supply a cognitive shortcut for human thought, allowing people to make decisions without complete information.[71] Whether it takes us away from truth or closer to it, metaphor reveals the embodiment of human thought, and shapes "what and how we experience, think, mean, imagine, reason, and communicate."[72]

As a language of law, then, the metaphor's distinctive force may be in legitimating and coordinating legal arrangements. Queues represent the outcome of an embodied knowledge, reprised in situations of fixed, but negotiable, ordering. They suggest a certain, perhaps inchoate, aspect of the Western "social imaginary":[73] one strikingly unlike the give and take of the market economy, or the status hierarchy of caste, but nevertheless a ubiquitous discipline in modern life.[74] This chapter argues that the queue metaphor can be understood first as a normative system, second as an allocative mechanism, and third as an aspect of state control. These three roles, described more fully below, explain the metaphor's appeal; and yet each, for different reasons, may contradict the promise of human rights.

First, as a normative system, the queue gives powerful, and graspable, content to the abstraction of rights. And yet it does so by supplanting the ethical justification of human rights by gesturing to rival notions of fairness and justice. Upholding the queue appears to be fair, as a matter of both equality and desert. Queues seem blind to the interpersonal differences that should be irrelevant to questions of distribution, such that gender, sexual orientation, race, ethnicity, religion, age, disability, socio-economic status, or other grounds become irrelevant to allocation. Moreover, the relevant

---

Goodhart, "Human rights and the politics of contestation," in Mark Goodale (ed.), *Human Rights at the Crossroads* (Oxford University Press, 2013), pp. 31–45 (suggesting a suspension of truth claims); see also Steven L. Winter, "Transcendental nonsense, metaphoric reasoning, and the cognitive stakes for law," *University of Pennsylvania Law Review*, 137 no. 4 (1989), 1105–1237, at 1231 (suggesting the meaning of rights is an imaginative, social construction that becomes real "for us").

[70] George Lakoff and Mark Johnson, *Metaphors We Live By* (Chicago, IL: University of Chicago Press, 1980). See also Raymond W. Gibbs Jr., *The Cambridge Handbook of Metaphor and Thought* (New York, NY: Cambridge University Press, 2008).

[71] Gary L. Blasi, "What lawyers know: Lawyering expertise, cognitive science, and the functions of theory," *Journal of Legal Education*, 45 no. 3 (1995), 313–397, at 338.

[72] Mark L. Johnson, "Mind, metaphor, law," *Mercer Law Review*, 58 n. 3 (2007), 845–868, at 846.

[73] Charles Taylor, *Modern Social Imaginaries* (Durham, NC: Duke University Press, 2004), at 2, 23 (referring to certain self-understandings, carried in images, stories and the like, that enable, "through making sense of, the practices of a society").

[74] Gray, "Property in a Queue," suggests the queue experience may be more deeply a part of the "software of the mind": at 166.

criterion of distribution or provision – the time of entry – appears to vindicate equality by treating equally every person's time.[75] And queues espouse the value of desert, since they allocate on the basis of a person's own conduct (arriving/filing/registering early, and waiting in line). This may have had a special appeal in South Africa in its effort to overcome the previous segregation of social spaces.[76]

Nonetheless, the ability of queues to deliver on such values is unreliable. More affluent participants often have the resources necessary to strategically adapt to early entry or waiting substitutes.[77] Gender, sexual orientation, race, ethnicity, religion, age, disability, and socioeconomic status are grounds that may determine, not only time and ability to wait in line, but also entry into the queue at all. And the lack of proportionality between effort (time invested) and result in different queueing systems means that they may flout a desert-based justification anyway.[78] This is evident in the South African context, where a person's age, race, and bureaucratic literacy determined entry onto the waiting list. Disassociated from the metaphor, rights offer a more sophisticated apparatus for understanding discrimination (and affirmative discrimination), and the questionable value of desert.[79] The metaphor's own presentation of fairness hollows out this conception.

Second, as an allocative mechanism, the queue is perceived as the device for realizing rights. In this respect, it provides a conceptual map for distribution that becomes powerful through a sensory-motor experience.[80] The queue

[75] Perry and Zarsky, "Queues in law," at 1611.
[76] Nadine Gordimer, "Standing in the queue," *Index on Censorship*, 23 no. 3 (1994), 128–130 (describing the new experience of waiting to vote in post-apartheid South Africa). Two decades later, record queues were again observed for those paying their final respects to Nelson Mandela: David Smith, "Nelson Mandela's lying in state draws queue of thousands to say goodbye," *The Guardian*, December 11, 2013.
[77] Rizwaan Jameel Mokal, "Priority as pathology: The *Pari Passu* myth," *Cambridge Law Journal*, 60 no. 3 (2001), 581–619, at 592 (noting reasons for departing from first-in first-out queues in bankruptcy).
[78] Perry and Zarsky, "Queues in law," at 1618. The investment of time may appear a poor desert base when government distribution should be guided by broader properties of virtue or effort. Cf. John Rawls, *A Theory of Justice* (Harvard University Press rev ed., 1971, 1999), pp. 88–89 (suggesting how this reward would resemble not desert but entitlement: "that those who, with the prospect of improving their condition, have done what the system announces it will reward are entitled to have their expectations met. In this sense the more fortunate have title to their better situation."
[79] Desert may fail to pass the required normative justification; and well as being an unreliable principle for identifying valued activities: Richard J. Arneson, "Egalitarianism and the undeserving poor," *Journal of Political Philosophy*, 5 no. 4 (1997), 327–350, at 331; Michael B. Katz, *The Undeserving Poor: From the War on Poverty to the War on Welfare* (New York, NY: Pantheon Books, 1989).
[80] Johnson, "Mind, metaphor, law," at 856.

therefore gains a cognitive advantage, alongside the time, journey, and container metaphors that are commonly applied to explicate different words or actions.[81] The physical experience of queueing may suggest that, in conditions of scarcity, lines can prevent chaos and disorder. Compared with other allocation methods, administrative costs are low because of the ease of explaining the method of allocation, monitoring compliance, and resolving disputes.[82] This brings obvious gains in efficiency.

Yet here, again, the queueing metaphor obscures – this time, the complexities of the distributive decisions that determine who has access to certain basic goods and services. In South Africa, just as elsewhere, access to housing is determined by a complex set of subsidies, upgrades, mortgage and finance regulation, rental protections, security of tenure, and zoning laws – factors that are obscured by a singular focus on the waiting list register. Access is also organized against the backdrop of a liberal market, in which owners enjoy the protection of their property rights, and their freedom to transact, with only limited restrictions.[83] The metaphor thus conjures order and efficiency in distribution that may not be borne out in practice,[84] and flattens out the complexity of any general market-ordered system.

Moreover, the perceived gains to order are culturally contingent. While queues represent "an overlapping, largely shared, common understanding of the right way to behave,"[85] this is not everywhere the same. Orderly queues may have particular resonance for Anglo, or at least for certain Western, consumers.[86] Different queueing norms are apparent elsewhere: in Nordic countries, for example, "time-outs" are often socially acceptable;[87] in Uganda queues are referred to as "hustling

---

[81] For examination, see Taylor, *The Language Animal*; Lakoff and Johnson, *Metaphors We Live By*.

[82] See e.g., Yoram Barzel, "A theory of rationing by waiting," *Journal of Law and Economics*, 17 no. 1 (1974), 73–95.

[83] Such limitations are, however, noteworthy, in setting out some critical protections: see, e.g., *Minister of Pub. Works v. Kyalami Ridge Envtl. Ass'n* 2001 (3) SA 1151 (CC); *Jaftha v. Schoeman* 2005 (1) BCLR 78 (CC); *President of the Republic of South Africa v. Modderklip Boerdery (Pty.) Ltd.* 2005 (5) SA 3 (CC); *Port Elizabeth Municipality v. Various Occupiers* 2005 (1) SA 217 (CC); *Blue Moonlight* (CC).

[84] See, e.g., Ryan Powell and John Flint, "(In)formalization and the civilizing process: Applying the work of Norbert Elias to housing-based anti-social behaviour interventions in the UK," *Housing, Theory & Society*, 26 no. 3 (2009), 159–178, at 171.

[85] Neil MacCormick, "Norms, institutions and institutional facts," at 301, 308–309.

[86] See, e.g., Joe Moran, *Queuing for Beginners: The Story of Daily Life from Breakfast to Bedtime* (Profile Books, 2008) (describing a social history of everyday British practices, including the queue). Gray, "Property in a Queue," at 178, points to the role of the English doctrine of "estates," and notes the absence of queue discipline in non-common-law based legal systems.

[87] MacCormick, "Norms, institutions and institutional facts."

practices."[88] Culture is a malleable concept, and cultural practices respond to institutional conditions. Queuing norms have undoubtedly changed in pre- and post-Communist Eastern Europe,[89] as they have in pre- and post-market Communist China.[90] Even where queueing norms do not follow first come first served, a preference for order is often expressed, which makes the cultural affinities more obscure.[91] These two distributive blind spots – of complexity and order – narrow the institutional possibilities of legal obligations to an idealized priority line.[92]

Third, as an aspect of state control, the queue contradicts a central justification for rights. While metaphors may reveal certain "cultural or personal truths,"[93] they are also often in the control of those in power.[94] It is worth questioning why politicians, officials and even courts, routinely invoke this expression in relation to housing rights. We know that queues are a recognizable medium for social integration,[95] and an incubator for developing important

---

[88] Henry J. Ssali, "Jumping the queue," *Africa News Service*, May 28, 2007, (comparing "hustling practices" in Uganda with respect for queues in the United Kingdom, Germany, and South Africa).

[89] See Vladimir Sorokin, *The Queue* (trans. Sally Laird) (New York, NY: New York Review Books, 2008). For other poignant examples in Eastern European literature, see, e.g., Stanisław Barańczak, *Breathing under Water and Other East European Essays* (Cambridge: Harvard University Press, 1990); Tadeusz Konwicki, *The Polish Complex* (trans. Richard Lourie) (Normal, IL: Dalkey Archive Press, 1982, 1998).

[90] Ian Johnson, "As Beijing becomes a supercity, the rapid growth brings pains," *New York Times*, July 19, 2015.

[91] Such preferences, in the face of contradictory cultural experience, apply to rights-talk as well, as recent anthropological studies make clear: see, e.g., Sally Engle Merry, *Human Rights and Gender Violence*, and the collection of Mark Goodale (ed.), *Human Rights at the Crossroads*.

[92] Similarly, the dislocation between the experience of rights and their appeal and legitimacy, does not undermine the strength of the discourse; Goodhart, "Human rights and the politics of contestation," at 40 (noting "repeated abuses of human rights ... may even have strengthened" the discourse). Compare with the position taken by Joseph Raz, "Human rights without foundations" in Samantha Besson and John Tasioulas, *The Philosophy of International Law* (Oxford and New York: Oxford University Press, 2010) pp. 321–339, at 322 (noting the hypocrisy of much human rights rhetoric does not invalidate rights arguments, although it may weaken them).

[93] Bernard J. Hibbitts, "Making sense of metaphors: Visuality, aurality, and the reconfiguration of American legal discourse," *Cardozo Law Review*, 16 no. 2 (1994), 229–356.

[94] Lakoff and Johnson, *The Metaphors We Live By*, at 157. For a helpful view of the inevitable constraints on which metaphors "stick," as law, see, e.g., Malcolm M. Feeley and Edward L. Rubin, *Judicial Policy Making in the Modern State* (Cambridge, UK: Cambridge University Press, 2000), p. 238; Lacey, "The Metaphor of Proportionality."

[95] E.g., Sorokin, *The Queue*; Gordimer, "Standing in the queue"; Nadine Beckmann and Janet Bujra, "The 'politics of the queue': The politicization of people living with HIV/AIDS in Tanzania," *Development & Change*, 41 no. 6 (2010), 1041–1064.

virtues such as patience, rule-compliance, and trust.[96] And if civility means regarding others, "including one's adversaries, as members of the same inclusive collectivity,"[97] queues can, in principle, provide a useful forum for learning and practicing it, and building norms of courtesy, cooperation, and institutional effectiveness.[98] These associations can be exploited, and yet not delivered, through queue-talk.

Indeed, the South African waiting list has been described as a "tool of political and social control."[99] In this way, queue-talk is able to undermine the democratic possibilities of rights-talk by creating enmity between rights-claimants who have otherwise solidaristic claims upon the state. This is because "queue jumpers" (as rights-claimants) are perceived as having misappropriated otherwise legitimate criteria – the criteria of need – and are therefore moving up the system of allocation illegitimately.[100] This perception connotes ideas of corruption and illegitimacy on the part of rights-claimants, producing a particularly disempowering effect. Queue jumping may thus be seen as a "blame frame" used by those who must be passive in the face of inequities of others,[101] but one that is peculiarly hostile to the political agency exercised by unpopular groups – in comparison with common tropes of "dependency,"[102] which invoke passivity,

---

[96] See, e.g., the values imputed to queues in, e.g., Ssali, "Jumping the queue"; Damian Barr, "The waiting game," *The Times* (London, England) November 28, 2009.

[97] Edward Shils, "The virtue of civil society" in Virginia A. Hodgkinson and Michael W. Foley (eds.), *The Civil Society Reader* (Hanover, NH: University Press of New England, 2003), pp. 292–306, at 300.

[98] For an analysis of the "episodic, single stranded, and anonymous" networks that may form from queues, and the very different social capital built into the "repeated, intensive, multistranded" networks of associations, see Robert D. Putnam, *Bowling Alone: The Collapse and Revival of American Community* (New York, NY: Simon & Schuster, 2000), p. 22.

[99] Tissington et al., "Jumping the queue," at 58. There is a related fear by some that the 'so-called database' may be used as evidence in court to evict people by claiming that people are "queue-jumping." Ibid. at 62.

[100] The corruption-through-payments also taints this perception, although it operates differently. See further Young, *Rights as Queues* (in particular, relating this to Canadian rights discourse).

[101] Jon D. Hanson and Kathleen Hanson, "The blame frame: Justifying (racial) injustice in America," *Harvard Civil Rights-Civil Liberties Law Review*, 41 no. 2 (2006), 413–480 (citing in particular Melvin J. Lerner and Dale T. Miller, "Just world research and the attribution process: Looking back and looking ahead," *Psychological Bulletin*, 85 no. 5 (1978), 1030–1051 (social psychology of understandings of fairness that is upheld through blaming victims of inequities and excuses perpetrators or passive observers).

[102] For examples of each, see Nancy Fraser and Linda Gordon, "A genealogy of dependency: Tracing a keyword in the U.S. welfare state," *Signs: Journal of Women in Culture and Society*, 19 no. 2 (1994), 309–336; (dependency); Joel Handler and Yeheskel Hasenfeld, *Blame Welfare: Ignore Poverty and Inequality* (New York: Cambridge University Press, 2007), p. 159 (noting that the "welfare queen" myth "is the joining of two stereotypes: race and the

rather than agency, as the source of blame. The consequence is to undermine the very norm of individual agency that the recognition of rights purports to mobilize.

As one housing rights movement in South Africa described the incapacitating effect of the "waiting patiently" mentality. "[T]his mind set has actually disempowered people over the last fifteen years or so, as it has undermined some community's [sic] ability or will power to get on with it themselves. In contrast, some of the social movements stand in contrast to this ("nothing for us without us")."[103] When government officials refer to the queue in making statements about housing rights, housing movements counter with another version of rights-talk. It offers, in effect, a counteridiom to the counteridiom.[104] In defending the politics of waiting, queue-talk may defend the politics of docility,[105] and its rejection leads to a more active embrace of rights-talk.

This chapter leans on law, not literature or sociology.[106] But revealing, in this respect, is a comment made about the ubiquitous lines we associate with Soviet Russia, where "[t]he collective body was steadily ritualized by queues. It was taught order and obedience, and rendered maximally governable.... [T]he line dissected the body into pieces, pacified and disciplined it, gave people time to think about the advantages of socialism and about the class struggle; and in the end they were rewarded with food and goods."[107] No less apt is current social commentary in the United States. One sociologist seeking to capture the divisions of a polarized polity described the perceptions felt by those living in

"underserving poor"); Ann Cammett, "Deadbeat dads & welfare queens: How metaphor shapes poverty law," *Boston College Journal of Law & Social Justice*, 34 no. 2 (2014), 233–265.

[103] Royston and Eglin, "Allocation thought piece for managed land settlement," at 4–5.

[104] One such movement engages a far-reaching political vision: Jacki Dugard, Tshepo Madlingozi, and Kate Tissington, "Rights-compromised or rights-savvy? The use of rights-based strategies to advance socio-economic struggles by Abahlali baseMjondolo, the South African shack-dwellers' movement," in Helena Alviar García, Karl E. Klare, and Lucy A. Williams, *Social and Economic Rights in Theory and Practice: Critical Inquiries*, pp. 23–43.

[105] For a recent contrast of South Africa's ambitions of transformation with its dangers of docility, see Justice Sisi Khampepe, "Meaningful participation as transformative process: The challenges of institutional change in South Africa's constitutional democracy," Lecture delivered at the Stellenbosch University Annual Human Rights Lecture, 6 October 2016. For further analysis of the stigma generated by other official registers, *see* Sandra Liebenberg, "Social rights and transformation in South Africa: Three frames," *South African Journal of Human Rights*, 31 no. 3 (2015), 446–472.

[106] But acknowledges, of course, the mutual constitution of each, and narrative's rich method of outlining this relation. For application to human rights, see Mark Goodale's discussion of Martin Luther King, Jr.'s "Letter from a Birmingham Jail," or Eleanor Roosevelt's "curious grapevine" of unfolding activism and debate: Mark Goodale, "Human rights and moral agency," in Cindy Holder and David Reidy (eds.), *Human Rights: The Hard Questions* (New York, NY: Cambridge University Press, 2013), pp. 418–436.

[107] Sorokin, *The Queue*, at p. 257.

conservative communities that expressed hostility to rights claimants – indeed, class conflict – through the metaphor of the queue.[108] Under this metaphor, Americans wait by "patiently standing in a long line leading up a hill,"[109] where lies the security and prosperity of the American Dream. Those in the middle of the line are "white, older, Christian, and predominantly male"; behind them are minorities and women. The line is moving slowly, if at all. As Hochschild describes it, those fixated on the line see minorities, women, immigrants, refugees, and public sector employees all cutting in to get ahead. The federal government is perceived as on the side of those unjustly "cutting in," while the free market is perceived as the unwavering ally of the "good citizens waiting in line."[110] In both Soviet Russia and the contemporary United States, the queue thus configures the social imaginary; it achieves the ethical, distributive, and political sleights of hand described above, despite operating against distinct ideological backdrops.[111]

HUMAN RIGHTS AND METAPHOR

Metaphor and narrative are both fundamental to law, via the need for rhetoric and persuasion – and cognitive understanding – to secure law's social acceptance.[112] To separate the two is somewhat artificial.[113] We might say that while narrative contextualizes, metaphor generalizes (and yet the two conspire in synthesis); or that metaphor stands in when literal words fail (and yet the mental modeling of metaphor runs on images that themselves generate script).[114]

---

[108] Arlie Russell Hochschild, *Strangers in Their Own Land: Anger and Mourning on the American Right* (New York, NY: The New Press, 2016), pp. 135–151.
[109] Ibid, at 136.   [110] Ibid, at 150.
[111] I discuss the queue's ideological changeability in Young, "Rights and queues." While one might compare the two excerpts alongside the traditionally espoused hostility to civil and political rights, in the Soviet example, and to economic, social, and cultural rights, in the American one, the comparison rests on divisions that are contested: see, e.g., Daniel J. Whelan and Jack Donnelly, "The West, economic and social rights, and the global human rights regime: Setting the record straight," *Human Rights Quarterly*, 29 no. 4 (2007), 908–949, and among multiple rejoinders, Alex Kirkup and Tony Evans, "The myth of western opposition to economic, social, and cultural rights?," *Human Rights Quarterly*, 31 no. 1 (2009) 221–237.
[112] This role of discourse, important alongside (and as part of) the coercion of law, was theorized in seminal terms by Robert Cover, "The Supreme Court, 1982 Term–Foreword: Nomos and narrative," *Harvard Law Review*, 97 no. 1 (1982), 4–68; "Violence and the Word," *Yale Law Journal*, 95, no. 8 (1986), 1601–1629.
[113] For a description of their overlap, and hybrid cases, see Stefán Snævarr, *Metaphors, Narratives, Emotions: Their Interplay and Impact* (Amsterdam; NY: Rodopi, 2010) (noting, however, the greater pervasiveness of narrative over metaphor and emotions in our cognitive and cultural worlds).
[114] Ibid. at 234 (describing the "storied structures" of metaphor).

Examining metaphor helps to understand "how culture necessarily works its way into law,"[115] an intriguing possibility in the transnational spaces occupied by human rights advocates, governments, treaty bodies, legislators, judges, interest groups, and social movements.

The analysis of metaphor has helped to ground a powerful human rights critique. In his seminal naming of "the metaphor of human rights," Makau Matua described the persistence of a "savages-victims-savior" triad, the parts of which comprised the "grand narrative" of the human rights movement. According to these metaphors, the state stands in for the savage, the human being for the victim, and human rights institutions, including the United Nations, Western governments, and international non-governmental organizations, for the savior. Each metaphor, suggests Matua, is deeply misleading, and underlines the colonial heritage of the human rights project.[116] Matua's study joins Joseph Slaughter's focus on the metaphorical "incorporation" of the human rights person into an artificial "rights-bearing unit."[117] Incorporation, for Slaughter, reveals the legalizing tendency of a Western project that correlates with the coming-of-age narrative of the *Bildungsroman*.[118] Such metaphors unsettle other accounts of the power of human rights,[119] in part by demonstrating the unreliability, and particularity, of human sentiment, even as the authors, themselves, marshal it.

In previous work, with Jeremy Perelman, to illustrate the constructive role of human rights, I deployed the metaphor of the "footprints" of human rights.[120] This study, like the present chapter, differs from those that anchor human rights in international legal practice – in the actions and statements of the United Nations system, international non-governmental organizations,

---

[115] Steven L. Winter, "Making the familiar conventional again," *Michigan Law Review*, 99 no. 6 (2001), 1607–1636, at 1635–1636.
[116] Makau Matua, "Savages, victims, and saviors: The metaphor of human rights," *Harvard International Law Journal*, 42 no. 1 (2001), 201–245.
[117] Joseph R. Slaughter, *Human Rights, Inc.: The World Novel, Narrative Form, and International Law* (New York, NY: Fordham University Press, 2007), p. 20.
[118] Ibid. at p. 7.
[119] Lynn Hunt, *Inventing Human Rights*; see also Beth Simmons, *Mobilizing for Human Rights: International Law in Domestic Politics* (Cambridge; NY: Cambridge University Press, 2009), 67; Ryan Goodman and Derek Jinks, *Socializing States: Promoting Human Rights through International Law* (Oxford, UK: Oxford University Press, 2013).
[120] Jeremy Perelman and Katharine G. Young, "Rights as footprints: A new metaphor for contemporary human rights practice," *Northwestern Journal of International Human Rights*, 9 no. 1 (2010), 27–58. The story is told in Jeremy Perelman and Katharine G. Young, "Freeing Mohammed Zakari: Footprints toward hope" in Jeremy Perelman and Lucie White (eds.), *Stones of Hope: How African Activists Reclaim Human Rights to Challenge Global Poverty* (Stanford, CA: Stanford University Press. 2011), pp. 122–149.

and powerful states.[121] Rather, it describes the ways in which a community in Ghana used the memory of, and storytelling about, a moment of resistance in order to mobilize an eclectic social movement over a period of years. The footprints metaphor revealed how human rights represents different things to different people. In this way, the emancipatory potential of human rights – in that case, the right to health[122] – was held together even as it conjured very different understandings. Like the processes of "vernacularization" described by Sally Engle Merry, human rights were translated across local and global domains without losing their power to change thoughts and actions. A metaphor coined by the community was able to capture this effect.[123]

This chapter, however, analyzes a metaphor that accompanies, but also contradicts, human rights law. In focusing on the constitutional guarantee of a right to access housing in South Africa, it traces ambiguous narratives and distorting conceptions of the right's institutional and juridical protection. The queue's appeal can be explained by its ubiquity in modern life.[124] We might further speculate on its resonance – on the sensory-motor experience of queueing, on its access to an emotional understanding of fairness, or even on its counterintuitiveness in an increasingly market-based world.[125] When the

---

[121] Compare, e.g., Raz, "Human rights without foundations." Another example of a non-positivist approach to human rights is the "metaphorical thinking" suggested by Benjamin Gregg, "Human rights as metaphor for political community beyond the nation state," *Critical Sociology*, 42 no. 6 (2015), 897–917.

[122] With its institutional complexity, the right to health is difficult to ground in a human rights narrative of state perpetrator and victim. Note the creation of multiple protagonists in the narratives invoked in Alicia Ely Yamin, *Power, Suffering, and the Struggle for Dignity: Human Rights Frameworks for Health and Why They Matter* (Philadelphia, PA: University of Pennsylvania Press, 2016). This is not to say that other human rights and their abuse are not also complicated by narrative: see a useful summary by James Dawes and Samantha Gupta, "On narrative and human rights," *Humanity*, 5 no. 1 (2014), 149–156, especially at 155–156 (comparing views on the apparent transparency of language, versus its inadequacy, in Richard Ashby Wilson, *Writing History in International Crime Trials* [Cambridge, UK; New York, NY: Cambridge University Press, 2011] and Lyndsey Stonebridge, *The Judicial Imagination: Writing after Nuremberg* [Edinburgh: Edinburgh University Press, 2011]).

[123] Compare with Edward L Rubin, *Beyond Camelot: Rethinking Politics and Law for the Modern State* (Princeton, NJ: Princeton University Press, 2005) (suggesting that metaphoric conceptions play into "negative" rights).

[124] Despite aspects of modernization and technology which have sought to reduce the need for queueing, other aspects (i.e. urbanization) have made it ever more inevitable. See further Young, "Rights and queues."

[125] Lacey, "The metaphor of proportionality," at 43 (making a similar point in relation to proportionality). Compare, e.g., with Sorokin, *The Queue*. Notwithstanding that most goods and services are traded, and not delivered in queue, we might inquire whether the patience (or docility) of recipients is not also a part of an exchange-based culture. See, e.g., Taylor, *Modern Social Imaginaries*, at p. 71 (citing the comment of Louis XIV, that "[t]he

queue configures politics and law – indeed, is given a legal classification – it unsettles and resettles the potential of human rights. As Lacey notes, "[O]ur evaluation of law's metaphors ... must not be confined to their conceptual structure, their discursive form or even their doctrinal elaboration: it must also attend to the institutional arrangements which provide the framework for their interpretation and enforcement, and to the interests and power relations which shape their development and implementation."[126] This goal can be achieved by examining how a metaphor might itself contradict the ambitions of what it represents. In this sense, we can see that the housing rights queue undermines human rights in South Africa just as it is, in part, required to institutionalize them.

CONCLUSION

In this essay, the metaphor of the queue has been shown to be both constitutive and suggestive of human rights. The queue configures the political contestations around housing rights by describing a waiting list that in fact operates more as a database of names than a mode of ordering; and a doctrinal requirement that in fact exists to rank need and administrative reasonableness rather than time spent waiting. In the analysis of metaphor, the important question is "not [its] truth or falsity ... but the perceptions and inferences that follow from it and the actions that are sanctioned by it."[127] Thus, the queue reveals the blind spots of human rights, in obscuring the ethical justifications, distributive decisions, and political freedoms that are vital to their realization. If human rights are indeed today's ethical lingua franca, we might ask how, and why, other language becomes prominent, and what meanings they, in turn, create.

---

deference and respect that we receive from our subjects are not a free gift from them but payment for the justice and protection they expect to receive from us").
[126] Ibid. [127] Lakoff and Johnson, *Metaphors We Live By*, at p. 158.

13

The Cutters and the Others

Bernadette A. Meyler

Katharine Young's fascinating paper, "Narrative, Metaphor and Human Rights Law: When Rights-Talk Meets Queue-Talk," makes a compelling case for the significance of the metaphors of the "queue" and "queue jumping" in understanding attitudes about access to social and economic rights and, concomitantly, in perpetuating a distorted vision of those rights. The essay is part of a larger project on the relationship between rights and queues in a number of countries that share legal origins in the common law.[1] The persuasiveness of Young's discussion of the role of queues in both shaping access to so-called "second generation" rights and in "legitimating and coordinating legal arrangements" within the South African, Canadian, and Australian contexts raises the question of why talk of queues remains so sparse within the American legal system. Even taking into account the fact that "line" is favored over "queue" in American English, the phrases "cut in line" or "cutting in line" appear surprisingly infrequently within judicial opinions – as metaphors, at least, rather than as descriptions of the source of some episode of violence. At the same time, the circumstances of the 2016 presidential election within the United States raised highly salient debates about the virtues and vices of literally and metaphorically standing in line and cutting in line. This response to Young's chapter briefly explores the settings in which line cutting has arisen in the United States context along with its larger cultural significance and speculates about the reasons for its traditionally lower profile and recent efflorescence in the public imaginary.

A search of federal cases since 2000 on Westlaw yields fewer than twenty in which the phrases "cutting in line" or "cut in line" were used metaphorically. Several of these pertain to creditors in bankruptcy and the claim that some

---

[1] Katharine G. Young, "Rights and queues: On distributive contests in the modern state," *Columbia Journal of Transnational Law*, 55 no.1 (2016), 65–137.

were jumping ahead of others[2]; others deal with civil procedure and "'cut[ting] in line' ahead of those litigants awaiting determination of their properly noticed and timely filed motions."[3] The set of cases closest to those that Young treats – particularly in the Australian asylum context – pertain to immigration.

The references to "cutting in line" in these instances all address the government's allegation that countenancing the claims of immigrants in the cases at issue would allow these individuals to bypass a legitimate queue and permit some an unfair benefit at the expense of others. Hence in *Dong* v. *Chertoff*, the Northern District of California addressed the claim on the part of defendant government officials – who were resisting an order of mandamus designed to force them to process immigrants' adjustment of status applications – that "allowing immigration applicants to use mandamus to 'cut in line' would open the floodgates for immigration-related mandamus actions. The use of mandamus in immigration matters would shorten the delay for some, only to lengthen it for others."[4] The court responded by pointing out that the plaintiffs had appeared to be displaced in the queue already, so that, rather than being allowed to "jump the queue," they were instead attempting to restore their positions in line:

> The court does not find this argument compelling. First, these plaintiffs have more than "waited their turn," having seen millions of later-filed applications processed before theirs. According to the documents submitted by the defendants, only 20 percent of FBI name checks take up to six months to resolve, and less than one percent remain pending for more than six months. See Docket No. 5, Ex. 1. The plaintiffs have been waiting close to two years for the completion of a name check. Thus, far from "cutting in line," or gaming for an unfair advantage vis-à-vis similarly situated applicants, the plaintiffs are simply asking to be placed back in the queue.[5]

Other courts considered nearly identical claims on behalf of the US Citizenship and Immigration Service ("USCIS").[6] Strikingly, these cases were all decided between 2005 and 2008 and all deployed the metaphor of cutting in line in response to government arguments raising the image in the first place. Here the claim of cutting in line appears to arise out of a

---

[2] *In re International Fibercom, Inc.*, 503 F.3d 933, 945 (9th Cir., 2007); *In re Xenerga, Inc.*, 2011 WL 52740 at *5 (M.D. Florida, 2011).
[3] *Cynthia L. Clark* v. *Bank of America*, 2013 WL 12119736 at *1 (C.D. California, 2013, internal citations omitted); *Aoki* v. *Gilbert*, 2013 WL 2474877 (unreported, C.D. California, 2013).
[4] *Dong* v. *Chertoff*, 513 F. Supp. 2d 1158, 1171 (N.D. Cal., 2007).   [5] Ibid.
[6] *Kashkool* v. *Chertoff*, 553 F. Supp. 2d 1131, 1145 (D. Arizona, 2008); *Saleh* v. *Hansen*, 2006 WL 2320232 *4 (unreported, S.D. Ohio, 2006).

litigation strategy on the part of the government designed to cut off federal courts of appeals' interventions in various immigration-related claims.

USCIS's reliance on this metaphor under President George W. Bush's tenure finds echoes in the president's own words in other immigration-related contexts and in statements by several republicans in Congress during the same period as well as subsequently. In describing his simultaneous opposition to amnesty and to rejecting all paths to citizenship by undocumented immigrants, President Bush advocated a "middle ground" that

> recognizes that there are differences between an illegal immigrant who crossed the border recently and someone who has worked here for many years, and has a home, a family, and an otherwise clean record. I believe that illegal immigrants who have roots in our country and want to stay should have to pay a meaningful penalty for breaking the law, ... to pay their taxes, ... to learn English ... and to work in a job for a number of years. People who meet these conditions should be able to apply for citizenship but approval would not be automatic, and they will have to wait in line behind those who played by the rules and followed the law.[7]

In the legislative arena, Senator Bill Frist repeated the President's words, asserting that "Law breakers should not be able to cut in line, as the President mentioned last night."[8] Years later, Representative Tom McClintock employed the metaphor as well, urging:

> [T]o those who say that we need a path to citizenship, I must point out we already have such a path that is followed by millions of legal immigrants who have obeyed all of our laws, who have respected our Nation's sovereignty, who've done everything our country's asked of them to do, including waiting patiently in line, and are now watching millions of illegal immigrants try and cut in line in front of them.[9]

While these uses may have different policy implications, all deprecate cutting in line and suggest that the immigration-related actions they reject would allow for this kind of inequity.

Line jumping found its way into the 2016 US Republican presidential primaries in a similar context. One of the candidates, Ohio Governor John Kasich, provisionally rejected an immediate grant of citizenship for undocumented immigrants residing within the United States, stating that "I don't

---

[7] President George W. Bush, "Bush's speech on immigration," *NY Times* (May 15, 2006), available at www.nytimes.com/2006/05/15/washington/15text-bush.html.

[8] 109th Congress, second session (Tues., May 16, 2006), S4572.

[9] Statement of Representative Tom McClintock, 113th Congress, first session (July 10, 2013), H4315.

favor citizenship because, as I teach my kids, you don't jump the line to get into a Taylor Swift concert."[10] The then president-elect, Donald Trump, did not display such reluctance to cut in line in his personal life. As one website reported the prelude of his attendance at an Adele concert, "Donald Trump is apparently, like us all, a fan of Adele. He expressed that fandom in an on-brand fashion Tuesday night, by cutting in front of hundreds of people to get into her show at Radio City Music Hall."[11]

Trump's behavior in this instance is not only the prerogative of potential presidents in the United States. Anyone who has waited in line at clubs or other such venues knows that VIPs – the wealthy or the famous – are often hastened in the door while others are left out in the cold. Airport security likewise permits those willing to invest more money in a preclearance service to circumvent long lines and early boarding can be purchased through special ticket categories on many airlines. Despite occasional grumbling, this kind of circumvention of lines through economic means appears perfectly acceptable to many.

While many bases for cutting in line may be subject to opprobrium in the United States, a certain kind of VIP status allows those possessing it to circumvent queues with impunity.[12] Furthermore, even if cutting in line is frowned up, the phenomenon of people waiting in line has itself been subject to scorn and disparagement. Perhaps partly as a consequence of longstanding cultural associations between Communism and standing in line,[13] the image of waiting in line is frequently associated with a critique of policies perceived as excessively socialist in nature. This kind of criticism has been voiced most frequently in the healthcare context.[14] Accounts of

[10] Tom LoBianco, "Kasich wants immigration crackdown, but leaves door open on pathway to citizenship," *CNN*, www.cnn.com/2015/08/12/politics/john-kasich-immigration (August 12, 2015). Accessed Oct. 26, 2016.
[11] Anna Merlan, "Adele superfan Donald Trump cut the line at her concert last night," *The Slot*, http://theslot.jezebel.com/adele-superfan-donald-trump-cut-the-line-at-her-concert-174323183 9 (Nov. 18, 2015). Accessed Oct. 26, 2016.
[12] In the *Wall Street Journal* article, "In Brazil, it's fine for seniors to cut the line," Marla Dickerson and Luciana Magalhaes describe the legal ability of senior citizens to go to the front of the line in Brazil as having the potential to "start a dust-up in the U.S. or England," while at the same time referring to "celebrit[ies] sauntering past a velvet rope" (Feb. 23, 2016), available at www.wsj.com/articles/in-brazil-its-fine-for-seniors-to-cut-the-line-1456276423.
[13] As Konstantin Bogdanov writes, "The queue was a constant and immediately recognisable attribute of Soviet everyday life." Bogdanov, "The queue as narrative," trans. Victoria Donovan in *Russian Cultural Anthropology after the Collapse of Communism*, Albert Baiburin, Catriona Kelly, and Nikolai Vakhtin eds. (London: Routledge, 2012), p. 77.
[14] As Jonathan Cohn wrote in 2009 in "Healthy Examples," "If President Obama and his supporters get their way, this argument goes, healthcare in America will start to look like

socialized medicine that emphasize waiting in line sometimes also lament the contingency of the lines, which, under these accounts, may never end in services. John Goodman writes, for example, in the course of debunking what he deems various myths of socialized medicine, that:

> If you're a citizen of Canada, you don't really have a right to any particular health care service. You don't have a right to heart surgery. You don't even have a right to a place in the waiting line. If you're the hundredth person waiting for heart surgery, you're not entitled to the hundredth surgery. Other people can and do get in ahead of you. From time to time, even Americans go to Canada and jump the queue, because Americans can do something that Canadians cannot — Americans can pay for care.[15]

Under this narrative, those waiting for healthcare in Canada seem less like responsible citizens fulfilling their social duty than dupes in some story spun by Kafka.

Based on this brief survey of the US context, I would like to suggest a few parameters for examining metaphors in disparate legal contexts. First, it is worth considering how pervasive the metaphor is – is its use widespread or does it emerge only in certain contexts as the result of the rhetorical choices of particular actors? In the United States, the metaphor of cutting in line shows up rarely and predominantly in the immigration setting, which allows one to trace its political and legal valences more concretely. In another cultural context, where the queue was a more dominant mode of social ordering, analyzing its appearance in law might suggest a widespread frame for understanding legal principles. Second, the metaphor may be applied to some populations and not others – examining who is included and who is exempted may reveal something significant about the surrounding political and legal system. For example, US legal materials suggest that those who are officially asked to wait in line are almost never ordinary citizens seeking rights protected under the US Constitution but instead immigrants looking for entrance into the country. This is possibly a result of general suspicion within the United States about systems that require waiting in line. Likewise, the relatively unproblematic quality in some contexts of lines differentiated by ability to pay perhaps reflects the

---

healthcare overseas. Yes, maybe everybody will have insurance. But people will have to wait in long lines. And when they are done waiting in line, the care won't be very good." *Boston Globe* (July 5, 2009), available at http://archive.boston.com/bostonglobe/ideas/articles/2009/07/05/healthy_examples_plenty_of_countries_get_healthcare_right/.

[15] John Goodman, "Five myths of socialized medicine," in *Cato's Letter* vol. 3, no. 1 (Winter, 2005), available at https://object.cato.org/sites/cato.org/files/pubs/pdf/catosletterv3n1.pdf.

pervasive acceptance of capitalism and its influence on legal and political arrangements within the country. More evidence would be required to substantiate any of these conclusions, but if we want to derive theses about our legal system from the metaphors it employs, we should be asking these questions.

CONVERSATION VIII
NARRATIVE AND METAPHOR IN CREATIVE WORK BY LAWYERS

Editors' Introduction

Michael Hanne and Robert Weisberg

All the other chapters in this volume are scholarly commentaries about the role of metaphor and narrative in law. This one is indeed a conversation between two scholars, Lawrence Joseph and Meredith Wallis, and it has a scholarly component. But its perspective is that of a creative writer (who is a lawyer) reflecting on the use of metaphor and narrative, and so the conversation crosses a genre boundary in the volume. Fittingly so, because its main subject is a non-scholarly book by the opening conversant here, Joseph's famed *Lawyerland*, which may be the most provocatively genre-defying work of literature ever written by a lawyer about law.

Lawyerland won great praise and yet caused great consternation on its arrival 20 years ago, because of its refusal to fit in any neat category of writing (Is it fiction? Play for voices? Documentary? Memoir? Philosophical reflection?[1]), and because it produced such wildly varied interpretations of the way it depicts the role of lawyers. Are they Bartlebys struggling in a professional hell-hole of meaninglessness? Are they the true poets of American society, the pulse readers of the national mood? Are they ethnographers of their profession? Are they bitter nihilists, or are they romantic idealists? In this chapter, Joseph takes the genre-bending further in offering a self-reflection on what he was accomplishing in his own book – and in his volumes of poetry, and we have literary scholar and lawyer Meredith Wallis responding with her own interpretation of Joseph's craft.

From one perspective, we can simply place our immediate subject somewhat mundanely under the heading of lawyers who become writers and write novels depicting law. But that category does not necessarily illuminate the role of metaphor or narrative in law in any distinct way. Lawyer novelists use metaphors just like anyone else, and the narration of legal events in their

---

[1] Pierre Schlag, "Jurisprudence Noire," *Columbia Law Review* 101 (2001), 1733–1742.

novels is not much different from what we get from non-lawyer writers, depicting events that are part of the general popular understanding of law. Lawyer-novelists obviously have some advantage in depicting the details of what lawyers do in the subtler mechanics of their practice, but these things are discoverable by close observers and researchers who are not lawyers. Instead, the unique potential contribution of a lawyer writing creatively about law is an intimate picture of how lawyers view themselves and their lives, about what it is like to live a life in the law. And no one has come close to Joseph in this endeavor.

Doubtless there are reflective lawyerly memoirs, but our premise is that imaginative literature can reveal more than autobiography. Alas, almost all the work in this latter category is what we would call popular fiction.[2] Some of it, as in the work of Lisa Scottoline, is perfectly respectable police procedural/trial drama mystery or thriller fiction, often relying on unabashed caricatures of real legal practice. Some of it, as in the work of Scott Turow, is written with a bit more of a pretense of being "serious" fiction but remains well within the realm of mystery genre work. As with another genre that curiously draws many lawyers to writing fiction – the romance novel[3] – lawyer novelists acknowledge that they turn to this pop fiction as a way of escaping law while still drawing on their knowledge of it. John Grisham is perhaps the high-end example of a lawyer using his legal knowledge to depict serious legal (and related social) issues and events, but his work is still more documentary entertainment than literary in any richer sense.[4] No one has delved into the secret spiritual and psychological life of lawyers as has Joseph.

In doing so, as he explains in his essay that follows, Joseph has explored the dual identity of the lawyer-writer, and is open about the importance of

---

[2] One recent list of famous lawyer-novelists includes only two who might be regarded as serious literary figures, one of whom, Henry Fielding, is not known for writing about law, and one who is ... Kafka. www.google.com/search?q=famous+lawyer+novelists&ie=utf-8&oe=utf-8.

[3] Authors describe their shift to romance novels as a mode of escape from what they dislike about law, but while their goal is to provide the happy endings that the legal world denies them, they stress that they draw on their analytic and writing skills from law to engineer these alternative outcomes. http://happyeverafter.usatoday.com/2014/04/23/daco-romance-authors-lawyers.

[4] The subject scope of these novels is pretty much limited to litigation, and of course especially criminal ligation. It is hard to find a roaring good yarn about transactional law, and indeed even one well-established transactional lawyer who turned to fiction, Sheldon Siegel, only writes about criminal trials. Some might cite Louis Auchincloss as an exception, since some of his novels deal with corporate business lawyers, but his subject really is more their lives as members of elite society than as working attorneys. (Perhaps a true exception is famed copyright scholar Paul Goldstein, whose very successful mystery novels are all about intellectual property matters).

self-consciousness about craft. That craft is evident in *Lawyerland* in ways that help us appreciate the unique power of that book, and what it adds to and how it challenges other notions about the role of metaphor and narrative in law that are discussed in this volume. The "interviewees" in *Lawyerland* are always telling narratives, but in a peculiar form designed to elicit the book's deeper revelations. The narratives are short bizarre exemplary tales of events that lawyers encounter, and they are usually offered as a kind of warmup to a promised answer to a big question (i.e., "What is law?"). The promised straight answer sometimes does not come. Instead, the story itself is the answer, in the form of a performance of the special art of observation that lawyers compulsively practice.[5] The narratives capture the searing half-self-conscious insights of the lawyers about the smoldering chaos that law just barely contains. The overall book has no narrative, no progress, no resolution, and the lawyers seem to live in a world without time, in a perpetual state of discomfort, of barely sustainable equilibrium.[6] If this sense of time and narrative seems to deny the drama of legal narrative (the investigations, the trials, the historical movements) that others proclaim, and if it seems like a pessimistic response to the view of many that narrative can improve and enrich law, well then Joseph would own these implications as the truth at least for the conscious daily laboring lawyers, as opposed to scholars.[7]

As for metaphor, of course Joseph's prolific poetry is all about metaphor, where shifting between legal and non-legal images is a key technique in capturing the double identity of the lawyer writer. In one poem he mentions in his essay, "Material Facts,"[8] he slyly twists a legal term to capture the impression of a wordless child, whose wry smile suggests he is withholding something very important, just as the lawyers in *Lawyerland* claim to know things unseen. Joseph has said in his own self-instructions, that he must use "high decibel language ... that visually pops off the page."[9] And the lawyer's common vulgar street language, which is of course carefully crafted to

---

[5] Robert Weisberg, "Civic Oratory in *Lawyerland*," *Columbia Law Review*, 101 (2001), 1782–1792, 1782–1783.

[6] Schlag, "Jurisprudence Noire," at 1736.

[7] One reason that Joseph offers us a different and unusually revealing sense of lawyer's experience of time is that he avoids the court-centrism of most legal commentary. Lawyers spend most of their time in random, chaotic conversations with clients and other lawyers, not in pushing cases through to resolution. David Luban, "The art of honesty," *Columbia Law Review*, 101 (2001), 1763–1774, 1766–1767.

[8] Lawrence Joseph, *Code, Precepts, Biases and Taboos: Poems* (New York: Farrar, Straus and Giroux, 2005), pp. 15–16.

[9] Lawrence Joseph, "Working rules for *Lawyerland*," *Columbia Law Review*, 101, no. 7 (2001), 1793–1796.

"seem authentic," finds in its slang vocabulary terms of considerable metaphoric power. But Joseph also shows how legal doctrinal terms become metaphoric and can evoke wondrous questions about reality, illusion, and deception when put in a catalytic relationship with non-legal terms. Metaphor is thus crucial for perhaps the key theme of *Lawyerland*, captured by two haunting bookends: the Rilke epitaph "Don't be confused by surfaces; in the depths everything becomes law" and in the final passage of the book, which tells us that small things and even large things are larger than we think.

Some of the key metaphors in *Lawyerland* are spatial. Joseph exploits the imagery of the blank address for Bartleby's law firm, N— Wall Street, to signify the blankness of some lawyers' lives.[10] (This was also a common device of the nineteenth century to create the effect of deleted reality as if for legality or privacy.) And perhaps most strikingly, as Meredith Wallis demonstrates in her conversation here with Joseph, the real estate of lower Manhattan is itself the key metaphor for the whole book. The book's redrawn "map" of lower Manhattan is not the real Manhattan but the true Manhattan of lawyers' consciousness, a purgatorial gray area between the speakers' law offices and the normal human non-work lives we can only hope they live somewhere else.[11]

In addition, Wallis uses the devilishly clever device of word-cloud to visualize the *Lawyerland* through its density of vocabulary. The key words become "know" and "lawyers," because the book is all about the obsession shared by many lawyers to show us the insights that are peculiar to their roles. She also derives a meta-image of the billable hour from the book's frequent use of "time" and "money" – the billable hour represents the pressure lawyers feel to race through their lives in a way that they experience as meaningless units, yet, again, they experience and possibly seek, unbilled time, the time for these interviews, where they can achieve some perspective.

Thus, narratives of the very Josephian sort, and the array of metaphors, are his tools for showing us how lawyers identify and define their unique role in the gritty world of human failure and conflict. The lawyer-writer tries to evoke the clumsy but indispensable work that law does. And addressing this failure and conflict requires metaphor and narrative to pique the reader's imagination to conceive of how big and ominous and immune to rational understanding

---

[10] David Skeel, Jr. "Lawyer as confidence man," *Columbia Law Review*, 101, no. 7 (2001), 1750–1762, 1757. Skeel also observes that the dash in the address signifies the use of dashes throughout the book to intensify the speakers' jagged compulsive speech.

[11] "[T]o a busy lawyer, Manhattan is barely located in space-time; it's merely a set of coordinates on which meeting rooms are strung..." Luban, "The art of honesty," at 1769.

are both the law and the world. They also are necessary for the book to fulfill the theme that some have ascribed to it – that the lawyers are not nihilists but rather that there is something redemptive about lawyers' capacity to see their own despair,[12] and that their motivation to keep working is at some level idealistic.

[12] Robin West, "Joseph in *Lawyerland*," *Columbia Law Review*, 101, no. 7 (2001), 1775–1781, 1776.

14

Through Narrative and by Metaphor: Creating a Lawyer-Self in Poetry and Prose

Lawrence Joseph

INTRODUCTION

First, by way of background, I've written six books of poems and two books of prose; I began seriously writing poetry in 1967 during my first year at the University of Michigan, where, in 1970, I received a degree in English Literature. I started law school at Michigan in 1973 after postgraduate studies in English Language and Literature at Magdalene College, University of Cambridge. Admitted to practice in Michigan in 1976, I've professionally been a lawyer continuously since, clerking for a justice on the Michigan Supreme Court, practicing as a litigator at a New York City law firm, and, mostly, as a law professor and legal academic, teaching and engaged in writing legal scholarship.[1]

Any creative or literary work requires aesthetic or formal choices. On a critical level, these choices present issues of narrative and metaphor. If a lawyer-self is to exist in poetry or prose, he or she will exist through narrative and by metaphor. In 1946, after completing her last book of prose *Brewsie and Willie*, Gertrude Stein wrote to a friend: "I think in a kind of way it is one of the best things I have ever done. You know how much I have always meditated about narration, how to tell what one has to tell, well this time I have written it, narration as the twentieth century sees it."[2] Issues of narrative or narration

---

[1] See Lawrence Joseph, *So Where Are We? Poems* (New York, NY: Farrar, Straus and Giroux, 2017); *Into it: Poems* (New York: Farrar, Straus and Giroux, 2005); *Codes, Precepts, Biases and Taboos: Poems 1973–1993* (includes *Shouting at No One, Curriculum Vitae* and *Before Our Eyes*) (New York, NY: Farrar, Straus and Giroux, 2005); *The Game Changed: Essays and Other Prose* (Ann Arbor: University of Michigan Press, 2011); *Lawyerland* (New York: Farrar, Straus and Giroux, 1997) (book of prose). See also St. John's University School of Law, Lawrence Joseph, Faculty Profile, http://www.stjohns.edu/academics/bio/lawrence-joseph.

[2] John Malcolm Brinnin, *The Third Rose: Gertrude Stein and Her World* (New York, NY: Grove Press, 1961), p. 391.

revolve around how to tell what one has to tell, the "how to tell" raising aesthetic or formal issues, the "what one has to tell" issues of content or substance. A poem's narrative is found in its composition; a poem is an aesthetically composed object, made of vocal expressions of a speaking self's interiorized and exteriorized realities. How you tell what you have to tell is the poem's form; a poem's telling is in the voice or voices of compressed, condensed thoughts, feeling, observations, and perceptions. As for metaphor and the multitude of critical definitions and descriptions surrounding it, I adhere to a notion derived from Nietzsche, who posits metaphor as prior to, and more basic than, literal speech. Metaphor is part of the common, imaginative core of human thought, a part of the cognitive process of how we relate one thing to another, the imaginative means by which we conceive the multiple relations of a complex world. Human thought itself is metaphor, through the act of sorting, ordering, and linking perceptions and experiences. The associative quality of thought, if expressed or formed into language, is "metaphoric" – the "carrying over" of thought into forms of expression.[3] Beginning with its title, a poem is, essentially, metaphoric, a deepening, associative cognitive mapping of human issues and transformations of intrinsically human domains by, in, and through expression. To write is to narrate; to form thoughts into spoken or written words is an act of metaphor.

THE LAWYER-SELF IN POETRY

From the beginning of my literary work I've been aesthetically concerned with the ways in which poetry raises issues and questions of identity, and, more basic to that, issues of the self, which include: the nature of the self and the speaking self; the types of language that deal with a sense of the self; and how a self or selves in a poem are constructed through various vocal languages that reflect personal and social identities in ongoing processes of narrative and metaphor. The core identity in my poems is the identity of the poet within the poem, making the poem. Other identities are expressed in the voices of a Catholic of Lebanese and Syrian descent, born and raised in Detroit, a resident of downtown Manhattan, who speaks within a complex set of personal and social realities, which encompass, among others, urban life in Detroit, the tension between high finance and the streets of New York, familial and religious ties to the Middle East, and issues of political economy. One self is also identified as a lawyer. Like William Carlos Williams, who spent his work

---

[3] See Steven L. Winter, "Death is the mother of metaphor," *Harvard Law Review* 105 (1992), 745–772.

life as both a doctor and a poet and author of literary prose, I've chosen to identify a lawyer-self who, within the poems, critically reflects not only on his life as a lawyer, but also on law itself, presenting a kind of lawyer's language alongside the other languages of identity.

A lawyer-self is introduced in Part 1 of *Shouting at No One*, my first book of poems, in "I Think About Thigpen Again." The poem's opening line repeats the title, in effect resetting its initial metaphorical cognitive mapping. The speaker of the poem's lawyer-identity is made known by "the record of the criminal court" that he sees, which, "[a]ccording to the pathologist," includes testimony that Thigpen's death

> ... was caused
> by massive tissue destruction,
> contusion and swelling of the brain.
> In the county morgue
> Thigpen's father whispered,
> "That's my baby son."

The poem's lawyer-self, "thinking of Thigpen again," thinks of him in the context of what he learns from the record of the criminal court and his relationship to Thigpen as a high school classmate and poet.[4]

In Part III, the lawyer-self appears again in "Do What You Can." At the end of the poem, the poem's speaker describes what he sees from his car at a stoplight: "Not far away, on Beaufait Street,"

> a crowd gathers to look at the steam
> from blood spread on the ice. The light red,
> I press the accelerator to keep the motor warm.
> I wonder if they know
> that after the jury is instructed
> on the Burden of Persuasion and the Burden of Truth,
> that after the sentence of twenty to thirty years comes down,
> when the accused begs, "Lord, I can't do that kind of time,"
> the judge, looking down, will smile and say,
> "Then do what you can."[5]

In my second book, *Curriculum Vitae*, the lawyer-self first appears in the title poem. Metaphorically, the poem is about identity, and starts with a chronological series of associative statements of self-identities:

> I might have been born in Beirut,
> Not Detroit, with my right name.

---

[4] Joseph, *Codes, Precepts, Biases and Taboos*, pp. 15, 16.   [5] Ibid., p. 58.

> Grandpa taught me to love to eat.
> I am not Orthodox, or Sunni,
> Shiite, or Druse. Baptized
> in the one true Church, I too
> was weaned on St. Augustine.
> Eisenhower never dreamed I wore
> corrective shoes, Ford Motor Co.
> never cared I'd never forgive
> Highland Park, River Rouge, Hamtramck.

Then, in a tonal shift toward the end of the poem: "After I applied Substance and Procedure / and Statements of Facts / my head was heavy, was earth" – an overt expression of a lawyer's language. Several lines of declarations of an evolving identity later, the poem's poet-lawyer-self hears himself say "What explains / the Bank of Lebanon's liquidity?" / think, "I too will declare / a doctrine upon whom the loss/ of language must fall regardless / whether Wallace Stevens / understood senior indebtedness/ in Greenwich Village in 1906," compressing legal-type language with a reference to the poet-lawyer Wallace Stevens.[6]

Law and lawyer-language appear throughout *Curriculum Vitae*. In "This is How It Happens," the poet speaks "a different tongue / in the Park where the two rivers / merge, or else by the oak benches / in some Court of Equity, your gaze / almost balanced";[7] and in "I've Already Said More Than I Should": "When, in this morning's paper, / the renowned poet and critic / professor is quoted decrying / the demise of English forms, / I write Esquire after my name."[8]

In "That's All," the poem's speaker does not deny "the court that rules/ my race is Jewish or Abyssinian."[9] In "Who to Deny," the poet describes himself "at his job, working volumes / of testimony, fleshing facts./ At the Capitol he argues strategy/ to use in opinions / he writes for the Chief Justice."[10] And in "An Awful Lot Was Happening," the speaker of the poem leans "again to embrace you. Uniform Commercial Code on the table"; "In the Law Quadrangle" is his peer, who "commanded Marines/ in the Anhoa Basin."[11]

In "Any and All," the lawyer-self occupies the language of the entire poem. The speaker, in a law office at "No. 54 Wall Street," hears the phone ringing. "You put Byrdman on hold," he says. "Polen / wants you in his office immediately.

> The lawyers from Mars and the bankers
> from Switzerland have arrived to close the deal,
> the money in their heads articulated

---

[6] Ibid., pp. 69, 70. [7] Ibid., p. 73. [8] Ibid., p. 76. [9] Ibid., p. 98. [10] Ibid., p. 99.
[11] Ibid., p. 103.

> to the debt of the state of Bolivia.
> How much later the Croatian woman
> who empties the wastebaskets laughs
> when you answer you've been better
> and you've been worse. How much sooner
> you're told not to tell anyone Byrdman's
> grandfather was a Jew. How much No. 54
> Wall Street, emblematic reality of extreme
> speculations and final effects.

After a series of images and declarations, the poem reaches the conclusion that "You're a monkey and you work for him, "you "decide for him whether his clauses should be restrictive, / whether to replace every 'any' with 'all.'"[12]

In my third book, *Before Our Eyes*, two poems early in the book signal a lawyer-self. The title of the poem "Material Facts" has overt legal meaning: in civil fraud actions, a fact is material if it is one to which a reasonable person would attach importance in determining his or her choice of action in the transaction in question. In the final ten-line stanza of the poem, "material facts" is presented in the context of

> A child again, who doesn't use
> words at all, says something
> by slightly turning a corner
> of his mouth, hiding material
> facts from your perception,
> standing beside a carp in a large
> iron tank swimming upside down
> in the window of Bank Central Asia
> on a corner in Chinatown."[13]

The title "Admissions Against Interest" also projects legal meaning. The title refers to a rule of evidence whereby a person's out-of-court statement, otherwise inadmissible as hearsay, may be used when the content of the statement is so prejudicial to the person making it that he or she would not have made it unless he believed it was true (and thus that it carries more reliability). In the second of the poem's four parts, the lawyer-self in the poem is made explicit:

> Now what type of animal asks after facts?
> —so I'm a lawyer. Maybe charming,
> direct yet as circumspect as any other lawyer
> going on about concrete forces of civil
> society substantially beyond anyone's grasp,

---

[12] Ibid., pp. 113, 115. [13] Ibid., 29, 130.

and about money. Things like "you too
may be silenced the way powerful
corporations silence, contractually"
attract my attention. The issue's
bifurcated. "Why divide the dead?"
the Foreign Minister asks, "what's one life
when you've lost twenty million?"
And if what has happened during my life
had been otherwise could I say
I would have seen it much differently?
Authority? Out of deep strata
illuminations. A lot of substance
chooses you. And it's no one's business
judging the secrets each of us needs:
I don't know what I'd do without my Double.[14]

Part IV of the eight-part poem "Variations on Variations on a Theme," later in the book, brings the lawyer-self again to the foreground: "And that's the law. To bring to light / most hidden depths. The juror screaming / defendant's the devil staring at her / making her insane. The intense strain / phrasing the truth, the whole truth, nothing / but sentences, endless sentences."[15] And in "Some Sort of Chronicler I Am," the poem's speaker again evokes Wallace Stevens, whose work as a surety-bond lawyer "covered high-risk losses" and who "knowingly chose / during the bank closings of early '33 / to suspend his grief between social planes / he'd transpose into thoughts, figures, colors."[16]

THE LAWYER-SELF IN POETRY AND PROSE, AND LAW, LANGUAGE, AND LITERATURE IN LEGAL SCHOLARSHIP

In the 1970s, while I was writing the poems that would appear in *Shouting at No One*, two books appeared – William Bishin's and Christopher Stone's *Law Language and Ethics: An Introduction to Law and Legal Method*,[17] and James Boyd White's *The Legal Imagination: Studies in the Nature of Legal Thought and Expression*[18] – which proved critical to my sense of the multitude of interrelationships between law and language, law and literature, and law and interpretation. In their Preface, Bishin and Stone write that *Law,*

---

[14] Ibid., p. 132. [15] Ibid., p. 155. [16] Ibid., p. 162.
[17] William R. Bishin and Christopher D. Stone, *Law, Language, and Ethics: An Introduction to Law and Legal Method* (New York, NY: The Foundation Press, 1972).
[18] James B. White, *The Legal Imagination: Studies in the Nature of Legal Thought and Expression* (Boston, MA: Little, Brown and Company, 1973).

Language and Ethics was "born of the belief that every legal problem has its roots and perhaps its analogue in traditionally philosophical realms ... about the nature of reality, of knowledge, of language." A lawyer, in her or his "day-to-day tasks of counseling, planning and contending," is engaged in activities that require "stating problems, clarifying questions, determining 'facts,' interpreting language, formulating and analyzing theories."[19] A quick look at the Table of Contents of *Law, Language and Ethics* shows, for example, excerpts from Herman Melville's *Billy Budd*; Norman O. Brown's *Apollo and Dionysius*; Felix S. Cohen's *Transcendental Nonsense and the Functional Approach*; Jerome Frank's *Fact Skepticism*; and passages from works by William James, Susan K. Langer, H. L. A. Hart, Thomas Aquinas, Learned Hand, Benjamin Cardozo, Karl Llewellyn, Paul Tillich, Jean-Paul Sartre, Erich Fromm, and Lionel Trilling. These texts are interspersed with legislation and mostly United States Supreme Court judicial opinions.[20]

James Boyd White's *The Legal Imagination* focuses entirely on issues of law, language, and literature. The book contains texts and questions about the texts under headings such as: "Learning the Language of Law"; "A Variety of Languages"; "Defining a Language System"; "Your Language in a Universe of Languages"; "The Law Among Other Possibilities for Expression"; "Defining Viciousness in Language and Imagination: The Rhetoric of the Death Penalty"; "How Should the Law Use the Language of Race"; "How Should the Courts Speak to the Police?"; "Making a Language of Judicial Criticism: How Should We Talk About Legal Judgment"; "The Narrative Imagination and the Claim of Meaning"; "Telling a Story"; and "The Force of Narrative;" "Is the Judge Really a Poet?"; "Reading the Poem: An Education of the Imagination," which includes poems by Robert Frost, John Donne, Andrew Marvell, George Herbert, Robert Browning, Emily Dickinson, Dylan Thomas, William Wordsworth, John Keats, and Walt Whitman.[21] In an abridged edition of *The Legal Imagination* published thirteen years later, White, in his Preface, writes that "the law is not merely a system of rules, or rules and principles; or reducible to policy choices based on markets; or reducible to political, class interests." It is, instead, "what I call a language—by which I do not mean just a set of terms and locutions, but habits of mind and expectations—what might also be called a culture." Law is "an enormously rich and complex system of thought and expression, of social definitions and practices, which can be learned and mastered, modified or preserved, by the individual mind ... The greatest power of law lies not in a set of particular rules or in decisions, but in its

---

[19] Bishin and Stone, p. vii. [20] Bishin and Stone, p. xi–xxix. [21] White, pp. vii–xviii.

language, in the coercive aspect of its rhetoric—in the way it structures sensibility and vision."[22]

During the 1980s, legal scholarship based on issues of law, language, literature, and interpretation exploded. Two articles in particular – Robert Cover's "The Supreme Court, 1982 Term – Foreword: Nomos and Narrative"[23] and Robin West's "Jurisprudence as Narrative: An Aesthetic Analysis of Modern Legal Theory"[24] – strongly influenced my thinking. "Nomos and Narrative" opens with an acknowledgment of the James Boyd White's work "for the ways in which he has explored the range of meaning-constituted functions of legal discourse."[25] White, Cover says, was the first to see that "no set of legal institutions or prescriptions exists apart from the narratives that locate it and give it meaning."[26] What a person knows about law "is determined by the person's connection with how he or she talks about it." Law is "a system of tension or a bridge linking a concept of reality to an imagined alternative, a connection between two states of affairs, both of which can be represented in their normative significance only through the device of narrative."[27]

"It is now commonplace that lawyers and legal theorists have much to learn from literature," West writes in "Jurisprudence as narrative." "We surely can learn something about the law from great works of literature that deal with legal themes, such as Kafka's *The Trial* and Melville's *Billy Budd*. But," West continues, "apart from the law depicted in literature, legal theory itself contains a substantial narrative component that can be analyzed as literature. It is not surprising that legal theory should rely so heavily upon narrative form."[28] Legal theorists "do not make law; they do not decide cases, vote on bills, or undertake to represent clients and hence the furtherance of those clients' interest. Consequently, legal theorists have the freedom that institutional responsibility does not allow; they *are* a step further removed from history than judges or legislators and practitioners. Legal theorists must exercise the freedom that their positions allow; they must acknowledge that legal theory and narrative, unlike politics and law, ultimately are forms of artistic play."[29]

In 1987, I joined the faculty at St. John's University School of Law and began to lecture and write on, among other legal subjects, law, literature, language,

---

[22] James B. White, *The Legal Imagination: Abridged Edition* (Chicago, IL: University of Chicago Press, 1986), p. xiii.
[23] Robert M. Cover, "The Supreme Court, 1982 Term—Foreword: Nomos and narrative," *Harvard Law Review* 97 no. 1(1983), 4–68.
[24] Robin West, "Jurisprudence as narrative: An aesthetic analysis of modern legal theory," *N.Y.U. Law Review* 60 (1985), 145–211.
[25] Cover, 6, 7. [26] Ibid., 4. [27] Ibid., 9. [28] West, 145, 146. [29] Ibid., p. 211.

and interpretation. In 1988, *Curriculum Vitae* was published, in 1993, *Before Our Eyes*; in 1993, "Theories of Poetry, Theories of Law," an essay on legal language viewed through the aesthetics of the language of poetry, appeared in the *Vanderbilt Law Review*.[30] In 1994, David Skeel, in "Practicing Poetry, Teaching Law," wrote an essay-review in the *Michigan Law Review* of *Before Our Eyes*, drawing comprehensively on law, language, and literature scholarship up to that time, including "Theories of Poetry, Theories of Law." Recognizing the development of a lawyer-self in *Shouting at No One, Curriculum Vitae, and Before Our Eyes*, Skeel placed my poetry critically within the various strands of law and literature, observing that "To an extent that is striking and at times uncanny," my "development as a poet and lawyer precisely tracks the emergence of the growth of law and literature."[31] By that point, I'd already begun to imagine my literary work not only as a subject of literary criticism, but also of legal scholarship. From the mid-nineties into the early 2000s, I wrote a series of scholarly pieces on law, language and literature, and law and interpretation.[32] In 1997, *Lawyerland*, variously described as a non-fiction novel or as documentary fiction, was published;[33] *Into It*, my fourth book of poems,[34] and *Codes, Precepts, Biases and Taboos: Poems 1973–1993*, a collection of my first three books of poems,[35] appeared in 2005.

Because of the earlier work and the critical work on my poetry in both literary and legal criticism, the lawyer-self is implicitly part of *Into It*'s narrative and evolving metaphors. The lawyer-self is brought expressly to the surface toward the end of the book in "The Game Changed," which begins:

> The phantasmic imperium is set in a chronic
> state of hypnotic fixity. I have absolutely
> no idea what the fuck you're talking about

---

[30] Lawrence Joseph, "Theories of poetry, theories of law," *Vanderbilt Law Review* 46 (1983), 1227–1254.

[31] David A. Skeel, Jr., "Practicing poetry, teaching law," *Michigan Law Review* 92 (1994), 1754–1775, 1755.

[32] See Lawrence Joseph, "Reflections on law and literature (imaginary interview), *Saskatchewan Law Review* 589 (1995), 417–430; "The language of judging," *St. John's Law Review* 59 (1996), 1–4; "On Kronman's rhetoric," *University of Cincinnati Law Review* 67 (1999), 719–725; "A year after the acquittal in the impeachment trial," in Leonard V. Kaplan and Beverly I. Moran (eds.), *Aftermath: The Clinton Impeachment and the Presidency in the Age of Political Spectacle* (New York, NY: New York University Press, 2001); "Working rules for Lawyerland," *Columbia Law Review* 101 (2011), 1793–1796; "The subject and object of Law," *Brooklyn Law Review* 67 (2001), 1023–1033.

[33] Lawrence Joseph, *Lawyerland* (New York, NY: Farrar, Straus and Giroux, 1997).

[34] Lawrence Joseph, *Into It* (New York, NY: Farrar, Straus and Giroux, 2005).

[35] Lawrence Joseph, *Codes, Precepts, Biases and Taboos: Poems 1973–1993* (New York, NY: Farrar, Straus and Giroux, 2005).

> was his reply, and he wasn't laughing,
> either, one of the most repellent human beings
> I've ever known, his presence a gross and slippery
> lie, a piece of chemically pure evil. A lawyer—
> although the type's not exclusive to lawyers.
> A lot of different minds touch, and have touched,
> the blood money in the dummy account
> in an offshore bank, washed clean, free to be
> transferred into a hedge fund or a foreign
> brokerage account, at least a half a trillion
> ending up in the United States, with more to come.
> I believe I've told you I'm a lawyer. Which has had
> little or no effect on a certain respect
> I have for occurrences that suggest laws
> of necessity.[36]

In 2009, the *University of Cincinnati Law Review* published "Law and Literature Symposium: 'Some sort of chronicler I am': Narration and the poetry of Lawrence Joseph,"[37] which included my "Notions of poetry and narration."[38] In 2010, in a personal essay "Being in the language of poetry, being in the language of law," I take the reader through various experiences of mine within the languages of both my literary work and legal work, including the various types of legal scholarship that I've written.[39] In 2011, *The Game Changed: Essays and Other Prose* appeared, the lawyer-self present, both explicitly and implicitly, throughout its twenty-four prose pieces.[40]

THE LAWYER-SELF IN *LAWYERLAND*

"Law" as metaphor in *Lawyerland* – which was written after *Before Our Eyes* – is overt and obvious from the title, infused in and throughout the book's carefully structured prose narrative. *Lawyerland* is entirely spoken by lawyers: an "I" who, biographically, resembles me, and the lawyers I meet and speak with in the book. The book's formal subject – what one has to tell – is what

---

[36] Joseph, *Into It: Poems*, p. 63.
[37] See "Law and Literature Symposium: 'Some sort of chronicler I am': Narration and the poetry of Lawrence Joseph," *University of Cincinnati Law Review*, 77 (2009).
[38] Lawrence Joseph, "Notions of poetry and narration," *University of Cincinnati Law Review*, 77 (2009), 941–968.
[39] Lawrence Joseph, "Being in the language of poetry, being in the language of law," *Oregon Law Review*, 88 (2009), 905–929.
[40] Lawrence Joseph, *The Game Changed: Essays and Other Prose* (Ann Arbor, MI: University of Michigan Press, 2011).

these lawyers think law is, and what they think about law in America. Everyone who speaks in the book is a lawyer; the entire field of language in the book is made up of the voices of lawyers, including the narrator's, talking to other lawyers about lawyers and the law. For a symposium on *Lawyerland* in the *Columbia Law Review*,[41] I wrote several of the "working rules" that I used in writing the book. Specifically, for the book's narrative strategies, in Rule 2 I note: "You know how much I have always meditated about narration, how to tell what one has to tell" – quoting Gertrude Stein; and, in Rule 3 I refer to Stein's *Wars I Have Seen*, which I describe as "Stories within stories within stories within .... (narration within narration within narration within ...). A means by which to broaden and deepen (and concentrate) time and space (including the temporal and spatial dimensions of language)." I also note my metaphorical strategy in Rule 1: "Don't be confused by surfaces; in the depths everything becomes law," a quotation from Rainer Marie Rilke's *Letters to a Young Poet*, which also serves as *Lawyerland*'s epigraph; and in Rule 11: "Only lower Manhattan settings: 'mapped-out'; the 'geographical' as metaphor (Harvey's *Justice, Nature and the Geography of Difference*): By condensing geographical space you pressure other metaphorical space (including the spatial dimension of language)."[42]

With these narrative and metaphorical strategies in mind, here are passages from the first three of *Lawyerland*'s eight chapters. The first passage is the book's opening paragraph, in a chapter entitled "Robinson's Metamorphosis." "I" am speaking with Robinson, a criminal defense lawyer whom I've known since law school:

> "Let me see. Lawyers." Robinson turned his chair around with his body and pulled a file off the shelf, then, swinging back, tossed a newspaper clipping across the desk. "Here"—he smiled—"you want lawyers? Here's a lawyer. A white shoe, metamerger, 'don't-you-love-the-Four- Seasons-Grill Room?' attorney- at-law. In a state of lament. He's lamenting! What is he lamenting? The demise. Of what? The profession? Why? Greed! That's what he says—greed! Two wives, four cars, three houses, two precociously gifted Ivy League children, driven to and from work down Park Avenue every day in a stretch limousine by some greasy-looking Green Card, when, one summer morning, our American Esquire awakens to—a vision! A veritable William Blake! In capital letters! LAWYERS AND GREED! Lawyers and greed! And you watch! Guaranteed! On the Op-Ed page of the paper of record. His visions will multiply! LAWYERS AND—God, what happened to—COMMON

---

[41] See "The *Lawyerland* essays," *Columbia Law Review*, 101 (2001).
[42] Lawrence Joseph, "Working rules for *Lawyerland*, *Columbia Law Review*, 101 (2010), 1793–1795.

SENSE! LAWYERS WHO—can you believe it?—SCREW THEIR CLIENTS! LAWYERS AND JUSTICE! Justice!"[43]

The second passage is the opening of the second chapter, "Something Split." Carl Wylie is a partner at a law firm at which "I" once worked:

> "I really don't care," Carl Wylie said, after I asked him what he thought law was.
> "Do you know what Holmes said it was," I asked.
> "What did Holmes say it was?"
> "A great anthropological document."
> "A great anthropological document. A great anthropological document. What? The millions of tons of paper generated every year by public offerings? The billions of words written by lawyers every day? How about the Supreme Court? The opinion declaring unconstitutional that Colorado law—the law approved by statewide referendum, by fifty-four percent of those voting. The one that says no preferential treatment for queers, no legislation privileging queers. I haven't read—I am never going to read it, are you? Who ever reads Supreme Court opinions? I know I don't. It's like when a friend of mine from college asked me what I thought money was. I told him I didn't know and didn't really care. He said it's a social institution. Now, that says a lot, doesn't it? Money is a social institution. Chaos. That's what interests me. Chaos. What did Holmes says about chaos?"
> "Chaos?"
> "Complexity so intricate no one can fathom it. Large things within small things, small things within large things—things encompassing things which would seem to be beyond them. Chaos."[44]

The third passages are from *Lawyerland*'s third chapter, "All Great Problems Come from the Streets." Celia Day is a federal district court judge in the Southern District of New York, located in downtown Manhattan. The narrator is meeting with her about a draft of a report for the New York City Bar Association on political criticism of a federal court decisions. The chapter begins:

> "A revolution," Judger Celia Day said.
> "A revolution?" I asked.
> "A revolution."
> "But who?"
>
> "Who? Everyone, that's who. The corruption's palpable. Everyone's sitting in front of their television sets watching it. Civility? No one believes there's any

---

[43] Joseph, *Lawyerland*, pp. 3, 4.   [44] Joseph, *Lawyerland*, pp. 31, 32.

anymore! Fragments—yes. But an integral part of the way that we do things? So what do you think happens when no one believes there's any real civility anymore? Politicians! It doesn't matter which side they say they're on—each of them backed by his own small army, and I mean army, too, of lobbyists and lawyers who haven't the slightest care for what is happening in people's lives . . . This time around," she added, "it's crime. Next time, what will it be? Blame the judges for not stopping a war? Drugs? Our fault! Social insanity? Our fault! As if *we* are the ones who make the laws."[45]

And the meeting in chambers over, the chapter ends, as Judge Day and the narrator "walked to the subway entrance under the arch of the Manhattan Municipal Building":

> . . . It was getting dark. The air had turned damp and cold. It had begun to rain . . . Day folded her arms around her trench coat. "It's gotten cold," she said, shaking her shoulders. She looked at me again, almost staring. "What if," she said, "just what if the law we have is the law we deserve?"
>
> She broke into a smile. "You're looking at me as if I'm out of my mind! I'm serious! It's a rather democratic concept, actually. I can see it on talk TV. 'Is the law we have the law we deserve?' How does it go?—from the Pledge of Allegiance? 'One nation, under God, indivisible.' But what if"—Day's voice changed tone—"it isn't indivisible? What if, in fact, it's very divisible—divided, dividing, all over the place? What if, instead, it's one nation of private militias, one of police, one of women, one of men, another of whatever race you are, still another one of your religion, one nation of armed forces, another of employers, one of employees, another of those who drug themselves, one nation of unemployed, of those who have had abortions, another of those who haven't, and then, of course, all those nations comprised of those either of upwardly mobile or mobile downward economic status. What, then, would be the law that we deserve? You tell me . . . What kind of law, what kind of lawyers, do you have when the civil order is, in fact, in a state of civil wars? What, for example, would have happened if the truck that exploded under the World Trade Center had been about two hundred feet away from where it was, an entire tower—all one hundred ten floors—collapsed? How many legal relationships—civil, criminal, federal, state, municipal. International—would have been affected? Tell me—who among those affected would have gotten what he deserved? Who would have gotten it for him? All great problems come from the streets. What happens when one of them—one small fraction of just one of them—enters the office of the United States Department of Justice? It can happen, you know. One day an Assistant United States Attorney receives a package in the

---

[45] Joseph, *Lawyerland*, pp. 61, 62.

mail. In it there's a briefcase just like this one I've got. Inside it, a sawed-off shotgun rigged to a device.

Day propped her briefcase on her knee and snapped it open. Her eyes widened. "Like this!" she said. "In the stomach! Do you know what happens if you're shot in the gut, a foot away, by a sawed-off shotgun? What if the briefcase is just a bit slanted—like this?" She turned her briefcase toward me. "*Whoosh!* There's not going to be much of your government attorney's head left, now, is there? It's what happened to Judge Lowenstein. The same way. Fortunately, in our case, an F.B.I. agent was with this assistant at the time. He told her that he'd better open it, that you never know. He opens it from the side—*pow!* A huge hole in the office wall."

Day closed her briefcase. "Tomorrow, first thing," she said, then paused to catch her breath. "A sentencing. Can I run it past you? Is that all right? Then I've got to be going. I know I'm keeping you." She shook her shoulders. "I should have worn my winter coat," she said. "Look. I appreciate it. I'll be fast. The facts." She took another breath. "A forty-year-old woman. She's— well, let's just say she's a citizen. She pays a lot of money to have her husband killed, but it doesn't come off. She's arrested and pleads guilty to conspiracy to murder. Under the sentencing guidelines I've no choice—nine years, no parole. I can reduce her sentence if there are mitigating circumstances. But I have to have really good reasons.

Suddenly a gust of wind blew rain near where we were standing. We moved farther under the Municipal Building arch, beside another pillar. Day continued. "Her lawyers have a psychiatric report done," she said. "First-rate. One of the best psychiatrists in the country. University of Chicago. Excellent. It so happens that this woman's marriage was arranged. It so happens, too, that every time this woman has sex with her husband, it's forced on her. The violence is graphic—you could even say perverse. Ugly stuff—sodomy, rape. This is on the record—the woman's never had an orgasm, which her husband attributes to her having affairs. So what does she do? More violence, under the guise of sex."

"Battered woman's syndrome," I said.

"Maybe that's what it is. I don't know. I've got to sentence her. This woman's pled to conspiracy to commit murder. She's going to go to prison. I have to decide how much of the next—at a minimum—nine years she's going to live in a federal penitentiary. But that's not all—there's more. Every single time the woman's been in court her husband's been with her. They sit beside each other. They talk. You'd think they were just like any other husband and wife. Oh, I almost forgot. The husband has never denied his wife's allegations ... Never. That's not all, either. Husband and wife are in business together. A very lucrative three-, four-million-dollar-a-year import business. There's a five-million-dollar life-insurance policy on the husband's life. Since the wife's been in jail, the business has been falling apart. She's the brains of the operation. Without her, the husband doesn't know how to run things. Finally—children. A boy and a girl. A ten and an eight-year-old. Beautiful children. There are pictures of both of them. They're part of the record."

Day stopped. She started walking toward the subway. "Let me know," she said over her shoulder, "when you're ready to go over the next draft of the report."[46]

THE LAWYER-SELF: A FINAL NOTE

A final note on the lawyer-self: in *So Where Are We?*, my book of poems published in 2017,[47] the lawyer-self identifies himself halfway through the book in the first part of the poem "In Parentheses," making himself distinctly present in the poem's remaining nine parts. Here is the poem in its entirety:

IN PARENTHESES

I
As I said, I'm a lawyer. Technically speaking,
is a head blown to pieces by a smart bomb a beheading?

II
Infinitely compressible, yet expandable time,
and curved space, in the preface to Lucretius's
first book of *De Rerum Natura* is a tribute to Venus,
in the last book a description of the plague.

III
Estimated one to two thousand militia, gangs,
really, of fifteen to three thousand
armed killers, in separate, overlapping
networks, difficult to differentiate, and now this,
to quote an anonymous State Department source,
what no one could have predicted, this phenomenon's,
the caliphate's, rise, nothing since the triumph
of the Vandals in Roman North Africa
this sudden, this incomprehensible.

---

[46] Joseph, *Lawyerland*, pp. 79–84.
[47] Lawrence Joseph, *So Where Are We? Poems* (New York, NY: Farrar, Straus and Giroux, 2017).

IV

In the technocapital sphere
absolute principles of profit growth,
of value accumulation, the absolute freedom
to recombine the production of raw materials
into virtual information
in spaces of time, info-time.

V

A theological-political fragment,
a mythographical, scriptural, text,
and sorrow, to understand the meaning
of sorrow, Saint Sorrow,
the addressee of my avowal,
Saint Sorrow's stern vigil necessary to keep.

VI

Hyperviolence is the word, of epic proportions,
a species thing, the point at which
violence becomes ontology,
these endless ambitious experiments of destruction,
a species grief.

VII

Quite often, almost daily,
in fact, I have strong impressions of eternity,
my ancestors are there, too,
in the shadows—my mother, my father,
grandmothers, grandfathers, whom I refuse
to let perish—whispering to me to be careful.

VIII

What's that about? Someone I heard say
that to say that Hispanics are East Asian
is sort of like saying that Arabs are white.

IX

Hear that, that man's face being stepped on,
skull being cracked by the baton stick, head
slammed against the concrete edge, blood
in his eyes, body limp, in the process now
of being handcuffed.

X
I am speaking of a law, now, understand,
that point at which bodies locked in cages
become ontology, the point at which
structures of cruelty, force, war,
become ontology. The analog
is what I believe in, the reconstruction
of the phenomenology of perception
not according to a machine,
more, now, for the imagination to affix to
than ever before.[48]

---

[48] Lawrence Joseph, *So Where Are We? Poems* (New York: Farrar, Straus and Giroux, 2017).

15

Secrets of Civility in *Lawyerland*[*]

Meredith Wallis

In his 1991 concurrence in *Rand v. Monsanto*, seventh circuit Judge Kanne composed a brief elegy to bygone professional rules, most of which he devoted to their cause of death: "With this case, we are merely observers of a current trend—one of a series of incremental steps away from ethical standards which set lawyers apart from entrepreneurs."[1] With this concurrence, however, he was more than merely an observer of a related trend, that is, a late-twentieth century spike in narratives lamenting the de-professionalization of law, or as it had become increasingly to be called, a *crisis of civility*.[2] Kanne goes on: "During the past 25 years there has been continuing pressure to convert the lawyer's 'professional calling' into a 'commercial enterprise' spurred on by egalitarian motives and an urge for unfettered market-place economics."[3] His passive construction leaves room for either a structural or an individual agent who is *pressuring* and *being spurred*; a gap Kanne closes in favor of the latter by the prophecy with which he

---

[*] For their help on earlier drafts, thank you to Sara Bernstein, Elise Chatelain, and Nathaniel Landry.
[1] *Rand v. Monsanto Company*, 926 F.2d 596, 603 (7th Cir. 1991) (holding that professional responsibility rules did not dictate that a named plaintiff in a class action must be willing to assume responsibility for *all* costs). Kanne is concerned with the parts of the opinion which describe a lessening in the prior ethical restrictions on attorneys participating financially in their cases.
[2] For one of the first public comments, see Chief Justice Warren E. Burger, "Opening remarks," *ALI Proceedings*, (1971), 21–31. For a representative sampling, see also: William H. Rehnquist, "Civility and freedom of speech," *Indiana Law Journal*, 49 (1973), 1–7; David Luban, "The Noblesse Oblige tradition in the practice of law," *Vanderbilt Law Review* 41 (1988), 736–740; Anthony T. Kronman, *The Lost Lawyer: Failing Ideals of the Legal Profession* (Cambridge, MA: Harvard University Press, 1993); Robert L. Nelson and David M. Trubek (eds.), *Lawyers' Ideals/Lawyers' Practices: Transformations in the American Legal Profession* (Ithaca, NY: Cornell University Press, 1992) (especially Part II and III). For contemporary critique, see the essays in Austin Sarat (ed.), *Civility, Legality, and Justice in America* (New York, NY: Cambridge University Press, 2014).
[3] *Rand v. Monsanto* (1991), 603.

concludes: "'law as a business' will fade as new generations of lawyers strive to retain attributes of service before self-interest which lie at the foundation of a traditional profession."[4] Less sanguine about the next generation's potential for self-interest-to-service alchemy, professional associations and courts attempted more direct formulas designed to give attorneys a self-interest in service, e.g. civility codes and procedural rules geared toward professionalism.[5] The thought being, when we, lawyers, aren't out to make a quick buck – or when the rest of our bucks are externally threatened if this impulse is followed – we can be (or at least can be made to act) civil.[6]

At the peak of popular saturation for the *crisis of civility* narrative – the late '90s – Lawrence Joseph published *Lawyerland*.[7] The book is eight chapters of a narrator-lawyer interviewing other New York lawyers about "what these lawyers think law is, and what they think about law in America," and given the year, it should come as no surprise that much of what they are thinking about is crisis. The first chapter's criminal lawyer imagines an addition to the Code of Professional Responsibility that mandated telling your clients that "becoming involved with the legal system is like three years of experimental chemotherapy, one hundred percent guaranteed not to work."[8] The commercial attorney from the sixth chapter asks: "what if the truth really is that your civilization, that your law, lawyer, really is an idea that becomes actualized—becomes real—only in terms of money?"[9] The third chapter's federal judge worries, "So what do you think happens when no one believes there's any real

---

[4] Ibid.

[5] For a history and assessment of these regulatory attempts, see Deborah L. Rhode, *In the Interests of Justice: Reforming the Legal Profession* (Oxford and New York: Oxford University Press, 2000) (especially Chapter 4) and Austin Sarat, "Enactments of professionalism: A study of judges' and lawyers' accounts of ethics civility in litigation," *Fordham Law Review* 67 (1998). See also: American Bar Association Commission on Professionalism, "'In the spirit of public service': A blueprint for the rekindling of lawyer professionalism," F.R.D., 112 (1986), 243, 261 and Marvin E. Aspen, "A specification of civility expectations and comments: Excerpts from the Seventh Circuit's Interim Report of the Committee on Civility," *Federal Bar News & Journal*, 39 (1992), 304–9. http://heinonline.org/HOL/Page?handle=hein.journals/vanlr54&div=73&g_sent=1&collection=journals.

[6] On the success of these measures: "The main obstacle ... involves enforcement. If bar regulatory structures cannot prevent widespread noncompliance, then strengthening ethical rules has limited value. And the current oversight system is inadequate to the task. Judicial sanctions are too intermittent, inconsistent and insignificant to deter abuse. Bar discipline for adversarial abuses is even less effective," Rhode, *In the Interests of Justice*, p. 94.

[7] For examples of its wide spread cultural proliferation, see Randall Kennedy, "State of the debate: The case against 'civility,'" *The American Prospect* (Nov.–Dec. 1998).

[8] Lawrence Joseph, *Lawyerland: What Lawyers Talk about When They Talk about Law* (New York, NY: Farrar, Straus and Giroux, 1997), p. 18.

[9] Ibid., p. 165.

civility anymore? ... lobbyists and lawyers who haven't the slightest care for what is happening in people's lives."[10] Page after page of money eroding values: *Lawyerland* seems immediately to be an exceedingly clever but solidly representative addition to the de-professionalization subgenre, one which is all the more effective by presenting the problem both in the content of its lawyer's speeches and in their crass and decidedly uncivil method of speech (e.g. "Of course the poor get fucked by the system. ... But lawyers make money off the poor").[11]

Lawyers both discussing and performing the crisis: this is, judging by reviews, the great success of the book, both popularly and aesthetically, that is, why it is both *liked* and *good*. Here readers can enjoy the familiar civility lament, but with "heat," as the ABA advertises in a book review section from 1998 promising "spicy treats for summer": "it's as honest and revelatory as glaring into the bathroom mirror at 3 in the morning. You may recognize yourself or your colleague. It'll hurt. And then you'll laugh."[12] More sophisticated versions of this can be found in the collection of essays on the book published in the *Columbia Law Review*, e.g. Robert Weisberg's conclusion: "Joseph's lawyers model and demonstrate how lawyers exquisitely experience and register, and just barely manage to resist, the disintegration of social relations and selfhood in a Hobbesian world of human rapacity."[13] Or Robin West: "law has become too hard a profession ... We need to cut it down to size, to make it human again ... But to do so, Joseph's lawyers tell us, we are going to have to humanize our civilization."[14] The commentaries – scholarly and otherwise – suggest a book that contains important, but not particularly revelatory, truths about lawyers and law, made more interesting by the method of relating its "dialect and streetwise syntax"[15] or, from the *New York Times* book review, its talent for "catching the way people talk and the details of their mannerisms" such that the characters "fairly jump off the page."[16] Is this, then, what works about *Lawyerland*: the stylish portrayal of attorneys equally rude and earnest calling for the humanization of their profession, a collection of Atticus Finches who you would actually want to get a beer with (but would probably have to drive home)?[17]

---

[10] Ibid., p. 60.   [11] Ibid., p.184.
[12] Richard Burst, Book Review, *American Bar Association Journal*, 84 (1998), 88–9.
[13] Robert Weisberg, "Civic Oratory in *Lawyerland*," *Columbia Law Review*, 101 (2001), 1782–1792, 1792.
[14] Robin West, "Joseph in Lawyerland," *Columbia Law Review* 101 (2001), 1775–1781, 1781.
[15] Burst, Book Review, 88.
[16] Christopher Lehmann-Haupt, "Tort and retort: Lawyers v. lawyers," *New York Times* (May 29, 1997).
[17] This is a reference to the two (gendered) archetypes that anchored opposing sides of the civility crisis, the Rambo and the Atticus Finch. For a history and critique of usage, see Amy Salyzyn,

I'm not convinced by that. Primarily because I'm not convinced by the artistic assumption underlying the idea, that is, that the true merit of a work is in its ability to reflect social conditions, the proverbial mirror to society which unmasks the hard truths we hide from ourselves. Lawyers being out to make a buck as big business shills or ambulance chasers is neither a hard nor a hidden truth, but even if it were, this is enough for a punchline, not a whole book, or, at the very least, not a particularly good book. For a piece of literature to resonate, for it to do something more than a newspaper, it can't just tell us how the world is. It has to provide us some satisfying way of being in that world. In other words, it has to function ideologically to make a conflict in our material environment more livable, a symbolic act that provides an "imaginary resolution to a real contradiction."[18] What satisfies readers about *Lawyerland* is not the knowledge of a crisis with which we were already familiar. It's some truth about how to live with it.

Assuming encomiums[19] can stand as proof of success, then, the question for this essay is how and in what way is *Lawyerland* making more comprehensible the crises to which it is so obviously addressed? Here, I think, we have to turn away from the almost uniform praise of lawyers to the complaints of one of the few non-lawyer critiques, the aforementioned *New York Times* review by

---

"John Rambo v Atticus Finch: Gender, diversity and the civility movement," *Legal Ethics* (2013), 97–118.

[18] Frederic Jameson, *The Political Unconscious: Narrative as a Socially Symbolic Act* (Ithaca, NY: Cornell University Press, 1981), p. 256.

[19] *Lawyerland* received extremely favorable reviews from magazines and journals. In addition, the majority of online reviews are positive. Almost all are from lawyers or law students who talk about the book as true or real or representative based on personal familiarity. Here are a few examples from different sites: "THE REALTRUTH about lawyers . . . I wish I'd had this book in law school. It would not have changed my plans, but it would have made the transition to real practice less jarring [because] . . . this is how we talk to and about each other, when there aren't any civilians around to be shocked," from Rebecca, comment on *Lawyerland*, Goodreads, comment posted March 6, 2010, www.goodreads.com/book/show/1642197.Lawyerland. "This is by far the best representation I have ever read of what happens when lawyers talk to lawyers . . . Professor Joseph has written the authoritative text on lawyers, and how practicing law brings about a certain life perspective that is shared only by lawyers. If you want to know what it means to practice law—not HOW to do it, but rather its very essence—stop watching all of the garbage on television, just read this book and get on with it," from JB, comment on *Lawyerland*, Amazon, comment posted May 21, 2015, www.amazon.com/Lawyerland-What-Lawyers-Talk-About/dp/0374184178/ref=pd_cp_0_1?_encoding=UTF8&psc=1&refRID=No75RA0QD8RE5T9TB6YV. Of the few critical appraisals, this one is most representative: "'What lawyers sometimes talk about when they indulge in aimless chatter.' Knowing a fair amount about lawyers, I was anxious to read the book. I kept waiting for the informative parts, but gave up halfway . . . maybe he was more interested in 'style' than information," J. Bandi, comment on *Lawyerland*, Amazon, comment posted November 5, 2001, www.amazon.com/Lawyerland-What-Lawyers-Talk-About/dp/0452279933.

journalist Christopher Lehmann-Haupt. The book has style, he concedes, at the level of dialogue and characterization, but turning to structure, Lehmann-Haupt finds fault: "Yet too often the points that 'Lawyerland' is driving at remain elusive ... parts of the essays often don't seem to fit together ... tangents that at first glance seem to mean something but on closer examination don't really make sense."[20] This "series of evocative vignettes," the reviewer suggests are a *formal* failure, because Joseph was unable to "link his images coherently" in order to convey a deeper meaning.[21] The tangents that don't fit together are pervasive, part of the pattern which each chapter follows where the interviewed lawyer, in a colloquial and direct manner, promises to answer the question about law, but then begins a series of narrative digressions – stories about their cases or someone else's cases or other lawyers – with each digression becoming more directly metaphoric and less narrative. Lehmann-Haupt is right to say it is unified. Here it just happens at the level of style. There is, first, the most obvious unification, which Joseph points out in the essay preceding this one: "The entire field of language in the book is made up of the voices of lawyers." Just how these voices are represented presents the most marked divide between popular and scholarly criticism. Popular commentary reports a high degree of verisimilitude e.g. "the conversations sound like something that could have been recorded in any closed-door,"[22] while most scholarly commentary finds the dialogue highly stylized, metaphoric, and, perhaps, aspirational, as the attorneys display a kind of casual erudition that strains credibility for a lunch meeting (a memorized Schlegel quote here, a Kafkaesque metaphor for the penal system there). "The fact is," David Luban writes, "that Joseph's lawyers talk the way that lawyers I know wish they could talk but in fact never do and cannot."[23] On one hand, the relationship between these two perceptions could just be that verisimilitude is evidence of effective stylization, that is, that it feels real because it conveys what lawyers mean rather than what they say. The same way Viktor Shklovsky explains the purpose of art to "make the stone stony," the artfulness employed by Joseph makes the lawyers lawyery.[24] A reasonable hypothesis, but if we step back for a moment from the close-read of all those metaphors and rhetorical devices, I think there is a simpler way in which *Lawyerland* achieves verisimilitude. Turning to one of the smallest units of the field of language – the word – here is a visualization of

---

[20] Lehmann-Haupt, "Tort and Retort."   [21] Ibid.
[22] Rebecca, Comment on *Lawyerland*, Goodreads.
[23] David Luban, "The art of honesty," *Columbia Law Review*, 101 (2001), 1763–1764, 1769.
[24] Victor Shklovsky, "Art as technique," in Julie Rivkin and Michael Ryan (eds.), *Literary Theory: An Anthology* (Oxford: Blackwell Publishers, 2004), p. 16.

FIGURE 15.1 Mindmap.

word frequency[25] in *Lawyerland*, which allows us to look at *what* is being said by *how much* it is being said:

What are lawyers *mostly* talking about when they talk about law? It turns out: themselves and each other. By far, the most frequent noun, especially when combined with its plural, is "lawyer," clocking in at 263 uses, almost twice as many as the 134 uses of "law."[26]

To really get a sense of what the field of language can tell us, though, we have to move from individual words to groupings. And here, "law" loses even more traction. The top groupings are: (1) lawyers (295 with the addition of related terms, e.g. prosecutor, attorney), time (98 alone, but with the

[25] This image was created using the software available from wordle.net, designed by Jonathan Feinberg. Wordle's code excludes common words (or "stop words"), which means that the actual most frequent words in *Lawyerland* are *the* (2,361), *a* (1,673), and *of* (1,251). Looking at stop words is still helpful for analysis even if it has limited value for visualization; for example, the fact that lawyer/s is used 263 is more impressive when we understand that this is just under the stop words *not* (266) and *my* (265) and over *have* (250), *her* (247), and *we* (239). Wordle assigns weights to word based on frequency and then allocates more space to higher frequency. In addition to stop words, I excluded proper nouns. Wordle does not do "stemming," which would count words that are variations of the same root or step as one word. For an explanation of how it works (including the parts of the source code information that did not belong to his former employer), see his piece "Wordle," in Julie Steele and Noah Illinsky (eds.), *Beautiful Visualization: Looking at Data through the Eyes of Experts* (Sebastopol, CA: O'Reilly Media, 2010).

[26] "Right" is used more than "law," but it is only used 13 times in its legal sense; more often, its use indicates colloquial style – "am I right? "right over there" – or to heighten setting – "turn right" "to the right of the courthouse."

addition of nouns like hourly, hour, etc. ... 281), and (3) money (147 including salary, dollars, billable, etc.). "The overwhelming feelings the lawyers in *Lawyerland* engender," Sarah Krakoff writes, "are alienation and despair."[27] Lawyers, time, money. This is more than a feeling of alienation, it is a style of one, which our practice has even combined into a single phrase: billable hour. Perhaps, then, even if on a microlevel, the dialogue of these lawyers, peppered with literary references and legal history and architecture, is too stylized, too metaphoric, to be how we really talk, on the macrolevel, the dominance of these three subjects lends formal support to the idea that what is being said is, in some resonant way, true-to-life – after all, what could be less artistic and more real to practicing attorneys than billables. This is heightened even more by verb frequency, as the lawyers in *Lawyerland* aren't just saying, but *knowing*. "Know" is used more than any verb except "be" and "said" (and only 100 times more than the latter, in a book made up of dialogue!). For comparison, in all of Oliver Wendell Holmes' *The Common Law*, "know" is used only 38 times.

Certainly, at a lexical level, what is being known – the *lawyers*, the *time*, the *money*, and finally, the *law* – seems un-romantically, depressingly real. The next most frequent noun is "people," and this makes sense, but then, with only three fewer uses is a more curious word: "streets," used 89 times in the book. If you've read it, you immediately know why. The interviews don't take place in a casually rendered sketch of an office; instead they are meticulously mapped around lower Manhattan. More specifically, below Houston St. Setting is not, or is not merely, backdrop. Where offices are, what you can see through their windows, where the lawyers walk to get food and where they eventually sit to eat it, where they will take taxis or subways to extra-textual locations – all of this takes up an impressive amount of narrative space, and like the digressions told by the lawyers, this space becomes increasingly metaphoric. Here is the map of *Lawyerland*:

This is not Manhattan. Or even Soho. This is a piece – a tiny, claustrophobic circle of the bottom of the island. We know that Judge Day, in Chapter 3, is going to the subway; the interviewer walks her toward it, but we don't know where she will go when she gets on. The world outside offices, courts, and where you eat while you are at either of these is completely missing from the map of *Lawyerland*, and, except for the picture of one lawyer's wife and kids on his desk and a mention of someone's wife in a hypothetical in another chapter – so are any of the relations symbolized by spaces outside of this.[28]

---

[27] Sarah Krakoff, "Does law and literature survive *Lawyerland?*" *Columbia Law Review* 101 (2001), 1742–1749, 1743.
[28] Joseph, *Lawyerland*, pp. 14 and 132.

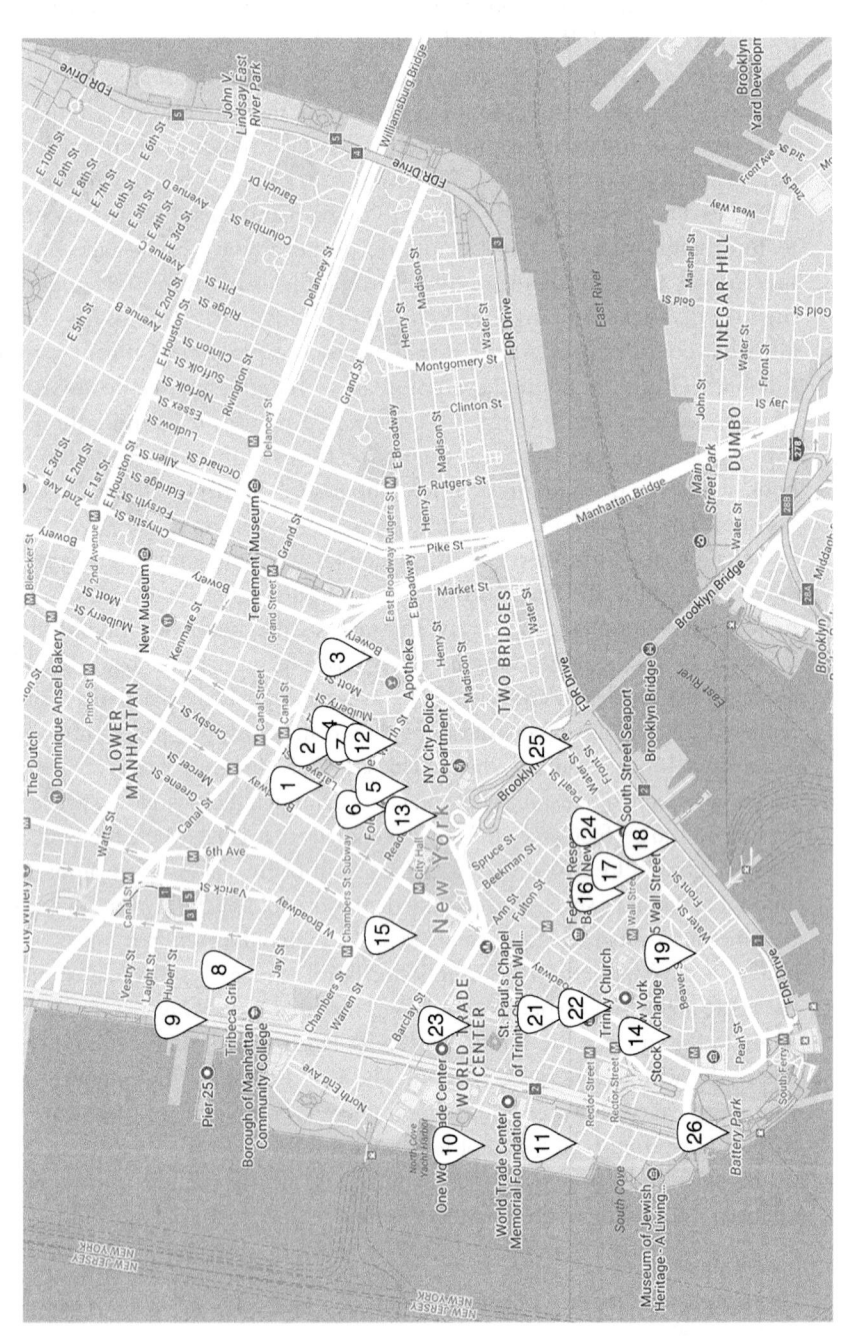

FIGURE 15.2 Manhattan map.

The mapping amplifies the style of alienation to the point of distortion; the force exerted by this closed circuit on the lexical multiplication of *lawyers, time, money* – when looked at spatially – is like a centripetal plot device: the insider feel of *Lawyerland* is achieved, in part, by subtracting anything and everything outside of it. In the *Columbia Law Review* volume mentioned above, Joseph provided his rules for writing, including this one: "Only lower Manhattan settings; 'mapped-out'; the 'geographical' as metaphor ... By condensing geographical space you pressure other metaphorical space (including the spatial dimension of language)."[29] The radical condensing of the geographical space does indeed pressure other metaphorical space, including language. What lawyers talk about when they talk about law depends on where they are talking. This is, in fact, one of the court's conclusions in *Rhem v. Malcom*, the federal case that closed The Tombs – bubble number 2 in the map above – mentioned in the first chapter as the criminal attorney and the interviewer are passing it and in the penultimate paragraph of the book. The court describes the "fortress-like" jail in detail before noting: "The character of the structure is of more than passing narrative interest, since many of the conditions which form the issues of this case flow from the character ... and the given fact of the building's character form the basis of defendants' justification of those conditions."[30]

A structure, of more than passing narrative interest, which, for its inhabitants, forms the conditions of their misery while providing their justifications ... as apt for The Tombs as the billable hour and the geographic totality of work which Joseph recreates stylistically. Lawyers endlessly circling around points they will never conclude while they physically circle the sites of labor they will never leave – here is the formal unification the *New York Times* missed, a vehicle through which the *crisis of civility* is both explained and critiqued. Complaints about the deprofessionalization of law are cyclical – not linear – they wax and wane corresponding with wider cultural anxieties about the contradictory processes at work in capitalism, i.e., how, in Albert Hirschman's neat summation, "the constant practice of commercial transactions generates feelings of trust, empathy for others ... but on the other hand ... such practice permeates all spheres of life with the element of calculation and instrumental reason."[31]

---

[29] Lawrence Joseph, "Working Rules for *Lawyerland*," *Columbia Law Review*, 101 (2001), 1793–1796, 1794.
[30] 371 F. Supp. 594 – Dist. Court, SD New York 1974 at 599.
[31] Albert O. Hirshman, "Rival interpretations of market society: Civilizing, destructive, or feeble?" *Journal of Economic Literature* 20 (1982), 1463–1484, 1483. For an explanation specific to the legal profession, see Amy R. Mashburn, "Professionalism as class ideology: Civility codes and bar hierarchy," *Valparaiso University Law Review* 28 (1993), 657–708.

Deprofessionalization prioritizes money, of course, but also clients. In locating its own critique structurally and in critiquing structure, *Lawyerland*'s style of alienation makes the commercialization of the bar more livable by removing the disproportionate and deceptive share of responsibility for the problem that traditional – and especially official – laments place on individuals. It tells us, then, a secret about *civility*: that its very use works to make a structural problem into an individual one, telling us we have to stop trying to make a quick buck instead of helping us figure out how to keep the quick buck from making us.

CONVERSATION IX
NARRATIVE AND METAPHOR IN LEGAL ACTIVISM

Editors' Introduction

Michael Hanne and Robert Weisberg

We close this volume with the perspective of a school of thought that declares itself a program of reformist advocacy as well as scholarly analysis, and which therefore uses metaphor and narrative in an especially (literally) provocative way: this is Critical Race Theory, one of whose leaders, Mari Matsuda, explains this perspective in an interview that supplies our final chapter. So, a review of the conversations that have led up to this finale is now in order.

Four of the conversations have explored the part played by narrative and metaphor in enabling a reconception – a "revisioning"[1] – of aspects of legal theory and practice. They are: the conversation between Roberto H. Potter and Robert Weisberg on innovations in legal thinking; the conversation between Linda Berger and Kathryn Stanchi on gender in the law; the conversation between Dahlia Lithwick and L. David Ritchie on public debate around crime and punishment; and the conversation between Katharine Young and Bernadette Meyler on narrative and metaphor in human rights law.

The conversation on "innovations in legal thinking" explored how the metaphorical lens of epidemiology enables us to examine the incidence of violence and crime in a place or at a time in a fresh way, and even to imagine remedies through policy narratives.

The "gender" conversation illustrated how traditional ways of collecting evidence, conducting a trial, and, especially, reaching judgment have omitted the perspectives and voices of women. It demonstrated how the same events could be retold in a radically different narrative form that would lead to a significantly different judicial outcome.

---

[1] The term "revisioning" was coined to refer to the achievement of a radically new vision of a topic. See, for instance, the volume of essays *Revisioning Gender*, edited by Myra Marx Ferree, Judith Lorber, and Beth B. Hess (Walnut Creek, CA; Lanham, MD; Oxford: Altamira Press, 2000).

The conversation about the "public debate around crime and punishment" highlighted the importance of the choice of metaphors and associated narratives by experts and the media for shaping the way in which public discussion runs and policy comes to be initiated.

The "human rights" chapter took up the issue of the role played by metaphors and narratives at every level of human rights discourse, as much in the everyday practical context ("queues" and "lines") as in the broad conceptual context.

Notably, most of these depictions of the roles of metaphor and narrative in law have been dynamic: they not only describe how literary depictions operate in or explain law, but they also induce us to imagine different legal regimes and to pursue change. But no recent strand of legal thought has so fully embraced the role of advocate for legal change as Critical Race Theory (CRT), and none has employed literary figurations in such a boldly dynamic way.

CRT, whose key leaders include Mari Matsuda, Patricia Williams, and Kimberlé Williams Crenshaw, might best be viewed against the background of a related school, Critical Legal Studies (CLS). CLS emerged in the 1970s to challenge the supposed deductive logic and determinacy of legal doctrine. The adherents of CLS drew on both the Legal Realism movement of earlier in the twentieth century and the Marxist intellectual tradition. They depicted lawmaking, especially by judges, as a rhetorical exercise using highly manipulable forms and terms and argued that law's supposed neutrality masked a commitment to highly contestable free-market values and a fiction of autonomous individualism.[2] CRT shares the goals of CLS in very broad terms, but strongly differentiates itself by its emphasis on how the interests of, indeed the basic recognition of, minority groups and women are suppressed by the traditional canons of legal discourse. Indeed one of the critiques of CLS advanced by exponents of CT, including Matsuda, has been that it has led only rarely to radical legal and social reform. Thus, CRT marries what might be called the deconstructive techniques of CLS with an unabashed social activism to underscore how law sustains white supremacy and racial power.[3] And in contrast to the drily abstract prose of most CLS writing, CRT also unabashedly uses narrative and metaphor.

Because CRT is in part a legal history discourse, it is probably more associated with the use of narrative than of metaphor. Critical Race scholars

---

[2] Mark G. Kelman, *A Guide to Critical Legal Studies* (Cambridge, MA: Harvard University Press, 1990).
[3] Kimberlé Crenshaw, Neil Gotanda, Gary Peller, and Kendall Thomas (eds.), *Critical Race Theory: The Key Writings that Formed the Movement* (New York, NY: The New Press, 1995).

and activists recount larger historical narratives around slavery and its aftermath, around the successes and failures of the civil rights movement, around the practices by which white supremacy has been maintained.[4] To achieve its goal, much of the work of CRT involves a narrative retelling of American legal history to precipitate the true motives of lawmaking. One striking example is the work of Mary Dudziak, who has demonstrated how the generally accepted and Whiggishly idealistic history of the American civil rights movement should be recast in large part as a pragmatic Cold War strategy. She argues that the US government's support for desegregation and racial equality in the 1960s was motivated at least as much by concern that they harmed the reputation of the US during early battles with the Soviet Union as by genuinely ethical commitment.[5]

But CRT also promotes and employs narrative on an individual level – literally the level of storytelling. Its legal activism frequently involves presenting scenarios that imagine the world operating differently. CRT "has an open and activist agenda, with an emphasis on storytelling and personal experience. It's about righting wrongs, not just questing after knowledge."[6] For CRT, despite the word "theory" in its name, narrative is capable of embodying individual and personal experience in a way that theory never can.[7] In its view, marginalized individuals and groups frequently lack the "voice" to ensure they are heard in civil society. Hence we get a new critical form of expression, the "voice of color." The "voice of color" consists of narratives and storytelling monologues used to convey personal racial experiences and to counter metanarratives that continue to maintain racial inequality.[8] Thus, Patricia Williams uses anecdotes and longer stories to illustrate issues around justice for the homeless and dispossessed.[9] Richard Delgado illustrates the potential of counterstorytelling in the form of five retellings of the story of a black professor applying and being rejected for a teaching job.[10] Gerald P.

[4] Michael A. Olivas, "The chronicles, my grandfather's stories, and immigration law: The slave traders' chronicles as racial history," *St Louis University Law Journal*, 34 (1990), 425–441.
[5] Mary L. Dudziak, "Desegregation as a Cold War imperative," *Stanford Law Review*, 41 (1988), 61–120.
[6] Will Oremus, "Did Obama hug a radical?" *Slate* (March 8, 2012).
[7] Richard Delgado, Jean Stefancic, "Critical race theory: An annotated bibliography," *Virginia Law Review*, 79 no. 2 (1993), 461–516.
[8] Alex M. Johnson, Jr., "The new voice of color," *Yale Law Journal*, 100 (1991), 2007–2064. A. Javier Treviño, Michelle A. Harris, Derron Wallace, "What's so critical about critical race theory?," *Contemporary Justice Review*, 11 no. 1 (2008), 7–10.
[9] Patricia Wright, "Commercial rights and constitutional wrongs," *Maryland Law Review*, 49 (1990), 293–313.
[10] Richard Delgado, "Storytelling for oppositionists and others: A plea for narrative," *Michigan Law Review*, 87 (1989), 2411–2441.

López has written fictional narratives to capture as vividly as possible how discrimination is experienced and the skills required by lawyers to represent clients in such cases.[11]

But, of course, narrative entails and is complemented by metaphor. So gender discrimination and racism are "engrained in the fabric" and system of American (but not only American, of course) law and society. Physical and spatial metaphors refer to discrimination as inherent in the "structure" of the society, and to categories of people being "marginalized" and "subordinated." Derrick Bell wrote of Black Americans occupying "the bottom rung of the socioeconomic ladder" and speculated that, after their departure, a new group would be assigned that status, lest a portion of the white population come to find that they may be next.[12]

Other examples abound, many of them explicitly using images of color. Cheryl I. Harris and Gloria Ladson-Billings propose the metaphor of "whiteness as property." They describe the "property functions of whiteness" as rights to disposition, rights to use and enjoyment, reputation and status property, and the absolute right to exclude grant – these are privileges to the owner that a renter (or a person of color) would not be afforded.[13] At the same time, one of the images that has been much debated is that of "color-blindness," with opposing views on whether the social and economic advancement of people of color is better served by disregarding color in selection for education, housing, employment, promotion etc. (on the basis that this will ensure greater equality of opportunity) or whether color-blindness tends rather to mask the existence of prejudice and discrimination.[14] (And to switch senses, a striking musical metaphor is employed by Milner S. Ball to suggest the desirability that the current "monophony" of the American story be replaced by "polyphony," in the form of a "plurality of consciousness, voices, and languages."[15])

---

[11] Gerald P. López, "Lay lawyering," *UCLA Law Review*, 32 (1984–85), 1–60; Gerald P. López, "Reconceiving civil rights practice: Seven weeks in the life of a rebellious collaboration," *The Georgetown Law Journal*, 77 (1989), 1603–1717.

[12] Derrick A. Bell, Jr., "After we're gone: Prudent speculations on America in a post-racial epoch," *St Louis University Law Journal*, 34 (1990), 393–405.

[13] Gloria Ladson-Billings, "Just what is critical race theory and what's it doing in a nice field like education?" in Laurence Parker, Donna Deyhle, Sofia Villenas, (eds.), *Race Is . . . Race Isn't: Critical Race Theory and Qualitative Studies in Education* (Boulder, CO: Westview Press, 1999), pp. 7–30.

[14] For instance, Eduardo Bonilla-Silva, *Racism without Racists: Color-Blind Racism and the Persistence of Racial Inequality in America*, 4th edition (Lanham, MD: Rowman and Littlefield, 2014).

[15] Milner S. Ball, "Stories of origin and constitutional possibilities, *Michigan Law Review*, 87 (1989). 2280–2319.

CRT has faced much skepticism. There has been a critique, from within, that invokes "the empathic fallacy," i.e., that exposing people to an alternative narrative is enough to radically shake racist beliefs and attitudes.[16] But most vociferous have been attacks from without, especially by Judge Richard Posner, who focuses precisely on CRT's reliance on narrative and other literary figurations:

> What is most arresting about critical race theory is that ... it turns its back on the Western tradition of rational inquiry, forswearing analysis for narrative. Rather than marshal logical arguments and empirical data, critical race theorists tell stories – fictional, science-fictional, quasi-fictional, autobiographical, anecdotal—designed to expose the pervasive and debilitating racism of America today. By repudiating reasoned argumentation, the storytellers reinforce stereotypes about the intellectual capacities of nonwhites.[17]

A fair rejoinder to the internal critique could be reference, within this volume, to such conversations as those between Young and Meyler, or Lithwick and Ritchie, or Potter and Weisberg, which show that literary figurations in public discourse do in fact cause rethinking of social values. And a rejoinder to the Posner critique might be to challenge his binary distinction between the tools of analytic reason and the figures of the imagination, that metaphor and narrative are not the enemy of good reasoning but help expose bad reasoning. A great source of that rejoinder is the classic article by Deirdre (formerly Donald) McCloskey that reveals that the economic reasoning that is Posner's positive paradigm relies heavily on rhetorical constructions to finesse the indeterminacy of its rational models.[18] And then there are the economists' metaphors: many have been the economists mesmerized by the imagery of "invisible hand" and the "free market" who have overlooked the complexity of human institutions. As McCloskey wryly observes, "To say that markets can be represented by supply and demand 'curves' is no less a metaphor than to say that the west wind is 'the breath of autumn's being.'" McCloskey emphasizes that these metaphors are often not ornamental or deceptive – they are essential to framing the economic analysis. This last rejoinder can serve as an argument for the theses of all the conversations in this volume.

The conversation with Mari Matsuda that follows illustrates the many purposes the activist finds for narrative in her writing and campaigning.

---

[16] Richard Delgado and Jean Stefancic, *Critical Race Theory: An Introduction*, 2nd edition (Critical America) (New York, NY: New York University Press, 2012), pp. 27–29.
[17] Richard A. Posner, "The skin trade, " *The New Republic*, 217 no. 15 (October 13, 1997), 40–43.
[18] Donald M. McCloskey, "The rhetoric of economics," *Journal of Economic Literature*, 31 (June 1983), 481–517.

These include: use of narratives which recount appalling events from the recent and more distant past, highlighting actions in the past which may be seen as inspiring, and envisaging progressive scenarios in the future. She argues that narrative is extraordinarily capable of capturing the complexity, the multidimensional character of many social and economic issues.

Metaphor figures equally as an activist tool for Matsuda. Her earliest writing insists on the importance of legal scholars "looking to the bottom," if they are to represent adequately the experience that the poor and disenfranchised have of the law. She writes of her preference for taking the long view and for the "slow-cooking school of theory building" and, a metaphor borrowed from Anna Scales, of the "ratchet principle" for achieving social change little by little. She speaks of the capacity of a well-chosen metaphor to communicate instantly, to get the listener to see a topic in a fresh way, whereas she argues that narrative is capable of greater complexity, of operating in several dimensions, of giving the full texture of relations and events.

16

A Conversation with Mari Matsuda

Michael Hanne

MICHAEL HANNE: This project focuses on the ways in which narrative and metaphor are deployed in every area of legal theory and practice: inside and outside the courtroom, by legal scholars, and in public discussion of the law. The hypothesis we are working with is that narrative and metaphor are everywhere in discourse within the law and that both actually exercise great influence on how we think about justice and the law, on how law is practiced in the United States and in the international context, on how we think and talk about crime and punishment, on how the law operates in areas related to gender and human rights, on how fresh metaphors and narratives disrupt the dominance of conventional narratives and metaphors in the legal context, and so on.

We approached you for this interview because we see you as having deployed narrative and metaphor brilliantly, not only in your contributions to developing Critical Race Theory in relation to the law, but, at least as importantly, as an activist who has worked on many different social, political and legal issues.

I'm going to ask you about some of the ways that you do that. I'm going to quote liberally from different works of yours and tease out with you some of the ways in which you use narrative and metaphor in your own work and ask how much you select and invent stories and metaphors by instinct and how conscious you are of the instruments you employ to develop your arguments and to persuade – because you use narrative and metaphor persuasively, to bring about change. You employ narrative and metaphor yourself in evocative ways, but you also critique dominant narratives and dominant metaphors with a view to undermining their dominance.

MARI MATSUDA: That is true.

MH: Can we start with some of the ways in which I see you as using narrative, then we'll move on to metaphor, then move on to how the two intersect with each other? One distinctive way in which I think you use narrative is in terms of stories of inspiration, or stories for inspiration, of outstanding actions by courageous people. You write about, for instance, two white women in 1868, acknowledging an African American as their nephew;[1] Japanese Americans interned during WWII, who then chose to fight in Europe for the United States;[2] young civil rights workers enrolling African Americans to vote in Alabama in the 1960s,[3] etc. Really inspiring, historical stories you tell. Can you say something about how you select those, because it is often not obvious which story you are going to select? How do you go about choosing those stories: they are obviously stories from your repertoire?

MARI MATSUDA: The twentieth century was my century. It's what I know, the book I know, so I'm pulling from that book and there are characters to fall in love with in that book, so if I'm in love with them, and they've moved me, then it stays in a file and I pull it out when I need it. But I think I am a pretty strategic person. There's this old labor song, "Which side are you on?" It's saying you have to make choices in this world and make the right one. Come on! Be on the justice side, it's a good side. When I'm writing, as opposed to teaching – in teaching I pull back a lot, because I want to draw out students' ideas – but in my writing, that's where I really am trying to say: "This world is in such terrible trouble and you can choose to be on the side of caring and changing it and making it a better place." So, I'll pull on those examples.

Sometimes it's very specific to the circumstance. You were talking about the story I used about the Grimké sisters. The back story to that is that there were women of color who were trying to organize around women of color and the law and there was conflict among allies. Some white feminists asked, "Where's our place in this?" Then, the push back, "You know what? This ain't about you." People who were really on the same side had taken on a huge, all-volunteer, national effort, and fights emerged. They were young. That's complicating it because the emotions tumble around when you are young and taking on world-changing work. I made a strategic choice to open with these white women at this conference in which some white women were saying "We are excluded," to say "No, you are right in the middle of this, and here's a way to be in the middle of it, to be a true sister in struggle."

---

[1] Mari Matsuda, "When the first quail calls: Multiple consciousness as jurisprudential method," *Women's Rights Law Reporter*, 14 no. 2–3 (Spring/Fall, 1992), 297–300.

[2] Mari Matsuda, "Looking to the bottom: Critical legal studies and reparations," *Harvard Civil Rights-Civil Liberties Review*, 22 (1987), 323–329.

[3] Mari Matsuda, "Admit that the waters around you have grown: Change and legal education," *Indiana Law Journal*, 89 (2014), 1381–1400.

The Grimké sisters were just a great example. They did this unthinkable thing of saying: "the Black children of our brother, born to an enslaved woman, are our kin." That was shocking, and wildly outside the safe zone of that period. It's one reason why I won't let suffragists like Susan B. Anthony off the hook for her opposition to full equality for Black Americans. People say, "Well, she was just a product of her time." She was of the same time as the Grimké sisters, and she made a different choice.

MH: I think what you also do in terms of inspiring your listeners and readers is imagine possible future situations and future stories. So, you say for instance that Rosa Parks "dared to imagine that a black woman could remain seated on a Montgomery bus while a white man stood."[4] That was Rosa Parks not simply taking her seat, but saying: that's how it could be in the future. Another time you write that "we imagine law to uplift and protect the sixteen-year old single mother on crack rather than law to criminalize her"[5] and that's saying, "Hey, the story we have is not the only story we could have."

MARI MATSUDA: What I've seen in my teaching is that the weakest intellectual tool in my students' toolkit is the visioning. They can't do it. They've been so beaten down by what, in theoretical terms, we call hegemony. There is no other possibility than what you are living with. Yeah, you have these horrible student loans – but, that's just the way life is. The ability to see that no, actually there's absolutely no reason why it has to be this way, is lost to them.

MH: It's like Bernie Sanders, just at the moment [February 2016, during the presidential primary campaigns] saying that it doesn't have to be like that.

MARI MATSUDA: And lo and behold a lot of people think, hey, that's right. I'm flying up to Kona next week to talk to people that are trying to protect fisheries and these are small subsistence fishermen that want to do something to keep the fishing stocks healthy in Hawai'i including moratoriums on fishing in certain places and being able to keep outsiders from coming into their areas. They are trying to organize around that and I've been thinking how I'm going to run this workshop. I want to open, not by talking about fish at all, but by saying: "What is it that you really want? What would a good world look like for your grandchildren," and just put up a piece of paper and have people holler out and push them to dream big. And then we'll talk about the fish!

---

[4] Matsuda, "Looking to the bottom," 323–329.
[5] Mari Matsuda, "Beside my sister, facing the enemy: Legal theory out of coalition," *Stanford Law Review*, 43 (1993), 1183–1192.

MH: At the same time, many of the stories that you tell are of appalling episodes from the past, stories, as you put it, of people living "at the bottom," and of the annexation of Hawai'i, or of police shooting young unarmed African Americans, just so many stories, reminding your audience that's just the way it has been in so many situations. Again, how do you see yourself working with those stories, the stories of the appalling, are you saying this is where we have come from, or are you saying this where we are, and there's got to be change? Or sometimes one, sometimes the other?

MARI MATSUDA: I was talking to my partner, Chuck Lawrence, who is also my co-author sometimes, and telling him I'm doing an interview on narrative and I asked him: "Why do you use narrative?" and he said: "It gets at the complexity." He planted that in my head. Telling the story of the people that we often forget about, part of it is just retrieval – so don't forget that there is a kid on this island who right now is hungry and doesn't have food. Beyond that, narrative gives the full texture to that story, including the mysteries and contradictions. Once I was on this panel about pragmatism and I think it was Richard Rorty on the same panel, some theory guy, and I was talking about how I really want to know the worldview and the opinions of this minimum-wage factory worker. This was back when we actually had factories. And he challenged me: "What if she's not thinking anything? She doesn't have time to think." He was right, in that she doesn't have time to read theoretical papers on pragmatism. But I wanted to show there's something complicated going on in her world of ideas. She might not be expressing her ideas and agency fully the way we would, because of the things that grind you down when you are poor, but it's not a story of her completely lacking a thought, or an act, or a desire. It's also not a story of the valorized working poor who have all the answers, it's: sometimes you get it, sometimes you don't. You are moving toward something, you know in your gut that something is wrong, but it's true that you've just to figure out how you're going to pay the bills and you don't have the time to go and campaign for Bernie Sanders. My Dad is a labor guy, so a lot of my politics I get from him and he believed that the workers were smarter, braver, they had all the answers, and he had a valorized view of the intellect of the working class. He was a working-class guy himself, so he comes to it honestly from all the people he met in factory and field. Sometimes I'm channeling that, but I think I'm also trying to see the sides of working-class life that might be self-defeating, self-destructive, but still retain respect for the full experience.

MH: Summing up what you have just said, may I quote a couple of sentences you wrote: "I try to remember always that there is a woman sitting at a bus stop somewhere, getting off a long shift cleaning rooms in a hotel like this one." (You were obviously at a conference when you first spoke these words.) "She pays taxes that help fund the university. Will her children go there?"[6] And again I was just thinking how important are the stories of people who have not had advantage in their lives, the stories they are telling. In a very early essay of yours, you suggest how dangerous abstraction is in talking about social issues and specifically John Rawls's use of abstraction,[7] and then you really seem to replace that with narrative. You say, hey, it's the stories of everyday people, that's what really counts and the abstractions we should be suspicious of. They "cloud the reality," you say. Do you still think that?

MARI MATSUDA: I do. In critical race theory, the bottom line is always actual lived effects of structures of oppression. We know oppression exists because we know the facts of people's lives, from police violence to lousy health outcomes. So material facts and experiences are my starting point. It's funny because often in my teaching, I'm trying to convince my students that they really need to stick with theory, when it's hard and complex, when it's abstract and dense, because there is value there. I don't want my commitment to lived experience read in an anti-intellectual kind of way. We need both.

Pronouncement from on high without any reference to the content of actual human suffering and human lives and human experience has gotten us into some really horrible places, this whole fantasy of the market, and how the wonderful market is going to free us, for example. Often when I would encounter one of these theorists of law and economics, and I would say "What about x, y, z," and insert some facts about what actually happens to people, they'd say something like "That's not part of my model." They have to take all the human out of it to make their numbers come out right. The way that human beings are not rational, and fool themselves, all of that has to come out. The way evil people can capture and distort markets and the entire democratic process. Of course, all of that is coming back into the conversation. It's hot now in economics to have suddenly discovered psychology and inequality and things like that.

MH: One of the other ways in which you suggest the significance of narrative is when you talk about the importance of genealogy for indigenous people, for Polynesians, for Native Americans. And following up on the topic of the need to avoid abstraction which is not grounded in concrete reality, you say:

---

[6] Mari Matsuda, "Who is excellent?" *Seattle Journal for Social Justice*, 1 (2003), 29–50.
[7] Mari Matsuda, "Liberal jurisprudence and abstracted visions of human nature: A feminist critique of Rawls' theory of justice," *New Mexico Law Review*, 16 (1986), 613–630.

"Not much time is wasted in communities of color and among feminists arguing over definitions of justice. Justice means children with full bellies sleeping in warm beds under clean sheets. Justice means no lynching, no rapes. Justice means access to livelihood. It means control over one's body. These kinds of concrete and substantive visions of justice flow naturally from the experience of oppression."[8] You are talking about notions of justice which come directly out of stories of experience.

MARI MATSUDA: I think it's important to talk about the fact that in Critical Race Theory narrative has been especially prominent and to ask why. Starting with Derrick Bell, who was one of the first people to just completely fictionalize how he was going to get his point across, and Patricia Williams who raised storytelling in legal analysis to an art form – critical race theorists used narrative to build insight and empathy. Narrative is home ground for communities of color. In our home cultures, there are griots and storytellers everywhere. When I grew up, all my moral instruction came in the form of stories. I think that's true in a lot of premodern cultures.

Critical race theorists used narrative to subvert a pack of lies told via liberalism: that law is color-blind, that legal processes are fair and therefore the results are fair, that a declaration of formal equality is the best thing the law can give you. We told stories to introduce a different way to understand justice and fairness.

All of my work to understand law and justice was influenced by people who are actually trying to make change in the world. So, in that passage you've just read I'm talking about actual people I know that are working in women's shelters, or organizing, or doing antipoverty work. My mother was part of War on Poverty, she was a Head Start trainer. The reason I have always known that there are children on this island going hungry is that she would tell me story after story of going to a house and with no food in the refrigerator.

MH: Can we take a sidestep now – that is a metaphor, of course – and talk about your use of metaphor. You are just so prolific in your use of striking metaphors, metaphors which really make the audience, the reader of your work, think about something in a different way. And, if you don't mind, I will quote more passages from your writing. The fundamental metaphor you employ is "Looking to the bottom" and related structures of society, with some people just managing "at the bottom." And then a really funny one, in the same article, is in your critique of Critical Legal Theory as you came to initiate the whole Critical Race Theory movement. You say, "Like a pack of

---

[8] Matsuda, "When the first quail calls," 297–300.

super-termites, these scholars eat away at the trees of legal doctrine and liberal ideals, leaving sawdust in their paths. That they do it so well and so single-mindedly, is compelling; it suggests that this is what the smartest are doing. Never mind that no one knows what to do with all the sawdust." And then another lovely metaphor – maybe this one you didn't create, I don't know – "the slow-cooking school of theory building."[9]

MARI MATSUDA: Yeah, I did invent that. The first one now feels too cheeky to me, but the context is: we were the new kids on the block, trying to shake up the deconstructionists left in the legal academy, to bring some new ideas in. So I don't know whether I still need it. I cook, so cooking metaphors slip in there. "Slow cooking" works. I still think that you see the need for that metaphor now. The kids who are organizing around Black Lives Matter, if you just look at it from the outside now, they are making such an amazing difference to the conversation in this country. All of a sudden, everybody is aware of police violence and the presidential candidates are talking about it, and the media are covering it in a way that has never happened before. And so you think "Wow, great success." But on the inside they are having a lot of struggles, it's hard to be in a movement. When I teach organizing or when I am talking to young people who are doing political work, I tell them it's never going to *not* be that way. You're trying to do something with other human beings, which is extraordinarily hard to do. When you mobilize large numbers of people, there is conflict, there is misunderstanding. There are those who think you're going too hard. There are those who think you are not going hard enough. There are people who are just fundamentally unhappy and they bring all their unhappiness to the table. It's never *not* like that. And you will have to stay up all night and build relationships and figure out who you need to cut off and figure out who you can still work with. It's going to be hard, hard, hard. There's just no way around it, you do it, and in the end when you really need it you will have your coalition in place. So that slow-cooking metaphor is pretty solid, I think, and it's one I still have to use.

MH: To what extent is the law a specific focus in the political and social organizing you do and the coaching you offer to other people working on major social issues? Are you particularly concerned with helping people make law changes or are you helping them to work their way around or through existing law for the moment?

MARI MATSUDA: Both and all. So, I don't see law as a primary target for change agents, but power under late capitalism is often packaged in law and often law

[9] Matsuda, "Beside my sister, facing the enemy," 1183–1192.

is useful as a focal point for struggle. Law is useful as a tool for struggle, and sometimes law is actually the problem. So, if there is some material change that you want and you see law as standing in the way of that change, you need a legal strategy built into your political strategy. But I've never seen law reform as the ultimate goal. My understanding of how law works in the world is that it is a product of economic, social and historical reality. It serves often to shore up a certain vision and it sometimes can be deployed to make change. So, often groups that I work with, or my students, are interested in challenging a specific law. But good law is not the end, it's the means to justice, and the by-product. A democratic, fair, equal, and compassionate society will probably generate some decent law.

MH: Can you talk specifically about hate speech, because that's an area you've done a lot of work on.

MARI MATSUDA: Well, that came out of work I was doing in the '70s with a group called the National Alliance against Racist and Political Repression. A major element of their campaign was to outlaw the KKK, because the Klan was standing in the way of a lot of things that were important for racial justice and labor organizing, terrorizing people who were trying to organize factories in the South, for example. So, I thought banning the Klan was a good idea. This comes right up against American legal doctrine that says you can't outlaw the Klan, and a set of free speech values that I am committed to. So, trying to work out that puzzle about why something that seemed so obviously necessary was considered so obviously impossible in the law, was how I came to that body of legal scholarship. We limit speech in all kinds of ways under Anglo-American law, so why is terroristic racist speech protected? That was an interesting question to ask.

MH: So interesting in the present climate of speech against Muslims, of pronouncements by some candidates for the Republican nomination for the [2016] presidential election about Muslims, and banning migration of Muslims to this country!

MARI MATSUDA: And there is an analogue in Europe. People are scared and anxious, understandably, and the easy route is hate, find somebody to scapegoat. That's a very old story.

MH: One of the things that you do strikingly with metaphor is bring into conjunction with each other areas about which people would probably think: "Oh, no, they don't fit together." So you say for instance "Homophobia is a building block for war."[10] That statement will really startle a lot of people. Yet, in my view it is so clearly right, because you are talking about ethnicity,

---

[10] Mari Matsuda, "Love, change," *Yale Journal of Law and Feminism*, 17 (2005): 185–203.

gender, class, poverty – and all these things need to be linked together. They can't be treated, and shouldn't be treated, separately. You are concerned also with international relations, and with war, which is sadly one of the prime manifestations of international relations.

MARI MATSUDA: One of the areas I started teaching in is peacemaking and this started after September 11, when students came to me and said: "We can't talk about this." If they didn't put an American flag in their window in the dorm, they were verbally attacked by other students and they felt that there was no space to ask very simple questions: "Where did this violence, where did this hatred, come from?" Even asking the questions was seen as disloyal. As a teacher, I said: "We can't *not* talk about this." I created this class to try and have a space to talk about it. One unexpected result that was interesting is that veterans and members of the armed services signed up for the class. They had questions about peace after their military experience, and taking this class over the years, they contributed significantly to the conversation. Adding an intersectional analysis to the class came naturally. When you look at the rhetoric surrounding the choice to go to war, it has patriarchy all over it. Sometimes it's laughable: the way we talk about it – the sexualization of weapons, for instance. The metaphor people could really have fun exploring this.

MH: I was asking you, though, about the way in which you bring together in your speaking and writing areas that other people don't think belong together.

MARI MATSUDA: That just comes from activist practice. Most people that are on the ground struggling to make change run up against the interconnection of all forms of subordination. I have a friend, Stephen Lerner, an amazing labor organizer – he ran the Justice for Janitors campaign in the United States. When I invited him to come to my organizing class, he kinda teased the students. He asked: "What would you do if you were trying to organize a factory and there were members of the Klan in the factory?" and they looked shocked, which was the set-up he needed to say: "You organize everyone in the factory – even the ones who are in the Ku Klux Klan – why are they in the Ku Klux Klan, what's their story and how do you give them a different story to replace the one they've been telling themselves that's about racial hatred?" The way that racism is a tool for entrenching class difference is just all over US history. It's not hard for anyone who's looked at that history to make these connections. I connect homophobia and war, make non-obvious links, on purpose. I dare you to tell me that these things are not connected.

And I dare you to tell me ordinary people can't get smarter about intersectionality. When I talk about retrieval, I want to find places in history when people who are supposed to hate each other came together to make change across their conflicting positions, because they came to see the bigger structure they needed to take on. In Hawai'i, that is the story of the ILWU organizing workers with the slogan "brothers under the skin," erasing decades of racial animosity that had broken strikes when plantation workers were divided into "Japanese camp," and "Filipino Camp." It's the Southern Tenant Farmers Union organizing white and Black sharecroppers in the south. It's the Marine Cooks and Stewards in the bay area organizing gay and straight, Black, Asian, Latino workers on cruise ships in the middle of the last century. What we learn is people can change, they can let go of deeply felt hatreds when their eyes open up to the ways in which bosses exploit those ancient hates in order to keep your paycheck small. History is a great narrative source, it can displace a story of the inevitability of conflict with a story of humans transcending hate.

MH: Yes, I think that is the provocation. Then there will be other times when you interweave a series of mini-narratives with some striking metaphors. So you introduce a recent essay[11] by recounting how young civil rights workers risked their lives to register voters in Lowndes, Alabama in 1965. And you say that those actions "brought forth a great fountain of law." Then you move forward to refer to the present crisis in the United States, saying: "It is shaking our windows and rattling our walls. It is the cruelties of wealth and inequality. It is city-swamping climate change. It is students seeing school loans as a life-long burden. It is hunger. Somewhere in your state, a parent is skipping a meal in order to make sure a child gets one." And this last mini-narrative – of the parent skipping a meal – is, of course, the most concrete, the most grounded one of all.

MARI MATSUDA: Shaking your windows is an allusion to Bob Dylan's "The times they are a changing," but no one gets my allusions anymore. I guess it becomes a metaphor then. I think I talk like that more the older I get. I've a mother-in-law who's 101 years old and basically all her speech is metaphor and parable, it's so distilled. In the beginning I had so many audiences, so some of this stuff you're reading to me is from my early work. I still had to get tenure, I had to get jobs, I had to get published. Now I don't care. I've got one goal: I'm trying to wake people up and get them to see that we can do something. And maybe that's why it comes out in that way with metaphor and narrative. How do you get someone to move from passive witness to active shaper of history? You get them to see what they already know. Something is horribly wrong, and only you can change it before it's

---

[11] Matsuda, "Admit that the waters around you have grown," 1381–1400.

too late. The facts are known: people know that the quality of their lives and their hopes for the future are degraded in a winner-take-all, everybody-for-themselves society. I try to find the right image, the right story, the right hook, to make them take what they know and turn it into action. This requires optimism, so anthems like Dylan's are important: he created a tone that said: "Smart people are on my side, change is inevitable."

MH: You say: "It is shaking our windows and rattling our walls." So it's nice to be able to quote Margaret Montoya, who used a similar metaphor, but to refer to your writing: "The tectonic plates of my identity have been shifted by Matsuda's work."

MARI MATSUDA: If my work did that, that's what I was trying to do. It's interesting because I talked to a young person who's doing some of this activist work on campus, and she was asked in an interview: "Aren't you just preaching to the choir?" (dusty old metaphor!) That just seemed to really miss the point. The choir is a primary audience. You are trying to get people who are like you to be as brave as you would like to be in your best self. That's hard. And that's important work, so I think my primary audience really was people like Margaret, who I think of as a lot like me. But the interesting thing is, particularly in the hate speech work, I had a lot of people tell me "You've changed my mind," and that was so interesting because I wasn't really trying to change minds, I was trying to get people to see what they already knew and give them permission to say it out loud. "I support free speech, and it is in the interest of free speech to consider limits on assaultive forms of speech that have the effect of silencing a much-needed voice." That was something you were not supposed to say if you wanted respect as a First Amendment scholar or civil libertarian. I wanted to give people permission to say it. I wasn't optimistic about converting anybody. But there are people who said: "This never happens to me, but I read your article and I changed my mind."

MH: But probably another thing you are doing is actually equipping people with tools – you might say weapons, but that would be a metaphor we would probably both want to avoid – tools to say some of the things they always knew but couldn't quite express.

MARI MATSUDA: Or just to see that it could be said by someone and lightning did not strike them dead.

MH: You use the lovely metaphor "the ratchet principle"[12] for achieving change, winding the device up and up.

---

[12] Mari Matsuda, "We the people: Jurisprudence in color," "Where is Your Body?" And Other Essays on Race Gender and the Law (Boston, MA: Beacon Press, 1987), pp. 21–27.

MARI MATSUDA: That is borrowed, from Ann Scales!

MH: Can we talk about the narrative-metaphor connection? You say that you haven't been particularly self-conscious about when you are creating a metaphor, or analyzing an existing metaphor, creating a narrative, or analyzing a narrative. Can you say something about how you see narrative and metaphor intersecting or interlinking with each other? Let me quote you again, if you don't mind. Two quotes I've got here from you. In the first one, you talk about wrapping fruit trees in leaves to protect them against frost, but then you link that to the war in Afghanistan: "The gesture of wrapping a tree in winter blankets of leaves is one a stranger from another land might recognize. It is done when there is hope that the sweet will come again, even though frost threatens. The pruning and watering and wrapping of trees was no doubt given up a while ago in Afghanistan to the wars and the scramble for today's food, water and shelter. I thought of parents tucking children into bed at night with that urgent, tender wish that they be safe until dawn's light. There I stood tucking in a tree, while somewhere in my name bombs fell on someone else's children."[3] That's an incredibly powerful juxtaposition of a story from one context with a story from another.

MARI MATSUDA: I think I was weeping when I wrote that, and I am again now. We've kind of gotten used to endless war since the time I wrote that. But on the eve of the Iraq invasion we were coming out of a period of relative peace and all of a sudden people were talking about: "We need to carpet-bomb Afghanistan." My Dad is a WWII vet, so I have a lot of very specific imagery of what happens when bombs fall. I think what happens with how I write is that I actually have in my mind what I want to say, but then I go work on something physical. I do a lot of work with my hands, so I was actually doing that act of tree-tending in the cold, icy DC winter, hauling leaves to bury the fig trees so that they would still be there in the spring. And while I'm doing that I'm thinking about what I want to say and how I want to say it. It's always been my goal to write things that are readable and persuasive and well-crafted. I read poetry before I write because poets are more careful than legal writers about the words they choose and the images and metaphors. And then it just kinda happens, the words that are the best way to make somebody really get it. How else are you going to do it? There are different ways of hooking people. A metaphor gets someone right away. They're with you, you're communicating, they know what you are trying to say. Any parent who reads about tucking in the children at night, they know what I'm

---

[3] Mari Matsuda, "Among the mourners who mourn, why should I among them be?' *Signs: Journal of Women in Culture and Society*, 28 no. 1 (2008), 475–477.

saying about looking at a sleeping child and needing, desperately, safety for that child.

With narrative is where you can tell a little more complicated story. When I was doing the hate speech work, I collected hundreds and hundreds of stories of people that were not able to do something they wanted to do because of a verbal assault. Let me just give you one example. I wrote an article and I made a little mention of gun control. I got a lot of threatening stuff on the internet because of that. I'm not now really so ready to talk about gun control any more. I don't know if I'm censoring myself, but if you called me up and you said: "I'm from network news, do you want to come on our show and talk about gun control?" I'd hesitate because of this ugly stuff that I got assaulted with the last time I spoke on the subject. It changed my willingness to speak. I collected hundreds of stories like that. How else do I explain to people that freedom is at stake here? The whole story of the First Amendment is freedom. We need to allow this horrible speech because that's how we protect freedom. And I was trying to say there is a freedom interest, there's a liberty interest on the other side. When people told me they changed their mind, they were affected by the stories. Their analysis changed because of specific stories, one person after another, that had to change where they lived, change where they worked, change how they behaved, change where they went to school because of verbal assaults. They could imagine their own speech stifled if they were targeted by a hate group with a history of violence. They got it. Narrative seems to draw empathy in that way. I don't know whether you want to call narrative an extended metaphor, or what, but it pulls people in so that they can imagine being in that position, and then all of a sudden they can see a claim where they didn't see one before.

One of the art pieces I have made was called the Next Dada Utopian Visioning Peace Orchestra and Manifesto of Radical Intersubjective Possibility. It consisted of instruments made of reclaimed trash, and amateur musicians gathered from all kinds of backgrounds. I wanted to create a preview of how we could live outside the market, making lovely, odd music in communal spaces. Law valorizes the objective, hard-edged thing called legal reasoning.Critical race theorists and feminist legal theorists have introduced a subjective, soft-edged thing called love. From earliest childhood we feel both the vulnerability and the embracing care that comes from living with others. Thank you, Mike, for making me think deliberately about how I have used narrative and metaphor. I see from this conversation that I have tried to find the words to get us to love one another. To see ourselves in the other, so that we can stop killing, and start making music.

Bibliography

Abrams, Kathryn, "Hearing the call of stories," *California Law Review*, 79 (1991), 971–1052.
Akers, Ronald L., *Social Learning and Social Structure: A General Theory of Crime and Deviance* (Boston, MA: Northeastern University Press, 1998).
Akers, Timothy P., Roberto H. Potter, and Carl V. Hill, *Epidemiological Criminology: A Public Health Approach to Crime and Violence* (San Francisco, CA: Jossey-Bass/ Wiley, 2013).
Allen, Ronald J. and Michael S. Pardo, "The problematic value of mathematical models of evidence," *Journal of Legal Studies*, 36 (2007), 107–140.
Altman, Meryl, "How not to do things with metaphors we live by," *College English*, 52 (1990), 495–506.
Al-Zahrani, Abdulsalam, "Darwin's metaphors revisited: Conceptual metaphors, conceptual blends, and idealized cognitive models in the Theory of Evolution," *Metaphor and Symbol*, 23 (2008), 50–82.
American Bar Association, *In the Spirit of Public Service: A Blueprint for the Rekindling of Lawyer Professionalism* (Chicago, IL: The Commission, 1986).
American Bar Association, *Perceptions of the US Justice System* (1999), pp. 94–95, www.abanet.org/media/perception/perceptions.pdf.
Amsterdam, Anthony G. and Jerome Bruner, *Minding the Law: How Courts Rely on Storytelling, and How Their Stories Change the Ways We Understand the Law – and Ourselves* (Cambridge, MA: Harvard University Press, 2000).
Anders, Jake et al., "Genetic research on wild rice and its cultural implications," May 6, 2004. www.d.umn.edu/~ande2927/Report.pdf. Accessed November 14, 2015.
Anderson, Bruce, *"Discovery" in Legal Decision-Making* (Dordrecht: Kluwer, 1996).
Anon, "What's-In-a-Name? German naming laws remain Byzantine," Spiegel Online, May 5, 2009. www.spiegel.de/international/germany/what-s-in-a-name-german-naming-laws-remain-byzantine-a-622912.html Accessed Feb. 17, 2017.
Appleton, Susan Frelich, "Toward a 'culturally cliterate' family law?" *Berkeley Journal of Gender Law and Justice*, 23 (2008), 267–337.
Aprill, Ellen P., "The law of the word: Dictionary shopping in the Supreme Court," *Arizona State Law Journal*, 30 (1998), 275–336.

Arenella, Peter, "Convicting the morally blameless: Reassessing the relationship between legal and moral accountability," *UCLA Law Review*, 39 (1992), 1511–1622.
Aristotle, *The Rhetoric of Aristotle*, Lane Cooper (trans.) (New York, NY: D. Appleton and Co., 1932).
Arneson, Richard J., "Egalitarianism and the undeserving poor," *Journal of Political Philosophy*, 5 no. 4 (1997), 327–350.
Arnold, Thurman, *The Folklore of Capitalism* (New Haven, CT: Yale University Press, 1937).
Aspen, Marvin E., "A specification of civility expectations and comments: Excerpts from the Seventh Circuit's Interim Report of the Committee on Civility," *Federal Bar News & Journal*, 39 (1992), 304–309.
Associated Press, "Navajos reclaim sacred mask at auction," December 16, 2014. www.cbsnews.com/news/navajo-indians-buy-back-sacred-masks-in-france-auction/. Accessed November 14, 2015.
Australian Government, "Australia's Resale Royalty Scheme Review," http://arts.gov.au/visual-arts/resale-royalty-scheme/review.
Averill, James R., "Emotions as mediators and as products of creative activity," in J. Kaufman and J. Baer (eds.), *Creativity across Domains: Faces of the Muse* (Mahwah, NJ: Erlbaum, 2005), 225–243.
Bachmann-Medick, Doris, *Cultural Turns: New Orientations in the Study of Culture*, trans. Adam Blauhut (Berlin; Boston, MA: de Gruyter, 2016).
Baker, Nicholson, *The Anthologist* (New York, NY: Simon & Schuster, 2009).
Ball, Milner S., *Lying Down Together: Law, Metaphor, and Theology* (Madison, WI; London: Madison, WI: University of Wisconsin Press, 1985).
Ball, Milner S., "Stories of origin and constitutional possibilities," *Michigan Law Review*, 87 (1989), 2280–2319.
Bandes, Susan, "Fear factor: The role of media in covering and shaping the death penalty," *Ohio State Journal of Criminal Law*, 1 no. 2 (2004), 585–597.
Banfield, Ann, *Unspeakable Sentences: Narration and Representation in the Language of Fiction* (London: Routledge, 1982).
Barańczak, Stanisław, *Breathing under Water and Other East European Essays* (Cambridge, MA: Harvard University Press, 1990).
Bar-Gill, Oren and Gideon Parchomovsky, "A marketplace for ideas?" *Texas Law Review*, 84 no. 2 (2005), 395–431.
Baron, Jane, "Law, literature, and the problems of interdisciplinarity," *Yale Law Journal*, 108 (1999), 1059–1085.
Baron, Jane, and Julia Epstein, "Is law narrative?" *Buffalo Law Review*, 45 (1997), 141–187.
Barr, Damian, "The waiting game: Are we losing the knack?," *The Times* (London), November 28, 2009.
Barsalou, Lawrence W., "Grounding symbolic operations in the brain's modal systems," in Gün R. Semin and Eliot R. Smith (eds.), *Embodied Grounding: Social, Cognitive, Affective, and Neuroscientific Approaches* (Cambridge, UK; New York, NY: Cambridge University Press, 2008), pp. 9–42.
Barthes, Roland, "L'Effet de réel," in *Le Bruissement de la langue* (Paris: Editions du Seuil, 1984), 167–174, trans.

Richard Howard, "The reality effect," in *The Rustle of Language* (New York: Hill & Wang, 1986), pp. 141–148.
Barzel, Yoram, "A theory of rationing by waiting," *Journal of Law and Economics*, 17 no. 1 (1974), 73–95.
Basic Law for the Federal Republic of Germany, trans. Christian Tomuschat, David P. Currie, Donald P. Kommers: www.bundestag.de/blob/284870/ceod03414872 b427e57fccb703634dcd/basic_law-data.pdf.
Battaglia, Debbora, "Retaining reality: Some practical problems with objects as property," *Man*, New Series, 29 no. 3 (1994), 631–644.
Beale, Sara Sun, "The news media's influence on criminal justice policy: How market-driven news promotes punitiveness," *William and Mary Law Review*, 48 no. 2 (2006), 397–481. http://scholarship.law.wm.edu/cgi/viewcontent.cgi?article=1103&context=wmlr.
Beazley, Mary Beth, *A Practical Guide to Appellate Advocacy*, 3rd edition (New York, NY: Wolters Kluwer Law and Business, 2010).
Beccaria, Cesare, *On Crimes and Punishments*, trans. David Young (Cambridge, MA: Hackett, 1986 [1764]).
Beckett, Katherine and Theodore Sasson, "Crime in the media," www.publiceye.org/defendingjustice/overview/beckett_media.html.
Beckmann, Nadine and Janet Bujra, "The 'politics of the queue': The politicization of people living with HIV/AIDS in Tanzania," *Development & Change*, 41 no. 6 (2010), 1041–1064.
Beeler, Nate, "Lady Justice and Lady Liberty embracing," *Columbus Dispatch* (2013). www.dispatch.com/content/cartoons/2013/06/beeler0627.html.
Beer, Gillian, *Darwin's Plots: Evolutionary Narrative in Darwin, George Eliot and Nineteenth-Century Fiction*, 3rd edition (Cambridge, UK; New York: Cambridge University Press, 2009).
Bell, Derrick A. Jr., "After we're gone: Prudent speculations on America in a post-racial epoch," *St Louis University Law Journal*, 34 (1990) 393–405.
Bennett, William, John DiIulio, and John P. Walters, *Body Count* (New York: Simon & Schuster, 1996).
Benveniste, Emile, "Subjectivity in language," in *Problems in General Linguistics* (Princeton, NJ: Princeton University Press, 1971), pp. 223–230.
Bergen, Benjamin, *Louder than Words: The New Science of How the Mind Creates Meaning* (New York, NY: Basic Books, 2012).
Berger, Benjamin L., "Trial by metaphor: Rhetoric, innovation, and the judicial text," *Court Review*, 39 no. 3 (Fall 2002), 30–38.
Berger, Linda L., "A revised view of the judicial hunch," *Legal Communication and Rhetoric: J. ALWD*, 10 (2013), 1–39.
Berger, Linda L., "Metaphor and analogy: The sun and moon of legal persuasion," *Journal of Law and Policy*, 22 (2013–2014), 147–195.
Berger, Linda L., "Metaphor in law as poetic and propositional language," Proceedings of the 13th conference of the International Society for the Study of European Ideas (ISSEI) (2012). http://lekythos.library.ucy.ac.cy/bitstream/handle/107 97/6172/ISSEIproceedings-Linda%20Berger.pdf?sequence=1&isAllowed=y

Berger, Linda L., "Of metaphor, metonymy, and corporate money: Rhetorical choices in Supreme Court decisions on campaign finance regulation," *Mercer Law Review*, 58 no. 3 (2007), 949–990.
Berger, Linda L., "Preface," *Journal of the Association of Legal Writing Directors*, 7 (2010), vii.
Berger, Linda L., "The lady or the tiger: A field guide to metaphor and narrative," *Washburn Law Journal*, 50 (2010–2011), 275–317.
Berger, Linda L., "What is the sound of a corporation speaking? How the cognitive theory of metaphor can help lawyers shape the law," *Journal of the Association of Legal Writing Directors*, 2 (2004), 169–208.
Berger, Vivian, "Payne and suffering: A personal reflection and victim-centered critique," *Florida State University Law Review*, 20 (1992), 21–65.
Bettelheim, Bruno, *The Uses of Enchantment: The Meaning and Importance of Fairy Tales* (New York, Alfred A. Knopf, 1976).
Bibas, Stephanos, "The story of Brady v. Maryland: From adversarial gamesmanship toward the search for innocence?" in Carol Steiker (ed.), *Criminal Procedure Stories* (New York: Foundation Press/Thomson/West, 2006), pp. 129–154.
Binder, Guyora, "Representing Nazism: Advocacy and identity at the trial of Klaus Barbie," *Yale Law Journal*, 98 (1989), 1321–1383.
Binder, Guyora and Robert Weisberg, *Literary Criticism of Law* (Princeton, NJ: Princeton University Press, 2000).
Binnie, Ian, "Interpreting the Constitution: The living tree vs. original meaning," *Policy Options* (October 2007), 104–110. http://irpp.org/assets/po/free-trade-20/binnie.pdf.
Bishin, William R. and Christopher D. Stone, *Law, Language, and Ethics: An Introduction to Law and Legal Method* (New York, NY: The Foundation Press, 1972).
Blackstone, William, *Commentaries on the Laws of England*, Book II, Ch. II, 19 (1765–69).
Blasi, Gary L., "What lawyers know: Lawyering expertise, cognitive science, and the functions of theory," *Journal of Legal Education*, 45 no. 3 (1995), 313–397.
Blumer, Herbert, "Social problems as collective behavior," *Social Problems* (1971), 298–306.
Bock, Gregory R. and Jamie A. Goode, *Genetics of Criminal and Antisocial Behaviour* (Chichester: Wiley, 1996).
Bogdanov, Konstantin, "The queue as narrative," trans. Victoria Donovan in Albert Baiburin, Catriona Kelly, and Nikolai Vakhtin (eds.), *Russian Cultural Anthropology after the Collapse of Communism* (London: Routledge, 2012), pp. 77–102.
Bonilla-Silva, Eduardo, *Racism without Racists: Color-Blind Racism and the Persistence of Racial Inequality in America*, 4th edition (Lanham, MD: Rowman and Littlefield, 2014).
Booth, Wayne C., "Metaphor as rhetoric," in Sheldon Sacks (ed.), *On Metaphor* (Chicago, IL: University of Chicago, 1979), pp. 47–70.
Borelli, Silvia and Federico Lenzerini (eds.), *Cultural Diversity: New Developments in International Law* (The Hague: Martinus Nijhoff, 2012).
Bosmajian, Haig, *Metaphor and Reason in Judicial Opinion* (Carbondale, IL: Southern Illinois University Press, 1992).
Bott, Ingo and Paul Krell, "Der Grundsatz 'nulla poena sine lege' im Lichte verfassungsgerichtlicher Entscheidungen," *ZJS* 6 (2010),694–700.

Bougher, Lori D., "Cognitive coherence in politics: Unifying metaphor and narrative in civic cognition," in Michael Hanne, William D. Crano, and Jeffrey Scott Mio (eds.), *Warring with Words: Narrative and Metaphor in Politics* (Claremont Symposium on Applied Social Psychology Series) (New York, NY; Hove, UK: Psychology Press, 2014), pp. 250–271.

Bradner, Eric, "Factcheck: Grim statistics on race and police killings," CNN Politics (December 3, 2014): http://edition.cnn.com/2014/12/02/politics/kristoff-oreilly-police-shooting-numbers-fact-check/index.html.

Brand, Danie, "The proceduralization of South African socio-economic rights jurisrprudence," in Henk Botha, Andre van der Walt, and Johan van der Walt (eds.), *Rights and Democracy in a Transformative Constitution* (Stellenbosch, South Africa: Sun Press, 2003), pp. 33–56.

Brand, Paul, "The language of the English legal profession: The emergence of a distinctive legal lexicon in insular French," in Richard Ingham (ed.), *The Anglo-Norman Language and Its Contexts* (York: York Medieval Press, 2010), pp. 94–101.

Bricker, Andrew (forthcoming), "Is narrative essential to the law? Precedent, case law and judicial emplotment," *Law, Culture & Humanities*.

Brinnin, John Malcolm, *The Third Rose: Gertrude Stein and Her World* (New York, NY: Grove Press, 1961).

Brooks, Peter, "Inevitable discovery—Law, narrative, retrospectivity," *Yale Journal of Law & the Humanities*, 15 (2003), 71–102.

Brooks, Peter, "Law and humanities: Two attempts," *Boston University Law Review*, 93 no. 4 (2013), 1437–1468.

Brooks, Peter, "Narrative in and of the law," in James Phelan and Peter J. Rabinowitz (eds.), *A Companion to Narrative Theory* (Malden, MA: Blackwell Publishing, 2005), pp. 415–426.

Brooks, Peter, "Narrative transactions—Does law need a narratology?" *Yale Journal of Law & Humanities*, 18 no. 1 (2006), 1–28.

Brooks, Peter and Paul Gewirtz (eds.), *Law's Stories: Narrative and Rhetoric in the Law* (New Haven; London: Yale University Press, 1996).

Brown, Michael F., "Culture, property and peoplehood," *International Journal of Cultural Property*, 17 no. 3 (2010), 569–579.

Bruner, Jerome, "Autobiography of the self," in *Acts of Meaning* (Cambridge, MA: Harvard University Press, 1990), pp. 99–138.

Bruner, Jerome, "Life as narrative," *Social Research*, 71 (2004), 691–710.

Bruner, Jerome, *Making Stories: Law, Literature, Life* (Cambridge, MA: Harvard University Press, 2003).

Bruner, Jerome, "The narrative construction of reality," *Critical Inquiry*, 18 no. 1 (1991), 1–21.

Burger, Chief Justice Warren E., "Opening remarks," *ALI Proceedings* (1971), 21–31.

Burke, Kenneth, "The range of rhetoric," in *A Rhetoric of Motives* (Berkeley and Los Angeles: University of California Press, 1969), pp. 3–46.

Burns, Robert, *A Theory of the Trial* (Princeton University Press, 1999), 172.

Burst, Richard, Book Review, *American Bar Association Journal*, 84 (1998), 88–89.

Burt, Robert A., "Constitutional Law and the Teaching of Parables," *Yale Law Journal*, 93 (1983–84), 455–502.

Bush, George W., "Bush's speech on immigration." *NY Times* (May 15, 2006), available at www.nytimes.com/2006/05/15/washington/15text-bush.html.
Cameron, Lynne, A talk "Metaphor and Empathy," www.open.ac.uk/researchprojects/livingwithuncertainty/sites/www.open.ac.uk.researchprojects.livingwithuncertainty/files/pics/d125010.pdf.
Cammett, Ann, "Deadbeat dads & welfare queens: How metaphor shapes poverty law," *Boston College Journal of Law and Social Justice*, 34 (2014), 233–265.
Cardozo, Benjamin, *The Growth of the Law* (New Haven: Yale University Press, 1934).
Carpenter, Kristen A., Sonia Katyal, and Angela Riley, "Clarifying cultural property," *International Journal of Cultural Property*, 17 no. 3 (2010), 581–598.
Carpenter, Kristen A., Sonia Katyal, and Angela Riley, "In defense of property," *Yale Law Journal*, 118 (2009), 1022–1125.
Carson, Clarence B., *A Basic History of the United States*, vol. II (Wadley, AL: American Textbook Committee, 1995).
Case, Mary Anne, "Of 'This' and 'That' in Lawrence v. Texas," *Supreme Court Review*, 55 (2003), 75.
Catalano, Theresa and Linda R. Waugh, "The ideologies behind newspaper crime reports of Latinos and Wall Street/CEOs: A critical analysis of metonymy in text and image," *Critical Discourse Studies*, 10 no. 4 (2013), 406–26. http://digitalcommons.unl.edu/teachlearnfacpub/140.
Cecconi, Elisabetta, "Witness narratives in 17th century trial proceedings," in Nicholas Brownlees et al. (eds.), *The Language of Private and Public Communication in a Historical Perspective* (Newcastle upon Tyne, UK: Cambridge Scholars Publishing, 2010), pp. 245–262.
Center for International Environmental Law, "The gap between indigenous peoples' demands and WIPO's framework on traditional knowledge" (September 2007). www.wipo.int/export/sites/www/tk/en/igc/ngo/ciel_gap.pdf. Accessed November 14, 2015.
Chambers, Ross, *Story and Situation: Narrative Seduction and the Power of Fiction* (Minneapolis, MI: University of Minnesota Press, 1990).
Charteris-Black, Jonathan, *Politicians and Rhetoric: The Persuasive Power of Metaphor* (Basingstoke; New York, NY: Palgrave-MacMillan, 2005).
Chen, Ronald and Jon Hanson, "Categorically biased: The influence of knowledge structures on law and legal theory," *Southern California Law Review*, 77 (2004), 1103–1254.
Chenwi, Lilian, "Democratizing the socio-economic rights enforcement process," in Helena Alviar García, Karl E. Klare, and Lucy A. Williams (eds.), *Social and Economic Rights in Theory and Practice: Critical Inquiries* (New York, NY: Routledge, 2015), pp. 178–197.
Chestek, Kenneth D., "Judging by the numbers: An empirical study of the power of story," *Journal of the Association of Legal Writing Directors*, 7 (2010), 1–35.
Chestek, Kenneth D., "The plot thickens: The appellate brief as story," *Legal Writing: The Journal of the Legal Writing Institute*, 14 (2008), 127–169.
Cohan, William D., "A clue to the scarcity of financial crisis prosecutions," *New York Times* (July 26, 2013). www.nytimes.com/2016/07/22/business/dealbook/a-clue-to-the-scarcity-of-financial-crisis-prosecutions.html.

Cohen, Deborah et al., "'Broken windows' and the risk of gonorrhea," *American Journal of Public Health*, 90 no. 2 (2000), 230–236.

Cohen, Ted, "Metaphor and the cultivation of intimacy," in Sheldon Sacks (ed.), *On Metaphor* (Chicago: University of Chicago Press: 1979), pp. 1–10

Cohn, Jonathan, "Healthy examples," *Boston Globe* (July 5, 2009), available at http://archive.boston.com/bostonglobe/ideas/articles/2009/07/05/healthy_examples_plenty_of_countries_get_healthcare_right/.

Cole, David, "Agon at Agora: Creative misreadings in the first amendment tradition," *Yale Law Journal*, 95 no. 5 (1986), 857–905.

Coleman, Renita and Esther Thorson, "The effects of news stories that put crime and violence into context: Testing the public health model of reporting," *Journal of Health Communication*, 7 no. 5 (2002): 401–425.

Collier, John Payne, *Criticisms on the Bar* (London: Simpkin, 1819).

Compstat: Its origins, evolution, and future in law enforcement agencies, 2013 by Police Executive Research Forum Bureau of Justice Assistance www.policeforum.org/assets/docs/Free_Online_Documents/Compstat/compstat%20-%20its%20origins%20evolution%20and%20future%20in%20law%20enforcement%20agencies%202013.pdf.

Connor, Steven, "Transcripts: Law, literature and the trials of the voice," *New Formations*, 32 (1997), 60–76.

Conrad, Peter and Joseph W. Schneider, *Deviance and Medicalization: From Badness to Sickness* (Philadelphia: Temple University Press, 1980 [2010]).

Coode, George, *On Legislative Expression; or, The Language of the Law* (London: Benning, 1845).

Corbett, Edward P.J. and Robert J. Connors, *Classical Rhetoric for the Modern Student*, 4th edition (New York, NY: Oxford University Press, 1999).

Cover, Robert, *Making Stories: Law, Literature, Life* (Cambridge, MA: Harvard University Press, 1990).

Cover, Robert, "*Nomos* and narrative," *Narrative, Violence and the Law* (Ann Arbor, MI: Michigan University Press, 1993 [1983]), 95–172.

Cover, Robert, "The Supreme Court, 1982 Term–foreword: Nomos and narrative," *Harvard Law Review*, 97 no. 1 (1982), 4–68.

Cover, Robert, "Violence and the word," *Yale Law Journal*, 95 no. 8 (1986), 1601–1629.

Coy, Peter, "Staggering drunks and fiscal cliffs: How *Bloomberg Businessweek* uses metaphors in the news." http://niemanreports.org/articles/staggering-drunks-and-fiscal-cliffs-how-bloomberg-businessweek-uses-metaphors-in-the-news/

Craig, Russell, Rawiri Taonui, and Susan Wild, "The concept of *Taonga* in Māori culture: Insights for accounting," *Accounting, Auditing and Accountability Journal*, 25 no. 6 (2012), 1025–1047.

Crenshaw, Kimberlé, Neil Gotanda, Gary Peller, and Kendall Thomas (eds.), *Critical Race Theory: The Key Writings that Formed the Movement* (New York, NY: The New Press, 1995).

Crisp, Peter, "Allegory, blending, and possible situations," *Metaphor and Symbol*, 20 (2005), 115–131.

Crisp, Peter, "Allegory: Conceptual metaphor in history," *Language and Literature*, 10 (2001), 5–19.

Crisp, Peter, "Between extended metaphor and allegory: Is blending enough?" *Language and Literature*, 17 (2008), 291–308.
Cunningham-Parmeter, Keith, "Alien language: Immigration metaphors and the jurisprudence of otherness," *Fordham Law Review*, 79 no. 4 (2011), 1545–1598.
Czarniawska, Barbara, *Writing Management: Organization Theory as a Literary Genre* (New York, NY: Oxford University Press, 1999).
Daes, Erica-Irene, *Protection of the Heritage of Indigenous Peoples* (New York, NY: United Nations, 1997).
Darling, John, "Education as horticulture: Some growth theorists and their critics," *Journal of Philosophy of Education*, 16 no. 2 (1982), 173–185.
Davis, Gerald F., Doug McAdam, William Richard, Scott Mayer, and Nathan Zald (eds.), *Social Movements and Organization Theory* (New York, NY: Cambridge University Press, 2005).
Dawes, James and Samantha Gupta, "On narrative and human rights," *Humanity: An International Journal of Human Rights, Humanitarianism, and Development*, 5 no. 1 (Spring 2014), 149–156.
Delgado, Richard, "Storytelling for oppositionists and others: A plea for narrative," *Michigan Law Review*, 87 no. 8 (August, 1989), 2411–2441.
Delgado, Richard and Jean Stefancic, "Critical race theory: An annotated bibliography," *Virginia Law Review*, 79 no. 2 (1993), 461–516.
Delgado, Richard and Jean Stefancic, *Critical Race Theory: An Introduction*, 2nd edition (Critical America) (New York, NY: New York University Press, 2012).
Del Mar, Maksymilian, "Exemplarity and narrativity in the Common Law tradition," *Law & Literature*, 25 (2013), 390–407.
Del Mar, Maksymilian, "Exemplarity and narrativity in the Common Law tradition: Exploring Williams v. Roffey," Queen Mary University of London, School of Law Legal Studies Research Paper No. 139/2013 (available at: http://ssrn.com/abstract=2247937).
Dershowitz, Alan M., "Life is not a dramatic narrative," in Peter Brooks and Paul Gewirtz (eds.), *Law's Stories: Narrative and Rhetoric in Law* (New Haven, CT: Yale University Press, 1996), pp. 99–105.
Dickerson, Marla and Luciana Magalhaes, "In Brazil, it's fine for seniors to cut the line," *Wall Street Journal* (Feb. 23, 2016), available at www.wsj.com/articles/in-brazil-its-fine-for-seniors-to-cut-the-line-1456276423.
Douard, John and Pamela D. Schultz, *Monstrous Crimes and the Failure of Forensic Psychiatry* (Dordrecht; Heidelberg; New York, NY; London: Springer, 2013).
Douglas, Mary, *In the Wilderness: The Doctrine of Defilement in the Book of Numbers* (Oxford, UK: Oxford University Press, 2001).
Douglas, Mary, *Thinking in Circles: An Essay on Ring Composition* (New Haven, CT: Yale University Press, 2010).
Dowdle, W., "The principles of disease elimination and eradication," *Morbidity and Mortality Weekly*, 48 (SU01, 1999), 23–27.
Dreisbach, Daniel, *The Mythical "Wall of Separation": How a Misused Metaphor Changed Church–State Law, Policy, and Discourse* (Washington, DC: Heritage Foundation Report, 2007).
Dubber, Markus, "Policing possession: The war on crime and the end of criminal law," *Journal of Criminal Law and Criminology*, 91 (2001), 829–996.

Dudziak, Mary L., "Desegregation as a Cold War imperative," *Stanford Law Review*, 41 (1988), 61–120.
Duffee, D., "Why is criminal justice theory important?" in E.M. Duffee (ed.), *Criminal Justice Theory: Explaining the Nature and Behavior of Criminal Justice*, 2nd edition (New York, NY: Taylor & Francis, 2015), pp. 5–26.
Dugard, Jackie, Tshepo Madlingozi, and Kate Tissington, "Rights-compromised or rights-savvy? The use of rights-based strategies to advance socio-economic struggles by Abahlali baseMjondolo, the South African shack-dwellers' movement," in Helena Alviar García, Karl E. Klare, and Lucy A. Williams (eds.), *Social and Economic Rights in Theory and Practice: Critical Inquiries* (New York, NY: Routledge, 2015), pp. 23–43.
Dugard, John, "The influence of international human rights law on the South African Constitution," *Current Legal Problems*, 49 (1996), 305–324.
Dulwich Centre, *Responding to Survivors of Torture and Suffering: Survival Skill and Stories of Kurdish Families* (Adelaide: Dulwich Centre Foundation International, 2012).
Durst, Ilene, "Nguyen v. INS," in Kathryn Stanchi, Linda L. Berger, and Bridget J. Crawford (eds.), *Feminist Judgments* (2016).
Dworkin, Ronald, "Rights as Trumps," in J. Waldron, (ed.), *Theories of Rights* (Oxford: Oxford University Press, 1984), pp. 153–167.
Dworkin, Ronald, *Law's Empire* (Cambridge, MA: Harvard University Press, 1986).
Ebrahim, Hassen, "The making of the South African Constitution," in Penelope Andrews and Stephen Ellmann (eds.), *The Post-Apartheid Constitutions* (Johannesburg: Witswatersrand University Press, 2001), pp. 85–103.
Edwards, Linda H., "The convergence of analogical and dialectic imaginations in legal discourse," *Legal Studies Forum*, 20 (1996), 7–50.
Edwards, Linda H., "Hearing voices: Non-party stories in abortion and gay rights advocacy," *Michigan State Law Review*, no. 4 (2015), 1327–1356.
Edwards, Linda H., "Once upon a time in law: Myth, metaphor, and authority," *Tennessee Law Review*, 77 (2010), 883–916.
Edwards, Linda H., *Legal Writing: Process, Analysis and Organization* (New York: Aspen/Wolters Kluwer Law and Business, 6th edition 2014, 1st edition 1996).
Eisen, Lauren-Brook and Oliver Roeder, *America's Faulty Perception of Crime Rates* (New York: Brennan Center for Justice, March 16, 2015), https://www.brennancenter.org/blog/americas-faulty-perception-crime-rates.
El Refaie, Elizabeth, "Metaphor in political cartoons: Exploring audience responses," in Charles J. Forceville and Eduardo Urios-Aparisi (eds.), *Multi-Modal Metaphor* (Berlin; New York, NY: Mouton de Gruyter, 2009), pp. 173–196.
El Refaie, Elizabeth, "Multiliteracies: How readers interpret political cartoons," *Visual Communication*, 8 (2009), 181–205.
Fable, Literary Devices.Net, http://literarydevices.net/fable/.
Fagan, Andrew, "Human rights," *The Internet Encyclopedia of Philosophy*, ISSN 2161–0002, www.iep.utm.edu, November 16, 2016.
Fagundes, David, "The social norms of waiting in line," (forthcoming) *Law and Social Inquiry*.
Farber, Daniel A. and Susanna Sherry, "Telling stories out of school: An essay on legal narratives," *Stanford Law Review*, 45 (1993), 807.

Farrington, Donald, "Developmental and life-course criminology: Key theoretical and empirical issues," 2002 Sutherland Award Address, *Criminology*, 19 no. 1 (2003), 221–256.
Fauconnier, Gilles and Mark Turner, "Conceptual integration networks," *Cognitive Science*, 22 no. 2 (1989), 133–187.
Fausey, Caitlin M. and Lera Boroditsky, "Subtle linguistic cues influence perceived blame and financial liability," *Psychonomic Bulletin & Review*, 17 (2010), 644–650.
Feeley, Malcolm M. and Edward L. Rubin, *Judicial Policy Making in the Modern State* (Cambridge University Press, 2000).
Fehling, Michael, Berthold Kastner, and Rainer Störmer (eds.), *Verwaltungsrecht: VwVfG – VwGO – Nebengesetze, Handkommentar, Vierte Auflage* (Baden-Baden: Nomos, 2016).
Feinberg, Jonathan, "Wordle," in Julie Steele and Noah Illinsky (eds.), *Beautiful Visualization: Looking at Data through the Eyes of Experts* (Sebastopol, CA: O'Reilly Media, 2010).
Felsenthal, Mark, "When is a housing crisis like venereal disease?" *Tales from the Trail* (Feb. 20, 2009). http://blogs.reuters.com/talesfromthetrail/2009/02/20/when-is-a-housing-crisis-like-venereal-disease/.
Ferguson, Rex, *Criminal Law and the Modernist Novel* (Cambridge University Press, 2013).
Ferguson, Robert, "Story and transcription in the trial of John Brown," *Yale Law Journal of Law and the Humanities* 6 (1994) 37–74.
Ferguson, Robert, "The judicial opinion as literary genre," *Yale Journal of Law & the Humanities* 2 (1990), 201–219.
Ferree, Myra Marx, Judith Lorber, and Beth B. Hess (eds.), *Revisioning Gender* (Walnut Creek, CA; Lanham, MD; and Oxford: Altamira Press, 2000).
Ferry, Leonard D.G., "Floors without foundations: Ignatieff and Rorty on human rights," *Logos: A Journal of Catholic Thought and Culture*, 10 (Winter 2007), 80–105.
Fineman, Martha Albertson, "The vulnerable subject: Anchoring equality in the human condition," *Yale Journal of Law and Feminism*, 20 (2008), 1–23.
Finley, Lucinda M., "Breaking women's silence in law: The dilemma of the gendered nature of legal reasoning," *Notre Dame Law Review*, 67 (1989), 886–910.
Finley, Lucinda M., "Geduldig v. Aiello," in Kathryn Stanchi, Linda L. Berger, and Bridget J. Crawford (eds.), *Feminist Judgments* (2016).
Fish, Stanley, *Is There a Text in This Class?* (Cambridge, MA: Harvard University Press, 1980).
Fisher, George, "The *Birth of the Prison* retold," *Yale Law Journal*, 104 (1995), 1235–1324
Fisher, Walter R., "The narrative paradigm: An elaboration," *Communication Monographs*, 52 (1985), no. 4, 347–367.
Fludernik, Monika, "A narratology of the law? Narratives in legal discourse," *Critical Analysis of the Law*, 1 no. 1 (2014), 87–109.
Fludernik, Monika, *The Fictions of Language and the Languages of Fiction* (London: Routledge, 1993).
Fludernik, Monika, Donald C. Freeman, and Margaret H., "Metaphor and beyond: An introduction," *Poetics Today*, 20 no. 3 (1999), 383–396.

Foley, Brian J. and Ruth Anne Robbins, "Fiction 101: A primer for lawyers on how to use fiction writing techniques to write persuasive facts sections," *Rutgers Law Journal*, 32 (2001), 459–483.
Forster, E.M., *Aspects of the Novel* (New York: Harcourt, 1927).
Fowler, Elizabeth, *Literary Character: The Human Figure in Early English Writing* (Ithaca, NY: Cornell University Press, 2003).
Frank, Jerome, *Law and the Modern Mind* (New York, NY: Brentano's, 1930).
Fraser, Nancy and Linda Gordon, "A genealogy of dependency: Tracing a keyword in the U.S. Welfare State," *Signs: Journal of Women in Culture and Society*, 19 no. 2 (1994), 309–336.
Freedom Charter of 26 June 1955: Reprinted in *Columbia Human Rights Law Review*, 21 (1989), 249–251.
Friedrichs, David O., *Trusted Criminals: White Collar Crime in Contemporary Society*, 4th edition (Belmont, CA: Wadworth, 2010).
Froebel, Friedrich, "The seed corn and the child: A comparison" in his *Pedagogics of the Kindergarten*: http://urweb.roehampton.ac.uk/digital-collection/froebel-archive/pedagogics-kindergarten/index.html.
Frost, Michael, "Greco-Roman analysis of metaphoric reasoning," *Legal Writing: The Journal of the Legal Writing Institute*, 2 (1996), 113–141.
Gaakeer, Jeanne, "The perplexity of judges becomes the scholar's opportunity," in Greta Olson and Franz Reimer (eds.), Special Issue on "Law's Pluralities" of the *German Law Journal*, 18 no. 2 (2017), no pag.
Gabel, Peter and Duncan Kennedy, "Roll over Beethoven," *Stanford Law Review*, 36 nos. 1–2 (1984), 1–55.
Gallagher, Catherine, "George Eliot: Immanent Victorian," *Representations*, 90 (2005), 61–74.
Gamson, William, *Talking Politics* (Cambridge, UK; New York, NY: Cambridge University Press, 1992).
Gargarella, Roberto, Pilar Domingo, and Theunis Roux (eds.), *Courts and Social Transformation in New Democracies: An Institutional Voice for the Poor?* (Burlington, VT; Aldershot, UK: Ashgate, 2006).
Garner, Bryan A., *A Dictionary of Modern Legal Usage*, 2nd edition (New York, NY; Oxford, UK: Oxford University Press, 1995).
Garry, Maryanne, Charles Manning, Elizabeth Loftus, and Steven Sherman, "Imagination inflation: Imagining a childhood event inflates confidence that it occurred," *Psychonomic Bulletin & Review*, 3 (1996), 208–214.
Geary, James, *I Is an Other: The Secret Life of Metaphor and How It Shapes the Way We See the World* (New York, NY: Harper, 2012).
Geertz, Clifford, *Local Knowledge* (New York, NY: Basic Books, 1983),
Gelber, Katherine, "A fair queue? Australian public discourse on refugees and immigration," *Journal of Australian Studies*, 27 no. 77 (2003), 23–30.
Gell, Andrew, *Art and Agency* (Oxford University Press, 1998).
Gendreau, Paul, Claire Goggin, and Francis T. Cullen, "The effects of prison sentences on recidivism," 4–5 (1999), Office of Justice Programs, available at www.prisonpolicy.org/scans/e199912.htm.

Gibbs, Raymond W. Jr., "Metaphor and thought: The state of the art" in Raymond W. Gibbs, Jr. (ed.), *The Cambridge Handbook of Metaphor and Thought* (New York, NY: Cambridge University Press, 2008), pp. 3–16.

Gibbs, Raymond W. Jr., "Metaphor interpretation as embodied simulation," *Mind and Language*, 21 (2006), 434–458.

Gibbs, Raymond W. Jr., "The allegorical character of political metaphors in discourse," *Metaphor and the Social World*, 5 (2015), 264–282.

Gibbs, Raymond W. Jr., "The allegorical impulse," *Metaphor and Symbol*, 26 (2011), 121–130.

Gibbs, Raymond W. Jr., *Embodiment and Cognitive Science* (New York, NY: Cambridge University Press, 2006).

Gibbs, Raymond W. Jr., *Metaphor Wars: Conceptual Metaphor in Human Life* (Cambridge, UK; New York, NY: Cambridge University Press, 2017).

Gibbs, Raymond W. Jr., *The Poetics of Mind: Figurative Thought, Language, and Understanding* (Cambridge, UK; Cambridge University Press, 1994).

Gibbs, Raymond W. Jr. and Natalia Blackwell, "Climbing the stairs to literary heaven: A case study of allegorical interpretation of fiction," *Scientific Study of Literature*, 2 (2012), 197–217.

Gibbs, Raymond W. Jr. and Erika Boers, "Metaphoric processing of allegorical poetry," in Zouhair Maalej (ed.), *Metaphor and Culture* (Tunis, Tunisia: University of Manouba Press, 2005).

Gibbs, Raymond W. Jr. and Herbert L. Colston, *Interpreting Figurative Meaning* (Cambridge, UK; New York, NY: Cambridge University Press, 2012).

Glenberg, Arthur and Michael Kaschak, "Grounding language in action," *Psychonomic Bulletin & Review*, 9 (2002), 558–565.

Glendon, Mary Ann, *Rights Talk: The Impoverishment of Political Discourse* (New York, NY: The Free Press, 1991).

Goldfarb, Phyllis, "Bradwell v. Illinois," in Kathryn Stanchi, Linda L. Berger, and Bridget J. Crawford (eds.), *Feminist Judgments* (2016).

Goodale, Mark, "Human rights and moral agency," in Cindy Holder and David Reidy (eds.), *Human Rights: The Hard Questions* (New York NY: Cambridge University Press, 2013), pp. 418–436.

Goodale, Mark (ed.), *Human Rights at the Crossroads* (Oxford; New York: Oxford University Press, 2013).

Goodhart, Michael, "Human rights and the politics of contestation," in Mark Goodale (ed.), *Human Rights at the Crossroads* (Oxford, UK; New York, NY: Oxford University Press, 2013), pp. 31–45.

Goodman, John, "Five myths of socialized medicine," *Cato's Letter*, 3 no. 1 (Winter, 2005), available at https://object.cato.org/sites/cato.org/files/pubs/pdf/catosletterv3n1.pdf.

Goodman, Ryan and Derek Jinks, *Socializing States: Promoting Human Rights through International Law* (Oxford, UK: Oxford University Press, 2013).

Gordimer, Nadine, "Standing in the queue," *Index on Censorship*, 23 no. 3 (1994), 128–130.

Gordon, Robert W., "Historicism in legal scholarship," *Yale Law Journal*, 90 (1981), 1017–1056.

Gould, M.W., "Suicide clusters: A critical review," *Suicide and Life-Threatening Behavior*, 19 no. 1 (2010), 17–29.

Grant, Daniel, "Artist resale royalties haven't hindered art trade or helped artists in the U.K.," *Huffington Post*, June 6, 2014.
Gray, Kevin, "Property in a queue," in Gregory S. Alexander and Eduardo M. Peñalver (eds.) (Oxford, UK; New York, NY: Oxford University Press, 2010), pp. 165–195.
Green, Melanie C., "Transportation into narrative worlds: The role of prior knowledge and perceived realism," *Discourse Processes*, 38 (2004): 247–266.
Green, Melanie C. and Timothy C. Brock, "The role of transportation in the persuasiveness of public narratives," *Journal of Personality and Social Psychology*, 79 (2000), 701–721.
Greene, Candace S. and Thomas D. Dresher, "The Tipi with battle pictures: The Kiowa tradition of intangible property rights," *Trademark Reporter*, 84 (1994), 418–433.
Greenhouse, Linda, "A Supreme Court hijacking," *The New York Times*, March 30, 2016.
Gregg, Benjamin, "Human rights as metaphor for political community beyond the nation state," *Critical Sociology*, 42 no. 6 (2016), 897–917.
Grey, Thomas C., *The Wallace Stevens Case: Law and the Practice of Poetry* (Cambridge, MA: Harvard University Press, 1991).
Gross, Donald, John F. Shortle, James M. Thompson, and Carl M. Harris (eds.), *Fundamentals of Queueing Theory*, 4th edition (Hoboken, NJ: John Wiley & Sons, Inc., 2008).
Grossman, Jonathan, *The Art of Alibi: English Law Courts and the Novel* (Baltimore, MD: Johns Hopkins University Press, 2002).
Grunewald, Ralph, "The narrative of innocence, or lost stories," *Law and Literature*, 15 no. 3 (2013), 366–389.
Gurnham, David, "Law's metaphors: Introduction," *Journal of Law and Society*, 43 (2016), 1–7.
Gusfield, Joseph R., *Symbolic Crusade: Status Politics and the American Temperance Movement* (Champaign, IL: University of Illinois Press, 1963).
Gusfield, Joseph R., *The Culture of Public Problems: Drinking-Driving and the Symbolic Order* (Chicago, IL: University of Chicago Press, 1981).
Haack, Susan, "Dry truth and real knowledge," in Jaakko Hintikka (ed.), *Aspects of Metaphor* (Dordrecht/Boston/London: Kluwer, 1994), pp. 1–22.
Halliday, Michael A.K., "Things and relations: Regrammaticising experience as technical knowledge," in James R. Martin and Robert Veel (eds.), *Reading Science: Critical and Functional Perspectives on Discourses of Science* (London; New York, NY: Routledge, 1998), 185–237.
Handler, Joel and Yeheskel Hasenfeld, *Blame Welfare: Ignore Poverty and Inequality* (New York, NY: Cambridge University Press, 2007).
Hanne, Michael, "An introduction to the 'Warring with Words' project," in Michael Hanne, William D. Crano, and Jeffery Scott Mio (eds.), *Warring with Words: Narrative and Metaphor in Politics* (New York, NY; Hove, UK: Psychology Press, 2015), pp. 1–50.
Hanne, Michael, "Crime and disease: Contagion by metaphor," in Catherine Stanton and Hannah Quirk (eds.), *Criminalising Contagion: Lethal and Ethical Challenges of Disease Transmission and the Criminal Law* (Cambridge, UK: Cambridge University Press, 2016), pp. 35–54.

Hanne, Michael, "Getting to know the neighbours: When plot meets knot," *Canadian Review of Comparative Literature*, 26 (1999), 35–50.
Hanne, Michael, "The binocular vision project: An introduction" in "Binocular Vision: Narrative and Metaphor in Medicine," special issue of *Genre: Forms of Discourse and Culture*, 44 no. 3 (Fall 2011), 223–237.
Hanne, Michael, William Crano, and Jeffery Mio (eds.), *Warring with Words: Narrative and Metaphor in Politics* (New York; Hove, UK: Psychology Press, 2015).
Hanson, Jon D. and Kathleen Hanson, "The blame frame: Justifying (racial) injustice in America," *Harvard Civil Rights-Civil Liberties Law Review*, 41 no. 2 (2006), 413–480.
Harcourt, Bernard, "From the asylum to the prison: Rethinking the incarceration revolution," *Texas Law Review*, 84 (2006), 1751–1786.
Harmon, Amy, "Indian tribe wins fight to limit research of its DNA," *New York Times*, April 21, 2010.
Harmon, William and Hugh Holman, *A Handbook to Literature*, 11th edition (Upper Saddle River, NJ: Pearson Prentice Hall, 2009).
Harris, Cheryl I., "Whiteness as property," *Harvard Law Review*, 106 (1993), 1707–91.
Harris, Randy Allen and Sarah Tolmie, "Cognitive allegory: An introduction," *Metaphor and Symbol*, 26 (2011), 109–120.
Harrison, Simon, "From prestige goods to legacies: Property and objectification of culture in Melanesia," *Comparative Studies in Society and History*, 42 no. 3 (2000), 662–679.
Hart, H.L.A., *Essays on Bentham: Studies in Jurisprudence and Political Theory* (Oxford: Clarendon Press, 1982).
Haste, Steve, *Criminal Sentences: True Crime in Fiction and Drama* (London: Cygnus Arts, 1997).
Haw, Kaye, "Risk factors and pathways into and out of crime, misleading, misinterpreted or mythic: From generative metaphor to professional myth," *Australian and New Zealand Journal of Criminology*, 39 no. 3 (2006), 339–353.
Hay, Bruce L., "The damned dolls," *Law & Literature*, 26 (2014), 321–342.
Haynes, John, "Metaphor and mediation." Unpublished manuscript. Available on www.mediate.com/articles.
Heller, Kevin, "The cognitive psychology of circumstantial evidence," *Michigan Law Review*, 105 (2006), 1–74.
Henderson, Greig, "The cost of persuasion: Figure, story, and eloquence in the rhetoric of judicial discourse," *The University of Toronto Quarterly*, 75 no. 4 (Fall 2006), 905–924.
Henderson, Lynne, "Getting to know: Honoring women in law and in fact," *Texas Journal of Women and Law*, 2 (1993), 41.
Henkin, Louis, "War and terrorism: Law or metaphor," *Santa Clara Law Review*, 45 (2005), 817–827.
Herdegen, Matthias, Art. 1 Abs. 1: in Maunz/Dürig (eds.) *Kommentar zum Grundgesetz* Band I (München: C.H. Beck, 2003).
Herman, David, *Story Logic: Problems and Possibilities of Narrative* (Lincoln, NE: University of Nebraska Press, 2002).
Herzog, Todd, "Crime stories: Criminal, society, and the modernist case history," *Representations*, 80 (2002), 34–61.

Herzog, Todd, *Crime Stories: Criminalistic Fantasy and the Culture of Crisis in Weimar Germany* (New York: Berghahn, 2009).
Hibbitts, Bernard J., "Making sense of metaphors: Visuality, aurality, and the reconfiguration of American legal discourse," *Cardozo Law Review*, 16 (1994), 229–356.
Higinbotham, Sarah, "Bloodletting and beasts: Metaphors of legal violence," *Wake Forest Law Review*, 49 (2014), 727–742.
Hills, Stuart L., *Demystifying Social Deviance* (New York, NY: McGraw-Hill Book Company, 1980).
Hirshman, Albert O., "Rival interpretations of market society: Civilizing, destructive, or feeble?" *Journal of Economic Literature*, 20 (1982), 1463–1484.
Hochschild, Arlie Russell, *Strangers in Their Own Land: Anger and Mourning on the American Right* (New York, NY: The New Press, 2016).
Hofstadter, Richard, *Social Darwinism in American Thought* (Boston, MA: Beacon Press 1944).
Hohfeld, Wesley N., *Fundamental Legal Conceptions*, in W. Cook (ed.) (New Haven, CT: Yale University Press, 1919).
Hohfeld, Wesley N., "Some fundamental legal conceptions as applied in judicial reasoning," *The Yale Law Journal*, 23 no. 1 (1913), 16–59.
hooks, bell, *Ain't I a Woman: Black Women and Feminism* (Boston, MA: South End Press, 1981).
Huchzermeyer, Marie, "Pounding at the tip of the iceberg: The dominant politics of informal settlement eradication in South Africa," *Politikon: The South African Journal of Political Science*, 37 no. 1 (2010), 129–148.
Hughes, Charles E. et al., "Mr. Justice Holmes," *Harvard Law Review*, 44 no. 5 (1931), pp. 677–696.
Huhn, Wilson R., "Use and limits of syllogistic reasoning in briefing cases," *Santa Clara Law Review*, 42 (2002), 813–862.
Hunt, Lynn, *Inventing Human Rights* (New York, NY: W.W. Norton & Company, 2007).
Hunter, John and Chris Jones, "Bioprospecting and indigenous knowledge in Australia: Implications of valuing indigenous spiritual knowledge," Bahá'í Library Online, 2006–7. http://bahai-library.com/hunter_jones_bioprospecting_australia. Accessed November 14, 2015.
Institute of Medicine & National Research Council, *Contagion of Violence: Workshop Summary* (Washington, DC: National Academies Press, 2013).
Iversen, Stefan and Henrik Skov Nielsen, "The politics of fictionality in documentary form, *The Act of Killing* and *The Ambassador*," *European Journal of English Studies*, 20 no. 3 (2016): 249–262.
Iyengar, Shanto, *Is Anyone Responsible? How Television Frames Political Issues* (Chicago, IL: University of Chicago Press, 1991).
Jackson, Bernard S., "Narrative theories and legal discourse," in Cristopher Nash (ed.), *Narrative in Culture* (London: Routledge, 1990), pp. 23–50.
Jackson, Vicki C., "Constitutions as 'Living Trees'? Comparative constitutional law and interpretive metaphors," *Fordham Law Review*, 75 (2006), 921–960.
Jameson, Frederic, *The Political Unconscious: Narrative as a Socially Symbolic Act* (Ithaca, NY: Cornell University Press, 1981).

Jamiol, Paul, "SCOTUS/Animal farm," www.juancole.com/2014/04/supreme-editor ial-cartoon.html, 2014.
Janusz, Sharon, "Feminism and metaphor, friend or foe," *Metaphor and Symbolic Activity*, 9 (1994), 289–300.
Jeffrey, Craig, "Guest editorial: Waiting," *Environment and Planning D: Society and Space*, 26 no. 6 (2008), 954–958.
Jeffrey, Craig, *Timepass: Youth, Class, and the Politics of Waiting in India* (Stanford, CA: Stanford University Press, 2010).
Jewkes, Yvonne, *Media and Crime* (Thousand Oaks, CA: Sage Publications, 2004).
Johnson, Alex M. Jr., "The new voice of color," *Yale Law Journal*, 100 (1991), 2007–2064.
Johnson, Ian, "As Beijing becomes a supercity, the rapid growth brings pains," *New York Times*, 19 July 2015.
Johnson, Mark L., *Moral Imagination: Implications of Cognitive Science for Ethics* (Chicago, IL: University of Chicago Press, 1994).
Johnson, Mark L., "Mind, metaphor, law," *Mercer Law Review*, 58 no. 3 (2007), 845–868.
Joseph, Lawrence, "A year after the acquittal in the impeachment trial," in Leonard V. Kaplan and Beverly I. Moran (eds.), *Aftermath: The Clinton Impeachment and the Presidency in the Age of Political Spectacle* (New York, NY: New York University Press, 2001).
Joseph, Lawrence, "Being in the language of poetry, being in the language of law," *Oregon Law Review* 88 (2009), 905–929.
Joseph, Lawrence, *Codes, Precepts, Biases and Taboos: Poems 1973–1993* (includes Shouting at No One, Curriculum Vitae and Before Our Eyes) (New York: Farrar, Straus and Giroux, 2005).
Joseph, Lawrence, *Into it: Poems* (New York: Farrar, Straus and Giroux, 2005).
Joseph, Lawrence, *Lawyerland: What Lawyers Talk about When They Talk about Law* (Farrar, Straus & Giroux, 1997).
Joseph, Lawrence, "Notions of poetry and narration," *University of Cincinnati Law Review* 77 (2009), 941–968.
Joseph, Lawrence, "On Kronman's rhetoric," *University of Cincinnati Law Review* 67 (1999), 719–725.
Joseph, Lawrence, "Reflections on law and literature (imaginary interview)," *Saskatchewan Law Review*, 589 (1995), 417–430.
Joseph, Lawrence, *So Where Are We? Poems* (New York, NY: Farrar, Straus and Giroux, 2017).
Joseph, Lawrence, "The language of judging," *St. John's Law Review*, 59 (1996), 1–4.
Joseph, Lawrence, "The subject and object of law," *Brooklyn Law Review*, 67 (2001), 1023–1033.
Joseph, Lawrence, "Theories of poetry, theories of law," *Vanderbilt Law Review*, 46 (1983), 1227–1254.
Joseph, Lawrence, "Working rules for *Lawyerland*," *Columbia Law Review* 101 (2001), 1793–1796.
Joseph, Lawrence, *The Game Changed: Essays and Other Prose* (Ann Arbor: University of Michigan Press, 2011).
Kahan, Dan M., "The cognitively illiberal state," *Stanford Law Review*, 60 (2007), 101–140.

Kahan, Dan M., David A. Hoffman, and Donald Braman, "Whose eyes are you going to believe? Scott v. Harris and the perils of cognitive illiberalism," *Harvard Law Review*, 122 (2009), 837–906.

Kalven, Harry, "Broadcasting, public policy and the First Amendment," *Journal of Law and Economics*, 10 (1967), 15–49.

Katz, Michael B., *The Undeserving Poor: From the War on Poverty to the War on Welfare* (New York, NY: Pantheon Books, 1989).

Kelling, George, "Crime and metaphor: Toward a new concept of policing," *City Journal* 1. www.city-journal.org/story.php?id=1577.

Kelling, George L. and William J. Bratton, "Why we need broken windows policing," *City Journal* (Winter 2015), www.city-journal.org:8080/html/why-we-need-broken-windows-policing-13696.html.

Kelling, George L. and James Q. Wilson, "Broken windows: The police and neighborhood safety," *The Atlantic Monthly* (March 1982), 29–38.

Kelman, Mark G., *A Guide to Critical Legal Studies* (Cambridge, MA: Harvard University Press, 1990).

Kendall-Taylor, Nathaniel, *Maze and Gears: Using Explanatory Metaphors to Increase Public Understanding of the Criminal Justice System and Its Reform* (Washington, DC: Frameworks Institute, 2013).

Kennedy, Randall, "State of the debate: The case against 'civility,'" *The American Prospect* (Nov.–Dec. 1998).

Kenney, Cortelyou C., "Reframing indigenous cultural artifacts disputes: An intellectual property-based approach," *Cardozo Arts & Entertainment Law Journal*, 28 (2011), 502–552.

Kerber, Linda K., "Separate spheres, female worlds, woman's place: The rhetoric of women's history," *Journal of American History*, 75 (1988), 9–39.

Kerr, Orin, "Searches and seizures in a digital world," *Harvard Law Review*, 119 (2005), 532–585.

Khampepe, Justice Sisi, "Meaningful participation as transformative process: The challenges of institutional change in South Africa's constitutional democracy," Lecture delivered at the Stellenbosch University Annual Human Rights Lecture, 6 October 2016.

Kirkup, Alex and Tony Evans, "The myth of western opposition to economic, social, and cultural rights?," *Human Rights Quarterly*, 31 no. 1 (2009), 221–237.

Klare, Karl E., "Legal culture and transformative constitutionalism," *South African Journal on Human Rights*, 14 no. 1 (1998), 146–188.

Klatzky, Roberta, James Pellegrino, Brian McCloskey, and Stephen Doherty, "Can you squeeze a tomato? The role of motor representations in semantic sensibility judgments," *Journal of Memory and Language*, 28 (1989), 56–77.

Konwicki, Tadeusz, *The Polish Complex* (trans. Richard Lourie) (Normal, IL: Dalkey Archive Press, 1982, 1998).

Krakoff, Sarah, "Does law and literature survive *Lawyerland?*" *Columbia Law Review*, 101 (2001), 1742–1749.

Krenberger, Verena and Greta Olson, "Durchsetzung und schutz von menschenrechten mit allen mitteln: Zur folterdebatte in Deutschland und in den Vereinigten Staaten" (Imposing and protecting human rights using all means? On the torture debate in Germany and the United States) in Monika Fludernik and Hans-Helmuth Gande (eds.), *Ethik des Strafens/The Ethics of Punishment* (Wuerzburg: Ergon, 2008), 177–210.

Kronman, Anthony T., *The Lost Lawyer: Failing Ideals of the Legal Profession* (Cambridge, MA: Harvard University Press, 1993).

Kuhn, Thomas S., *The Structure of Scientific Revolutions* (Chicago, IL: University of Chicago Press, 1962).

Kuruk, Paul, "Protecting folklore under modern intellectual property regimes: A reappraisal of the tension between individual and communal rights in Africa and United States," *American University Law Review*, 48 (1999), 769–849.

Lacey, Nicola, "The metaphor of proportionality," *Journal of Law and Society*, 43 no. 1 (2016), 27–44.

Ladson-Billings, Gloria, "Just what is critical race theory and what's it doing in a nice field like education?" in Laurence Parker, Donna Deyhle, Sofia Villenas, *Race Is . . . Race Isn't: Critical Race Theory and Qualitative Studies in Education* (Boulder, CO: Westview Press, 1999), pp. 7–30.

Lakoff, George interviewed by Lois Beckett January 31, 2011. http://timtyson.us/word press/wp-content/uploads/2011/pdfs/Explain-Yourself-George-Lakoff.pdf.

Lakoff, George, "Mapping the brain's metaphor circuitry: Metaphorical thought in everyday reason," *Frontiers of Human Neuroscience* (December 16, 2014). http://jou rnal.frontiersin.org/article/10.3389/fnhum.2014.00958.

Lakoff, George, "The contemporary theory of metaphor," in Andrew Ortony (ed.), *Metaphor and Thought*, 2nd edition (Cambridge University Press, 1993).

Lakoff, George, *Moral Politics: How Liberals and Conservatives Think*, 3rd edition (Chicago, IL: University of Chicago Press, 2016).

Lakoff, George, *The Political Mind* (New York, NY: Penguin, 2008).

Lakoff, George and Mark Johnson, *Metaphors We Live By* (Chicago, IL: University of Chicago Press, 1980).

Lakoff, George and Mark Johnson, *Philosophy in the Flesh: The Embodied Mind and Its Challenge to Western Thought* (New York, NY: Basic Books, 1999).

Lamond, Grant, "Precedent and analogy in legal reasoning," in Edward N. Zalta (ed.), *The Stanford Encyclopedia of Philosophy*. https://plato.stanford.edu/entries/legal-re as-prec/. Accessed March 15, 2017.

Landau, Mark, Daniel Sullivan, and Jeffrey Greenberg, "Evidence that self-relevant motives and metaphoric framing interact to influence political and social attitudes," *Psychological Science*, 20 (2009), 1421–1427.

Langbein, John, "The German advantage in civil procedure," *University of Chicago Law Review* (Fall 1985), no pag. http://chicagounbound.uchicago.edu/uclrev/vol52/iss4/1/. Accessed Feb. 17, 2017.

Laufer-Ukeles, Pamela, "Muller v. Oregon," in Kathryn Stanchi, Linda L. Berger, and Bridget J. Crawford (eds.), *Feminist Judgments* (2016).

Lave, Tamara Rice, "Campus sexual assault adjudication: Why universities should reject the Dear Colleague Letter," *Kansas Law Review*, 64 (2016) 915–962.

LeBon, G., *The Crowd: A Study of the Popular Mind*. Digireads.com. (1896 [2008]).

Lee, Jieun, "Interpreting reported speech in witnesses' evidence," *Interpreting*, 12 (2010), 60–82.

Lehmann-Haupt, Christopher, "Tort and retort: Lawyers v. lawyers," *New York Times*, May 29, 1997.

Lemon, Joseph L. Jr., *Federal Appellate Court Law Clerk Handbook* (Chicago: ABA, 2007).
Lerner, Melvin J. and Dale T. Miller, "Just world research and the attribution process: Looking back and looking ahead," *Psychological Bulletin*, 85 no. 5 (1978), 1030–1051.
Leval, Pierre N., "Judicial opinions as literature," in Peter Brooks and Paul Gewirtz (eds.), *Law's Stories* (New Haven, CT: Yale University Press, 1996).
Levitt, Steven, "Understanding why crime fell in the 1990s: Four factors that explain the decline and six that do not," *Journal of Economic Perspectives*, 18 no. 1 (2004), 163–190.
Liebenberg, Sandra, "Social rights and transformation in South Africa: Three frames," *South African Journal on Human Rights*, 31 no. 3 (2015), 446–472.
Liebenberg, Sandra, *Socio-Economic Rights: Adjudication under a Transformative Constitution* (Claremont, South Africa: Juta & Co., 2010).
Light, Alfred R., "Civil procedure parables in the first year: Applying the Bible to think like a lawyer," *Gonzaga Law Review*, 37 no. 2 (2001), 282–313.
Lightowlers, Jenni, "Australian law relating to communal indigenous intellectual property," *Lexology* (February 12, 2013). www.lexology.com/library/detail.aspx?g=07 3fdf42-e293-4566-bd7e-f93604e66ae1. Accessed August 10, 2015.
Lindquist, Stefanie A. and Frank B. Cross, "Empirically testing Dworkin's chain novel theory studying the path of precedent," *NYU Law Review*, 80 (October 2005), 1156–1206. www.nyulawreview.org/sites/default/files/pdf/NYULawReview-80-4-Lindquist-Cross.pdf.
Llewellyn, Karl N., "Remarks on the theory of appellate decision and the rules or canons about how statutes are to be construed," *Vanderbilt Law Review*, 3 (1950), 395–406.
LoBianco, Tom, "Kasich wants immigration crackdown, but leaves door open on pathway to citizenship," CNN.com, available at www.cnn.com/2015/08/12/politics/john-kasich-immigration (August 12, 2015).
Loke, Margaret, "Sacred and secular clash at auction," *New York Times*, December 3, 1998.
Lombroso, Cesare, *Criminal Man*, trans. Mary Gibson and Nicole Hahn Rafter (Durham, NC: Duke University Press, 2006 [1876]).
López, Gerald P., "Lay lawyering," *UCLA Law Review*, 32 (1984–85), 1–60.
López, Gerald P., "Reconceiving civil rights practice: Seven weeks in the life of a rebellious collaboration," *The Georgetown Law Journal*, 77 (1989), 1603–1717.
Lopez, Ken, "Lists of analogies, metaphors and idioms for lawyers," *The Litigation Report*, 2012. www.a2lc.com/blog/bid/54079/Lists-of-Analogies-Metaphors-and-Idioms-for-Lawyers.
Lopez, Ken, "10 Videos to help litigators become better at storytelling," *The Litigation Report*, 2012. www.a2lc.com/blog/bid/53536/10-Videos-to-Help-Litigators-Become-Better-at-Storytelling.
Lorde, Audre, "Poetry is not a luxury," in *Sister Outsider: Essays & Speeches* (Trumansburg, NJ: Crossing Press Feminist Series, 1984).
Lorde, Audre, "The Black Unicorn," in *The Black Unicorn: Poems* (New York, NY: Norton, 1978).
Lorde, Audre, "The master's tools will never dismantle the master's house," in *Sister Outsider: Essays & Speeches* (New York, NY: Crossing Press Feminist Series, 1984), pp. 110–113.

Loughlin, Patricia, "Pirates, parasites, reapers, sowers, fruits, foxes . . . The metaphors of intellectual property," *Sydney Law Review*, 28 (2006), 211–226.

Luban, David, "The art of honesty," *Columbia Law Review*, 101 (2001), 1763–1764.

Luban, David, "The *Noblesse Oblige* tradition in the practice of law," *Vanderbilt Law Review*, 41 (1988), 736–740.

Lynch, M.B., "Crime as pollution? Theoretical, definitional and policy concerns with conceptualizing crime as pollution," *American Journal of Criminal Justice*, 40 (2015), 843–860.

MacCormick, Neil, "Coherence in legal justification," in Aleksander Peczenik et al. (eds.), *Theory of Legal Science* (Dordrecht: Springer, 1984), pp. 235–251.

MacCormick, Neil, "Norms, institutions and institutional facts," *Law & Philosophy*, 17 no. 3 (1998), 301–345.

MacKinnon, Catharine A., "On difference and dominance," in *Feminism Unmodified: Discourses on Life and Law* (Cambridge, MA: Harvard University Press, 1987).

MacKinnon, Catharine A., *Only Words* (Cambridge, MA: Harvard University Press, 1993).

Madoff, Ray D., "The new grave robbers," *New York Times*, March 27, 2011.

Makela, Finn, "Metaphors and models in legal theory," *Les Cahiers de droit*, 52 nos. 3–4 (Sept.–Dec. 2011), 397–415.

Maquet, Jacques, *Introduction to Aesthetic Anthropology*, 2nd edition (Malibu, CA: Undena Publications, 1979).

Mashburn, Amy R., "Professionalism as class ideology: Civility codes and bar hierarchy," *Valparaiso University Law Review*, 28 (1993): 657–708.

Matlock, Teenie, "Fictive motion as cognitive simulation," *Memory & Cognition*, 32 (2004), 1389–1400.

Matlock, Teenie, "Framing political messages with grammar and metaphor," *American Scientist*, 100 (2012), 478–483.

Matlon, Amina Para, "Safeguarding Native American sacred art by partnering tribal law and equity: An exploratory case study applying the *Bulun Bulun* equity to Navajo sandpainting," *Columbia Journal of Law and Arts*, 27 (2003–4), 211–247.

Matsuda, Mari, "Admit that the waters around you have grown: Change and legal education," *Indiana Law Journal*, 89 (2014), 1381–1400.

Matsuda, Mari, "Among the mourners who mourn, why should I among them be?" *Signs: Journal of Women in Culture and Society*, 28 no. 1 (2008), 475–477.

Matsuda, Mari, "Beside my sister, facing the enemy: Legal theory out of coalition," *Stanford Law Review*, 43 (1993), 1183–1192.

Matsuda, Mari, "Liberal jurisprudence and abstracted visions of human nature: A feminist critique of Rawls' theory of justice," *New Mexico Law Review*, 16 (1986), 613–630.

Matsuda, Mari, "Looking to the bottom: Critical legal studies and reparations," *Harvard Civil Rights-Civil Liberties Review*, 22 (1987), 323–329.

Matsuda, Mari, "Love, change," *Yale Journal of Law and Feminism*, 17 (2005), 185–203.

Matsuda, Mari, "We the people: Jurisprudence in color," in *"Where is Your Body?" And Other Essays on Race Gender and the Law* (Boston, MA: Beacon Press, 1987), pp. 21–27.

Matsuda, Mari, "When the first quail calls: Multiple consciousness as jurisprudential method," *Women's Rights Law Reporter*, 14 no. 2–3 (Spring/Fall, 1992), 297–300.

Matsuda, Mari, "Who is excellent?" *Seattle Journal for Social Justice*, 1 (2003), 29–50.

Matua, Makau, "Savages, victims, and saviors: The metaphor of human rights," *Harvard International Law Journal*, 42 no. 1 (2001), 201–245.

Maus, Derek, "The changing metaphors of education," in course notes at Potsdam: www2.potsdam.edu/mausdc/class/601/metaphor.html.

Mays, Thomas D. et al., "*Quid Pro Quo*: Alternatives for equity and conservation," in Stephen B. Brush and Doreen Stabinsky (eds.), *Valuing Local Knowledge: Indigenous People and Intellectual Property Rights* (Washington, DC: Island Press, 1996), pp. 259–280.

McAdam, Jane, "Editorial: Australia and asylum seekers," *International Journal of Refugee Law*, 25 no. 3 (2013), 435–448.

McCloskey, Donald, "Storytelling in economics," in Cristopher Nash (ed.), *Narrative in Culture: The Uses of Storytelling in the Sciences, Philosophy and Literature* (London; New York: Routledge, 1990), pp. 5–22.

McCloskey, Donald M., "The rhetoric of economics," *Journal of Economic Literature*, 31 (June 1983), 481–517.

McGinley, Ann, "Oncale v. Sundowner Offshore Services," in Kathryn Stanchi, Linda L. Berger, and Bridget J. Crawford (eds.), *Feminist Judgments* (2016).

McMurtry-Chubb, Teri, "Loving v. Virginia," in Kathryn Stanchi, Linda L. Berger, and Bridget J. Crawford (eds.), *Feminist Judgments* (2016).

Menkel-Meadow, Carrie, "The trouble with the adversary system in a postmodern, multicultural world," *William and Mary Law Review*, 38 (1996–7), 5–44.

Mercy, James A. and W. Rodney Hammond, "Preventing homicide: A public health perspective," in M. Dwayne Smith and Margaret A. Zahn (eds.), *Studying and Preventing Homicide* (Thousand Oaks, CA: Sage, 1999), pp. 274–294.

Mercy, James A. and Patrick W. O'Carroll, "New directions in violence prevention: The public health arena," *Violence and Victims*, 3 no. 4 (1988), 285–301.

Merlan, Anna, "Adele superfan Donald Trump cut the line at her concert last night," *The Slot*, available at http://theslot.jezebel.com/adele-superfan-donald-trump-cut-t he-line-at-her-concert-1743231839 (Nov. 18, 2015).

Merry, Sally Engle, *Human Rights and Gender Violence: Translating International Law into Local Justice*, Chicago Series in Law and Society (Chicago, IL: University of Chicago Press, 2006).

Metzger, O., "Making the doctrine of *Res Extra Commercium* visible in United States law," *Texas Law Review*, 74 (1996), 615–653.

Meyer, Philip N., *Storytelling for Lawyers* (New York, NY: Oxford University Press, 2013).

Meyler, Bernadette, "The myth of law and literature," *Legal Ethics* 8 (2005), 318–325.

Miller, J. Hillis, "Narrative," in Frank Lentricchia and Thomas McLaughlin (eds.), *Critical Terms for Literary Study*, 2d edition (Chicago, IL: University of Chicago Press, 1995), pp. 66–79.

Miller, Russell A., "Germany's German constitution," *Virginia Journal of International Law* 57 (forthcoming).

Mills, David and Robert Weisberg, "Corrupting the harm requirement in white collar crime," *Stanford Law Review*, 60 (2008), 1371–1446.

Mink, Louis O., "Narrative form as a cognitive instrument," in Robert H. Canary and Henry Kosicki (eds.), *The Writing of History: Literary Form and Historical Understanding* (Madison, WI: University of Wisconsin Press, 1978), pp. 129–149.

Mio, Jeffery, "Political metaphors and persuasion," in Jeffery Mio and Albert N. Katz (eds.), *Metaphor: Implications and Applications* (1996), pp. 127–146.

Mitchell, John B., "Narrative and client-centered representation: What is a true believer to do when his two favorite theories collide?" *Clinical Law Review*, 6 (1999), 85–126.

Mitchell, W.J.T. (ed.), *On Narrative* (Chicago, IL: University of Chicago Press, 1981).

Moffitt, T., "Adolescent-limited and life-course-persistent antisocial behavior: A developmental taxonomy," *Psychological Review*, 100 (1993), 674–701.

Mokal, Rizwaan Jameel, "Priority as pathology: The *Pari Passu* myth," *Cambridge Law Journal*, 60 no. 3 (2001), 581–619.

Moran, Joe, *Queuing for Beginners: The Story of Daily Life from Breakfast to Bedtime* (London: Profile Books, 2008).

Morgan, Gareth, *Images of Organization*, 4th edition (Thousand Oaks, CA: Sage, 2006).

Morgan, Mary S., "Case studies: One observation or many? Justification or discovery?" *Philosophy of Science*, 79 (2012), 667–677.

Moseneke, Deputy Chief Justice, "The fourth Bram Fisher Memorial Lecture – transformative adjudication," *South African Journal on Human Rights*, 18 no. 3 (2002), 309–319.

Mullins, Anne E., "Subtly selling the system: Where psychological influence tactics lurk in judicial writing," *University of Richmond Law Review*, 48 (2014), 1111–1156.

Murdoch, Iris, *Sartre* (Cambridge, UK: Bowes & Bowes, 1953).

Mureinik, Etienne, "Beyond a charter of luxuries: Economic rights in the Constitution," *South African Journal on Human Rights*, 8 no. 4 (1992) 464–474.

Murphy, Bruce Allen, "Justice Antonin Scalia and the Dead Constitution," *New York Times*, February 14, 2016. www.nytimes.com/192016/02/15/opinion/justice-antonin-s calia-and-the-dead-constitution.html.

Murray, James E., "Understanding law as metaphor," *Journal of Legal Education*, 34 (1984), 714–730.

Musolff, Andreas, *Metaphor and Political Discourse: Analogical Reasoning in Debates about Europe* (London; New York: Palgrave Macmillan, 2004).

Musolff, Andreas, "Metaphor scenarios in public discourse," *Metaphor and Symbol*, 21 (2006), 23–38.

Mutua, Makau W., "Savages, Victims, and Saviors: The Metaphor of Human Rights," *Harvard International Law Journal*, 42 no. 1 (2001), 201–245.

Nagel, Thomas, "Moral luck," in Thomas Nagel (ed.), *Mortal Questions* (New York, NY: Cambridge University Press, 1976), pp. 24–38.

Nassim, Omar W., "Toward an Islamic aesthetic theory," *The American Journal of Islamic Social Studies*, 15 no. 1 (1998), 71–90.

Nelson, Robert L. and David M. Trubek (eds.), *Lawyers' Ideals/Lawyers' Practices: Transformations in the American Legal Profession* (Ithaca, NY: Cornell University Press, 1992).

Newton, Nell Jessup, "Memory and misrepresentation: Representing Crazy Horse in tribal court," in Bruce Ziff and Pratima V. Rao (eds.), *Borrowed Power: Essays on*

Cultural Appropriation (New Brunswick, NJ: Rutgers University Press, 1997), pp. 195–224.
Nidditch, Peter H. (ed.), *John Locke: An Essay concerning Human Understanding* (Oxford: Clarendon Press, 1975).
Nielsen, Henrik Skov and Simona Zetterberg Gjerlevsen, "Distinguishing fictionality," in C. Maagaard, M.W. Lundholt, and D. Schäbler (eds.), *Fictionality and Factuality: Blurred Borders in Narrations of Identity* (Berlin: Walter de Gruyter, forthcoming).
Nussbaum, Martha, *Cultivating Humanity* (Cambridge, MA: Harvard University Press, 1997).
Nye, Andrea, "Woman clothed with the sun: Julia Kristeva and the escape from/to language," *Signs: Journal of Women in Culture and Society*, 12 (1987), 664–686.
O'Neil, Moira, Nathaniel Kendall-Taylor, and Andrew Volmert, *New Narratives: Changing the Frame on Crime and Justice* (Washington, DC: Frameworks Institute, 2016).
Oldfather, Chad M., "The hidden ball: A substantive critique of baseball metaphors in judicial opinions," *Connecticut Law Review*, 27 no. 1 (Fall 1994), 17–52.
Oldfield, Sophie and Saskia Greyling, "Waiting for the state: A politics of housing in South Africa," *Environment and Planning A*, 47 no. 5 (2015), 1100–1112.
Olivas, Michael A., "The chronicles, my grandfather's stories, and immigration law: The slave traders' chronicles as racial history," *St Louis University Law Journal*, 34 (1990), 425–441.
Olson, Greta, *Criminals as Animals from Shakespeare to Lombroso* (Amsterdam: De Gruyter, 2014).
Olson, Greta, "Narration and narrative in legal discourse," in *Living Handbook of Narratology* (Hamburg: Hamburg University Press, 2014). www.lhn.uni-hamburg.de/article/narration-and-narrative-legal-discourse.
Olson, Greta, "Towards a comparative and localized study of Brazilian law and literature," in Sonja Arnold and Michael Korfmann (eds.), *Direito e Literatura na Virada do Milênio/ Law and Literature at the Turn of the Millennium* (Porto Alegre: Editora Dublinese, 2014), pp. 15–38.
Olson, Greta and Sarah Copland, "Towards a politics of form," *European Journal of English Studies*, 20 no. 3 (2016), 207–221.
Onwuachi-Willig, Angela, "Meritor Savings Bank v. Vinson," in Kathryn Stanchi, Linda L. Berger, and Bridget J. Crawford (eds.), *Feminist Judgments* (2016).
Oremus, Will, "Did Obama hug a radical?" *Slate* (March 8, 2012).
Orwell, George, *Animal Farm* (New York, NY: Harcourt, Brace & World, 1946).
Orwell, George, "Politics and the English language," *Horizon*, 13, no. 76 (1946), pp. 252–265.
Otsuka, Michael, *Libertarianism without Inequality* (New York, NY: Oxford University Press, 2003).
Ottati, Victor C. and Randall A. Enstrom, "Metaphor and persuasive communication: A multifunctional approach," *Social and Personality Compass*, 4 (2010), 783–794.
Pan, Zhongdang and Gerald M. Kosicki, "Framing analysis: An approach to news discourse," *Political Communication*, 10 (1993), 59–79.
Pearson, Thomas W., "'Life is not for sale': Confronting free trade and intellectual property in Costa Rica," *American Anthropologist*, 115 no. 1 (2013), 58–71.

Pelletier, Benoît, "The case of the Treasures of L'Ange Gardien: An overview," *International Journal of Cultural Property*, 2 no. 2 (1993), 371–382.

Pennington, Nancy and Reid Hastie, "A cognitive theory of juror decision making: The story model," *Cardozo Law Review*, 13 (1991), 519–557.

Perelman, Jeremy and Katharine G. Young, "Freeing Mohammed Zakari: Footprints toward hop," in Jeremy Perelman and Lucie White (eds.), *Stones of Hope: How African Activists Reclaim Human Rights to Challenge Global Poverty* (Stanford, CA: Stanford University Press. 2011), pp. 122–149.

Perelman, Jeremy and Katharine G. Young, "Rights as footprints: A new metaphor for contemporary human rights practice," *Northwestern Journal of International Human Rights*, 9 no. 1 (2010), 27–58.

Perry, Ronen and Tal Z. Zarsky, "Queues in law," *Iowa Law Review*, 99 no. 4 (2014), 1595–1620.

Peters, Julie Stone, "Law, literature, and the vanishing real: On the future of an interdisciplinary illusion," *PMLA*, 120 (2005), 442–453.

Petersilia, Joan, *Understanding California Corrections* (Berkeley, CA: California Policy Research Center, 2006).

Petersilia, Joan, *When Prisoners Come Home: Parole and Prisoner Reentry* (New York, NY: Oxford University Press, 2009).

Petroski, Karen, "Fictions of omniscience," *Kentucky Law Review*, 103 (2015), 477–528.

Petty, Richard E. and John T. Cacioppo, *Attitudes and Persuasion – Classic and Contemporary Approaches* (Dubuque, IA: W. C. Brown, 1981).

Pew Center on the States, *Public Safety Performance Project, Risk /Needs Assessment 101: Science Reveals New Tools to Manage Offenders*, Sept. 2011. www.pewtrusts.org/~/media/legacy/uploadedfiles/pcs_assets/2011/pewriskassessmentbriefpdf.pdf.

Pfuhl, E., *The Deviance Process*, 2nd edition (Belmont, CA: Wadsworth Publishing Company, 1986).

Phelan, James, *Living to Tell about It: A Rhetoric and Ethics of Character Narration* (Ithaca, NY: Cornell University Press, 2005).

Phelan, James, "Narratives in contest; or, another twist in the narrative turn," *PMLA*, 123 (2008): 166–175.

Philippopoulos-Mihalopoulos, Andreas, "Flesh of the law: Material legal metaphors," *Journal of Law and Society*, 43 (2016), 45–65.

Philp, Rowan and Nashira Davids, "South Africa: Jumping the Housing Queue," Africa News Service, May 9, 2005, available at http://allafrica.com/stories/200505091640.html

Polkinghorne, Donald, *Narrative Knowing and the Human Sciences* (Albany, NY: SUNY Press, 1988).

Pollak, Jessica M. and Charis E. Kubrin, "Crime in the news: How crime, offenders and victims are portrayed in the media," *Journal of Criminal Justice and Popular Culture*, 14 no. 1 (2007), 59–83.

Pollock, Sir Frederick and Frederic William Maitland, *The History of English Law before the Time of Edward I*, 2 vols. (Cambridge, UK: Cambridge University Press, 1895).

Posner, Richard A., "Judges' writing styles (and do they matter)," *University of Chicago Law Review*, 62 (1995), 142–149.

Posner, Richard A., "The skin trade," *The New Republic*, 217 no. 15 (October 13, 1997), 40–43.

Potter, Roberto H., *Pornography: Group Pressures and Individual Rights* (Sydney: The Federation Press, 1996).
Potter, Roberto H., Jails, Public Health and Generalizability. *Journal of Correctional Health Care*, 16 no. 4 (2010), 263–272.
Potter, Roberto H. and Jeanne H. Krider, "Teaching about violence prevention: A bridge between public health and criminal justice educators," *Journal of Criminal Justice Education*, 11 (2000), 339–351.
Potter, Roberto H. and Jeffrey W. Rosky, "The iron fist in the latex glove: The intersection of public health and criminal justice," *American Journal of Criminal Justice*, 38 (2013), 276–282.
Powell, Ryan and John Flint, "(In)formalization and the civilizing process: Applying the work of Norbert Elias to housing-based anti-social behaviour interventions in the UK," *Housing, Theory & Society*, 26 no. 3 (2009), 159–178.
Prasad, Vinay, "The folly of big science awards," *New York Times*, October 2, 2015.
Predpol, "5 Myths about predictive policing," www.predpol.com/5-common-myths-predictive-policing-predpol/.
Presser, Lois and Sveinung Sandberg (eds.), *Narrative Criminology: Understanding Stories of Crime* (New York, NY; London: New York University Press, 2015).
Price, Vincent, David Tewksbury, and Elizabeth Powers, "Switching trains of thought: The impact of news frames on readers' cognitive responses," *Communication Research*, 24 (1997), 481–506.
Prince, Gerald, "The disnarrated," *Style*, 22 (1988), 1–8.
Prince, Richard, "How media have shaped our perception of race and crime," *The Root* (September 4, 2014), www.theroot.com/blogs/journalisms/2014/09/how_media_have_shaped_our_perception_of_race_and_crime.html.
Putnam, Robert D., *Bowling Alone: The Collapse and Revival of American Community* (New York, NY: Simon & Schuster, 2000).
Quintilianus, Marius Fabius, *Institutio Oratoria*, H.E. Butler (trans.), 3 vols. (Cambridge, MA: Harvard University Press, 1954).
Raack, David, "'To preserve the best fruits': The legal thought of Chancellor James Kent," *American Journal of Legal History*, 33 (1989), 320–366.
Radin, Max, "The theory of judicial decision: or how judges think," *American Bar Association Journal*, 11 (1925), 357–362.
Ransford, Charles, Candice Kane, and Gary Slutkin, "Cure violence: A disease control approach to reduce violence and change behavior," in Eve Walermauer and Timothy A. Akers (eds.), *Epidemiological Criminology: Theory to Practice* (New York, NY: Routledge, 2013), pp. 232–242.
Rawls, John, *A Theory of Justice* (Cambridge, MA: Harvard University Press rev. ed., 1971, 1999).
Raz, Joseph, "Human rights without foundations," in Samantha Besson and John Tasioulas (eds.), *The Philosophy of International Law* (Oxford, UK; New York, NY: Oxford University Press, 2010), pp. 321–339.
Raz, Joseph, *The Morality of Freedom* (Oxford, UK: Oxford University Press, 1986).
Raz, Joseph, *Value, Respect and Attachment* (Cambridge, UK: Cambridge University Press, 2001).
Reaves, Brian A., *Felony Defendants in Large Urban Counties, 2009-Statistical Tables* (Washington, DC: Bureau of Justice Statistics, 2013).

Reddy, Michael J., "The conduit metaphor: A case of frame conflict in our language about language," in Andrew Ortony (ed.), *Metaphor and Thought*, 2nd edition (New York, NY: Cambridge University Press, 1993), 164–201.
Rehnquist, William H., "Civility and freedom of speech," *Indiana Law Journal*, 49 (1973), 1–7.
Reich, Robert B., "Entrepreneurship reconsidered: The team as hero," *Harvard Business Review*, 65 no. 3 (May/June 1987), 77–83.
Reinarman, Craig and Harry G. Levine, "The crack attack: Politics and media in America's latest drug scare," in Joel Best (ed.), *Images of Issues: Typifying Contemporary Social Problems* (New York, NY: Aldine de Gruyter, 1989), pp. 115–137.
Rezek, Natalie, "Is self-harm by cutting a constitutionally protected right?" *Quinnipiac Health Law*, 12 (2009), 303–331.
Rhode, Deborah L., *In the Interests of Justice: Reforming the Legal Profession* (Oxford, UK; New York, NY: Oxford University Press, 2000).
Rhodes, Tim, "Risk environments and drug harms: A social science for harm reduction approach," *International Journal of Drug Policy*, 20 no. 3 (2009), 193–201.
Rich, Adrienne, "Aunt Jennifer's Tigers," in *Collected Early Poems: 1950–1970* (New York, NY: Norton, 1995).
Rich, Adrienne, "The burning of paper instead of children," in *The Will to Change: Poems 1968–1970* (New York, NY: Norton, 1971).
Ricoeur, Paul, "The metaphorical process as cognition, imagination, and feeling," *Critical Inquiry*, 5 (1978), 143–159.
Ricoeur, Paul, *The Rule of Metaphor: Multidisciplinary Studies of the Creation of Meaning in Language* (Toronto: University of Toronto Press, 2004).
Ricoeur, Paul, *The Rule of Metaphor: The Creation of Meaning in Language* (London: Routledge, 1977).
Ricoeur, Paul, *Time and Narrative*, trans. Kathleen McLaughlin and David Pellauer, 4 vols. (Chicago, IL: University of Chicago Press, 1984).
Rideout, J. Christopher, "Applied legal storytelling: A bibliography," *Legal Communication and Rhetoric: JALWD*, 12 (2015), 247–264.
Rideout, J. Christopher, "Penumbral thinking revisited: Metaphor in legal argumentation," *JALWD*, 7 (2010), 155–91.
Rideout, J. Christopher, "Storytelling, narrative rationality, and legal persuasion," *Journal of Legal Writing*, 14 (2008), 53–86.
Ritchie, David T., "The centrality of metaphor in legal analysis and communication: An introduction," *Mercer Law Review*, 58 (Spring 2007), 839–843.
Ritchie, L. David, "'Born on third base': Stories, simulations, and metaphor comprehension." Presented at the annual conference of Researching and Analyzing Metaphor, Cagliari, Italy (2014).
Ritchie, L. David, "'Everybody goes down': Metaphors, stories, and simulations in conversations," *Metaphor and Symbol*, 25 (2010), 123–143.
Ritchie, L. David, "Justice is blind": A model for analyzing metaphor transformations and narratives in actual discourse," in *Metaphor and The Social World*, 1 (2011), 70–89.
Ritchie, L. David, *Metaphorical Stories in Discourse* (New York, NY: Cambridge University Press, 2017).

Ritchie, L. David and Lynne Cameron, "Open hearts or smoke and mirrors: Metaphorical framing and frame conflicts in a public meeting," *Metaphor and Symbol*, 29 (2014), 204–223.

Ritchie, L. David and Min Zhu, "'Nixon stonewalled the investigation': Potential contributions of grammatical metaphor to conceptual metaphor theory and analysis," *Metaphor and Symbol*, 30 (2015), 118–136.

Roach, Kent, "Polycentricity and queue jumping in public law remedies: A two-track response," *University of Toronto Law Journal*, 66 no. 1 (2016), 3–52.

Robbins, Ruth Anne, "Harry Potter, Ruby Slippers and Merlin: Telling the client's story using the characters and paradigm of the archetypal hero's journey," *Seattle University Law Review*, 29 (2006), 767–802.

Rodensky, Lisa, *The Crime in Mind: Criminal Responsibility and the Victorian Novel* (New York, NY: Oxford University Press, 2003).

Röhl, Klaus F. and Stefan Ulbrich, *Recht anschaulich: Visualisierung in der Juristenausbildung* (Köln: Halem, 2007).

Rosch, Eleanor, "Natural categories," *Cognitive Psychology*, 4 (1973), 328–350.

Rose, George, "Literature and the bar," *Law Notes*, 5 (1901), 107–110.

Rose, Mark, *Authors and Owners: The Invention of Copyright* (Cambridge, MA: Harvard University Press, 1993).

Rosen, Lawrence, *Law as Culture: An Invitation* (Princeton, NJ: Princeton University Press, 2006).

Rosenberg, M.L., "Let's be clear: Violence is a public health problem," *Journal of the American Medical Association*, 267 (1992), 3071–3072.

Rosenbury, Laura, "Griswold v. Connecticut," in Kathryn Stanchi, Linda L. Berger, and Bridget J. Crawford (eds.), *Feminist Judgments* (2016).

Rothman, David, *The Discovery of the Asylum: Social Order and Disorder in the New Republic* (Boston, MA: Little, Brown, 1971).

Roux, Theunis, "Understanding Grootboom—A response to Cass R. Sunstein," *Constitutional Forum*, 12 no. 2 (2002), 41–51.

Royston, Lauren and Ronald Eglin, "Allocation thought piece for managed land settlement," unpublished draft (Dec. 5, 2011), available at www.incrementalsettlement.org.za/files/uploads/files/1323332855-allocation-thought-piece-for-managed-land-settlement.pdf.

Rubin, Edward L., *Beyond Camelot: Rethinking Politics and Law for the Modern State* (Princeton, NJ: Princeton University Press, 2005).

Sacco, Vincent F., "Media constructions of crime," *Annals of the American Academy of the Political and Social Sciences*, 539 (1995), 141–154.

Sachs, Albie, "The creation of South Africa's Constitution," *New York Law School Law Review*, 41 no. 2 (1996), 669–701.

Sachs, Albie, *The Strange Alchemy of Life and Law* (Oxford, UK; New York, NY: Oxford University Press, 2009).

Sacks, Sheldon (ed.), *On Metaphor* (Chicago, IL: Chicago University Press, 1979).

Sage, Alexandria, "U.S. foundation buys Hopi masks at auction to return to tribe," Reuters, December 11, 2013. www.reuters.com/article/2013/12/11/us-france-auction-idUSBRE9B80QJ20131211. Accessed November 14, 2015).

Sahlins, Marshall D., *Tribesmen* (Englewood Cliffs, NJ: Prentice-Hall, 1968).

Saleh, Matt, *Great Minds Speak Alike: Inter-Court Communication of Metaphor in Education Finance Litigation*. PhD dissertation. Columbia University (2015).

Salyzyn, Amy, "John Rambo v Atticus Finch: Gender, diversity and the civility movement," *Legal Ethics* (2013), 97–118.

Sampson, Robert J. and John H. Laub, "Life–course desisters? Trajectories of crime among delinquent boys followed to age 70," *Criminology*, 41 (2003), 319–339.

Sandberg, Sveinung, "What can 'lies' tell us about life? Notes towards a framework of narrative criminology," *Journal of Justice Education*, 21 no. 4 (2010), 447–465.

Sarat, Austin (ed.), *Civility, Legality, and Justice in America* (New York, NY: Cambridge University Press, 2014).

Sarat, Austin, "Enactments of professionalism: A study of judges' and lawyers' accounts of ethics civility in litigation," *Fordham Law Review*, 67 (1998), 809–835.

Scafidi, Susan, *Who Owns Culture? Appropriation and Authenticity in American Law* (New Brunswick, NJ: Rutgers University Press, 2005).

Schaffer, Kay and Sidonie Smith, *Human Rights and Narrated Lives: The Ethics of Recognition* (New York, NY: Palgrave Macmillan, 2004).

Schank, Roger C. and Robert P. Abelson, "Knowledge and memory: The real story," in Robert. S. Wyer, Jr. (ed.), *Knowledge and Memory: The Real Story*. Advances in Social Cognition, vol. 8 (Hillsdale, NJ: Lawrence Erlbaum Associates 1995), pp. 1–86.

Schapp, Wilhelm, *In Geschichten verstrickt* (Frankfurt: Klostermann, 1953).

Schauer, Frederick, *Thinking Like a Lawyer* (Cambridge, MA: Harvard University Press, 2009).

Scheingold, Stuart, *The Politics of Rights: Lawyers, Public Policy and Political Change* (New Haven, CT: Yale University Press, 1974).

Schilling, Vincent, "Oglala Sioux Tribe's alcohol lawsuit dismissed without prejudice," *Indian Country*, October 3, 2012.

Schlag, Pierre, "Jurisprudence Noire," *Columbia Law Review*, 101 (2001), 1733–1742.

Schlesinger, Philip and Howard Tumber, *Reporting Crime: The Media Politics of Criminal Justice* (Oxford, UK: Clarendon Press; New York, NY: Oxford University Press, 1994).

Schön, Donald, "Generative metaphor: A perspective on problem-setting in social policy," in Andrew Ortony (ed.), *Metaphor and Thought*, 2nd edition (Cambridge, UK; New York, NY: Cambridge University Press, 1993), pp. 137–163.

Schultz, Vicki, "Reconceptualizing sexual harassment," *Yale Law Journal*, 107 (1999), 1683.

Schüssel, Stuart, "Copyright protection's challenges and Alaska Natives' cultural property," *Alaska Law Review*, 92 no. 2 (2012), 313–340.

Sehon, Scott R., *Free Will and Action Explanation: A Non-Causal, Compatibilist Account* (Oxford, UK: Oxford University Press, 2016).

Sen, Amartya, *Development as Freedom* (New York, NY: Oxford University Press, 1999).

Sen, Amartya, "Elements of a theory of human rights," *Philosophy & Public Affairs*, 32 no. 4 (2004), 315–356.

Sheley, Joseph F. and Cindy D. Ashkins, "Crime, crime news, and crime views," *Public Opinion Quarterly*, 45 no. 4 (1981), 492–506.

Sherwin, Richard, "Law frames: Historical truth and narrative necessity in a criminal case," *Stanford Law Review*, 47 (1994), 39–83.

Shils, Edward, "The virtue of civil society," in Virginia A. Hodgkinson and Michael W. Foley (eds.), *The Civil Society Reader* (Hanover, NH: University Press of New England, 2003), pp. 292–306.

Shklovsky, Victor, "Art as technique," in Julie Rivkin and Michael Ryan (eds.), *Literary Theory: An Anthology* (Oxford: Blackwell Publishers, 2004).

Simmons, Beth, *Mobilizing for Human Rights: International Law in Domestic Politics* (Cambridge, UK; New York, NY: Cambridge University Press, 2009).

Simon, Dan, "A third view of the black box: Cognitive coherence in legal decision making," *University of Chicago Law Review*, 71 (2004), 511–586.

Simon, Jonathan, "Governing through crime metaphors," *Brooklyn Law Review*, 67 (2001), 1035–1070. http://scholarship.law.berkeley.edu/facpubs/1342.

Skeel, David A. Jr., "Lawyer as confidence man," *Columbia Law Review*, 101 (2001), 1750–1762,

Skeel, David A. Jr., "Practicing poetry, teaching law," *Michigan Law Review*, 92 (1994), 1754–1775.

Slaughter, Joseph R., *Human Rights, Inc.: The World Novel, Narrative Form, and International Law* (New York, NY: Fordham University Press, 2007).

Slutkin, Gary, *Violence is a Contagious Disease* (Chicago, IL: Cure Violence, 2012).

Smith, David, "Nelson Mandela's lying in state draws queue of thousands to say goodbye," *The Guardian*, December 11, 2013.

Smith, Michael R., *Advanced Legal Writing: Theories and Strategies in Persuasive Writing* (New York: Aspen/Wolters Kluwer Law and Business, 3rd edition 2013, 1st edition 2002).

Smith, Michael R., "Crafting effective metaphors," in *Advanced Legal Writing: Theories and Strategies in Persuasive Writing*, 3rd edition (New York, NY: Wolters Kluwer Law and Business, 2013), pp. 217–246.

Smith, Michael R., "Levels of metaphor in persuasive legal writing," *Mercer Law Review*, 58 (2007), 919–947.

Snævarr, Stefán, *Metaphors, Narratives, Emotions: Their Interplay and Impact* (Amsterdam; NY: Rodopi, 2010).

Sorokin, Vladimir, *The Queue* (trans. Sally Laird) (New York, NY: New York Review Books, 2008).

Spearing, A.C., "What is a narrator? Narrator theory and medieval narratives," *Digital Philology*, 4 (2015), 59–105.

Spector, Malcolm, *Constructing Social Problems* (Hawthorne, NY: Walter de Gruyter, 1987).

Spector, Malcolm, "Social problems: A reformulation," *Social Problems*, 21 no. 2 (1973), 145–159.

Spencer, Alexander, "The social construction of terrorism: Media, metaphor and policy implications," *Journal of International Relations and Development*, 15 no. 3 (2012), 393–419. www.palgrave-journals.com/jird/journal/v15/n3/pdf/jird20124a.pdf.

Spender, Dale, *Man Made Language* (Chicago, IL; Pandora, 1998).

Ssali, Henry J., "Jumping the queue," *Africa News Service*, May 28, 2007.

Stanchi, Kathryn M., "Feminist legal writing," *San Diego Law Review*, 39 (2002), 387–436.

Stanchi, Kathryn M., Linda L. Berger, and Bridget J. Crawford (eds.), *Feminist Judgments: Rewritten Opinions of the United States Supreme Court* (New York, NY: Cambridge University Press, 2016).

Steen, Gerard, "Developing, testing and interpreting Deliberate Metaphor Theory," *Journal of Pragmatics*, 90 (2015), 67–72.

Steen, Gerard S., W. Gudrun Reijnierse, and Christian Burgers, "When do natural language metaphors influence reasoning? A follow-up study to Thibodeau and Boroditsky," *PLoS One*, 9 no. 12 (2014). www.plosone.org/article/info%3Adoi%2F10 .1371%2Fjournal.pone.0113536 (2013).

Stern, Simon, "Law and literature," in Markus Dirk Dubber (ed.), *The Oxford Handbook of Criminal Law* (Oxford, UK; New York, NY: Oxford University Press, 2014), pp. 111–130.

Stern, Simon, "Literary evidence and legal aesthetics," in Austin Sarat, Matthew Anderson, and Catherine O. Frank (eds.), *Teaching Literature and Law: MLA Approaches to Teaching Series* (New York, NY: Modern Language Association, 2011), pp. 244–252.

Stern, Simon, "Legal and literary fictions," in Elizabeth Anker and Bernadette Meyler (eds.), *New Directions in Law and Literature* (Oxford, UK: Oxford University Press, 2017), pp. 313–326.

Stern, Simon, "The third party doctrine and the third person," *New Criminal Law Review*, 16 (2013), 364–412.

Stiritz, Susan Ekberg, "Cultural cliteracy: Exposing the contexts of women's not coming," *Berkeley Journal of Gender, Law and Justice*, 23 (2013), 243–66.

Stonebridge, Lyndsey, *The Judicial Imagination: Writing after Nuremberg* (Edinburgh: Edinburgh University Press, 2011).

Strathern, Marilyn, *The Gender of the Gift: Problems with Women and Problems with Society in Melanesia* (Berkeley: University of California Press, 1988).

Strathern, Marilyn, *Kinship, Law and the Unexpected: Relatives Are Always Unexpected* (New York, NY: Cambridge University Press, 2005), pp. 58–61.

Strawson, Galen, "Against narrativity," *Ratio*, XVIII (2004), 428–452.

Strydom, Janke and Sue-Mari Viljoen, "Unlawful occupation of inner-city buildings: A constitutional analysis of the rights and obligations involved," *Potchefstroom Electronic Law Journal*, 17 no. 4 (2014), 1206–1261.

Suk, Jeannie, "'The look in his eyes': The story of *State v. Rusk* and rape reform," (Harvard Law Sch. Pub. Law & Legal Theory Working Paper Series, Paper No. 10–23, 2010), published in Donna K. Coker and Robert Weisberg (eds.), *Criminal Law Stories* (New York, NY: Foundation Press, 2012).

Surette, R., "Cause or catalyst: The interaction of real world and media crime models," *American Journal of Criminal Justice*, 38 no. 3 (2013), 392–409.

Surette, R., *Media, Crime, and Criminal Justice: Images, Realities and Policies* (Belmont, CA: Cengage, 2015).

Sutherland, Edwin H., *Principles of Criminology*, 4th edition (Philadelphia: Lippincott, 1947).

Swales, John, *Genre Analysis: English in Academic and Research Settings* (Cambridge, UK; New York, NY: Cambridge University Press, 1990).

Szubert, Rafal, "Ein beitrag zur metapher in der rechtssprache: Am beispiel 'juristische person,'" *Zeitschrift des Verbandes Polnischer Germanisten*, 4 no. 2 (2015), 141–157.

Taber, Charles S., "Political cognition and public opinion," in Robert Y. Shapiro and Lawrence R. Jacobs (eds.), *The Oxford Handbook of American Public Opinion and the Media* (Oxford, UK; New York, NY: Oxford University Press, 2011), pp. 368–383.

Tasioulas, John, "The moral reality of human rights," in Thomas Pogge (ed.), *Freedom from Poverty as a Human Right: Who Owes What to the Very Poor ?* (Paris: UNESCO; Oxford; New York: Oxford University Press, 2007), pp. 75–103.

Taylor, Charles, *Modern Social Imaginaries* (Durham, NC: Duke University Press, 2004).

Taylor, Charles, *The Language Animal: The Full Shape of the Human Linguistic Capacity* (Cambridge, MA: Harvard University Press, 2016).

Thibodeau, Paul H., "Extended metaphors are the home run of persuasion: Don't fumble the phrase," *Metaphor & Symbol*, 31 (2016), 53–72.

Thibodeau, Paul H., "Is crime a virus or a beast? When describing crime, Stanford study shows the word you pick can frame the debate on how to fight it." http://news.stanford.edu/news/2011/february/metaphors-crime-study-022311.html.

Thibodeau, Paul H. and Lera Boroditsky, "Measuring effects of metaphor in a dynamic opinion landscape," *PLoS ONE*, 10 no. 7 (2015): pone.0133939.

Thibodeau, Paul H. and Lera Boroditsky, "Metaphors we think with: The role of metaphor in reasoning," *PLoS ONE*, 6 no. 2 (2011): e16782.

Thibodeau, Paul H., Peace O. Iyiewuare, and Lera Boroditsky, "Metaphors affect reasoning: Measuring effects of metaphor in a dynamic opinion landscape" (2016), *CogSci* (2015).

Thornburg, Elizabeth G., "Just say 'No fishing': The lure of metaphor," *University of Michigan Journal of Law Reform*, 40 (Fall 2006), 1–65.

Thornburg, Elizabeth G., "Metaphors matter: How images of battle, sports, and sex shape the adversary system," *Wisconsin Women's Law Journal*, 10 (1995), 225–281.

Tiegreen, Sara and Elana Newman, "The effect of 'news frames,'" http://dartcenter.org/content/effect-news-frames.

Tissington, Kate, Naadira Munshi, Gladys Mirugi-Mukundi, and Ebenezer Durogaye, "'Jumping the queue', waiting lists and other myths: Perceptions and practice around housing demand and allocation in South Africa," report, Community Law Centre, University of the Western Cape & Socio-Economic Rights Institute of South Africa (2013).

Todorov, Tzvetan, *The Poetics of Prose*, trans. Richard Howard (Ithaca, NY: Cornell University Press, 1977).

Tracy, Karen, "Interactional trouble in emergency service requests: A problem of frames," *Research on Language and Social Interaction*, 30 (1997), 315–343.

Treviño, A. Javier, Michelle A. Harris, and Derron Wallace, "What's so critical about critical race theory?" *Contemporary Justice Review*, 11 no. 1 (2008), 7–10.

Tribe, Lawrence H., "Trial by mathematics: Precision and ritual in the legal process," *Harvard Law Review*, 84 (1971), 1329–1393.

Turner, Mark, *The Literary Mind* (Princeton, NJ: Princeton University Press, 1996).

Tushnet, Mark, *Weak Courts, Strong Rights* (Princeton, NJ: Princeton University Press, 2008).

Vallentyne, Peter and Hillel Steiner, *Left Libertarianism and Its Critics: The Contemporary Debate* (New York, NY: Palgrave Macmillan, 2000).

Vasquez, Juan Gabriel, "In Colson Whitehead's latest, the underground railroad is more than a metaphor," *New York Times Book Review*, August 5, 2016.

Velleman, J. David, "Narrative explanation," *Philosophical Review*, 112 (2003), 1–25.

VG Göttingen, Urteil von 25 April 2012, Az. 4 A 18/11. Web. Accessed Feb. 17, 2017.

Waldron, Jeremy, "Rights and needs, the myth of disjunction," in Austin Sarat and Thomas Kearns (eds.), *Legal Rights: Historical and Philosophical Perspectives* (Ann Arbor, MI: University of Michigan Press, 1996), pp. 87–110.

Walsh, Richard, *The Rhetoric of Fictionality: Narrative Theory and the Idea of Fiction* (Columbus, OH: Ohio State University Press, 2007).

Weatherall, Kimberlee, "Culture, autonomy and *Djulibinyamurr*: Individual and community in the construction of rights to traditional designs," *The Modern Law Review*, 64 (2001), 215–242.

Weigend, Thomas, "Is the criminal process about truth? A German perspective," *Harvard Journal of Law and Public Policy*, 26 (2003), 157–173,

Weisberg, Richard, *Poethics and Other Strategies of Law and Literature* (New York: Columbia University Press, 1992).

Weisberg, Robert, "Civic Oratory in *Lawyerland*," *Columbia Law Review*, 101 (2001), 1782–1792.

Weisberg, Robert, "Meanings and measures of recidivism," *Southern California Law Review*, 87 (2014), 785–804.

Weisberg, Robert, "Proclaiming trials as narratives: Premises and pretenses," in Brooks and Gewirtz (eds.), *Law's Stories* (1996), pp. 61–83.

Weisburd, David and Lorraine Green Mazerolle, "Crime and disorder in drug hot spots: Implications for theory and practice in policing," *Police Quarterly*, 3 (September 2000), 331–349.

Welsh, Alexander, *Strong Representations: Narrative and Circumstantial Evidence in England* (Baltimore, MD: Johns Hopkins University Press, 1992).

Wenar, Leif, "Rights," *The Stanford Encyclopedia of Philosophy* (Fall 2015 Edition), Edward N. Zalta (ed.), http://plato.stanford.edu/archives/fall2015/entries/rights/.

Wessner, David R., "The origins of viruses," *Nature Education*, 3 no. 9 (2010), 37.

West, Robin, "Jurisprudence as narrative: An aesthetic analysis of modern legal theory," *N.Y.U. Law Review*, 60 (1985), 145–211.

West, Robin, "Joseph in *Lawyerland*," *Columbia Law Review*, 101 (2001), 1775–1781.

Western, Bruce, *Punishment and Inequality in America* (New York: Russell Sage Foundation, 2006).

Whelan, Daniel J. and Jack Donnelly, "The West, economic and social rights, and the global human rights regime: Setting the record straight," *Human Rights Quarterly*, 29 no. 4 (2007), 908–949.

White, Hayden, "The value of narrativity in the representation of reality," *Critical Inquiry*, 1 (1980), 5–27.

White, James B., *The Legal Imagination: Abridged Edition* (Chicago, IL: University of Chicago Press, 1986).

White, James B., *The Legal Imagination: Studies in the Nature of Legal Thought and Expression* (Boston, MA: Little, Brown and Company, 1973).

White, James Boyd, *Heracles' Bow: Essays on the Rhetoric and Poetics of the Law* (Madison, WI: University of Wisconsin Press, 1985).

Whitehead, Colson, *The Underground Railroad* (New York: Doubleday, 2016).

Wikipedia, "Indigenous intellectual property," *Wikipedia*. https://en.wikipedia.org/wiki/Indigenous_intellectual_pr.

Wikipedia, "Personality Rights," *Wikipedia*. https://en.wikipedia.org/wiki/Personality.

Williams, Bernard, "Moral luck," *Proceedings of the Aristotelian Society*, 1 (1976), 115–135.
Williams, Joan C., "Reconstructive feminism: Changing the way we talk about gender and work thirty years after the PDA," *Yale Journal of Law and Feminism*, 21 (2009), 79–117.
Williams, Patricia J., *The Alchemy of Race and Rights* (Cambridge, MA: Harvard University Press, 1991).
Wilson, James Q., *Thinking about Crime* (New York, NY: Basic Books (rev. ed. 1983).
Wilson, James Q. and Joan Petersilia (eds.), *Crime and Public Policy* (New York, NY: Oxford University Press, 2011).
Wilson, Nicole and Raymond W. Gibbs, Jr., "Real and imagined body movement primes metaphor comprehension," *Cognitive Science*, 31 (2007), 721–731.
Wilson, Richard Ashby, *Writing History in International Crime Trials* (Cambridge, UK; New York, NY: Cambridge University Press, 2011).
Wilson, Stuart, "Curing the poor: State housing policy in Johannesburg after Blue Moonlight," *Constitutional Court Review*, 5 (2013), 280–296.
Winnett, Susan, "Coming unstrung: Women, men, narrative and principles of pleasure," *PMLA*, 105 (1990), 505–518.
Winter, Stephen, *A Clearing in the Forest: Law, Life, and Mind* (Chicago, IL: University of Chicago Press, 2001).
Winter, Steven L., "Death is the mother of metaphor," *Harvard Law Review*, 105 (1992), 745–772.
Winter, Steven L., "Making the familiar conventional again," *Michigan Law Review*, 99 no. 6 (2001), 1607–1636.
Winter, Steven L., "Re-embodying law," *Mercer Law Review*, 58 (2006), 869–897.
Winter, Steven L., "The cognitive dimension of the agon between legal power and narrative meaning," *Michigan Law Review*, 87 (1989), 2276–2277.
Winter, Steven L., "Transcendental nonsense, metaphoric reasoning, and the cognitive stakes for law," *University of Pennsylvania Law Review*, 137 no. 4 (1989), 1105–1237.
Wolf, Werner, "Narratology and media(lity): The transmedial expansion of a literary discipline and possible consequences," in Greta Olson (ed.), *Current Trends in Narratology* (Berlin; New York, NY: De Gruyter, 2011), pp. 145–180.
Wright, Laura, "Third person plural present tense markers in London prisoners' depositions, 1562–1623," *American Speech*, 77 (2002), 242–263.
Wright, Patricia, "Commercial rights and constitutional wrongs," *Maryland Law Review*, 49 (1990), 293–313.
Yamin, Ely, *Power, Suffering, and the Struggle for Dignity: Human Rights Frameworks for Health and Why They Matter* (Philadelphia, PA; University of Pennsylvania Press, 2016).
Yano, Lester I., "Protection of the ethnobiological knowledge of indigenous peoples," *UCLA Law Review*, 41 (1993), 443–486.
Yong, Ed, "Dormant viruses can hide in our DNA and be passed from parent to child" (2010). Retrieved from http://blogs.discovermagazine.com/notrocketscience/2010/0 3/27/dormant-viruses-can-hide-in-our-dna-and-be-passed-from-parent-to-child/.
Young, Katharine G., *Constituting Economic and Social Rights* (Oxford: Oxford University Press, 2012).
Young, Katharine G., "Rights and queues: On distributive contests in the modern state," *Columbia Journal of Transnational Law*, 55, no. 1 (2016), 65–137.

Young, Katharine G., "The minimum core of economic and social rights: A concept in search of content," *Yale Journal of International Law*, 33 no. 1 (2008), 113–175.

Young, Katharine and Jeremy Perelman, "Rights as footprints: A new metaphor for contemporary human rights practice," *Northwestern Journal of International Human Rights*, 9 no. 27 (2010), 27–58.

Ziman, John, *Real Science: What It Is and What It Means* (Cambridge, UK; New York, NY: Cambridge University Press, 2000).

Zunshine, Lisa, *Why We Read Fiction: Theory of Mind and the Novel* (Columbus, OH: Ohio State University Press, 2006).

Zwaan, Rolf A., "Embodiment and language comprehension: Reframing the discussion," *Trends in Cognitive Sciences*, 18 (2014), 229–234.

Index

Abelson, Robert P., 286
Activism. *See* Legal activism, narrative and metaphor in
Adele, 322
"Admissions Against Interest" (Joseph), 336–337
Advanced Legal Writing: Theories and Strategies in Persuasive Writing (Smith), 57
Aeneid (Virgil), 76–77, 94–95
Affordable Care Act, 164
Akers, Timothy A., 211–212
Allegory, 97–99
American Bar Association, 262, 351
American Civil Liberties Union, 191
America's Most Wanted (television program), 261
Amsterdam, Anthony G., 1, 2–3, 60, 146
"An Awful Lot Was Happening" (Joseph), 335
Anderson v. Litzenberg (1997), 77–78
Animal Farm (Orwell), 273, 281
The Anthologist (Baker), 102–104
Anthony, Casey, 252
Anthony, Susan B., 369
Antiquities Act, 48–49
"Any and All" (Joseph), 335–336
Apollo and Dionysius (Brown), 338
Applied Legal Storytelling, 59
"Applied Legal Storytelling" (conference), 2
Aquinas, Thomas, 338
Aristotle, 84, 255
Arizona State University, 48
Arnold, Thurman, 197
Art works, 39–40, 41–42
Ashkins, C.D., 254
Assault weapon laws, 232

Attorneys, narrative and metaphor and. *See also* "Lawyer-self"
overview, 327–331
civility and, 349–358
Auchincloss, Louis, 328
"Aunt Jennifer's Tigers" (Rich), 160–161
Australia
indigenous peoples in, 41–42, 45
"queue jumping" in, 307

Bachmann-Medick, Doris, 22
Baker, Nicholson, 102–104
Baldwin v. Seelig (1935), 31
Ball, Milner S., 7, 169, 364
Bandes, Susan, 262
Barthes, Roland, 123, 127–128, 135–136, 137, 140, 143, 145, 225–226
Beale, Sara Sun, 260, 261, 263
Beckett, Katherine, 262
Before Our Eyes (Joseph), 336–337, 340
Bell, Derrick, 372
Benveniste, Emile, 124
Berger, Benjamin, 114
Berger, Linda L., 7, 9, 62–63, 64, 119–120, 153–156, 275, 276, 361. *See also* Gender, narrative and metaphor and
Berkey v. Third Avenue Railway Co. (1927), 30
Berne Convention for the Protection of Artistic and Literary Works, 42–43
Bibas, Stephanos, 63
Biblical parables, 94
Billy Budd (Melville), 338, 339
Binder, Guyora, 2–3, 117, 119
"Binocular vision," 20
"Birth" metaphor, 276
Bishin, William R., 337–338

Index

Black, Hugo, 116
Black Lives Matter, 373
Blackstone, William, 52
"Black Unicorn" (Lorde), 160
Blumer, Herbert, 211–213
Bogdanov, Konstantin, 322
Booth, Wayne C., 97, 255
Booth v. Maryland (1987), 140–141
Boroditsky, Lera, 198, 255–256, 263–264, 277, 279–280, 283
Bosmajian, Haig A., 7, 113–115
Bowers v. Hardwick (1986), 276–277
Bradley, Joseph, 171–172, 174
Bradwell, Myra, 171, 176
Bradwell v. Illinois (1873), 171–172, 174, 175, 177
Brandeis, Louis, 5
Brazil, "queue jumping" in, 322
Brennan, William, 164
Brewsie and Willie (Stein), 332
Breyer, Stephen, 5, 142
Bribery, 240
Brock v. State (1989), 234
"Broken windows" metaphor, 205, 236
Brooks, Peter, 2–3, 16, 20, 118–120, 126, 155. *See also* Judicial opinions, narrative and metaphor in
Brown, Norman O., 338
Brown v. Board of Education (1954), 23–24, 35, 118, 119, 187, 188
Bruner, Jerome, 1, 2–3, 8, 21, 60, 147
Bryant, Kobe, 252
Bulun Equity Principle, 49–50
Burgers, Christian, 279–280
Burns, Robert, 59
Bush, George H.W., 247, 274
Bush, George W., 321

Cacioppo, John T., 285
California Resale Royalties Act, 39–40
Cameron, Lynne, 245–246, 270–271
Canada
  Canada Health Act, 307
  Constitution, 16
  health care in, 322–323
  "queue jumping" in, 307, 322–323
"Captive audience" metaphor, 95
Cardozo, Benjamin N., 5, 30–31, 33, 36, 52–53, 109, 115–116, 149, 338
Carpenter, Irving, 89, 93–94
Case, Mary Ann, 182
Cash transaction reporting laws, 231

Castile, Philandro, 145
Catalano, Theresa, 259–260
Centers for Disease Control and Prevention, 210, 215
"Chain of evidence" metaphor, 95
Chambers, Ross, 59, 154
Charon, Rita, 2
Chilkat Indian Village v. Johnson (1989), 43
"Chilling effect" metaphor, 95
Cismaru v. Radisson Seven Seas Cruises, Inc. (2001), 73–74
Citizenship and Immigration Service (USCIS), 320–321
Citizens United v. Federal Election Commission (2010), 30–31, 281
Civility among attorneys, 349–358
Civil law systems
  common law systems versus, 21, 33–34
  metaphor in, 32
  narrative in, 25–28
Clark, Kenneth, 187–188
A Clearing in the Forest: Law, Life, and Mind (Winter), 7, 9
Clement, Paul, 164
Codes, Precepts, Biases and Taboos: Poems 1973–1993 (Joseph), 340
Cohen, Felix S., 338
Cohen, Ted, 154
Cohn, Jonathan, 322–323
Coleman, Renita, 246
Colleges, sexual assaults in, 240–241
"Color blind" metaphor, 178–179, 364, 372
Columbia Law Review, 342, 351, 357
Columbia University, 2, 264–265
The Common Law (Holmes), 355
Common law systems, civil law systems versus, 21, 33–34
Community policing, 236
Compstat, 236–237
"Conception" metaphor, 202–204
Concepts of justice, narrative and metaphor in
  overview, 15–18
  covenant metaphor, 16
  indigenous peoples (*See* Indigenous peoples)
  legal discourse (*See* Legal discourse, narrative and metaphor in)
  "living tree doctrine," 16
Conceptual Metaphor Theory, 271–273
Constitution, metaphors regarding, 114–115
Contagion theory, 206
"Containment" metaphor, 227–228

Contraception, 184–186
"Control" metaphor, 207
Conventional metaphors, 63, 107–108
Convention on Economic, Social and Cultural Rights, 44
Convention on the Rights of Persons with Disabilities, 303
Coode, George, 134
Cops (television program), 261
"Copycat" effect, 206–207
Copyrights, 40, 42–43, 50
Corcoran v. Astrue (2011), 87
Counterfactuals, 125
"Covenant" metaphor, 16
Cover, Robert, 21, 24, 339
Coy, Peter, 256, 267–268
Coyle v. Texas (1985), 66–67, 68, 71, 81, 82, 83, 92–93
Crazy Horse, 43–44
Crenshaw, Kimberlé Williams, 362
Crimes against humanity, 294–295
Criminal law, narrative and metaphor in
  overview, 53, 195–199
  assault weapon laws, 232
  bribery, 240
  "broken windows" metaphor, 205, 236
  cash transaction reporting laws, 231
  colleges, sexual assaults in, 240–241
  community policing, 236
  deterrence and, 246–247
  drug paraphernalia laws, 232
  HIV transmission as assault, 233
  loitering, 234
  mass incarceration, 229–230, 237–238
  media reporting of crime (See Media reporting of crime, narrative and metaphor in)
  medical metaphor (See Medical metaphor of crime)
  "narrative criminology," 248–249
  pathological model, 247
  "rational actor" model, 246–247
  scientific criminology, 210–211
  selective incapacitation, 236–237
  suicide, 206–207, 229
  "superpredators," 222, 247
  white collar crime, 239–240, 259–260, 279
Critical Legal Theory, 3, 362, 372
Critical Race Theory, 3, 196, 361, 362–364, 365, 367, 371, 372, 379
Crowning, Robert, 338

The Crucible (Miller), 97–98, 100
Cultural appropriation, 50
Curriculum Vitae (Joseph), 334–336, 340

Darwin, Charles, 195
Dead metaphors, 5, 107–108
DeBose, Cynthia Hawkins, 185
Defense of Marriage Act, 280–281
Defoe, Daniel, 42
Delgado, Richard, 3, 363
Dershowitz, Alan, 92
Dickerson, Maria, 322
Dickinson, Emily, 338
Dickinson v. Texas (1984), 66–67, 93
Differential Association/Social Learning (DA/SL) perspective, 207–208
"Dirty laundry" metaphor, 181
Discourse. *See* Legal discourse, narrative and metaphor in
Disease metaphor of crime. *See* Medical metaphor of crime
Disnarration, 125–126
"Dolls study," 187–188
Dong v. Chertoff (2007), 320
Donne, John, 338
Douard, John, 257
Dowdle, Walter R., 207
Dreisbach, Daniel, 116
Droit de suite, 39–40
Drug paraphernalia laws, 232
Dudziak, Mary, 363
Duke University, 256
Durst, Ilene, 173–174
Dworkin, Ronald, 1–2, 17, 232, 294
Dylan, Bob, 376–377

Editorial cartoons, reporting of crime and, 280–282
Edwards, Linda H., 57, 59, 60, 162, 275, 276–277
Eighth Amendment, 227–228, 238
Eisenstadt v. Baird (1972), 184
"Elimination" metaphor, 207
El Refaie, Elizabeth, 281–282, 283
Embodied metaphor
  overview, 90–92, 109–110
  allegory and, 97–99
  interpretation of parable via embodied simulation, 100–104
  legal narrative, parable in, 92–97
  literary versus legal parable, 108
  persuasion and, 104–109

woodcutter parable and, 92–93, 100, 106–107
Emotional resonance, 186–192
"Empathic fallacy," 365
Epidemiological Criminology (Akers, Potter, and Hill), 211–212
Equitable copyright, 50
"Eradication" metaphor, 207
Ethos, 84–85, 226
Extended metaphor, metaphoric parable versus, 77–80

Fable, metaphoric parable versus, 74–75
Fabula (story), 129, 146
Fact Skepticism (Frank), 338
Facts versus law, 131–132
Fauconnier, Gilles, 29–30
"Federal citizens," 175–177
Federal Rules of Civil Procedure, 63, 131–132
Feinberg, Jonathan, 354
Female sexuality, narrative and metaphor and, 184–186
Feminist Judgments Project, 154, 170–174, 182–186, 188–192
Feminist Legal Theory, 3, 379
Fictionality, 35–36
Fielding, Henry, 130–131
Fifth Amendment, 236
Finley, Lucinda, 173
First Amendment, 49–50, 61, 245
Fish, Stanley, 127
Fisher, Walter, 186
"Fishing" metaphor, 63
Flaubert, Gustave, 145
Fludernik, Monika, 27–28
"Footprints" metaphor, 316–317
Forster, E.M., 133
Fourteenth Amendment, 171, 175–177
Fourth Amendment, 142, 233, 236
Frameworks Institute, 248–249
Framing, 35–36
Frank, Jerome, 338
Frank, John Paul, 276
Frankfurter, Felix, 114
Fresh metaphors, 62–63
Frist, Bill, 321
Froebel, Friedrich, 196
Fromm, Erich, 338
Frontiero v. Richardson (1973), 164
Frost, Robert, 338
"Fruit of the poisonous tree" metaphor, 61

Fuller, Lon, 88–89

Gaakeer, Jeanne, 27–28
Gallagher, Catherine, 131
"The Game Changed" (Joseph), 340–341
The Game Changed: Essays and Other Prose (Joseph), 341
Gamson, William, 269
Geduldig v. Aiello (1974), 173
Geertz, Clifford, 46
Gell, Andrew, 46
Gender, narrative and metaphor and
  overview, 153–156, 157–159, 361
  allusive nature of, 169
  contraception and, 184–186
  in decision making, 168
  "dirty laundry" metaphor, 181
  discrimination and, 364
  disruptive use of, 170
  emotional resonance and, 186–192
  female sexuality and, 184–186
  feminist advocacy, contribution to, 168–170
  Feminist Judgments Project and, 154, 170–174, 182–186, 188–192
  feminist persuasion, relationship with, 159–162
  interracial marriage and, 188–192
  judicial opinions and, 119–120
  lack of constraints on, 168–169
  in legal argument, 162–163
  male homosexuality and, 182–184
  novel metaphors, use of, 174–177
  oppression, as tool of, 159–162
  persuasion by, 165–167
  politicization of law and, 159–162
  pornography and, 161
  "separate spheres" metaphor and, 170–174, 177
  sexual harassment and, 179–181
  significance of, 163–165
  social justice advocacy, contribution to, 168–170
  structure of logical reasoning, 167
  tacit knowledge and, 166
  thought processes as metaphoric, 166
  unconscious assumptions and inferences and, 166
Genetic predisposition, medical metaphor of crime and, 226–229
Germany
  metaphor in, 32
  narrative in, 25–28

Germany (cont.)
    rules of legal application in, 33–34
In Geschichten verstrickt: Zum Sein von Mensch und Ding (Schapp), 28
Gewirtz, Paul, 2–3
Gibbs, Raymond W., Jr., 8, 57, 60–61, 64, 154.
    See also Embodied metaphor
Ginsburg, Ruth Bader, 164
Glossip v. Gross (2015), 5
Goldberg, Irving, 78–79
Goldfarb, Phyllis, 172, 174–177
Goldman Sachs, 259, 279
Goldstein, Paul, 328
Goodman, John, 322–323
Good Samaritan parable, 94
Gordon, Robert W., 197
Grimké sisters, 368–369
Grisham, John, 328
Griswold v. Connecticut (1965), 182, 184–186
Grossman, Jonathan, 131
Grunewald, Ralph, 197
Gurnham, David, 6
Gusfield, Joseph, 211–212, 213–214

Haack, Susan, 195
Hand, Learned, 338
Handler, Alan, 76–77, 94–95
Hanne, Michael, 10, 20, 221, 224, 233
Harcourt, Bernard, 238
"Hardball" (television program), 101–102
Harrell, Glenn, 77–78
Harris, Cheryl I., 191, 364
Hart, H.L.A., 338
Hate speech, 374
Hay, Bruce L., 187
Health care
    in Canada, 322–323
    as human right, 317
    "queue jumping" and, 322–323
    "queue" metaphor and, 322–323
Heller, Kevin, 59–60
Henderson, Greig, 113, 119
Herbert, George, 338
Herdegen, Matthias, 32
"Hidden agenda" metaphor, 274
Hightower, Jim, 274
Hill, Carl V., 211–212
Hill v. Komar (2006), 68–70, 71
Hirschman, Albert, 357
HIV transmission as assault, 233
Hochschild, Arlie Russell, 314–315

Hogan, Thomas, 87–88
Holmes, Oliver Wendell, 355
hooks, bell, 181
Hoover, J. Edgar, 276
Horton, Willie, 247
"Hotspots," 236–237
Housing
    as human right, 317–318
    mortgage crisis, 240
    South Africa, guarantee of housing in, 297–299, 317–318
Human rights, narrative and metaphor in
    overview, 291–292, 362
    crimes against humanity and, 294–295
    definition of "right," 292
    dispute resolution, 294
    existential rights, 293
    "footprints" metaphor, 316–317
    health care, 317
    housing, 317–318
    indigenous peoples and, 296
    infringement of, 294
    intellectual property and, 44
    literature and, 295
    metaphors for rights, 292–294, 308–309, 315–318
    narratives of rights, 294–296
    property, rights as, 292–293
    "queue" metaphor (*See* "Queue" metaphor)
    wealth redistribution and, 293
    weapons and, 293–294
Hunt, Lynn, 295

Image, right to, 43
Immigration, "queue jumping" and, 319–324
Immigration law, narrative and metaphor in, 53
Indigenous peoples
    in Australia, 41–42, 45
    collective ownership, assumptions regarding, 45–46
    cultural appropriation, 50
    culturally significant objects, 46–47
    diversity of, 52
    genetic material of, 48
    human rights and, 296
    intellectual property and, 39, 41–42, 43, 51–52
    legal protections, 47–48
    Matsuda on, 371–372
    metaphor and, 51–53

in New Zealand, 45
open source licensing and, 49
plants and, 48
property and, 38
United Nations Declaration on the Rights of Indigenous Peoples, 44
"In Parentheses" (Joseph), 346–348
Intellectual property
  overview, 44
  agricultural metaphor, 40–41
  art works, 39–40, 41–42
  copyrights, 40, 42–43, 50
  diversity and, 52
  droit de suite, 39–40
  equitable copyright, 50
  human rights and, 44
  image, right to, 43
  indigenous peoples and, 39, 41–42, 43, 51–52 (*See also* Indigenous peoples)
  moral rights, 42–43
  open source licensing, 49
  patents, 40, 41, 50
  paternity metaphor, 42
  personality, right to, 43
  software, 49
  trademarks, 40
  World Intellectual Property Organization, 44
International Covenant on Civil and Political Rights, 303
International Covenant on Economic, Social and Cultural Rights, 303
International Longshore and Warehouse Union (ILWU), 376
Interracial marriage, 188–192
Into It (Joseph), 340
"Iron fist in velvet glove" metaphor, 217–218
"I Think About Thigpen Again" (Joseph), 334
"I've Already Said More Than I Should" (Joseph), 335
Iversen, Stefan, 35
Iyengar, Shanto, 248, 269–270

Jakobson, Roman, 29
James, William, 338
Jameson, Fredric, 8
Jefferson, Thomas, 61, 116
Jeter, Mildred, 188–192
Johannesburg Metropolitan Municipality v. Blue Moonlight Properties (2012), 305–307

Johnny Lynn Old Chief v. U.S. (1997), 147–149
Johnson, Lyndon, 258, 276
Johnson, Mark, 8, 29, 167, 271
Joseph, Lawrence, 327–331, 349–358. *See also Lawyerland* (Joseph); "Lawyer-self"
Judicial opinions, narrative and metaphor in
  overview, 113–120
  absence of narrative, 118–119
  counterfactuals and, 125
  dangers of, 115–116
  disnarration and, 125–126
  fabula and, 129, 146
  gender law and, 119–120
  incorporation of narrative features, 126–127
  judgments, 128–131
  "legality effect," 137
  legal scholarship, narrative in, 123–128
  literary narrative, legal narrative versus, 121–123
  multiple plots, 131–135
  "penumbral rights," 114
  quasi-character, 135
  quasi-plot, 118, 122–123, 133–135, 138
  "reality effect," 118, 123, 135–139, 140–149
  "reasonable person" and, 124–125
  sjuzhet and, 129, 146
  victim impact statements and, 140–141
  videos and, 141–146
  visual narratives and, 140–149
  "wall of separation" metaphor, 116
  "watertight compartments," 114
Justice for Janitors, 375

Kafka, Franz, 339
Kalven, Harry, 37
Kanne, Michael, 349–350
Kasich, John, 321–322
Keats, John, 338
Kelling, George L., 236, 266–267
Kennedy, Anthony, 5
Kennedy, Robert F., 191
Kent, James, 232
Kerber, Linda, 171
Kerper v. Kerper (1989), 88
King, Rodney, 143
Kitsuse, John, 211–213
Krakoff, Sarah, 355
Krider, Jeanne, 211
Kubrin, Charis E., 253–254
Kuhn, Thomas, 195
Ku Klux Klan, 374, 375

Lacey, Nicola, 308, 318
Ladson-Billings, Gloria, 364
Lakoff, George, 8, 29, 167, 255, 266, 267, 271
Lambert v. California (1957), 114
Landau, Jack, 72–73
Langbein, John, 26
Langer, Susan K., 338
Langley v. Boyter (1984), 88–89
Latinos, media reporting of crime and, 259–260, 279
Laufer-Ukeles, Pamela, 173
Law Language and Ethics: An Introduction to Law and Legal Method (Bishin and Stone), 337–338
Lawrence, Chuck, 370
Lawrence v. Texas (2003), 34–35, 182, 235
"Law's Metaphors" (conference), 6
Law's Stories (Brooks and Gewirtz), 21
Law versus facts, 131–132
Lawyerland (Joseph)
  overview, 327–331, 340
  civility in, 349–358
  "lawyer-self" in, 341–346
  reviews of, 351, 352
"Lawyer-self"
  overview, 327–331, 332–333, 346–348
  in *Lawyerland*, 341–346
  in legal scholarship, 339
  in poetry, 333–341
  in prose, 337–339
Le Bon, Gustave, 206
Legal activism, narrative and metaphor in
  overview, 361–366
  connection between narrative and metaphor and, 378–379
  Critical Race Theory and, 361, 362–364, 365, 367, 371, 372, 379
  metaphor, 378
  narrative, 372
  peacemaking, 374–375
  "ratchet principle," 366, 377–378
  "shaking our windows and rattling our walls" metaphor, 376–377
  "slow-cooking school of theory building," 366, 373
Legal discourse, narrative and metaphor in
  overview, 19–20, 36
  "binocular vision," 20
  in civil law systems, 25–28, 32, 33–34
  different aspects of narrative, 23–25
  discourse, 24–25
  distortive nature of narrative, 34–35
  fictionality, 35–36
  framing, 35–36
  in Germany, 25–28, 32, 33–34
  narration, 23–24
  narrative turn, 20–23
  narrativity, 25
  narrativization, 25
  in rules of legal application, 33–34
  specificity of narrative, 25–28
  story, 24–25
  universality of metaphor, 29–33
The Legal Imagination: Studies in the Nature of Legal Thought and Expression (White), 3, 9, 337, 338–339
"Legality effect," 137
Legal persuasion, narrative and metaphor in
  overview, 57–64
  abstract topics, metaphor and, 61–62
  closing arguments, 58
  commercial cases, 62
  conventional metaphors, 63
  embodied metaphor (*See* Embodied metaphor)
  "fishing" metaphor, 63
  fresh metaphors, 62–63
  intimacy, metaphor and, 60–61
  metaphoric parable (*See* Metaphoric parable)
  multiple narratives, 60
  opening statements, 58
  sporting metaphors, 63
Legal scholarship
  "lawyer-self" in, 339
  narrative in, 123–128
Legal Writing: Process, Analysis, and Organization (Edwards), 57
Le Goulven, Katell, 50
Lehmann-Haupt, Christopher, 352–353
Lerner, Stephen, 375
Letters to a Young Poet (Rilke), 342
Lewin, Kurt, 211
Literal parable, metaphoric parable versus, 71–74
Literature
  human rights and, 295
  "lawyer-self" in (*See* "Lawyer-self")
  literary allusion versus metaphoric parable, 76–77
  literary narrative versus legal narrative, 121–123

literary parable versus legal parable versus, 108
poetry, "lawyer-self" in, 333–341
prose, "lawyer-self" in, 337–339
Lithwick, Dahlia, 116, 155, 198, 239, 240, 248, 249, 269, 271, 277–279, 287, 361, 365. *See also* Media reporting of crime, narrative and metaphor in
"Living tree doctrine," 16
Llewellyn, Karl, 338
Lochner v. New York (1905), 172
Locke, John, 308
Logos, 80–82, 226
Loitering, 234
Lombroso, Cesare, 210–211
López, Gerald P., 363–364
Lopez, Ken, 57–58, 62
Lorde, Audre, 160
Loving, Richard, 188–192
Loving v. Virginia (1967), 188–192
Lowie, Robert, 47
Luban, David, 353
Lying Down Together: Law, Metaphor, and Theology (Ball), 7

MacKinnon, Catharine, 160, 161
Madison, James, 38
Magalhaes, Luciana, 322
Magdalene College, 332
Male homosexuality, narrative and metaphor and, 182–184
Mandela, Nelson, 310
Marginalized persons, narrative and metaphor and, 177–178
Marine Cooks and Stewards Union, 376
"Marketplace of ideas" metaphor, 61, 95, 276
Marvell, Andrew, 338
Maryland v. Rusk (1981), 146–147
Mass incarceration, 229–230, 237–238
"Material Facts" (Joseph), 329, 336
Matsuda, Mari. *See also* Legal activism, narrative and metaphor in
generally, 11, 156, 196, 365–366
on "color blind" metaphor, 372
on connection between narrative and metaphor, 378–379
Critical Race Theory and, 361, 362, 367, 371, 372, 379
on hate speech, 374
on Hawai'ian fisheries, 369
on indigenous peoples, 371–372
on law, 373–374
on Muslim ban, 374
on peacemaking, 374–375
on police shootings, 370, 373
on "ratchet principle," 366, 377–378
"shaking our windows and rattling our walls" metaphor, 376–377
on "slow-cooking school of theory building," 366, 373
Matthews, Chris, 101–102
Matua, Makau W., 295, 316
McCarthyism, 97–98
McClintock, Tom, 321
McCloskey, Deirdre, 8–9, 365
McCutcheon v. Federal Election Commission (2014), 281
McFadden, Joseph, 89
McGinley, Ann, 182–184
McMurtry-Chubb, Teri, 188–192
Media reporting of crime, narrative and metaphor in
overview, 245–250, 251–253, 269–271, 287, 362
analysis of, 282–284
"birth" metaphor, 276
Conceptual Metaphor Theory and, 271–273
crime versus law, 263
criminal justice system as metaphor, 266–267
editorial cartoons and, 280–282
frames, 269–271
"hidden agenda" metaphor, 274
influence on public thinking, 262–265
Latinos and, 259–260, 279
in legal journalism, 277–278
metaphorical stories, 273–274, 276–277
metaphors about crime, 255–260, 278–280
methods of reporting, 260–262
misperception of crime levels and, 253–254
"monster" metaphor, 257, 279
in newspapers, 265
newsworthiness and, 253
print versus broadcast news, 265
recommendations for improvement, 266–268, 284–286
"rescue" metaphor, 276–277
scenarios, 269
selection of stories, 253–255
"smoke out" metaphor, 273–274
story metaphors, 275–276, 278–282
on television, 260–261, 265

Media reporting of crime (cont.)
    terrorism and, 258–259
    values, 270
    victims and, 258
    "war on crime" metaphor, 258, 279
    white collar crime and, 259–260, 279
    "yellow journalism," 253
Medical metaphor of crime
    overview, 200–201, 218–219, 220–221, 242, 361
    aging and, 230, 238
    assessment of, 208–209
    "conception" metaphor, 202–204
    contagion theory and, 206
    "containment" metaphor, 227–228
    "control" metaphor, 207
    "copycat" effect, 206–207
    courts, role of, 231–235
    dangers of, 216
    Differential Association/Social Learning (DA/SL) perspective and, 207–208
    "elimination" metaphor, 207
    "eradication" metaphor, 207
    genetic predisposition and, 226–229
    government agencies and, 220–221
    "hotspots" and, 236–237
    "iron fist in velvet glove" metaphor, 217–218
    law of possession and, 232–234
    legislatures, role of, 231–235
    "life-course" analysis, 202
    literal versus figurative, 224–225
    mass incarceration and, 229–230, 237–238
    police, role of, 235–237
    priority between narrative and metaphor, 220, 221–231
    prisons, role of, 237–238
    "psychopaths" and, 227
    public health model, 211–212, 214–215
    "reproduction" metaphor, 204–205
    scientific criminology and, 210–211
    sexual assaults in colleges and, 240–241
    social constructionist approach, 212–213
    social problems theory approach, 209–216
    status politics and, 213–214
    "superpredators" and, 222
    symbolic crusades and, 213–214
    "vaccine" metaphor, 205–207
    "vaccine thinking," 216–217
    white collar crime and, 239–240
"Medicated Goo" (Traffic song), 209
Melville, Herman, 338, 339

Menendez brothers, 252
Mercer University, 6
Meritor Savings Bank v. Vinson (1986), 179–181, 185
Merry, Sally Engle, 317
Metaphor. *See specific topic*
"Metaphor: The Conceptual Leap" (conference), 8
Metaphor and Reason in Judicial Opinions (Bosmajian), 7, 113–114
Metaphorical stories, 273–274, 276–277
Metaphoric parable
    overview, 65–68, 86
    ethos function of, 84–85
    examples of, 86–89
    extended metaphor versus, 77–80
    fable versus, 74–75
    general characteristics, 68–70
    literal parable versus, 71–74
    literary allusion versus, 76–77
    logos function of, 80–82
    pathos function of, 82–84
    rhetorical style function of, 85–86
    as stylistic device, 70–71
    woodcutter parable and, 66–67, 81, 82, 83
Metaphor in law, 4–9. *See also specific topic*
Metonymy, 304
Meyler, Bernadette, 153, 156, 296, 361, 365. *See also* "Queue" metaphor
Miller, Arthur, 97–98
Miller, J. Hillis, 132–133
Mink, Louis O., 7–8
Miranda, Ernesto, 276
Miranda v. Arizona (1966), 276
"Monster" metaphor, 257, 279
Monstrous Crimes and the Failure of Forensic Psychiatry (Douard and Schultz), 257
Montanans for Multiple Use v. Barbouletos (2008), 87–88
Montoya, Margaret, 377
Morrison v. Olson (1988), 95–96, 105–106
Mortgage crisis, 240
Muller, Russell, 25
Muller v. Oregon (1908), 5, 172–173, 177
Murray, James E., 114
Musolff, Andreas, 269
"My Love is a Mountain" (Simone), 29

Narration, 23–24
Narrative. *See specific topic*

"Narrative: The Illusion of Sequence" (conference), 8
"Narrative criminology," 248–249
Narrative in law, 1–4. *See also specific topic*
"Narrative/Metaphor Nexus" (conference series), 9–10
"Narrative therapy," 295
Narrativity, 25
Narrativization, 25
National Alliance against Racist and Political Repression, 374
National Center for Injury Prevention and Control, 210, 215
Native American Graves Protection Act, 39
Native Americans. *See* Indigenous peoples
Neiman, Kenneth, 87
New Jersey v. Irving (2011), 94–95
New Jersey v. Muhammad (1996), 76–77
New Jersey v. Smith (1993), 234
Newspapers, reporting of crime in, 265
New York Times, 351, 352–353, 357
New York University School of Law, 2
New Zealand, indigenous peoples in, 45, 47–48
Next Dada Utopian Visioning Peace Orchestra and Manifesto of Radical Intersubjectivity Possibility (Matsuda), 379
Nguyen v. INS (2001), 173–174
Nielson, Henrik Skov, 35
Nietzsche, Friedrich, 333
Nixon, Richard, 258
Nussbaum, Martha, 245–246, 295

Obama, Barack, 101–102, 322–323
Oldfather, Chad, 115
Olson, Greta, 2–3, 16–18, 58, 257. *See also* Legal discourse, narrative and metaphor in
Oncale, Joseph, 182–184
Oncale v. Sundowner Offshore Services (1998), 182–184
Only Words (MacKinnon), 161
On Metaphor (Sacks ed.), 8
On Narrative (Mitchell ed.), 8
Onwauchi-Willig, Angela, 179–181, 185
Open source licensing, 49
Opinions. *See* Judicial opinions, narrative and metaphor in
Ortony, Andrew, 8
Orwell, George, 251, 266

Pacific Telegraph Act of 1860, 301
Papachristou v. Jacksonville (1972), 234
Parable
 allegory and, 97–99
 Biblical parables, 94
 embodied metaphor (*See* Embodied metaphor)
 Good Samaritan parable, 94
 literary versus legal parable, 108
 metaphoric parable (*See* Metaphoric parable)
 woodcutter parable, 66–67, 81, 82, 83, 92–93, 100, 106–107, 108
Parks, Rosa, 369
Patents, 40, 41, 50
Pathos, 82–84, 226
Payne v. Tennessee (1991), 140–141, 145
"Penumbral rights," 114
People v. Zackowitz (1930), 149
Perelman, Jeremy, 316
Personality, right to, 43
Persuasion. *See* Legal persuasion, narrative and metaphor in
Peterson, Scott, 252
Petty, Richard E., 285
Phelan, James, 128–129
Philippopoulos-Mihalopoulos, Andreas, 24
The Pilgrim's Progress (Bunyan), 273
Plants
 ideas as, 90–91, 96
 indigenous peoples and, 48
Plessy v. Ferguson (1896), 187, 188
Poetry, "lawyer-self" in, 333–341
Police shootings, 145–146, 252, 370, 373
Polkinghome, Donald, 134
Pollak, Jessica M., 253–254
Pornography, 161
Posner, Richard, 119, 365
Possession, law of, 232–234
Potter, Roberto H., 11, 155, 198–199, 220–221, 229, 361, 365. *See also* Medical metaphor of crime
Powell v. Bunn (2005), 72–73
Powell v. Georgia (1998), 34–35
Powers, Elizabeth, 270
Presser, Lois, 248–249
Price, Vincent, 270
Prince, Gerald, 125–126
Privileges and Immunities Clause, 175, 176
Prohibition, 214

Property
    indigenous peoples and, 38 (*See also* Indigenous peoples)
    intellectual property (*See* Intellectual property)
    metaphors regarding, 38
    rights as, 292–293
    "whiteness" as, 364
Prose, "lawyer-self" in, 337–339
Prosecutors, 240
"Psychopaths," 227

Quasi-character, 135
Quasi-plot, 118, 122–123, 133–135, 138, 225
"Queue" metaphor
    overview, 297–299, 318, 362
    abstraction of rights and, 309–310
    as allocative mechanism, 310–312
    doctrinal nature of, 302, 304–305
    health care and, 322–323
    ideological changeability of, 315
    institutional nature of, 302, 303–304
    as normative system, 309–310
    "queue jumping," 298–299, 300–302, 307, 319–324
    realization of rights and, 310–312
    in Soviet Union, 314–315
    state control and, 312–314
    in United States, 314–315
Quinn, Brian, 73–74

Race, narrative and metaphor and, 178–181
    "color blind" metaphor, 178–179, 364, 372
    Critical Race Theory, 3, 196, 361, 362–364, 365, 367, 371, 372, 379
    "dirty laundry" metaphor, 181
    discrimination and, 364
    Latinos, media reporting of crime and, 259–260, 279
    police shootings, 145–146, 252, 370, 373
    sexual harassment and, 179–181
    "whiteness" as property, 364
Racketeer Influenced and Corrupt Organizations Act, 239
Ramsay, JonBenet, 258, 263
Rand v. Monsanto Company (1991), 349–350
"Ratchet principle," 366, 377–378
"Rational actor" model, 246–247
Ratzlaf v. U.S. (1994), 231
Rawls, John, 310, 371
"Reality effect," 118, 123, 135–139, 140–149
"Reasonable person," 124–125

Reed v. Reed (1971), 164
Refugee Convention, 307
Rehnquist, William, 140–141, 145
Reijnierse, W. Gudrun, 279–280
Reno, Janet, 258
"Reproduction" metaphor, 204–205
"Rescue" metaphor, 276–277
"Revisioning," 361
Rhem v. Malcolm (1974), 357
Rhetorical style function of metaphoric parable, 85–86
Rhode, Deborah L., 350
Rich, Adrienne, 159–161
Ricoeur, Paul, 8–9, 118, 122–123, 127–128, 133–135, 138, 225–226
Rideout, Chris, 59–60
Rilke, Rainer Maria, 330, 342
Ripeness, 114
Ritchie, David T., 6
Ritchie, L. David, 9, 116, 155, 198, 222, 223–224, 248, 249–250, 270–271, 361, 365. *See also* Media reporting of crime, narrative and metaphor in
Rodensky, Lisa, 131
Roe v. Wade (1973), 114, 184
Röhl, Klaus F., 31–32
Rolling Stone, 256
Romney, Mitt, 101–102
Rorty, Richard, 295, 370
Rosch, Eleanor, 25
Rose, Mark, 42
Rosen, Lawrence, 9, 18, 153–154, 296. *See also* Indigenous peoples
Rosenberg, Mark, 210
Rosky, Jeff, 211
Rusk v. Maryland (1979), 146–147

Safe Streets Act, 258
Sahlins, Marshall, 37–38
St. John's University School of Law, 339–340
Salem Witch Trials, 97–98
Sandberg, Sveinung, 248–250
Sanders, Alex, 88–89
Sanders, Bernie, 369, 370
Sarbin, Theodore, 8
Sartre, Jean-Paul, 338
Sasson, Theodore, 262
Scales, Anna, 366, 377–378
Scalia, Antonin, 5, 95–96, 105–106, 108, 115, 142, 143, 144, 145, 182, 183
Scarry, Elaine, 295
Schank, Roger C., 8, 286

Schapp, Wilhelm, 28
Schön, Donald, 195–196, 208–209, 266
Schultz, Pamela D., 257
Schwarzenegger, Arnold, 237
Scientific criminology, 210–211
Scottoline, Lisa, 328
Scott v. Harris (2007), 141–145, 146–147, 149
Seattle University Law School, 2
Selective incapacitation, 236–237
"Separate spheres" metaphor, 170–174, 177
Serial (podcast), 255
Sessions v. Southern California Edison (1941), 75
Sexual assaults in colleges, 240–241
Sexual harassment, 179–181
Shafer, Jack, 261–262
"Shaking our windows and rattling our walls" metaphor, 376–377
Shanley v. Northeast Indiana School District (1972), 78–79
Sheley, Joseph F., 254
Shklovsky, Viktor, 353
Shouting at No One (Joseph), 334, 337, 340
Siegel, Sheldon, 328
Simon, Jonathan, 258
Simone, Alina, 29
A Simple Heart (Flaubert), 145
Simpson, O.J., 92, 252, 263
Sjuzhet (discourse), 129, 146
Skeel, David, 330, 340
Slaughter, Joseph, 22, 316
Slaughter-House Cases (1873), 175
Sloviaczek v. Puckett (1977), 89
"Slow-cooking school of theory building," 366, 373
Smith, Michael R., 6, 30, 32–33, 57, 64, 92–93, 94–95, 97, 154, 223–224. *See also* Metaphoric parable
"Smoke out" metaphor, 273–274
Software, 49
"Some Sort of Chronicler I Am" (Joseph), 337
Souter, David, 147–149
South Africa
  Constitution, 297–298, 301
  governmental obligation to provide housing, 297–299
  guarantee of housing in, 297–299, 317–318
  housing register, 302, 303–304
  National Housing Code, 306
South Africa v. Grootboom (2001), 303
Southampton University Law School, 6
Southern Tenant Farmers Union, 376

Soviet Union, "queue" metaphor in, 314–315, 322
So Where Are We? (Joseph), 346–348
Sparling, Jon, 66–67, 68, 70, 71, 80, 81, 82, 83, 92–93, 100, 106–107, 108
Spector, Malcolm, 211–213
Spencer, Alexander, 258–259
Sporting metaphors, 63
Stalin, Josef, 281
Stanchi, Kathryn M., 119–120, 153–156, 361. *See also* Gender, narrative and metaphor and
Standing, 114
Stanford University Law School, 9–10
Status politics, 213–214
Steen, Gerard S., 279–280, 283, 286
Steffens, Lincoln, 260
Stein, Gertrude, 332, 342
Sterling, Alton, 145
Stern, Simon, 22, 118–120, 140, 146, 149, 155, 222, 225–226. *See also* Judicial opinions, narrative and metaphor in
Stevens, John Paul, 142, 143–144, 146–147
Stock narratives, 5
Stone, Christopher D., 337–338
Story, 24–25
Story metaphors, 275–276, 278–282
Strawson, Galen, 21, 22
Suicide, 206–207, 229
"Superpredators," 222, 247
Swift, Taylor, 321–322
Symbolic crusades, 213–214
Szubert, Rafal, 32

Taylor, Sidney, 179–181
Television, reporting of crime on, 260–261, 265
Terrorism, 258–259
Tewksbury, David, 270
"That's All" (Joseph), 335
A Theory of the Trial (Burns), 59
Thibodeau, Paul H., 198, 255–256, 263–264, 277, 279–280, 283
"This is How It Happens" (Joseph), 335
Thomas, Dylan, 338
Thornburg, Elizabeth, 63
Thorson, Esther, 246
Tillich, Paul, 338
Tinker v. Des Moines Independent Community School District (1969), 78–79
Tocqueville, Alexis de, 171
Todorov, Tzvetan, 122–123, 127–128, 132–133
Tom Jones (Fielding), 130–131
Tracy, Karen, 270
Trademarks, 40

Transcendental Nonsense and the Functional Approach (Cohen), 338
The Trial (Kafka), 339
Trilling, Lionel, 338
Trojan horse allusion, 76–77, 94–95
Trump, Donald, 322
Truth and Reconciliation Commissions, 294–295
Turner, Mark, 29–30, 97
Turow, Scott, 328
20/20 (television program), 261

Ulbrich, Stefan, 31–32
The Underground Railroad (Whitehead), 158–159
Underground railroad metaphor, 158–159
United Nations Declaration on the Rights of Indigenous Peoples, 44
University of British Columbia, 47
University of Cambridge, 332
University of Chicago, 8
University of Cincinnati Law Review, 341
University of Michigan, 332
University of Minnesota, 48
University of Virginia, 252, 256
University of Virginia Law School, 2
U.S. v. Hudson (2013), 86–87
U.S. v. Windsor (2013), 5
"Using Metaphor in Legal Analysis and Communication" (conference), 6

"Vaccine" metaphor, 205–207
Vanderbilt Law Review, 340
"Variations on Variations on a Theme" (Joseph), 337
Velleman, David, 126
"Vernacularization," 317
Victim impact statements, 140–141
Videos
 cognitive bias and, 142
 judicial opinions and, 141–145
 of police shootings, 145–146
Vinson, Mechelle, 179–181
Virgil, 76–77
Visual Artists Rights Act, 43
Vratil, Kathryn H., 86–87

Wallis, Meredith, 327–331
"Wall of separation" metaphor, 61, 95, 116
"War on crime" metaphor, 258, 279

Warren, Earl, 118, 119, 187, 188–189, 191
Wars I Have Seen (Stein), 342
Washington Post, 265
"Watertight compartments," 114
Waugh, Linda R., 259–260
Wealth redistribution, 293
Weigend, Thomas, 197
Weisberg, Robert, 2–3, 11, 117–118, 119, 120, 155, 198–199, 351, 361, 365. *See also* Medical metaphor of crime
Weishann v. Kemper (1928), 89
Welsh, Alexander, 130–131
Wenar, Leif, 293
West, Robin, 339, 351
White, Byron, 136
White, Hayden, 8, 21–22
White, James Boyd, 3, 9, 117, 119, 120, 337, 338–339
White, Terry, 143
White collar crime, 239–240, 259–260, 279
Whitehead, Colson, 158–159
"Whiteness" as property, 364
Whitman, Walt, 338
"Who to Deny" (Joseph), 335
Williams, Patricia, 161, 362, 363, 372
Williams, William Carlos, 333–334
Wilson, James Q., 236
Winter, Steven L., 7, 9, 82, 161, 163, 292
Wolf, Werner, 20
"Wolf in sheep's clothing" metaphor, 95–96, 105–106
Woodcutter parable, 66–67, 81, 82, 83, 92–93, 100, 106–107, 108
Wood v. Lucy, Lady Duff-Gordon (1917), 31
Woodward, Louise, 252
Wordle, 354
Wordsworth, William, 338
World Intellectual Property Organization, 44
Worldwide Volkswagen Corporation v. Woodson (1980), 125
Wright v. Crane (1825), 234

Yaeger v. Murphy (1987), 88
"Yellow journalism," 253
Young, Katharine, 7, 153, 156, 296, 319–320, 361, 365. *See also* "Queue" metaphor

Zimmerman, George, 252
Zubik v. Burwell (2016), 164
Zwaan, Rolf A., 285–286